Regional Economic Integration and the Global Financial System

Engin Sorhun
Istanbul 29 Mayis University, Turkey

Ümit Hacıoğlu
Istanbul Medipol University, Turkey

Hasan Dinçer
Istanbul Medipol University, Turkey

A volume in the Advances in Finance, Accounting, and Economics (AFAE) Book Series

BUSINESS SCIENCE Reference
An Imprint of IGI Global

Managing Director: Lindsay Johnston
Managing Editor: Austin DeMarco
Director of Intellectual Property & Contracts: Jan Travers
Acquisitions Editor: Kayla Wolfe
Production Editor: Christina Henning
Development Editor: Erin O'Dea
Typesetter: Cody Page
Cover Design: Jason Mull

Published in the United States of America by
Business Science Reference (an imprint of IGI Global)
701 E. Chocolate Avenue
Hershey PA, USA 17033
Tel: 717-533-8845
Fax: 717-533-8661
E-mail: cust@igi-global.com
Web site: http://www.igi-global.com

Library of Congress Cataloging-in-Publication Data

CIP Data

Regional economic integration and the global financial system / Engin Sorhun, Umit Hacioglu, and Hasan Dincer, editors.
pages cm
Includes bibliographical references and index.
Summary: "This book addresses recent trends in regional integration projects and the strides that such projects are making on the road toward globalization, focusing on a range of economic projects, emerging supranational units, and possible implications for future trends"-- Provided by publisher.
ISBN 978-1-4666-7308-3 (hardcover : alk. paper) -- ISBN 978-1-4666-7309-0 (ebook) -- ISBN 978-1-4666-7311-3 (print & perpetual access) 1. International economic integration. 2. Economic interest groupings. 3. International finance. I. Sorhun, Engin, 1979- editor.

HF1418.5.R442 2015
337.1--dc23

2014036389

This book is published in the IGI Global book series Advances in Finance, Accounting, and Economics (AFAE) (ISSN: 2327-5677; eISSN: 2327-5685)

British Cataloguing in Publication Data
A Cataloguing in Publication record for this book is available from the British Library.

For electronic access to this publication, please contact: eresources@igi-global.com.

Advances in Finance, Accounting, and Economics (AFAE) Book Series

Ahmed Driouchi
Al Akhawayn University, Morocco

ISSN: 2327-5677
EISSN: 2327-5685

Mission

In our changing economic and business environment, it is important to consider the financial changes occurring internationally as well as within individual organizations and business environments. Understanding these changes as well as the factors that influence them is crucial in preparing for our financial future and ensuring economic sustainability and growth.

The **Advances in Finance, Accounting, and Economics (AFAE)** book series aims to publish comprehensive and informative titles in all areas of economics and economic theory, finance, and accounting to assist in advancing the available knowledge and providing for further research development in these dynamic fields.

Coverage

- Economics of Innovation and Knowledge
- Statistical Analysis
- Finance and Accounting in SMEs
- Labor Economics
- Finance
- Economics of Agriculture and Biotechnology
- Macroeconomics
- Evidence-Based Studies
- Development Economics
- Ethics in Accounting and Finance

IGI Global is currently accepting manuscripts for publication within this series. To submit a proposal for a volume in this series, please contact our Acquisition Editors at Acquisitions@igi-global.com or visit: http://www.igi-global.com/publish/.

The Advances in Finance, Accounting, and Economics (AFAE) Book Series (ISSN 2327-5677) is published by IGI Global, 701 E. Chocolate Avenue, Hershey, PA 17033-1240, USA, www.igi-global.com. This series is composed of titles available for purchase individually; each title is edited to be contextually exclusive from any other title within the series. For pricing and ordering information please visit http://www.igi-global.com/book-series/advances-finance-accounting-economics/73685. Postmaster: Send all address changes to above address.

Titles in this Series

For a list of additional titles in this series, please visit: www.igi-global.com

Green Economic Structures in Modern Business and Society
Andrei Jean-Vasile (Petroleum-Gas University of Poiesti, Romania) Ion Raluca Andreea (Bucharest Academy of Economic Studies, Romania) and Turek Rahoveanu Adrian (University of Agronomic Sciences and Veterinary Medicine, Bucharest, Romania)
Business Science Reference • copyright 2015 • 325pp • H/C (ISBN: 9781466682191) • US $195.00 (our price)

Handbook of Research on Behavioral Finance and Investment Strategies Decision Making in the Financial Industry
Zeynep Copur (Hacettepe University, Turkey)
Business Science Reference • copyright 2015 • 473pp • H/C (ISBN: 9781466674844) • US $245.00 (our price)

Agricultural Management Strategies in a Changing Economy
Gabriel Popescu (Bucharest Academy of Economic Studies, Romania) and Andrei Jean-Vasile (Petroleum - Gas University of Ploiesti, Romania)
Business Science Reference • copyright 2015 • 439pp • H/C (ISBN: 9781466675216) • US $225.00 (our price)

Handbook of Research on In-Country Determinants and Implications of Foreign Land Acquisitions
Evans Osabuohien (Covenant University, Nigeria & German Development Institute, Germany)
Business Science Reference • copyright 2015 • 430pp • H/C (ISBN: 9781466674059) • US $265.00 (our price)

Handbook of Research on Strategic Developments and Regulatory Practice in Global Finance
Özlem Olgu (Koç University, Turkey) Hasan Dinçer (Beykent University, Turkey) and Ümit Hacıoğlu (Beykent University, Turkey)
Business Science Reference • copyright 2015 • 430pp • H/C (ISBN: 9781466672888) • US $235.00 (our price)

Urbanization and Migration as Factors Affecting Global Economic Development
Denis Ushakov (International College Suan Sunandha Rajabhat University, Thailand & Russian Academy of National Economy and Public Administration–South branch, Russia)
Information Science Reference • copyright 2015 • 317pp • H/C (ISBN: 9781466673281) • US $215.00 (our price)

Handbook of Research on Developing Sustainable Value in Economics, Finance, and Marketing
Ulas Akkucuk (Bogazici University, Turkey)
Business Science Reference • copyright 2015 • 550pp • H/C (ISBN: 9781466666351) • US $345.00 (our price)

Handbook of Research on Economic Growth and Technological Change in Latin America
Bryan Christiansen (PryMarke, LLC, USA)
Business Science Reference • copyright 2014 • 504pp • H/C (ISBN: 9781466662247) • US $295.00 (our price)

IGI GLOBAL
DISSEMINATOR OF KNOWLEDGE
www.igi-global.com

701 E. Chocolate Ave., Hershey, PA 17033
Order online at www.igi-global.com or call 717-533-8845 x100
To place a standing order for titles released in this series, contact: cust@igi-global.com
Mon-Fri 8:00 am - 5:00 pm (est) or fax 24 hours a day 717-533-8661

Editorial Advisory Board

Table of Contents

Detailed Table of Contents

The subprime mortgage crisis, which started in the United States in 2008, turned into a global crisis in a short time. Following the policies to reduce and mitigate the impacts of the global crisis, a sovereign debt crisis began that led to tremendous increases in government deficits and debt stock in the European Union region and made government financial systems unsustainable. This debt crisis, which started in the second half of 2009 in Greece, has resulted in a spillover effect for every EU member country. The ongoing crisis has rendered the future of Economic and Monetary Union uncertain. This chapter aims to determine the root causes of sovereign debt crisis in the EU and the economic and financial effects of and precautions for the crisis. This study also discusses the degradation of the EU's economic and political integration as a result of the sovereign debt crisis.

Unemployment has become an increasingly serious economic and social problem in many European countries. Theoretically, unemployment has a negative effect on economic growth and development. This chapter examines the impact of unemployment on economic growth in 15 EU countries from 1984 to 2012 by using several panel data techniques. Panel unit root tests suggest that the series employed in the study are stationary at first differences. In other words, the series are integrated of order one, I(1). Panel cointegration tests show that the variables are cointegrated over the period implying a long-run relationship between the variables. Panel OLS estimations show that the impact of unemployment on economic growth is negative and statistically significant. This indicates that unemployment decreases economic growth in these countries. Finally, Granger causality tests based on vector error correction model suggest that there is a bi-directional causality between the variables in the short and long run. The findings may provide some policy implications.

Since the inception of the European integration process, the Franco-German axis is considered to be a major driving force. Even today, Europe moves faster in the presence of an entente between France and Germany. However, the harmonization of German and French positions is not quasi-automatic as it used to be. The desynchronization that occurred over time is based on various factors such as the German unification, the EU's enlargements, and the change in German self-perception. One of the contexts in which the divergences between Paris and Berlin can be seen is related to the Euro zone rescue operations. Germany came to the fore in the resolution process and made clear her preferences, which are not always truly supported by France. The drifting-apart that started after the end of the Cold War thus continues.

The European Community/Union has always been a controversial issue in the UK. At present, the probability of an in-or-out referendum makes it all the more divisive. Eurosceptics see a brighter future for their country outside the union both in political and economic terms. Pro-Europeans, on the other hand, maintain that British membership brings up benefits that outweigh the costs. Both sides have their arguments. The former seek success through social mobilizations and debates. The latter believe that the anti-EU stance may be costly in economic and political terms. Hence, the public must be convinced before the referendum – if it ever takes place.

The concept of integration expresses an extremely fundamental and complicated formation. Despite such important and complicated issues and problems, Europe has made considerable progress and developments and been able to form the European Economic Community first and then the European Communities, and finally the European Union. It is necessary to precisely and smoothly complete the three stages of integration in order to mention about an exact integration. These stages, economic integration, fiscal integration, and political integration are discussed within this chapter. The first stage, economic integration, can be achieved only with the integration of the trade among the elements of the integration. Hence, it is required to seek for the fiscal harmonization of the tax legislation that is the most important competition breaker element in the field in question. A complete economic integration will be possible only by providing this fiscal harmonization.

Although not openly identified in treaties until the Maastricht Treaty, health has always been a crucial area for the European Union (EU), since freedoms provided and regulations brought by common market also dealt with several sections of the health sector. All concerning parts of health sector have to be subject to both freedoms and regulations of single market system. Despite the value given to health and related issues, a separate or supranational policy dealing with health issues has not been formed by the EU. The member states keep their privilege on health policies. However, the EU does not stay completely aside of health issues; on the contrary, the EU got involved in certain areas of health, especially the ones which have cross-border implications. In this chapter, the matter of to what extent the EU got involved in health issues is researched and the question of if the EU has a concrete health policy is analyzed.

Dental health expenditures are a big part of general health expenditures. In Turkey, oral health services are provided by both private practitioners and government sections. In 2012, approximately 7 million fillings were made by government clinics. According to Turkish Dental Association data, in the same year, the number of fillings that Turkish citizens needed was 247 million. Even if the entire budget of the Health Ministry of Turkey were spent for these fillings, it is impossible to handle this demand. In 2012, in the European Union with 24 member countries, dental health spending was close to 74 billion Euro. Because of this financial burden, Turkey and the other countries are trying to find cost-effective methods to minimize dental health spending. This chapter emphasizes dental health conditions of both Turkey and European Union, firstly, and then successful and cost-effective strategies are discussed.

SMEs form 90% of commercial businesses in Turkey and the support given to SMEs means support directly given to the real sector in a vast scale. SMEs have some problems currently that are accepted as structural throughout Turkey, such as that they were constituted in form of family companies, that they do not use financial instruments sufficiently, that they do not work with professional executives, their commercial activities without invoice, etc. There could be other common problems that SMEs can meet with as related to sector or location. The main duties of Development Agencies is to mobilize commercial potential in region, to support sectors that have the potential to grow, and thus, to decrease the difference of development between regions. This chapter explores SMEs in Turkey.

Section 3
New Dynamics in Globalization

The aim of this chapter is to investigate the cointegration and causal relationship between financial development, trade openness, and economic growth in Turkey for the period of 1980-2012. To analyze the data, the bounds testing and Johansen-Juselius approaches to cointegration and Granger causality test based on vector error-correction model are employed. The cointegration tests suggest that there is a long-run relationship between the variables. The Granger causality test reveals long-run bidirectional causality between trade openness and economic growth. The findings also indicate unidirectional causality running from financial development to trade openness and economic growth in the long run as well as a bi-directional causality between financial development and economic growth in the short run. The results support supply-leading and trade-led growth hypotheses. Therefore, it can be suggested that Turkey can accelerate its economic growth by improving its financial systems and encouraging foreign trade.

The managerial model of cooperation and dialogue-driven, international, and supranational efforts during the past half-century form one of the most important topics within the "sustainable development" concept. Rapidly growing human population, together with the unsustainable pattern of consumption of renewable natural resources for future generations, also leads to the transfer of resources. The concept of development in keeping with ecological concerns about the impact of the dynamic approach should be reformulated. Faced with such dilemmas, these debates illustrate the need for a rational approach. Without jeopardizing the needs of future generations, to meet the demands of today's resource usage, the authors envision a sustainable development approach that seeks to balance protection and use. This approach should be addressed in the context of an understanding.

This chapter analyzes the impact of trade openness on environmental pollution in the newly industrialized countries that have focused on trade over the period 1971-2010 by using recently developed panel unit root, cointegration, and causality tests. The results indicate a cointegration relationship between the variables. The results also show that trade openness increases carbon dioxide emissions with the elasticity of 0.53 and there is a Granger causality running from trade openness to carbon dioxide emissions in the long run. These findings may provide some policy implications. Without taking into account impact of trade on pollutions, optimistic environmental Kuznets curve hypothesis would be invalid. Therefore, policymakers who decide on environment policies should pay attention to not only growth effects but also trade effects on pollutions. Future empirical analysis would expose the new evidences for governmental policies and environmental regulations to change these effects positively.

This chapter reviews the financial crisis of 2008-09 and its impacts on the international trade in terms of regionalism and globalism. The chapter glances over different aspects of globalism and regionalism as well as looks on historical pattern and recent developments of regionalism and globalism. The data used in the chapter indicates that the financial crisis of 2008-09 negatively affected both globalization and regionalization trends. In addition, the EU has experienced an interesting transformation from regionalism to globalism. This chapter suggests that the issue is not only related with the great trade collapse of 2008-09 but also the sovereign debt crisis of 2010-12.

The colossal economic transformations and political intrusions had been affecting brutally China and the Soviet Union in the final decades of the twentieth century. Currently, Russia is a gigantic power struggling to rebuild its economic base in an era of globalization. On the other hand, the economic rise of China has attracted a great deal of attention and labeled as a success story by the Western world. China and Russia have made a number of efforts to strengthen bilateral ties and improve cooperation on a number of economic/political/diplomatic fronts. Since the mid-1990s, the Shanghai Cooperation Organization (SCO) has been an important feature of Eurasian politics and a vehicle to forge a new sort of cooperation between China and Russia. A number of issues related to geopolitics, security, the economy, and regional politics have been handled by the SCO member states.

Preface

In the second half of the twentieth century, two dynamic changes shaped the world economy: Globalization and Regionalism. First, regional economic integration, in which a group of countries eliminates barriers to trade and competition on a regional rather than a global scale, became increasingly popular after World War II. This trend manifested itself at various strata from preferential trade agreement to economic union. The WTO estimates there are about 190 Regional Trade Agreements (RTA), 10 customs unions, 6 common markets, and 2 monetary unions. The OECD (2013) estimates RTAs cover more than half of international trade. Second, the unprecedented speed of liberalization of markets in the last quarter of the century has fueled globalization as mobility of goods, labor, and financial instruments increased. Trade relative to world output has grown faster than ever before. McKinsey & Company (2008) reports in the prelude of the Global Crisis that the world's financial assets are four times as large as the world's GDP.

The European Union is the most successful example for the regional economic integration when the WTO is the pioneering attempts of globalisation.

However, the interaction between globalism and regionalism that had been considered for long as competitor presents today a different challenge: Globalization of Regionalism. This is the third dynamic change that the new millennium gave rise to in economic integration. There are two innovations that support this challenge:

First, the trend of economic integration is about to enter another phase: integration of different regional supranational organizations. Can the Transatlantic Trade and Investment Partnership (TTIP) project potentially be the core of this future trend? Can integration of different regional supranational units be a transitional stage towards complete globalization?

Second, another innovation in economic integration results from the interaction among international and regional economic institutions. Both global integration and regional integration have their own institutions and regulations. However, the last global economic crisis explicitly revealed that these institutions are not sufficiently capable of dealing with the problems alone. In the absence of fundamental judiciary basis, the crisis compelled global and regional integration institutions to pragmatic collaborations while sharing the responsibility (IMF as a global institution and ECB as a regional institution collaborated to bail out some indebted EU members). This situation demonstrates that global integration and regional integration may contribute to the world economy as long as they complement each other.

The primary objective of this book is to discuss the latest advances in the economic integration and the interaction between globalization and regional integration from an interdisciplinary perspective. This book set out to illustrate the impacts on driving forces, changing strategies of international and regional institutions, and emerging new supranational units. Finally, the book explores the new trends in regional integration and globalization and provides insights on potential gains and losses of the new economic integration projects.

The authors of these chapters have accepted inclusion of their respective manuscripts. This book, consisting of 21 chapters, is divided into 4 sections: "Crisis in EU Regionalism," "New Dynamics in EU Regionalism and Enlargement," "New Dynamics in Globalization," "Globalization of Regionalism."

A brief description of each of the chapters follows.

Chapter 1 identifies the root causes of sovereign debt crisis in the EU and the economic and financial effects of and precautions for the crisis. In this globalizing world, countries that cannot compete on their own in all areas form common markets by establishing regional blocks, and to form common political, legal, and social systems. The EU, as one of the foremost regionally integrated markets, seems to be a gradually growing supranational organization. Thus, this study also discusses the degradation of the EU's economic and political integration as a result of the sovereign debt crisis.

Chapter 2 examines the impact of unemployment on economic growth in 15 EU countries from 1984 to 2012 by using several panel data techniques. Panel unit root tests suggest that the series employed in the study are stationary at first differences. In other words, the series are integrated of order one, I(1). Panel cointegration tests show that the variables are cointegrated over the period implying a long-run relationship between the variables. Panel OLS estimations show that the impact of unemployment on economic growth is negative and statistically significant. This indicates that unemployment decreases economic growth in these countries. Finally, Granger causality tests based on vector error correction model suggest that there is a bi-directional causality between the variables in the short and long run. The findings may provide some policy implications.

Chapter 3 discusses the Franco-German axis in the EU and debates about the weakening of this axis during Eurozone Crisis. Since the inception of the European integration process, the Franco-German axis is considered to be a major driving force. Even today, Europe moves faster in the presence of an entente between France and Germany. However, the harmonization of German and French positions is not quasi-automatic as it used to be. The desynchronization that occurred over time is based on various factors such as the German unification, the EU's enlargements and the change in German self-perception. One of the contexts in which the divergences between Paris and Berlin can be seen is related to the Euro zone rescue operations. Germany came to the fore in the resolution process and made clear her preferences which are not always truly supported by France. The drifting-apart that started after the end of the Cold War thus continues.

Chapter 4 questions the Euroscepticism in UK where the government suggests a referendum for the EU. The European Community/Union has always been a controversial issue in the UK. At present, the probability of an in-or-out referendum makes it all the more divisive. Eurosceptics see a brighter future for their country outside the Union both in political and economic terms. Pro-Europeans, on the other hand, maintain that British membership brings up benefits that outweigh the costs. Both sides have their arguments. The former seek success through social mobilizations and debates support. The latter believe that the anti-EU stance may be costly in economic and political terms. Hence, the public must be convinced before the referendum –if it ever takes place.

Chapter 5 analyzes the fiscal factors and political objectives and means to overcome obstacles within the EU. And it focuses on the fiscal harmonization of the tax legislation that is the most important competition breaker element in the field. The chapter concludes that a complete economic integration will be possible only by providing this fiscal harmonization.

Chapter 6 draws a comprehensive frame for European Financial Integration throughout debates about a European Banking Union. In 2012, the European Commission created a roadmap towards a European banking union. The aim of this EBU is to ensure financial stability in Europe. The proposed framework by the European Commission is based on three pillars: a Single Supervisory Mechanism (SSM), a Single Resolution Mechanism (SRM), and a single deposit guarantee mechanism. The EBU project is a step towards a better functioning EMU in the future. However, there are several controversies on this project. The main concerns are conflicts of interest between monetary policy and banking supervision, and cooperation between ECB and other banking authorities. If the EBU is a necessary step, it is not a sufficient one to resolve all financial issues in the EMU and in Europe.

Chapter 7 provides some background information on the progress of each candidate and potential candidate country (Turkey, Iceland, Serbia and the Former Yugoslav Republic of Macedonia) on the way to EU accession and compares them with the current EU28 members in order to emphasize the main similarities and the differences.

Chapter 8 examines the economic profit of the EU in the case of Turkey's membership to the Union. Even though Turkey has become sixth largest economy in the Europe, there are still hesitations in the EU due to Turkey's low profile performance in the past. However, in last decade the country has a significant rise in economy by carrying out market economy and privatizations successfully. This give rise to a greater potential gain for the EU members that will get when Turkey joint the Union.

Chapter 9 deals with EU health policy. All parts of health sector (health insurances, health care services, health workforce, cross-border patients and medication, etc.) have to be subject to both freedoms and regulations of common market/single market system. Despite the value given to health and related issues, a separate or supranational policy, such as the common agricultural policy, dealing with health issues has not been formed by the EU. The member states keep their privilege on health policies. However, this does not mean that the EU stays completely aside of health issues, contrary, in the course of time, the EU got involved in certain areas of health especially the ones which have cross-border implications. This chapter analyzes to what extent the EU is involved in health issues and question whether the EU has a concrete health policy.

Chapter 10 analyzes the cost-effective spending on dental health expenditure, which is the biggest share in total health expenditure, by comparing the cases in Turkey (as a candidate country) and EU members. Because of this financial burden, Turkey and the EU countries are trying to find cost-effective methods to minimize dental health spending. This chapter emphasizes dental health conditions of both Turkey and European Union firstly, and then successful and cost-effective strategies will be discussed.

Chapter 11 deals with the problems of Small-Medium Enterprises (SME) in Turkey, which is a candidate country for EU membership. The majority of SMEs, accounting for 90% of commercial businesses in the country, are established in form of family companies. This causes some problems such as insufficiently use of financial instruments, leak of professional executives, informal economy, etc. To overcome these problems, Development Agencies, being in the first place, and some other public institutions may be a remedy for SMEs. This chapter explain how the institutions in question will act to support SMEs.

Chapter 12 examines the government intervention during the three major global crises. And deregulation is diagnosed as principal reason for these crises. However, it points out that the reasons of the crises are the unethical and irrational behavior of homo economicus. This chapter concludes that it require regulation policies to be applied in order to overcome the last global crisis as it was done for the past crises.

Chapter 13 establishes a link between fiscal paradises and the 2008 economic crisis and investigate the role of G-20 as a global actor in regulating the fiscal paradises problem. Fiscal Paradises are described as the "dark side of globalization" because of the negative role they have been playing in global economy. Today they are an extremely important reason of tax evasion and tax avoidance, financial instability, money laundering, terrorist finance, issues. Recent actions by G-20 have focused on fiscal paradise countries, targeting tax evasion and avoidance issues, because of the fact that the economic crisis in 2008 has shown the importance of destructive influence of fiscal paradises in the economy not only on national but also on international level. This chapter aims to explain what has been achieved regarding the fiscal paradises problems at G-20 summits since the economic crisis of 2008.

Chapter 14 reviews the Historical Development of Financial Transaction Taxes from J.M. Keynes's idea of excising the security transactions to J. Tobin's thought of excising the speculative capital movements. Then the feasible alternatives as two-staged Tobin tax of P.B. Spahn were suggested. Today, the effects occurring due to the global finance crisis has resulted in forcing the EU to review the mechanisms that will be activated during the crisis. In this context, an implementation of financial transactions tax that has been drafted to be implemented across the EU has been brought to the agenda. In this study, it is aimed to discuss financial transaction taxes in the context of the European Union and Turkey from a historical view.

Chapter 15 aims to investigate the cointegration and causal relationship between financial development, trade openness and economic growth in Turkey for the period of 1980-2012. To analyze the data, the bounds testing and Johansen-Juselius approaches to cointegration and Granger causality test based on vector error-correction model are employed. The cointegration tests suggest that there is a long-run relationship between the variables. The Granger causality test reveals long run bidirectional causality between trade openness and economic growth. The findings also indicate unidirectional causality running from financial development to trade openness and economic growth in the long run as well as a bi-directional causality between financial development and economic growth in the short run. The results support supply-leading and trade-led growth hypotheses. Therefore, it can be suggested that Turkey can accelerate its economic growth by improving its financial systems and encouraging foreign trade.

Chapter 16 threats sustainable development approach in Economy-Ecology dilemma. The managerial model of cooperation and dialogue-driven, international and supranational efforts in the past half-century period which is the subject of one of the most important topics of "sustainable development" concept. Rapidly growing human population, due to the unsustainable pattern of consumption of renewable natural resources for future generations also leads to transfer of resources not worry. The concept of development with ecological concerns with the impact of the moving approach should be reformulated has become a concept. "Despite the economy, ecology?" or "Despite the economy, ecology?" Fed from such dilemmas, these debates illustrate the need for a rational approach. Without jeopardizing the needs of future generations, to meet the needs of today's resource usage envisioning a sustainable development approach seeks to balance protection and use should be addressed in the context of an understanding.

Chapter 17 analyzes the impact of trade openness on environmental pollution in the newly industrialized countries that have focused on trade over the period 1971-2010 by using recently developed panel unit root, cointegration and causality tests. The results indicate a cointegration relationship between the variables. The results also show that trade openness increases carbon dioxide emissions with the elasticity of 0.53 and there is a Granger causality running from trade openness to carbon dioxide emissions in the long run. These findings may provide some policy implications. Without taking into account impact of trade on pollutions, optimistic environmental Kuznets curve hypothesis would be invalid. Therefore, policy makers who decide on environment policies should pay attention to not only growth effects but also trade effects on pollutions. Future empirical analysis would expose the new evidences for governmental policies and environmental regulations to change these effects positively.

Chapter 18 reviews the financial crisis of 2008-09 and its impacts on the international trade in terms of regionalism and globalism. The chapter glances over different aspects of globalism and regionalism as well as looks on historical pattern and recent developments of regionalism and globalism. The data used in the chapter indicates that the financial crisis of 2008-09 negatively affected both globalization and regionalization trends. In addition, the EU has experienced an interesting transformation from regionalism to globalism. This chapter suggests that the issue is not only related with the great trade collapse of 2008-09, but also the sovereign debt crisis of 2010-12.

Chapter 19 deals with China-Russia relationship throughout the Shanghai Cooperation Organization (SCO). Relations between China and Russia have evolved dramatically throughout the twentieth century. However, during the past decade China and Russia have made a number of efforts to strengthen bilateral ties and improve cooperation on a number of economic/political/diplomatic fronts. Since the mid-1990s, the Shanghai Cooperation Organization (SCO) has been an important feature of Eurasian politics and a vehicle to forge a new sort of cooperation between China and Russia. A number of issues related to geopolitics, security, economy and regional politics have been handled by the SCO member states. It would be fair to argue that the SCO achieved noteworthy results in the past decade. The organization, today, appears as a solid and inclusive multilateral regional organization, very active in terms of promoting economic development and security in Eurasia.

Chapter 20 reviews political, economic, institutional, and natural conditions for a successful economic integration. And the Transatlantic Trade and Investment Partnership (TTIP) and the Shanghai Cooperation Organization (SCO) are evaluated in the light of these success conditions. The last global economic crisis has prompted new dynamics in the scope of economic integration: on the one hand, the USA and the EU, which is together the largest and wealthiest market in the world; on the other hand, Shanghai Cooperation Organization (SCO) recently adopted the economic vision for forming a free trade area and initiating an economic integration. Since these two integration projects were recently launched, the concerned policymakers, academicians, NGOs, etc. have a very limited scientific resource. This study is intended to make a small contribution to fill the gap in this field.

Chapter 21 deals with the impact of regionalism and globalization on metropolitan governance schemes of Turkey from political economy perspective. This chapter tackles with different dimensions of the Turkish metropolitan policymaking within the context of Law No: 6360, namely, the administrative aspects, the public financial characteristics along with the political dimensions. The problematization of the work simply follows how regionalism and globalization have come and interacted to render such a reform in Turkish local management units, under the rule of the Justice and Development Party (JDP-Adalet ve Kalkınma Partisi). The effort shall also tackle with the philosophy and the rational of new system in reference to regionalism and globalization with the need to underline the ramifications of the implementation of the new scheme in Turkey.

The impacts of globalization and the 2008-2009 financial crisis on global economic activity have been sufficiently examined in the literature. However, a politic approach to economic integration has not been sufficiently connected to strategic issues in the literature yet. Therefore, it is important to develop an innovative and strategic approach to issues in the international political economy. In this regard, regional economic integration and globalization issues in the international political economy have been assessed from an interdisciplinary perspective. The authors of these chapters developed models and strategies for innovative solutions to regional and global issues in the international political economy by assessing critical empirical studies and theories.

Engin Sorhun
Istanbul 29 Mayıs University, Turkey

Ümit Hacıoğlu
Istanbul Medipol University, Turkey

Hasan Dinçer
Istanbul Medipol University, Turkey

REFERENCES

Lejárraga, I., & Shepherd, B. (2013). *Quantitative evidence on transparency in regional trade agreements (OECD Trade Policy Papers No. 153)*. Paris: OECD. doi:10.1787/18166873

McKinsey & Company. (2008). *Mapping global capital markets: Fifth annual report*. Retrieved from http://www.mckinsey.com/insights/global_capital_markets/mapping_global_capital_markets_fifth_annual_report

Section 1
Crisis in EU Regionalism

Chapter 1
The Impact of Sovereign Debt Crisis on the EU Economy:
Is This the End of the Dream?

Serkan Cura
Celal Bayar University, Turkey

ABSTRACT

The subprime mortgage crisis, which started in the United States in 2008, turned into a global crisis in a short time. Following the policies to reduce and mitigate the impacts of the global crisis, a sovereign debt crisis began that led to tremendous increases in government deficits and debt stock in the European Union region and made government financial systems unsustainable. This debt crisis, which started in the second half of 2009 in Greece, has resulted in a spillover effect for every EU member country. The ongoing crisis has rendered the future of Economic and Monetary Union uncertain. This chapter aims to determine the root causes of sovereign debt crisis in the EU and the economic and financial effects of and precautions for the crisis. This study also discusses the degradation of the EU's economic and political integration as a result of the sovereign debt crisis.

INTRODUCTION

The European Coal and Steel Community (ECSC) was founded with the Schuman Declaration in 1951 following World War II, by six members: Belgium, Federal Germany, Luxembourg, France, Italy and the Netherlands. In 1957, all six members signed the Treaty of Rome to establish the European Economic Community (EEC), which was based on free movement of labor, goods, and services (European Central Bank, 2011). As a result of rapid globalization and the acceptance of the idea that political partnership would be more beneficial for regional development, growth, and peace, the EEC, which was an economic partnership, ultimately became the European Union (EU) in its final stage of regional integration. (Gökbunar et al., 2008).

The idea of the Economic and Monetary Union (EMU) stems from the very first Werner Report in 1970, though the EMU was not formed until a decade later. It has been suggested that this delay was due to a lack of sufficient support from EU members and the recession following the first oil crisis in 1973 (Akçay, 2013). In 1979, The

DOI: 10.4018/978-1-4666-7308-3.ch001

European Monetary System (EMS), which aimed to overcome the instability among the member states' currencies, was established to combat the economic instabilities of the 1970s (European Central Bank, 2011). The ratification of the Single European Act by the member states (and later revised by the European Council in 1986) meant that both the single market and the EMU were brought into being. The Delors Report, which laid the groundwork for the EMU, was signed in 1992 as the Maastrict Treaty (Dellas, 1997). The Maastricht Treaty aimed to create fiscal convergence among the member nations and put forth a three-stage implementation process designed for the EMU (Vallée, 2014). The first stage (1990-1993) was the creation of an EU with a single market; the second stage (1994-1998) was the establishment of the European Monetary Institute (EMI) to accelerate the fiscal harmonization process among member states; and third stage (1999-onward) was use of single currency (the euro), transfer of national authority on monetary and currency policies to the European Central Bank (ECB), and finally the establishment of the 'Eurozone' (European Central Bank, 2011). There are presently 17 EU member states in the third stage. The EU is in the process of political integration—the natural result of trade integration based on a single market and a single currency. It is a major project with the goal of solidifying Europe's position by eliminating the costs of globalization.

Since the removal of obstacles to the movement of capital in the 1980s, capital and capital movements have become more global. As stated by Tobin (2000), the globalization of financial markets affects assets, debt, bank loans, and real capital. The globalization of capital in particular has caused an increase of liquidity in international markets, as well as a decrease in fund costs, the emergence of new financial instruments, and the internationalization of alternate financial institutions (Tobin, 2000). Nevertheless, financial globalization and the integration of markets also lead to denser capital movements and deeper financial crises (Ureche-Rangau & Burietz, 2013).

Together with the liberalization of capital movements and globalization, economic crises in developed economies have caused ripples throughout the entire world. The subprime mortgage crisis, starting in the US following the bankruptcy of Lehman Brothers in September 2008, is among the best examples of this phenomenon (Lane, 2012). With farther-reaching repercussions than the Great Depression of 1929, the US subprime mortgage crisis caused the Eurozone to enter sovereign debt crisis.

This paper discusses the underlying causes of the sovereign debt crisis; the economic and financial effects of the crisis and the measure taken to counteract it; as well as the continuity of the EU, with its ultimate goal of political union.

EUROZONE SOVEREIGN DEBT CRISIS

Literature Review

Tanzi & Schuknecht (2000) identifies that public budgets were either balanced or had surpluses in countries that supported institutional limitations in the period between the beginning of 1900s and the 1960s. Since the 1980s, the increases in fiscal deficits have also caused an increase in sovereign debts. Consequently, sovereign debts are now not only an important public finance resource, but also a public revenue type among fiscal policy instruments that are used for classifying countries based on metrics of sustainability of public finance (Teica, 2012).

There are many studies on sovereign debt crisis in the EU and elsewhere, one being the study by Tanzi & Schuknecht (2000) that states that chronic high sovereign deficits create an unsustainable debt burden, especially in countries where real interest rates of government borrowing are high and growth rate is low. They asserted that this would result in crowding out in private sector activities and investments in the long run. Manganelli & Wolswijk (2009) and Lane (2012) stated that the rapid decrease in the interest rates of ten-year German state bonds after the third stage of the EMU, which created Eurozone, resulted in a spending increase throughout the Eurozone without tight fiscal policy controls, and that public deficits and public debt stock increased as a result of spending. The study by Reinhart & Rogoff (2010) analyzed the countries in Africa, Asia, Europe, Latin America, North America and Oceania between 1800-2009 years. The study reveals a strong correlation between banking crises and sovereign default. Roman & Bilan (2012), Alter & Schüler (2012) and Kollmann et al. (2013) said that there were inter-correlations among sovereign debt crisis, banking crisis and real sector in Eurozone; and that the ECB should take these three elements into consideration when adjusting its monetary policy. Kollmann et al. (2013) used New Keynesian Model, which evaluated banks, to research effectiveness of fiscal policy of the Eurozone. They found out that the sovereign spending increases stabilized the Gross Domestic Product (GDP), while increasing sovereign debt stock and crowding-out consumption and investments. Ferry (2013) revealed the weaknesses of the EMU before the crisis in the Eurozone. Especially balance of payments crises before the crisis indicated the undervaluation of the relation between bank crisis and sovereign debt crisis.

Causes and Development of the Crisis

There are allegations that some structural problems, referred to as the pre-crisis factors in the EU, which still continue, have been ignored (Puig & Rivero, 2014).

Some of the studies that analyze the structural problems of the EU and Eurozone are Lane (2012), Ali (2012), Roman & Bilan (2012), Ferry (2013), Glencross (2014), Santis (2014), Puig & Rivero (2014), Honkapohja (2014) and Constancio (2014). When these studies in the literature are analyzed; we can summarize the structural problems, which are referred to as pre-crisis factors in the EU and Eurozone, as below;

- The fact that public finance management was left to the initiative of the members, when monetary policy management on behalf of all members was transferred to the EMU during the process of forming a common economic zone in Europe, resulted in divergence from fiscal discipline, an increase in the public deficits, and increase of the public debts in order to finance these increasing deficits;
- With the decrease of interest rates in countries in Eurozone, the opportunity for banking sector in these countries to borrow money expanded. Consequently, spending opportunities increased in these countries and fiscal instabilities emerged.
- Development level and economic competition power differences among the Eurozone countries stand in their way of forming a coherent economy policy and this caused financial and current account imbalances.
- Maastricht Treaty did not create any crisis mechanism. In addition to this, in the pre-crisis era, the Eurozone countries had already started not to comply with some of the Maastricht criteria (such as ratio of public budget deficit not to exceed 3% of the GDP and ratio of public debt stock not to exceed 60% of the GDP) as stated in the Stability and Growth Pact (SGP).

Subprime mortgage crisis primarily affected banking and insurance sectors and then investment and trade fields, following the bankruptcy of Lehman Brothers in the second half of 2008 in the States and then turned into a global financial crisis. The main reason is that financial markets of the developed countries, including Eurozone bond market, were heavily affected from the process after Lehman Brothers' bankruptcy. The contagion effect of the crisis was not only limited to finance field: it also deeply affected the real sector (Kousenidis et al., 2013).

The first effect of global crisis in the EU and Eurozone was the recession of real GDP growth rate in 2009, respectively 4.5% and 4.4%. Similarly, in Table-2, the unemployment rates for people between the ages of 15-64 was 9% in the EU, whereas it was 9.6% in Eurozone in 2009.

The ECB decided to act in unison with the FED (American Central Bank) in the fight against the global financial crisis affecting the whole world since the end of 2008, put emissions to the markets (Lane, 2012). Furthermore, expansionary fiscal policy implementations in order to eliminate the tightening of growth for the purposes of rectification of macroeconomic instabilities resulting from the crisis in European countries, rescue operations for banks threatened by solvency, and increases in the current accounts all contributed to the sovereign debt crisis (Baum et al., 2013). Following sovereign debt crisis of Greece, the crisis spread over to Italy, Ireland, Portugal and Spain as of the last quarter of 2009 (Bhanot et al., 2014 ; Mink & De Haan, 2013). Consequently, the importance of sovereign debt crisis in Greece, Italy, Ireland, Portugal and Spain (GIIPS) lies in the fact that it is the very first crisis in Eurozone and the deepest crisis in the EU after the EMU crisis (Constancio, 2014 ; Puig & Rivero, 2014 ; Kollmann et al., 2013). With the impact of the global financial crisis that started in the States, the EU and Eurozone saw unstable growth rates until 2013, under the influence of sovereign debt

Table 1. Real GDP growth rate (%)

	2008	2009	2010	2011	2012	2013
EU	0.4	-4.5	2	1.6	-0.4	0.1
Eurozone (EU 17)	0.4	-4.4	2	1.6	-0.7	-0.4
Greece	-0.2	-3.1	-4.9	-7.1	-7	-3.9
Italy	-1.2	-5.5	1.7	0.4	-2.4	-1.9
Ireland	-2.2	-6.4	-1.1	2.2	0.2	-0.3
Portugal	0	-2.9	1.9	-1.3	-3.2	-1.4
Spain	0.9	-3.8	-0.2	0.1	-1.6	-1.2

Source: Eurostat

Table 2. Unemployment rate (%)

	2008	2009	2010	2011	2012	2013
EU	7.1	9	9.7	9.8	10.6	11
Eurozone (EU 17)	7.6	9.6	10.1	10.1	11.3	12
Greece	7.8	9.6	12.7	17.9	24.5	27.5
Italy	6.8	7.9	8.5	8.5	10.8	12.4
Ireland	6.1	12.2	14.1	14.9	15	13.3
Portugal	8.1	10	11.4	13.4	16.4	17
Spain	11.4	18.1	20.2	21.8	25.2	26.5

Source: Eurostat

crisis that had started in GIIPS in the last quarter of 2009 and expanded to the whole zone, in terms of contracting real GDP growth rates (see Table-1).

The factors that led to GIIPS' ongoing sovereign debt crisis show that, although the crisis resulted from debt obligation of public sectors, each country experienced their own sovereign debt crisis due to separate reasons. We can summarize the reasons of sovereign debt crisis for each country as follows (Bhanot, 2014 ; Santis, 2014 ; Ali, 2012 ; Lane, 2012; Oliveira et al., 2012 ; Arghyrou & Kontonikas, 2011); Public budget deficiencies and public debt stock, which increased as a result of current account deficits in Greece; high debt stock level and insufficient growth expectations in Italy; increases in public sector borrowings as a result of serious problems in banking sector in Ireland; low growth rates in Portugal; and increase in loans and property prices in Spain were the causes of sovereign debt crisis in GIIPS. Greece has had the deepest hit from the crisis in the EU and Eurozone, in terms of real GDP growth rate (Table-1) and unemployment rates (Table-2). Spain, Italy, Portugal and Ireland followed Greece in this order.

Table 3 presents an important data set in terms of determining the scale of sovereign debt crisis in the EU and Eurozone. With the global crisis and following sovereign debt crisis, although there is not any amelioration in total government revenue for the EU, Eurozone and GIIPS, the increase rate of total government expenditures as of the end of 2009 reached tremendous amounts. Having higher public expenditure than revenue for years caused general government deficits in public fiscal management. Public expenditure of GDP share in GIIPS, which are going through sovereign debt crisis, has been over the EU and Eurozone average.

The increase of general government deficit in the EU and Eurozone in 2009, compared to the previous fiscal year, is the basic indicator that the zone has not reached the fiscal discipline yet. Especially expansionary fiscal policy implementations and rescue operations for banks for diminishing effects of global crisis has resulted in an inevitable rise of fiscal deficits. Greece is the country that has the highest fiscal deficit in the GIIPS group, with -15.7% in 2009. And emergence of fiscal deficits is the basic variable that increases the sovereign debt stock.

In coherence with the instability in the tables of public finance indicators (Table-3 and Table-4), the sovereign debt of GDP rate, for especially GIIPS and then EU and Eurozone, increased consistently during 2008-2013 period. This means that it is inevitable for the EU to be generally among the highly indebted countries group, and that the main determinant of the instability is the high public debts. Tremendous amounts of fiscal deficits

Table 3. Public revenue and expenditure (% of GDP)

	2008		2009		2010		2011		2012		2013	
	PR	PE	PR	PE	PR	PE	PR	PE	PR	PE	PR	PE
EU	44.6	47	44.1	51	44.1	50.6	44.6	49	45.4	49.3	45.7	49
Eurozone (EU 17)	45.1	47.2	44.9	51.2	44.8	51.1	45.4	49.5	46.3	50	44.8	49.8
Greece	40.7	50.6	38.3	54	40.4	51.4	42.2	51.9	44.4	53.4	45.8	58.5
Italy	45.9	48.6	46.5	51.9	46.1	50.5	46.1	49.7	47.7	50.6	47.7	50.6
Ireland	35.4	42.8	34.5	48.2	34.9	65.5	34	47.1	34.5	42.6	35.9	42.9
Portugal	41.1	44.8	39.6	49.8	41.6	51.5	45	49.3	40.9	47.4	43.7	48.7
Spain	36.9	41.4	35.1	46.2	36.7	46.3	36.2	45.7	37.2	47.8	37.8	44.8

Source: Eurostat

Table 4. General government deficit/surplus (% of GDP)

	2008	2009	2010	2011	2012	2013
EU	-2.4	-6.9	-6.5	-4.4	-3.9	-3.3
Eurozone (EU 17)	-2.1	-6.4	-6.2	-4.1	-3.7	-3
Greece	-9.8	-15.7	-10.9	-9.6	-8.9	-12.7
Italy	-2.7	-5.5	-4.5	-3.7	-3	-3
Ireland	-7.4	-13.7	-30.6	-13.1	-8.2	-7.2
Portugal	-3.6	-10.2	-9.8	-4.3	-6.4	-4.9
Spain	-4.5	-11.1	-9.6	-9.6	-10.6	-7.1

Source: Eurostat

Table 5. Government consolidate gross debt (% of GDP)

	2008	2009	2010	2011	2012	2013
EU	62	74.4	79.9	82.4	85.2	87.1
Eurozone (EU 17)	70.1	80	85.5	87.4	90.7	92.6
Greece	112.9	129.7	148.3	170.3	157.2	175.1
Italy	106.1	116.4	119.3	120.7	127	132.6
Ireland	44.2	64.4	91.2	104.1	117.4	123.7
Portugal	71.7	83.7	94	108.2	124.1	129
Spain	40.2	54	61.7	70.5	86	93.9

Source: Eurostat

for GIIPS, which have caused the sovereign debt crisis to spill-over to other Eurozone countries and government consolidated gross debt of GDP rate, especially for Greece, Italy, Ireland and Portugal, caused their results to be much higher than the average of the region.

Measures Taken after Eruption of Sovereign Debt Crisis

When we look at the global financial crises, the hardest decision the countries have to make is what economic measures they will take in their fight against the crisis. The reason for this is that the contractionary policies that can be implemented against crisis cause recession and then an increase in the unemployment rates. Likewise, contractionary measures taken in GIIPS resulted in recession and an increase in the unemployment rates as well (Table-1 and Table-2).

The EU is an economically integrated regional block. It is not enough when only GIIPS countries implement measures. Therefore, taking measures for the whole EU is a more rational method (Glencross, 2014 ; Honkapohja, 2014 ; Lane, 2012).

Sovereign debt crisis, which started at the end of 2009, caused discussions on three differing perceptions in the EU and the EU decided what measures to take in lien with these three differing perceptions. The first of these perceptions was to form tools for crisis management and resolution. The second one was to take the fiscal management into the agenda again. The third one was the perception that it was necessary to meet more systematic reform needs. (Ferry, 2013).

Table 6 summarizes measures taken against and mechanisms formed in face of the sovereign debt crisis

According to Table 6, the main objectives of the measures taken and mechanisms formed, are to effectively lower the cost of debts for countries that face financial problems, to increase competitiveness of the EU and to strengthen the economic governance in EU.

Future of the EU: Is This the End of the Dream?

The ultimate goal of the EU is to reach political integration stage in the integration incentive that started in 1951 at the center of Europe with six countries at the North-south axis and has reached to 28 members at the end of expansion processes.

Sovereign debt crisis, which affected the EU and Eurozone, both economically and politically, started a discussion regarding the end of the EU. The facilitating factor for these discussions is the presence of pre-crisis structural problems in the EU and Eurozone. The focus of discussions, which created concerns about the future of the EU, is on the distinction between core and periphery countries and also on the economic integration/political fragmentation paradox (Öniş & Kutlay, 2012).

The development level and economic competitiveness differences among Eurozone countries result in core and periphery distinction. The distinction is between the core countries, which have

Table 6. Measures and mechanisms against sovereign debt crisis

• In order to protect EU members and Eurozone by ensuring refinancing of public debts, Eurozone countries and the IMF agreed to establish a common financial assistant mechanism through a bailout package for Greece, Ireland and Portugal. On April 11, 2010, Finance Ministers of Eurozone countries approved the decision of allocating the first tranche of emergency assistance of an amount of 30 billion to Greece. Greece was allocated with a total of 110 billion Euros within the scope of three-year long emergency assistance package. On November 28, 2010, Ireland applied to the EU because of the banking sector problems and a bailout package was ratified with the support of the EU and IMF. Portugal applied to the EU and a total of 78 billion Euros worth bailout package for Portugal in cooperation with IMF was ratified on April 6, 2011. Furthermore, austerity programs were initiated in the above-mentioned countries in order to decrease the sovereign debt stock. • The ECB declared reduction of policy interest in order to minimize economic contraction caused by the crises. As of May 2010, the ECB started to buy public bonds at secondary market for a lower bond margin and to increase trust for Eurozone bonds, which were under the pressure of the market. • The EU decided to let the member countries to give warranties to the banks that were affected from the debt crisis and to continue to provide loans that were necessary for the banks to create growth and employment. • *Balance of Payments Facility* was established as the facility in charge of solving problems that could occur in balance of payments of 10 EU member states, which are out of Eurozone. • *Pooled Loans-Greek Loan Facility* is a one-time-only mechanism, established to give loans to Greece. It is a pool of loans, which is composed of 80 billion Euros supplied by Eurozone countries through European Commission and 30 billion Euros supplied by the IMF. • *European Financial Stability Mechanism-EFSM* was established when various EU member states had financial problems after the global financial crisis. The EFSM gives financial assistance to financially troubled EU countries in order to assure fiscal stability of the EU and Euro. It provides loans from the markets and submits these loans to the use of beneficiary member state on behalf of the EU. • *European Financial Stability Facility-EFSF*, was established in June 2010 as a limited liability corporation. Its main objective is to give temporary support to Eurozone states which have various loan problems. • *European Stability Mechanism-ESM* is a permanent mechanism that replaced EFSM which was established in June 2013 to take place of temporary EFSM. ESM's objective is to ensure stability of Euro and it has a 700 billion Euro capital base. • *Six Pact* is the pack that entered into force on December 13, 2011 in order to strengthen budget discipline in EU member states through fiscal compact and to create strong economic policy coordination. It also developed stability tools for short-term problems. • *The Europe 2020 Strategy* was adopted by the European Commission in June 2010 in line with smart, sustainable and inclusive growth objectives. It is the successor of the Lisbon Strategy. It has determined three growth objective: ensuring fiscal discipline in the EU member states, harmonization of fiscal policies, and production of common solution in terms of employment, environment, education and technology fields.

Source: (Honkapohja, 2014 ; Ioannou & Stracca, 2014; Eurostat, 2013; Ferry, 2013; Mink & De Haan, 2013; Roman & Bilan, 2012; Wignall, 2011).

the capacity for current account surplus (such as Germany) and periphery countries, which have current account deficit problems and excessive loans (such as GIIPS group countries) (Ferry, 2013). During the sovereign debt crisis, which started in Greece and then spilled over to other periphery countries, core countries ignored the structural problems in the EU and accused GIIPS group countries for being unstable economies. The core countries criticized the periphery countries claiming that they were in the crisis due to their own unstable economies. A core country group emerged, a group that threatened Greece, Ireland and Portugal with bailout packages. For instance, German Chancellor Merkel, whose country has the biggest economic power in the EU and contributes the biggest amounts to bailouts, openly announced her ideas on what bailouts should include and how they should be implemented. (Glencross, 2014). Eurozone, which was established after transition to a single currency and transfer of monetary policy authorities to the ECB, resulted in economic and financial integration. However, the fact that fiscal policy implementations were left to nation states resulted in a limiting situation for federal Europe idea, which was defined as political integration. So much so that, mutual accusations and discontentment rose among the citizens of the countries which financially supported the bailouts and those whose countries benefited from these bailouts. Economic integration and political disintegration dilemma also suggests why Eurozone sovereign debt crisis has taken so much longer (Glencross, 2014 ; Ferry, 2013 ; Glencross, 2014 ; Öniş & Kutlay, 2012 ; Bickerton, 2011).

Studies from different point of views present three different scenarios regarding the pre-crisis structural problems in the EU and Eurozone, which will also affect the future of the EU. The first scenario is called 'dissolution'. Dissolution is when every member country goes back to its own previous currency and exchange parity fluctuations become free of control as result of unsolved structural problems. Such a situation could cause EU, which is the second biggest block after NAFTA, to lose its current position in the global economy. Second scenario is called 'restructuring'. Restructuring is to make reforms in order to solve structural problems that prevent Eurozone from becoming optimal currency area. Regulations that will assure fiscal harmonization predominantly stand out in the reforms. When we analyze the importance attributed to nation state norm by the EU member states, it is suggested that 'restructuring' scenario will have hard time in keeping Eurozone alive. The third scenario is referred to as 'reshaping'. It is seen as the alternative scenario that falls in-between the first and second scenarios. This scenario proposes to exclude periphery countries in Eurozone, which have economic and financial weaknesses, and to continue its way with economically and financially stronger and more stable core countries. It is likely that the idea of a new union within the EU might emerge as a result of this scenario. And this might result in a function that could disrupt political integration stage of the EU (Ferry, 2013; Öniş & Kutlay, 2012 ; Lane, 2012 ; Gökbunar et al., 2008).

CONCLUSION AND REMARKS

US born global financial crisis, which triggered a global recession in 2008, resulted in a sovereign debt crisis that reached a level to affect first the GIIPS group in the Eurozone, then all Eurozone and the EU.

The reason why sovereign debt crisis in the EU reached to serious levels in a short period is neither limited to economic and financial factors nor was the GIIPS group countries were the only responsible countries for this crisis. Despite measures taken and mechanisms applied against crisis since 2009, many EU member countries, and especially GIIPS group countries, still have very high fiscal deficits and sovereign debt stocks (Table-4 and Table-5). The main reason for this is the presence of structural problems within the EU and Eurozone.

As long as structural problems within the EU and Eurozone are not solved, the future is not going to be bright for the EU and Eurozone. Scenarios born from discussions about the future of the EU should be evaluated carefully. If the EU stays in the economic integration process without presence of political integration, it is highly likely that the EU will face a danger of disintegration in the long run. As a result, sovereign debt crisis, which still have devastating effects, is not a single country's problem, but rather the problem of the whole EU and Eurozone. Based on this, we can say that it is necessary to form and implement regulations for removing structural problems. Otherwise, the dream of the EU, which is one of the biggest blocks in the world, will turn into a nightmare.

REFERENCES

Akçay, B. (2013). Avro Bölgesinin Yapısı ve Yönetimi. In B. Akçay (Ed.), *Avrupayı Saran Kriz Avro Bölgesi* (pp. 31–52). Ankara: Seçkin Yayıncılık.

Ali, T. M. (2012). The impact of the sovereign debt crisis on the eurozone countris. *Procedia: Social and Behavioral Sciences*, *62*, 424–430. doi:10.1016/j.sbspro.2012.09.069

Alter, A., & Schüler, Y. S. (2012). Credit spread interdepencies of European states and banks during the financial crisis. *Journal of Banking & Finance*, *36*(12), 3444–3468. doi:10.1016/j.jbankfin.2012.08.002

Arghyrou, M. G., & Kontonikas, A. (2011). *The EMU-sovereign debt crisis: Fundemantals, expectetion and contagion*. Brussels: European Commision.

Baum, A., Westphal, C. C., & Rother, P. (2013). Debt and growth: New evidence for the euro area. *Journal of International Money and Finance*, *32*, 809–821. doi:10.1016/j.jimonfin.2012.07.004

Bhanot, K., Burns, N., Hunter, D., & Williams, M. (2014). News spillovers from the Greek debt crisis: Impact on the Eurozone financial sector. *Journal of Banking & Finance*, *38*, 51–63. doi:10.1016/j.jbankfin.2013.09.015

Bickerton, C. J. (2011). Crisis in the Eurozone: Transnational governance and national power in European integration. *Political Geography*, *30*(8), 415–416. doi:10.1016/j.polgeo.2011.03.004

Constancio, V. (2014). The European crisis and the role of the financial system. *Journal of Macroeconomics, 39* (Part B), 250-259.

Dellas, H. (1997). European monetary union: A new approach. *Journal of International Money and Finance*, *16*(4), 581–594. doi:10.1016/S0261-5606(97)00019-3

European Central Bank. (2011). *The Eurosystem: The European system of the central banks*. Luxembourg: European Central Bank.

Eurostat. (2013). *Smarter, greener, more inclusive? Indicators to support the Europe 2020 strategy*. Luxembourg: Eurostat.

Ferry, J. P. (2013). The known unknowns and unknown unknowns of European Monetary Union. *Journal of International Money and Finance*, *34*, 6–14. doi:10.1016/j.jimonfin.2012.11.002

Glencross, A. (2014). The Eurozone crisis as a challenge to democracy and integration in Europe. *Orbis*, *58*(1), 55–68. doi:10.1016/j.orbis.2013.11.003

Gökbunar, R., Yanıkkaya, H., & Cura, S. (2008). *Avrupa Birliği'nin Türkiyeli Geleceği Umutlar ve Korkular*. Ankara: Nobel Yayıncılık.

Honkapohja, S. (2014). The Euro area crisis: A view from the north. *Journal of Macroeconomics*, *39*, 260–271. doi:10.1016/j.jmacro.2013.08.004

Ioannou, D., & Stracca, L. (2014). Havethe euro area and EU governance worked? Just the facts. *European Journal of Political Economy*, *34*, 1–17. doi:10.1016/j.ejpoleco.2013.11.009

Kollmann, R., Ratto, M., Roeger, W., & Veld, J. i. (2013). Fiscal policy, banks and the financial crisis. *Journal of Economic Dynamics & Control*, *37*(2), 387–403. doi:10.1016/j.jedc.2012.09.007

Kousenidis, D. V., Ladas, A. C., & Negakis, C. I. (2013). The effects of the European debt crisis on earnings quality. *International Review of Financial Analysis*, *30*, 352–362. doi:10.1016/j.irfa.2013.03.004

Lane, P. R. (2012). The European sovereign debt crisis. *The Journal of Economic Perspectives*, *26*(3), 49–68. doi:10.1257/jep.26.3.49

Manganelli, S., & Wolswijk, G. (2009). What drives spreads in the Euro area government bond market? *Economic Policy*, *24*(58), 191–240. doi:10.1111/j.1468-0327.2009.00220.x

Mink, M., & De Haan, J. (2013). Contagion during the Greek sovereign debt crisis. *Journal of International Money and Finance*, *34*, 102–113. doi:10.1016/j.jimonfin.2012.11.006

Oliveira, L., Curto, J. D., & Nunes, J. P. (2012). The determinants of sovereign credit spread changes in the Euro-zone. *Journal of International Financial Markets, Institutions and Money*, *22*(2), 278–304. doi:10.1016/j.intfin.2011.09.007

Öniş, Z., & Kutlay, M. (2012). Ekonomik Bütünleşme/Siyasal Parçalanmışlık Paradoksu: Avro Krizi ve Avrupa Birliğinin Geleceği. *Uluslararası İlişkiler*, *9*(33), 3–22.

Puig, M. G., & Rivero, S. S. (2014). Causality and contagion in EMU sovereign debt markets. *International Review of Economics & Finance*, *33*, 12–27. doi:10.1016/j.iref.2014.03.003

Reinhart, C. M., & Rogoff, K. S. (2010). *From financial crash to debt crisis*. Cambridge, MA: NBER Working Paper No.15795.

Roman, A., & Bilan, I. (2012). The Euro area sovereign debt crisis and the role of ECB's monetary policy. *Procedia Economics and Finance*, *3*, 763–768. doi:10.1016/S2212-5671(12)00227-4

Santis, R. A. (2014). The euro area sovereign debt crisis: Identifying flight-to-liquidity and the spillover mechanisms. *Journal of Empirical Finance*, *26*, 150–170. doi:10.1016/j.jempfin.2013.12.003

Tanzi, V., & Schuknecht, L. (2000). Public spending. In *The 20th century a global perspective*. Cambridge, UK: Cambridge University Press. doi:10.1017/CBO9780511625800.017

Teica, R. A. (2012). Analysis of the public debt sustainability in the economic and monetary union. *Procedia Economics and Finance*, *3*, 1081–1087. doi:10.1016/S2212-5671(12)00277-8

Tobin, J. (2000). Financial globalization. *World Development*, *28*(6), 1101–1104. doi:10.1016/S0305-750X(00)00008-5

Ureche-Rangau, L., & Burietz, A. (2013). One crisis, two crises...the subprime crisis and the European sovereign debt problems. *Economic Modelling*, *35*, 35–44. doi:10.1016/j.econmod.2013.06.026

Vallée, S. (2014). From mutual insurance to fiscal federalism: Rebuilding the Economic and Monetary Union after the demise of the Maastricht architecture. *Inter Economics*, *138*, 49–62. doi:10.1016/j.inteco.2013.11.003

Wignall, A. B. (2011). Solving the financial and sovereign debt crisis in Europe. *Financial Market Trends- OECD Journal*, (2), 1-23.

KEY TERMS AND DEFINITIONS

Economic and Monetary Union: The Economic and Monetary Union is the cooperation of the European Union towards achieving use of a single currency within a Single Market.

Eurozone: Eurozone is the group of the European Union Member States, which accepts Euro as their common currency and the sole legal tender.

Fiscal Discipline: It refers to a budget where public revenues are equal to the public spending.

Fiscal Policy: Fiscal policy is a government policy that uses all public spending, public revenue and public borrowing instruments to achieve economic stability through economic development and growth.

Integration: The act of combining parts with different characteristics together to form a whole.

Maastricht Criteria: Maastricht Criteria are all the economic and financial conditions that the European Union Member States are required to meet in order to join the Economic and Monetary Union.

Public Deficit: Public deficit is the amount by which public expenditure of a state exceeds its public revenue over a fiscal year. It increases public borrowing.

Subprime Mortgage Crisis: It is the global financial crisis that started in the US in the second half of 2008, following the Lehman Brothers' bankruptcy. This crisis had negative impacts on banking and insurance sectors, and then investments and trade in the US, before influencing the whole World.

Chapter 2
Unemployment and its Impact on Economic Growth in the European Union:
An Evidence from Panel Data Analysis

Murat Cetin
Namik Kemal University, Turkey

Hakan Cavlak
Namik Kemal University, Turkey

Davuthan Gunaydın
Namik Kemal University, Turkey

Birol Topcu
Namik Kemal University, Turkey

ABSTRACT

Unemployment has become an increasingly serious economic and social problem in many European countries. Theoretically, unemployment has a negative effect on economic growth and development. This chapter examines the impact of unemployment on economic growth in 15 EU countries from 1984 to 2012 by using several panel data techniques. Panel unit root tests suggest that the series employed in the study are stationary at first differences. In other words, the series are integrated of order one, I(1). Panel cointegration tests show that the variables are cointegrated over the period implying a long-run relationship between the variables. Panel OLS estimations show that the impact of unemployment on economic growth is negative and statistically significant. This indicates that unemployment decreases economic growth in these countries. Finally, Granger causality tests based on vector error correction model suggest that there is a bi-directional causality between the variables in the short and long run. The findings may provide some policy implications.

INTRODUCTION

Recently, unemployment and economic growth are among the most discussed topics in European countries (Christopoulos, 2004; Adanu, 2005; Tatoglu, 2011; Dogru, 2013). Firstly, the problem of unemployment has increasingly deepened from the second half of the 2000s. The dimension of this problem can be expressed by some statistics. According to EUROSTAT (2014), unemployment has raised from 4% in the 1960s to over 10% in the 2000s. The number of persons unemployed

DOI: 10.4018/978-1-4666-7308-3.ch002

reached 26.553 in November 2013. Compared to a year ago, unemployment increased by 278.000 in the EU28. Among the Member States, the highest unemployment rates were registered in Greece (27.4%), Cyprus (17.3%), Portugal (15.5%), Italy (12.7%), Ireland (12.3%) and Latvia (12.0%) in October 2013. These developments emphasize the need to introduce measures overcoming unemployment both at the national and the European level.

According to the macroeconomists, unemployment which is a main socio-economic problem adversely affects the process of economic growth. It can be said that the countries which witness the largest decreases in growth rate are nearly the same countries having the highest unemployment rates. The highest decreases in growth rate were recorded in Cyprus (-5.4%), Greece (-3.9%), Italy (-1.9%) and Portugal (-1.4%) between 2012 and 2013 (EUROSTAT, 2014). The relationship between unemployment and economic growth brings to mind the Okun's law which is well known as a major macroeconomic theory.

The main purpose of this paper is to examine the link between unemployment and economic growth. Applying several panel data techniques, we investigate the cointegration and causal relationships between unemployment and economic growth in European countries. We consider 15 EU countries from 1984 to 2012. For this purpose, we firstly examine the stationarity of the variables. So, several panel unit root tests developed by Maddala & Wu (1999), Breitung (2000) and Im, Pesaran & Shin (IPS) (2003) are employed. Using several panel cointegration techniques presented by Pedroni (1999), Kao (1999), Maddala & Wu (1999), we secondly examine the presence of long run relationship between the variables. Thirdly, we estimate the long run parameter through the panel OLS method. Finally, we investigate the existence of the long and short run causal relationship between the variables by employing panel vector error correction model (PVECM). Empirical results obtained from this paper may provide policy implications.

The remainder of the paper is organized as follows. We discuss the economic theory related to the Okun's law in Section 2. We also discuss the empirical literature in this section. Section 3 deals with the model and data. Section 4 examines econometric methodology used in this paper. Empirical results obtained from several tests are presented in Section 5. Finally, Section 6 provides conclusions and some policy implications.

LITERATURE REVIEW

The law developed by Okun (1962) implies the presence of an inverse link between the unemployment rate and real GDP. Basically, Okun (1962)'s law states that a one percentage point change in unemployment rate reveals three percent inverse change in the real output. Therefore, Okun's law suggests a statistical relationship between unemployment and economic growth. In the next section, the specifications used by Okun will be explained in detail.

Empirically, a number of studies have investigated the relationship between unemployment and real output (Freeman, 2001; Christopoulos, 2004; Adanu, 2005; Huang & Lin, 2008; Villaverde & Maza, 2009; Ceylan & Sahin, 2010; Tatoglu, 2011; Dogru, 2013; Elshamy, 2013). Using panel seemengly unrelated regressions, Freeman (2001) try to analyze the Okun's law for 10 industrialized countries during the period 1962-1995. In this study, the evidences supporting the validity of Okun's law are found in all countries.

Applying several panel unit root and cointegration techniques, Christopoulos (2004) analyzes the Okun's law in Greece at a regional level over the period 1971-1993. The empirical results obtained from the study suggest that there is a long-run relationship in 6 out of 13 regions and Okun's law is valid for these regions.

Using a novel smooth-time-varying-parameter approach, Huang & Lin (2008) estimate the Okun's coefficients in USA over the period 1948:Q1-

2006:Q1. Empirical results reveal that the mean estimates related to the Okun's coefficients indicate large variations for the period. Empirical results also reveal that the findings of classical fixed-parameter model may be incorrect.

Villaverde & Maza (2009) examine the Okun's law for the Spanish regions from 1980 to 2004. The results of regression analysis indicate that the Okun's law is valid for most of the regions considered in this study. The paper shows that the presence of different coefficients across regions are somewhat attributed to differences in productivity growth.

Ceylan & Sahin (2010) examine the validity of Okun's law for Turkish economy from 1950 to 2007 by employing time series data. The study uses cointegration methodology based on TAR and M-TAR models. The results reveal an empirical evidence that Okun's law is valid for Turkey.

Tatoglu (2011) examines the long and short run relationships between unemployment rate and real output in European countries from 1977 to 2008. Several time-series and panel techniques are employed in the study. Estimation results provide an empirical evidence supporting the Okun's law in most of European countries.

Dogru (2013) investigates the relationship between unemployment rate and real output in Euro Area by employing annual data over the period 2000-2012. This study uses panel error correction model and cointegration method to test the Okun's law. Empirical results reveal a long run relationship between the variables. Empirical results also reveal an evidence in favor of Okun's law in most of European countries.

Elshamy (2013) attempts to empirically test the Okun's law in Egypt for the period 1970-2010 by using CDRW and error correction model. The results show a long run relationship between the variables. The results also show that the Okun's coefficient is statically significant and negative in the short and long runs.

MODEL AND DATA

Okun (1962) considers two classical models called "first-difference" and "gap" specifications. The first-difference model can be expressed as follows:

$$y_t - y_{t-1} = \alpha + \beta\left(u_t - u_{t-1}\right) + \varepsilon_t \tag{1}$$

where y_t and u_t denote the logarithm of real output and unemployment rate, respectively. α is the intercept, ε is the error term, β is Okun's coefficient and expected to be less than zero. This coefficient measures the impact of changes in unemployment rate on real output. On the other hand, the gap model is given by

$$y_t - y_t^* = \alpha + \beta\left(u_t - u_t^*\right) + \varepsilon_t \tag{2}$$

where y^* and u^* are the corresponding potential values. In this specification, $y_t - y_t^*$ and $u_t - u_t^*$ represent the output gap and unemployment gap, respectively. Using panel form, Okun's law can be expressed as follows

$$ln\left(\frac{y_{it}}{y_{it}^*}\right) = \beta_i ln\left(\frac{u_{it}}{u_{it}^*}\right) + \varepsilon_{it}\; i = 1,2,\ldots\ldots,N;\; t = 1,2,\ldots\ldots,N \tag{3}$$

Equation (3) requires information about the values of y_{it}^* and u_{it}^* variables. Therefore, Prachowny (1993) suggests an alternative model in relation to Okun's law. We use this specification expressed as follows:

$$lny_{it} = \alpha_i + \gamma_i t + \beta_i lnu_{it} + \varepsilon_{it} \tag{4}$$

where *t* is the time variable and captures the long-run growth which cannot be explained by the model. y_{it} and u_{it} represent real GDP and unemployment rate, respectively. We use annual data covering the period of 1984 to 2012 gathered from World Bank's World Development Indicators, 2014. The variables are converted to natural logarithms. The countries considered in this study are Germany, Austria, Belgium, Denmark, Finland, France, Netherland, Ireland, Spain, Italy, Luxemburg, Portugal, Greece, Sweden and United Kingdom. Since the logarithm of y_{it} and u_{it} are potentially non-stationary variables, the long run relationship may be examined between the variables. According to Engle & Granger (1987), if y_{it} and u_{it} are both $I(1)$ the cointegration relationship may exist between the variables.

Table 1 presents the variables and their descriptive statistics. The cross-sectional dimension is 15 units and the time dimension is 29 years. In total, there are 435 observations for each variable. On the other hand, the plots of y_{it} and u_{it} series in natural logarithm are presented in Figure 1.

ECONOMETRIC METHODOLOGY

We conduct a panel data analysis which has several major advantages over a time-series analysis. Our econometric strategy consists of four steps to investigate the cointegration and causality relationships between unemployment rate and real GDP. In the first step, the order of integration in the variables is examined. The second step tests for panel cointegration. The Okun's coefficient is estimated in the third step. The Granger causality based on PVECM is tested in final step.

In this study, we use several panel unit root tests presented by Maddala & Wu (1999), Breitung (2000) and Im et al. (2003) to investigate the integration degree of the variables. All the methods are well known as first-generation panel unit root tests. Maddala & Wu (1999) suggest the use of a Fisher-type test well known as ADF-Fisher. This test can be expressed as follows:

$$p_{\lambda} = -2\sum_{i=1}^{N} \log_{e} \pi_{i} \tag{5}$$

The test is based on combining the p-values of the test-statistic for a unit root in each cross-sectional unit. The test is asymptotically χ^2 distributed with $2N$ degrees of freedom. An advantage of this test is that it may overcome unbalanced panels. In this test, N can be finite or infinite. The null and alternative hypotheses are the same as in the IPS test. Applying the ADF estimation equation in each cross-section, the ADF t-statistic for each individual series are computed and then the corresponding p-value from the empirical distribution of ADF t-statistic are found. Finally, the Fisher-test statistics are compared with the appropriate χ^2 critical values.

Breitung (2000) and IPS (2003) tests uses the following ADF specification:

$$y_{it} = \alpha y_{it-1} + \sum_{j-1}^{pi} \beta_{ij} \Delta y_{it-j} + X_{it}' \delta + \varepsilon_{it} \tag{6}$$

Table 1. Descriptive statistics

Balanced panel: N=15, T=29, Observations=435						
Variable	**Unit**	**Mean**	**Median**	**Std. Dev.**	**Min.**	**Max.**
$\ln y_{it}$	Gross domestic product, 2005=100, $	28.544	28.570	0.150	28.241	28.753
$\ln u_{it}$	Unemployment rate	2.039	2.054	0.216	1.589	2.424

Figure 1. The Plots of $\ln y_{it}$ *and* $\ln u_{it}$ *series*

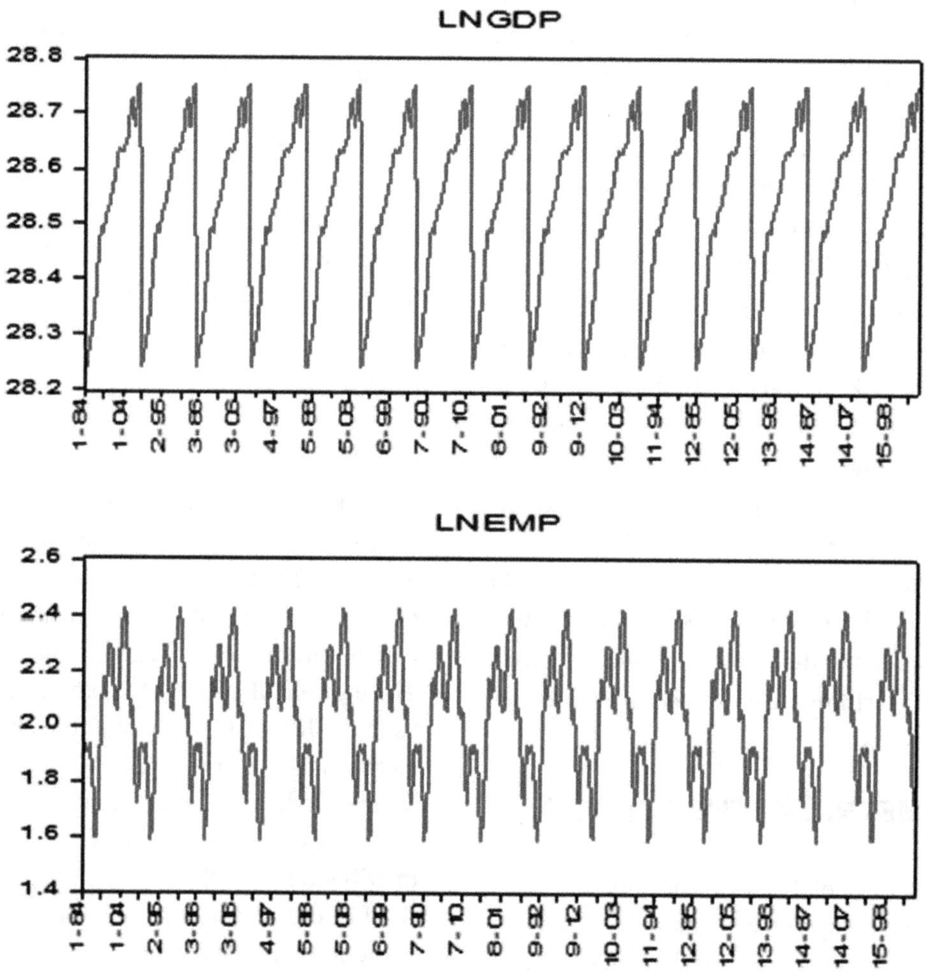

In Breitung test, $\alpha = \rho - 1$. The null and alternative hypotheses for the tests can be written as:

$H_0 : \alpha = 0$ there is a unit root
$H_1 : \alpha < 0$ there is no unit root

In IPS test, the null and alternative hypotheses can be expressed as:

$H_0 : \alpha = 0$ for all *i*
$H_1 : \alpha_i < 0$ *i=1,..,N₁*
$H_1 : \alpha_i = 0$ *i=N₁+1,...,N*

IPS test allows for heterogeneity in the value of the autoregressive coefficient. In this test, the *t*-statistic is an average and can be computed as:

$$\bar{t} = \frac{1}{n} \sum_{i=1}^{N} t_i \quad (7)$$

where t_i is the individual ADF *t*-statistics for the unit root test.

IPS and ADF-Fisher tests allow for individual unit root processes. In these tests, we can obtain a panel-specific result by combining of individual unit root tests. Fisher-type test has several advantages over the IPS test. Firstly, it does not require a balanced panel. Secondly, it can use different lag lengths in the individual ADF regressions.

In this study, we use Kao (1999), Pedroni (1999) and Johansen-Fisher panel cointegration methods to examine the presence of cointegration relationship between the variables. The null hypothesis for these panel cointegration tests is that there is no cointegration in cross-sectionally independent panels.

Kao (1999) suggests two different cointegration tests such as the DF and ADF types in panel data methodology. For the ADF test, the following regression is considered

$$\hat{u}_{it} = \delta\hat{u}_{it-1} + \sum\nolimits_{j=1}^{p}\psi_j\Delta\hat{u}_{it-j} + v_{it} \quad (8)$$

With the null hypothesis of no cointegration, Kao (1999) constructs the ADF test statistics as follows:

$$ADF = \frac{t_{ADF} + \sqrt{\dfrac{6N\hat{\sigma}_v}{2\hat{\sigma}_{0v}}}}{\sqrt{\dfrac{\hat{\sigma}_{0v}}{2\hat{\sigma}_v^2} + \dfrac{3\hat{\sigma}_v^2}{10\hat{\sigma}_{0v}^2}}} \quad (9)$$

where t_{ADF} is the t statistics of ρ, $\widehat{\sigma}_v^2 = \sum_{yy} - \sum_{yx}\sum_{xx}^{-1}$ and $\widehat{\sigma}_{0v}^2 = \widehat{\Omega}_{yy} - \widehat{\Omega}_{yx}\widehat{\Omega}_{xx}^{-1}$. $\widehat{\Omega}_i$ denote long run variance of the residuals. The asymptotic distributions of ADF converge to a standard normal distribution $N(0, 1)$.

Pedroni (1999) presents seven Philips-Perron type tests for cointegration in a panel context. Of these seven statistics, four are within-dimension statistics and three are between-dimension statistics. All these tests allow for heterogeneity. These test statistics are distributed asymptotically as a normal distribution.

Pedroni (1999) firstly computes the residuals from the following cointegration regression:

$$y_{it} = \alpha_i + \delta_i t + \beta_{1i}x_{1it} + \beta_{2i}x_{2it} + \ldots + \beta_{Mi}x_{Mit} + e_{it}$$
$$t = 1,\ldots, T\,;\, i = 1,\ldots,N \quad (10)$$

where T, N and M represent the number of observation over time, the number of the individual members in the panel and the number of regression variables. x and y are assumed to be integrated of order one. $\beta_{1i}, \beta_{2i}, \ldots\ldots, \beta_{Mi}$ are the slope coefficients and α_i is specific intercept. To estimate the residuals from equation (10), the seven statistics developed by Pedroni are used. After the computation of the test statistics, Pedroni indicates that the standardized statistic is asymptotically normally distributed.

Finally, we also employ the Johansen-Fisher based tests proposed by Maddala & Wu (1999) to investigate the long run relation between the variables. This panel cointegration methodology is based on Johansen's cointegration trace test and maximum eigenvalue test.

The cointegration tests do not provide information about the existence and direction of causal relationship between the variables. Therefore, we employ a PVECM to investigate the presence and direction of causality between the variables. This model considers the augmented VAR system. This system includes the Error-Correction Term (ECT) to the classical VAR model as an additional variable. The main characteristic of the model is that it can distinguish the short-run and long-run causality. A PVECM can be expressed as follows:

$$\Delta Y_{it} = \theta_{1i} + \delta_{1i}ECT_{it-1} + \sum\nolimits_{k=1}^{p}\theta_{12ik}\Delta_{it-k} + \varepsilon_{it} \quad (11)$$

where Δ, ECT and p refer the first difference of the variable, the error-correction term and the lag length, respectively. ECT are the residuals estimated from the long-run model, $\delta_{1i}\, ECT_{it}$ refers the long-run equilibrium relationship among the variables. If θ_{12} or δ_{1i} are not equal to zero, there is a short/long run causal relationship.

EMPIRICAL RESULTS

Table 2 presents the results of IPS, ADF-Fisher and Breitung panel unit root tests. The results reported in this table reveal that the null hypothesis cannot be rejected implying that all the variables are non-stationary at the level. The results also reveal that the null hypothesis can be rejected implying that the variables are stationary at the first difference. Thus, the series are integrated of one.

The results obtained from Pedroni, Kao and Johansen-Fisher cointegration tests are reported in Table 3. Pedroni panel-v and panel-ADF tests reveal that there is a long run relationship between unemployment rate and real GDP at the 1% and 10% significance levels, respectively. Kao ADF-*t* test shows that there is a long run relationship between the variables at the 5% significance level. Johansen-Fisher tests indicate a similar result at the 1% significance level. Thus, we find a long run relationship between the variables over the period.

After determining the cointegration relationship between the variables, we estimate Okun's parameter through the panel OLS method. The parameter is found negative and statistically significant at the 1% level. The results show that there is a negative relationship between the variables. The results provide an evidence supporting the validity of Okun's law. The diagnostic tests such as the Breusch-Pagan heteroscedasticity and Baltagi-Lee serrial correlation test are conducted. The results show that there are serial correlation and heteroscedasticity problems in the model. Therefore, in the study the process of AR(1) and the correction of White cross-section are performed to overcome these problems.

Panel findings reveal that unemployment is an important determinant of economic growth in these countries over the period. This is in agreement with Okun (1962), Christopoulos (2004), Villaverde & Maza (2009), Ceylan & Sahin (2010), Elshamy (2013) and Dogru (2013).

Finally, we apply the Granger causality test based on PVECM. The Granger causality results are presented in table 5. The coefficients of ECT's are found negative and statistically significant as expected. The results imply that there is a bi-directional causal relation between the variables in the long run. The results also imply that there is a bi-directional causal relation between the variables in the short run.

Table 2. Panel unit root test results

Variables	IPS Test Statistics	ADF-Fisher Test Statistics	Breitung Test Statistics
Panel A: Level			
$\ln y_{it}$	1.747	11.517	1.093
$\ln u_{it}$	0.414	18.849	-1.159
Panel B: First Difference			
$\Delta \ln y_{it}$	-10.934 [a][0.000]	156.975 [a][0.000]	-15.538 [a][0.000]
$\Delta \ln u_{it}$	-6.440 [a][0.000]	91.604 [a][0.000]	-11.640 [a][0.000]

Note: Δ is the first difference operator. The *p*-values are given in parenthesis. AIC is used to select the optimal lag length. [a] denotes significance at the 1% level. The tests contain the results of the model with intercept and trend.

Table 3. Panel cointegration test results

Cointegration Tests	Test Statistics
Panel A: Pedroni	
Panel-v	12.151 a[0.000]
Panel-ADF	-1.445 c[0.074]
Panel B: Kao	
ADF-t	-1.803 b[0.035]
Panel B: Johansen-Fisher	
None (Trace)	84.66 a[0.000]
At most 1 (Trace)	25.71 [0.689]
None (Maximum-eigen)	85.70 a[0.000]
At most 1 (Maximum-eigen)	25.71 [0.689]

Note: The *p*-values are given in parenthesis. [a] and [b] denote significance at the 1 and 5% level, respectively. Pedroni and Johansen-Fisher cointegration tests results include the model with trend.

Table 4. Panel estimation results (Dependent variable: $\ln y_{it}$*, Method: Panel OLS)*

Variables	Coefficients	T-Statistics	Standard Errors
$\ln u_{it}$	-0.103	-12.815 [a][0.000]	0.008
Constant	30.093	16.425 [a][0.000]	1.832
AR(1)	0.968	47.797 [a][0.000]	0.020
TREND	-0.016	-0.704 [0.481]	0.024
Diagnostic tests			
R^2		0.988	
Adjusted- R^2		0.987	
F statistic		11468.27 [a][0.000]	
Durbin-Watson statistic		2.067	
Breusch-Pagan statistic		262.435 [a][0.000]	
Baltagi-Lee statistic		292.695 [a][0.000]	

Note: The *p*-values are given in parenthesis. [a] denotes significance at the 1% level.

CONCLUSION AND POLICY IMPLICATIONS

In recent times, unemployment has been a main problem of the European Countries. According to the macroeconomists, unemployment decreases economic growth. So, it can be said that there is a negative relationship between the variables. In this study, the relationship between unemployment and economic growth is investigated for

Table 5. Panel granger causality test results

	Short Run	Long Run	Joint (Short Run and Long Run)
Dependent Variable: $\Delta \ln y_{it}$, Lag 4			
$\Delta \ln u_{it}$	33.089 [a][0.000]		
ECT_{it-1}		-0.201 [a][0.000]	
$\Delta \ln u_{it}$ /ECT			48.625 [a][0.000]
Dependent Variable: $\Delta \ln u_{it}$, Lag 4			
$\Delta \ln y_{it}$	31.782 [a][0.000]		
ECT_{it-1}		-0.397 [a][0.000]	
$\Delta \ln y_{it}$ /ECT			51.429 [a][0.000]

Note:Δ is the first difference operator. The *p*-values are given in parenthesis. AIC is used to select the optimal lag length. [a] denotes significance at the 1% level.

15 European countries. We use panel data from 1984 to 2012. Our econometric strategy includes four stages. In the first stage, the stationarity of the variables is examined by panel unit root tests. The presence of the cointegration relationship between the variables is analyzed in the second stage. The parameter's estimation is conducted in the third stage. The short and long run causal relations between the variables are investigated in the final stage.

Employing panel unit root tests, we find that the variables are integrated of order one. This allows for applying panel cointegration tests. The results of panel cointegration tests reveal that there is a long term relationship between unemployment and economic growth. According to panel OLS estimations, there is a negative and statistically significant relationship between the variables with the elasticity of -0.10. Finally, we find that there is a bi-directional causality between the variables in the short and long run.

We can infer some policy implications from the empirical results. The main empirical result is that unemployment has a negative impact on economic growth over the period. So, the governments should decrease the unemployment rate if they want to increase economic growth and welfare. First of all, there is a structural unemployment in most of European countries. In this respect, several reforms based on the tax and benefit system could be applied. So, it is possible to increase work incentives and wage flexibility. Additionally, labor mobility could be enhanced to fall in unemployment in these countries.

REFERENCES

Adanu, K. (2005). A cross-province comparison of Okun's coefficient for Canada. *Applied Economics*, *37*(5), 561–570. doi:10.1080/0003684042000201848

Breitung, J. (2000). The local power of some unit root tests for panel data. In B. Baltagi (Ed.), *Nonstationary panels, panel cointegration, and dynamic panels, advances in econometrics, 15* (pp. 161–178). Amsterdam: JAI. doi:10.1016/S0731-9053(00)15006-6

Ceylan, S., & Sahin, B. Y. (2010). Asymmetry in the relationship between unemployment and economic growth. *The Journal of Dogus University, 11*(2), 157–165.

Christopoulos, D. K. (2004). The relationship between output and unemployment: Evidence from Greek regions. *Regional Science, 83*(3), 611–620. doi:10.1111/j.1435-5597.2004.tb01928.x

Dogru, B. (2013). The link between unemployment rate and real output in Eurozone: A panel error correction approach. *Procedia: Social and Behavioral Sciences, 99*, 94–103. doi:10.1016/j.sbspro.2013.10.475

Elshamy, H. (2013). The relationship between unemployment and output in Egypt. *Procedia: Social and Behavioral Sciences, 81*, 22–26. doi:10.1016/j.sbspro.2013.06.381

Engle, R. F., & Granger, C. W. J. (1987). Co-integration and error correction: Representation, estimation and testing. *Econometrica, 55*(2), 251–276. doi:10.2307/1913236

EUROSTAT. (2014). *Selected principal European economic indicators*. Retrieved April 22, 2014, from http://epp.eurostat.ec.europa.eu/cache/ITY_PUBLIC/3-08012014-BP/EN/3-08012014-BP-EN.PDF

Freeman, D. G. (2001). Panel tests of Okun's law for ten industrial countries. *Economic Inquiry, 39*(4), 511–523. doi:10.1093/ei/39.4.511

Huang, H. C., & Lin, S. C. (2008). Smooth-time-varying Okun's coefficients. *Economic Modelling, 25*(2), 363–375. doi:10.1016/j.econmod.2007.06.009

Im, K. S., Pesaran, M. H., & Shin, Y. (2003). Testing for unit roots in heterogeneous panels. *Journal of Econometrics, 115*(1), 53–63. doi:10.1016/S0304-4076(03)00092-7

Kao, C. (1999). Spurious regression and residual-based tests for cointegration in panel data. *Journal of Econometrics, 90*(1), 1–44. doi:10.1016/S0304-4076(98)00023-2

Maddala, G. S., & Wu, S. (1999). A comparative study of unit root tests with panel data and a new simple test. *Oxford Bulletin of Economics and Statistics, 61*(Special Issue), 631–652. doi:10.1111/1468-0084.61.s1.13

Okun, A. (1962). Potential GNP: Its measurement and significance. American Statistical Association. In *Proceedings of the Business and Economic Statistics Section* (pp. 98-104). Academic Press.

Pedroni, P. (1999). Critical values for cointegration tests in heterogeneous panels with multiple regressors. *Oxford Bulletin of Economics and Statistics, 61*(s1), 653–670. doi:10.1111/1468-0084.61.s1.14

Prachowny, M. F. J. (1993). Okun's law: Theoretical foundations and revised estimates. *The Review of Economics and Statistics, 75*(2), 331–336. doi:10.2307/2109440

Tatoglu, F. Y. (2011). The long and short run effects between unemployment and economic growth in Europe. *The Journal of Dogus University, 12*(1), 99–113.

Villaverde, J., & Maza, A. (2009). The robustness of Okun's law in Spain, 1980-2004 regional evidence. *Journal of Policy Modeling, 31*(2), 289–297. doi:10.1016/j.jpolmod.2008.09.003

World Bank World Development Indicators Database. (2014). Retrieved May 5, 2014 from http://data.worldbank.org/data-catalog/world-development-indicators

KEY TERMS AND DEFINITIONS

Economic Growth: Economic growth implies the continuous improvements in per capita real GDP or real GDP. The differences in growth rates and the drivers of economic growth have been important topics discussed by many theorists and politicians. The increases in economic growth rates has positively affected economic development process. For example, it can be said that there is a significant relation between energy use, employment rate, productivity, foreign trade and economic growth.

European Union: The final stage of economic integration is economic and political union. European Union (EU) is an ideal example of this integration. Today, there are the 28 member countries that belong to the Union.

Panel Cointegration Methods: In investigating of the long run (cointegration) relationship between the variables, panel cointegration methods are employed. After determining the presence of long run relationship, next step is to estimate the long run relationship between the variables.

Panel Data Analysis: Panel data are a type of longitudinal data at different points in time. We can use this data which belong to states, companies, individuals, countries to investigate their relations. Fixed effects and random effects are well known as panel data techniques.

Panel Unit Root Tests: Panel unit root tests are used to investigate the stationarity properties of the panel data. It is the first step of the panel regression, panel cointegration or panel causality analyses.

Panel Vector Error Correction Model (PVECM): This model is first developed by Engle & Granger in the form of time series. Afterward, this technique adopted to the panel data. To examine the long run or short run causal relations between the variables, this method is usually applied.

Unemployment: Unemployment is accepted as one of the main macroeconomic problems for nearly all the countries. The causes, consequences and solutions for unemployment has been debated in many theoretical and empirical studies. An increase in unemployment rate decreases Gross Domestic Product (GDP) of a country. Therefore, there exists a negative relation between unemployment rate and economic growth.

Chapter 3
The Weakening of the Franco-German Tandem in Light of the Eurozone Crisis

Armağan Gözkaman
Beykent University, Turkey

ABSTRACT

Since the inception of the European integration process, the Franco-German axis is considered to be a major driving force. Even today, Europe moves faster in the presence of an entente between France and Germany. However, the harmonization of German and French positions is not quasi-automatic as it used to be. The desynchronization that occurred over time is based on various factors such as the German unification, the EU's enlargements, and the change in German self-perception. One of the contexts in which the divergences between Paris and Berlin can be seen is related to the Euro zone rescue operations. Germany came to the fore in the resolution process and made clear her preferences, which are not always truly supported by France. The drifting-apart that started after the end of the Cold War thus continues.

INTRODUCTION

Franco-German reconciliation was the biggest objective of the European construction. The two nations have even wanted to go further, by opting for a multi-dimensional rapprochement throughout the decades, thanks to the structures built together. The Franco-German Office of Youth, the famous couples of statespersons (from Mitterrand-Kohl to Merkozy) are the concrete manifestations of such efforts. Moving forth with new projects reveals the mutually perceived interest in preserving the tandem.

Compromise between Paris and Bonn (and later on, Berlin) has been a key to the progress in the European construction. But there have been occurrences in which the quasi-automaticity of this compromise was challenged. Besides, the Franco-German tandem does not veritably seem indispensable for the future of the European Union –in contrast to what was the case for decades. At this point, it is important to underscore that the positions of both sides do not always coincide. This is due to a change in time as a result of a multitude of factors (I) and exposed by the diverging positions in light of the Euro crisis (II).

DOI: 10.4018/978-1-4666-7308-3.ch003

THE LOWERING OF THE SYMMETRY BETWEEN FRANCE AND GERMANY

Despite her inglorious past, Germany has started to gain a privileged position in the European Community/Union to the detriment of her partner. To understand this change, one should look at the internal dynamics of Germany and the external factors, which include economic aspects.

Change of German Position in the European Union

Whereas the Franco-German tandem was traditionally led by the French, from 1990s on Germany has seen herself in an ostensibly different position. The latter is, first and foremost, the inevitable consequence of the unification. With a bigger population and gross domestic product (GDP) and with decades-long commitment to the principles of democracy, the new Germany had every right to see herself released from the restrictions of the history.

This reality was certainly perceived by the neighbors of Germany as well. The necessity to alleviate the fears of their partners was hence a necessity for Germany. As a consequence, the decision of unification has been simultaneous with the decision of further commitment to the "European" idea. This choice has inevitably been materialized by a firm position in the European monetary system which has also been a relief for Germany's European partners that feared the domination of a stronger Deutsche Mark.

Another important factor that has led to a new German position within the European structure is external to Germany. Every time they occurred, the successive enlargements tilted the center of gravity of the Community/Union in favor of Germany, both in economic and political terms. Just to give an example, the enlargement to Central and Eastern European countries was expected to result in an annual increase of 0,6% in German gross domestic product. This additional wealth, combined with a political re-positioning of Germany, could provide a discernible advantage to Berlin.

A change in German self-perception merits to be underscored as well. Gradually after the unification, Germany has felt free to pursue assertive politics in the international platform. The self-confident stance has been particularly salient with Gerhard Schröder's chancellorship between 1998 and 2005. The leader of the social democrat party displayed his predilections at the early stage of his term by refusing to attend the First and the Second World War commemorations. He delivered an unprecedented speech at the 60th anniversary of the *D-day* in which he stated that whereas the memories of France and Germany on Normandy landings were different, peace was the common belief shared by both sides, and that his country had found the path of civilized international community ("Commemorating 60th anniversary", 2004). The guilt of the Second-World-War remorse seems to have depleted.

A striking development directly linked to the 'new' German stance is witnessed during the negotiations that led to the Treaty of Nice. Back then, the French still had the nostalgia of the old days of European construction (when Paris was superior to Bonn in the political field and both capitals adhered firmly to the 'parity') while Germany claimed (and obtained) the abandonment of parity of votes in the Council because of its demographic superiority. To nobody's surprise, German request of a higher vote weighting did not meet with the sympathy of French delegation. The demand was in fact not unjustified, because Germany's population was 20 million greater than France. The reason why France objected was based on the principle of parity with Germany that had been maintained since the inception of the European Community. As a scholar makes the point, the firm stance of the then-Chancellor G. Schröder resulted in deep bilateral conflicts that had not been witnessed since Charles de Gaulle's empty chair policy of mid-1960s (Schild, 2011).

One of the reasons why the European Commission's proposal of a 'dual majority' system failed was French objection. Paris did not accept that a majority of member states and population be simultaneously imposed as a decision-making rule (Beach, 2006). During the negotiations on the Treaty Establishing a Constitution for the European Union and the Treaty of Lisbon, however, France consented to the double majority voting rule (55% of member states and 65% of the EU's population) in the Council. The alliance that Paris and Berlin could establish during these negotiations explains the change in French attitude (Krotz & Schild, 2013: 128).

Hence, the arrangements of 2000 stipulated the irreversible change in the Franco-German parity and the asymmetry has continued to reveal itself in the relations of the couple. This would indeed have an impact on the future relations between the two states in general, and the discussions concerning the management of the Euro crisis in particular. In addition to the broken symmetry, the economic superiority would put German authorities in a more advantageous position to determine the rules of the game so as to suit their national interests.

A Better Economic Performance: An Advantage for Germany

The macroeconomic landscape shows that Germany performs better than France. Figure 1 exposes the yearly change in the GDP growth: Although France has experienced a better growth rate than Germany in the period 1995 – 2005, the trend reversed from 2006 on –with the exception of the year 2009, when both economies were seriously hit by the crisis in Eurozone.

As revealed by Figure 2, the crisis in the Eurozone has a negative impact upon the balance between governmental expenditures and public revenue. In the period 2002-2007, France performed better than Germany in terms of governmental debt. However, from 2008 on, Germany outperformed France. It is worth noting that the gap between the two states widened continuously after this date.

Sales to the outside world constitute another variable that can be taken to demonstrate a disadvantage that France has vis-à-vis Germany. Two observations can be made on the statistical data of exports. The first one is about the comparison

Figure 1. Annual GDP growth rate in France and Germany

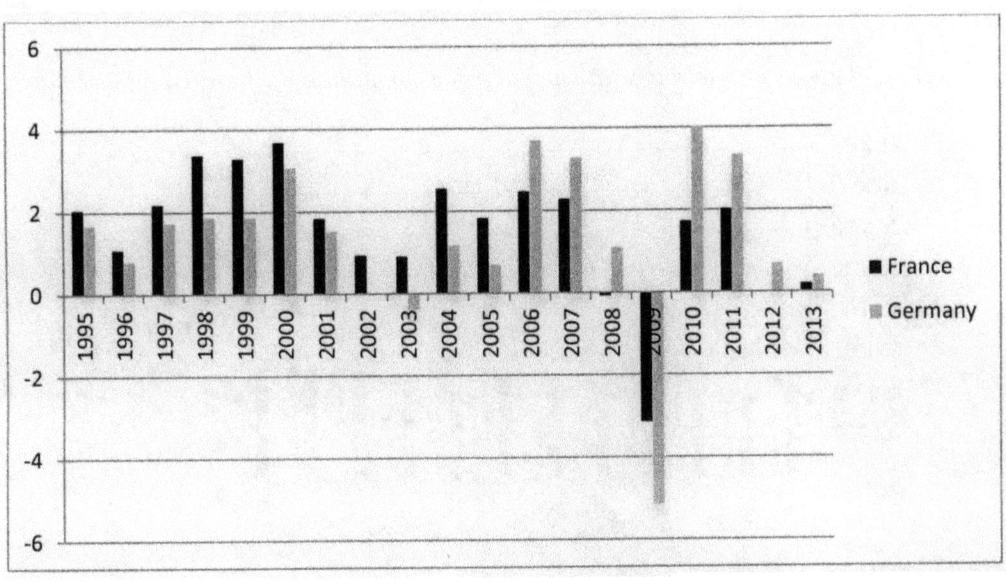

Figure 2. General government gross debt - annual data (percentage of GDP)

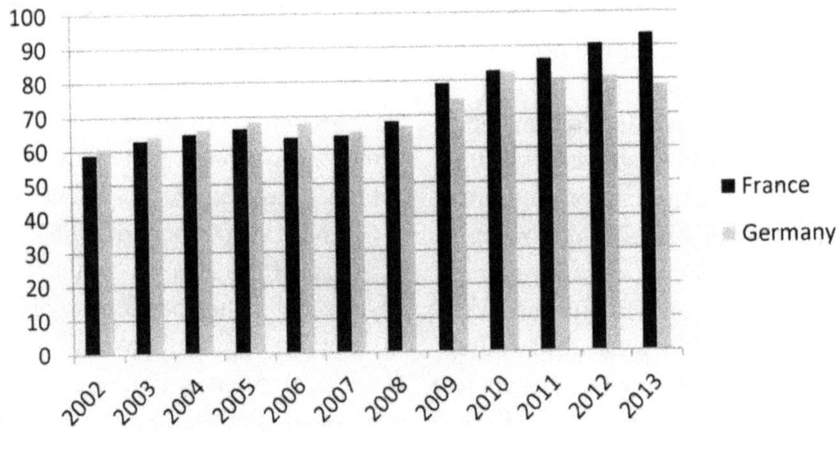

of the export volumes of the two countries. Obviously, Germany has been in a better situation vis-à-vis France.

In addition, the Germany/France divergence of exportation has tended to increase in time, and the trend is even more perceptible after 2008 despite a literally negligible decrease in 2013. As shown by the table below (built upon the data provided by Figure 3), there has been a steady increase for the period 2002-2012, and in 2013, there was also a negligible decrease in the ratio.

The second observation concerns the similarity of the fluctuation of the export levels. Between 2002 and 2008, one can speak of a constant increase in German exports. The situation is slightly different on the other side of Rhine. France underperformed in 2003 compared to 2002. Both countries share the trend of increase of exportations from 2009 on.

Further remarks can be made by taking into consideration the overall consequence of foreign trade. The difference between the exports and the imports -as evidenced by Figure 4- suggests once again a better performance in the German case. France has a negative balance sheet from 2005 on, despite some improvement after the nadir

Figure 3. Exports of goods and services (at current prices in million €), France and Germany

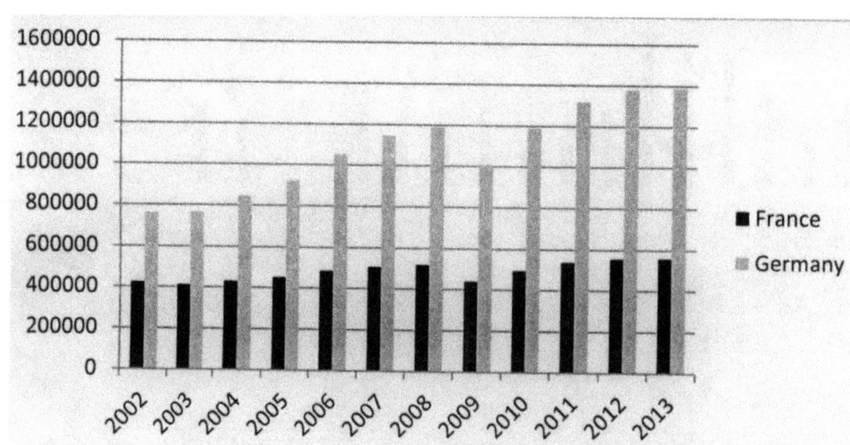

Table 1. The change in the export ratio (Germany/France) between 2002 and 2013

Year	2002	2003	2004	2005	2006	2007	2008	2009	2010	2011	2012	2013
Ratio	1,792	1,864	1,956	2,029	2,167	2,260	2,286	2,288	2,404	2,455	2,477	2,476

she reached in 2011. In Germany, however, the revenue generated by the exportations has not been less than the import value.

The partial conclusion is that Germany did better than France in dealing with the Eurozone crisis in all three criteria taken above: Exportation, balance of payments and governmental debt. This "loss of the race" to Germany has further materialized after the decrease of international credibility in French economy.

Confirmation of the Degradation in French Economy by Standard and Poors

On 13 January 2012, Standard & Poor's (S&P) Ratings Services reduced the credit ratings of nine euro zone countries on the grounds that European policymakers were not capable of fully addressing the systemic stresses in the Eurozone ("Standard & Poors", 2012). This move deprived France of the AAA rating, the highest possible grade that can be given to a country. It consequently spurred a political debate in French domestic scene and abroad.

If the new rating points to a lower rank (which is deemed inacceptable for the then *hyperprésident* Sarkozy, it does not signify a considerable deterioration of French economy. This argument constituted the immediate reaction of French government. Nevertheless, the loss of the triple-A status had national as well as European-level implications. What is lost is in fact a *national treasure*: France scored AAA since 1975.

On the eve of the presidential race, Sarkozy would have liked to see the rating unchanged, for the negative evaluation of French economy could be an argument for the Socialist party to use against him. That is exactly what happened: The opposition severely criticized Sarkozy administra-

Figure 4. Balance of payments (at current prices in million €), France and Germany

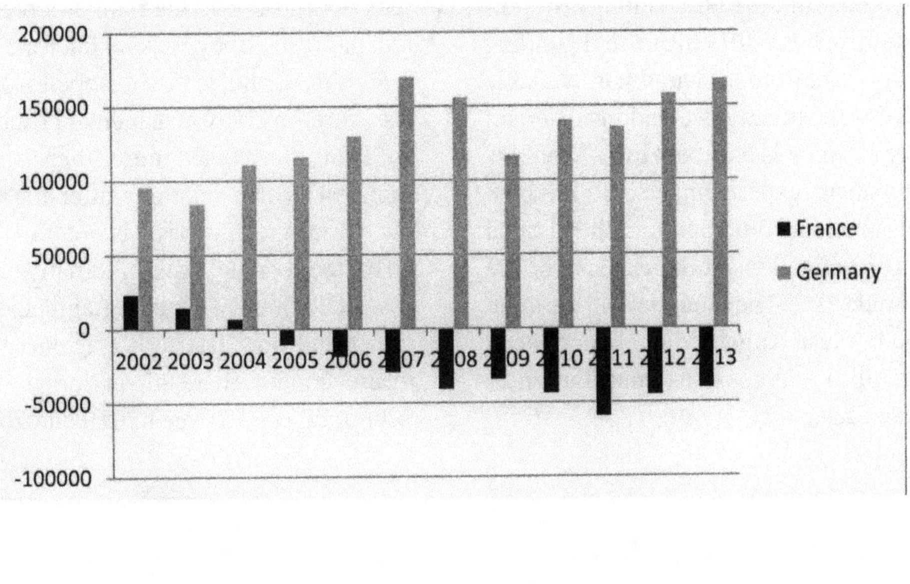

tion. For François Hollande, it was a policy that was degraded and not France herself. According to Jean-Marc Ayrault, member of the Socialist Party (PS), the downgrade has led to a feeling of humiliation. A parallel view was expressed by another PS member, Jean-Marie Le Guen: A considerable failure for N. Sarkozy, with grave consequences for France ("Perte AAA", 2012).

The second type of repercussions touched upon the status and prestige of France in the European level. Franco-German symmetry is important for France. On this account, the loss of a triple-A credit rating has been bad news for French authorities. This was especially important for having a say on financial and economic questions in the European Union. The note was in fact a veritable national treasure, in the words of Alain Minc, Sarkozy's advisor ("Alain Minc", 2011).

It was expected that the downgrade of nine EU member states by the S&P would eventually have an effect for the European Financial Stability Facility (EFSF) as well, simply because the fund's rating is based on the ratings of the countries that provide guarantees for capital. It is also important to note that the downgrade of France and Austria, which are among the biggest contributors of the fund, deprived the fund of an adequate number of guarantors to maintain its AAA rating. Thus, to nobody's surprise, S&P concluded that the EFSF should be cut to AA+ from AAA.

The downgrade of the EFSF's rating is important because it will be difficult to find funding for EU members in trouble. The funds available for the EFSF were already deemed insufficient; with a lower rating, it is expected to be even less effective. Financial experts underscore the possibility that investors could opt for bonds issued by other top-rated nations at the expense of the EFSF (Yousouf, 2012) The situation is all the more problematic because Angela Merkel announced that Berlin will not increase its contribution to the European fund.

Operational since August 2010, the EFSF aims to safeguard financial stability in Europe by extending financial assistance to euro zone states. In order to achieve this objective, the EFSF issues bonds or other debt instruments on the capital markets.

FRANCO-GERMAN DIVERGENCES IN DEALING WITH THE EURO CRISIS

The differences of opinion between the French and German decision-makers concern the solutions that they emphasise. This leads, indeed, to different approaches on banking arrangements and the system of Euro loans.

The Differing Views of Solutions to the Crisis

Historical legacy, economic cultures and not-always-overlapping priorities result in a difference of approach between Germany and France (Pisani-Ferry, 2006). It has resurfaced again when economic governance was on top of the European agenda after the sovereign debt crisis. Germany firmly subscribes to the Stability and Growth Pact (SGP) and welcomes the idea to add new rules to the game so as to evaluate and to guarantee the competitiveness of the Eurozone members. France sees politics above the market forces and wants that national policy-makers interpret the existing rules to coordinate fiscal policies and have the last word on crisis management (Schild, 2011).

That there was more than one stage of Franco-German relations after the breakout of the sovereign debt crisis is noteworthy. Up until 2010, the 'couple' seeks alternative partners and has difficulties of reaching agreements on how to act and how fast to act against the growing macroeconomic hardship in Europe (Stark, 2012; Schild, 2011). Between 2010 and 2012, the two states concurred on the revitalisation of the SGP, the necessity of a European semester, the controversial Competitiveness Pact and the adoption of a new intergovernmental treaty for a budgetary discipline (Stark, 2012; Willis, 2011, "France and Germany", 2011; Willsher & Chu, 2011).

The election of François Hollande to the post of president in 2012 opened a new era. Yet, again, this period can be divided in two. Until the grand coalition of Christian Democrats and the Social Democrats, it had been difficult to reach unity of German and French positions. To talk about the re-building of the 'couple' was easier after this period, possibly due to the existence of a political component in the government which belongs to the same political line as the French ruling party. Hence, in February 2014, Hollande and Merkel had the willingness to give an image of a couple more united than ever. This attitude was remarked by the unity on foreign policy issues such as Ukraine and Africa and some *rapprochement* and pledge of cooperation on the delicate topics including the taxation of financial transactions and the widening of energy transition (Biseau & Alemagna, 2014).

Against this background, there have been many cases on which Hollande's and Merkel's positions opposed each other, as witnessed through the concept of 'economic government' with a budget, a right to borrow, an integrated fiscal system and a veritable president asserted by the French president ("Hollande proposes Eurozone", 2013). As will be shown below, German stance is mostly against the projects of pooling European debt. Merkel prefers rather a 'common understanding' in the European Union ("Split persists", 2013). What she has in mind reflects the need of reform that will provide the EU with a remedy to the crisis.

Merkel's 'common understanding' can be qualified as a way of making the EU strong and generating its growth. The essence of the concept exposes the difference between the two leaders: While F. Hollande has a predilection to favor policies of spending to realize growth, Merkel focuses more on austerity as a means to make growth sustainable. For Merkel, EU member states must agree upon a common definition of what will make a state competitive ("Les gouvernments européens", 2013).

As Pierre Lellouche reminds, the last years have witnessed an infertile dialogue between Paris and Berlin: The former defended the solidarity with southern European states without having the means to accomplish it while the second insisted on the fact that rigor and growth were not in antagonism (2011). While sticking to this position, Germany has sometimes been criticized for maximizing her own interests before those of the EU. This created the basis upon which the discussions on the German *diktat* came to the fore. The French Minister of Productive Recovery went as far as accusing Germany to have committed several egoist acts that were "dangerous for France, absurd for Germany and suicidal for Europe" (Montébourg, 2011).

Mixed Reactions to Banking Arrangements

In December 2013, EU member states could make an important move of financial solidarity by agreeing on the Single Resolution Mechanism (SRM). In the European Commission's view, the latter was a key to a stronger single market and a stronger monetary union. The logic of the SRM laid on the impossibility to supervise banks while leaving the resolution of banking problems to national authorities ("Banking Union").

With a rescue fund that would reach 55 billion by 2024, the SRM was not really a panacea for future crises. Neither were its prerogatives significant compared to the US Federal Deposit Insurance Corporation. Nevertheless, reaching an agreement on a topic where divergences prevailed was a success by itself (Gould, 2014). Besides, it was a step forward towards the banking union ("Banking Union"). The SRM was in line with the commitment reached at the European Union's

Brussels summit of October 2012 (European Council Conclusions, 2012). Back then, the deal could satisfy Paris and Berlin simultaneously. For the former, it was a good thing that the mechanism provided for the possibility to monitor all of the banks in the Eurozone. The fact that no exact starting date was fixed was in conformity with the German preference of a cautious progress. For Merkel, the quality of supervision was more important than its speed (Jackson, 2012).

Within the framework drawn above, the SRM can be considered a case in which Franco-German agreement could be grasped by the reconciliation of diverging stances into the same European-level agreement. Nevertheless, it did not mean a total satisfaction for these two states. The funding will be ensured by a tax paid by the banks equaling to 1% of covered deposits. France will be the main contributor under a national target with 21% of the total funding whereas Germany's share will reach 35% in case of a European calculation. Paris recommends that the European target level be phased in, on the grounds that the national contributions spread over a decade. In such a case, the percentage of German contribution will decline to 28%, leading still to a difference of an approximate four billion Euros between the two sides of the Rhine. (Barker, 2014). This proposal aims to reduce German resistance to the European target level and prevent a massive loss to French top lenders.

A common attitude of the two states has been much easier to reach against European Commission project for banning the EU's biggest banks from speculative trading. The plan was to prevent the banks from proprietary trading, a method wherein they use their own funds for higher profit, rather than customers' deposits ("Barnier launches EU bid", 2014). Michel Barnier, the EU's Commissioner for internal market and services, explained the purpose of the initiative as follows:

This legislation deals with the small number of very large banks which otherwise might still be too-big-to-fail, too-costly-to save, too-complex-to-resolve. The proposed measures will further strengthen financial stability and ensure taxpayers don't end up paying for the mistakes of banks." ("Structural reform, 2014).

The European Commission defended its initiative by stating that the proprietary trading involved many risks with no "tangible benefits for the bank's clients or the wider economy" ("Structural reform", 2014). Yet, the initiative has been subject to criticism. In fact, proprietary trading had been severely reduced after the financial crisis of 2008 ("Europe backs down", 2014). Besides, some observers questioned the proposal's effectiveness because of the split between investment and retail. Its bureaucratic nature and a high number of exceptions have also been opposed ("Banks' riskier trading", 2014). Because France and Germany have – naturally – had the reflex to protect their biggest lenders, they created a united front against the European Commission's initiative.

As of 2014, the banking arrangements constitute a topic with mixed results in Franco-German relations. The banking union is within reach despite the seemingly irreconcilable attitude of the two states: The French are sympathetic to the supervision of and – more importantly – intervention in the banking sector while German officials tend to avoid them. Michel Barnier had to yield before France and Germany and give up on the project to isolate a sort of risky trading by the big banks ("New EU banking rules", 2014).

It seems pertinent to recall that Germany – unlike France – was not keen on approving a resolution fund as a rescue for the banks. On various occasions, Berlin pointed to the necessity of treaty changes at the EU level in order to realize banking union (Brunsden & Christie, 2013). The green light that finally came out in 2014 was in fact coloured by the German impact upon the formulation of a mechanism which was particularly salient through the absence of a European taxing system as a safety net. Thus, if the bankruptcy of the bank entails a financial intervention which goes beyond the capacity of the rescue fund, then it will fall to the hosting nation to fill the gap. In this provision, the German refusal of shouldering the financial burden at the European level is plain to see.

Disagreement on the Eurobonds

The idea of a European system of loans is not new. Reports and researches on Eurobonds can be traced back to 1970s (Collignon, 2011). Jacques Delors had suggested to use that instrument in order to finance the EU's budget ("Growth, competitiveness", 1993). At the early stages of the European sovereign debt crisis, Eurobonds have been recalled again as a remedy. Since François Hollande declared – shortly after his election as French president – his intention to bolster the issuance of Eurobonds, discussions on the Euro loans have become widespread (Stewart, 2012).

Eurobonds consist of an effort to collectivize sovereign debt. Hence, it aims to provide for the possibility to borrow at more affordable interest rates. Such a possibility would ease the difficulties faced by states which have found themselves in a financial bottleneck. A study on Portugal shows how significant the impact of Eurobonds can be: Her annual repayments would fall by €15bn (an amount that equals approximately 9% of its GDP) if the interest rate applied to her were to fall to the Eurozone average (Inman, 2012).

The divergence on the Eurobonds is twofold. On the one hand, François Hollande believes that Eurobonds constitute an option for dealing with the sovereign debt crisis in Europe maintaining that they will lead to growth in the Eurozone. With this idea in mind, he declared his will to see Eurobonds circulate in the nearest future possible within Eurozone territory ("Mini-sommet", 2012). However, admitting that they would not be issued rapidly, he expressed his desire to substitute them with the short-term Euro-bills for the time being ("Hollande, Monti", 2012). The fact that Germany is not the only EU member state to oppose Eurobonds explains Hollande's attitude.

The Franco-German divergence of views on how to ensure the growth within the EU territories is discussed above. Suffice to underline, therefore, that Merkel strongly rejects the possibility of sustaining growth via financial instruments in lack of budgetary discipline. She affirmed clearly that Eurobonds would "not make any contribution to stimulating growth" (Traynor & Wintour, 2012). Merkel's position is clear: It is not possible to achieve growth through more debt (Fow News, 2012).

The second field of disagreement concerns the legality of the Eurobonds –a point that is frequently made by German officials. For them, a treaty change must occur in order to make of Euro loans an acceptable option. As a specialist of the Eurozone reminds, Eurobonds are in opposition with the spirit of Maastricht Treaty which established a distinction between monetary union and budgetary power. The latter, according to the Treaty, must remain in the competence of member states. It is very likely to see Germany resisting to a transfer of sovereignty that will prevent her from issuing her national bonds (Seibt, 2011).

There seems to be more than a legal dimension. For Merkel, Eurobonds have two aspects that can possibly jeopardize German interests. First, they can lead to a lethargy of heavily indebted EU member states. The chancellor of Germany maintains that they risk decreasing the pressure on these states to take the necessary financial measures. Second, they can result in an augmentation of borrowing costs for Germany –and for all other EU members which have a better-performing fiscal system. It is therefore not surprising to hear the German deputy finance minister saying that the Eurobonds would be "a prescription at the wrong time with the wrong side-effects" and reiterating his government's assertion that the budget-discipline pact is something that "Merkel [has] championed and Hollande has criticized" ("Germany insists", 2012).

On the scheme drawn above, Hollande has been campaigning for the adoption of Eurobonds, but Angela Merkel stubbornly rejects the idea. He is not the only European to support the project: Italian and Spanish prime ministers have joined his battle to convince the anti-Eurobonds states such as Germany, Finland and Austria on the advantages of the latter (Inman, 2012). That Olli Rehn, member of the European Commission who is responsible for economic affairs, has called for a roadmap to put in place Eurobonds is also noteworthy (Pratley, 2012).

A remark deserves to be made on Merkel's change of attitude, however. Reluctant to provide for financial support to those states which suffer from the financial deadlock, Merkel could join the proponents of the EU-level rescue fund. She could also give a green light for a debt relief –with the proviso of successful structural reforms (Rickens, 2013). The chancellor had also provided support to the European Central Bank's bond-buying program (Boston, 2012).

EPILOGUE

The weakening of the Franco-German tandem is not a new process. The end of the Cold War, the renewed self-perception and the economic success have provided momentous gains for Germany. The consequent top-status that Germany has acquired was something that went to the detriment of France.

Then came the Euro crisis, a big blow to political and economic relations within the European Union. Neither the member states nor the institutions were ready to cope with a financial problem of such extent. Besides, a polarisation took place after the crisis: The Community/Union spirit was replaced by the groups of creditors and debtors. The new environment was suitable for the strongest actor (re-)set the rules of the game. That's what Germany has chosen to do, having intermittently made choices that disturbed others.

The dominant position further increased the gap with the partner. In the current context, there are significant divergences between Paris and Berlin. Stakes are high for both capitals: The monetary union must function and sustained economic growth must be ensured. German preferences are most likely to colour the common positions that they will reach in the future.

REFERENCES

Banking Union – Single Resolution Mechanism (SRM). (n.d.). *European Commission*. Factsheet. Retrieved June 1, 2014, from http://ec.europa.eu/internal_market/finances/docs/banking-union/dg-markt-factsheets-srm_en.pdf

Banks' Riskier Trading Activities to be Curbed, EU Proposes. (2014, January 29). *BBC*. Retrieved April 20, 2014, from http://www.bbc.com/news/business-25941075

Barker, A. (2014, March 17). France and Germany squabble over who pays for EU banking union. *Financial Times*. Retrieved April 20, 2014, from http://www.ft.com/intl/cms/s/0/4ab7c61a-adcb-11e3-9ddc-00144feab7de.html

Barnier Launches EU Bid to Ban Risky Bank Trades. (2014, January 29). *EUobserver*. Retrieved May 12, 2014, from http://euobserver.com/news/122919

Beach, D. (2006). The commission and the council secretariat: How they gained some influence. In F. Laursen (Ed.), *The treaty of Nice: Actor preferences, bargaining and institutional choice* (pp. 369–406). Leiden: Martinus Nijhoff Publishers.

Biseau, G., & Alemagna, L. (2014, February 19). Hollande et Merkel, plus unis que jamais. *Libération*. Retrieved May 12, 2014, from http://www.liberation.fr/politiques/2014/02/19/hollande-et-merkel-toujours-plus-proches_981468

Boston, W. (2012, September 18). Merkel backs bond-buying program. *The Wall Street Journal*. Retrieved April 24, 2014, from http://online.wsj.com/news/articles/SB10000872396390444450004578002150260399228

Brunsden, J., & Christie, R. (2013, July 10). EU unveils bank-crisis plan with 55 billion-Euro fund. *Bloomberg*. Retrieved June 12, 2014, from http://www.bloomberg.com/news/2013-07-09/eu-steels-for-battle-over-bank-resolution-plans-led-by-germany.html

Collignon, S. (2011, March 24). Eurobonds: The financial equivalent of the single currency. In *Eurobonds: Concepts and implications: Compilation of notes for the monetary dialogue*. European Parliament, Directorate-General for Internal Policies. Retrieved June 20, 2014, from http://www.europarl.europa.eu/document/activities/cont/201201/20120130ATT36516/20120130ATT36516EN.pdf

Commemorating 60th Anniversary of Allied Landing on D-Day. (2004). *Deutsche aussenpolitik*. Retrieved May 12, 2014, from http://www.deutsche-aussenpolitik.de/daparchive/dateien/2002/06082004xxx24.html

Europe Backs Down in Bid to Tackle Mega-Banks. (2014, January 29). *Reuters*. Retrieved April 14, 2014, from http://uk.reuters.com/article/2014/01/29/uk-eu-banks-idUKBREA0S0PY20140129

European Council Conclusions. (2012, October 9). *EUCO 156/12*. Retrieved June 1, 2014, from http://www.consilium.europa.eu/uedocs/cms_data/docs/pressdata/en/ec/133004.pdf

France and Germany Propose EU 'Competitiveness Pact'. (2011, February 4). *BBC*. Retrieved June 12, 2014, from http://www.bbc.co.uk/news/world-europe-12368401

GDP Growth (Annual %). (n.d.). *The World Bank*. Retrieved June 4, 2014, from http://data.worldbank.org/indicator/NY.GDP.MKTP.KD.ZG/countries?display=default

Germany Insists no Eurobonds to Solve Debt Crisis. (2012, May 21). *Fox News*. Retrieved May 19, 2014, from http://www.foxnews.com/world/2012/05/21/germany-insists-no-eurobonds-to-solve-debt-crisis/

Gould, J. E. (2014, January 8). Roadmap to a banking union. *The Financialist*. Retrieved May 18, 2014, http://www.thefinancialist.com/roadmap-to-a-banking-union/

Growth, Competitiveness, Employment: The Challenges and Ways Forward into the 21st Century. (1993, December 5). *European Commission*. White Paper. COM(93) 700.

Hollande, M. (2012, June 22). Merkel et Rajoy tentent de s'accorder avant le sommet Européen. *France24*. Retrieved May 18, 2014, from http://www.france24.com/fr/20120622-zone-euro-sommet-plan-anti-crise-rencontre-monti-merkel-hollande-rajoy/

Hollande Proposes Eurozone 'Government' as Differences with Merkel Show. (2013, May 17). *Deutsche Welle*. Retrieved June 1, 2014, from http://www.dw.de/hollande-proposes-eurozone-government-as-differences-with-merkel-show/a-16819966

Inman, P. (2012, May 24). Eurobonds: An essential guide. *The Guardian*. Retrieved May 18, 2014, from http://www.theguardian.com/business/2012/may/24/eurobonds-an-essential-guide

Jackson, A. (2012, October 26). *The Financialist*. Retrieved June 10, 2014, http://www.thefinancialist.com/euro-area-banking-union-gains-momentum-axel-lang-credit-suisse/

Krotz, U., & Schild, J. (2013). *Shaping Europe: France, Germany, and embedded bilateralism from the Elysée Treaty to twenty-first century politics*. Oxford, UK: Oxford University Press.

Lellouche, P. (2012). France-allemagne: Le double déni. *Politique Etrangere*, *4*(Hiver), 739–754. doi:10.3917/pe.124.0739

Les Gouvernements Européens ont une Marge de Manoeuvre Limitée pour Stimuler la Croissance – Merkel. (2013, June 28). *Les Echos*. Retrieved June 5, 2014, from http://bourse.lesechos.fr/infos-conseils-boursiers/actus-des-marches/infos-marches/les-gouvernements-europeens-ont-une-marge-de-manoeuvre-limitee-pour-stimuler-la-croissance-merkel-892386.php

Minc, A. (2011, August 23). *Le Figaro*. Retrieved April 14, 2014, from http://www.lefigaro.fr/conjoncture/2011/08/23/04016-20110823ARTFIG00548-alain-minc-le-aaa-de-la-france-est-un-tresor-national.php

Mini-Sommet de la Zone Euro: 130 Milliards Pour la Relance. (2012, June 22). *La Chaine Info*. Retrieved June 22, 2014, from http://lci.tf1.fr/economie/conjoncture/merkel-hollande-rajoy-et-monti-s-accordent-sur-la-croissance-7380147.html

Montébourg, A. (2011). *Votez pour la démondialisation*. Paris: Flammarion.

New EU Banking Rules Without Teeth; EU Banking. (2014, January 29). *Business World*. Retrieved June 1, 2014, from http://www.businessworld.ie/livenews.htm?a=3136310

Perte, A. A. A. (2012, January 13). L'opposition fustige Sarkozy, la majorité temporise. *Le Nouvel Observateur*. Retrieved April 14, 2014, from http://tempsreel.nouvelobs.com/chronique-du-triple-a/20120113.OBS8761/video-perte-aaa-l-opposition-fustige-sarkozy-la-majorite-temporise.html

Pisani-Ferry, J. (2006). Only one bed for two dreams: A critical retrospective on the debate over the economic governance of the Euro area. *Journal of Common Market Studies*, *44*(4), 823–844. doi:10.1111/j.1468-5965.2006.00664.x

Pratley, N. (2012, 23 May). Germany and its Eurobonds resistance. *The Guardian*. Retrieved June 12, 2014, from http://www.theguardian.com/business/nils-pratley-on-finance/2012/may/23/why-germany-doesnt-want-eurobonds

Real GDP Growth Rate – Volume. (n.d.). *Eurostat*. Retrieved June 10, 2014, from http://epp.eurostat.ec.europa.eu/portal/page/portal/product_details/dataset?p_product_code=tec00115

Rickens, C. (2013, 26 August). Aid debate: Merkel leaves door open to greek debt cut. *Der Spiegel*. Retrieved April 14, 2014, from http://www.spiegel.de/international/europe/merkel-declines-to-rule-out-greek-debt-cut-a-918560.html

Schild, J. (2011). 20 ans après: La France et l'Allemagne dans la nouvelle Europe. *Regards sur l'Economie Allemande*, *100*, 11-25.

Seibt, S. (2011, August 16). Les Euro-obligations sont-elles le remède miracle à la crise? *France24*. Retrieved June 8, 2014, from http://www.france24.com/fr/20110816-sommet-franco-allemand-sarkozy-merkel-zone-euro-crise-eurobond-obligation-dette-marche-speculation/

Split Persists between Berlin and Paris. (2013, May 17). *Der Spiegel*. Retrieved June 3, 2014, from http://www.spiegel.de/international/europe/germany-and-france-will-not-create-joint-statement-ahead-of-eu-summit-a-900514.html

Standard & Poor's Takes Various Rating Actions on 16 Eurozone Sovereign Governments. (2012, 13 January). *S&P*. Retrieved May 19, 2014, from http://www.standardandpoors.com/ratings/articles/en/us/?articleType=HTML&assetID=1245327294763

Stark, H. (2012). Le couple Franco-Allemand à l'épreuve de la crise de la zone Euro. *Questions Internationales, 54*(March-April), 76–78.

Stewart, H. (2012, May 22). Hollande pushes case for Eurobonds. *The Guardian*. Retrieved June 19, 2014, from, http://www.theguardian.com/business/2012/may/22/eurozone-crisis-eurobonds-hollande-merkel

Structural Reform of the EU Banking Sector. (2014, January 29). *European Commission*. Retrieved April 18, 2014, from http://europa.eu/rapid/press-release_IP-14-85_en.htm?locale=FR

Traynor, I., & Wintour, P. (2012, May 24). Eurozone crisis: Germany and France clash over Eurobonds at summit. *The Guardian*. Retrieved May 19, 2014, from http://www.theguardian.com/business/2012/may/23/eurozone-crisis-france-germany-divide

Volkery, C. (2012, May 24). *France dominates EU summit: Hollande steals the show from Merkel*. Retrieved April 15, 2014, from http://www.spiegel.de/international/europe/euro-bond-discussion-dominates-european-union-summit-a-834865.html

Willis, A. (2011, February 4). Franco-German 'pact for competitiveness' hits immediate opposition. *EUobserver*. Retrieved April 14, 2014, from, http://euobserver.com/economic/31755

Willsher, K., & Chu, H. (2011, December 5). France, Germany see budget discipline as key in crisis. *Los Angeles Times*. Retrieved May 22, 2014, from, http://articles.latimes.com/2011/dec/05/world/la-fg-eu-merkel-sarkozy-20111206

Yousouf, H. (2012). S&P downgrades Europe bailout fund. *CNN International*. Retrieved April 15, 2014, from http://money.cnn.com/2012/01/16/markets/sandp_efsf_downgrade/index.htm

KEY TERMS AND DEFINITIONS

Banking Union: The transfer of national banking policy prerogatives to the European Union, ongoing since 2012, as a remedy for the Eurozone crisis.

Competitiveness Pact: A Franco-German plan that touches upon such sensitive areas as wage indexation, pension ages, corporate tax and debt brakes. It also envisages a national monitoring process and a yearly summit.

Eurobonds: The controversial idea of bonds, advanced by the European Commission, that should be issued by the Eurozone states.

European Financial Stability Facility (EFSF): An instrument that aims to preserve financial stability in the Eurozone by providing assistance to member states in financial difficulty.

Eurozone Crisis: A sovereign debt crisis that has been affecting the Eurozone countries since 2009.

Franco-German Tandem: A particular relationship between France and Germany, two founding members of the European Communities, which has had a key place in the European integration.

Single Resolution Mechanism (SRM): A mechanism built to deal with failing credit institutions and investment firms.

Stability and Growth Pact (SGP): A safeguard mechanism that focuses on the national fiscal policies of the EU members.

Chapter 4
Perspectives on the United Kingdom's Withdrawal from the European Union

Armağan Gözkaman
Beykent University, Turkey

ABSTRACT

The European Community/Union has always been a controversial issue in the UK. At present, the probability of an in-or-out referendum makes it all the more divisive. Eurosceptics see a brighter future for their country outside the union both in political and economic terms. Pro-Europeans, on the other hand, maintain that British membership brings up benefits that outweigh the costs. Both sides have their arguments. The former seek success through social mobilizations and debates. The latter believe that the anti-EU stance may be costly in economic and political terms. Hence, the public must be convinced before the referendum – if it ever takes place.

INTRODUCTION

Since Britain joined the then European Community in 1973, policy-makers of both wings of the political spectrum had to face the question of their country's place in Europe. At present, the question is all the more significant in the Union of 28 members that moved forward in economic and political integration. In this context, Britain's exit from the European Union (EU), known as Brexit or Brixit, seems to be a probability considerable enough to spark serious discussions.

A member state leaving the EU has never been witnessed before, but it is legally possible since the Treaty of Lisbon entered into force in 2009. Bold as it may seem, the decision can be taken if there is enough public support for it. Consequently, it seems pertinent to advocate the consideration of pro and con arguments while reflecting on the possibility of Brexit –Britain's withdrawal from the European Union. Thus, the first part of the study will be allotted to the factors that make Brexit possible while the second will focus on those that make it seem unlikely.

DOI: 10.4018/978-1-4666-7308-3.ch004

THE CIRCUMSTANCES IN FAVOR OF BRITISH WITHDRAWAL

There are basically three pillars that fuel the Eurosceptic stance in Britain. First, the public opinion is divided over but increasingly supportive of the idea of quitting the European Union. Second, and in close connection with the previous point, social mobilizations have gained momentum especially in the last few years. Third, the debates on Brexit are held around the fears of people.

British Public Opinion on Parting Ways with the EU

Historical experience and national interest, combined, provide for varying degree of sympathy to regional integration schemes. In Britain's case, the perception of the EC/EU integration has not been very positive due to the peculiarities that have been forged in time (Aspinwall, 2000; Wallace, 1991). Parliamentary divisions on the accession to the common market in 1970s, along with the low rate of support measured by opinion polls, reflect the difficulty posed by the European question for British policymakers (Gifford, 2014; Lazer, 1976). The mobilization against the Treaty of Maastricht characterized by alliances involving intra and extra-parliamentary groupings also proved the extent of Euroscepticism in the country (Gifford, 2006).

Hence, one can legitimately argue that the discussions on Brexit (or Brixit) have a historical background. In 2013, they took another dimension when the PM promised to let the British people decide on whether or not to stay in the EU. The referendum is thus expected to take place in 2017 if, indeed, the Conservative Party wins the legislative elections of 2015. The referendum project is bolstered by the UK Independence Party, British National Party, the Green Party of England and Wales as well. Nevertheless, the majority of the Labour Party members oppose the idea of a referendum unless the UK is forced to give up on more of its sovereignty in favor of the European Union ("EU referendum", 2014). The number of Labour MPs taking part in the movement calling on party leadership to back the EU referendum is less than 20 (http://labourforareferendum.com). Liberal Democrats form another group which will seek referendum only if questions of sovereignty transfer arise (Watt, 2014).

Obviously, Cameron wants to negotiate for an enhanced British position within the EU before holding the in-or-out referendum (Bentley & Glaze, 2012). After a "real change in terms of Europe", British people will have the opportunity to make the "real choice" (Wintour, 2012). This attitude reflects in fact the PM's anti-Brexit stance, perhaps difficult to perceive after his parting ways with the center-right European People's Party. If Tories have joined the ranks of Eurosceptic and anti-federalist European Conservatives and Reformists, the majority of party members do not wish to see their country leaving the EU. Hence, Cameron has consented to the in-or-out referendum because he aimed to appease the non-negligible anti-EU voices in Britain. In his opinion, "British national interest is to reform the EU, to organize a referendum over this reform and to recommend that [Britain] remains [in the EU]" (Albert, 2014).

The British PM's move seems to serve at least three purposes simultaneously. The first (and most obvious) one is related to the maximization of national interests: Cameron wanted to seize the opportunity to meet the widely-shared British demand to negotiate with Brussels for better terms of membership. The second one concerns the political gain he can reap for conservatives: The referendum will take place only if his party can renew its term in 2015. He therefore uses a strong public demand as an opportunity to increase his chances for re-election. The fact that Labour will not seek referendum makes the bid all the more meaningful. The third benefit he can expect is more personal: the consolidation of his leadership by responding to a contagious discontent within Tory ranks.

Since the perspective of a public vote on the UK's exit from the European Union opened at the governmental level, discussion on the issue gained momentum. Nevertheless, it is not possible to foresee an absolute triumph for Europhiles. Polls indicate that British people are split on the EU membership. A survey conducted in June 2014 shows that 44% of the interviewed would vote in favor of British membership while 36% would vote for the withdrawal. According to the same survey, the undecided (15%) and those who wouldn't vote (5%) constitute one fifth of the sample. Yet, 57% affirmed to vote for the continuation of the EU membership if the Cameron government renegotiates with the EU and succeeds to protect the UK's interests against 22% who would vote against (YouGov, 2014).

In this regard, British support to Cameron's antagonism to the nomination of Jean Claude Juncker to the European Commission is indicative. M. Juncker is known and disliked in the UK for his federalist vision of Europe. Cameron's stance was supported by 43% and opposed by 13% of the voters according to the survey undertaken jointly by Financial Times and Populus ("GB: Risques accrus", 2014).

Various Mobilizations in Favor of the Withdrawal

In what regards the initiatives launched as a support to Brexit, the legislative one – which proves that the United Kingdom's withdrawal from the EU is not just a matter of rhetoric –should indeed be the first to cite. In 2013, conservative members of the British parliament drafted a bill to provide for the guidelines of the referendum. Hence, the *European Union (Referendum) Act 2013* foresees a referendum that will be organized before the year 2017 ends ("European Union (Referendum) Bill", 2013). The Prime Minister (PM) maintained that only his party offers a "clear choice" about his country's future in the EU, implying that the other two major parties were not eager to hear what British people say ("David Cameron: EU Referendum", 2013).

J. Wharton, Tory member of the parliament since the general election of 2010, has been the one to take forward the draft as a private members bill. The bill's first and second readings in the House of Commons took place in summer 2013. Subsequently, it was introduced to the House of Lords where the popular disagreement on the referendum was once again proven: The legislation process terminated with the rejection of 180 Lords against 130 (Rigby & Pickard, 2014).

If the result has been disappointing for the conservatives, Cameron did not fail to use the opportunity to give two political messages. First, he made known his will to carry on the endeavor of legislation on the issue. Hence, a new bill can be drafted next year. Second, he asserted that the referendum was not dependent on the success of the private member's bill, underlining that it could take place if he were to be elected prime minister again ("Cameron says Tories", 2014). These messages show that the issue will continue to be on the agenda despite the defeat imposed to Cameron by the House of Lords.

Mobilizations at the citizen level pull also focus in what regards the critical referendum on the UK's European Union membership. The People's Pledge is among the most salient ones. With cross-party backing of more than 60 members of the parliament, the political campaign aims to let voters sign a petition to support the referendum (Hall, 2012). Its motto is "People not politicians should decide our future with the European Union" (www.peoplespledge.org).

Another campaign that captured public attention is the one set out in 2010 by Nikki Sinclaire for a public vote calling on a referendum. Two years later, the independent MP handed in a petition signed by 120.000 people to 10, Downing Street ("Nikki's petition drive", 2012). Her 'Have Your Say' battle bus continued to travel across the country afterwards with the same mission ("EU poll battle bus", 2012). Perhaps the significant number of the referendum supporters has bolstered the drafting of the European Union Act 2013.

The momentum witnessed since Cameron's promise of an EU referendum is also colored by an event that spurred attention in the media: a competition to design the best plan for pulling out of the European Union. In this respect, it seems important to underscore that the contest was more than an ordinary populist activity. It was launched by the Institute of Economic Affairs, a right-leaning prestigious think tank that was depicted by Andrew Marr as "the most influential [one] in modern British history" (2007). Among the jury that would determine the winner, there were prominent figures such as Lord Nigel Lawson (Chancellor of the Exchequer under the Thatcher government) who served as the chairman of the judging panel.

In April 2014, it rewarded Iain Mansfield with a € 100.000 prize for his entry named "A Blueprint for Britain: Openness not Isolation". Mansfield refused to be qualified as pro-Brexit, but he claimed to set guidelines that would "maximize the potential for an open, prosperous and globally engaged UK" in case the people of Britain take such a decision. Nigel Lawson's comments on the triumphant proposal show parallelism with Mansfield's assertion:

The British people have been promised a referendum on whether the UK should leave the European Union. There are few more important decisions than this. In advance of that decision the issues need to be fully debated, and an essential element of the debate will be an understanding of how the UK might conduct itself if and when we leave. Iain Mansfield's prize-winning entry provides an excellent starting point for this important debate. ("Iain Mansfield named winner," 2014)

The issue is more than whether or not the winner or the jury supports the UK's withdrawal. As Mansfield himself made the point, his paper does not hold a normative position on the issue of exit. The importance of the blueprint is mainly ontological. In an environment increasingly colored by Euroscepticism, the decision to launch a competition with a highly-considerable reward is of particular meaning.

A Debate Going Around Fears and Limitations

The institutional and policy-related evolution of the European Union generally followed the lines that suited British preferences (Schnapper, 2010). The United Kingdom has secured opt-outs in a panoply of fields ranging from justice and home affairs to economic and monetary union so as to better protect its interests. Yet, at the domestic level, the fears of Europe persist. An important part of the anti-EU propaganda has developed around the financial aspect of the EU membership. One of the building blocks of this discourse is the 'net contributor' status of the UK: In 2012, British taxpayers contributed a sum of 8,468 billion pounds to the EU's budget ("European Union finances", 2013). An additional economic benefit of the withdrawal could lead to a growth of 1,1% in British gross domestic product (GDP) as Mansfield estimated – with the proviso that the UK continues to have access to European single market (2014).

Cameron's pledge to protect the *City* should also be interpreted in the same vein. According to the Tory leader, the European Union's regulative power must not grow at the expense of the UK's national interests. That is the reason why Cameron refused a new treaty calling for tighter economic discipline and fiscal integration ("Entre les marchés", 2011). The same reasoning explains why Cameron advocates for the modification of Lisbon Treaty in a way to prevent Eurozone members to impose financial service regulations on Britain. No doubt, the sovereign debt crisis, along with the decrease of competitiveness in the EU, intensified the reflex to preserve the City.

The economic arguments are not the only ones that motivate Eurosceptics. Getting rid of European regulations, too, has been among the major battle cries of anti-EU politicians. A research paper submitted to the House of Commons stipulates that, from 1997 to 2009, around 7% of primary and 14% of secondary legislations aimed to implement EU obligations in varying degrees of involvement. The study also points to the increase in the range of areas touched by the European Community/Union (Miller, 2010). Those who subscribe to the necessity of overcoming EU regulations want to repatriate legislative sovereignty to Westminster. Because there is a wide-spread impression that growth and entrepreneurship are constrained by these regulations (Collomp, 2014).

In his famous speech on the EU, the PM himself expressed the requirement for examining "whether the balance is right in so many areas where the European Union has legislated" by referring particularly to the environment, social affairs and crime. He further put forward British people's resentment on European interference in daily lives by "what they see as unnecessary rules and regulation". In addition, he pointed to the necessity of a new framework of relations with the EU so as to free his country from "the spurious regulation which damages Europe's competitiveness" ("David Cameron's EU speech", 2013).

The challenge of immigration is also used for criticism against the European Union. In times when job opportunities have become scarcer than ever, it seems easy to use this argument for opposing further integration in the European continent. The following statement of the British PM is illustrative:

January 1, the people of Romania and Bulgaria will have the same right to work in the UK as other EU citizens. I know many people are deeply concerned about the impact that could have on our country. I share those concerns. (Cameron, 2013).

In the words of Laszlo Andor, the EU commissioner for employment, social affairs and inclusion, the free movement of persons is "a guiding principle" of the European integration. Unlike Cameron, and in conformity with the position he fills, he believes that access to labor markets improves employment opportunities (Miller Llana, 2014). Obviously, this idea does not really appeal to all EU citizens. 82% of the British people want to impose restrictions on the citizens of Romania and Bulgaria; 52% want to put an end to the free movement of persons against 29% who wish to see it preserved (Albert, 2013).

The distance of the EU from its citizens exacerbates further the problems cited in this section. The 'democratic deficit' plays into the hands of anti-EU campaigners: The technocrats in Brussels have prerogatives that outweigh those of the democratically elected members of the parliaments at home. As Cameron affirms, the EU is considered something that is done to people whereas it was meant to be acting on their behalf. The situation is worsened by the bitter measures taken for dealing with economic and financial hardship. The frustration caused by the austerity measures and additional taxation grows bigger when they affect people living "on the other side of the continent" (Cameron, 2013).

THE FACTORS THAT PLAY AGAINST BRITISH WITHDRAWAL

The points made in the previous section are, indeed, difficult to neglect in what regards the future of UK-EU relations. However, there are also possibilities that undermine the idea that Brexit will suit British interests: expectations of benefit may not materialize, negative political repercussions may occur and the UK's requests may be met by its European partners.

The Possibility of Unfulfilled Expectations

Whether the United Kingdom will benefit from or lose because of a withdrawal from the EU is controversial. A report elaborated by British parliamentarians reminds that an irrefutable demonstration of the withdrawal's net effects is an extraordinarily arduous task. Thus, there is not a definitive report stating the exact costs and benefits of the UK's European Union membership. Nevertheless, borrowing from the report's sectoral conclusion, one can maintain that Brexit will bear considerable impact upon many sectors of the economy and upon the regions that benefit from the EU's funding (Thompson & Harari, 2013).

A research focused on the economic benefits brought about by EU membership came up with impressive results. According to their findings, taking part in the European integration generated an additional *per capita* income of 12% for the members –Greece being the only exception. In Britain's case, the percentage reached 24% (Campos et al., 2014; "Economic benefits of EU membership"). Based on this research, one may have concerns whether a future outside the EU might reverse this growth.

An attempt to answer the question above has been the objective of some scholarly research. A group led by G. Ottaviano focused on costs and benefits of leaving the EU and concluded with attention-grabbing numbers. Reminding that more than half of Britain's exports are to EU member states – amounting to nearly 15% of its GDP – researchers point to the reduction of trade volume due to tariff and non-tariff barriers. They have come up with two forecasts: The pessimistic scenario indicated an income loss that would reach 3,1% of the GDP –approximately 50 billion pounds. Optimistic estimations indicated a loss of 1,1%. When it comes to productivity, lower growth would result in losses nearing at least 2,2% of the GDP. Gloomier expectations situate the rate between 6.3% and 9.5% (Ottaviano et al., 2014). Another analysis suggests that British GDP, at constant prices, would decline by 2,25% in case of a withdrawal from the EU (Pain & Young, 2004).

Foreign direct investment (FDI) is another area that will considerably be affected by Brexit. An enlarged market – as the one created by the EU – gives the possibility to do trade in a bigger territory, making thus a bigger capital accumulation possible. Most research support that the European integration process – mostly thanks to the Single Market – boosts intra and extra-regional FDI despite varying impact upon different industries (HM Treasury, 2010). Since 1999, the EU has had a prominent place in the UK's inward and outward FDI transactions. At the end of 2003, European investments into the UK were above 341 billion pounds while the EU received nearly 390 billion pounds of investment from the UK. There are grounds to believe that Brexit would have momentous impact on FDI flows in the medium to long term (HM Treasury, 2010; Pain & Young, 2004).

The belief that the withdrawal will have negative repercussions on the economic growth in Britain is also discernible in business circles. The general director of the Confederation of British Industry, John Cridland, publicly criticized the calls on a legislative act to pave the way for an EU referendum:

The recent tussle presents an inward-looking picture of British politics to the outside. For those in the business world, it feels like a diversion from what we should be doing in Europe which is restoring growth, through trade deals, and championing the reforms that we want to make all of Europe more competitive. Let [us] be clear. Being a member of a reformed EU is the best way to preserve market access (Davies & Wintour, 2013).

A survey suggests that political risks due to a potential EU referendum are a bigger source of concern for the UK's biggest companies than financial issues such as high interest rates. A prominent example of a sector that vehemently opposes the UK exit from the EU is the automotive industry. According to the report prepared by KPMG and released by the Society of Motor Manufacturers and Traders, the UK has no choice but to "play a key role in shaping EU policies, budgets and regulations". The same report notes that 92% of car companies are in favor of staying in the EU ("UK must maintain", 2014). A further difficulty for the sector may be the re-examination of investments in the UK's territory by foreign companies such as Nissan, Ford and Toyota (Bounds, 2014).

Polls also show that less than 20% of businesses want to stay in the EU while 10 to 15% of them opt for a withdrawal. Yet, one can not ignore that the support is conditional. According to the survey launched by the Institute of Directors, 60% of members linked their endorsement of EU membership to reforms, while 34% insisted on substantial repatriation of powers from Brussels (Vina, 2013; Groom, 2014).

Possible Political Repercussions

As mentioned earlier, part of the population believes that the EU must not quit the European Union. Lord P. Mandelson (former First Secretary of State under Brown), Ken Clarke (Cameron's minister since 2012) and Danny Alexander (liberal democrat MP since 2005 and Chief Secretary to the Treasury since 2010) formed a new campaign group through the manifesto of "British Influence". The latter states that Britain should not only stay in the EU, but also be a leading nation by highlighting an important message: Taking part in the European Union is something that gives power within and outside the continent ("Brexit or Brinfluence?", 2013).

The opinion is shared by other British people as well. According to Sajjad Karim, the leader of British conservatives in the European Parliament, there is a risk for the United Kingdom to lose power on the world stage if it withdraws from the EU. He even envisages the possibility for such a move to cost the UK its permanent member status in the United Nations Security Council: The referendum can put an end to the United Kingdom if Scotland leaves because of Brexit. Karim makes the point by stating that Scottish, Wales and Northern Irish people will vote for the EU if a referendum is held in 2017 ("Brexit could cost UK", 2014). In this scenario, if the referendum result is negative, it will be due to the English rejection of the EU.

It seems pertinent to maintain that the unity of the nation will be called into question if "no" comes out of the referendum. The Scottish position is delicate because of the simultaneous desires of leaving the United Kingdom (a point on which the population is split) and becoming a member of the EU. Before September 18, 2014, there were worries that the perspective of Brexit could have a serious impact upon the Scottish independence decision. Yet, 55,3% of the Scottish voters answered "no" to their country's independence at the referendum ("Scotland decides", 2014). This does not mean, however, that a similar plebiscite will not resurface again.

Another political consequence will concern the relations between the UK and the United States. The EU is seen by the US administration as a 'force multiplier'. Therefore, Washington has openly voiced concern on the possibility of Brexit and warned Britain that its position in the international arena could be jeopardized (Spillius, 2012). In the words of Philip Gordon, the US assistant secretary responsible for European affairs:

Britain has been such a special partner of the United States – that shares our values, shares our interests, has significant resources to bring to the table. More than most other, its voice within the

European Union is essential and critical to the United States. (…) [A]s a broad and general theme, we value a strong UK voice in a strong European Union. (…) We have a growing relationship with the [EU] as an institution which has a growing voice in the world – and we want to see a strong British voice in that [EU]. That is in the American interest (Blair, 2013).

The assistant secretary emphasized that the 'special relationship' between the two states would continue regardless of the decision that British authorities will take on the EU. Yet, some interpreted Gordon's remarks as a warning that the existing relationship would be devalued in the eyes of Washington if London were to leave the EU (Borger et al, 2013). The argument seems reasonable, in light of the emphasis made by Gordon on British presence within the EU.

Last, but not least, Brexit risks damaging the UK's foreign policy interests. As a government-sponsored report implies, a force multiplication effect of the EU is also perceptible through the common security and defense policy. The EU provides for more international influence to the UK in various ways. The EU, which does not have a colonial history, is perceived by third countries as a neutral actor. In addition, it provides for synergies that maximize member states' national interests. The possibility to further promote human rights and political reconciliation through commercial links is one of them. A better allocation of scarce resources thanks to a large panoply of foreign missions and operations launched within the EU framework is another example (Report, 2013).

Optimism Concerning UK-EU Negotiations

There are reasons to believe that the UK withdrawal will profoundly change the EU. As Tim Oliver of the German Institute for International and Security Affairs claims, a Brexit could bring protectionism to the fore, aggravate differences among the member states and lead to the disentanglement of the Union. Some also argue that it could put one of the most uncooperative members outside the Union and result in moving on with integration more comfortably (Oliver, 2013).

It would be commonsensical to assume that both the United Kingdom and the European Union risk to pay a high price because of the breakup. The Eurozone crisis far from over, losing a – big – member would lead to a huge traumatism for the European integration. The criticism of key figures in the EU is, at least partly, due to this possibility. As Angela Merkel justly affirms, it is "certainly not all the same" whether or not Britain leaves the EU (Wagstyl et al., 2014). She is cautiously open to the idea of negotiating with the UK: While she declared her readiness to discuss Britain's wishes on the European Union, she also reminded that there were other states with wishes, and that a balanced compromise should be sought ("UE: Berlin prêt", 2013). The president of the European Commission, José Manuel Barroso, described Britain as a "special" case while emphasizing that "Europe is stronger with the UK as its member and (…) the UK is stronger as a member of the European Union than on its own" (Parker & Fontanella-Khan, 2014).

Some reactions, however, have reflected an indisposition to a sort of *à la carte* Europe. Both François Hollande and his foreign minister Laurent Fabius expressed their desire to see the UK remaining in the EU while implying that membership entails responsibilities. In their view, Europe should be taken as it is ("Hollande à Cameron", 2013). The most severe criticism came from the former president of the European Commission, Jacques Delors. He openly suggested to the UK to quit the EU by stating that the British are "solely concerned about their economic interests" and that they could be offered "a different form of partnership" ("Jacques Delors", 2012).

Delors' view is not widespread among the European politicians. Therefore, in light of European reactions, it seems plausible to maintain the possibility to expect positive outcome from the future negotiations between London and Brussels. Even Jean-Claude Juncker, after his appointment to the European Commission's presidency, called David Cameron to say that he would commit to finding a solution for the UK's political worries (Albert, 2014). Indeed, the negotiations may not be very easy. Besides, in today's Europe, there is not a strong willingness to re-negotiate the treaties. Nevertheless, the problematic points Cameron exposed at his Europe speech are not impossible to deal with. A 'new settlement' with the EU can be within reach.

Another point that leads to optimism for the future of UK-EU relations is related to the possible losses of London. Even an award-winning project leans too much towards preserving ties with the EU under circumstances that favor London. However, no one can guarantee such a construction. The EU, abandoned by the UK, may not be willing to give the UK what it wants. The former European Commissioner for Justice, Fundamental Rights and Citizenship, Viviane Reding, makes the point: "It is difficult to see why the other member states would grant the UK unfettered access to their markets without requiring it to apply the EU's rules" (O'Donnel, 2014).

In this context, one can expect that both sides will be disposed to lead the relations to success. Like all negotiations, political and economic interests will determine the course. For the UK, many uncertainties about the outcome of alternative scenarios necessitate a prioritization of the European option. The 27 members of the EU, on the other hand, may have a constructive attitude and provide the UK with the possibility to give an acceptable European perspective to its nation on the eve of a possible referendum. As the Labour leader aptly observes, British PM is strained from all sides and has to commit a "delicate balancing act" so as to reach, after negotiations, a satisfactory settlement for the UK to remain in the EU (Miliband, 2014).

EPILOGUE

Despite all the discussion, the UK is part of Europe. She did too much for Europe and she received too much from it. In time, history, geography and identity have determined her relations with the old continent. As of now, she has a particular status in the EU with all the opt-outs and rebates.

For some time now, European decision-makers (including, of course, the British) have been pondering on the future of UK-EU relations. What is new is the possibility that the people of Britain may be asked to decide on a Shakespearian dilemma of remaining or not remaining in the EU. The answer will depend on at least two factors.

First, the British government must be able to offer a set of new relations with the European Union. As mentioned earlier, the task is not impossible to fulfill. There is much at stake for both London and the 27 European capitals.

Second, people must be better informed on the European project – a necessity that holds valid for all EU countries. The benefits of being within the EU must be better explained to them. The consequences of an inadequate public diplomacy may be grave, because the rising Euroscepticism gives the possibility to benefit from the lack of information. Worse still, they can use this vacuum for misinforming the voters.

REFERENCES

Albert, E. (2013, November 29). Londres défie l'Union européenne sur la libre circulation. *Le Monde*. Retrieved July 3, 2014, from http://www.lexisnexis.com/hottopics/lnacademic

Albert, E. (2014, July 1). Londres pris dans l'engrenage du "Brexit". *Le Monde*. Retrieved July 3, 2014, from http://www.lemonde.fr/europe/article/2014/06/30/londres-pris-dans-l-engrenage-du-brexit_4447850_3214.html

Aspinwall, M. (2000). Structuring Europe: Powersharing institutions and British preferences on European integration. *Political Studies*, *48*(3), 415–442. doi:10.1111/1467-9248.00268

Blair, D. (2013, January 9). US publicly voices concerns over Britain leaving EU. *The Telegraph*. Retrieved July 5, 2014, from http://www.telegraph.co.uk/news/worldnews/europe/eu/9791484/US-publicly-voices-concerns-over-Britain-leaving-EU.html

Borger, J., Traynor, I., & Watt, N. (2013, January 10). Britain should stay in European Union, says Obama administration. *The Guardian*. Retrieved July 2, 2014, from http://www.theguardian.com/world/2013/jan/09/us-warns-uk-european-union

Bounds, A. (2014, June 30). Pro-EU strategy at risk of failing, warns head of Siemens UK. *Financial Times*. Retrieved July 14, 2014, from http://www.ft.com/intl/cms/s/0/b172bf28-fe1a-11e3-b4f1-00144feab7de.html#axzz37QWUcfdo

Brexit Could Cost UK its UN Security Council Seat, Warns Leading Tory. (2014, June 20). *Euractiv*. Retrieved June 30, 2014, from http://www.euractiv.com/sections/uk-europe/brexit-could-cost-uk-its-un-security-council-seat-warns-leading-tory-302920

Brexit or Brinfluence? Britain and Europe. (2013, July 17). *The Economist*. Retrieved June 30, 2014, from http://www.lexisnexis.com/hottopics/lnacademic

Cameron, D. (2013, November 26). Free movement within Europe needs to be less free. *Financial Times*. Retrieved July 7, 2014, from http://www.ft.com/cms/s/0/add36222-56be-11e3-ab12-00144feabdc0.html#axzz37SWR98FG

Campos, N. F., Coricelli, F., & Moretti, L. (2014, April 5). The eye, the needle and the camel: Rich countries can benefit from EU membership. *Vox*. Retrieved July 12, 2014, from http://www.voxeu.org/article/how-rich-nations-benefit-eu-membership

Collomp, F. (2014, June 30). Le Royaume-Uni peut-il quitter l'UE? Argument de négociation agité par Londres face à ses partenaires européens, la perspective d'un « Brexit » (British exit) n'est pas seulement rhétorique. *Le Figaro*. Retrieved July 1, 2014, from http://www.lexisnexis.com/hottopics/lnacademic

David Cameron's EU Speech – Full Text. (2013, January 23). *The Guardian*. Retrieved June 12, 2014, from http://www.theguardian.com/politics/2013/jan/23/david-cameron-eu-speech-referendum

Davies, C., & Wintour, P. (2013, May 17). CBI chief John Cridland issues warning over European Union exit. *The Guardian*. Retrieved July 12, 2014, from http://www.theguardian.com/politics/2013/may/17/cbi-john-cridland-european-union-exit

Economic Benefits of EU Membership – Vox Views with Nauro Campos. (n.d.). *Vox*. Retrieved July 12, 2014, from http://www.voxeu.org/content/economic-benefits-eu-membership-vox-views-nauro-campos

Entre les marchés et l'Europe, le Royaume-Uni a choisi. (2014, December 10). *RTL*. Retrieved July 14, 2014, from http://www.rtl.fr/actu/international/entre-le-marche-et-l-europe-le-royaume-uni-a-choisi-7740381990

EU Poll Battle Bus in Town. (2012, May 16). *Birmingham Evening Mail*. Retrieved July 14, 2014, from http://www.lexisnexis.com/hottopics/lnacademic

EU Referendum 'Unlikely' under Labour, says Ed Miliband. (2014, March 12). *BBC*. Retrieved July 9, 2014, from http://www.bbc.com/news/uk-politics-26538420

European Union Finances 2013: Statement on the 2013 EU Budget and Measures to Counter Fraud and Financial Mismanagement (2013, November). *HM Treasury*. Retrieved July 12, 2014, from https://www.gov.uk/government/uploads/system/uploads/attachment_data/file/259692/EU_Finances_2013.pdf

GB. risques accrus d'une sortie de l'UE après la défaite de Cameron contre Juncker. (2014, June 28). *Agence France Presse*. Retrieved June 30, 2014, from http://www.lexisnexis.com/hottopics/lnacademic

Gifford, C. (2006). The rise of post-imperial populism: The case of right-wing Euroscepticism in Britain. *European Journal of Political Research*, *45*(5), 851–869. doi:10.1111/j.1475-6765.2006.00638.x

Gifford, C. (2014). The people against Europe: The Eurosceptic challenge to the united kingdom's coalition government. *JCMS: Journal of Common Market Studies*, *52*(3), 512–528.

Groom, B. (2014, July 7). Political risks top concerns for UK company finance chiefs. *Financial Times*. Retrieved July 14, 2014, from http://www.ft.com/intl/cms/s/0/bf097006-037d-11e4-9195-00144feab7de.html#axzz37QWUcfdo

Hall, M. (2012, January 31). MPs urged to back EU referendum ballots. *The Daily Express*. Retrieved July 14, 2014, from http://www.express.co.uk/news/uk/299080/MPs-urged-to-back-EU-referendum-ballots

Hollande à Cameron: "Pas possible de négocier l'Europe". (2013, January 23). *Le Figaro*. Retrieved July 15, 2014, from http://www.lefigaro.fr/international/2013/01/23/01003-20130123ARTFIG00343-fabius-previent-cameron-pas-d-europe-a-la-carte.php

Iain Mansfield named winner of €100.000 IEA Brexit Prize. (2014, April 8). Retrieved July 8, 2014, from http://www.iea.org.uk/in-the-media/press-release/iain-mansfield-named-winner-of-%E2%82%AC100000-iea-brexit-prize

Jacques Delors suggère au Royaume-Uni de quitter l'UE. (2012, December 28). *Le Monde*. Retrieved July 15, 2014, from http://www.lemonde.fr/europe/article/2012/12/28/jacques-delors-suggere-au-royaume-uni-de-quitter-l-ue_1811217_3214.html. http://labourforareferendum.com. Retrieved July 9, 2014.

Lazer, H. (1976). British populism: The Labour Party and the common market parliamentary debate. *Political Science Quarterly*, *91*(2), 259–277. doi:10.2307/2148412

Mansfield, I. (2014). A blueprint for Britain: Openness not isolation. *IEA Brexit Prize*. Retrieved June 20, 2014, from http://www.iea.org.uk/sites/default/files/publications/files/Brexit%20Entry%20170_final_bio_web.pdf

Marr, A. (2007). *A history of modern Britain*. Macmillan.

Miller, V. (2010, October 13). How much legislation comes from Europe? *House of Commons*. Research Paper 10/62. Retrieved July 8, 2014, from http://www.parliament.uk/business/publications/research/briefing-papers/RP10-62/how-much-legislation-comes-from-europe

Miller Llana, S. (2014, May 1). A decade after the EU's first expansion, open borders still rankle. *The Christian Science Monitor*. Retrieved July 14, 2014, from http://www.lexisnexis.com/hottopics/lnacademic

Nikki's Petition Drive. (2012, May 11). *Solihull News*. Retrieved July 14, 2014, from www.lexisnexis.com/hottopics/lnacademic

O'Donnel, J. (2014, February 17). EU's Reding warns Brexit would isolate London's city. *Reuters*. Retrieved July 14, 2014, from http://www.reuters.com/article/2014/02/17/us-eu-britain-city-idUSBREA1G17C20140217

Oliver, T. (2013, September). *Europe without Britain*. SWP Research Paper. Stiftung Wissenschaft und Politik / German Institute for International and Security Affairs. Retrieved June 21, 2014, from http://www.swp-berlin.org/fileadmin/contents/products/research_papers/2013_RP07_olv.pdf

Ottaviano, G., Pessoa, J. P., Sampson, T., & van Reenen, J. (2014, May 13). *The costs and benefits of leaving the EU*. London School of Economics Centre for Economic Performance. Retrieved July 13, 2014, http://cep.lse.ac.uk/pubs/download/pa016_tech.pdf

Pain, N., & Young, G. (2004). The macroeconomic impact of UK withdrawal from the EU. *Economic Modelling*, *21*(3), 387–408. doi:10.1016/S0264-9993(02)00068-8

People's Pledge. (n.d.). Retrieved from www.thepeoplespledge.org

Schnapper, P. (2010). Le Royaume-Uni et l'Europe: Toujours un malentendu? Hérodote. *Revue de Géographie et de Géopolitique*, *137*, 135–147.

Scotland Decides. (2014). *BBC*. Retrieved September 25, 2014, from http://www.bbc.com/news/events/scotland-decides/results

Spillius, A. (2012, December 18). Britain will be weaker without EU, says USA. *The Telegraph*. Retrieved July 5, 2014, from http://www.telegraph.co.uk/news/worldnews/europe/eu/9754042/Britain-will-be-weaker-without-EU-says-USA.html

Thompson, G., & Harari, D. (2013, September 17). *The economic impact of EU membership on the UK*. House of Commons. SN/EP/6730. Retrieved July 8, 2014, from http://www.parliament.uk/business/publications/research/briefing-papers/SN06730/the-economic-impact-of-eu-membership-on-the-uk

Treasury, H. M. (2013). *European Union finances 2013: Statement on the 2013 EU budget and measures to counter fraud and financial mismanagement*. Retrieved July 13, 2014, from https://www.gov.uk/government/uploads/system/uploads/attachment_data/file/220966/foi_eumembership_fdi.pdf

UE. Berlin prêt à discuter avec Londres. (2013, January 23). *Le Figaro*. Retrieved July 15, 2014, from http://www.lefigaro.fr/flash-eco/2013/01/23/97002-20130123FILWWW00450-ue-berlin-pret-a-discuter-avec-londres.php

UK must maintain a strong voice in Europe says automotive industry. (2014, April 2). *SMMT*. Retrieved July 14, 2014, from http://www.smmt.co.uk/2014/04/uk-automotive-industry-europe/

Vina, G. (2013, April 14). Almost one in five U.K. companies favor leaving EU. *Businessweek*. Retrieved July 7, 2014, from http://www.businessweek.com/news/2013-04-14/almost-one-in-five-u-dot-k-dot-companies-favor-leaving-eu

Wagstyl, S., Parker, G., & Barker, A. (2014, June 4). Angela Merkel seeks to dispel fears of Brexit. *Financial Times*. Retrieved July 15, 2014, from http://www.ft.com/intl/cms/s/0/f091232e-ec05-11e3-a9e3-00144feabdc0.html#axzz37QTMXh00

Wallace, W. (1991). Foreign policy and national identity in the United Kingdom. *International Affairs*, *67*(1), 65–80. doi:10.2307/2621219

Watt, N. (2014, July 1). Nick Clegg defeats Lib Dem bid to guarantee EU referendum. *The Guardian*. Retrieved July 9, 2014, from http://www.theguardian.com/politics/2014/jul/01/clegg-lib-dems-no-in-out-referendum-eu

Wintour, P. (2013, January 4). Cameron promises voters 'a real choice' over relations with Europe. *The Guardian*. Retrieved July 7, 2014, from http://www.theguardian.com/politics/2013/jan/04/cameron-promises-real-choice-eu

YouGov / The Sun Survey Results. (2014). Retrieved July 1, 2014, from http://yougov.co.uk/news/categories/politics/

KEY TERMS AND DEFINITIONS

A La Carte Europe: The idea that the European Union's integration levels on various policy areas should be different for each member state.

Brexit (Brixit): A merger of the words "Britain" and "exit" which refers to the possibility of the United Kingdom's withdrawal from the European Union.

The City: The financial and commercial center of London.

Confederation of British Industry: UK business organization formed out of a merger of the Federation of British Industries, the British Employers' Confederation and the National Association of British Manufacturers.

Democratic Deficit: The deficiency of democratic accountability and control over the decision-making processes.

Eurosceptic: A person who believes that their country had better not be a member of the European Union.

Foreign Direct Investment: An investment made in one country by an entity based in another country.

Chapter 5
Fiscal Integration and Harmonization:
European Union Integration from Fiscal Perspectives - Objectives, Means, Obstacles, and Politics

Yalçın Alganer
Marmara University, Turkey

Güneş Yılmaz
Trakya University, Turkey

ABSTRACT

The concept of integration expresses an extremely fundamental and complicated formation. Despite such important and complicated issues and problems, Europe has made considerable progress and developments and been able to form the European Economic Community first and then the European Communities, and finally the European Union. It is necessary to precisely and smoothly complete the three stages of integration in order to mention about an exact integration. These stages, economic integration, fiscal integration, and political integration are discussed within this chapter. The first stage, economic integration, can be achieved only with the integration of the trade among the elements of the integration. Hence, it is required to seek for the fiscal harmonization of the tax legislation that is the most important competition breaker element in the field in question. A complete economic integration will be possible only by providing this fiscal harmonization.

INTRODUCTION

The European Union has already followed the politics of fiscal harmonization aforementioned in a planned and systematical way since the first stage, in other words The Treaty of Rome of the European Economic Community. Although it has achieved considerable successes about this subject, it has been unable to place the system and fiscal harmonization within the relevant legislation of the acquis communautaire completely and as necessary; moreover, it could not apply the regulations it has made in the activity and direction it has desired.

DOI: 10.4018/978-1-4666-7308-3.ch005

As a matter of course, significant progresses and developments have been procured and a specific harmonization has been provided in terms of fiscal rules.

If successes considered as important had not been achieved in this stage, fiscal and political integrations which are the next stages could not have come to the fore and the EU could not have reached their current level.

The issues we will discuss and assess in the article will be the addressing processes of the taxational obstacles in the way passed to come to this level in terms of the tax approximations first and then tax harmonization. These stages will ensure to institute the tax coordination and remove the tax competition that is upper final objective.

Can these objectives be provided as required and desired?

We will seek for an answer to this question in the article here, and we will try to analyze and assess the causes and results of the developments in positive and/or negative way.

Both the primary legislation and secondary legislation regulations and application will be explained within the context of the EU acquis communautaire and the issue will be sophisticatedly discussed within the context of the indirect taxations and direct taxations.

Consequently, the recent state will be presented by generally synthesizing, and expectations and suggestions will be included.

BACKGROUND

Fiscal Integration is one of the main stages to achieve Union Integration. Union concept has economical, fiscal and political processes. European Union, at the first step, tried to construct the primary stage with fiscal approximations and harmonizations. The role and the consequences of the Neumark Committee (1960) and Neumark Report (1962) were very important and considerable. Avoiding tax competition is very important for the concept and for the spirit of common market. Otherwise tax harmonisation is inevitable to construct the base of the desired and preformed system. So the acquis communautaire, founder treaties, their legislations and especially their fiscal rules, are very important. But at the same time, the application of the mentioned issues is very sensitive as well. The authors believe that, tax harmonization is indispensable and even essential. Once the tax harmonization was rightly and notably applied on the indirect taxation, especially in Value Added Tax (VAT) system, it brought success. In spite the success of indirect taxation, the direct taxation experience was at the time and unfortunately still at present, has been insufficient and unsuccessful.

The authors also propose that, if the European Union members can regulate, apply commonly and act in full harmonization their corporate and income tax systems, than European Union will be much more significant.

CHRONOLOGICAL PROCESS OF THE EUROPEAN UNION INTEGRATION

In our time basis of social relations is the economic relations. These economic desicions and problems are also the determiners of countries, standards of living and policies which will be followed by the governments. Wars which were won depending on human power, concessions (privileges and capitulations) obtained by political skills of experienced diplomats have out lived their validity. In our day the power of production has taken the seat of the power of war. Economy and finance policies have become the factor of this economic power in a sense. State government has been based upon economic and financial applications within the context of legal rules and legislation. Missions, visions, manners and applications of the governments have changed parallel to this. Throughout the history, uniting european governments and efforts on european integrations have been carried out by voluntary and / or warfighting union and integration methods.

Europe (Europa) throughout the history has been the symbol of cultural accumulation and formation. Europa was the name of the daugther of the king of phoenica, Phoenix, and has been used in the meaning of sunset place as well. Thoughts and movements of European Union date back to very old times, but in real terms they had started in the middle ages. European union movements which took centuries (including all the bloody wars), had brought in some significant successful conclusions as late as the twentieth century. Many noted philosophers had aimed for this goal. From Immanuel Kant in his Perpetual Peace: A Philosophical Sketch (Kant, 1795) to Victor Hugo in his Project which he had presented in Congres de la Paix- International Peace Congress in Paris on 21 st August 1849, (Viegnes, 2005; Hugo, n.d.), from Montesquieu and Proudhon to Voltaire, Saint-Simon and to many more philosophers and people had made declerations, given pieces and made a big effort within the direction of this goal. All of these declerations, pieces and efforts had become very influential and even it were late they had come up with the results. European integration / union thought dealing with the european peace as the main theme have made big progresses (For further information: Alganer & Çetin, 2007)

Works and efforts in order to the reach the goal of European Union had continued increasingly and finally on 18 th April 1951 Paris Treaty were signed which had founded european cool and European Cool and Steel Community and can be considered as the first official and legal step in this subject. This treaty entered into force on 23 rd July 1952; and exactly 50 years after ended on 23 rd July 2002. With this treaty European Cool and Steel Community – ECSC, Communauté Européenne de Charbon et d'Acier – CECA) has been established. The six country which were the parties of this agreement have been remembered as the six in the literature (Germany, France, Italy, Belgium, Holland and Luxembourg). They wanted to carry this association to other fields. Taking courage from positive developments, after this important beginning step, in 1955 they had organised Messina Conference. After this conference on 25 th March 1957 Treaties of Rome were signed. In these treaties which entered into force on 1 st January 1958, European Atomic Energy Community (EURATOM) and European Economic Community (EEC) - Communauté Economique Européenne (CEE), have been established and so the integration period had properly been stated (Waal, 2014; Hansen, 2001; Office for Offical Publications of the European Communities, 1987).

Right of these treaties "The Six" had aimed to establish Customs Union which was the solid state of the integration Project and they succeeded in 1968. 60's has also been the years in which significant steps were taken in order to develop Common Agricultural Policy.

Only one counsil and one commission for all of the communities have been formed with Merger Treaty – Brussels Treaty which were signed on 8 th April 1965 and entered into force on 1 st July 1967. Thus European Communities - EC had started to take important steps in the wake of economic union and consolidation of organizational and economic structures.

70's had been the years for EC aiming at the foundation of European Monetary Union – EMU. Works started in this field with Lahey (Hague) Summit in 1969, had resulted with Werner Report which had been completed in 1970. In 1971, although works and progresses had been interrupted because of the economic problems in Europe, it has never been brought to an end. Intensive work had been pursued insistently and finally in 1979 European Monetary System – EMS- could had been formed. Besides being considered as an unsuccessful experience, EMS which took almost twenty years had been the basis of foundation of EMU (Cini & Perez -Borragan, 2013).

As a neccesity of European Integration, realization of enlargement, meaning the participation of new member governments has been counted as very important, even indespensable. In this respect 70's and 80's are assumed as important years for the enlargement of Europe. With the participation of England (United Kingdom), Denmark and Ireland in 1973, Greece in 1981, Spain and Portugal in 1986, number of EC had increased to 12. Thus, it had been tried to carry out economical and political integration paralel to each other and they had succeeded in this.

The Single European Act – SEA which was signed on 17 th February 1986 in Luxembourg and in Hague on 28 th February 1986 as well and entered into force on 1 st July 1987 has been considered as one of the main establishing treaties of the European Union today. SEA which includes provisions and items forming emendators on the treaties which established EC, includes also significant clauses providing collaboration between member governments in the field of foreign politics.

EC, has made very big progress which even lays the foundation of EU today for the sake of economic and political integration within the period starting from 1951 to Treaty on European Union – Maastricht Treaty which was signed on 2 nd February 1992 and entered into force on 1 st November 1993.

Treaty of Amsterdam had been signed on 2 nd October 1997 and entered into force on 1 st May 1999. Especially considering the new participants EU had reorganized its institutions. This also can be considered as a very important arrangement fort he integration.

Stability and Growth Pact (SGP) which was first approved in 1997 (with substantial reforms agreed to it in 2005 and 2011), was created enforce fiscal discipline in member state budgeting by imposing rules and target numbers, and attach effective warnings and sanctions to them. SGP did not prove to be an efficient way to ensure fiscal discipline and sustainable output growth before the crisis. The 2011 reform is known by the name of the "six pack", as it package of six legislative changes to the SGP to ensure credible commitment to the goals of fiscal consilidation and competitiveness. The SGP reform also introduced the Macroeconomic Imbalances Procedure (MIP) to prevent and correct macro-imbalances (Polyak, 2013)

Treaty of Nice which was signed on 26 th February 2001 and entered into force on 1 st February 2003 had reformed institutions of European Union of which the member number would reach to 25. Particularly it had arranged composition of the Commission and the voting system of the Council.

After a long and arguing period Treaty of Lisbon had finally been signed on 13 th December 2007 and entered into force on 1 st December 2009. This treaty had merely brought to EU a constitutional system. Setting out goal had been EU constitution but as the out come of the referendum was negative, concessions had firstly been reduced to Reform Treaty, and then being a little more modified it had taken its final structure as Treaty of Lisbon (Bomberg, Peterson & Corbett, 2012)

After shortly touching upon the role and the importance of basic founding treaties over EU integration process, we can move into our essential analyze topic which is integration research and development.

EUROPEAN UNION INTEGRATION FROM FISCAL PERSPECTIVES: OBJECTIVES, MEANS, OBSTCLES, AND POLITICS

Integration besides seeming as a general term as of its concept, when it is started to be examined throughly it becomes a concept of which the aspects can no easily be formed. As follows:

The field of integration (union – integration) has its political, economical, fiscal, military and social aspects. As soon as all of these parameters can exactly fit into their places it will be possible to make mention of a whole integration. Let's analyze all of these parameters now. Firstly economic integration; success in this field can only be by removing all of the obstacles to trade. If the elements preventing trade can be eliminated, it means that trade integration is provided and this is an important coloumn of economical integration. Another parameter is the integration of the factors. In the case that factors of production can freely move in a composition, then it means this base is reached as well. Also national economic policies should be accomodated. There is consensus about economic integration in three different literatures. One, that economic integration refers basically to division of labor; two, that economic integration involves mobility of goods or factors or both; and three, that it is related to discrimination or nondiscrimination in the treatment of goods and factors (Machlup, 1975).

This attendantly puts forward the subject of fiscal harmonization which we will consider as indispensable. Moreover economic integration can only be provided by fiscal harmonization. If fiscal harmonization can not be provided economic integrations are always obliged to go-off half-cooked. We will dwell on the subject of fiscal integration, more tangible fiscal harmonization, in more detail later. This will attribute us to the subject of tax competition. Let's now we drop the subject with the harmonization of national economical policies. If also this parameter is procured we can talk about a whole economic integration. This will probably take us to foreign trade zone, customs union and common market and next to economic union and finally to a whole economic integration.

If the countries which are the members of the union and are trying to be integrated, can bind their national money the others with fixed exchange rate system than they can pass into one monetary unit and of course to application of only one central bank. This shows us the second coloumn fiscal integration is succeeded.

If economic and fiscal integration have been provided and then monetary integrations has been procured now the political integration which is the ultimate goal will be tried to be put into practice. This step is absolutely the most difficult and the most problemetical step, but at least it could be reached theoretically and it would be aimed to be reached as the next higher goal. The main founding treaties have been directive, regulatory and even supervisory in this respect. For example, with Maastricht Treaty (Treaty on European Union) it has tried to establish a kind of United States of Europe in such a way that:

One monetary unit has been put into the system. EU citizenship has been put into the model; it has been agreed upon the topics of mutual foreign and security policy and cooperation in the fields of justice and home affairs and desicions of acting in unison coordinately and making necessary adjustments have been made. (Cini et al., 2013).

Fiscal integration requires the coordination of fiscal policies. In this respect, fiscal union enables a federal state or a federation of several countries to conduct a coordinated fiscal policy and typically shows several (but not necessarily all) of the following components:

1. A common set of fiscal rules
2. Mechanisms for crisis intervention
3. Fiscal equalisation and transfer mechanisms between countries
4. A common budget

While most of these components may be both preventive and reactive in nature, depending on the specific design, (1) is clearly preventive and (2) clearly reactive. Points (3) and (4) are found solely at the national level. The extent to which these components should be integrated into the architecture of the eurozone is a matter of dispute, however (Hoffman & Speyer, 2013).

Here it has to be indicated that when we look at the historical progress and consider the models within the national borders fiscal integrations have usually been carried out after political integrations. And the economic integrations have progressed differently depending on time and ground. While in Germany economic integration has been carried out before political integration, in Italy economic integration has occured after political integration. It is still built up a formula even it is flexible in some aspects. As follows:

In order to build a political integration, the field of trade and its regulations in the widest sense have to be developed in an economical signification. The main substance and first closest goal of EU (EEC) was this. Secondly sociological formations play a big role such as cultural identities, language and religion factors. We think that these parameters are secondary but important for the formation of union. And the third parameter is to conflict against common enemy or enemies. We think that this also is one of the main indicators and requirements to form the union.

In the case that all of these parameters become real, the union should be adorned with common benefits. There is the need of a qualified legal superstructure. This structure or the authority will be above national states and be centralized. In other words it should be supranational. Thus beyond economic goals it will provide an infrastructure for the rule " to build up tigher relations between the member governments". This concept is the second item of Treaty of Rome which established EEC. We shortly mentioned above the important developments about this subject. The ultimate goal has sensitively carefully and meticulously been carried out and positive results have already be taken. Important difficulties and obstacles have been faced, blockings have been seen and even there has been the danger of a breakdown, economic and fiscal problems have occured but, hopes, efforts and researches for the ultimate goal have never faded.

Now we can dwell with the fiscal aspect of the matter. Here fiscal policies, tax applications, coordination of taxes, tax approximations and tax harmonizations have come into prominence. And the ultimate goal in this field is to reduce tax competition as to minimum as possible and to resolve if possible (For more information Yılmaz et al., 2010).

Today globalization is a solid ever-developing fact. EU has tried to take place in globalization with its sui generis structure. With its structure today EU is neither a federation nor a confederation. It has desicion making and executive organs with its parliament acceded with voting, council, comission and comittees. Because of these specification EU can be considered as a supranational union of nation states.

Because of its relation with our topic, within the context of integration in EU which we mentioned above, financial instruments especially the taxes which are the most efficient ones among these instruments have an important and different place. It has been required to start the work with the adjustments which will effect tax systems of the member governments. But this is a very sensitive and critical matter that its level and dimensions have to be adjusted accurately. It has gained currency and has been adopted to eliminate tax barriers and to form more coordinating tax system by without renouncing sovereignty rights in cross border processes of EU member governments, keeping these rights as much as possible. It is reported that it was hard but not impossible. And this formation is called tax coordination.

In a foundation like EU, tax competition comes the first among the factors which can prevent to reach goals. Tax coordination will try to minimize tax competition but the real effecting factor of the process are low tax rates, exceptions and exemptions, discounts, other tax-related supports and privileges. Taking these elements into account, foreign capital will call out its decisions and make investments. And because of this a big competition will occur. All of the players will try to take the biggest, predominant share of the cake. And this process is called tax competition. In this respect preferential taxes and /or discriminatory tax applications have an important place, making cost and benefit analysis as essential as loss and justice analysis.

How will these delicate balances be overcome, what kind of a structure or a system should be activated to reach to the lowest loss and fairest solutions and as a result to the ultimate upper goals as EU. Two important concepts and regulations come into effect here. First stage of these regulations will be tax approximation. This regulation is the work of approximations related to direct taxes taken from especially natural persons and legal entities in national base within the domestic market.

The most efficient regulation and parameter of reaching the ultimate goal in terms of these works and fiscal integration will be tax harmonizations. It comprises the process of according tax systems of the member govenments having different tax systems. This is a general statement but it is possible to mount this to EU. It means the according of the tax systems of the member governments by bringing tax related arrangements which can prevent competition as much as possible, providing purification of tax legislation from tax-related injustice. Tax harmonization aims to prevent double taxation which is one of the most problematic subject of our days, abusements in transfer pricing and international evasion of taxes and to minimize and even to remove inconsistency costs of different tax systems.

We will try to give answers to the questions like at what level these goals could be reached, in which accordances we have succeeded and could expected progresses be achieved, in this last part of our article.

We want to emphasize that tax competition has taken the place of accordance of direct taxation in EU. The goal in this field is to provide the mobility, in other words free circulation, of the people, capital and the trade by at least minimizing and then removing the unequality of competition. Member governments agrees upon reducing two sided effects of the taxes over economy to the lowest in all member governments by seting aside the advantages and disadvantages arising from different tax applications because of different tax systems of the member governments.

This is the iner part of the matter. And there is also the outer part and that is:

As being EU countries it is aimed to build a specific EU market and EU marketing systems for the contries outside EU. If this can be provided, it will also provide an infrastructure for EU companies in order to establish a superiority or an advantage in competition at a general level. This is the first goal desired.

Tax harmonization in another aspect, limits and brings restrictions for the usage of fiscal policies which are among the most efficient instruments of financial policies of the countries in accordance with the revenues they desire. Because of this it has a specific cost for the countries. The system will be connected to certain fiscal rules, their ability to use tax mechanism will possibly decrease; or at least will loose their previous strengths.

The subjects of harmonization and tax competition are of vital importance for EU because of these reasons we have already mentioned. All of these EU acquis communautaire, in other words primary legislations which are composed of founder treaties, their annexes, protocols, emendator treaties and the secondary legislations comprising of regulations, directives, decisions, opinions and recommendations, are organized in a rule-bound and active process.

CONCLUSION

EU tax harmonization policies are a very important and effective means to reach the main objectives of the agreement that establishes EEC. The Neumark Committee constituted in 1960 and Neumark Report presented in 1962 which are the most important studies and stages about harmonization do not suggest that the tax systems of countries are combined and turned into only one tax system and are applied in this form. EEC also suggests harmonization policies instead of a common tax policy. This matter is both very significant and striking. While it suggests to ensure a relative balance in the total tax incidences in national incomes, it also suggests to equalize the tax and similar incidences in cost prices as much as possible. In the model, the final stage is to incrementally harmonize the tax systems. It is emphasized that the regulation of the indirect taxes which are taken on especially goods and services must be harmonized in order to ensure that the objective Common Market operates without any problem. For this purpose, a regulation arrangement has been made in terms of turnover taxes, excise duties and other indirect taxes. The most successful harmonization in terms of indirect taxes has been in VAT (Value Added Taxes) that is nearly turned into an EU tax.

The second significant and effective study about tax harmonization has been performed in Excise Duties. It has been aimed to be applied especially manufactured tobacco products, alcoholic beverages, energy products (motor fuels, and heating fuels, such as petrol and gasoline, electricity, natural gas, coal and coke).

The positive and successful improvements in direct taxes, could not be achieved in the harmonization of indirect taxes. There are some problems about the structure of the tax, investment and capital activities of the companies and institutions to be solved. We think that it is necessary to harmonize the economy and finance policies, the structures of national economies and even cultural and social life standards as much as possible in order to achieve the goal exactly.

Here we want to emphasize that these topics are still the question in debate in EU. It has been put forward that a decrease in competition between the people in Europe may reduce the life quality, change the way of living and social and cultural habits and in long term may cause poverty. Competition element in economy, trade, industry, in other words, competition in business life is the expression of liberty and wealth. Regulations for tax harmonization and fiscal rules will hamper central administrations and can reduce the competition in EU. This is the subject of the argument among EU institutions—especially European Parliament—and the economists—especially the financiers—in general.

REFERENCES

Alganer, Y., & Çetin, M.Ö. (2007). Avrupa'da birlik ve bütünleşme hareketleri-I, *Journal of Marmara University İ.İ.B.F., 23*(2), 285-309.

Bomberg, E., Peterson, J., & Corbett, R. (2012). *The European Union: How does it work?* (3rd ed.). Oxford University Press.

Cini, M., Perez, N., & Borragan, S. (2013). *European Union politics* (4th ed.). Oxford University Press.

IMF Country Report. (2012). *Euro area policies - 2012 article IV consultation- No.12/181.* Washington, DC: Author.

de Waal, M. (2014). *The choice for Euro: the treaty on stability, coordination and governance through a liberal intergovernmentalist lens (2012-2014).* (Unpublished master dissertation). University of Twente, Faculty of Management and Governance, Netherland.

Deutsche Bank- DB Research. (2013). *Do all roads lead to fiscal union? Options for deeper fiscal integraton in the Eurozone.* Frankfurt am Main: Author.

Hansen, E. D. (2001). *European economic history.* Copenhagen Bussines School Press DK.

Hugo, V. (n.d.). *Les états-Unis d'Europe, Discours prononcé le 21 août 1849 lors du Congrès de la paix.* Retrieved June 8, 2014, from http://www.oasisfle.com/culture_oasisfle/etats_unis_d_europe.htm

IMF Working Paper. (2012). *Fiscal rules in response to the crisis—Toward the "next-generation" rule.* Washington, DC: Author.

International Monetary Fund (IMF) Working Paper. (2001). *Is fiscal policy coordination in EMU desirable?* Washington, DC: Author.

Kant, I. (1795). *Perpetual peace: A philosophical sketch.* Retrieved June 7, 2014, from http://isites.harvard.edu/fs/docs/icb.topic248058.files/March%2017%20readings/Kant%20Perpetual%20Peace%20section%20II.pdf

Machlup, F. (1975). *The history of thought on economic integration.* New York: New York University Press.

Miller, V. (2011). *The EU's acquis communautaire.* Retrieved May 20, 2014, from www.parliament.uk/briefing.../sn05944.pdf

Office for Offical Publications of the European Communities. (1987). Treaties establishing the European Communities (ECSC, EEC, EAEC). Brussels: Author.

Organisation for Economic Co-operation and Development. (n.d.). *Better regulation in Europe: An OECD assessment of regulatory: Capacity in the 15 original member states of the EU.* Paris: OECD. Retrieved July 11, 2014, from http://www.oecd.org/gov/regulatory-policy/44952782.pdf

Polyak, P. (2013). *Fiscal unification going unnoticed? Trends in the European Union's involvement in national tax policies in the onset of the Euro crisis.* (Unpublished master dissertation). Central European University.

Steichen, A. (2002). Tax competition in Europe or the taming of leviathan. *General Report at the EATLP Seminar.* Retrieved July 12, 2014, from http://www.eatlp.org/uploads/Members/GeneralReportSteichen.pdf

EU Treaties. (n.d.). Retrieved July 10, 2014, from http://europa.eu/about-eu/basic-information/decision-making/treaties/index_en.htm

Velayos, F., Barreix, A., & Villela, L. (2008). *Regional integration and tax harmonization: issues and recent experiences.* Retrieved July 12, 2014, from http://siteresources.worldbank.org/INTTPA/Resources/Velayos-Villela-Barreix.pdf

Viegnes, M. (2005). The French vision of Europe from Victor Hugo's United States of Europe to the no to the constitution. *Europe's Journal of Psychology.* Retrieved May 30, 2014, from http://ejop.psychopen.eu/article/view/376/279

Yılmaz, G., & Alganer, Y. (2010). Avrupa Birliği müktesebatı bağlamında katma değer vergisinde yakınlaştırma ve uyumlaştırma çalışmaları. *Journal of Marmara University İ.İ.B.F., 27*(1), 135-160.

KEY TERMS AND DEFINITIONS

Acquis Communautaire: The Acquis Communautaire is the accumulated body of European Union (EU) law and obligations from 1958 to the present day. It comprises all the EU's treaties and laws (directives, regulations, decisions), declarations and resolutions, international agreements and the judgments of the Court of Justice. It also includes action that EU governments take together in the Area of Freedom, Security and Justice and under the Common Foreign and Security Policy (Miller, 2011).

Fiscal Coordination: Need for national governments to closely coordinate decisions on the overall fiscal stance (Beetsma, Debrun & Klaassen, 2001).

Fiscal Integration: Fiscal integration means stronger governance arrangements that help to ensure fiscal behavior in accordance with commonly agreed standards (IMF Country Report, 2012).

Fiscal Rules: Fiscal rules impose a long-lasting constraint on fiscal policy through numerical limits on budgetary aggregates (Schaechter, Kinda, Budina & Weber, 2012).

Primary and Secondary Legislation: Regulations enacted by the legislature (parliament or congress). At the European level, the treaties constitute the EU's 'primary legislation. Secondary regulation can be enacted by a body authorized to do so by primary legislation (legislation enacted by the legislature). It may also be known as subordinate regulation (OECD, n.d.).

Tax Approximation: Tax approximation may be defined as a situation driven by EU legislation driving tax systems and tax rates closer together, without becoming identical (Steichen, 2002).

Tax Harmonization: The process of adjusting national fiscal systems to conform with a set of common economic aims (Velayos, Barreix & Villela, 2008).

Tax Competition: Tax competition may be defined as a process leading to a result that involves the fiscal decisions of one country affecting the economic welfare of another (Steichen, 2002).

Treaty of Lisbon: Signed: 13 December 2007; Entered into force: 1 December 2009.

Purpose of Treaty of Lisbon: To make the EU more democratic, more efficient and better able to address global problems, such as climate change, with one voice. Main changes: more power for the European Parliament, change of voting procedures in the Council, citizens' initiative, a permanent president of the European Council, a new High Representative for Foreign Affairs, a new EU diplomatic service ("EU Treaties", n.d.).

Treaties of Rome: EEC and EURATOM treaties. Signed: 25 March 1957; Entered into force: 1 January 1958. Purpose of Treaties of Rome: to set up the European Economic Community (EEC) and the European Atomic Energy Community (EURATOM). Main changes: extension of European integration to include general economic cooperation ("EU Treaties", n.d.).

Section 2
New Dynamics in EU Regionalism and Enlargement

Chapter 6
Does the Regional Economic Integration Lead to Banking Union?
The European Case

Christophe Schalck
ESG Management School, France

ABSTRACT

In 2012, the European Commission created a roadmap towards a European Banking Union. The aim of this EBU is to ensure financial stability in Europe. The proposed framework by the European Commission is based on three pillars: a Single Supervisory Mechanism (SSM), a Single Resolution Mechanism (SRM), and a single deposit guarantee mechanism. The EBU project is a step towards a better functioning EMU in the future. However, there are several controversies on this project. The main concerns are conflicts of interest between monetary policy and banking supervision, and cooperation between ECB and other banking authorities. If the EBU is a necessary step, it is not a sufficient one to resolve all financial issues in the EMU and in Europe.

INTRODUCTION

The global financial and economic crisis in 2009 has pointed out failures of financial services supervision. In Europe, this crisis was first reflected by a banking crisis. Europe has implemented a broad rescue plan for banks in the amount of 1,700 billion euros, or 13.6% of European GDP. This plan has mainly included guarantees of interbank loans and funds to recapitalize banks. The global crisis was also reflected by a sovereign debt crisis in Europe caused by deterioration in public accounts: the EU public deficit increased from 0.9% of GDP in 2007 to 6.5% of GDP in 2010, and the EU public debt increased from 58.9% of GDP to 80,7% of GDP in the same period. Thus, these crises have highlighted the weaknesses of the European governance, in particular for the Economic and Monetary Union (EMU). The first responses of European authorities concerned fiscal policies:

DOI: 10.4018/978-1-4666-7308-3.ch006

within the European Semester, the new reforms of the Stability and Growth Pact (SGP) tend to increase fiscal discipline and improve enforcement mechanisms. The European Commission analyses the fiscal and structural reform policies of every Member State, provides recommendations, and monitors their implementation. To strengthen the implementation of the European Semester, the Commission may rely on two European legislative package called "Six pack" and "Two pack". The Commission has now the opportunity to request corrections to projects of Member States and to apply sanctions more easily. Moreover, the European monitoring now includes global imbalances. The Macroeconomic Imbalance Procedure (MIP) is a surveillance mechanism that aims to identify potential risks early on, prevent the emergence of harmful macroeconomic imbalances and correct the imbalances that are already in place. Parallel to this monitoring and to respond to the crisis, the EU has established a European system of financial crisis management in the euro area: the European Stability Mechanism (ESM) is a permanent firewall for the eurozone to safeguard and provide instant access to financial assistance programs for member states of the eurozone in financial difficulty, with a maximum lending capacity of €500 billion. It replaced two earlier temporary EU funding programs: the European Financial Stability Facility (EFSF) and the European Financial Stabilization Mechanism (EFSM).

However, the issue of banking sector was not dealt so deeply until 2012. The chosen way was an intermediate step with the founding of the European System of Financial Supervisors (ESFS) in 2011. The ESFS is made up of: i) the European Systemic Risk Board (ESRB) which is in charge of monitoring and analyzing any risks to the stability of the financial system arising from macroeconomic developments and developments within the financial system as a whole (macro prudential supervision); ii) the three European Supervisory Authorities (ESAs) which interact with the existing national supervisory authorities in order to ensure the financial soundness of the financial institutions themselves and to protect users of financial services (micro prudential supervision). Owing to this fragmented structure and face to a deeper fiscal and monetary integration, the European Commission proposed a European Banking Union (EBU) to reach a Genuine Economic and Monetary Union (Van Rompuy, 2012). This proposition is based on a single supervisory mechanism for banks led by the European Central Bank (ECB), a single bank resolution mechanism and a common deposit protection. On 15 April 2014, the European Parliament adopted several texts launching the EBU.

This chapter addresses the relevance of the EBU: Does the EBU can prevent and mitigate the crisis? How would the EBU affect the monetary policy? The chapter is organized as follows: section 1 provides an overview of theoretical and empirical justifications of the EBU, section 2 presents the EBU, and the section 3 debates on the EBU highlighting controversies and limits.

THEORETICAL AND EMPIRICAL JUSTIFICATIONS OF THE EBU

Ensure Financial Stability

The final aim of the EBU is to contribute to the financial stability objective. Financial stability can be defined as a condition in which the financial system is resistant to economic shocks and is fit to smoothly fulfil its basic functions: the intermediation of financial funds, management of risks and the arrangement of payments. The recent economic and financial crisis is a global crisis which emphasized the role of systemic risk on the conditions of an international financial system. Under these conditions, an international supervision seems to be relevant. Cechetti, Fender, and McGuire (2010) concern the necessity of international exchange information and a larger framework for statistical reporting. According to Saveanu (2012), an architectural supervision package in which the microeconomic supervision components mix with the macroeconomic ones can create the financial stability. The need for international supervision to ensure financial stability is all the more justified by the existence of cross-border interbank networks in Europe: in 2012 for EMU, 16% of total banking assets corresponded to cross-border activities and the cross-border banking businesses with Britain are stronger (Schoenmaker & Peek, 2014). Schoenmaker and Wagner (2013) find that the countries with the largest banking centers, the UK and Germany, are well diversified. By contrast, the New Member States are highly dependent on a few West European banks and vulnerable to contagion effects. The Nordic and Baltic regions are closely linked with little diversification. At the system level, the EU banking system is weakly diversified, with an overexposure to the United States and an underexposure to Japan and China. This explains why the recent US-originated financial crisis had such a significant impact on European banks.

With an increasing financial integration, the pursuit of national financial policy would not lead to financial stability. Since national policies seek to improve national welfare, they do not taking account externalities of their supervisory practices on other countries. This leads to an under-provision of financial stability (Holthausen & Ronde, 2004). In the same way, Goodhart and Schoenmaker (2009) show that ex-post coordination among different national supervisors leads to an under-provision recapitalization of cross-border banks after a banking problem.

The EBU explicitly connects the tiered banking and financial stability. Therefore, it completes the overview of the various institutions and mechanisms that have been implemented in the EMU after the crisis for a greater integration (Figure 1).

Figure 1. The new framework of the EMU
EBU: European Banking Union; ECB: European Central Bank; ESM: European Stability Mechanism; ESFS: European System of Financial Supervisors; SGP: Stability and Growth Pact.
Source: Author's conception

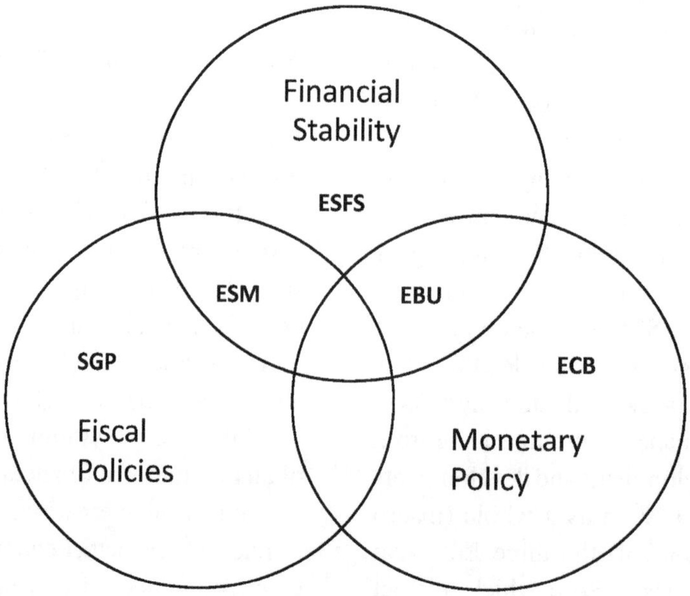

The Fragmentation of Financial Markets

The EBU could delink sovereigns and banks markets (Turliuc & Popovici, 2013). With the euro crisis, there is close relationship of banks to sovereign debt and the view of the rating agencies because European banks continue to hold large amounts of bonds from their home governments. This ties the fates of the sovereign and the banks together, leading to the disruptive self-reinforcing feedback loops that brought the euro area to the brink of collapse (Gros, 2013). This loop is driven by bank bail outs (or bail-out expectations) that Members states will have to rescue, which then increases borrowing costs for countries and further drives up costs for banks. Thus the sovereign debt crisis has led to a fragmentation of credit and government bonds markets.

The fragmentation of financial markets is reflected in a significant increase of the heterogeneity in financial conditions within the euro area. Since the start of the EMU, some degree of national differentiation in the financial conditions has existed, but the financial crisis marked the reemergence of differentiated financial conditions within the Eurozone. In some countries, changes in ECB interest rate are being passed on fully by banks, in others, because bank funding is tight, interest rate changes are being passed on hardly at all. This is making credit very hard to come by or unduly expensive in some parts of the euro area. Table 1 presents some retails rates in the EMU and shows these ongoing slippages in interest rates on loans and deposits, especially for consumer loans. This fragmentation has impaired the transmission mechanism of monetary policy, since it requires an appropriate level of financial integration that ensures well performing cross border money markets. Therefore, the EBU could restore the effectiveness of the monetary policy, in particular by creating enhanced confidence in the national banking sectors' solvency and liquidity situations. Moreover, early supervisory action limits the necessity to access central banks' financing.

Dealing with Some Specific Banking Sector Features

The last main reason for the establishment of the EBU is avoiding national bias in supervision. A single and independent supervisor could rebuild investor confidence since it could not be suspected of allowing banks to hide bad assets in some countries. This will reduce the moral hazard of banks otherwise encouraged to take risks under the insurance of being bailed out by their State. The shift of supervision from the domestic to the supranational level could eliminate national bias because supervisors should be free from local pressures and interest. This ensures shorter delays for the implementation of bankruptcy or resolution procedures.

This point could be crucial because some European countries have not an efficient baking sector. The number of "bad loans" greatly increased since 2008, especially in peripheral countries, and reached 9.5% of GDP in the euro area. The share of these "bad loans" to total assets would be high in Spain (16%) and Italy (10%) and low in Germany (3%) (Breuss, 2013). Another issue is the too large banking sector in small countries that made them greatly vulnerable. It is particularly true for Luxembourg, Malta, Ireland and obviously Cyprus, which known a dramatically crisis and benefited of European intervention (Figure 2).

THE EBU: A THREE-PILLAR FRAMEWORK

The "Van Rompuy Plan" in December 2012 stipulated that the banking union will be built in three stages. First, a single supervisory mechanism

Table 1. Average bank retail rates in the euro area countries over the 2003-2010 period

	Consumer Loans	Real Estate Loans	Household Deposits	Loans to Firms < 1m€	Loans to Firms > 1m€	Firm Deposits
Austria	5.47	4.03	2.43	3.93	3.35	2.42
Belgium	7.94	4.02	2.03			2.22
Finland	4.67	3.43	2.59	4.03	3.39	2.25
France	6.57	4.18	2.56	4.31	3.33	2.40
Germany	6.68	4.6	2.37	4.78	3.83	2.28
Greece	9.29	4.34	3.08			2.77
Ireland	6.41	3.86	2.36	4.97	4.40	2.37
Italy	8.63	4.16	1.86	4.40	3.41	2.39
Netherlands		4.56	2.93	4.42	3.40	2.37
Portugal	9.05	3.77	2.47	6.21	4.28	2.60
Spain	8.61	3.84	2.78	4.43	3.44	2.60

Source: ECB

Figure 2. Size of banking sector in euro area countries
Source: Author's computation from ECB database

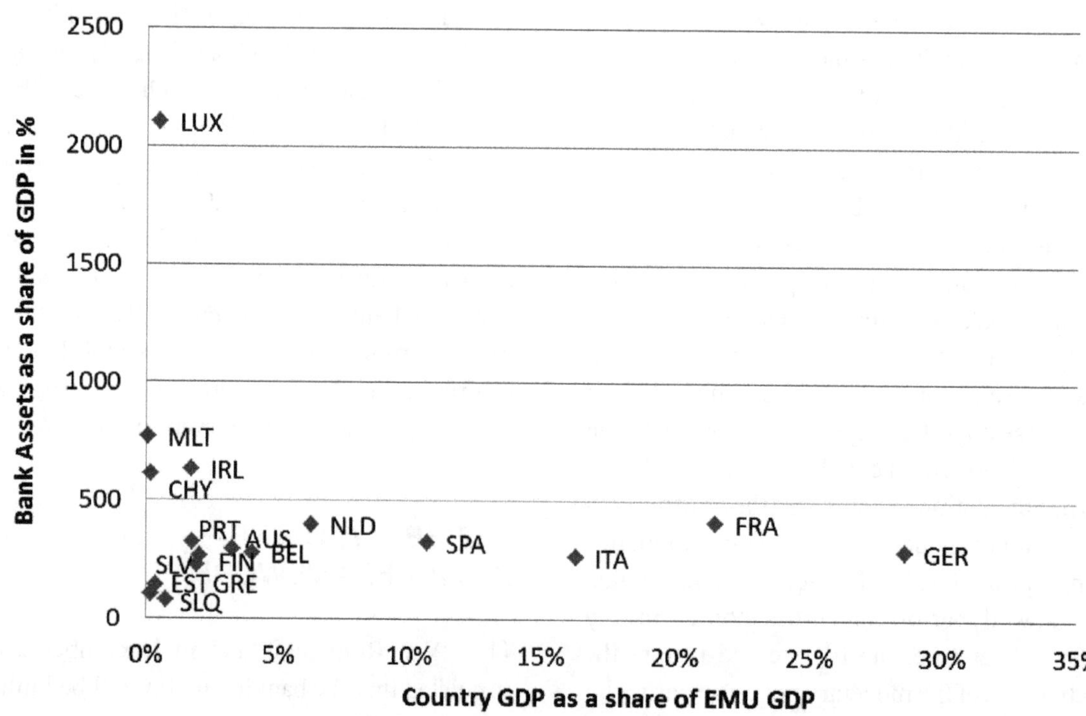

(SSM) will be implemented as soon as possible, later a single resolution mechanism (SRM) should follow and in the end a single deposit guarantee mechanism would complete the scheme.

The first pillar of the banking union is the Single Supervisory Mechanism (SSM), which would grant the European Central Bank (ECB) a supervisory role to monitor financial stability of all members' states banks. It will ensure compliance with provisions on leverage and liquidity, impose constitution of capital buffer or the introduction of correctives measures as deemed necessary. Thus, the ECB should facilitate the implementation of the common scheme of crisis resolution, by acting by in normal times and on times of crisis for the resolution of bankruptcy procedures. Furthermore, the ECB will directly supervise large banks (200 banks on a total of 6 000 banks in Europe), i.e. banks with assets amounting to more than 30 billion euros or at least 20% of GDP of the home country. While all banks in EMU will be under the supervision of the ECB, this will be carried out in cooperation with national supervisors.

The Single Resolution Mechanism (SRM) is a proposed pillar that would centrally implement the common rulebook's Bank Recovery and Resolution Directive in participating Member States. The scheme has five pillars (Avaro & Sterdyniak, 2014). The first one is to improve prevention by requiring banks to provide strategies for recovery. The second gives the European banking authorities the power to implement recovery plans and to change bank managers if the bank does not meet the capital requirements. The third indicate that, if a bank fails, national authorities will be able to take control of it and use instruments of resolution such as the transfer of activities, the creation of a "bad bank" or the bail-in. In the event of a bank failure, shareholders will be affected first, and then subordinated claims. The fourth pillar requires Member States to set up a resolution fund, which must amount within 10 years, to 1% of the covered deposits of all credit institutions, which would have to finance it. The found would provide temporary support to institutions under resolution. According to the fifth, Member States shall ensure that the institutions maintain a sufficient aggregate amount of own funds and eligible liabilities. This scheme implies two institutions at the European level: a Single Resolution Board (SRB) and a Single Bank Resolution Fund (SBRF). The SRM would work as follows:

- The ECB would signal when a bank in the euro area or established in a Member State participating in the Banking Union was in severe financial difficulties and needed to be resolved.
- The SRB, consisting of representatives from the ECB, the European Commission and the relevant national authorities, would prepare the resolution of the bank.
- On the basis of the SRB' recommendation, the European Commission would decide whether and when to place a bank into resolution and would set out a framework for the use of resolution tools and the fund.
- Under the supervision of the SRB, national resolution authorities would be in charge of the execution of the resolution plan.
- The SRB would oversee the resolution. It would monitor the execution at national level by the national resolution authorities and, should a national resolution authority not comply with its decision, it could directly address executive orders to the troubled banks.
- The SBRF would be set up under the control of the SRB to ensure the availability of medium term funding support while the bank was restructured. It would be funded by contributions from the banking sector

The last pillar is a European deposit guarantee scheme. A deposit guarantee system protects savers in case of bank failure by refunding their deposits up to a certain ceiling. It is one of the sovereign tasks of the State to provide citizens with a risk free instrument of payment and saving. Customers do not exactly know their bank's financial health. They are subject to information asymmetries which, in normal times, promote confidence in credit institutions. In a banking crisis, information asymmetries between depositors and towards banks strengthen the contagion of panic and cause a rush of investors seeking to withdraw their deposits massively. Then liquidity crises turn into solvency crises threatening to spillover to the entire banking system. A bank failure deteriorates stakeholders' confidence on the interbank market and decreases credit supply; therefore, it has a negative impact on the real economy halting activities that depend on these credits and causing a sudden stop of investments. The harmonization of the deposit guarantee level in Europe would avoid that some countries attract deposits from their neighbors by offering a full guarantee if deposits knowing that this full guarantee may have heavy consequences for the population of the country concerned.

EBU: A CONTROVERSIAL TOOL?

How EBU Have Helped During The Crisis?

According to ECB Board, problems in the banking sector might originate at the national level, but are more and more likely to affect other countries of the euro area as well, and may quickly threaten the stability of the entire euro area banking system. Such developments and the underlying financial structures can be best assessed by a central authority rather than through cooperation between national ones (Constancio, 2013).

Under this view, the recent economic and financial crisis could have been prevented by a European banking union. A banking union would not have halted the sovereign debt crisis in some countries, but it could have substantially weakened the adverse sovereign-bank-growth spirals, maintained depositor confidence and attenuated the liquidity and funding freezes that followed (Turliuc & Popovici, 2013). Within a banking union, the rate cuts of the ECB would more likely have fed through to lower borrowing costs for the private sector. Had a single European supervisor existed prior the crisis, it could have spotted the unsustainable growth in private sector debt and the excessive leveraging of banks' balance sheets (such as Spain, Ireland and Cyprus), and taken early preventative measures.

The efficiency of the EBU is related to the resolution mechanisms: what could be the favored mechanism by the ECB? Breuss (2013) presents different resolution mechanism:

- **Home Rule Bank Rescue:** A national bank is rescued via home measures by the national government, which plays as lender of last resort. This solution has the advantage to be flexible but it would be the least efficient one since the link between sovereign debts and bank failures is maintained.
- **SRM Rescue within the EBU:** The burden of the bank rescue in one country would be share by all members of the EBU. Hence, the stabilization of a country with the failing bank can succeed better, but the impact in the remaining Euro area would be worse than in the case of a national rescue operation in the periphery alone. The main advantage of this solution is to break the link between banks failures and sovereign debts.
- **Direct Recapitalization via ESM:** This would be an alternative measure to the EBU. But in this case, the burden of the bank rescue is only shared by EMU countries. The question whether the ESM bank rescue or the SRM bank rescue would be better to stabilize the economies is still open.

- **Mixed Resolution Mechanism with Bail-In Approaches:** Such solution would shift the losses from the EBU member states more to the deposit holders of failed bank and would therefore reduce the stabilization effect of SRM solution.

A Particular Situation for the ECB

The attribution of unified banking supervision powers to the ECB seems to be relevant in a first look. The ECB has an established reputation of political independence. The ECB has the advantage to already have a good knowledge of the interbank market and situation of each large bank. Nevertheless, this attribution of powers may raise several problems.

Triple Objectives

According to the Treaty on the Functioning of the European Union, the primary objective of the ECB is to maintain price stability. Thus, the ECB aims to keep inflation below, but close to, 2% over medium term. Since the launch of the EMU, this objective has been considered as the most important, the only one, on which the European monetary policy is based on. With the crisis, an implicit objective has become increasingly important: the financial stability. The ECB took several unusual measures and play the role as lender of last resort while this mission it is not explicitly asked. This mission is crucial, especially for the sovereign debt market because they suffer a liquidity risk which may lead to macroeconomic instability (Buiter & Rahbari, 2012). The mandate of the ECB should explicitly mention the role as lender of last resort, which would clarify the necessity of closer coordination between governments and ECB. Finally, the EBU will impose that ECB conducts banking supervision within the single supervisory mechanism.

This multiple mandate could lead to governance issues. According to Tinbergen principle, each objective must be achieved by independent instrument. The objective of price stability is achieved by changing the key interest rate, that financial stability is based on a macro-prudential policy and banking supervision is based on micro-prudential policy. Therefore, the ECB should be segmented. Masciandaro (2007) shows, on a dataset of 89 countries, that if the central bank involvement in supervision and its reputation are high, the unification level likely to be low, and vice versa, confirming also the robustness of the central bank fragmentation effect.

Moreover, some studies showed that the central bank supervision should be limited to macro-prudential aspects only (e.g. Boyer & Ponce, 2012). If on the one hand, micro-prudential aspects allow to know the situation of the intermediary on an ongoing basis, on the other hand, they also source of potential conflicts of interest. According to Repullo (2000), the deposit guarantee must be separate from the function of lender as last resort. Otherwise, there may be a fear that the ECB uses excessively money creation to recapitalize banks, so that the monetary policy targets and support to banks could be in conflict. Consequently, the ECB will have to structure itself into two separate areas (both preparatory and executive activities), one for monetary task, which will continue to be carried out with full independence, and the other for banking supervision, which will be accountable to the European Parliament and Council.

Coordination with Others Institutions

Because the SSM for banks was proposed to be lead by the ECB, it raises several problems of co-existence with other institutions. The first problem arises with the Eurozone's national supervision authorities, which will continue to carry out usual activities for the preparation and implementation of the ECB's decisions. Indeed, national supervisors will continue to play an important role since all tasks not conferred on the ECB will remain with them. For example, national supervisors will remain in charge of consumer protection and the fight against money laundering, and the supervision of third country credit institutions establishing branches within a Member State. Nevertheless, the implementation of the SSM implies a delegation of activities for national supervisors. This delegation could be bound by rules and standards, and the ECB could retain the power to decide on a case-by-case analysis.

The second issue regarding coexistence arises with the European Banking Authority (EBA), which has already powers of supervision and responsibility over the entire European Union. The EBA should elaborate a common legal framework for surveillance through a single rulebook for banking supervision in Europe. It should also provide the texts of laws that will govern the management of banking crisis in the euro area. Finally, it should ensure regular stress tests on European banks. According to the European Commission (2012), the ECB and the EBA are expected to work closely within the European Systemic Risk Board, responsible for alerting the European authorities about banking and financial instability risks in Europe. But it is not certain that this committee will have an effective role (Avaro & Sterdyniak, 2014). Moreover, it seems there are some tasks overlaps and divergence between the ECB and the EBA. The ECB will carry out stress tests for banks while it is previously the exclusive competence of the EBA. Since the weight of Eurozone countries, the ECB could have an incentive to favor them, while the EBA will have broader view. Since bank's operative practices are influenced by the supervisors (the ECB), the task of the EBA to avoid fragmentation of the single markets risks becoming limited. In addition, the supervisory activities of the ECB and the delegated national bodies may indicate the need to introduce new rules or modify those already contained in the single rulebook, with the possibility for collaboration as well as conflict between the two European authorities.

The Role of the Non Euro Area Banks

With the centralization of the SSM at the ECB, the banking union will first apply to all members of the euro area. Thus, the EBU will plant divisive element in the European Union. If not all risks or spill-over risks are covered by the SSM, it is incomplete and open to new crises. Although this centralization, the European Commission (2012) proposed that EU member states that have not adopted the euro can also participate in the SSM. But the mechanism for that provision and conditions whereby non-euro area member states could participate are not clear. Supervisory authorities of the non-EMU countries may sign an agreement of cooperation with the ECB and be represented in supervisory council. The diversity of situations of non-euro area will prevent to implement the one single scheme that the ECB can develop. It will result in differential treatments, which will reflect in several different agreements. In this case, the management of the European supervision will be more complex and difficult.

Winners and Losers of Joining EBU

In a cost-benefit analysis, Schoenmaker and Siegmann (2013) calculate the benefits of switching from a national bail-out to a European level bail-out mechanism and compare this improvement with the costs to join EBU. The initial issue is the following: a decision must be made whether a failed bank will be bailed out or whether it is closed. Under efficient resolution, a bail-out takes place when the aggregate benefits exceed the total costs. The study covers top 25 European banks in 2011. The assets of these banks amount to about half of total EU banking assets and the European cross-border assets counts for 71% of overall cross-border assets within the EMU. The authors compute the resolution under a supranational authority in the EBU and under a home country approach and compare the obtained results. The difference between the EBU resolution and that of home country resolution indicates the improvement of efficiency of bank resolution. Results are presented in Table 2. For EMU countries, the net effect (benefits minus costs) is only positive for two countries (Spain and the Netherlands) and close to zero for four countries (Malta, Cyprus, Luxembourg, and Estonia). The biggest losers of the EMU would be biggest country: Germany, France, and Italy. For the non-EMU countries, the net effect is positive for three countries (United Kingdom, Sweden, and Denmark) and negative for seven countries (especially for Poland). Interestingly, the largest beneficiaries in non-EMU countries from the EBU would be those that do not wish to join the banking union (UK and Sweden). These results challenge EBU efficiency.

Others results challenge this efficiency. Cervellati and Fioriti (2007) describe the three main theoretical supervisory models proposed in the literature (vertical, horizontal, centralized) and considering the actual supervisory systems are the result of the different legal frameworks of the Member States. They conclude that differences still exist among the EU systems male more difficult to achieve a real European integration in financial supervision. Considering the importance of banking competition in the EU[1], Stoica and Scântee (2012) analyze the impact of financial supervision on banking competition in the EU countries with different financial supervision arrangements. Their findings suggest that there are not significant differences in the main indicators of banking concentration in countries with different types of financial supervision. The supervisory function is being performed by a variety of institutions (one, two or three institutions), there is no significant influence on banking sector and on banking competition; this underlines the fact that changing the structure of the financial system does not guarantee better supervision.

Table 2. Net effect for European countries of joining banking union

EMU Countries	Net Effect	Non-EMU Countries	Net Effect
Spain	10.9	UK	12.9
Netherlands	3.1	Sweden	8.6
Malta	-0.1	Denmark	0.3
Cyprus	-0.1	Latvia	-0.3
Luxembourg	-0.2	Lithuania	-0.4
Estonia	-0.2	Bulgaria	-0.9
Slovenia	-0.3	Hungary	-1.4
Slovakia	-0.7	Czech Republic	-1.5
Ireland	-0.7	Romania	-2.5
Finland	-1.3	Poland	-4.9
Belgium	-1.6		
Portugal	-1.8		
Austria	-1.9		
Greece	-2.0		
France	-2.8		
Italy	-3.9		
Germany	-6.7		

Source: Schoenmarker and Siegmann (2013)

FUTURE RESEARCH DIRECTIONS

Because the EBU is something new, future research will be necessary. In particular, it would be interesting to know how the ECB has managed its triple objective and coordination with other institutions. Besides this point, several complementary points could be discussed.

The first issue is related to the bank model in Europe. A choice needs to be made between the universal banks and banking specialization. On the one hand, the crisis questioned the relevance of universal bank model where deposits finance and guarantee market activities. On the other hand, the crisis has shown the fragility of specialized institutions which had an insufficient deposit base and depended heavily on markets for refinancing. The universal bank model has shown a better resilience during the financial crisis. The heavy losses of markets and investments banks activities have been offset by their retail bank activities. However, these losses have reduced banks' own funds. The link between banking activities has also contributed to the development of suspicion on the stability of the European banking system. Thus, a better regulation in the EU banking system requires the separation within banks of activities with different logics, procedures and risks. This is the reason why this proposition is supported by Liikanen Report (2012).

The second issue is related to the fiscal union. Van Rompuy (2012) set out the main building blocks towards deeper economic and monetary integration. One of them concerns banking union but another refers to an integrated budgetary framework to ensure sound fiscal policy making at the national and European levels, encompassing coordination, and commensurate steps towards common debt issuance. By this way, Van Rompuy called for a fiscal union. Several studies support the case for a fiscal union in the euro area. There are various proposals for the design of this fiscal union: an interregional fiscal transfer mechanism as insurance against asymmetric shocks, an increase in the European budget to establish a horizontal fiscal equalization mechanism, and the introduction of Eurobonds backed by all member countries. The EBU remerges the question about the relevance of a fiscal union in Europe.

CONCLUSION

In 2012, the European Commission created a roadmap towards a European banking union. The aim of this EBU is to ensure financial stability in Europe, in particular by breaking the link between banks failures and sovereign debts. The maintenance of a stable and reliable financial system is the essential prerequisite to keep the confidence and consistency in the European banking environment. Taking into consideration the fact that the banks were the origins of the crisis, the European Union clearly need better tools to address the problems in banks more effectively. The proposed framework by the European Commission is based on three pillars: a single supervisory mechanism (SSM), a single resolution mechanism (SRM), and a single deposit guarantee mechanism. The existence of a true banking union would have made a difference both before and during the current crisis. Thus, the EBU project is a step, and a necessary step, towards a better functioning EMU in the future.

However, the EBU project has several dark sides which could compromise efficiency of the banking union. The main concern is the role of the ECB. The attribution of unified banking supervision powers to the ECB raises several problems. In particular, it leads to potential conflicts of interest between monetary policy and banking supervision, and imply strong cooperation between ECB and other European and national authorities. This should be concerned the European Parliament and the European Commission. If the EBU is a necessary step, it is not a sufficient one to resolve all financial issues in the EMU and in Europe. It should be completed by a broader analysis on the European bank model and on the European integration via a fiscal and/or a political union.

REFERENCES

Avaro, M., & Sterdyniak, H. (2014). Banking union: A solution to the Euro Zone crisis? *Revue de l'OFCE*, *132*, 195–241.

Boyer, P., & Ponce, J. (2012). Regulatory capture and banking supervision reform. *Journal of Financial Stability*, *8*(3), 206–217. doi:10.1016/j.jfs.2011.07.002

Breuss, F. (2013). European banking union. *WIFO Working Papers*, No 454.

Buiter, W., & Rahbari, E. (2012). The European Central Bank as lender of last resort for sovereigns in the Eurozone. *Journal of Common Market Studies*, *50*, 6–35. doi:10.1111/j.1468-5965.2012.02275.x

Cechetti, S., Fender, I., & McGuire, P. (2010). Towards a global risk map. *Bank for International Settlements Working Papers*, No 309.

Cervellati, E., & Fioriti, E. (2007). *Financial supervision in EU countries*. Paper presented at the EFMA Annual Meeting, Vienna, Austria.

Constancio, V. (2013). *Speech of Vice-President of the ECB*. Paper presented at the 2nd FIN-FSA Conference "Banking and Supervision under Transformation", Helsinki, Finland.

European Commission. (2012). *A roadmap towards a banking union, COM(2012)510*. Retrieved from http://ec.europa.eu/internal_market/finances/banking-union/index_en.html

Goodhart, C., & Schoenmaker, D. (2009). Fiscal burden sharing in cross-border banking crisis. *International Journal of Central Banking*, *5*(1), 141–165.

Gros, D. (2013). Banking union with a sovereign virus. *Inter Economics*, *48*(2), 93–97. doi:10.1007/s10272-013-0449-8

Holhausen, C., & Ronde, T. (2004). Cooperation in international banking supervision. *ECB Working Paper*, No 245.

Liikanen, E. (2012). *Final report of the high-level expert group on reforming the structure of the EU banking section*. Retrieved from http://ec.europa.eu/internal_market/bank/docs/hihl-level_expert_group/report_en.pdf

Masciandaro, D. (2007). Divide et impera: Financial supervision unification and central bank fragmentation effect. *European Journal of Political Economy*, *23*(2), 285–315. doi:10.1016/j.ejpoleco.2006.02.001

Repullo, R. (2000). Who should act as lender of last resort? An incomplete contracts model. *Journal of Money, Credit and Banking*, *32*(3), 580–605. doi:10.2307/2601196

Saveanu, C. (2012). For and against a new framework for banking supervision. *Ovidius University Annals*, *12*(1), 278–289.

Schoenmaker, D., & Peek, T. (2014). The state of the banking sector in Europe. *OECD Working Papers*, No 1102.

Schoenmaker, D., & Siegmann, D. (2013). Efficiency gains of a European Banking Union. *Tinbergen Institute Discussion Papers*, No 13-026/IV/DSF51.

Schoenmaker, D., & Wagner, W. (2013). Cross-border banking in Europe and financial stability. *International Finance*, *16*(1), 1–22. doi:10.1111/j.1468-2362.2013.12026.x

Stoica, O., & Scântee. (2012). Financial supervision and banking competition in European Union. *Acta Universitatis Danubius*, *8*(6), 56–67.

Tuliuc, D., & Popovici, A. (2013). Towards the European Banking Union. *SEA Practical Application of Science*, *1*(1), 221–229.

Van Rompuy, H. (2012). Towards a genuine economic and monetary union. *Report by President of the European Council*. Retrieved from http://www.consilium.europa.eu/uedocs/cms_data/docs/pressdata/en/ec/134069.pdf

KEY TERMS AND DEFINITIONS

Bail-In: Tool of the prudential supervision of financial institutions, in the case of a bank which have solvency problem, to impose certain creditors to convert their debts into shares and/or a reduction of such claims.

Banking Regulation: Formulation and issuance by authorized agencies of specific rules or regulations, under governing law, for the conduct and structure of banking.

Financial Stability: Condition in which the financial system is resistant to economic shocks and is fit to smoothly fulfil its basic functions: the intermediation of financial funds, management of risks and the arrangement of payments.

Fragmentation of Financial Markets: Refers to how financial markets are structured. Markets where financial conditions are unusual different.

Lender of Last Resort: Act of the Central bank as the ultimate source of credit. It extends loans to solvent but illiquid depository institutions whose failure to obtain credit would have a destabilizing effect on the national or regional economy.

Macro-Prudential Regulation: Oversight that focuses on the stability of a financial system as a whole, rather than on its components. The need for macro-prudential regulation of the system arises because the actions of individual companies acting prudently within guidelines may collectively result in the instability of a financial system.

Macro-Prudential Regulation: Supervision that focuses on the stability of the component parts of a financial system.

Sovereign Debt: Bonds issued by a national government in order to finance the issuing country's growth. Sovereign debt is generally a safer investment.

ENDNOTE

1 Competition is a fundamental condition of the market economy and also is considered one of the most important factors for economic progress.

Chapter 7
The European Union: Another Round of Enlargement?

Yontem Sonmez
Manchester Metropolitan University, UK

ABSTRACT

In spite of the recent rise in Euroscepticism across most of Europe, owing to the recent Eurozone crisis and reflected by the European Parliament elections of May 2014 where far-right parties gained strength, there is little evidence to suggest that the enlargement of the EU will soon stop. The membership negotiations have started with Turkey, Iceland, Serbia, and the Former Yugoslav Republic of Macedonia. In terms of both economic and physical size, Turkey is more influential than the rest of the candidate countries. Therefore, the purpose of this chapter is to provide some background information on the progress of each candidate and potential candidate country on the way to EU accession and compare them with the current EU28 members in order to emphasize the main similarities and the differences. Finally, a literature survey of the economic implications of a potential Turkish EU membership is also provided as a case study.

INTRODUCTION

European Union, with twenty eight member states, a surface area of four million km^2 and a population of more than five hundred million people, has experienced seven enlargements and thus, is the world leader in international economic integration. It has been widening and deepening for more than sixty years, growing from the original six members (of Belgium, France, West Germany, Italy, Luxembourg and the Netherlands) to the current twenty eight[1] in order to bring economic, political and social stability to Europe.

In spite of the recent rise in Euroscepticism across most of Europe, owing to the recent Eurozone crisis and reflected by the European Parliament elections of May 2014 where far-right parties gained strenght, there is little evidence to suggest that the enlargement of the EU will soon stop. Just after the challenging eastern enlargement process and the recent Croatian membership, it has embarked upon negotiations about the pos-

DOI: 10.4018/978-1-4666-7308-3.ch007

sible EU accessions of Turkey, Montenegro and Iceland. Moreover, the Former Yugoslav Republic of Macedonia and Serbia are candidate countries. The latest deveopment was on 27thJune 2014 when the European Commission also granted Albania the candidate status (EU Commission, 2014*b*).

The aim of this chapter is firstly to summarise the evolution of regionalisation mainly in Europe by briefly explaining the EU's enlargement experience together with the conditions for EU membership. Secondly, some background information on each candidate country will be provided, comparing candidate and potential candidate countries with the current EU28 members to emphasize the similarities as well as the differences in population, GDP, per capita GDP and economic growth rates. Since Turkey is the largest candidate country in terms of the population, there will be a literature survey of the economic implications of a potential Turkish EU membership as the final section of this chapter.

BACKGROUND: REGIONALISATION IN EUROPE

Regionalisation is the process of liberalising trade, in most cases not only by tariff-cutting, but also by the harmonisation of rules and regulations shaping the trade policies as well as the regional rules on investment, competition, labour, etc. as a result of the mutual negotiations of such commitments. According to Bhagwati et al. (1999, p.3), regionalisation can be defined broadly as 'preferential trade agreements among a subset of nations'.

Bhagawati et al. (1999) argue that the main reasons for the second wave of regionalism or to the revival of regionalism in the 1980s, is due to the conversion of the United States of America (USA) to regionalism, although it had always been a supporter of multilateralism previously. The establishment of the Single European Market (SEM) in 1993 and the eastern enlargement of the EU in 2004 were also important steps in the second wave of regionalisation.

The major characteristic of the second wave of regionalism, also called new regionalism, is the growing number of agreements across regional groupings, as well as across developed and developing countries, their deep integration, i.e. not only by reducing or eliminating the trade barriers in commodities but with real and financial capital mobility, free labour mobility, domestic tax and subsidy policy harmonisation, macro policy harmonisation, institution reforming and building, communications and transportation infrastructure development, legal rules and regulations harmonisation for markets and monetary union (Lawrence, 1996; Burfisher, Robinson, & Thierfelder, 2003; Whalley, 2008).

During the global recession of 2008-2009 global trade decreased by 29%, that was at a faster rate than the global GDP (Eaton, Kortum, Neiman, & Romalis, 2013). One of the reasons for the reduction in the global trade volume was argued to be the tendency of the national governments to re-introduce protectionist measures in order to deal with the negative consequences of the global recession (Brock, 2009). It is also estimated by Fontagné et al. (2014) that the share of trade within major regional trade agreements might decline in the future as the trend towards increased regionalism could be reversed (WTO, 2014*a*).

However, in spite of the negative implications of the global recession on trade flows, there has been an increase in the number of regional trade agreements (RTAs); By 2005, 330 RTAs had been notified to the World Trade Orginisation but by January 2014 this number had increased to 538 and there were 377 RTAs in force (WTO, 2014*b*, 2014*c*).

The Enlargement Experiences of the EU

Treaty of Rome established the root of the European Union with the formation of the European

Economic Community by the six original members in 1956. In addition to that, two other European Communities; European Coal and Steel Community (ECSC) and EURATOM were also established by these six founding members in 1951 and 1958 respectively.

This small community has grown in size from the original six to current twenty eight members as a result of the six successive enlargements. The Union experienced its first enlargement, when Denmark, Ireland and the UK joined in 1973. It was followed by the second enlargement, when Greece joined in 1981 and the third one when Spain and Portugal joined in 1986. Fourth enlargement was in 1995 when Austria, Finland and Sweden joined (Nello, 2012). Amongst all, the Eastern enlargement of 2004, when 10 new members[2] joined, eight being the Central and Eastern European countries[3] (CEECs) was the most challenging one regarding the size and the diversity of the countries that has joined. The Eastern enlargement process has been successfully completed, when Bulgaria and Romania became EU members in 2007. The final enlargement was when Croatia joined this unique political and economic partnership in July 2013 (European Commission Online, 2013*a*).

Conditions for Enlargement

Given that the European Union is ready to integrate another member, in order to be considered for the EU membership, a county should respect and promote the democratic EU values and must meet the key criteria for accession referred to as Cophenagen criteria. Although originally they were laid out for the CEECs' membership by the European Council, the Cophenagen Criteria of 1993 are still applied today (European Council, 1993; Baldwin & Wyplosz, 2012). In order to fulfill the Cophenagen Criteria, the member countries need to:

- Have a functioning market economy with a capacity to cope with market forces and competition in the EU;
- Achieve stability of institutions to guarantee democracy, rule of law, human rights and respect for and protection of minorities;
- Be able to take on and implement the obligations of membership effectively and at the same time adhere to the aims of political, economic and monetary union.

When the European Council recognises a country as a candidate, they agree on how and when they would be adopting, implementing and enforcing all current EU rules, i.e. *acquis communautaire*. For example, on 4th June 2014, the European Commission confirmed its recommendation to grant Albania candidate status at the European Council in 26th June 2014 (European Commission, 2014*a*).

Membership negotiations can only start if as a result of a unanimous decision by the EU Council, all EU governments agree on a framework for negotiation which will take place between ministers and ambassadors of the EU governments and the candidate country.

The duration and speed of accession negotiations depend on the candidate country's ability to transpose the *acquis communautaire* into their national legislation, i.e. candidate country's progress. All chapters should be negotiated and closed before the accession so that the *Community acquis* could be implemented from the moment of accession.

Adoption and implementation of the cumulative body of European Community laws, rights and obligations, i.e. *Community acquis*, which is binding on all the EU countries are made up of thirty five policy fields/chapters covering every single area from the free movement of workers to company law, energy to science & research, etc., and are the basis of the negotiations (European Commision, 2012*a* ; European Commission, 2013*a*; European Commission, 2013*b*).

CANDIDATE COUNTRIES: A BRIEF BACKGROUND INFO

After the EU membership of Croatia in July, 2013, there are currently five countries- Turkey, Iceland, Montenegro, Serbia and Former Yugoslav Republic of Macedonia- on the way to EU accession. Moreover, it is expected that a sixth county, Albania, will also gain the candidate status by the end of June 2014. In addition, Kosovo and Bosnia and Herzegovina are the potential candidates (European Commission, 2014*b*).

Serbia

Serbia applied for EU membership in December 2009 and in March 2012, it was granted the candidate status by the European Commission. Since December 2009, visa requirements were lifted for Serbs traveling to Schengen countries. A Stabilisation and Association agreement between Serbia and the EU entered into force in September 2013. The main aims of this agreement were to contribute to political, economic and institutional stability, to promote peace in the region preserving regional stability and also to support Serbia while it is trying to complete its transition into a competitive market economy (European Commision, 2014*c*).

It was decided to open the accession negotiations between Serbia and the EU by the European Council in 2013. Following that, the 1st Intergovernmental Conference took place between the two parties which acted as a formal signal of the start of Serbia's accession negotiations.

Montenegro

It was in 2006 when Montenegro seperated from the State Union of Serbia and Montenegro and emegered as an independent country. Montenegro applied for EU membership in 2008 and two years after that it was granted candidate status in 2010 after the Commission identified 7 key priority areas for Montenegro to address before the negotiations could begin. Following that, in June 2012, accession negotiations started between the two parties and the first chapter- Science and Research- was opened and provisionally closed in six months (European Commision, 2014*d*).

Former Yugoslav Republic of Macedonia

FYRM applied for EU membership in March 2004. It was 2005 when it was granted candidate country status. The opening of negotiations between FYRM and the EU was recommended by the European Commision in October 2009 but they have not started yet. Shortly after that, visa liberalisation entered into force between the two parties in December 2009. The latest development between the EU and FYRM was in 2012 when the European Commission launched a High Level Accession Dialogue with this country (European Commsion, 2014*e*).

Iceland

Iceland applied for EU membership in July 2009 and the accession negotiation started in a year in July 2010 after 'screening', i.e. technical preperations for the negotiations, was concluded in June 2011. Although the accession negotiations started in July in 2010, as a consequence of the recent elections which brought a eurosceptic party into power, negotiations were put on hold by the Icelandic government in May 2013. At the time of that decision, of the 27 negotiating chapters opened, 11 had been provisionally closed (European Commission, 2014*f*).

Turkey

Turkey is not a newcomer to Europe although her journey on the way to EU accession has been slow and rough. One of her major aims was to benefit from the static and dynamic effects of economic integration as a result of participating in a new and larger market. Another aim was to benefit from the structural and investment funds, which are a part of EU's regional policy aimed at development of backward regions. Finally, Turkey did not want to miss the opportunity of being part of one of the strongest economic unions of the era. For the EU, Turkey is important due to her strategic and demographic location (Dura & Atik, 2003).

Turkey's EU journey started when she made her first application to join the EU – then the European Economic Community in 1959, when Ankara applied for associate membership. However, the answer was negative; the main argument was that in comparison to the other EEC members Turkey was economically and socially underdeveloped.

Four years later in 1963, she became an associate member of the EU with the Ankara Association Agreement. Turkey's membership motivation was both economic and political. Two of the aims listed in that agreement were, firstly, an introduction of the gradual bilateral elimination of trade taxes and secondly, the harmonization of the economic policies between both parties. Another agreement was signed in 1970 detailing Turkey and EU's mutual commitments to each other as well as the details of the free mobility of factors of production between the two parties. Turkey-EU relations were frozen in 1976 for eleven years due to the economic disadvantages to Turkey caused by EU-EFTA free trade area during 1972-1973 and the growing trade deficit of Turkey's with the EU. Another factor was EU's plans of lowering the Common Customs Tarrif to 6%, which was interpreted by the Turkish government of that era as more of an economic burden than an advantage. With the generalized system of preferences, EU granted preferential access to some of the developing countries of the world to the EU market, to some other third countries as a result of Lomé agreement and to the Mediterranean countries with some other trade agreements. Turkey believed that the economic privileges that she had with the EU before were overshadowed as a result of all those agreements. As a result, all Turkey-EU relations were frozen until 1987, when Turkey once again applied for the EU membership. After 1980's military coup, when a liberal party came to power in 1983, one of the major objectives was economic liberalization and therefore re-establishing economic relations with the EU. Thus, in 1987, the country formally applied for full EEC membership.

However, due to the internal changes within the EU, particularly due to the preparations for the 1992 Single European Market Programme and as a result of the developments in Eastern Europe and the Soviet Union, the answer was once again negative; the accession negotiations could not be undertaken (DTM, 2007; Hoekman & Togan, 2005). Instead, a CU agreement was signed between the two parties in 1995 to be finally phased in by 2001.

It was only in 1999, 40 years after her first application that Turkey was recognized as a candidate country. Historically speaking, no other issue has ever been that important for Turkey's external trade relations (Bacik & Aras, 2004). After a summit in December 2004, the European Council decided to open the membership negotiations with Turkey officially. Membership negotiations between Turkey and the EU started in 2005. The membership negotiations entail a complex process, incorporating, implementing and enforcing EU's treaties, regulations, legal system and policies. Irrespective of whether EU accepts Turkey as a member or not, Turkey will be better off as a result of this process which has already dramatically upgraded its economic and democratic credentials as she undergoes comprehensive legal and political changes, also increasing the stability of the Turkish economy (Akcapar, 2006).

Because of the Cyprus problem, Turkey does not apply the Additional Protocol of the Ankara agreement to the Republic of Cyprus as it does not recognise it. Because of that eight chapters of the Community acquis can not be opened for negotiation (European Commision, 2014*g*).

Throughout Europe, the debate around Turkey's projected EU accession revolves around a series of issues, ranging from demographic through geographic to cultural, political and economic as well as historical and religious (Hughes, 2004; Euroactiv, 2006). Akcapar (2006, p.2) argues that although Turkey is said to be 'too big, too poor and too Muslim' to join the EU, these should not be the main stumbling blocks on the way to EU accession but instead the way Turkey will deal with these should be decisive; how well Turkey adopts and implements the EU's rules and regulations. Moreover, one of the thorniest issues is the EU's capacity to absorb Turkey.

Turkey: EU Customs Union

The establishment of the Customs Union has been the most important development regarding Turkey's foreign economic and commercial relations.

Turkey became a part of the common EU Customs Territory since the entering into force of the EU-Turkey Customs Union in 1996. Tariffs and quantitative restrictions on trade between Turkey and the EU have been gradually removed. This agreement covers industrial products and processed agricultural goods. Traditional agricultural products will be included in the Customs Union only after Turkey's adaptation to the Community's Common Agricultural Policy (CAP).

"The EU-Turkey CU represents a clear example of new regionalism" (Zahariadis, 2005, p.1) as it constitutes the deep integration measures with a wider perspective and context rather than only being restricted to conventional border controls. The Customs Union Decision (CUD) covers a wide range of legislation and policies, involving all aspects of trade. Harmonisation to the competition policy and to the technical standards of the EU, "participation in several conventions on intellectual, industrial and commercial property rights" and harmonisation to some other administrative procedures are among the CUDs (DTM, 2007). Turkey is the first and only country, which has experienced such a deep form of integration without actually being a full member.

As a result of the Eastern enlargement of the EU15 in 2004, Turkey started to implement the same trade duties on the imports and exports to/from the CEECs and Malta. Turkey has also adopted the Common Customs Tariff of the European Union, resulting in lower tariffs for imports from third countries. According to the estimates by the Turkish government, the average tariff rate for industrial imports from the EU and EFTA countries, which used to be at 10%, was eliminated in 1996. In the same year, for products imported from third countries the tariff rates have declined from about 16% to 5.6%. An average protection rate for industrial products was 4.2% in 2005, whereas some agricultural goods still remain protected by steep tariffs. The tariff rate for products imported from the poorest countries of the world is zero, whereas it is around 2.86% for the developing countries (Baygun, 2005).

The EU is now by far Turkey's biggest trading partner. As well as covering industrial products together with processed agriculture, the scope of this Customs Union also entails alignment by Turkey with certain EU competition and commercial policies, such as technical regulation of products and intellectual property law. Turkey also needs to harmonise its external trade relations in parallel to EU's. In other words, Turkey has to have preferential trade relations with the countries that the EU already has.

EU28, Candidate and Potential Candidate Countries: A Macro Comparison

Since European Union is made up of twenty eight member states it would be naive to expect that all those countries would be similar to each other. Indeed, the EU28 is made up of nations which are different from one another.

The population of the European Union is more than 500 million, which is relatively larger than the population of USA (318 million) and Japan (127 million) combined.

As it can be seen from Figure 1, EU28 countries as well as the candidate countries vary enormously in terms of population. For example, Germany has the largest number of people with 80.5 million, followed by Turkey which is a candidate country with a population of around 76 million people. Within EU28, Germany is followed by France, UK, Italy and Spain which are the core countries of the EU. Poland, who became part of the EU as a result of the Eastern enlargement of 2004, on the other hand, is also one of the big EU nations with a population of 38.5 million.

In addition to the big nations, there are also the tiny nations with the lowest number of people. For example, Malta with a population of about 421,000 and Luxembourgh with 537,000 people, followed by Cyprus with a population of 865,000 are the tiny nations of EU28. Among the candidate countries, Iceland has the lowest population with 321,000 people.

GDP and GDP Per Capita in Euro

In line with the enormous differences in the level of population, both GDP and GDP per capita levels of EU28 and the candidate countries also vary enormously.

According to table 1, the German GDP is almost as high as the combined GDPs of the twenty smallest countries of EU28 (i.e. around 2.7 million). Given that importance of the German GDP for the EU as a whole, the dominant position of Germany in EU decision making is not surprising. France, UK, Italy and Spain are also important players as they also have relatively higher levels of GDP.

Turkey, which is the candidate country with the largest population, also has the highest level of GDP among the candidate countries whereas Iceland has the lowest level of population but the lowest GDP level is the Montenegron GDP.

According to figure 2, the richest country is Luxembourgh with a GDP per capita of 67,100

Figure 1. EU28, candidate and potential candidate countries' population, (in millions), 2013
Source: Eurostat, 2014. Albania 2009 data, Bosnia and Herzegovina provisional.

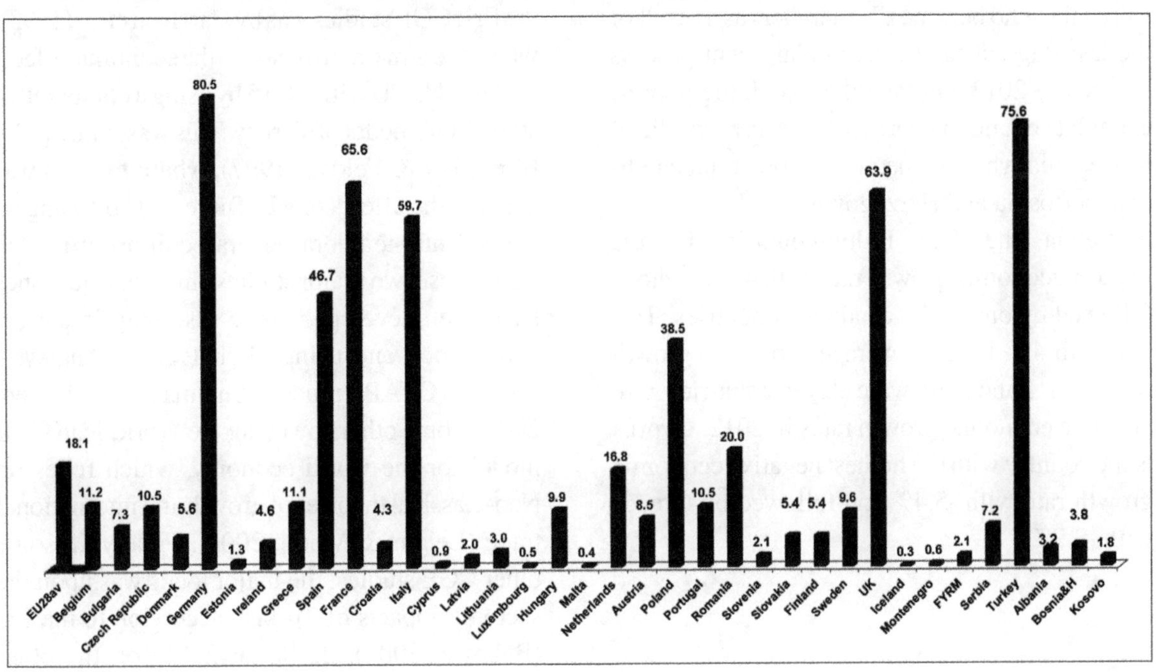

Table 1. EU28, candidate and potential candidate countries' GDP (in Euros), 2012

Germany	2,666,400	Austria	307,004	Croatia	43,904	Iceland	10,567
France	2,032,296	Denmark	245,252	Luxembourg	42,899	Albania	9,372
UK	1,929,581	Greece	193,749	Bulgaria	39,668	FYRM	7,454
Italy	1,567,010	Finland	192,541	Slovenia	35,319	Malta	6,829
Spain	1,029,002	Portugal	165,107	Lithuania	32,940	Montenegro	3,149
Turkey	611,967	Ireland	163,938	Serbia	29,932	EU28av	463,132
Netherlands	599,338	CzechR.	152,926	Latvia	22,257		
Sweden	407,714	Romania	131,747	Cyprus	17,720		
Poland	381,204	Hungary	96,968	Estonia	17,415		
Belgium	375,881	Slovakia	71,096	Bosnia&H	13,907		

Source: Eurostat, 2014.

Euros. Luxembourgh is twice as rich as the second richest EU28 country which is Austria with 33,100 Euros. Austria is closely followed by Ireland, Netherlands, Sweden, Denmark, Germany, Belgium and Finland.

Iceland, which is one of the candidate countries, is also relatively rich in comparison to both the rest of the EU28 and the other candidate countries. For example, its GDP per capita is higher than the level of GDP per capita both in France and the UK.

The poorest EU28 countries are Bulgaria and Romania, who became EU members as a result of the last stage of the Eastern enlargment process in January 2013. On the other hand, the poorest candidate country is Former Yugoslav Reublic of Macedonia whereas the poorest potential candidate is Bosnia and Herzegovinia.

Latvia, one of the Baltic countries, has the highest economic growth rate with 4.1%, who is followed by one of the candidate countries, Turkey with 4%. EU28's average economic growth rate is 0.1% and there were eleven countries with negative economic growth rates in 2012. Cyprus is the country with the highest negative economic growth rate with -5.4% and followed by Greece with -3.9%.

A Literature Survey of the Impacts of EU Membership: A Case Study of Turkey

Although there have been several general equilibrium studies regarding the Turkish economy in general (Celasun, 1986; Yeldan, 1989; Harrison, Rutherfold, & Tarr, 1993) there have been only a handful of CGE studies studying the impact of Turkey-EU CU as well as the economic implications of Turkey's potential EU accession. One of the first CGE studies was by Harrison et al. (1993), where the aim was to measure the economic effects of Turkey's CU with EU15 by using a comparative static CGE model of Turkey. This was followed by Mercenier & Yeldan (1997), where the aim was to study the effects of EU-Turkey CU by using an applied inter-temporal general equilibrium model. After those two major studies only a few new ones have been developed some assuming imperfect competition and using Global Trade Analaysis Project (GTAP) model (Sulamaa & Widgren, 2005), some others by using the WorldScan CGE model for the world economy, which relies on Neo-classical theories of growth and international trade (Lejour & Mooij, 2005). Finally, in some other CGE studies, the major focus was upon the sectoral impacts of Turkish accession to the EU (Bekmez, 2002). de Santis(2001) on the other

Figure 2. EU28, candidate and potential candidate countries' GDP per capita, (in thousands), 2012
Source: Eurostat, 2014. Real Expenditure per capita in PPS_EU28

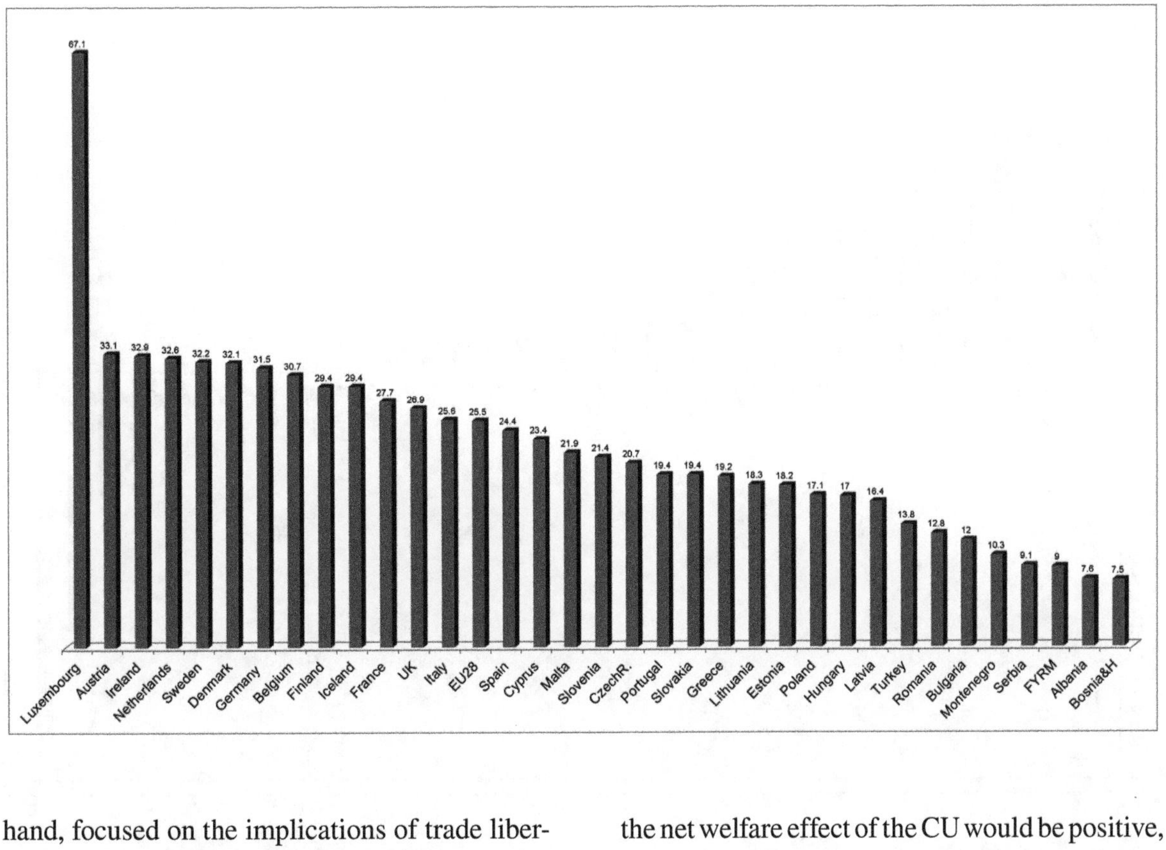

hand, focused on the implications of trade liberalisation policy of Turkey, including the CU, on income inequality by using a static CGE model. Zahariadis (2005) and Ulgen & Zahariadis (2004) extended a CGE model and used it to analyse the economic impacts of Turkey-EU deep integration scenario. A vast majority of the literature regarding Turkey's EU accession has been done with the use of econometric analysis, particularly by using the gravity models (Francois, 2005; Togan, 2005; Hoekman & Togan, 2005; Danzinger, Felicitaz, Inmaculada, & Vollme, 2005; Eruygur & Cakmak, 2005).

According to Harrison et al. (1996) Turkey will gain from 1-1.5% of her GDP per year from the CU agreement, whereas it will lose about 1.4% of GDP as a result of the loss of tariff revenue. One of the important findings of this study is that if the Value Added Tax is applied uniformly, then the lost tariff revenue will be compensated and the net welfare effect of the CU would be positive, increasing the welfare gain as well as the gain to a net gain of 1.1% of the GDP. It is also argued that another way of replacing the lost tariff revenue can be the reduction of export subsidies which can both compensate the lost tariff revenue, given the limitations of other types of taxes and improve the fiscal deficit of Turkey's and at the same time meet the efficiency goals (Harrison et al., 1993, 1997*a*). Another important argument is that the biggest economic gains for Turkey will come from the application of EU's Common Customs Tariff on imports from third countries, which would typically be reciprocal, giving improved access to third country markets (Harrison et al., 1996). A later study by the same authors, Harrison et al. (1997*b*) argue that by this way the gains to Turkey will be about 1.1% of her GDP per year.

By using an applied inter-temporal general equilibrium model, with the assumptions of in-

Figure 3. EU28, candidate and potential candidate countries' GDP growth rate (in %s), 2013
Source: Eurostat, 2014.

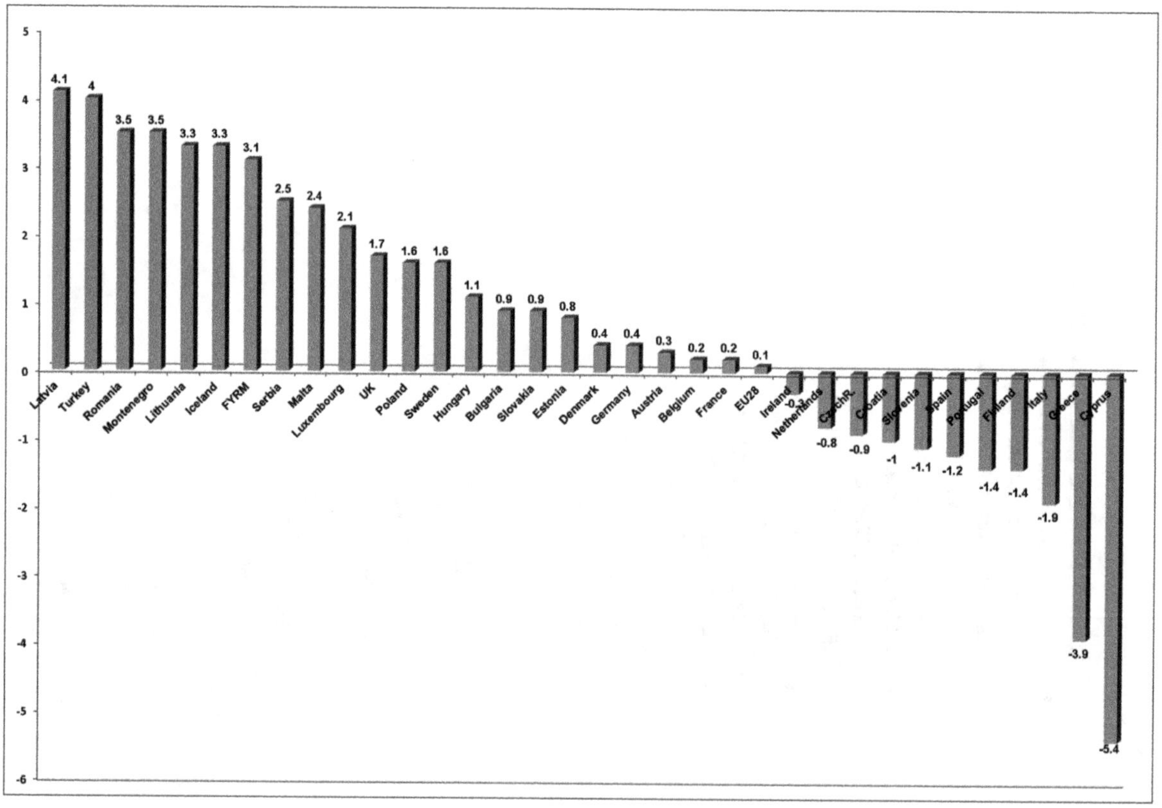

creasing returns to scale and oligopolistic market structures, Mercenier & Yeldan (1997) state that the Turkey-EU CU, where there is only simple harmonization of the tariff system, would generate negative welfare effects. It is welfare improving only when this initial phase is complemented with further reforms, eliminating all forms of non-tariff barriers. The domestic consumers are better off with lower prices in domestic Turkish market, when Turkish and the European firms are assumed to switch from the previous price-discriminating strategy to a single-pricing one. With a higher degree of competition, domestic prices are cut, efficiency increases, increasing capital accumulation and causing an induced expansion of demand. It is argued that the efficiency gains by the second-phase of reform vary between 12-19% (Mercenier & Yeldan, 1997).

Sulamaa & Widgren (2006) evaluate the economic implications of Turkish-EU CU by using a GTAP model with imperfect competition and scale economies only on non-agricultural sectors. Their results clearly confirm the results from previous studies; it is argued that Turkish EU membership is beneficial for Turkey without significant negative effects for the rest of the world. The aggregate effects are larger with the assumption of scale economies. In comparison to earlier studies, the positive effect for Turkey is smaller in terms of both the output and welfare. According to Francois (2005), the main reason for relatively small gains is the fact that bilateral tariffs on imports between the two parties have already been reduced or eliminated as a result of the CU agreement of 1996.

Francois (2005) argues that due to the already established CU between the two parties, the trade effects of Turkish EU membership is expected to be very small. By using a global CGE model based on Francois et al. (2003), the economic impact of the CU is found to be over an increase of 1.3% relative to the baseline income level with MFN industrial tariffs., which corresponds to an increase in real GDP of US$2.2 billion.

In addition to Francois (2005), Ulgen & Zahariadis (2004) also argue that due to the CU there is already a "considerable convergence" in trade between Turkey and EU. This is why potential economic implications of eliminating the non-tariff barriers have also been analysed by various studies (Zahariadis, 2005; Ulgen & Zahariadis, 2004).

Lejour & de Mooij (2005), on the other hand, use the gravity model and CGE analysis together in order to evaluate Turkish EU accession. Firstly, potential trade between two parties are derived by using a gravity model. Then, the potential trade is compared to the actual trade and the difference is treated as the tariff equivalent of the remaining trade barriers. After that, a CGE analysis is done by simulating Turkey's accession to EU's internal market by removing those remaining non-trade barriers. It is also argued that as a result of Turkey's implementation of *acquis communautaire* institutions will be reformed and improved, increasing competition. A second experiment is simulated to account for the trade effect of the change in institutions. At the same time, labour market implications of the potential accession are also simulated with their CGE model. As a result of this study, it is argued that Turkey's accession to the internal market will increase her GDP by 0.8% in the long-run and incumbent EU countries' only marginally. This result is mainly due to Turkey's relatively smaller share in EU trade and EU's large share in Turkish trade flows. When the institutions are improved, Turkish GDP will increase by 5.6% and as a result of the migration simulation in which around 2.7 million Turks migrate to current EU members, Turkish GDP declines between 1.8% and 2.2% while EU15's increase between 0.5% and 0.7%.

Bekmez (2002) analyses the impacts of Turkish accession to the EU by using a single-country, multi-sector CGE model with imperfect competition in the Turkish manufacturing sector. His main finding is similar to Mercenier & Yeldan (1997) and Sulamaa & Widgren (2006); based on domestic production, domestic sales and private income, Turkey will benefit the most as a result of a full membership (Bekmez, 2002). Sectoral impacts of Turkish accession has also been analysed in this study. Under the Customs Union scenario, a decrease in domestic prices is observed as a result of the tariff reduction which causes a decrease in domestic production, particularly in tobacco industry by 6.6%, petroleum industry by 2.3% and in transportation equipment by 5.2%. Similar changes are observed in trade with the rest of the world although the changes are not as big as in case of EU. The highest increases in Turkish exports will be in wearing apparel by 16.6% and in textile, leather and fur products by 15%. Turkish exports to the rest of the world also increase with the exception of the metal industry and the machinery as well as transport equipment. In the full accession scenario, agricultural and service sectors are also included in the tariff harmonisation process together with the removal of the non-tariff barriers. Under this full membership scenario, domestic production increases in all manufacturing sectors with the exception of tobacco, paper and publishing, petroleum, non-metallic products, electrical machinery and transportation equipment. In this scenario, the increase in Turkish exports to EU is greater than the CU scenario with the exception of transportation equipment sector, the biggest increases being in Turkish exports of wearing apparel by 20.7%, textiles by 18.6%, leather and fur products by 18.5% and agriculture-related sectors by 16.8% (Bekmez, 2002).

CONCLUSION

There has always been a debate about the pros and cons of multilateral trading system against bilateral trade liberalisation and the regional trade agreements. Initially, regional trade agreements were not very popular, as they were established due to political reasons rather than economic and thus, did not help to the development of the economies much. It was with the second wave of regionalisation, when the countries started to engage in deep integration with other countries and started to realise the major economic gains from regionalisation.

European Union has been one of the most successful examples of economic integration in Europe. Particularly with the Eastern enlargement, the number of Union members has grown from 15 to 27, adding to the economic and physical size of the Union as well as its population and the diversity of the cultures under the same roof. After the challenging Eastern enlargement, the EU has continued to make preparation to accept more members. Hence, the membership negotiations have started with Turkey, Iceland, Serbia and the Former Yugoslav Republic of Macedonia. In terms of both economic and physical size, Turkey is more influential than the rest of the candidate countries. This is why a potential Turkish EU membership is expected to cause a bigger impact on both the EU28 and on the Turkish economy in comparison to the EU membership of the rest of the candidate countries.

REFERENCES

Akcapar, B. (2006). Perspectives on Turkey's EU accession: The long road from Ankara to Brussels. *Yale Journal of International Affairs*, *1*(2), 50–57.

Bacik, G., & Aras, B. (2004). Turkey's inescapable dilemma: America or Europe? *Alternatives: Turkish Journal of International Affairs*, *3*(1), 56–74.

Baldwin, R., & Wyplosz, C. (2012). *The economics of European integration*. London: McGraw-Hill.

Baygun, S. (2005). *EU – Turkey customs union*. Retrieved from: http://www.dtm.gov.tr/ab/ingilizce/gbnot.htm

Bekmez, S. (2002). Sectoral impacts of Turkish accession to the European Union. *Eastern European Economics*, *40*, 57–84.

Bhagwati, J., Krishna, P., & Panagariya, A. (1999). *Trading blocs: Alternative approaches to analysing preferential trade agreements*. Cambridge, MA: MIT Press.

Brock, W. (2009). Comments in collapse in world trade: A symposium of views. *The International Economy*, (2009), 28-38.

Burfisher, M., Robinson, S., & Thierfelder, K. (2003). Regionalism: Old and new, theory and practice. In *Proceedings of Conference of International Agricultural Trade Research Consortium (IATRC)*. Capri, Italy: IATRC.

Celasun, M. (1986). A general equilibrium model of the Turkish economy. *SIMLOG-1 METU Studies in Development, 13*(1-2), 29-64.

Danzinger, N. L., Felicitaz, D. H., Inmaculada, M. Z., & Vollme, S. (2005). The impact of a customs union between Turkey and the EU on Turkey's exports to the EU: A reassessment of the paradox. *DIW's Working Papers Series*, No. 483.

de Santis, R. A. (2001). The 1990 trade liberalisation policy of Turkey: An applied general equilibrium assessment. *International Economic Journal*, *15*(2), 115–132.

DTM. (2007a). *Turkiye'nin Dis Ticareti ve AB'nin Payi*. Retrieved from: http://www.dtm.gov.tr/dtmweb/index.cfm?action=detay&yayinID=376&icerikID=475&dil=TR

Dura, C., & Atik, H. (2003). *Avrupa Birligi, Gumruk Birligi ve Turkiye*. Ankara: Nobel Yayin Dagitim.

Eaton, J., Kortum, S., Neiman, B., & Romalis, J. (2013). Trade and the global recession. NBER *Working Paper*, No:16666.

Eruygur, H. O., & Cakmak, E. H. (2005). Trade implications of extending Turkey-EU customs union to agricultural products. In *Proceedings of the Conference of 'Middile East and North African Economies: Past Perspectives and Future Challenges*. Brussels, Belgium: Academic Press.

Euroactiv. (2006). *EU-Turkey negotiations*. Retrieved from: http://www.euractiv.com/en/enlargement/eu-turkey-negotiations/article-145219

European Commission. (2013a). *Enlargement: Chapters of the acqius*. Retrieved from http://ec.europa.eu/enlargement/policy/conditions-membership/chapters-of-the-acquis/index_en.htm

European Commission. (2013b). *From 6 to 28 members*. Retrieved from http://ec.europa.eu/enlargement/policy/from-6-to-28-members/index_en.htm

European Commission. (2013c). *Steps towards joining*. Retrieved from http://ec.europa.eu/enlargement/policy/steps-towards-joining/index_en.htm

European Commission. (2014a). *EU-Albania: Solid argument for candidate status*. Retrieved from http://ec.europa.eu/commission_2010-2014/fule/headlines/news/2014/06/20140604_en.htm

European Commission. (2014b). *Countries preparing to join*. Retrieved from http://ec.europa.eu/enlargement/countries/check-current-status/index_en.htm

European Commission. (2014c). *Detailed country information: Serbia*. Retrieved from http://ec.europa.eu/enlargement/countries/detailed-country-information/serbia/index_en.htm

European Commission. (2014d). *Detailed country information: Montenegro*. Retrieved from http://ec.europa.eu/enlargement/countries/detailed-country-information/montenegro/index_en.htm

European Commission. (2014e). *Detailed country information: Former Yugoslav Republic of Macedonia*. Retrieved from http://ec.europa.eu/enlargement/countries/detailed-country-information/fyrom/index_en.htm

European Commission. (2014f). *Detailed country information: Iceland*. Retrieved from http://ec.europa.eu/enlargement/countries/detailed-country-information/iceland/index_en.htm

European Commission. (2014g). *Detailed country information: Turkey*. Retrieved from http://ec.europa.eu/enlargement/countries/detailed-country-information/turkey/index_en.htm

European Council. (1993). *Press release: Copenhagen criteria*. Retrieved from http://europa.eu/rapid/press-release_DOC-93-3_en.htm?locale=en

Fontagne, L., Foure, J., & Keck, A. (2014). Stimulating world trade in the decades ahead: Driving forces and policy implications. *World Trade Organisation Working Paper* ERSD-2014-05.

Francois, J. (2005). Accession of Turkey to the EU: Implications for the transport sector. In Turkey economic reform and accession to the European Union. Washington, DC: The World Bank.

Francois, J. F., McQueen, M., & Wignaraja, G. (2003). An overview of EU FTAs. In *Proceedings of the Vienna World Economic Institute Workshop on WTO Issues*. Vienna: Academic Press.

Harrison, G., Rutherfold, T., & Tarr, D. (1997b). Quantifying the Uruguay round. *The Economic Journal*, *107*(444), 1405–1430. doi:10.1111/j.1468-0297.1997.tb00055.x

Harrison, G. W., Rutherford, T. F., & Tarr, D. G. (1993). Trade reform in the partially liberalised economy of Turkey. *The World Bank Economic Review*, *7*(2), 191–217. doi:10.1093/wber/7.2.191

Harrison, G.W., Rutherford, T.F. & Tarr, D.G. (1996). *Economic implications for Turkey of a customs union with the European Union.* The World Bank, International Economics Department, International Trade Division.

Harrison, G. W., Rutherford, T. F., & Tarr, D. G. (1997a). Economic implications of Turkey of a customs union with the European Union. *European Economic Review*, *41*(3-5), 861–870. doi:10.1016/S0014-2921(97)00043-3

Hoekman, B. M., & Togan, S. (2005). *Turkey: Economic reform & accession to the European Union*. Washington, DC: World Bank and the Centre for Economic Policy Research. doi:10.1596/978-0-8213-5932-0

Hughes, K. (2004). Turkey and the European Union: Just another enlargement. *A Friends of Europe Working Paper*.

Lawrence, R. Z. (1996). *Regionalism, multilateralism and deeper integration*. Washington, DC: Brookings Institute.

Lejour, A., & de Mooij, R. A. (2005). Turkish delight: Does Turkey's accession to the EU bring economic benefits? *Kyklow*, *58*(1), 87–120. doi:10.1111/j.0023-5962.2005.00279.x

Mercenier, J., & Yeldan, E. (1997). On Turkey's trade policy: Is a customs union with Europe enough? *European Economic Review*, *41*(3-5), 871–880. doi:10.1016/S0014-2921(97)00044-5

Nello, S. S. (2012). *The European Union: Economics, policies and history*. McGraw-Hill.

Sulamaa, P. &Widgren, M. T. (2005). Turkish EU membership: A simulation study on economic effects. *VATT Discussion Papers from Government Institute for Economic Research*, No. 410.

Togan, S. (2005). Economic implications of EU accession for Turkey. In Turkey economic reform and accession to the European Union. Washington, DC: The World Bank.

Ulgen, S., & Zahariadis, Y. (2004). The future of Turkey-EU trade relations: Deepening vs widening. *CEPS EU-Turkey Working Papers*, 5.

Whalley, J. (2008). Recent regional agreements: Why so many, why so much variance in form, why coming so fast and where are they headed? *World Economy*, *31*(1), 31–66.

WTO. (2014a). *The trend towards increased regionalism could be reversed, new WTO research suggests*. Retrieved from http://www.wto.org/english/news_e/news14_e/rese_23apr14_e.htm

WTO. (2014b). *Regional trade agreements*. Retrieved from http://www.wto.org/english/tratop_e/region_e/region_e.htm

WTO. (2014c). *Regionalism: Friends or rivals?* Retrieved from http://www.wto.org/english/thewto_e/whatis_e/tif_e/bey1_e.htm

Yeldan, E. (1989). Structural adjustment and trade in Turkey: Investigating the alternatives beyond export-led growth. *Journal of Policy Modeling*, *11*(2), 273–296. doi:10.1016/0161-8938(89)90018-5

Zahariadis, Y. (2005). The economic implications of deep integration in the EU-Turkey customs union. *GTAP Paper Resource*. No 1668.

KEY TERMS AND DEFINITIONS

Acquis Communautaire: The whole body of EU legislation, rules and regulations.

Copenhagen Criteria: Accession criteria that needs to be fulfilled by the candidate countries in order to be eligible for EU membership.

Customs Union: Elimination of bilateral trade duties within a group of countries and imposition of a common external tariff as well as common trade policies towards third countries.

European Union: An economic and political union of twenty eight European states aiming to bring economic, political and social stability to Europe.

Regionalisation: Liberalisation of trade among a group of nations in a specific region.

ENDNOTES

1 Austria, Bulgaria, Croatia, Cyprus, Czech Republic, Denmark, Estonia, Finland, Greece, Hungary, Ireland, Latvia, Lithuania, Malta, Poland, Portugal, Romania, Slovakia, Slovenia, Spain, Sweden, United Kingdom.

2 Cyprus, Malta and the CEECs

3 Czech Republic, Estonia, Hungary, Latvia, Lithuania, Poland, Slovakia, Slovenia

Chapter 8
An Analysis of Potential Economic Benefits of Turkey's Full EU Membership

Hakan Ay
Dokuz Eylül University, Turkey

Eren Alper Yilmaz
Dokuz Eylül University, Turkey

ABSTRACT

Even though Turkey has become the sixth largest economy in Europe, there are still hesitations and economic problems for the EU due to Turkey's rising population, low rate of GDP, budget deficit, migration, etc. In recent political history—before 2000s—Turkey failed in its economic liberalization policy. However, the country has seen a significant increase in the economy by developing a market economy and privatizations successfully in the last decade. There is no doubt that Europe would profit from the accession of Turkey to the EU in terms of internal market factors, agriculture, manufacturing industry, trade relations, tourism, and so on. For this reason, instead of looking for faults within the Turkish economy, the EU should try to see positive developments in the Turkish economic system and it should follow a policy that could overcome ongoing problems by mutual negotiations with Turkey. Approval of Turkey's membership to the EU would bring serious economic profits to Europe.

INTRODUCTION

The first step in European integration started with the foundation of the European Coal and Steel Community in 1951 by six states. Following this, was the creation of the European Economic Community (EEC) in 1957, and European Atomic Energy Community in 1958. While the other states in Europe were approaching cautiously, Turkey was the second state admitted to the EEC after Greece in 1959. This application brought the next largest modernization movement after the Republic, so Turkey was moving forward decisively at this stage. However, the European Community asserted that Turkey's level of development for full membership was not sufficient enough, so it proposed a partnership agreement. Thereupon, Turkey signed an agreement named the "Ankara

DOI: 10.4018/978-1-4666-7308-3.ch008

Agreement" with the European Economic Community in 1963 which explicitly envisaged full membership. This agreement formed the basis of the partnership between the European Economic Community and Turkey (Ay, 2013: 16).

This agreement, which aimed to accelerate the development of Turkey both economically and in terms of trade relations between the two sides, envisaged three stages: the preparatory period, the transitional period, and the final period (T.C Avrupa Birliği Bakanlığı, 2011). Following the transitional period, it was planned to finish "Customs Unions" and in 1973 an Additional Protocol was entered into force. It consisted of topics such as free movement of goods, capital, services and persons, transport and competition, taxation and approximation of legislation, and harmonization of trade policies. It was considered as an agreement to regulate the period before full membership (Ay, 2013: 74-75).

The EEC, which was perceived mainly as an intergovernmental organization similar to NATO, aimed to develop an economic relationship with Turkey despite being negative at the time of Turkey's application. The EEC, which changed into the European Union after a while, put many obstacles in terms of politics, social affairs, and "economics", which forms the main debate of this essay. The EC's stance at this time was based on low economic growth, budget deficits, high interest rates, low per capita income, low Gross Domestic Product, failure in the application of economic liberalization, and high unemployment rates, all of which were considered important economic barriers that pointed to an unready economic situation. Nevertheless, the completion of the Customs Union in 1995 enhanced Turkey's economic integration with the EU. Turkey, as a first phase of integration with the European Union, signed the Customs Union in March 1995 and with the decision of Association Council entered into the Customs Union on 1 January 1996. Upon completion of the Customs Union, Turkey came a long way for integration with the EU. At least, the Turkish economy and industry proved that they were able to cope with the process. Then, the acknowledgment of its candidate status in 1999 in the Helsinki Summit initiated a comprehensive reform process in the country. With this summit, a new period started in relations between Turkey and the EU, following which an Accession Partnership was prepared in order to determine policies that could help toward membership.

Turkey's economic situation was seen in a positive manner, such as being the sixteenth largest economy in the world and sixth largest in Europe at that time. There is no doubt that Turkey will affect the size of the EU's internal market, develop trade relations and provide a large economic gain from tourism in the EU, which also depends on its growing industry, production and export rates. If the Turkish economy is further liberalized successfully and provides stability inside and outside, the EU will certainly gain economically from Turkey`s membership if doors are fully opened to Turkey.

ECONOMIC PROBLEMS WHICH DISTURB THE EU

It is possible to claim that Turkey's economic situation has been creating a problem for several years on the way to full integration into the EU. Even though Turkey became a member of the Customs Union in 1995, and the aim of developing economic relationship with the EU was recognized with candidate status in 1999 at the Helsinki Summit that promoted a comprehensive reform process, Turkey has not been successful enough in carrying out liberalization according to the EU. Because of the fact that the country's economy is so different from that of EU countries – as well as other candidate countries – in many ways, it is problematic for Turkey to be given full membership to the EU. Beyond any doubt, the increase in population is one of the major contributions to economic progress for Turkey. For instance, the population of candidate countries ranges from 388,000 people (Malta) to 67.8 million (Turkey) (Eder, 2003: 219-244). According to the Turkey Statistical Institute (TUIK), the total population of Turkey in 2013 reached 76. 667. 864 people, an increase of 13.7% (Türkiye İstatistik Kurumu, 2014). If granted full membership, Turkey would become the most populous country after Germany. In this situation, the EU would have to allocate more budget and transfer more funds to Turkey. For this reason, the EU can deviate from its target of a "single market" which is a part of "Deepening Process" in case it allows a populous Turkey to join (Atik, 2013).

The second disadvantage of a populous country is that in parallel with a rising population, the young and dynamic people also increase in percentage, in contrast to high average age of Europe. Therefore, the Turkish population is able to have more capability and, thus, power to do more work in less time. Due to the population growth and young population of Turkey, the unemployment rate would potentially increase across Europe as a consequence of migration from Turkey to the other European countries for work. Even now, without being the member of the EU, there are approximately 2.7 million Turks live in Germany (Strüning, 2012). Apart from that, Turks are able to find wider work areas and business districts in many part of Germany, especially in Berlin, with a higher wage than they get in Turkey. There are 350,000 people working in nearly 78,000 Turkish companies which are owned by Turkish immigrants in Germany. The investment of these companies is over 10 billion euros and their annual return is about 35 billion Euro (HSCB Bank A.ş, 2013). So, if the accession to the EU takes place, more Turks would migrate towards European countries and obtain residence without any visa procedure. In case of Turkey's full membership, free movement of the labor force could cause a problem for the EU as although additional migration is accepted by EU countries due to requirement, accomplishment of this cannot be exactly pre-determined without further arguments (Ulchenko, 1988: 141). Thus, the EU fears that Turkish employees could supplant European workers because of their young and dynamic population, causing Europeans to lose their jobs and creating conflicts between employees and employers. All in all, it is seen as an economic threat that could lead to unemployment in Europe from the perspective of the EU.

On the other hand, the EU thinks that Turkey is not still ready in terms of economic position due to the low rate of GDP, official exchange rate, GDP per capita, budget deficit, high interest rates, low real growth rates, etc. Looking at the economic variables of Turkey, real GDP growth has exceeded 6% for many years. But, this strong expansion was interrupted by sharp declines in output in 1994, 1999, and 2001. After the 2008 economic crisis, GDP real growth rate of Turkey was at the ratio of -4.8% in 2009. Despite the rise after 2009 to the nearly 9%, GDP growth rate fell to 2.2 in 2012 and to 3.8% in 2013 (The World Bank, 2014). In these conditions, Turkey has been ranked 86th worldwide (Central Intellligence Agency, 2013). Another important measure that shows the weak side of Turkish economy is low GDP per capita. Comparing to 2007 and 2008 levels, the 2009 GDP per capita of Turkey was low at around $8,561. However, in 2013, the GDP per capita rate increased three times reaching $10,783 (T.C.Ekonomi Bakanlığı, 2014: 9). Nevertheless, Turkey was ranked 90th worldwide (Central Intellligence Agency, 2013). All these indicators are regarded as economic barriers by the Union, so the EU wants Turkey to overcome these problems and reach a more stabilized economy with the help of economic reforms to become a fully ready member among themselves.

Despite EU complaints about an inadequate Turkish economy, some views from the inside the union accept the contradictions about Turkish economic system. Even though Turkey has had a remarkable experience with a market economy for years, compared to the other candidate countries in Eastern Europe, the country faces serious dilemmas and challenges on the way to achieving successful economic criteria (Eder, 2003: 219). A high inflation rate is one of the serious dilemmas of the Turkish economy that must be solved. In 1998, the average Consumer Price Index of 12 months increased annually to 1.3% in the Europe. This number was 84.6% in Turkey in the same year. As of 2000, only three countries, Turkey, Romania and Slovakia, had more than 10% inflation rate (TISK – Confederation of Turkish Employers Union, 2002: 35). For instance, headline inflation driven due to mostly unprocessed food prices increased from 6.2% in December 2012 to 7.3% in March 2013 (European Commission, 2013: 111). Moreover, Turkey pays one of the highest real interest rates among the other candidate countries, so it causes a current deficit. A strategy of expansion based on import with the low rate of exchange, but high interest rate, established sensitivity in the economy. Also, Turkey's debt decrease in proportion to national income allows the country to pay less real interest, which is a term free from inflation, much more than the economic real growth rate and inflation. In this context, if the real interest rates exceed the economic growth rate, it would not be possible to consider economic stability of Turkey from the perspective of the EU.

FAILURE IN LIBERALIZATION POLICY

The Effects of Customs Union on Turkey

On the way to integration into the EU, Turkey faced a very important proposal named the "Copenhagen Criteria" that regulates the economic, political and social affairs of a country. Touching on the economical elements of the proposal, it aims for a transition to an effective market economy, applying neoliberal policies into the economic system, accelerating privatization, creating competition in the EU, supporting new entrepreneurs, etc. Since that time, Turkey started to accelerate the liberalization process and create a free market economy, limiting state intervention to hasten integration into the EU. Moreover, it became the member of Custom Union in 1995 without accession to the EU for strengthening the economic bounds with the EU and to take a position of an open market. However, it is not absolutely right to claim that Turkey has been applying liberalization policy since its accession to the Custom Union. Analyzing the results of the first years of the Turkey-EU Custom Union, it is clearly seen that Turkish industry was not competitive with that of the EU. A special study was conducted in Turkey in 1995 in which were submitted three levels of competitive ability for Turkish industrial enterprises: high, equal to EU enterprises and low. The low level meant full absence of competitive force. In the group of large enterprises, those with high and equal competitive ability constituted 57%. In the group of medium enterprises, 47%, and in the group of small enterprises only 35% (TMMOB, 1996: 57-59). Thus, the Turkish economy might have difficulties in joining the European single market initially.

The other failure of Turkey in implementing liberalization is that Turkey has recently begun to move forward with public sector reforms. Because of the demanding legacy of populism and patronage politics, it was difficult for the Turkish government to engage in policy reforms with short-term costs and long-term benefits, which are EU- related economic reforms. These populist pressures and patronage politics have eliminated all the incentives for public sector reforms, limiting Turkey's view on carrying out the Copenhagen criteria. Therefore, state spending increased and public deficits grew in the second half of the 1980s (Eder, 2003: 223). Related to this point, Sunar mentions that there are two fundamental factors available that explain the failure of public sector reform; one of them is an ongoing problem about rent distribution, the other one is the reason behind the populist strategies of sequential governments (Sunar, 1990: 745-757).

Another barrier from the perspective of the EU is income distribution. Since the beginning of the liberalization process, income distribution levels were very low in Turkey. Looking at the statistics on income according over the years, whereas the income share in the lowest 20 percent of households fell from 5.23% in 1987 to 4.86% in 1994, the share of income in the highest 20 percent increased from 49.93% to 54.88% (Cizre & Yeldan, 2000: 488). Nowadays, it is still possible to see the gap in income distribution in Turkey with the wealthy living in better conditions, and much of the middle class living hand to mouth with an insufficient wage for life.

For Europe, unemployment is a very serious problem for Turkish economic development. In Turkey, the unemployment rate has been high for decades despite a small decrease in recent years. Looking at the economic table of Turkey after 2001 domestic economic crisis and 2008 global crisis, the unemployment rate rose from 8.4% (2001) to 10.3% (2002), and from 11.0% (2008) to 14.0% (2009); a very remarkable jump (Uysal, 2014). As we saw in the 2013 European Commission Turkey Progress Report, while the unemployment rate between 20-64 years of age was 8.8% in 2011, this rate fell to 8.2% and employment rose by 3% in 2012. Parallel to the economic growth rate in the first six months of 2013, average employment accelerated at a growth rate of 4.1% year-on-year. Nevertheless, the average unemployment rate increased 0.4% year-on-year, because the labour force rose faster than employment (European Commission, 2013: 19). Based on these statistics, unemployment is seen as a barrier that must be overcome by the Turkish economy.

Turkey's Economic Rise After 2000s

Nevertheless, the EU would benefit in the case of Turkey's full membership due to her improving economy after Custom Union, especially during 2000s. The influence of neo-liberal economic policies has accelerated the Turkish economy to integrate into the EU by fulfilling economic criteria in Copenhagen. Especially, at the period of AKP, Turkey has followed a stronger market economy, promoted privatizations in public areas, supported entrepreneurship, private sector and competitiveness in markets with regard to Copenhagen criteria. The Turkish economy has been very dynamic in recent years. Between the period of 2000 and 2005, economic growth was significantly higher than EU25, despite being lower than new member states, Bulgaria and Romania. Looking at the basic economic indicators for Turkey and the EU, in 2005, Turkey's GDP and GDP per capita rate were higher than Bulgaria and Romania (Lammers, 2006: 282).

It should be accepted that the structure of the Turkish economy is different from many Central and Eastern European countries due to its entrepreneurial ability, dynamic labor force, sector structure, and welfare level. In today's global world, the deepening processes of EU, the changing global dynamics of the world and common interests make Turkey-EU integration indispensable for both sides. Between 2001 and 2006, it is possible to show that Turkish growth was more rapid than other EU candidate countries and there was a considerable decrease in the rate of inflation (Us, 2007: 123). Moreover, Turkey has been placed the sixth largest economy in Europe and occupied top rank in Europe in terms of growth with a rate of 8.5% in 2011 and 2.2% in 2012 (Ministery of Foreign Affairs, 2014). In this context, the EU does not want to ignore a country enlarging day-by-day and achieving stable economic power. There is no doubt Europe would gain economically from the accession of Turkey to EU.

PROFITS OF THE EU FROM TURKEY'S ACCESSION

Internal Market Factor

During the 1980s, the EU applied a deepening process which changed the external economic environment for Turkey. As a result of the enlargement process, which included Mediterranean countries like Spain, Portugal and Greece as new members of the EU, the deepening process started to move towards the realization of an internal market policy by the end of 1992 (Müftüler, 1995: 86). Now, a fundamental economic effect of Turkey's membership to the EU refers to the accession into the internal market. There is no doubt that this would affect the economies of both Turkey and EU members via trade, domestic investment, FDI, and so on. Looking at the benefits on the EU side, Turkey's accession to the EU would increase the size of the European internal market, as well as the competitiveness of the EU in the global economy.

Since the Customs Union, Turkey has proposed to participate in the internal market of the EU in terms of industrial goods and materials. Within the framework of the Customs Union, Turkey had the right to movements of goods, industrial and intellectual property rights, policy of competition related to internal market acquis. In addition to that, Turkey is a large and growing consumer market which has a serious strategic position. It also bring possibilities of increasing investments opportunities in infrastructure and the energy area (Avrupa Birliği Genel Sekreterliği, 2014: 27). Therefore, Turkey's participation would absolutely increase the size of the internal market of Europe and strengthen the ability of relative competitiveness of the EU in the global economy (Ministery of Foreign Affairs, 2014).

One of the former directors of the State Planning Institute's European Community Department has explained the impact of the EC on Turkey:

In order to overcome the economic obstacles that lay in the way of economic integration between Turkey and the Community, the government has sought to create a new economic order since 1980 through structural changes, new infrastructure, economic liberalization and trade reforms. These reforms have been motivated by the Turkish anxiety of being left out of the new European order that is in the making since the adoption of the internal market programme (Turkish State Planning Institute, 1990: 15-16).

Agriculture and Manufacturing Industry

Considering the wide agriculture and manufacturing area of Turkey, Europe would benefit from the trade of agricultural products in the case of Turkey's full membership by being exposed to a welfare-increasing effect in trade. Despite negativity in Turkey's total balance of foreign trade with the EU, the balance of agricultural products has a surplus (calculated in accordance with Dış Ticaret İstatistikleri, 1995: 191-220). Due to the fact that exports are higher than imports in Turkey, despite the existence of protective measures, Turkey can be shown as a large production industry that could meet the requirements of many EU countries. Considering that Turkey's manufacturing industry has 93.4% shares in its total export, thanks to Turkey's membership, the EU could become fully self-sufficient in imports of agricultural products such as tea, nuts, seeds, corn, citric fruits and so on. In addition to that, Turkey's modern industries have a serious place in Europe. For instance; Turkey is the number one maker of TVs, DVD players and buses, the second biggest commercial vehicle and cement manufacturer, and the third biggest producer of steel and ceramic tiles in Europe. In world rankings, Turkey is also the top producer of boron, second of glass, and fourth of large luxury yachts (S&S Group of Companies, 2011).

Trade Relations

Another issue we must touch on is trade relations, which would increase after the full accession of Turkey to the EU. On 17 October 1991, Turkey signed an agreement with the European Free Trade Association (EFTA) countries with the aim of integrating itself into the economic area of Europe. The neoliberal form of globalization involved trade liberalization, removal of limitations on the movements of capital, service and goods, closer integration into the transnational networks of production through FDI, and partnerships in many areas between Turkish companies and multinational companies (MNCs) (Önder, 2008: 89). In that case, it is possible to consider that trade openness is the basic measure of participation of Turkey in neoliberal globalization. Thanks to the Customs Union, preparation of Turkish industry for EU membership became a fundamental part of trade liberalization. Because of the fact that restrictions on imports were removed, Turkey could buy products from outside without any barriers. Also, export-promotion played a major role in Turkey's further integration into the global economy. In the case of the EU accepting the membership of Turkey, the EU would provide economic gains and benefit from the high level of exports with the USA, Russia and Middle East countries.

After the decisions made on 24 January 1980, which showed Turkey's shift from "mixed capitalism" to a free market economy, Turkey's international expansion policy was carried out intensely between the 1980-1995 period. This increased average export by 12% annually and import from the EU rose by 15% (Ay, 2013: 237). While in 1996, the year Customs Union was carried in Turkey, total foreign trade volume was 66,851 million dollars, this amount reached 243,054 million dollars by the end of 2009. During the same period, looking at the general viewpoint on trade relations between Turkey and the EU, while Turkey's exports amounted to 12,569 million dollar in 1996, they rose to 46,984 million dollars by the end of 2007, a 374% increase (Ay, 2013: 239). In goods and services, Turkey's international trade grew from the annual average of 6.9% of GDP in 1975-79 to 16.8% in 1990-94. Also it rose to 30.2 percent during the period of 2000-04 (Önder, 2008: 90). According to OECD statistics, Turkey's international trade integration rose faster than many other OECD countries' trade integrations related to share of trades (OECD Macro Trade Indicators, 2006). Due to all these trade capabilities of Turkey, the EU would gain a significant measure of economic benefit from the trade relations inside Europe and grow its export rate due to selling goods and materials to USA and Eastern-block countries.

Tourism and Cultural Organizations

Lastly, Turkey is one of the major destinations for tourism in terms of historical and cultural architecture, water sports, environmental beauty and so on. Thus, the country receives many tourists from all parts of the world every year. Istanbul, particularly, is the heart of Turkey that attracts the attention of tourists due to its geographic position. Some important events such as Formula 1, Eurovision, and the Basketball World Cup Championships raised the importance of Istanbul and made it a favorite city with tourists. Looking at the statistics, Turkey is the eighth most popular tourism destination in the world and Istanbul, the "European Capital of Culture 2010", is the seventh most visited city in the world (S&S Group of Companies, 2011). In 2009, tourist numbers visiting Turkey were 25.5 million and the country surpassed many European countries with 21.3 billon dollars income from tourism (Kültür ve Turizm Bakanlığı: 3). Table-1 shows tourism receipts obtained from foreign visitors in first 3 months of 2013 and 2014. Also, there was 4648.8 million dollars total income from tourism in 2013. This amount rose to 4807.8 million dollars in 2014 (Kültür ve Turizm Bakanlığı, 2014).

Table 1. Tourism receipt (Million $)

Aylar Months	Kültür Ve Turizm Bakanliği + Türkiye Istatistik Kurumu + Merkez Bankasi / Ministry of Culture and Tourism + Turkstat + Central Bank				Kültür Ve Turizm Bakanliği + Türkiye Istatistik Kurumu + Merkez Bankasi / Ministry of Culture and Tourism + Turkstat + Central Bank			
	2013				2014			
	(*)	(**)	(***)	TOPLAM (Total)	(*)	(**)	(***)	TOPLAM (Total)
OCAK-January	975.4	462.9	12.6	1451	1 090.3	417.9	12.2	1 520.4
ŞUBAT-February	944.5	429.1	10.1	1383.7	1065.6	365.3	11.4	1 442.3
MART-March	1350.2	451.9	12.2	1814.2	1 476.5	354.4	14.3	1 845.2
3 AYLIK TOPLAM 3 Months Total	3270.1	1343.8	34.9	4648.8	3 632.4	1 137.6	37.8	4 807.8

Source: TurkStat, Central Bank, Ministry of Culture and Tourism
(*) Receipts obtained from foreign visitors
(**)Receipts obtained from citizen residing in abroad
(***) GSM Roaming Spendings and Marina Service Spendings

According to all these statistics, tourists coming from many parts of the world bring foreign currency to the country and contribute significantly to the Turkish economy. In other words, it has become an inward money flow. State or private actors can save or use this money on new investments for public or individual's benefit. Such a country definitely provides benefit for the EU by pulling tourists towards itself, so that foreign currency could flow into the Union and contribute to the Europe economy. All in all, the Union would become richer and have an opportunity to spend on new investment for the sake of member states.

CONCLUSION

To conclude, Turkey's time has been wasted for more than 40 years by coming up with many economic obstacles such as low GDP rates, wrong liberal policies and unemployment. Indeed, some of these preventions originate from the fear of the EU with regard to rising population and dynamic human power of Turkey. It makes the accession process to the EU difficult for Turkey over time. However, there are some points that the EU ignores about Turkey's rising dimension of economy in recent years. A strong possibility of becoming an internal market for the EU, increasing production capacity in agricultural area, manufacture and export of goods to outside, stronger trade relations inside and outside of the EU are all the factors which show the economic power of Turkey, especially after Customs Union. These will create a stronger EU in economic area against outside such as the USA and the Eastern block. Also, tourism opportunities of Turkey bring foreign currency into the EU reserves, so that the EU both will be able to get more receipt from tourism. Furthermore, it is able to advertise Europe's tourism areas more strikingly such as "holiday paradise Europe" and improve its image in a positive way. To sum up, the EU should find a way to facilitate the membership of Turkey instead of imposing the same obstacles for years.

REFERENCES

Atik, H. (2013). AB Türkiye'yi Neden Tam Üyeliğe Kabul Etmiyor? *Ankara Strateji Enstitüsü.* Retrieved from http://www.ankarastrateji.org/yazar/prof-dr-hayriye-atik/ab-turkiye-yi-neden-tam-uyelige-kabul-etmiyor/

Avrupa Birliği Bakanlığı, T. C. (2011). *Türkiye-AB İlişkilerinin Tarihçesi*. Retrieved from http://www.abgs.gov.tr/index.php?p=111&l=1

Avrupa Birliği Genel Sekreterliği. (2010). *Türkiye'nin Üyeliği Perspektifinden Kaynaklanan Hususlar*. Retrieved from http://www.mfa.gov.tr/data/AB/etki_degerlendirme.pdf

Ay, H. (2013). *AB Mali Yapısı* (p. 237). İzmir: Kanyılmaz Matbaası.

Calculated in Accordance with Dış Ticaret İstatistikleri: 1995. (1997). Ankara, pp. 191-220. quoted from Natalia Ulchenko, p. 140.

Central Intelligence Agency. (2013). *The world factbook: Turkey*. Retrieved from https://www.cia.gov/library/publications/the-world-factbook/geos/tu.html

Cizre, Ü., & Yeldan, E. (2000). Politics, society and financial liberalization: Turkey in the 1990s. *Development and Change, 31*(2), 488.

Economic and Financial Affairs - European Commission. (2013). *Turkey from soft landing to renewed upturn*. Retrieved from http://ec.europa.eu/economy_finance/eu/forecasts/2013_spring/cc_turkey_en.pdf

Eder, M. (2003). Implementing the economic criteria of the EU membership: How difficult is it for Turkey? *Turkish Studies, Vol, 4*(1), 219–244. doi:10.1080/714005711

Ekonomi Bakanlığı, T. C. (2014). Ekonomik Görünüm Nisan 2014: Kişi Başına Düşen GSYH Oranları. Academic Press.

European Commission. (2013). *Turkey 2013 progress report*. Retrieved from http://ec.europa.eu/enlargement/pdf/key_documents/2013/package/brochures/turkey_2013.pdf

HSCB Bank A.ş. (2013, March). Almanya Türk Yatırımcısına Büyük Fırsatlar Sunuyor. *Turkish Time Global Export*, p. 5.

Lammers, K. (2006). The EU and Turkey – Economic effects of Turkey's full membership. *Inter Economics, 41*(5), 282–288. doi:10.1007/s10272-006-0198-z

Ministery of Foreign Affairs. (n.d.). *Turkey-EU relations*. Retrieved from http://www.mfa.gov.tr/relations-between-turkey-and-the-european-union.en.mfa

Müftüler, M. (1995). Turkish economic liberalization and European integration. *Middle Eastern Studies, 31*(1), 86.

Önder, N. (2007). The Turkish political economy: Globalization and regionalism. *Perspectives on Global Development and Technology, 6*(1), 242–243.

Önder, N. (2008). The Turkish project of globalization and new regionalism. *Turkish Journal of International Relations, 7*(2-3), 89.

S&S Group of Companies. (2011). *About Turkey: Turkey to Europe's future*. Retrieved from http://www.ssgroupofcompanies.com/en/index/turkey.php#

Strüning, F. (2012). Turks in Germany in 2012: Study on German-Turkish life and values. *Citizen Times*. Retrieved from http://www.citizentimes.theEU/2012/08/23/turks-in-germany-2012/

Sunar, İ. (1990). Populism and patronage: The democrat party and its legacy in Turkey. Academic Press.

TC. (n.d.a). Kültür ve Turizm Bakanlığı. 2011-2014 Turizm Gelir, Gider ve Ortalama Harcamaları: Turizm Gelirleri. Academic Press.

TC. (n.d.b). Kültür ve Turizm Bakanlığı: Turizm Raporları: Dünya'da ve Türkiye'de Turizm 2009. Araştırma ve Değerlendirme Daire Başkanlığı. Academic Press.

The World Bank. (2014). *Table: GDP growth rate of all countries (2009 – 2013)*. Retrieved from http://data.worldbank.org/indicator/NY.GDP.MKTP.KD.ZG

TISK (Confederation of Turkish Employers Union). (2002). *Comparative report on candidate countries to the EU*. Ankara: Author.

TMMOB. (1996). 95 Sanayi Kongresi, Bildiriler Kitabı. Academic Press.

Turkish State Planning Institute. (1990, March). Article. *European Communities Bulletin*, *1*(3/4), 15–16.

Türkiye İstatistik Kurumu. (2014). *Adrese Dayalı Nüfus Kayıt Sistemi Sonuçları: 2013. No:15974*. Retrieved from http://www.tuik.gov.tr/PreHaberBultenleri.do?id=15974

Ulchenko, N. (1988). Turkey-EU economic relations: problems and prospects. *The Turkish Yearbook of International Relations*, *18*, 141.

Us, V. (2007). Türkiye-AB Bütünleşmesi Sürecine İlişkin Karşılaştırmalı Analiz: EMR2 İçin Yol Haritası. *Ankara Çalışmaları Dergisi*, *6*(2), 123.

Uysal, Y. (2014). *Temel Ekonomik Göstergeler: Türkiye Ekonomisine İlişkin Temel Göstergeler*. Retrieved from http://kisi.deu.edu.tr/yasar.uysal/site/temel-gostergeler.html

Chapter 9
EU Health Policy:
To What Extent the EU Got Involved in the Field of Health?

Hakan Cavlak
Namık Kemal University, Turkey

Abdülkadir Işik
Namık Kemal University, Turkey

Davuthan Günaydin
Namık Kemal University, Turkey

ABSTRACT

Although not openly identified in treaties until the Maastricht Treaty, health has always been a crucial area for the European Union (EU), since freedoms provided and regulations brought by common market also dealt with several sections of the health sector. All concerning parts of health sector have to be subject to both freedoms and regulations of single market system. Despite the value given to health and related issues, a separate or supranational policy dealing with health issues has not been formed by the EU. The member states keep their privilege on health policies. However, the EU does not stay completely aside of health issues; on the contrary, the EU got involved in certain areas of health, especially the ones which have cross-border implications. In this chapter, the matter of to what extent the EU got involved in health issues is researched and the question of if the EU has a concrete health policy is analyzed.

INTRODUCTION

This study analyses the influence of the European Union (EU) on health policies of the member states. Despite the common belief; health care systems in member states are not apart from EU impact (Hervey & McHale, Health law and the European Union, 2004). The clear statements of Article 168 of the Lisbon Treaty, which underlines health as an area of national governments' competence, and the inherent implication of the subsidiarity, do not mean that health is excluded from EU interference. The 1998 Kohll and Decker cases[1] have opened the way for many EU citizens seek health treatment elsewhere their home countries as a right entailed from European Community rules for free

DOI: 10.4018/978-1-4666-7308-3.ch009

movement of goods and services. These cases have shown that health policy, although it is stated otherwise in the Treaties, cannot escape from the free movement rules of the EU. Thus, maybe not empowered by the treaties, the EU got involved in the health area. The level of EU's competences in the health field and new pressures in the area of health from the EU after the Kohll and Decker cases are the two main questions of this paper concerned. In answering such questions, it have to be considered that there are three EU policy types i.e. Market building policies, which are regulatory usually and leaded by EU institutions, e.g. internal market, commercial policy ; market correcting policies, which aims to avoid negative impacts of market forces on citizens and producers and generally subject to intergovernmental bargaining, e.g. common agricultural policy; and finally there are also market-cushioning policies, that are also regulatory and having intention to decrease the loss given to individuals by economic activities of which the competences in this policy type are shared between EU and member states, e.g. environmental policy and social and health policies (Sbragia & Stolfi, 2008). Economic integration has started with market building policies, however through the time some unexpected and negative effects of integration have been addressed by market correcting and cushioning policies.

Health Policy in the EU faces a serious dichotomy. On the one hand the Treaty explicitly states that the area of Health is specifically within the responsibility of national governments (EC, 2009); on the other hand health systems of member states are dealing with people (e.g. professionals and patients), goods (e.g. medicines and medical devices) and services (e.g. insurance systems) which have been granted free movement by the same treaty (EC, 2009). So, many of the health systems of the national governments are subject to EU law and policy. In buying or selling pharmaceuticals or medical devices or recruiting health professionals the decisions are mainly made according to EU policies. Moreover, the citizens of the member states may travel to other member states and get their treatments there and their expenses would be refunded by their national authority; thus, the national health systems are officially excluded from the EU competence, however, they are subject to EU law in the fields of financing, delivery and provisions. Additionally, the EU has been bounded by the 1992 Maastricht Treaty "to contribute to the attainment of a high level of health protection" for the citizens of the EU. The question of how the EU executives expected to provide measures to comply with this treaty provision without being involved in the health policies of the national governments remains unanswered. The EU thus faces a challenge of either promoting free movements for the sake of integration or recedes from health policies to let member states to provide more social security (Scharpf, 2002). However, as it is in the case of health policy area, the EU can expand its influence in areas which have not been exclusively defined in EU competences standing on the rules stated in the EC Treaty. Furthermore, the EU does not want to leave health policy to the market forces, instead the commission tried, for example, to issue directives in the years of 2006 and 2008 about patient mobility, however, these initiatives did not welcome by some of the member states and those directives could not have been adopted.

In evaluating the integration of health policies in the EU, an old but effective theory of integration "Neo-Functionalism" (Haas, 1958) would be applied in this study as an explanatory tool. In explaining integration in the EU, the Neo - functionalist theory offers a coherent and a stringent explanation of this development. As Sweet (2012, p. 1) stated: "The theory is dynamic; it explicitly seeks to explain market and political integration over time, and provides appropriate concepts, specifies mechanisms of institutional change, and generates testable hypotheses, and it has supported an ongoing, productive stream of empirical research confirming the theory's core propositions." The opposite approach to European integration is intergovernmentalism and its basic argument is: the structure and influence of the EU can be explained by the decisions made by the member states. Other general theories cannot reach its explanatory power. Although the neo-functionalist theory is considered by many contemporary researchers as an outdated approach, it is claimed in this paper that it is still very useful in understanding many aspects of European integration including the area of health policies.

As mentioned above, the Treaty clearly states that the field of health is falling under the exclusive competence of member states and the principle of subsidiarity inherently implied in the concerned article on how the issues relating health would be dealt. However, it would be argued that there is substantial integration and EU impact in health issues despite the statements in the Treaty and this can be explained by the "spillover effect" argument of the Neo-functionalist theory (Haas, 1958). The EU seems abstained from the area of health when the official documents, especially the Treaty, are taken into consideration, but other rules and provisions of acquis, such as free movements of goods, services, persons and capital, and social policy principles, enable and even force the EU to take measures on health issues. So it can be observed that although there are no special intentions of the national governments to create a common health policy, the spillover effect in the integration forms an implicit health policy for the EU.

RESEARCH DESIGN AND METHODOLOGY

In order to assess the involvement of the EU in the integration of health policies, the main question formed in this study is: 'does the EU have an effect on the integration of the health policies of the member states?' The neo-functionalist theory has been chosen as the explanatory tool to answer this question. The EU involvement, especially in the fields of health workforce, mobility of patients and cross border functioning of health insurances would be taken as the cases to prove the argument of this study. In order to carry out the research more systemically four secondary questions have been formulated. First: what are neo functionalism and its main premises? Second: How the role of the EU is defined in the EU's official documents? Third: What are the evidences that demonstrate the EU involvement in health issues? Fourth: How these evidences prove that the neo functionalist theory is still effective in explaining integration in various areas? Thus the main aim of this paper is to determine to what extent the EU is involved in the integration of the health policies of the member states. The hypothesis of the study is "despite the apparent statement of the EU of not interfering the health policies of the member states, it is involved the concerned area." Thus, the dependent variable of this research would be the level of integration in the field of health in member states; the independent variable would be the effect of the EU's involvement into the health issues of member states through different policies and EU law. In order to accomplish this research the literature on neo-functionalism would be attentively reviewed; recent articles and books written on health policy would be evaluated; the EU's publications and reports on health policy would be assessed; additionally, the EU Treaties, directives, regulations and case law would be revised. Thus, both primary and secondary sources about the subject would be analyzed and the information gathered through those sources would be combined and applied to the study to enrich it and prove above mentioned argument.

AN OLD BUT STILL EFFECTIVE TOOL OF EXPLAINING EUROPEAN INTEGRATION: NEO-FUNCTIONALISM

The neo-functionalism had been formulized as an alternative to International Relations' (IR) mainstream theories by Ernest Haas in 1950s. Haas considered Realism's power centered view on to the international system and Idealism's ideal of a Kantian legal order to surpass conflict problematic (Haas, 1958). The main arguments of neo-functionalism have been offered by Haas, especially in his book named: "Uniting of Europe" (Haas, 1958). Besides opposing two grand theories of IR, neo-functionalism has been emerged as a critique of functionalism and an attempt to explain the brand new integration occurring in Europe. The time when Haas offered neo-functionalism was overlapped with the initiative of creating a more comprehensive European integration from the Coal and Steel Community to European Economic Community. Thus, neo-functionalism has been a pioneer attempt for the theorization of European integration, that is, at that time, the only serious economic integration effort in the world. As an international integration theory the neo-functionalism looks for reaching a political entity greater than the nation-state and tries to understand the conditions in which this type of political entity will develop. Neo-functionalism reminds federalism with this feature. Both approaches target a model of a supranational state or political entity. Nevertheless, their methods are quite distinctive. Although, the final point projected by neo-functionalism and federalism seems similar; the method used by neo-functionalism is derived from functionalism. Neo-functionalism offers, unlike federalism, but similar to functionalism, a gradual method for reaching the final goal of creating a supranational political entity by beginning from economics and diffusing the integration to other areas, especially to the political sphere (Bergmann & Niemann, 2013). So, it can be argued that neo-functionalism is a combination of federalism and functionalism as it derived its method from functionalism and its fundamental objective from federalism.

The concept of "political community" has been the startup of neo-functionalism's theoretical structure. The political community is defined as "a condition in which specific groups and individuals show more loyalty to their central political institutions than to any other political authority, in a specific period of time and in a definable geographic space" (Haas, 1958, p. 8). So, Haas views institutions and loyalty to them as central points of political community; and Haas continued that the set of conditions given in a certain time and space, shape people's loyalty to the political institutions. Accordingly, the conditions that shape the people's loyalty may change and, therefore, people's loyalty may also change from one central political institution to another. The underlying forces of this shift from national state to a larger entity and terms of development of a regional integration were demonstrated in Haas's book. The "supranational community" is a greater political entity compared to national state according to neo-functionalist theory. According to the neo-functionalist theory the States joining the regional integration would constitute a supranational domain of which is above their national authorities. The domain of this supranational entity would be governed by a supranational institution exercising supranational power. The neo-functionalism argues that at the first phase integration, a supranational institution gathers nation states within its supranational authority and then this supranational authority would spread over to the domains of national sovereignties at the expense of national authority. This process of authority diffusion is considered as almost an instinctive one by the neo-functionalists and named as "Spillover". It is endorsed by the neo-functionalists that integration in an economic sector would comprise other sectors through the means of interdependence. This process named as "Spillover" and it is the main tool of explanation in neo-functionalism (Haas, 1958, pp. 12-13). Lindberg made the definition of Spillover as follows: "situation in which a given action, related to a specific goal, creates a situation in which the original goal can be assured only by taking further actions, which in turn create a further condition and a need for more action, and so forth" (Lindberg, 1963, p. 1). Haas employed this concept to demonstrate integration of an economic sector, e.g. coal and steel community, would unavoidably lead to the integration of other economic sectors. According to neo-functionalists, an integration started in a limited economic sector would spread over other economic sectors and at the end whole body of the economies of the nation states joined the supranational organization would get integrated. Haas claims that the realization of such a supranational agency is quite difficult and requires a strong compromise between the concerned states built on the conviction that certain interests of the states cannot be achieved in any alternative way (Haas, 1958, p. 4). Along with the neo-functionalist understanding of integration, once a supranational organization which promotes the interests of nation states is founded this will end up with more integration in different sectors and enlargement of the supranational organization's sovereignty.

The neo-functionalism formulized their conception of change by the term of Spillover. The concept of Spillover has usually been identified with three types as: functional Spillover, political Spillover and cultivated Spillover (Tranholm-Mikkelsen, 1991). The influence of functional Spillover occurs when a specific target can be secured only by furthering the integration (Tranholm-Mikkelsen, 1991, p. 10). The source of the influence is the policy sectors' and concerned areas' interdependency. According to Haas, the certain sectors and issue areas are so interdependent that it is almost impossible to isolate them from the rest (1958, pp. 267,283). Thus, the tensions, contradictions occurred between various policies, politics and polity within the EU cause the policy makers to take further integrative actions in achieving their original objectives. Political Spillover describes the situation whereby national elites believe that crucial interests cannot be reached at the domestic level and therefore requires supranational assistance. So national elites would promote more integration and add more political incentives to the integration. Cultivated Spillover explains the role of supranational institutions which are concerned to increase their power and become an important agent in the integration process and thus benefit from the development of the integration process. As observed in various examples, once a supranational institution is formed it is quite difficult to control them even for their original founders. Supranational institutions may promote further integration through numerous ways, such as acting as policy initiators.

In neo-functionalist thought the area of politics is viewed by two separate parts as high and low politics. Starting integration in High Politics such as diplomacy, strategy, defense and ideologies is quite difficult. Nation states demonstrate resistance to give up their sovereignty in high political issues. Hence, according to neo-functionalism, the integration has to be initiated in the fields of low politics, such as, economic and technical domains (Pentland, 1973, p. 109). The integration process in low politics would certainly lead integration in high politics. The identification of people would be switching from the national level to the supranational level once the supranational organization achieves a full integration of national economies and markets.

According to neo-functionalism the nation state does not consist of a single structure, instead it is an amalgamation of different interests and areas that are various interest groups, elites, bureaucrats, politicians; and in line with neo-functionalist approach those diverse groups may cooperate on building coalitions for maximizing their interests. Moreover, they also act together with their international counterparts (Pentland, 1973). Hence, integration is defined by Haas as switching coalitions of the various interests of which bureaucrats, interest groups and elites represent (1958, p. 4). Haas anticipated that as the integration proceeds benefits of various groups would be redefined in line with regional level interests instead of only national level interests (1958, p. 5). This phase, according to Haas, has the crucial importance as economic integration would convert into a political one at this stage of integration. The concept of "political integration" is defined by Haas as: "process whereby political actors in several distinct national settings are persuaded to shift their loyalties, expectations and political activities toward a new center, whose institutions possess or demand jurisdiction over the pre-existing nation-states" and claims that "the end-result of a political integration process is a new political community, superimposed over the pre-existing ones" (1958, p. 13).

The key arguments of neo-functionalism could be stated as follows:

1. Integration is a process which develops over time and creates its own dynamic.
2. Regional integration is influenced by various, diverse and altering actors who also build coalitions (Haas, 1958, p. 68).
3. Rational and self-interested actors act as decision makers (Haas, 1958, p. 291).
4. Step by step decision making is chosen instead of grand designs where relatively small arrangements are usually caused by the unintended consequences of previous decisions.

The opposite approach to European integration is intergovernmentalism and its basic argument is: the structure and influence of the EU can be explained by the decisions made by the member states. The most known intergovernmentalist Andrew Moravcsik derived his assumptions from IR theory and argues that the EU or similar international institutions are founded because they allow the founder states benefit and such institutions make intergovernmental bargains more efficient.

To conclude the theoretical review of neo-functionalism, it can be stated that the neo-functionalists expect to reach a federal or confederal entity at the end of the integration process. To reach this end the neo-functionalist authors offer a system which begins with integration in low politics i.e. economics under the authority of a supranational framework. The supranational framework would be founded on the principal of delegating sovereignty from national authorities to supranational one. Neo-functionalists assume that after this process of delegation is started and integration in economic sector pursued, these would lead further integration in national economies and markets and thus the loyalty of people would shift from national authorities to supranational authority. Finally, a regional, i.e. European, political entity which transcends the limits of nation states would emerge.

Testing the basic ideas of neo-functionalist and the contrary approach of intergovernmentalism in the field of health policy can simply be accomplished. There are essentially three areas that both neo-functionalists and intergovernmentalists seek to enlighten: the role of the EU that the member states have determined, the extent of the EU role in a certain policy and if the role of the developed into a broader one with the effect of such a policy (Greer, 2006). According to intergovernmentalists, there would be no EU Health Policy if the member states wish not to have one. However, neo-functionalists claim the opposite; according to them a policy could emerge despite the preferences of member states, thus, a health policy would emerge if the conditions are suitable enough without requiring member states' intentions. It is argued that there is no evidence of member states wishing to have a separate area of health policy. Therefore, according to intergovernmentalists there would not be significant health policy in the EU. Contrary, neo-functionalists anticipate that, regardless of the open preference of member states, there would be the influence of Spillover which would help emerging of an EU health policy.

Health in Treaties

Health policy of the EU has been founded upon a dilemma. On the one hand the leaders of the EU desired the EU to be perceived as doing something about sensitive and relatively significant issues for the citizens, like health. On the other hand, the health policy is considered so substantial for the national governments that they don't want the EU to get involved in it. Although health never been excluded from the treaties, the EU had never got a serious competency on health issues until recent times (Randall, 2001). Health councils have been held since 1970s and some common actions initiated by the EU as "Europe against Cancer" in 1987 or a program against AIDS which began in 1991. The situation started to change with the signing of the Single European Act (SEA) in 1986; the EU gained some authority to legislate on health issues which have connection to internal market. Mutual recognition of degrees (initiated in 1975) took a new phase after SEA, which meant free movement of medical professionals across borders. It also gave the EU the chance to decrease potential negative effects of the market and prevent discrimination. The treaty of Maastricht has introduced some particular clauses about health policy. The article 129 (now part of article 168) has been inserted into the Treaty, which stated that "the Community shall contribute towards a high level of human health protection by encouraging co-operation between Member States and, if necessary, lending support to their action". This clause obliged the EU to take health protection into consideration in all of its activities. The social dimension of the EU was extended by the incorporation of 'social charter' into the Treaty of Amsterdam of 1997. Thus, in the clause 1 of article 152 of the Amsterdam Treaty, the EU ensured 'a high level of human health protection in the definition and implementation of all EU policies' and 'working with member states to improve health, prevent illness and obviate sources of danger to human health'. However, the actual power delegated for this clause remained very vague and the mean for this statement has been a simple recommendation. Moreover, the clauses of 4 and 5 of article 152 of the Amsterdam Treaty clearly stated that 'harmonization of public health legislation of member states is strictly prohibited' and the EU was instructed to 'respect the member states' responsibilities for the organization and delivery of health services and medical care'. The Lisbon Treaty of 2009 proposes a more coherent health protection competence for the EU. Regulation of medical devices, measures to address cross-border risks and authorization for spending programs and recommendations for public health is included in the competencies of the EU according to the Lisbon Treaty. However, the areas of 'management of health services and medical care and the allocation of resources assigned to them' remained exclusively under the authority of the member states. Thus, the general overview of health policy in the EU demonstrates evidences both for the neo-functionalists (i.e. Expansion of competencies of the EU, especially in public health and EU's responsibility in considering health protection in all EU policies) and intergovernmentalists (i.e. Insistence on reserving the authority of member states in administration and resource allocation of health services and medical care). However, in the following section, the evidences supporting neo-functionalist arguments would be presented. It is going to be seen that although there are some clear statements on the exclusive competence of member states on health issues, in reality the intergovernmentalist arguments have not a robust stand. If states are in control of health policies, there would not be a significant occurrence in this field. However, this is not the case; the decisions made by the European Court of Justice (ECJ) have extended the role of the EU on health issues. The influence of the EU on health issues come from its responsibilities and powers for regulating and designing the internal market. The decisions of the ECJ intended to achieve the objectives of the internal market proven to alter the competences in the area of health policy. The main characteristic of the decisions of the ECJ is to eliminate discrimination about nationality and replacing the national rules with European ones. The outcome of this process is the realization of new EU competencies which the national governments did not intend.

Neo-Functionalism Over Again: "Unintended" European Integration in Health Policy

Free movement of persons has been one of the key aspects of the European integration since the establishment. In the case of health, the directive on mutual recognition of professions (Directive 93/16/EEC) has been the main issue since the time this directive has come into force (Nichols, 2004). Although there are some controversial issues such as the fate of health professionals educated outside the EU, but licensed by a member state, the general position of the ECJ about these cases can be summarized as health professionals are health professionals disregard to their origin of state or education. In other words, according the principle of non-discrimination, disregarding to the quality of education or profession in a given country, any person licensed in an EU country has to be treated equally. Although the effect of this situation is quite limited in the EU, it somehow annoys the member states and they are in an attempt to harmonize their medical education and licensing procedures (Nickless, 2001, p. 81). In accordance with the arguments of neo-functionalists without the intention of the national governments the competence of the EU has been expanded in this area of the health.

The EU law strictly prohibits any kind of discrimination on the basis of citizenship. Accordingly, the ECJ narrows down the member states' rights to limit entrance to their welfare systems. According to ECJ rulings workers have the right to have access to social security systems of any member states and this is getting expanded incrementally for any person in the EU (Weathill & Beaumont, 1999, pp. 620,714). This is also true for the field of health. Member states desire to keep cross-border movements of patients in order to limit their potential of health tourism and keep the resource in their country. The two important cases on this issue have been the cases of Kohll and Decker both held in 1998. According to the decisions made by ECJ, they have the right to have treatment at any member state and the home member state have to fund the treatment as it is held in its own country (Case of Kohll and Decker, 1998). This means that any member state cannot force or bound their citizens to health institutions based only in their country. Agencies in any member state have to make a contract with health providers all over the EU. Actually there are no big numbers of patients crossing the borders for treatment except for the situations of geographical proximity, or interest in specific treatments. There are many reasons why the patients do not prefer to cross border for medical treatment such as difference in language or customs in health care etc. However, the point that has to be accounted in the decision of the ECJ is that national governments cannot restrict their residents to flow for health care treatment on any basis to other member states and concerning agencies of the member states are mandated to take the responsibility to tackle with this situation. In order to comply with these rules national governments changed their legislations and the concerned agencies seek health care providers all around the EU to make contracts. Spillover effect driven by the decisions made by the ECJ can easily be found in the case of patient movement. The member states strictly tried to secure their security and welfare systems from the outsiders, but again the basic principles of the EU applied by the ECJ decisions and force member states to integrate and bolster them to create a European standard in health care and health insurances.

The health area does not consist of only health professionals and patients; it also includes purchasing of goods and services such as real estate, pharmaceuticals, and medical devices. The European Union has influence on these issues at least in two ways: Constraints of the EU on public purchasing and EU harmonization of standards that limits the authority of national governments on what can be sold to their national health systems. For instance a directive dated back in 1965 (Directive 65/65/EEC) opened way to the EU to interfere medical purchasing. According to this directive no member state can purchase or sell medicines without an approval of an appropriate body. After the Single European Act, numerous new directives were issued in order to regulate the purchasing and selling of pharmaceuticals and medical devices that have had the intention of harmonizing medical standards and protecting internal market through facilitating cross-border sales (Hervey, 2002, pp. 89-91). Thus, the EU intervened in the medical market and broke down the national rules in this field and brought EU wide rules. However, this did not realized easily since many of the member states objected the role of the EU, accusing the EU as ignoring the different standards of regulatory bodies, setting too low standards thereby letting ineffective and dangerous technologies to insert into their markets. A European market for pharmaceuticals and medical devices has been formed despite the complaints from the member states. The EU responded to these complaints of the member states by establishing the European Medicines Evaluation Agency in 1995. It is mandatory for many new products to be authorized by this agency before it can be sold in the EU market. Consequently, the EU has an expanded role in technology assessment, pharmaceutical control and medical device regulation as a result of pressure from the rules of the single market despite the reluctance of many member states. Here again the neo-functionalist Spillover effect could be observed as the EU has a quite substantial role in the health related market even though the member states desires the opposite and the Treaty contains clauses in line with the claims of the national governments.

Anything inserted into the field of health have been originated from the rules of the single market. This is how the area of health is shaped via EU rules despite the refusal of national governments to form competence of the EU in Health Policy. This situation does not mean only the demonstration of the results of the single market policies. This also changes the debates on the policies. The effects foreseen by the neo-functionalism do not always create an inevitable integration. Besides, the consequences might be unwelcome by the agents in the system and might create a negative reaction (Haas, 1958). Even, the ones who feel harmed by the de facto or de jure situation created by the supranational organization might get organized against the new situation and counterattack to regain their former rights and privileges. However, this is not the case for European Health Policy, at least not yet. In addition, the European Commission also interested to extend its authority on health issues by the means of problems and opportunities created by the ECJ. Three different Directorate-Generals (DGs) seek to get involved in health area: DG responsible for Health and Consumer Protection, DG responsible for Internal Market and Services and DG responsible for Employment, Social Affairs and Equal Opportunities. The DG for Health and Consumer Protection holds the name health and it is responsible especially for the issues related public health and the statement of the Treaty that indicates "every policy or action shall take protection of human health into account". However, its authority is restricted to the above mentioned areas and it has very limited legislative and financial resources to get involved other issues related to health despite it desires vice versa (Greer, 2006). The DG for Internal Market and Services is one of the most eager institutions that desire to interfere in the health area since it has a substantial power of legislating internal market which is one of the oldest and important pillars of the European integration. They are trying to intervene the field of health by the means of Directive on Services of General Interest (COM(2011) 900 final), which has the objective of consolidating legislation concerning general interest including health services. Finally DG for Employment, Social Affairs and Equal Opportunities, it views itself as the guardian of the European social model which includes also health, and tries to reserve issues concerning social model from internal market and ECJ. It offers a different tool for policy making in areas such as health, namely the open method of coordination (OMC). Thus, it wants to protect health issues from the strict rules of the internal market and to some extent from the rulings of the ECJ.

CONCLUSION

In order to answer the central question of this study, i.e. 'does the EU have an effect on the integration of the health policies of the member states?' this paper offered three sections. In the first section, the neo-functionalist theory and its components and arguments were discussed. In the second section, the articles concerning the health area in the treaties were revised and in the third section the evidences of EU involvement in the health care area were presented. Eventually, the answer to the main question, based on the research carried out in all sections, appeared as "there is a substantial EU effect on health policies of the member states".

The impact of the EU on health policies of the member states is evaluated in this study through the means of neo-functionalism. As it is argued, health care systems of national governments are not apart from the integration process. Although, the article 168 (formerly 152) of the Treaty on the Functioning of the European Union reserved health care policies exclusively to the competence of the member states, the EU gets involved in these policies as a result of the integration dynamics. The cases presented against member states in the ECJ opened the way of EU interference to the health care systems of the national governments generally based on the rules of the internal market. It is presented in this paper that, although implicitly, the effect of the EU on national health care systems is relatively high and new pressures, especially from supranational bodies, can be accounted. In other words, both the market correcting and market building policies of the EU have influenced the health policies of the EU. As the movements of goods, services, capital and persons concerning health faced the rules of the internal market, the member states, thus, have to reconsider their authority in the field and consequently comply with the EU rules in the sake of European integration. Moreover, the EU does not desire to leave health issues to the market forces and issued several directives, this also expanded the role of the EU in the health area, despite the unwillingness of some member states.

The theory of neo-functionalism applied to explain the gradual expansion of the EU role in health policy. Although, it is considered an old fashioned approach by various scholars of European integration, neo-functionalism offers a "coherent and stringent" explanation about the evolution of health policy as an EU dominated field. The arguments of the rival theory, i.e. intergovernmentalism, appeared to be insufficient, as the member states imposed their reluctance several times in not leaving authority to the EU on health issues through the Treaties, the incidents demonstrate the opposite. In spite of the arguments of intergovernmentalism as the core decision makers in European integration are national states, the neo-functionalist statement of integration initiated in the fields of economics and markets would eventually affect the other areas and force them to be integrated proved to be more accurate. The "spillover effect" of the integration on the health care area through ECJ cases and EU directives asserted the accuracy of the neo-functional arguments.

REFERENCES

Bergmann, J., & Niemann, A. (2013). Theories of European integration and their contribution to the study of European foreign policy. In *Proceedings of 8th Pan-European Conference on International Relations*. Warsaw: Academic Press.

Case of Kohll and Decker, C-120/95; C-158/96 (ECJ 4 28, 1998).

COM(2011) 900 final (a Communication on a Quality Framework for Services of General Interest (SGI) in the EU 12 20, 2011).

Directive 65/65/EEC (Council Directive on the approximation of provisions laid down by Law, Regulation or Administrative Action relating to proprietary medicinal products 1 26, 1965).

Directive 93/16/EEC (Council Directive to facilitate the free movement of doctors and the mutual recognition of their diplomas, certificates and other evidence of formal qualifications 4 5, 1993).

EC. (2009). Lisbon Treaty. *Article 168*.

EC. (2009). Lisbon Treaty. *Article 18, 39, 43, 28 and 49*.

Greer, S. (2006). Uninvited Europeanization: Neofunctionalism and the EU in health policy. *Journal of European Public Policy*, *13*(1), 134–152. doi:10.1080/13501760500380783

Haas, E. B. (1958). *The uniting of Europe: Political, social, and economic forces, 1950-1957*. Stanford, CA: Stanford University Press.

Hervey, T. (2002). Mapping the contours of European Union health law and policy. *European Public Law*, *8*(1), 69–105. doi:10.1023/A:1014542608569

Hervey, T., & McHale, J. (2004). *Health law and the European Union*. Cambridge, UK: Cambridge University Press. doi:10.1017/CBO9780511617553

Lindberg, L. N. (1963). *The political dynamics of European economic integration*. Stanford, CA: Stanford Univeristy Press.

Nichols, S. (2004). The challenges of the free movement of health professionals. In *Health policy and European Union enlargement*. Maidenhead, UK: Open University Press.

Nickless, J. (2001). The internal market and the social nature of health care. In *The impact of EU law on health care systems*. Brussels: Peter Lang.

Pentland, C. (1973). *International theory and European integration*. London: Faber and Faber.

Randall, E. (2001). *The European Union and health policy*. Basingstoke, UK: Palgrave.

Sbragia, A., & Stolfi, F. (2008). Key policies. In E. Bomberg, J. Peterson, & A. Stubb (Eds.), *The European Union: How does it work?* Oxford, UK: Oxford University Press.

Scharpf, F. (2002). The European social model: Coping with the challenges of diversity. *Journal of Common Market Studies*, *40*(4), 645–670. doi:10.1111/1468-5965.00392

Sweet, A. S. (2012). Neofunctionalism and supranational governance. *Faculty Scholarship Series*, 1.

Tranholm-Mikkelsen, J. (1991). Neo-functionalism: Obstinate or obsolete? A reappraisal in the light of the new dynamism of the EC millennium. *Journal of International Studies*, *20*(1), 1–22.

Weathill, S., & Beaumont, P. (1999). *EU law*. London: Penguin.

KEY TERMS AND DEFINITIONS

Common Market: Group formed by countries within a geographical area to promote duty free trade and free movement of labor and capital among its members.

European Union: an association of European nations formed in 1993 for the purpose of achieving political and economic integration.

Integration Theories: Any theories have emerged which attempt to explain the process and outcome of integration in Europe. They try to clarify how and why the European Union came about and how it is today.

Intergovernmentalism: An approach to integration that treats States and national Governments in particular, as the primary actors in the integration process.

International Relations: The study of relationships among countries, the roles of sovereign states, inter-governmental organizations, international non-governmental organizations, non-governmental organizations, and multinational corporations.

Neo-Functionalism: Describes and explains the process of regional integration with reference to how three causal factors interact with one another: (a) growing economic interdependence between nations, (b) organizational capacity to resolve disputes and build international legal regimes, and (c) supranational market rules that replace national regulatory regimes.

Single Market: A single market is a type of trade bloc which is composed of a free trade area (for goods) with some common policies on product regulation, and freedom of movement of the factors of production (capital and labor) and of enterprise and services.

ENDNOTES

1. *Raymond Kohll v Union des Caisses de Maladie and Nicolas Decker v Caisse de Maladie de Employés Privés* the European Court of Justice applied EC law on the free movement of goods and services to extensively extend a patient's options for receiving non-emergency health care in another Member State at the expense of his/her social health care system.

Chapter 10
An Evaluation of Oral and Dental Health Services in Turkey and in the Member States of the EU in Terms of Economy

Abdülkadir Işık
Namık Kemal University, Turkey

Özge Selvi Yavuz
Namık Kemal University, Turkey

Seda Suat
Sevgi Dental Clinic, Turkey

Gamze Yıldız Şeren
Namık Kemal University, Turkey

Berkay Habiboğlu
Thrace Development Agency, Turkey

ABSTRACT

Dental health expenditures are a big part of general health expenditures. In Turkey, oral health services are provided by both private practitioners and government sections. In 2012, approximately 7 million fillings were made by government clinics. According to Turkish Dental Association data, in the same year, the number of fillings that Turkish citizens needed was 247 million. Even if the entire budget of the Health Ministry of Turkey were spent for these fillings, it is impossible to handle this demand. In 2012, in the European Union with 24 member countries, dental health spending was close to 74 billion Euro. Because of this financial burden, Turkey and the other countries are trying to find cost-effective methods to minimize dental health spending. This chapter emphasizes dental health conditions of both Turkey and European Union, firstly, and then successful and cost-effective strategies are discussed.

INTRODUCTION

Every year thousands of Turkish Liras (TL) are spent for dental health. In this study, we will discuss how to use the resources more effectively. We will be explaining the dental health services in the EU and in Turkey and will mention the projects applied to reduce the economic effects of dental health services before the conclusion part.

DOI: 10.4018/978-1-4666-7308-3.ch010

COST ITEMS IN ORAL AND DENTAL HEALTH SERVICES

Calculating properly the cost of a service plays a role not only in the control and audit of the costs, but also in the efficient allocation of resources. Various cost centers appear in health care units and this issue prevents to calculate the costs exactly. Therefore, the classification method started to be used in determining the cost of health care. Generally costs are divided into three groups as follows: direct costs, indirect costs and immaterial costs (Elliott& Payne 2008):

- **Immaterial Costs:** Immaterial costs are the most difficult ones to express monetarily. Costs of pain due to tooth decay take part in immaterial costs.
- **Indirect Costs:** Indirect costs occur because of the loss of work force of the patient or of the person who takes care of the patient.
- **Direct Costs:** Direct costs are the costs related to the medical care services and can be calculated at market prices. Direct costs are divided into two groups, direct medical costs and direct non-medical costs. This separation can be made in oral and dental health services as follows: Direct dental costs and direct non-dental costs.
    - **Direct Non-Dental Costs:** These costs include foods, drinks, transportations and accommodations.
    - **Direct Dental Costs:** Direct dental costs are divided into three groups:
- **Fixed Costs:** The building where the service is provided, building-related expenses and service investments are included in this group. Dental units, all equipment, instruments and systems are included in this group.
- **Semi Fixed Costs:** Personal expenses are included in this group.
- **Variable Costs:** Drugs and consumables used for treatment are included in this group.

ORAL AND DENTAL HEALTH PROFILE OF TURKEY

In Turkey, oral and dental health problems are among the most important health problems. Oral diseases affect 96% of the individuals and the losses suffered by the country's economy is quite large.

According to Turkish Dental Association's report published in 2011, there are 24.203 dentists working actively. Turkish population was 74.724.269 in 2011. So in 2011 there were 3087 patients per dentist. The distribution of the dentists actively employed is, 60% of them work in private clinics, 29% of them work for the Ministry of Health, 10% of them work at faculties, and 1% for other institutions (Table 1).

We can see the current situation below in terms of the number of treatments provided and the number of treatments needed. But considering the number of treatments needed in our country, these numbers seem very low (Figure 1).

In February 2010, the first results of "Health for your mouth" project were published. 3040 persons from 7 different regions and from 9 different age groups participated in this project, which was ongoing for four years. The results of the project are:

1. 1 of every 3 people in Turkey do not have the habit of brushing their teeth.
2. In a year a person has less than one toothbrush.
    a. Annual consumption of toothpaste is 440 grams, it is 870 grams in France, 703 grams in Germany.
3. Frequency of going to the dentist is 0.9 per a year, it's 5 times a year in the European Union countries

Table 1. The number of treatments provided by dentists working for the Ministry of Health in 2010

Name of Treatment	Number
Filling	4.739.103
Root canal operation	752.206
Detertraj	4.954.240
Tooth extraction	6.369.715
Removable denture	944.276
Fixed partial denture	3.043.235

Table 2. The number of treatments in 2010

Name of Treatment	Number
Filling	247.000.000
Tooth extraction	35.000.000
Root canal operation	8.700.000
Detertraj	39.500.000

Figure 1. The distribution of dentists who are actively employed

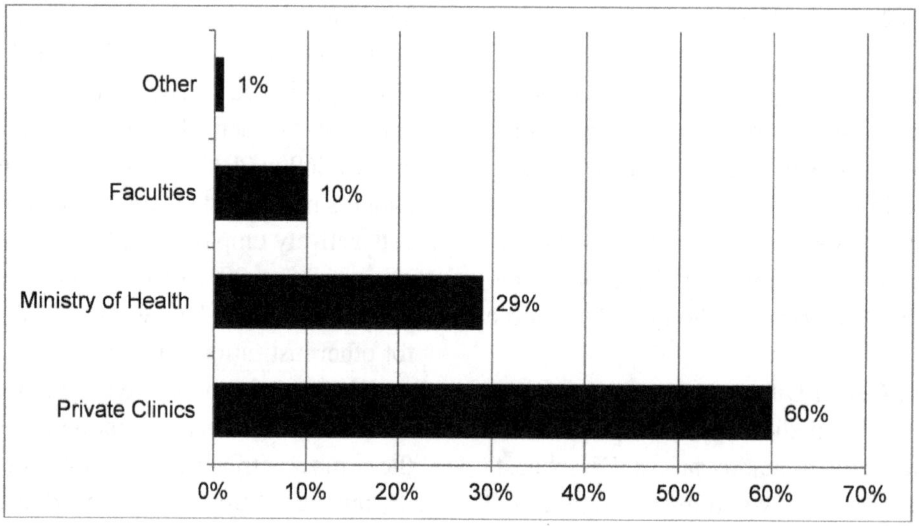

4. While the tooth decay ratio is 35% for 0-4 age group, it's 90% for 10-15 age group.
   a. Evaluating the results of the project, it's obvious that in oral and dental health services, our country is far more behind than the developed countries.

ORAL AND DENTAL HEALTH PROFILES OF EU MEMBER COUNTRIES

Distribution of Oral Diseases in EU Member Countries

In the last 30 years, the percentage of young adults and children who have tooth decays highly reduced. Simultaneously the percentage of individuals who lost their teeth reduced too. These developments are the result of better life conditions, changed nutrition habits, augmented usage of fluoride and fluorinated toothpaste and the emergence of new oral hygiene techniques.

However, the averages based on population may hide the disequilibrium in oral health. The researches show that even if the childhood tooth decays dropped, there's a disequilibrium among some minority-ethnic groups and some social classes (Watt & Sheiham 1999, Locker 2000, Sabbah 2007). In the east of Europe, tooth decay is a serious problem for lots of groups that are socio-economically behind all of the member countries (Figure 2 and Table 1). For example, in Spain, the number of tooth decays of young adults who are the members of lower socio-economic classes are twice more than the ones who are the members of upper socio-economic classes (Spanish Dental Association 2010).

The researches show that especially the tooth decay ratios of children coming from lower socio-economic classes are much more than the ones coming from other classes and they generally are not treated (Droz 20006). A research done in Denmark showed that the oral and dental health disequilibrium is obvious between the families migrated to Denmark and the ones living in Denmark for more than one generation.

When we look at Table 1 and Figure 2, we see that during the last 30 years, the tooth decay prevalence of 12 years old groups dropped obviously. In the Eastern European countries, the drop is less obvious.

Europe's Situation in Periodontal Health

Even if there are lots of research about Europe's periodontal situation, gathering trustful information is still a serious problem. Advanced periodontitis impacts 5-20% of the adult population worldwide and is the main cause of teeth losses (Petersen 2005, Philstrom 2005, Jin 2011). In Europe, more than 50% of the population are suffering from periodontitis and 10% of the population from advanced periodontitis (König, 2011). Here appears the misleading part: When the older population has more tooth in mouth, the number of teeth having periodontal problems increases. Also, when the population consists of individuals who lose their teeth in early ages, periodontal diseases appear rarely since there's no tooth.

Europe's Situation in Oral Cancers

Oral cancer is globally the 8th most common cancer type (Johnson, 2011). In 2008, there was 132.000 head and neck cancer. 62.800 of them ended with the death (Ferlay, 2010).

Figure 2. Number of treatments needed in Turkey in 2010

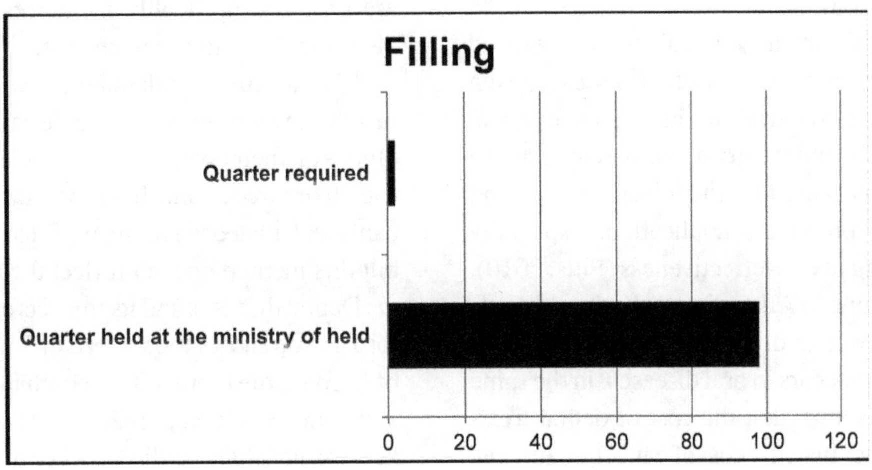

There's a strong relation between oral cancer incidence and socio-economic situation. The most disadvantaged, poorest groups face with highest cancer ratios (Menvielle 2005, Conway 2007, Conway 2008, Warnakulasuriye 2009).

Oral cancer incidences are differences among the EU countries, this is because of the regional differences in being exposed to risk factors. The highest incidence speed in 100.000 persons belongs to Spain with 6,7 and to Hungary with 9,4 (Figure 3)

Figure 4 shows the mortality in Europe. While Slovakia, ABD and Hungary have the highest mortality, Cyprus and Iceland have the lowest (IARC 2012c). In many countries of Europe and Asia, mortality due to oral cavity cancers declined seriously (Garavello 2010).

Survival rates change obviously upon geographical regions for oral cavity and oropharynx cancers. The survival rates of rich people are higher like in the other cancer types (Edwards & Jones, 1999). Researches in this area shows that five-year survival rate in Eastern Europe countries is 23% while it's 51% in North Europe countries (Zigon, 2011).

The Cost of Oral Diseases in Europe

In EU member countries, the general health expenditures including dentistry are directly related to the country's welfare which is measured by gross national income.

Expenditures made for oral diseases exceed the expenditures caused by other diseases, even in high-income countries. It's interesting to spend lots of money in order to treat tooth decays and the complications caused by them instead of taking into account preventive applications especially when thinking of cost-effectiveness (Pitts, 2010). A research done in Australia emphasizes that after cardiac vascular diseases, the second highest treatment cost occurs in oral diseases. In the same research it's shown that the cost of dental treatments is higher than the cost of cancer treatments (Australian Institute of Health and Welfare 2010). Other researches indicate that the more expensive treatment is dental treatment in industrialized countries (Schneider 1998, Bauer 2009).

In 2009, 5% of total health expenditures and 16% of private health expenditures are dental expenditures in OECD countries (OECD 2011).

In 2000, in the former European Union countries (15 countries), the total cost of services and treatments provided by dentists was 54 billion Euros (Widstrom & Eaton 2004). In the current EU, this number is about 79 billion Euros. This number is expected to be 93 billion Euros by 2020.

The regulations in patient contributions and dentists' tariff of fares directly impact the number and the cost of treatments. Since private dentists are more common in oral and dental health services, every regulation, treatment prices, payment plans and contributions of the state have a direct impact on dentists' and patients' needs for treatment.

Additionally, OECD reports show that people's own dental expenditures change upon the country's dental health system. In member countries, for example in Spain, oral health services are provided by private clinics and patients pay all the treatment costs. However, poor people have difficulties to pay for the service in such a system. In Denmark, the service is free for children under 18, however, adults pay for the treatment to the private clinics with the support of the state. In the other countries like France and Germany, preventive treatments are provided by health insurances and patients also contribute to the payments.

It's difficult to calculate the oral and dental health expenditures since people pay to the private clinics on their own. In most of the member countries like Greece and Italy, private expenditures can be calculated via the forms filled with patients, but this method doesn't reflect the exact data.

Dental diseases and its impacts are very costly for a person and for the society. In England, the cost of keeping the tooth in the mouth increases more and more (Steele Report 2009). Also, it should be kept in mind that oral diseases because the indirect

Figure 3. The comparison of dmft scores of 12 years old group in 1980S and in 2000S (who 2012B)

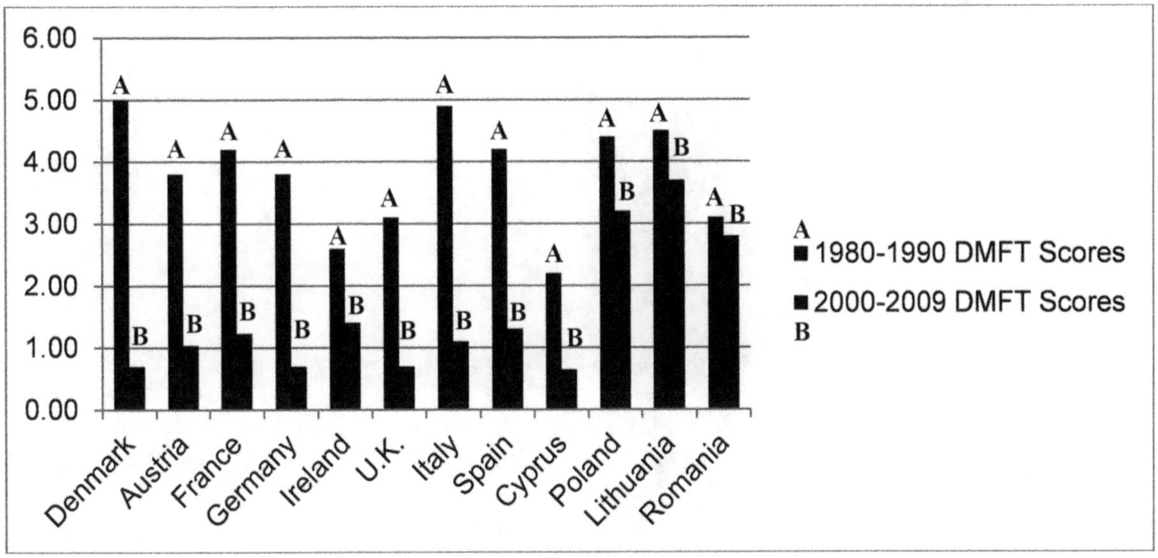

Figure 4. Lid and oral cavity cancer incidence speed of EU member countries among 100.000 persons (IARC 2012b, GLOBOCAN 2008)

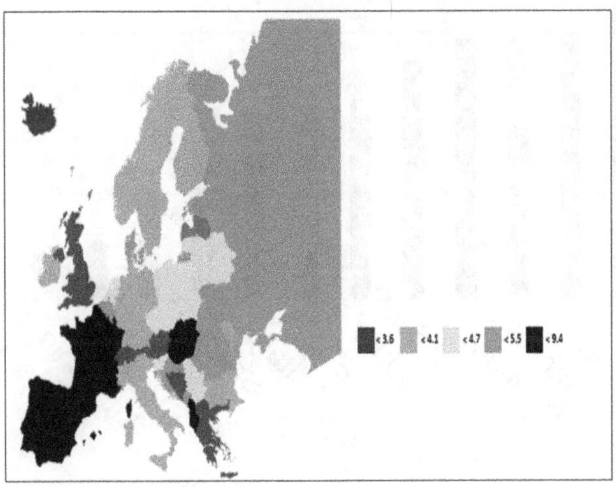

costs like workforce loss. These problems emerge more and more with the aging population.

Preventive applications' importance of health economics are accepted in the literature. Lots of researches accepts that preventive applications, avoiding tooth decays are more profitable and useful than treating them (Oscarson 2007, Burt 1998). Also the usage of tooth paste including fluoride is one of the best methods considering its cost-effectiveness (Davies 2003, Yee 2004).

Sweden and Denmark managed to diminish the prevalence of oral diseases and the dental expenditures by concentrating on preventive applications (Wang, 1998).

Figure 5. Lid and oral cavity cancer mortality speed of EU member countries among 100.000 persons (IARC 2012b, GLOBOCAN 2008)

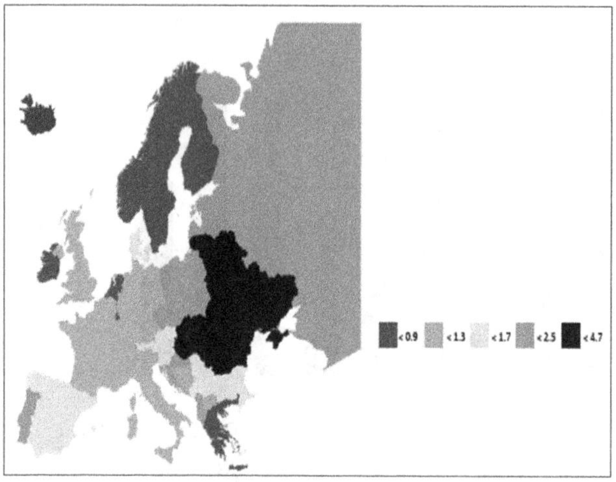

Figure 6. GNI per person in 2010, World Bank 2012
Source: World Bank, 2012

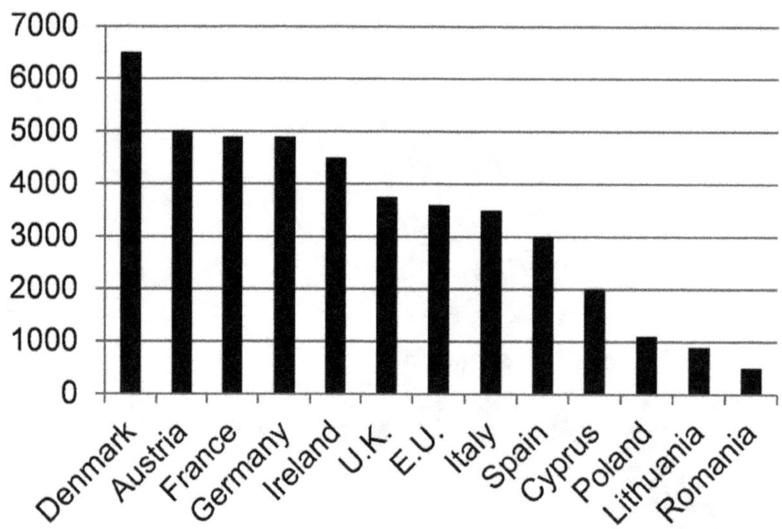

Finally, a research analyzed the global situation as follows: "A system which primarily focuses on the treatment of a disease cannot be economically and socially supported by people and it's not ethically true. The most effective method is to concentrate on preventive applications" (Gooch 2009, Truman 2002, Tomar 2010).

Inequalities in the Treatment of Oral Diseases in Europe

The World Health Organization's 'Commission on Social Determinants of Health (CSDH)' states that: "The inequalities of health are mainly because of the inequalities of power, income and services" (CSDH, 2008).

Figure 7. Health Expenditures per person in 2010, World Bank 2012
Source: World Bank, 2012

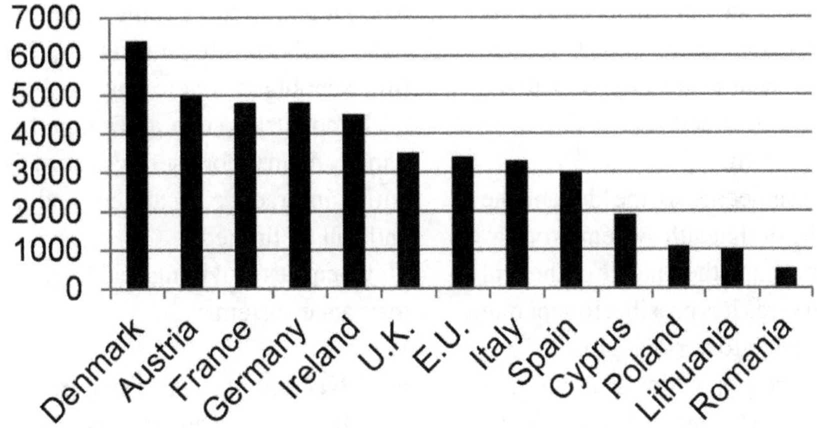

European Parliament declared via "Resolution on Reducing Health Inequalities in the EU": "Among the countries that are member of EU, there's an increasing physical and mental health inequality (2011). In these countries, health inequalities generally occur between high and low income groups and also between highly educated and not-well educated groups.

In addition to economic, social and environmental factors, health is also affected by individuals' lifestyle and service providers. Lower socio-economic groups have a tendency to unhealthy nutrition, smoke, drink alcohol. With combination of all these factors disease occurrence is inevitable.

Considering the socio-economic status, age, sex, general health status there is a serious inequality in oral health between EU countries. This inequality is more obvious at lower income levels of the society, such as

- People living in social deprivation areas (Marmot & Bell 2010)
- Those stays in psychiatric hospitals (Vigild, 1993)
- Elderly population (Griffin,2012)
- Convicts (Walsh, 2008)
- Homeless people (Depalma 2005)
- Refugees (Angelilo 1996)
- Immigrants (Heidmann 1985)
- Frequent traveler populations (Edwards 1997)
- Minority groups affected by social disadvantage (Christensen 2010)
- Adults with learning disabilities (Glassman 2003)

The groups listed above have extremely poor oral health and they have difficulties in accessing dental services. There groups usually apply to the medical institutions when it is an emergency.

Tooth Brushing Habits in Europe

In Europe, children around 12 years old who brush their teeth more than once a day tend to continue this behavior as a habit (Koivusilta, 2003).

A study about the 11 years old children's tooth brushing habits all across Europe shows that there is a direct relation between the family's income and brushing habits of children (HSBC 2010).

Another study conducted in Scotland about tooth brushing habits shows that familial factors have an important role in gaining tooth brushing habits (Levin & Currie 2010).

Access to Dental Services

Accessing to dental service units in an equal and fair way is a very important factor about to reduce the inequality in oral health. Reaching easily or not to the dental treatment services is the basic substructure of the system.

Government grant is needed for the kids and the deprived ones for the oral health system process. Considering the supply and the finance of the oral and dental health services it is possible to separate the EU Member States into various groups.

Cyprus: 80% of the population (all children of primary school age, low income individuals, civil servants, national security forces, and police) can take advantage of the free dental treatment services in State-owned clinics. Despite this, a large part of the population pay for the treatment in the private clinics.

Ireland: Children up to the age of 16 can receive a free service in the State-owned dental services. The others need to pay for the treatment in the private clinics.

Spain: All dental treatment services are provided by the private sector, all adult patients pay for expenses themselves. In some autonomous regions, taking advantage of the tax system, treatments of the children between the ages of 7-14 can be provided.

In Cyprus, Italy and Spain, state's contribution to the system is due to local taxes or in national revenue, but the given services are limited to only certain groups.

Denmark: Oral health services are being provided in schools and free until the age of 18. Free treatment service exists for the disadvantaged groups in the population (especially for old and poor individuals).

Italy: In theory, children under the age of 14 and disadvantaged groups may have free dental services, but in practice in most regions, only the emergency treatments are covered by the State.

England: Some groups' treatment expenses like the children under the age of 18, pregnant women and breastfeeding mothers, low income individuals and students under 19 who have part time school are covered by the State.

In countries such as Denmark, Italy, United Kingdom, in theory services exist for all citizens, while, in practice, treatment options can change and can be limited.

Countries providing health services with social insurance systems:

- **Germany:** A large majority of the population's treatment expenses is covered by the non-profit funds. There are State's dental clinics but they are just for the medical examination, medical diagnosis, and protecting implementations.
- **Austria:** Compulsory health insurance includes basic restorative and protecting dental treatments. Some protecting implementations are applied during education. Parents' health insurance covers their children's dental treatment expenses.
- **France:** Protecting implementations applied for the kids until 12 years old and also children between 6 and 18 can have free dental checkup at school. Other age groups have to cover their treatments under insurance on their own.
- **Lithuania:** State covers all oral treatments and dental treatments freely of the individuals up to 18 years. Adults between 18 and 65 can receive their treatments at the state-owned dental clinics with contribution payments.
- **Poland:** State has limitations about covering dental treatment expenses, only covers annual check-ups. Young adults and pregnant may have enhanced treatments.
- **Romania:** Government health insurance also covers oral health care expenses.

Dental treatments are free for those under the age of 18 and they have annual examinations. Despite unemployed, pregnant women, nursing mothers, military personnel, veterans and prisoners exempt from paying insurance, they are part of it.

Admission rates for dental health services are higher in developing member countries whose expenses met by the state than developed member countries which do not cover the dental health expenses. For example, in Catalonia there are no state support for oral and dental health services, having dental health service rates were, 32% of men, 38% of women in 2006 (Casals, 2007). In Belarus, state support is quite serious, 60% of the population went to the dentist in 2007 (Tserakheva, 2011). Before 1989, EU member Eastern European countries generally covered children's treatment expenses in schools. But today, because of increasing privatization of oral and dental health services, many public health programs has been stopped.

Each member country of the European Union supports the idea that each individual must be included in the state insurance or social insurance funds for the health care systems since it's a constitutional right.

Differences in Access to Dental Services

There are some recommended deadlines for regular dental examinations, the incidence of these periods varies between EU member countries.

Via the survey made by Eurobarometer, people have been asked that if they have visited a dentist in the last 12 months. Here are the results.

Compared with other regions in Europe, the values are higher in these countries. On the other hand, despite mandatory dentist controls are being held every 6 months and annually, these values are interestingly low (Eurobarometer 2010).

Visit rates in Eastern European Countries have lower values, Lithuania is % 46, Poland is %44, and Romania is % 34. Also Spain is % 43 and Portuguese is % 46 that can be counted in the same group. The rest of the countries have values like this, Austria is %56, Ireland is % 54, Cyprus is % 54, Italy is % 52, and France is % 52.

Differences in Dental Treatment

Differences do exist in the process of therapeutic and preventive treatment. In the countries such as Austria, France, Italy, operative treatment rates are higher. On the other hand countries such as Sweden, Denmark, Switzerland, and Netherlands have lower operative treatment rates than preventive treatment rates.

THE STRATEGIES THAT CARRY ORAL AND DENTAL HEALTH SERVICES TO A BETTER LEVEL AND THE EVALUATION IN TERMS OF COST EFFECTIVENESS

In Turkey, there is an insufficient source in terms of the expenditures that is made in the oral and dental health services. We may compare some examples from foreign sources to understand the size of spending over oral and dental health services. In the United States with a population of 308.000.000, 108 billion dollars were spent for dental services in 2010. In Canada with a population of 33.000.000, 12.6 billion dollars were spent for dental services in 2009. Oral and dental health-related problems also create a loss such as the loss of a work/school day that we cannot explain financially. In Canada, 2.26 million school days, 4.15 million work days became loss due to the dental treatments or dental problems in 2010.

In Turkey, among all health expenditures, the part allocated to dental health is between 5-6%. In our country, almost all of the oral and dental health services which are given by the public sector consist of therapeutic services, namely 2nd step treatment services. According to the data of Social

Security Institution for 2008-2009, dental treatment constitutes 33,8% of the dental applications. The proportion is 70% in West European countries. 60% of the oral and dental health services which is a large proportion, is provided by the private clinic and polyclinics where the services are mostly therapeutical. The cost of the first step, in other words, preventive health services' costs are much lower. The rosthodontic and restorative applications are mostly seen in the individuals who are not performed Preventive Dentistry applications and the financial burden to the Government is quite high. It is declared by the World Health Organization (WHO) that the DMFT (average number of teeth with decays-filling per individual and average number of lost teeth due to decay per individual) is the highest in the countries which have the dentistry services based on restorative applications, and again these countries at the same time, have the highest number of "toothless young age" individual. It is determined that the DMTF begins decreasing structurally in the countries that constitute their systems based on preventive philosophy and preventive applications. To explain with an example, the number of fillings that is needed in our country is 247.000.000 that has been revealed by the table 3 from the previous page. In the price list which has been determined by the Turkish Dental Association for 2012, the price of the filling for a tooth is 80 TL, the required amount of the all necessary fillings is 19.760.000.000 TL and this is the amount that is required for just one treatment method. The amount allocated to the Ministry of Health is 17.000.000.000 TL for 2011.

Although the tooth decays are one of the most widespread chronic diseases, they can be prevented. The cost may become lower with the some preventive measures. Here are some of the preventive measures that we'll be examining to lower the cost of oral and dental health services:

Fluor Varnish Application and Projection Example

Studies have shown that 80% of the dentistry applications is limited by 20% of the population. This proportion of 20% expresses as high risk caries and they, from the first years of their lives, tend to have continuous exposure to dental decay. Systematic early detection and prevention program of these risk groups is significant for not only the community health but also the economic

Table 3. The comparison of daft scores of 12 years old group in 1980's and in 2000's. (WHO, 2012b)

Country	80s' DMFT Scores	2000s' DMFT Scores
Austria	3.8 (1984)	1.04 (2002)
Cyprus	2.2 (1990)	0.65 (2003-2004)
Denmark	5 (1980)	0.7 (2008)
France	4.2 (1987)	1.23 (2006)
Germany	3.8 (1989)	0.7 (2005)
Ireland	2.6 (1984)	1.4 (2001)
Italy	4.9 (1986)	1.1 (2004-2005)
Lithuania	4.5 (1983)	3.7 (2005)
Poland	4.4 (1985)	3.2 (2003)
Romania	3.1 (1986)	2.8 (2000)
Spain	4.2 (1984)	1.3 (2005)
England	3.1 (1983)	0.7 (2008-2009)

Figure 8. Dental treatment habits in EU

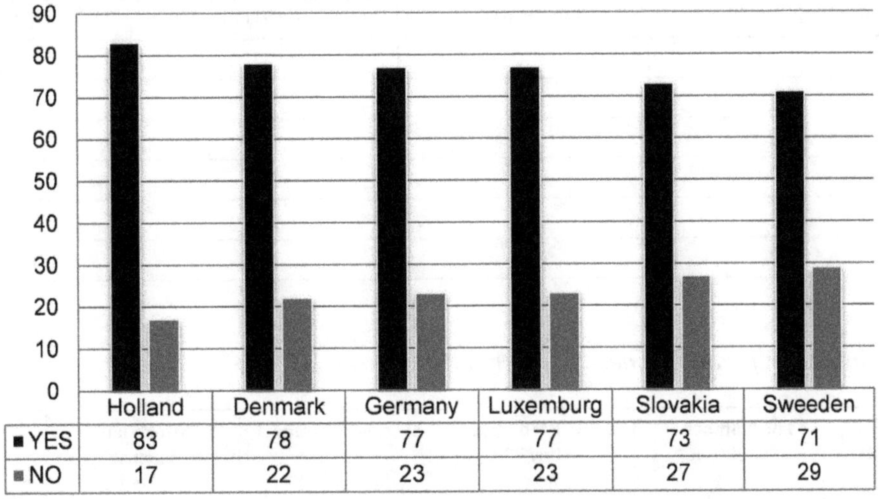

terms. Early childhood decay (ECD) means that there is decay on the at least one surface of the teeth in children with up to the month of 71. ECD refers to permanent decay in the medium and long term; in other words, the children with ECD are the high risk groups of the future. Because of this reason, ECD related numbers are very important for making estimated tooth decay projections and correspondingly potential cost analysis. A projection work related to this subject has been made by D.Doğan and his friends. In this study, between the years of 2009-2010, in two different city centers, between 5-60 months old 499 children have been evaluated in terms of ECD prevalence and there have been evaluated the amount of decays, necessity treatments and the costs.

According to the studies, it is set that milk tooth of the 94% of the children with the tooth decay in their permanent tooth have also decay. It is declared that 83% of the children with no decay in their milk tooth have also no decay when they become 12 years old. It is seen that in comparison with the children who have no decay in their milk tooth, the children with decay in their milk tooth have 3 times more decay in their permanent teeth. In the projection based on of this study, 499 children have been examined and it is foreseen that 255 children out of 303 children who have decay will have a decay in their permanent tooth when they become 12 years old; however 33 children out of 196 children without any decay will have hardly

Table 4. Recommended Frequency in EU

Recommended Frequency	Member Country
Every six months	Poland
Once between nine and twelve months	Denmark
Yearly	Austria Cyprus France Germany Ireland İtaly Lithuania Romania
In case of need	England
Unclear	Spain

Table 5. Dental costs for treatment types

Treatment Types	Total Number	Unit Cost (TL)	Total Cost (TL)
Surface Covering	40	32	1280
Filling to one surface	999	73	72.927
Filling to two or more surface	169	77	13.013
Extracting	9	54	486
Crown	105	224	23.520
Total			**111.226 TL**

Table 6. Medium-term prediction decay and treatment cost

The Number of Decayed Tooth	The Number of Children	%85 Predictive Value/ The Number of Children who have Possibly Tooth Decay at 12 Years Old	Average Treatment Cost DMTF=2 (TL)	After Flour Varnish Application the Number of Children who have Possibly Tooth Decay at 12 Years Old	Average Treatment Cost (TL)
Without decay	196	33	33x146=4818	3	3x146=438
1-2 decays	106	93	93x146=13.578	28	28x146=4.088
3-4 decays	79	67	67x146=9.872	27	27x146=3.942
5 and more decays	115	98	98x46=14.308	59	59x146=8.164
Total	499	291	42.486	117	17.082

a decay in their permanent tooth. The following is a table of the medium-term prediction decay and treatment cost:

The result of the study shows that even though it is expected that 58% of the 499 children have tooth decay when become 12 years old, thanks to fluor varnish application the amount may be decreased to 23%. In terms of cost, again with the fluor varnish application, the total cost may decrease from 42.486 TL to 17.082 TL. These results are noteworthy in terms of the country's economy and oral and dental health and it is stated with the simple but continuous applications such as flour varnish which could be applied to the children between the ages of 0-3, significant results could be achieved with regards to medium-long term decay prevalence and treatment cost

Fluoridation of Drinking Water

In drinking water, there has been fluoride naturally; on the other hand, this quantity is not at the optimal value. The optimal value that protects teeth from decay is 0.7- 1.2 ppm. All over the world, more than 40 countries and more than 300 million people consume their drinking water with fluorally. Only in USA 145 million people consume water which has been processed fluorally. In comparison with the other preventive applications, fluoridation has the lowest cost. Although it differs according to the population it is provided, the average cost of drinking water fluoridation annual per capita is between 20-50 cents. According to studies published by the CDC, the settlement which has a population of about 20.000 people or more, in response to every allocated 1 dollar for fluoridation, there occurs 38 dollars gain. Explaining with an example, in California average filling price is 14 dollars, fluoridation cost per capita is 50 cents, so it corresponds to 2 dollars for a family of four persons.

SOME SUCCESFUL COST-EFFECTIVE PROJECTS APPLIED IN EU TO PREVENT DENTAL DISEASES

- **Fluoridation of Water:** It's the process of the fluoridation of city water. It's safe, cheap and effective. In Europe England, Ireland, Spain and Poland are among the countries using this system.
- **Usage of Fluoridated Salt:** It's useful for the healthy development of children's permanent tooth. (Yeung, 2011). This program has been applied in Switzerland, Germany, Czech Republic and Slovakia.
- **Usage of Fluoridated Milk:** A method used in Bulgaria and England for children (The Borrow Foundation 2012, CED 2009). It's appropriate for regions in which fluoride cannot be provided via salt or water.
- **Childsmile Program, Scotland:** It's applied in regions in which the city water is not fluoridated. Oral health educations has been realized in all elementary and nursery schools, free tooth brushes and pastes have been distributed, families have been educated, fluoride polish applications have been made (CHILDSMILE 2012). DMFT scores of children participated to this program dropped from 1,86 in 2008 to 1,52 in 2010 (NDIP 2010).
- **Denmark's Preventive Oral Health Model:** In 1974, oral and dental health clinics were established under every municipality. Every person under 18 was obliged to be educated in these clinics. They were examined and benefited from preventive treatment.
- **Programs in Community Centers:** It's based on informing especially the migrated families in community centers in Sweden. This program contains the education of families, brushing and hygiene educations, nutrition advices and prescribing fluoride tablets for children (Wenhall 2008).
- **Oral Health Education Provided by Students:** This method is being used in some poor regions of Germany and Ireland. In Germany, the 4th grade students who took before an extensive oral hygiene education educated 1st grade students. A similar program applied also in Ireland.
- **The Addition of Oral Examinations to General Health Controls for Old People:** This is a method used in England.
- **Raise Awareness for Oral Hygiene Habits:** This is a method applied in Sweden. First, an education is given to the participants, then they gain the ability to diagnose bacterial plaque. During the program, there's an education every two months and dental controls every 3-12 months.
- **Cancer Screenings for high Risk Groups:** It started as a pilot application in Hungary. Media has been used to inform people. People have been invited to dental check-up and free examinations made for high-risk groups.
- **National Preventive Program Realized in Order to Rise the Frequency of Dental Visits of People in Adolescence Period:** Applied in 1997 in France. Within this program, free check-up right was given to people who were between 15-18 years old.

- **Supporting the Sugar-Free Products:** With lots of researches, it is proven that the sweetening (xylitol, sorbitol, mannitol etc.) avoid tooth decays (Deshponde 2008, Ly 2008). The sales of sugar-free products are encouraged in countries like Germany and Switzerland.
- **Imposing Restrictions on the Sales of Sugared Products / Encouraging the Labelling of Some Products:** This is made for giving more detailed information about the product contents. Some restrictions can also be imposed in order to reduce the sugar content of some products.

CONCLUSION

In the developing countries, the increasing cost of oral and dental health treatment compels the social security institutions. In this respect, it is quite substantial to identify the risky individuals from the early periods, launch applications for protection, provide training for the parents and to determine the prevalence of this type of individuals in the community and to make medium and long term cost projections.

Tooth decay, which are the most widespread and the most harmful among the oral illnesses, are periodontal diseases and oral cancers. Decays have been started being restrained with preventive programs which have been executed by various countries. On the other hand, it still poses a serious problem for the poor or deprived groups. The periodontal diseases have become more destructive by affecting more than 50% of the European population. The situation has seemed more desperate, the highest incidence of oral cancer is in Europe after South Asia.

It is obvious that the preventive applications are much more effective and cheaper than the therapeutic applications. In contrast, it is not clear that which applications are the most effective and necessary methods. The methods for enhancing and encouraging the health of the mouth are required to identify and explain in a good way. The determination of the best preventive applications will enable researchers to advance in that way and it will decrease the amount of money and time that are spent for the ineffective methods.

REFERENCES

Abuhanoğlu, H. C., & Ayanoğlu, Y. (2011). Mezuniyet Oncesi Tıp Egitimi Maliyetlerinin Belirlenmesi: Tıp Fakültesinde Bir Uygulama. *Sağlıkta Performans ve Kalite Dergisi, 4.*

Amariei, C., & Eaton, K. A. (2009). Systems for the provision of oral health care in the Black Sea countries part 1: Romania. *Oral Health and Dental Management in the Black Sea Countries, 8*, 3–6.

Angelillo, I. F., Nobile, C. G., & Pavia, M. (1996). Oral health status and treatment needs in immigrants and refugees in Italy. *European Journal of Epidemiology, 12*(4), 359–365. doi:10.1007/BF00145298 PMID:8891539

Araujo, M. W., Dermen, K., & Connors, G. (2004). 0ral and dental health among inpatients in treatment for alcohol use disorders: A pilot study. *Journal of the International Academy of Periodontology, 6*, 125–130. PMID:15553979

Australian Institute of Health and Welfare. (2010). *Australia's health in 2010: Twelth biennial health report of the Australian Institute of Health and Welfare.* Retrieved from: www.aihw.gov.au/W0rkArea/DownloadAsset.aspx?id=6442452962 on O1/07/2012

Bauer J., Neumann T. & Saekel R. (2009). *Zahnmedizinische Versorgung in Deutschland.* Verlag: Hans Huber.

Blot, W. J., McLaughlin, J. K., Winn, D. M., Austin, D. F., Greenberg, R. S., & Preston-Martin, S. (1998). Smoking and drinking in rela-tion to oral and pharyngeal cancer. *Cancer Research*, *4*(23282), 7.

Borrow Foundation. (n.d.). Retrieved from: http://wwwborrowfoundation.org/why-fluoridate-milk

Boyle, P., & Levin, B. (2008). *World cancer report*. Lyon: International Agency for Research on Cancer.

Çalışkan, Z. (2009). Saglık Hizmetlerinde Önceliklerin Belirlenmesinde Ekonomik Degerlendirme Yontemi Olarak Maliyet-Etkililik Analizi. *Süleyman Demirel Üniversitesi İktisadi ve İdari Bilimler Fakültesi Dergisi*, *14*, 311–332.

Childsmile. (n.d.). Retrieved from: http://www.child-smile.org.uk

Christensen, L., Twetman, S., & Sundby, A. (2010). Oral health in children and adolescents with different socio-cultural and socio-economic backgrounds. *Acta Odontologica Scandinavica*, *68*(1), 34–42. doi:10.3109/00016350903301712 PMID:19878044

Chuang, S. C., Jenab, M., Heck, J. E., Bosetti, C., Talamini, R., Matsuo, K., & Hashibe, M. et al. (2012). Diet and the risk of head and neck cancer: A pooled analysis in the INHANCE consortium. *Cancer Causes & Control*, *23*(1), 69–88. doi:10.1007/s10552-011-9857-x PMID:22037906

Colak, H., Serdaroglu, L., & Dulgergil, C. (2010). Temel Agız Ve Dis Saglıgı Hizmetinde Restorasyon Uygulamalarının Yeri Önemi ve Sonucları. *Saglıkta Performans ve Kalite Dergisi*, (1).

Commission of the European Communities. (2009). *Reducing health inequalities in the EU. COM(2009) 567*. Retrieved from: http://ec.europa.eu/health/ph_determinants/socio_economics/documents/com2009_en.pdf

Corbet, E. (2007). Public health aspects of oral diseases and disorders — Periodontal diseases. In C. Pine & R. Harris (Eds.), *Community oral health* (2nd ed.). Surrey, UK: Quintessence.

Council of European Chief Dental Officers. (n.d.). *Database*. Retrivied from: http://www.cecdo.org/pages/database%20intro.html

Council of European Dentists. (2009). *EU manual of dental practice: Version 4.1*. Retrivied from: http://www.eudental.eu/index.php?lD=35918 on O2/04/2012

Council of European Dentists. (2011). *CED resolution 'for better oral health ofall EU citizens: Mutual integration of oral and general health*. Retrivied from: http://wwweudental.eu/inde><.php?lD=2741 on 25/O3/2012

Deshpande, A., & Jadad, A. R. (2008). The impact of polyol-containing chewing gums on dental caries: A systematic review of original randomized controlled trials and observational studies. *The Journal of the American Dental Association*, *139*(12), 1602–1614. doi:10.14219/jada.archive.2008.0102 PMID:19047666

Doğan, B. G. (2007). Toplum Agız ve Dis Saglıgı Göstergeleri. *Toplum Hekimligi Bulteni*, *26*(2).

Droz, D., Guéguen, R., Bruncher, P., Gerhard, J. L., & Roland, E. (2006). Epidemiological study of oral dental health of 4-year-old children in french nursery schools. *Archives of Pediatrics & Adolescent Medicine*, *13*, 122Z–9. PMID:16860544

Eaton, K. A., Newman, H. N., & Bulman, J. S. (2003). National mean DMFF scores for Western European 12 year-olds — Are they Comparable? *Journal of Dental Research*, *82*(519), 334. PMID:12709497

Edwards, D. M., & Watt, R. G. (1997). Oral health care in the lives of Gypsy travellers in east Hertfordshire. *British Dental Journal*, *183*(252), 7. PMID:9364092

Ericsson, J. S., Abrahamsson, K. H., & Ostberg, A. L. (2009). Periodontal health status in Swedish adolescents: An epidemiological, cross-sectional study. *Swedish Dental Journal*, *33*, 131–139. PMID:19994563

Eurobaromoter 72.3 Oral Health. Special Eurobarometer 330. (2010). Retrivied from: http://eceuropa.eu/public_opinion/archives/ebs/ebs_330_en.pdf

Ferlay, J., Parkin, D. M., & Steliarova-Foucher, E. (2010). Estimates of cancer incidence and mortality in Europe in 2008. *European Journal of Cancer*, *46*(4), 765–781. doi:10.1016/j.ejca.2009.12.014 PMID:20116997

Glassman, P., & Miller, C. E. (2003). Preventing dental disease for people with special needs: The need for practical preventive protocols for use in community settings. *Special Care in Dentistry*, *23*(5), 165–167. doi:10.1111/j.1754-4505.2003.tb00305.x PMID:14965180

Gooch, B. F., Griffin, S. O., Gray, S. K., Kohn, W. G., Rozier, R. G., Siegal, M., & Zero, D. T. et al. (2009). Preventing dental caries through school-based sealant programs: Updated recommendations and reviews of evidence. *The Journal of the American Dental Association*, *140*(11), 1356–1365. doi:10.14219/jada.archive.2009.0070 PMID:19884392

Hashibe, M., Brennan, P., & Chuang, S. C. (2009). Interaction between tobacco and alcohol use and the risk of head and neck cancer: Pooled analysis in the INHANCE consortium. *Cancer Epidemiology, Biomarkers & Prevention*, *18*, 541–550. PMID:19190158

Işık, A., & Mutlu, A. (2011). *Saglık Ekonomisine Giris*. Ekin Basım Yayın.

Koivusilta, L., Honkala, S., Honkala, E., & Rimpela, A. (2003). Toothbrushing as part of the adolescent lifestyle predicts education level. *Journal of Dental Research*, *82*(5), 361–366. doi:10.1177/154405910308200507 PMID:12709502

Konig, J., Holtfreter, B., & Kocher, T. (2010). Periodontal health in Europe: Future trends based on treatment needs and the provision of periodontal services-position paper. *European Journal of Dental Education*, *1*, 4–24. doi:10.1111/j.1600-0579.2010.00620.x PMID:20415972

Levin, K. A., & Currie, C. (2010). Adolescent toothbrushing and the home environment: Sociodemographic factors, family relationships and mealtime routines and disorganisation. *Community Dentistry and Oral Epidemiology*, *38*(1), 10–18. doi:10.1111/j.1600-0528.2009.00509.x PMID:19845713

Ly, K. A., Milgrom, P., & Rothen, M. (2008). The potential of dental-protective chewing gum in oral health interventions. *The Journal of the American Dental Association*, *139*(5), 553–563. doi:10.14219/jada.archive.2008.0215 PMID:18451371

Marinho, V. C. C., Higgins, J. P. T., Logan, S., & Sheiham, A. (2003). Fluoride toothpastes for preventing dental caries in children and adolescents. *Cochrane Database of Systematic Reviews*, 1.

OECD Library. (2011). *HealthataGlance 2011: OECDindicators*. Retrivied from http://www.oecd-ilibrary.org/sites/health_glance2011en/06/06/index.html;jsessionid=3dln9sdrovedm.delta?cOntentType=&itemld=/content/chapter/health_glance201157n&containerltemld=/content/seriaI/19991312&accessltemlds=/content/book/health_glance-2011-en&mimeType=text/html on 02/04/2012

Ozgen H., Tatar M. (2008). *Saglık Sektorunde Bir Verimlilik Degerlendirme Teknigi Olarak Maliyet-Etkililik Analizi ve Turkiye'de Durum.*

Pihlstrom, B. L., Michalowicz, B. S., & Johnson, N. W. (2005). Periodontal diseases. *Lancet*, *366*(9499), 1809–1820. doi:10.1016/S0140-6736(05)67728-8 PMID:16298220

Reinhardt, C. H., Lopker, N., Noack, M. J., Klein, K., & Rosen, E. (2009). Peer tutoring pilot program for the improvement of oral health behavior in underprivileged and immigrant children. *Pediatric Dentistry*, *31*, 481–485. PMID:20108738

Sabbah, W., Sheiham, A., & Bernabé, E. (2010). Income inequality and periodontal diseases in rich countries: An ecological cross-sectional study. *International Dental Journal*, *60*, 370–374. PMID:21141210

Sahinoz. T., Sahinoz. S. (2012). Demografik ve Bazı Saglık Gostergeleri Acısından Turkiye'nin Dunyadaki Durumu. *Gumushane Universitesi Saglık Bilimleri Dergisi, 1*.

Sahyoun, N. R., Lin, C. L., & Krall, E. (2003). Nutritional status of the older adult is associated with dentition status. *Journal of the American Dietetic Association*, *103*(1), 61–66. doi:10.1053/jada.2003.50003 PMID:12525795

Scully, C., & Bagan, J. (2009). Oral squamous cell carcinoma overview. *Oral Oncology*, *45*(4-5), 301–308. doi:10.1016/j.oraloncology.2009.01.004 PMID:19249237

Sheiham, A. (2006). Dental caries affects body weight, growth and quality of life in preschool children. *British Dental Journal*, *201*(910), 625–626. doi:10.1038/sj.bdj.4814259 PMID:17128231

Sheiham, A., & Nicolau, B. (2005). Evaluation of social and psychological factors in periodontal disease. *Periodontol*, *Z00039*(1), 118–131. doi:10.1111/j.1600-0757.2005.00115.x PMID:16135067

Shiau, H. J., & Reynolds, M. A. (2010). Sex differences n destructive periodontal disease: Exploring the biologic basis. *Journal of Periodontology*, *81*(11), 1505–1517. doi:10.1902/jop.2010.100045 PMID:20594052

Tserakhava T., Shakavets N., & Smirnoy A. (2011). Systems for the provision of oral health care in the black sea countries part 9: Belarus. *Oral Health and Dental Management, 10*, 115-118.

Turk Dishekimleri Birligi Dishekimlerinin Calısma Sekilleri. (n.d.). *Kurumlarda ve Ilcelerde.*

Vereecken, C. A. (2005). The Relative influence of individual and contextual socioeconomic status on consumption of fruit and soft drinks among adolescents in Europe. *European Journal of Public Health*, *15*(3), 224–232. doi:10.1093/eurpub/cki005 PMID:15905182

Watt, R., & Sheiham, A. (1999). Inequalities in oral health: A review of the evidence and recommendations for action. *British Dental Journal*, *187*, 6–12. PMID:10452185

Watt, R., & Sheiham, A. (2012). Integrating the common risk factor approach into a social determinants framework. *Community Dentistry and Oral Epidemiology*, *40*(4), 289–296. doi:10.1111/j.1600-0528.2012.00680.x PMID:22429083

Widstrom, E., & Eaton, K. A. (2004). Oral healthcare systems in the extended European Union. *Oral Health & Preventive Dentistry*, *2*, 155–194. PMID:15641621

World Bank. (n.d.). *World databank*. Retrivied from http://databank.worldbank.org

World Health Organisation. (2012a). *Oral health fact sheet N°318*. Retrivied from: http://www.who.int/media-centre/factsheets/fs318/en/index.html on 14/04/2012

World Health Organisation. (2012b). Oral health country/area profile programme. WHO Collaborating Centre, Malmo University, Sweden. Retrivied from: http://www.mah.se/CAPP/Country-Oral-Health-Profiles/EURO/

Yeung, C. A. (2011). Efficacy of salt fluoridation. *Evidence-Based Dentistry*, *12*(1), 17–18. doi:10.1038/sj.ebd.6400776 PMID:21436859

Yıldırım I., Dulgergil C., & Serdaroglu. (2010). Aile Hekimligi Uygulamalarında Erken Donem Koruyucu Dis Hekimligi Uygulamaları ve Önemi. *Saglıkta Performans ve Kalite Dergisi, 2.*

Zigon, G., Berrino, F., Gatta, G., Sanchez, M. J., Van Dijk, B., Van Eycken, E., & Francisci, S.EUROCARE Working Group. (2011). Prognoses for head and neck cancers in Europe diagnosed in 1995-1999: A population-based study. *Annals of Oncology*, *22*(1), 165–174. doi:10.1093/annonc/mdq306 PMID:20587510

KEY TERMS AND DEFINITIONS

Economics: Economics is the science which tries to give the most appropriate answer to the 'How to satisfy the unlimited wants with limited ressources?' question.

Gingival Diseases: Gingival diseases occur as a result of the infection of supportive tissues such as gingival and bones.

Health: According to the World Health Organization (WHO), "health is more than just the absence of illness or disability, but also is phsical, spiritual and social well-being." This definition explains all dimensions of health. Lately, "Living socially and economically a productive life" has been added to this definiton.

Health Economics: Health economics can be defined as the application of the rules of economics to the health services. It can also be defined as the efficient use of the ressources allocated to the health sector.

APPENDIX: MAIN RISK FACTORS FOR ORAL DISEASES

Oral diseases are generally preventable. Some harmful habits for general health increase the risk to catch oral diseases. These are:

- **Insufficient Nourishment/Malnutrition:** There's a close relation between insufficient nourishment/malnutrition and poor oral health (Nowjack-Raymer ve Sheiham 2003, Sahyoun ve Krall 2003).
- **Insufficient Oral Hygiene:** Brushing the theeth with toothpaste containing fluoride is effective in preventing the tooth decays and periodontal diseases (Marinho 2003, Wong 2011).
- **Cigarette/Tobacco Consumption:** Cigarette has been defined as an important risk factor for periodontal diseases (Johnson ve Guthmiller 2000). Cigarette is also one of the main causes of oral cancers.
- **Alcohol Consumption:** There's a well defined relation between excessive and wrong consumption of alcohol and oral diseases.
- **Oral Cancers:** Oral cancers are arising from tissues in and around the mouth such as tongue, lip, gingival and cheek.
- **Oral and Dental Health:** According to WHO, "Oral health is a state of being free from chronic mouth and facial pain, oral and throat cancer, oral sores, birth defects such as cleft lip and palate, periodontal (gum) disease, tooth decay and tooth loss, and other diseases and disorders that affect the oral cavity." Oral health can be divided into 3 groups: Tooth decays, periodontal diseases and oral cancers.
- **Tooth Decays:** Tooth decay is an illness which occurs with the resorption/perforation of tooth enamel.

Chapter 11
Development Agencies, Grant System, and Financial Support for SMEs in Turkey

Hasan Dinçer
Istanbul Medipol University, Turkey

Ümit Hacıoğlu
Istanbul Medipol University, Turkey

Abdullah Önder Özkul
Beykent University, Turkey

ABSTRACT

SMEs form 90% of commercial businesses in Turkey and the support given to SMEs means support directly given to the real sector in a vast scale. SMEs have some problems currently that are accepted as structural throughout Turkey, such as that they were constituted in form of family companies, that they do not use financial instruments sufficiently, that they do not work with professional executives, their commercial activities without invoice, etc. There could be other common problems that SMEs can meet with as related to sector or location. The main duties of Development Agencies is to mobilize commercial potential in region, to support sectors that have the potential to grow, and thus, to decrease the difference of development between regions. This chapter explores SMEs in Turkey.

INTRODUCTION

Countries aim to provide their citizens a life convenient to age's standards despite of concepts of which contents may vary such as changing population, level of income, level of education, health standards, technology, political changes. Development is a dynamic process which emerging countries try to realize with different methods. That makes the need of development urgent and unavoidable is the periods in which countries implement intense development programmes following a period of war, natural disasters and anti-democratic political regimes. The success of development moves that were implemented in these periods is in line with that they were designed

DOI: 10.4018/978-1-4666-7308-3.ch011

as convenient to the reality of country, they are far away from populist implementations and they were organised through effective implementation and control mechanisms.

One of factors that make the concept of development difficult one is that the country having central government is to try producing their policies without being able to analyse the realities, potentials and development axes properly. For instance, public incentives implemented in Turkey in various times are designed in its every re-implementation. The changing of 4-region-incentive-system into 6-region-incentive-system is a concrete example of this situation.

Development Agency is not field service of Ministry of Development. Agencies are governed through directorates. Members of board are formed by the governors, mayors, Chairman of Chambers of Commerce and Industry and Presidents of City General Assemble of cities in which agency operates. The chairman of directorate is the governor. The aim in the model is decentralisation.Non-profit organisations and NGOs can benefit from, depending on the features of support programmes, support mechanisms of Development Agencies. In addition, the biggest proportion of agencies in annual support budgets usually belongs to programmes towards SMEs. The annual budgets and financial support programmes is finalized through confirmation of Ministry of Development. That ministry and development agencies separate the biggest proportion of their budgets for SME support programmes, in the sense of national politics, shows that the priority is given to the private sector to carry development.

This chapter begins with a literature review on grant system and the structure of development agencies in Turkey. The implementations of development agency in World and Turkey have been studies in the second part. This chapter concludes with the SME profile and grants provided by support programmes and agencies as financing tool.

LITERATURE REVIEW

Main important developments observed in World economy regarding regional development and economical geography is the fact of localisation tendencies in economy and urban economies. While experienced developments in communication, transport, technology in the process experienced decreases importance of traditional parameters of settlement theory such as raw material and proximity to markets, it becomes possible that a product produced at any region of the world is able to be sold in any region of the world. (Kaya, 2007)

Development process is the result of acquisitions that countries obtained from historical process they passed. Institutional infrastructure of countries in historical process has a big share in forming of their institutional structures today. Tabellini suggests in his study that beside that institutional culture is formed by the effects of institutional culture, regional development is also in a firm correlation with past in the same way. In the same way it is suggested that with the reason of low labour force efficiency, economically disadvantaged regions cannot advance through income transfer, that poor regions in terms of economy and culture need to benefit from education investment, from cheap financing source born with local initiative and from localization of government. (Tabellini, 2014)

The sensibility of economy management in Turkey to manage and decrease debt stress of country has lead that the fact of growth remained at the second plan. Rational distribution of sources relevant with the concept of growth and productivity in production cannot be ensured. That Turkey adopts growing depending on production and efficiency as a strategy is urgent. With this reason, necessary regulations to make performance of growth stable in short term is needed. Sufficient condition is the establishment of R&D and industrial infrastructure based on human capital as a requirement of definition of sustainable growth. (Yiğidim, 2012)

Development agencies can play a very important catalyser role as institutions producing efficient solutions to special problems with their flexible structure and in forming common development targets through public and private sector cooperation, partnerships and network relations. These institutions that will be able to ensure social and economic development from bottom to top can develop activity fields through channel of decision processes that resident and have community support and thus, they can maximize benefit they could provide to the fact of export under the global competition conditions. Turkey is in the situation to put her all potential forward to stand in a changing competition environment under globalisation; for this regional development policies need to be developed and it has to adapt more sensitive approaching about its correct implementation. In our country in this context, it has been thought that increasing numbers and activities of development agencies operating regionally is helpful in terms of sustainability of regional development and growth of export in a regular and planned way. (Yardımcıoğlu, Kocamaz, & Sezal, 2012)

The reason of development agencies become prominent as efficient institutions is that their duties and structures have changed according to the features of locality in which they were found. The situation watched in the examples of world, development policies toward long term targets is realised by increasing local capacity through cooperation constituted between local actors and institutionalization containing coordination and with a multi-layered system of governance. Development Agencies will be the first institutions aiming economic development in local scale in a sense for Turkey. If Development Agencies provides internal development with efficient use of local sources within cooperation and coordination with local actors, this target can be achieved. (Kayasü & S.Yaşar, 2006)

According to the Geradin who takes development agencies in his study, that the number of agencies over national and European levels is one of the most important regulations for development in structural organisation of European Union and member states. Agencies with their special structures play a helpful role, with their scientific, technic and observer functions on the name of commission in general. But for the sake of strengthening the institutional structures, various steps such as being facilitator, being interaction with each other and being administered by a good institutional management can be taken. (Geradin, 2014)

It has been observed in the implementations of development agencies in Turkey that grant toward SMEs is given priority. It is aimed that move of development is realized through private sector promoted by state. Similar policies can be met in world implementations. Tambunan, in his study that investigates SMEs supports, suggests that defenders of SMEs policy have attributed the support of government to SMEs to three basic arguments. First of arguments is that SMEs develop competition and entrepreneurs while they form exterior benefit such as efficiency, innovation and total efficiency in general economy. When viewed from this aspect, development programmes designed particularly for supporting SMEs provide social benefits like more competition and entrepreneurs. Secondly, institutional recovery has positive effects on economic growth and development which will be realized on it. Thirdly, most of SMEs operates in labour intensive fields, the rise of employment in these fields as a result of developing of SMEs is a kind of tool to struggle with poverty. (Tambunan, 2014)

Banks have recently noticed that businesses which are at the bottom of SMEs segment cannot benefit from credit market sufficiently and started competing with each other to include businesses in this group in their credit portfolio by forming retail banking departments. Altman, Sabato and

Nicholas who stressed importance of information which is not financial in lending to SMEs suggest that credit and risk analysis of these SMEs considered to be under retail banking segment of banks have to be formed with criteria peculiar to themselves as separate from normal commercial credit segment. SMEs took place in this group is the most common type of company in OECD countries. (I.Altman, Sabato, & Wilson, 2014)

Development Agencies that accept the most important policy field to remove development differences as SMEs give the biggest slice of its sources to SMEs programmes. According to Guiso, Sapienza and Zingalese who mentions of necessity of development at the level of regions in financial sense too, financial development is an important need for big and small firms. This situation is originated not only from relationship between some reel economic variables or from local financial development, it also appears as some economic effects of financial integration. Europe and the world become increasingly more integrated. Big firms move independently from conditions and local financial system while small firms have to live with these limitations. Therefore, distribution network of small firms at the beginning level is the only tool for reaching to foreign funds. If local financial markets find political support, they can survive, otherwise this markets disappears and world becomes more integrated financially. (Guiso, Sapienza, & Zingales, 2014)

The support of development agencies towards SMEs are financial supports, in essence. For SMEs, these funds provided in form of grant is in the quality of an alternative financial source to the methods of containing foreign source such as using credit or borrowing from markets. Therefore, it is an indirect public intervention on finance market. According to Zhuang and his friends investigating relation between finance and market in their study, there is a functional relationship between financial system and decreasing poverty and economic growth. In addition, financial system contains some risks too. According to some opinions, financial system leads to speculation and price inflation, it increases the risk of rising volatility economic crisis. Therefore how a financial market providing economic growth and decreasing poverty is to be developed enters into financial stability. Financial crisis experienced has revealed the importance of macro economical management such as forming effective financial control and regulation mechanisms, making structural regulation for financial system of emerging countries. (Juzhong Zhuang, 2014)

Development agencies organised on 26 areas of level 2 in Turkey provide support to SMEs in their regions while they are centres watching closely potential of commerce and production regionally. Activities such as sectorial clumping, business incubators, forming technology centres are preferential fields on which development agencies work, too. Development agencies are local centres supporting commercial network in national sense. According to Itoh and Urata, the importance of local production networks, naturally, reveals the question whether or not there is a connection between being formed of such a network and national supports. This situation is an initiative about themselves of SMEs rather than national politics. At the same time national support is a concept that got into daily routine of SMEs through important activities such as information exchange and accession to financial sources Unless there are national supports, activities of SMEs would be somehow restricted. Some policies such as gathering firms at certain regions and providing interaction between firms courage SMEs. (Itoh & Urata, 2014)

The structure of Development Agencies organised in all cities in Turkey functions as a network operating well between SMEs and public authority. Many businesses in under developed regions have a very restricted capacity in terms of institutional operating. This situation creates a gap between SMEs and finance market. Basilico who stresses the importance of institutional management of SMEs states that institutional management of SMEs is a very important matter and that SMEs on the scale of institutionalization can obtain funds than finance market easier. At the same way, Basilico stated that value of credit of SMEs coordinated by a single executive is lower in the rating systems of banks. (Basilico, Maestroni, & Mantovani, 2014)

THE IMPLEMENTATIONS OF DEVELOPMENT AGENCY IN WORLD AND TURKEY

The effects that Great Depression lasting from 1929 to 1939 created could be removed through Keynes' economics policies relying on state intervention. Keynesian economic policies lasting until stagflation crisis in 1970's has expanded public space in expanded in terms of both macroeconomic variables and on subjects of growth, development and foreign expansion and increased the power of state institutions in front of local bodies. In line with this, regional development policies before 1970's have taken a centralist Outlook. (Akiş, 2011)

Regional Development Agencies are indicators of transition to an entrepreneur reason from governmentalize mind in search of regional policy. In 1960's and 70's, policies relying on improvement of infrastructure and incentives programmes were prevail under rule of central government. Since middle of 1970's, it has been seeing that an understanding of regional policy relying on local resources, developed bottom to top and as a result of this, regional development agencies started out. First regional development agency, Tennessee Valley Authority was founded in USA in 1933. After Great Depression, it was founded as a part of the move of new participant started by President F. D. Roosevelt in USA, of New Deal, with the aim to support different enterprises in land in valley of Tennessee that lost its value because of excessive farming. Agency which is expected to be "strong as government but flexible and aggressive as private sector" has ensured that efficiency has increased in agriculture and was successful in attracting many firms to the region. (Filiztekin, 2008)

According to Ozen's study regarding institutional structure of Regional Development Agency, regional development agencies founded in UK and USA were established by the cooperation of private and public sectors and had partly autonomy while they were designed as bodies trying to solve the problems of relatively under-developed regions with long term development programmes in Japan and France examples. GAP (Southeast Anatolian Project) in Turkey has similarity with model implemented in Japan and France. In frame of new developmentalist thought appearing in 1990's, international institutions (such as funds and loans of World Bank, EBRD, EIB, UNDP, EU) have made possible development agencies that have different features to be established all over the World. Development agencies have experienced important structural changes together with World economic conjuncture. Many development agencies that all have different structural features and fund sources from each other were founded in 1990's. (Özen, 2005)

Though difference of regional development exists nearly on entire world, policies to be implemented can show differences. According to a research by Harvard Institute of Economic Research on difference of regional development and implementations of development, there are many explanations about regional inequalities and that even sometimes they can last for centuries. There are much confusion about what should be understood of these opinions and what should be done. What is clear on this matter is that a model used successfully in a country does not give the same result in other countries. For example, China has opened her some shore regions directly to the foreigner investors and these special regions formed a rapid commercial activity. On the other hand, Mongolia has determined the whole country as a free trade region for foreign capital towards the end of 1990's but it has realised only a small rise when compared with China. (Demurger, et al., 2014)

Development including education, opportunity and human honour and welfare with its all other aspects is the most important priority of emerging countries. But development is difficult. All the economy policies, including competition, should be arranged according to development. (Fox, 2012)

The fact of development, whether it is carried out with local structures like agency or rather more centralist national institution, preserves always its place on the world agenda. With decreasing dominancy of socialist regimes in World politics, development policies planned and implemented in local regions became prominent.

According to Shah who argues the necessity of financial localisation, transition periods economies and emerging countries' economies, with the central planning paradigms in last 50 years, have a more centralist structure than those of advanced countries had in past. Transition period economies has completed their transformation process from central planning to market focused economies rapidly but emerging countries goes ahead in this transition period very slowly. The possibility of national governments to ensure macro-economic balance is increasingly low together with globalisation and localisation. Localisation continues with different variables such as political, administrative and financial subjects. (Shah, 2014)

Turkey's preferences in the adventure of development have been in line with world politics. First Five-Year-Industrialisation-Plan (1934) accepted as first planning example and First-Five-Year-Development Plan which is the first development plan have been designed as centralist implementations as a result of conjuncture of their periods. GAP (Southern Anatolian Project) was first planning implementation that was planned in central level but gives the priority to the development of locals in 1980's. In 2000's, other local development plans in level of sub-regions (such as DAP-Eastern Anatolian Development Project-, DOKAP-Eastern Black See Development Plan-Yesilirmak Basin Plan) were planned in centre and put into practise in locals. Development Agencies are the last link of this planning process and its difference from other planning enterprises is that region plans is done in locals through locals and development policies is implemented by being designed according to the this regional plans.

EU And Development Agencies

According to Arslan who mentions in his study that first examples of development agencies in Europe in historical process started out in the countries such as Italy and UK where difference of regional development was high, development agencies have started being established to remove the damage II. WW has given and to provide development in Austria, France, Ireland and Belgium in 1950's, Germany, UK, Italy, Holland, Scotland and Wales in 1960's and Greece, Spain, Denmark and Finland in 1980's. (Arslan, 2010)

EUNIDA (European Union Development Agency- EUNIDA) was established by member countries of union to improve member countries' capacities and determine the sustainable development strategies in June 2006. (EUNİDA, 2013)

While the structure in form of company in development agency in Europe is prominent, structure of agency in form of public institution, council enterprise and foundation exists.

Development Adventure in Turkey and Implementations of Development Agency

The Turkey of Republic which lost her capital and human resources in wars has tried to establish her development strategy through private sector at her

Table 1. Legal structure of RDA's in Europe 1999

Countries	Legal Status of RDA's
Germany	Semi-autonomy public companies
Spain	Public companies subject to private law
France	Mix economical companies
Belgium	Inter-councils companies
Romania, Denmark	Foundations
Czech Rep., Estonia, Slovakia, Poland	Public-Private sector companies
Sweden	Limited company
Holland, Italy, Ireland, Portugal	Public limited company
England	Mon-ministry public institution/ autonomy organization
Lithuania	Non-profit organisation
Greece	Council enterprises

Source: EURADA, *Creation, Development and Management of RDAs*, 1999, 4, (Date of Accession 24/01/2014).

first ten year but she failed. The reason she failed is that private entrepreneurs that time preferred commercial activities which is composed of solely purchasing and selling goods instead of manufacturing. In a conjuncture there is no possible infrastructure, the private entrepreneurs of time has made its preference and it wasn't interested in activities regarding industry. In 1930's, strategy was changed and economical system has started being constituted through statist policies. Financial institutions were established, a big change was introduced in tax system (dime levy was removed) and planning development method was tried by adopting a five-year-industrialization-programme.

In Turkey, seeking of industrialization through state is not an implementation peculiar to 1930's. In time of Ottoman State, in particularly second constitutional period, state has made some attempt to establish industrial business. The leaders of Republic have grown up among these kinds of practices. Most of these leaders were started out from cycles of soldiers and administrators. It was plausible that a control system from top to bottom on economy seems to be easier to these leaders. (Sahin, 1998)

The most important decision taken, in terms of economic development of country, is the decision to remove tithe tax in Ottoman era taken as 10% of products that farmers produced. One of the most important revenues of Ottoman state could take place as an important source of revenue among beginning conditions of Turkish Republic. Preference made here is the preference to collect taxes via consumer rather than producer as we would confront later more frequently. (Gonul, 2010)

Hasanoglu and Aliyev who mentions about historical process of development agencies in Turkey have stated that Regional Development Agencies have taken seriously into the agenda first time at the end of 1999 Helsinki summit in which Turkey's status was confirmed as a member candidate and that the establishment of Regional Development Agencies have taken place in arrangements that need to be done in middle-term under Accession Partnership Document.

The Bill Regarding Establishment, Coordination and Duties of Development Agencies was prepared by Ministry of Development and passed in 25/01/2006. (Anonymous, 2006)

The implementation of Turkey has started with 2 pivot regions (Izmir Development Agency and Cukurova Development Agency) and its organization was realized with the establishment of further 26 development agencies between 2006 and 2009.

Development Agencies were organized in Turkey as in Table 2 on the base of Level 2 Statistical Region Unit as a result of Article 5449.

Geographical proximity is not only the factor in specifying level 2 region units; factors such as socio-economic and cultural structure have played their role in specifying of region units.

Organisational Structure of Development Agencies in Turkey

Organisation scheme of development agencies has been shown in Figure 1. As it would be understand from the figure itself, directorate of agency has been designed in a way that it will be run under a two-fold directorate which is an

Table 2. Regional organisation of development agencies in Turkey

L.N.	Agency Name	City of Operating
1	Ankara Development Agency	Ankara
2	Izmir Development Agency	Izmir
3	Istanbul Development Agency	İstanbul
4	Bursa, Bilecik, Eskişehir Development Agency	Bursa, Eskisehir, Bilecik
5	Trakya Development Agency	Tekirdag, Edirne, Kırklareli
6	South Marmara Development Agency	Balıkesir, Canakkale
7	South Aegean Development Agency	Aydin, Denizli, Muğla
8	Karacadag Development Agency	Sanliurfa, Diyarbakir
9	East Marmara Development Agency	Kocaeli, Sakarya, Duzce, Bolu, Yalova
10	Mevlana Development Agency	Konya, Karaman
11	West-Anatolian Development Agency	Antalya, Burdur,Isparta
12	Nort-East Anatolian Development Agency	Erzurum, Erzincan, Bayburt
13	Middle Mediterranean Development Agency	Hatay, Kahramanmaras, Osmaniye
14	Cukurova Development Agency	Adana, Mersin
15	Middle Anatolia Development Agency	Kayseri, Sivas,Yozgat
16	West Blacksea Development Agency	Zonguldak, Karabuk, Bartin
17	North Anatolia Development Agency	Kastamonu, Cankiri, Sinop
18	Middle Blacksea Development Agency	Samsun, Corum, Tokat, Amasya
19	East Blacksea Development Agency	Ordu, Giresun, Trabzon, Rize, Artvin, Gumushane
20	Zafer Development Agency	Manisa, Afyon, Kutahya, Usak
21	Firat Development Agency	Malatya, Elazığ, Bingol, Tunceli
22	East Anatolia Development Agency	Van, Hakkari, Mus, Bitlis
23	Ipekyolu Development Agency	Gaziantep, Adıyaman, Kilis
24	Ahiler Development Agency	Kırıkkale, Aksaray, Nigde, Nevsehir, Kırsehir
25	Dicle Development Agency	Mardin, Sırnak, Batman, Siirt
26	Serhat Development Agency	Kars, Ardahan, Agri, Igdir

Source: RT Ministery of Development, http://www.kalkinma.gov.tr/bolgesel.portal (Date of Accession 29/11/2013)

executive board body and Development Board which is on advisory position. The element of directorate which takes place actively in current reel operation but not in organisation scheme is the Ministry of Development. Funds that agencies provide for SMEs and other support users come from ministry's budget. The proportion of funds given to the agencies serving to metropolis such as Istanbul, Ankara, Izmir, Bursa etc. is relatively less. The reason of this is shares that councils, special provincial administrations and commerce and industry chambers have to transfer to agency budget as the 19th article of Act 5449. Since these shares are relatively higher in metropolises than other cities, agencies in bigger cities can operate their activities with this revenue as long as they collect it.

Board of Development

Development Boards are advisory and consultation bodies of agencies. Development Boards is a council in which cities agency operates have a balanced number of members and which consists of at most 100 members. The membership of board is confirmed by a cabinet decree while representatives of public organisations, private sectors and NGO (Non-governmental Organisations) can become member of board.

Development Board can choice a chairmen within itself, elected chairman does not have right to vote and membership in directorate. That the chairman of development board is a member of directorate would function as a tie between two different directory boards.

Directorate

Directorate board is the active decision body of agency, there are four representatives in board from each city that agency operates. Governor, Mayor, Chairman of Chambers of Commerce and Industry and President of City General Assembly are members of board. One of members is on chairman position while others keep merely member position. Only governors can be chairman while this duty changes among Governors in board. Board is gathered once in a month.

On the name of functionality of board rising, the suggestions that Development Board chairman, university rectors and Agency Secretary General are able to have the right to vote in directorate conveyed to those concerned.

Figure 1. Organisation structure of development agencies
Source: Karacadag Development Agency, http://www.karacadag.org.tr/organizasyon-yapisi.asp, (Date of Accession 24/01/2014).

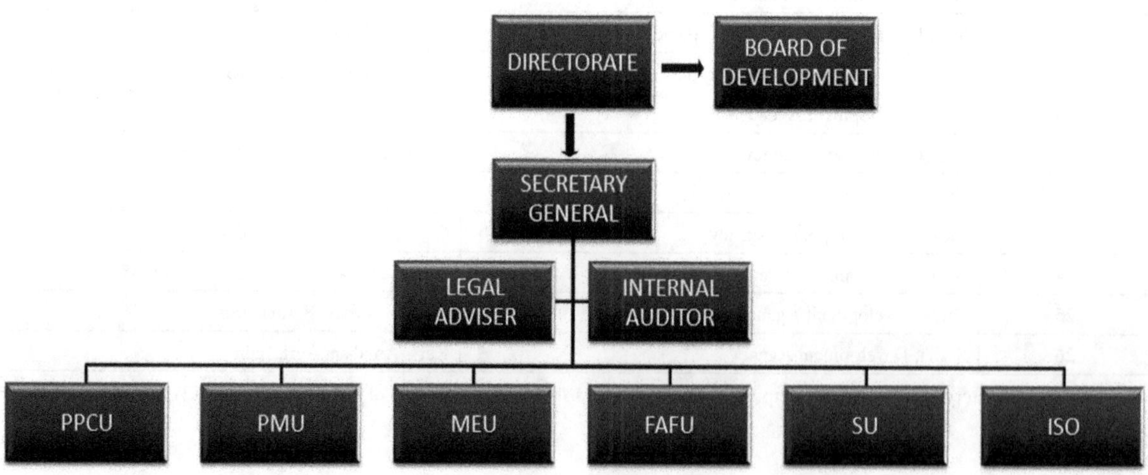

Secretary General

Secretary General is the executive body of agency. Top executive chief of secretary general and investment support offices is secretary general. Secretary General is responsible against directorate. (Republic, 2006)

Sources of Development Agencies In Turkey

Budget that Development Agencies used for support mechanisms and commercial expenditure have two main sources. Main source are funds transferred from the budget of Ministry of Development annually. Another important source is contribution margins that are transferred by Municipality, Chambers Of Commerce And Industry and City Special Administrations that are obliged to pay a contribution margin at a certain rate by the law.

Support Mechanisms of Development Agencies in Turkey

Development agencies implement their programme with the model of support that can be counted as limited which exists in its guide. Agencies need to diversify their support instruments in order them to gain a more comprehensive feature in their region. For example, there is no mechanism such as Business Angels to support new entrepreneurs. Support models should be designed such as exporter supports, R&D supports.

Directly Financial Support, Directly Operation Support and Technical Support programmes are support tools of agencies actively. Interest support and Loan without Interest Support tools have not yet been used by agencies actively though they exist in guide.

Directly Financial Support

The support model in which agency supports that are the main focus of study have effects on SMEs and agencies can have effect on SMEs is Directly Financial Support Model.

Directly Financial Support model's beneficiary is not only SMEs. With the decision of directorate, financial support programmes that have different beneficiaries can be built on. In some programmes, only non-profit organisations is declared as applicants while in some programmes only profit-oriented applicant is declared as convenient applicant.

In this type of support, agency transfer a certain rate of financial support to Project owner as grant, rest of the financing is provided with the support of co-financing contribution of beneficiary within Project time.

Figure 2. Funds sources of development agencies
Source: Adopted from Development Agencies Project and Active Support Guide

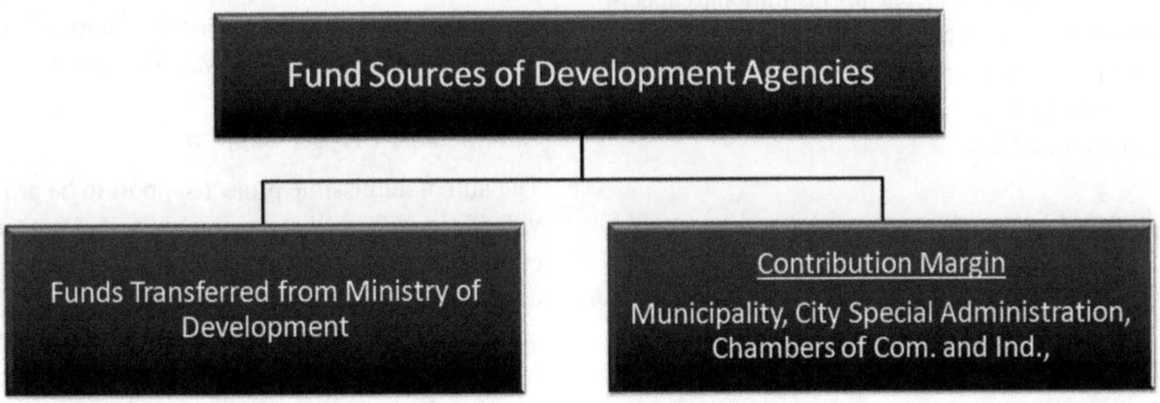

Figure 3. Support mechanisms of development agencies
Source: It has been adopted from Development Agencies Project and Active Support Guide

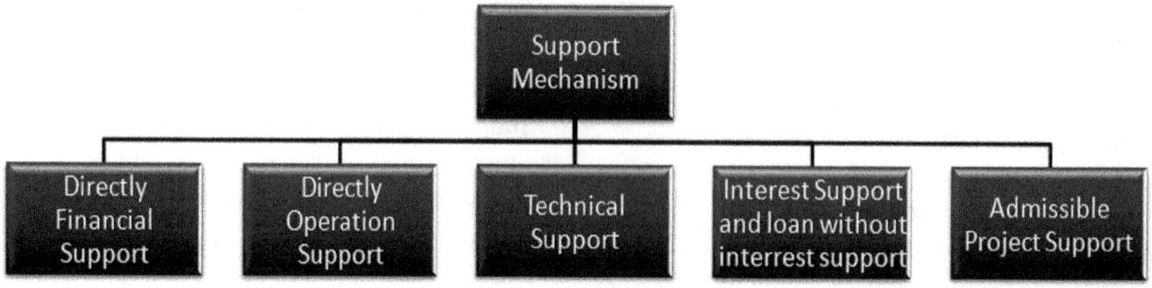

Directly Operation Support

In this type of support, project offer calling method is not applied, agencies provide financial support to activities that non-profit organisation and NGOs operate in subjects such as making research, feasibility, regional sectorial report on based of region or making inventory. The rate of support might go up to 100%.

Technical Support Programme

Through technical support programmes, it is initially aimed to form the region's capacity to prepare and execute project . In this context, through "Projects Cycle Management Education" (PCM), it is the most basic education provided to applicants. "Entrepreneurs Educations" is implemented with the cooperation of KOSGEB and trainees who get their certificates by joining to educations that agency funds gain the right to apply entrepreneurs support of KOSGEB.

With the aim of increasing institutional capacities of regions, other educations provided under this programme are the educations on technical subjects that vary according to the areas of expertise of NGOs.

Interest Support

Interest support is a complimentary aid that foreseeing that the cost of interest that SMEs will pay in return of credits, they will get from relevant medium institutions for their projects in quality stated in the protocol to be signed between Agency and relevant medium institutions. (Tamer, 2012)

This model that is available on the guide of Development Agencies is a model that was available on the guide of KOSGEB that is another public institution providing support for SMEs like agencies but was not used since 2010.

Interest Free Credit Support

Interest-free credit support, uses by for-profit oriented real and legal persons. Relevant intermediary organization and the Agency will be signed the protocol and specified qualifications for the potential projects. And than Related intermediary organizations gives loan to applicant and beneficiary repay the found in specified periods. (Tamer, Legislation Of Development Agencies, 2012)

This model, as different directly financial support model, is designed in a way that the capital of credit that will be given to SMEs following protocol with medium organisation (bank) is to be charged in a certain time. At the moment, no development agency did activate this model.

Addmissible Project Support

The aim of admissible project support to be provided by agency is that agency becomes Pioneer of projects that are important in terms of speeding up regional development, strengthening competitiveness of region and making environment of business better and that agency undertakes the coordination. (Tamer, Legislation Of Development Agencies, 2012)

SMEs AND PROFILE OF SMEs IN TURKEY

The term consisting of capital letters of small and medium sized Enterprises (SMEs) have gained an important place for itself in business World and literature recently. Commercial institutions that have financial size and number of worker stated in law are accepted as SME.

SMEs in Turkey consists 99,9% of number of enterprises, 77,8% of employment, 51,5% of wages, 64,8% of turning in, 55,5% of contribution value with factor cost, 41.1% of gross investment regarding material goods. (TUIK, 2013)

SMEs that consists 99% of current companies and 77% of employment in their body are accepted as skeleton of economy. The whole problems such as unemployment, export, registered economy, collecting tax that official authorizes of economy of country try to solve are all about SMEs and therefore decision makers are interested in the concept of SME.

Definition of SME

The definition of KOBI in Turkey: Businesses whose annual gross sale turnover or Financial Balance does not excess 40 million TL and whose number of employee is under 250 are accepted as SME. With relevant guide, SMEs are divided into three subtitles within itself;

"Micro business: Businesses that employ less than ten annual employee and have less than one million TL annual gross sale turnover or financial balance

Small business: Businesses that employ less than fifty annual employee and have less than eight million TL annual gross sale turnover or financial balance Medium sized business: That employs less than 250 annual employee and that has less than forty million TL annual gross sale turnover or financial balance

Medium-scaled SMEs: Businesses that employ less than two hundred and fifty people and have less than forty million TL annual net sales revenue or any of the financial balance" (EU, 2013)

There is no only one recognized definition of SMEs. Countries use different definitions with different reasons. In order to gauge the concepts of small and medium size, the size of firm and volume of economic activities is relied on. In addition, in some countries the legal and statistical definitions of SMEs vary. But definition generally requires SMEs to be independent and predicates on the size of firm in terms of number of full-time employee. Besides, the definition of SMEs sometimes takes financial performances of firm such as annual turnover and annual size of balances as threshold. (Cruz & Stamps, 2014)

SMEs definition accepted in Turkey shows similarity with that of EU in terms of parameters chosen even though numeric threshold values are different (Table 4).

Parameters used in different geographies of the world for determining SMEs shows big similarities even though their numeric thresholds are different (Table 5).

Table 3. SMEs classification in EU legislation

Criteria	Micro-Scaled SMEs	Small-Scaled SMEs	Medium-Scaled SMEs
Number of Working Personnel	<10	<50	<250
Gross Net Sale Turnover	≤ 2 Million Avro	≤ 10 Million Euro	≤ 50 Million Euro
Annual Financial Balance	≤ 2 Million Euro	≤ 5 Million Euro	≤ 43 Million Euro

Source: European Commission, The new SME Definition. (Date of Accession:30/12/2013).

Table 4. SMEs definition USA, EU, Australia and Canada

Nation /Region	Criteria	All Manufacturing Companies and Service Sector Firms that do not Export.	Exporter Service Sector Firms		Farms
USA	Number of employee	<500	<500		<500
	Annual Revenue	Non-applicable	≤ $ 7 Mio	≤ $ 25 Mio	≤ $ 250,000 Mio
EU	Number of employee	< 250			
	Annual Turnover (or)	≤ € 50 million			
	Balance Total	≤ € 43 million			
Australia	SMEs (non-farm) Number of employee	≤ 200			
	SMEs (non-farm) Number of employee SMEs (Farm) App. Value of Transactions	$ 18.866,00– $ 335.400,00			
Canada	Number of employee	< 250			
	Annual Revenue	< $ 48 Million			

Source: USITC, Small and Medium-sized Enterprises: Overview of Participation in U.S. Exports, 2010.

SMEs are quite important structures in terms of subjects such as growth, real economy, employment. The shares of SMEs within country economy are given in Table 6.

Structural Problems of SMEs in Turkey

99% of trading in Turkey is carried out by businesses that are within definition of SMEs. Certain subjects that businesses cannot place into their vision are subjects such as not being able to become more professional, organisation in form of family, out of registered selling, purchasing and partnerships, financing institution and unwillingness at point of working with banks, marketing and management. Each of problems specified are problems that need to be investigated in their peculiarity at more depth.

Illegal working is a very important problem of SMEs, this matter should be taken in a wide perspective from public financing due to high rate of taxes to the point in which firms adopt an excessively conservative attitude about sharing information belong to commercial activities of businesses. Even if that businesses do not have register of their activities provides some advantages for short term, in reaching to financing companies that their balances do not reflect current situation is confronted with disadvantage of their this attitudes in working of banks.

By the way, main criticism that is done against banks regarding activities of SMEs is that they preferred assurance banking instead of Project banking. As one of the main obstacles in front of SMEs reaching to credit is that banks do not deploy necessary limit for businesses because of insufficient assurance.

Operation done by bank while giving decision of credit is to decide if business can repay credit on time by investigating financial tables and morality details of company. At this point the subject that makes an obligation for the bank to take assurance is that tables of SMEs that are customer of credit do not reflect reel situation.

Table 5. The shares of SMEs in the economy of country

Country	Its Share in All Companies	Its Share in Employment	Its Share in Contribution Value
USA	98.9	57.9	50
India	97.3	66.9	-
Japan	98.2	66	49.3
Korea	99.9	87.7	49.2
Brazil	99.9	67	-
Malaysia	99.9	65.2	31.2
EU 27	99.9	67.4	57.7
England	99.6	54.1	51
Germany	99.5	60.4	53.6
Italy	99.9	81.1	71.3
Turkey	99.9	78	55

Source: KOSGEB 2011-2013 SME Strategy and Action Plan, p.29.

Table 6. Financial sources of firms in Turkey and world

	Bank Credit	Bill of Exchange	Resource	Seller's Credit
G-7	0.23	0.08	0.63	0.06
Rising Economies	0.27	0.21	0.40	0.12
Turkey	0.30	0.00	0.43	0.27

Source: Mümin Hakkı Ay, Esra Talaşlı, Selçuk Üniversitesi Karaman I.I.B.F. Journal. (Special Issıe, 2007)

SMEs' Viewing of Capital Markets

Many structural problems such as institutionalization, companies tendency to work illegally due to excessive tax burden, unhealthy financial tables, intense usage of accounts of debts to partners and receivables from debtors because of that company safe is to be thought as the pocket of firm-owner, financial movements between group companies is followed closely and fictive debt/receivable balances within group is available etc. which are among most basic problems of SMEs in Turkey, functions as a barrier between SMEs and capital market an even Money market.

Most basic and determinative factor in assessing of SMEs by any institution that is creditor and providing grant is financial tables. Recently, banks and similar organisations and organisation providing grant demand official financial tables confirmed by tax Office particularly and they do not accept financial tables that do not rely on tax declaration as reliable. On the other hand financial tables in tax declaration of SMEs are regulated as financial tables showing profitableness at minimum level to pay less tax depending upon high tax rates. This limits accessibility of SMEs to credit market.

Capital market might provide funds to businesses with lower costs compared with funds that banking sector provided.

SMEs Stock Market and Its Practibility in Turkey

Markets that businesses will be able to obtain foreign source are mainly Money markets (through credit supplying) and capital markets (through fund supplying). Only market that SMEs can obtain foreign source in Turkey is, generally speaking, Money market while fund source is credit. Mostly, SMEs in Turkey do not have a vision to get fund from capital market.

Under Borsa Istanbul two markets have institutionally been established under names of Second National Market and Improving Businesses Market for SMEs.

- **Second National Market:** Small and medium sized companies, companies that are permanently or temporarily removed from National Market and that cannot meet the conditions of quotation and trading necessary for National Market. (İstanbul, 2014).
- **Improving Businesses Market:** Improving Businesses Market (GIP) has been established as a separate market under Borsa Istanbul with the aim of creating a transparent and regular environment in which stock and shares that companies that can't meet the conditions of quotation but have the potential to improve and grow are to export to obtain fund from capital market can be in trading. (İstanbul, 2014).

In financing from capital markets, there is no obligation to make repayments that might constrain cash flow of businesses while capital structure of businesses is to be strengthening. Beside, together with increasing capital rates borrowing capacity of businesses also rises and it becomes easier for them to find credit. Therefore, opening to the stock exchange is a convenient method for businesses that want to grow. (Yüksel, 2011)

The data in Table 6 shows lack of capital market in terms of SMEs financing. As understood from data in table, SMEs in Turkey benefit from market mechanism in financing more than compared other country groups.

Advantages And Disadvantages Of Being SMEs

In almost every country of world, the most common company type in business life is companies that remain within frame of SMEs definition.

Being SMEs provides companies advantages in many fields together with a series of difficulties. Advantages that are brought by being SMEs are flexibility in choose of operation matter, that trading relies on small capital and labour, that the effects of commercial losses suffered is more minimal, that practicality of new commercial activities in different field following a short period of recovery as a result of fail, that financial squeeze might be exceed with the support of family members, that making position adjustment is possible by developing a strategy rapidly against outer economic changes since diameter of its commercial activities is small, that company deploys most rational strategy within market mechanism through direct relation with customer and supplier. Small organisational structure and less number of staff increase motivations and culture of winning together.

Disadvantages of being SMEs are features such as irregularity of financial tables and limited possibility of accession to financing depending on insufficient liquidity; that commercial activities can be practised depending on only equity capital because of limited credit possibilities, that company is not long-lived because of proportion of shares in structures in form of family company, that professional management and executive are not used when diameter of commercial activities exceed the cultural level of company owner, that needed credit channels cannot be opened depending on lack of assurance in countries like Turkey where assurance banking is common, that qualify staff is not employed depending on lack of capital, all trading cycle is limited with a person's working and vision.

SMEs have similar problems in many countries against financial markets. Baas and Schrooten has mentioned of problems that SMEs experienced against financial institutions. SMEs are experiencing in accessing to outer financial resources in whole world. Banks are usually able to act unwillingly while supplying credit to businesses in this class, the result of this is that they have limited information about these firms. Their need of official accountancy is limited while firm owners have a low vision about detailed investment information. (Baas & Schrooten, 2014)

According to Aidis who mentions of weak side of businesses operating in the scale of SMEs, stable macro-economic environment is generally characterized by low purchasing power, decreased consumer demand, lack of fund and incapacities of SMEs owners to improve their businesses. Even if the lack of information alone is not accepted as very important this situation gains importance when it comes together with legal obstacles, limit of abilities and SMEs owners working with low turnovers. In a similar way, management problems starts being important when it comes together with environmental obstacles, informal obstacles and SMEs run with high turnovers. (Aidis, 2014)

Development Agencies' the most important tool that its effects are most measurable is grant support programmes towards SMEs. SMEs to receive support might make an application for project in certain sectors determined by agency according to priorities. The value of applicant SMEs at the point of receiving grant is carried by an a few phased evaluation system. Agencies do not make evaluation of SMEs programme through its own staff, it gets independent evaluators that it employs through purchasing of service to make it. In the guide of evaluating they given to independent evaluators, the frame of evaluating process and rating system is transferred to evaluators and agency coordinates the process. The perfection of individuals who made evaluation is very important. SMEs projects are rated through a type of rating system. Each one of SMEs who wins right to make an application to the programme passes through from the same evaluation system whether or not it gets grant. The rating system implemented in this stage needs to show differences in terms of sector and scale of firm. Recently it has been argued that different rating models need to be implemented in banking system through which SMEs pass from evaluation process. Rikkers and Thibeault, in their study arguing that rating systems need to be varied, suggest that there are models such as spot time ous rating, cycle rating, mixed rating and it is very important to decide which one to be used. (Rikkers & Thibeault, 2014)

In terms of banks, financing of SMEs, particularly that of SMEs in the segment of micro and small enterprises (Those which have an active total and gross selling less than 8 million TL) is more risky than normal commercial businesses. According to Choe who mentions of that process of lending to SMEs should be different than other businesses; firstly, while amount given as debt rise when scale economies are available in lending, follow up activity of each unit decreases therefore borrowing cost is higher for SMEs under this segment. Secondly, the fact that banks have difficulties to obtain the information necessary in lending process as scale of firm gets smaller increases the cost of follow-up costs. (Choe, 2014)

Public authorities should undertake the duty to remove the rupture between SMEs in the segment of micro and small enterprises and financial market. Funding SMEs through Development Agencies might be considered as an action taken in this direction.

Management theory and strategy researches remind us concepts of entrepreneurs and creative aspects of management on some occasions in which SMEs are confronted with a wild and dynamic competition, a complex and turbulent business life and demanding and strong customers. Actually, improving a reliable strategy is not too easy for SMEs after business world has taken their all energy. Still, the potential of innovation, flexible structure of organisation, its independence on remote management, deep effect being owner of business brought are the features in literature. These formed the perception in us that SMEs are not weak, rather SMEs have many options in order to overcome their market problems. (Freiling, 2014)

INSTITUTION THAT PROVIDES GRANT TO SMEs IN TURKEY AND PUBLIC FUNDED GRANTS THAT IS A NEW FINCANCING TOOL

Recently, particularly in the process of EU funds are used by SMEs, fund in form of grant is provided to projects SMEs prepared in case of they are proved to be successful.

Main institutions and organisations that implement these support mechanisms;

KOSGEB; In the coordination of Ministry of Development, Development Agencies; Institution of Supporting Agriculture and Rural Development (TKDK); Ministry of food, agriculture and livestock; Ministry of science, industry and technology; IFAD(International Food Agriculture Development); CFCU (central finance and contracting unit);

Even though that grant mechanisms of institution and foundations stated contains some sectorial, regional, functional differences, they are systems providing fund flowing to SMEs for their projects to extent that study is concerned. Establishing the efficiencies of funds given to SMEs through different institutions in the eye of public is a matter that has being discussed recently.

The Effects Of Direct Financing Support (Grant) On SMEs

Direct Financing Support is a model that development Agencies use in supplying funds to the SMEs. In the budgets of Development Agencies, the biggest share is usually taken by programmes implemented towards SMEs in an annual basis.

Support might change in the band of 50.000,00 TL - 500.000,00 TL, since support might be maximum 50% project value, SMEs preparing the project obtain financing out of support from its own equity capital or borrowing.

Additiveness

Beside results are sometimes realized as independent from intervention, sometimes a series of results which is not convenient to the target of intervention can be obtained. This points should be considered in evaluation, it should be tried to determine whether or not changes aimed by intervention is created. Now, the grade of occurring gross changes that interventions aimed is called as additiveness. In this context, gross changes derive from public interventions are expressed as addictive changes. (Ersayin, 2012)

The Evaluation of Effect Analysis

That wants to be expressed by the concept of effect analysis is whether or not instrument used with the aim of providing support has produced results observed or results that is unexpected to be observed.

Activities in groups which is respondent to support is not only limited with support budget. SMEs which are sample taken in this particular study and beneficiary of similar public supports are constitution operating within a market mechanism that has extremely dynamic parameters. As independent of support mechanisms, they contain many differentiating factors in their body such as capital, credibility, human source, commercial experience.

Therefore even in the level maximum equals (the same sector, the same amount of support, the same location...) Support that SMEs received will not give the same results. Financing obtained and objective benefits together with it (production speed, number of production, new product etc.) is relevant with the capacity of company to form these benefits and effects created by support will be different in every SME.

This point, contrary to what Ersayin suggested, it has been thought that it is a less measurable concept when compared with effect analysis. In the analysis which will be carried by waiting a reasonable time for effects to appear at the end of support process the effect of support can be analysed with parameters such as financial tables, information of production capacity, and number of workers. But it has been considered that it would not be rational to establish additiveness aiming a measurement like what the role of public support granted in the effect appeared by separating it from other parameters SMEs have.

CONCLUSION

There is no single model that its correctness and sustainability was proved in advanced and emerging countries in the field of development. However, there is also no even general model about methodology of development. The form and implementing performance of plans prepared for development depending on political conjuncture of the world and countries vary. In the periods central government models have weight, models planned by centre, having limited auditability in terms of its comprehensiveness and results and level of success remains very low.

Mentality in development policies has changed together with republican and democratic regimes; concepts such as regional development, local development, rural development etc. have started having their places in the literature. This change has brought with itself that a transition towards to a mentality of regional development and regional planning by giving up an understanding of planning at central level in the phase of planning too for getting expected efficiency from development moves.

In implementations of development, there realized a transition from central organisations coordinating development process toward institutional structures found on local and watching implementations from first hand.

In Turkey, initially a development focused on private sector was designed but this approach has been replaced by the policy of realizing a development move through state since technical and financial accumulation of private sector of that time could not slot into this policy. Designed plans of industrialization could not be implemented as wished due to political conjuncture of that period.

1960's have been accepted in the history of Turkish economy as years when planned development has started. Plans that are formed under State Planning Organisation is criticized due to some of its aspects such as that it cannot be implemented by political decisions, that it does not addresses to rural areas since it was done from central etc. GAP (South-east Anatolia Project) which is first example of regional development in 1980's was put into practice but actions planned cannot be realized fully so far. Together with the process of EU integration at the beginning of 2000's, the concept of regional development which started far ago in the world has got enter in the agenda of Turkey more actively. Beside regional development administration like GAP, development agencies were established as most extensive move. These organisations that its institutional organisation is different than those in the world as a result of her administration order try to be recognized within administration order. Development agencies attract attentions on itself since the day it was found through supports it provided and in terms of efficiency and correctness of these supports.

The biggest source in the budget of Development Agencies is separated for support programmes. Grants given towards SMEs has a direct effect on SMEs and 50% of cost of machinery equipment that is demanded by SME under the extension of project it prepared is financed through grant transferred under project.

Without any doubt, increasing or modernisation of machinery equipment forms objective benefits on SMEs such as increasing of capacity, quality, number and quality of staff, export etc. Beside this, it brings many benefits together with itself such as being able to get support from a public institution, preparing and carrying a project, working legally, taking place in activities like domestic or abroad fair, business travelling in organisations of agency, obtaining financial possibilities depending on cooperation of agency with financial institutions.

Many SMEs that gets support from development agencies, particularly in under-developed cities, involves in an institutional implementation first time together with agency support process. It practices a project that has time and budget limitation, makes various reporting and in addition to the benefit it obtained, it also gains a feeling of self-confidence about practising a project.

Besides providing support, development agencies organised on 26 areas in Turkey are information centres knowing SMEs found on their region closely, watching sectorial condensations and needs at the level of region closely.

REFERENCES

Aidis, R. (2014). *Why don't we see more small- and medium-sized enterprises (SMEs) in Lithuania? Institutional impediments to SME development.* Retrieved, May 17, 2014, from http://papers.ssrn.com/sol3/papers.cfm?abstract_id=314201

Akiş, E. (2011). In the process of globalization developments in regional development approach and regional development agencies. *Journal of Sociology Conference*, (s. 239).

Altman, E., Sabato, G., & Wilson, N. (2014, May 20). *The value of non-financial information in SME risk management*. Academic Press.

Anonymous. (2006). *The law abaout the establisment coordination and duties of development agencies*. Author.

Arslan, E. (2010). Development agencies and development agency expected contribution to the economy of Turkey. *Kamu İş*, 93.

Baas, T., & Schrooten, M. (2014). *Relationship banking and SMEs: A theoretical analysis*. Retrieved, May 17, 2014, from http://papers.ssrn.com/sol3/papers.cfm?abstract_id=788344

Basilico, E., Maestroni, M., & Mantovani, G. M. (2014). *The relation between corporate governance, firm performance and the merit of credit in SMEs*. Retrieved, May 25, 2014, from http://papers.ssrn.com/sol3/papers.cfm?abstract_id=2403166

Choe, C. (2014). *The political economy of SME financing and Japan's regional bank problems*. Retrieved, May 21, 2014, from http://papers.ssrn.com/sol3/papers.cfm?abstract_id=902791

Cruz, J. D., & Stamps, J. (2014). *Small and medium-sized enterprises: U.S. and EU export activities, and barriers and opportunities experienced by U.S. firms*. Retrieved, January 4, 2014, from http://www.usitc.gov/publications/332/pub4169.pdf

Demurger, S., Sachs, J. D., Woo, W. T., Bao, S., Chang, G., & Mellinger, A. (2014). *Geography, economic policy and regional development in China*. Retrieved, May 16, 2014, from http://post.economics.harvard.edu/hier/2002papers/2002list.html

Ersayin, Z. (2012). Assessment of additiveness in public intervention. In *Assessment of additiveness in public intervention*. Ankara, Turkey: Ministery of Development.

EU. (2013). *The new SME definition*. Retrieved, December 30, 2013, from http://ec.europa.eu/enterprise/policies/sme/files/sme_definition/sme_user_guide_en.pdf

EUNİDA. (n.d.). Retrieved, October 30, 2013, from http://www.eunida.eu/

Filiztekin, A. (2008). *Regional differences and policies in Turkey. (s. 97)*. TUSİAD.

Fox, E. M. (2012). Competition, development and regional integration: In search of a competition law fit for developing countries, law & economics research paper series working paper. *Economic Research Paper Series Working Paper*, s. 2-3.

Freiling, J. (2014). *SME management – What can we learn from entrepreneurship theory?* Retrieved, May 21, 2014, from http://papers.ssrn.com/sol3/papers.cfm?abstract_id=984658

Geradin, D. (2014). *The development of european regulatory agencies: What the EU should learn from Amerıcan experience*. Retrieved, May 24, 2014, from http://papers.ssrn.com/sol3/papers.cfm?abstract_id=877922

Gonul, F. D. (2010). Economy of development. In F. D. Gonul içinde (Ed.), Economy of development (pp. 237-298). Ankara: Efil Bookstore.

Guiso, L., Sapienza, P., & Zingales, L. (n.d.). *Does local financial development matter*. Retrieved, May 17, 2014, from http://papers.ssrn.com/sol3/papers.cfm?abstract_id=308569

İstanbul, E. (2014). Retrieved, January 07, 2014, from http://borsaistanbul.com/urunler-ve-piyasalar/piyasalar/pay-piyasasi

Itoh, M., & Urata, S. (2014). *Small and medium size enterprise support policy in Japan*. Retrieved, May 25, 2014, from http://papers.ssrn.com/sol3/papers.cfm?abstract_id=604918

Juzhong Zhuang, O. (2014). *Financial sector development, economic growth, and poverty*. Retrieved, May 21, 2014, from http://www.adb.org/publications/financial-sector-development-economic-growth-and-poverty-reduction-literature-review

Kaya, K. (2007). *A new model of regional development*. Ankara: Develeopment Agencies and Applicability in Turkey.

Kayasü, S., & Yaşar, S. S. (2006). *Development policies in the EU accession process: Legal and institutional transformation*. Paper presented at the Regional Development and Governance Symposium, Ankara, Turkey.

Özen, P. (2005). *Regional development agencies*. Ankara: TEPAV. Retrieved, December 23, 2013,from http://www.tepav.org.tr/upload/files/1271245092r8246.Bolgesel_Kalkinma_Ajanslari.pdf

Republic, T. O. (2006). Retrieved, December 30, 2013, from http://www.kosgeb.gov.tr/Pages/UI/Baskanligimiz.aspx?ref=2

Rikkers, F., & Thibeault, A. E. (2014). *The optimal rating philosophy for the rating of SMEs*. Retrieved, May 20, 2014, from http://ssrn.com/abstract=966322

Sahin, H. (1998). *Economy of Turkey*. Bursa: Ezgi Bookstore.

Shah, A. (n.d.). *Fiscal decentralization in developing and transition economies*. Retrieved, May 21, 2014, from http://elibrary.worldbank.org/doi/book/10.1596/1813-9450-3282

Tabellini, G. (n.d.). *Culture and institutions: Economic development in the regions of Europe*. Retrieved, May 20, 2014, from http://SSRN.com/abstract=754086

Tambunan, T. (n.d.). *SME development in Indonesia: Do economic growth and government supports matter*. Retrieved, May 16, 2014, from http://ijaps.usm.my/?page_id=312

Tamer, A. (2012). *Legislation of development agencies*. Ankara: Adalet Bookstore.

TUIK. (n.d.). *News bulletin*. Retrieved, December 30, 2013, from http://www.tuik.gov.tr/PreHaberBultenleri.do?id=13146

Yardımcıoğlu, M., Kocamaz, H., & Sezal, N. (2012). *Regional development policiy and development in Turkey*. Paper presented at the *Regional Development and Governance Symposium*, Kahramanmaraş, Turkey.

Yiğidim, A. (2012). *Growing policy: Evaluation in terms of Turkey economy*. Retrieved, January 10, 2014, from http://www.tek.org.tr/dosyalar/buyume6.pdf

Yüksel, A. (2011). *Access to bank loans of SMEs in Turkey*. Ankara, Turkey: Minister of Development.

KEY TERMS AND DEFINITIONS

Additiveness: That term is more specific scale than effect analysis. Additiveness is the determination of the effect of per given money on beneficiary.

Development Agencies: The agencies is the local offices of the central development autorities. Regional development plans is prepared by that units. In addition local and national funds gives by the agencies to beneficiaries. These beneficiaries should be work at determined sectors which have development potential according to the regional development plan.

Directly Financial Support: That support tool's may be uses by company and other non-profit beneficiaries according to program criteria. And the agencies give the high portion of the grants with that support mechanism.

Effect Analysis: The development agencies, do effect analysis for their programme to scale the effect of the programme. According to result of the analysis the agency does needful regulation on programme.

Garant System: This system is the most prominent tools of the Develeopment agencies. That model's specialty is that, co-finansing. In other words beneficiary has to add co-finans for project.

Regional Development: The economic and demographic differencies between regions is the main difficulties of the development. For that reason, regional development policy is inevitable to responsible policy makers.

SMEs: The SME criterias determined by related law, almost 90% of the companies located at that group.To specify the group,there are some scales, like balance sheet value and the number of employee.

Section 3
New Dynamics in Globalization

Chapter 12
Global Crisis and Government Intervention:
Economic Crisis

Hakan Ay
Dokuz Eylül University, Turkey

Öznur Uçar
Dokuz Eylül University, Turkey

ABSTRACT

The authors look at the three major global crises; they see state intervention in causes and solutions. The causes of the crisis were deregulation. To resolve the crises, again regulation policies have been applied. Although the causes of the crises seem to have been regulation policies, in fact, the main problem was homo economicus. In conclusion, the authors see that when we analyze the reasons for the three big global crises and the ways to overcome crisis, the reasons are the unethical and irrational behavior of homo economicus. That is why homo economicus must be constrained and obey constitutional financial and monetary rules.

INTRODUCTION

The aim of our study is to research the role of government intervention in the causes and result of the global crisis and to investigate and find the solution. The 1929, 1973 and 2008 crises have been examined. Between 1929 and 2008 the cause of the crises was deregulation policy;It was observed that regulatory policies were used to exit from the crisis. The crisis of 1973 has lead to the understanding that the state's share in the economy was far away from optimal due to the policies of regulation and has provided again return to the policies of deregulation.

At the end of our study we've noticed that government intervention in the crisis was not the main problem. The main problem was moving away from an ethical Homo Economicus. Many experiments showed us that Homo Economicus does not interfere with the motive of earning further after a certain point, but it can lead to risky decisions and / or unethical behavior. This move away from optimum has caused the economic crisis. Also, the inexistence of Homo Economicus has caused

DOI: 10.4018/978-1-4666-7308-3.ch012

a move away from the the ideal situation. At this point, the solution is the human model known as "Zoon Politikon" by Ariston,and the "moderate human" by Nasurid Tusi and Kınalızade Ali Efendi. Moderation to ensure the effective functioning of humans and markets must be competitive to the extent that competition as well as ethical motives should limit the extent to which limits are exceeded. This limit can be achieved by binding rules on the constitutional level.

With our research, we have approached the question of the most ancient history of economic thought from a different angle, may be the solution that we sought could be approachable.

BACKGROUND

Knowledge is cumulative. Our article is the work of cumulative knowledge. We thank thinking people who made important contributions with their knowledge and ideas.

Economic Crisis

Crisis derives from the Greek word "krisis" meaning sudden decision-making, and refers to a deteriorating situation. An economic crisis suddenly occurs and is an adverse condition that affects both state and market players. It acts on the three main variables of the economy; the general level of prices, economic growth and unemployment. In the literature, a few problems generated with different combinations of these three variables a few problems have been identified. They are: inflation, deflation, stagflation, recession, depression, and slumpflasyo.

APPROACHES OF SCHOOLS OF ECONOMIC THOUGHT

Economic crises are evaluated in terms of different economic schools of thought. One of them is a school of classical economics. In 1776, classical economics begins with Adam Smith's book *Wealth of Nations* and was active until the 1930s. Until 1930, the economy was believed to be in balance thanks to the invisible hand and to re-balance itself in the future economy, despite deviation from equilibrium. Likewise, the economy has come back into balance after eight crises experienced in the 19th century and three crises experienced in the 20th century until the Great Depression. However, the economic crisis of 1929 led to the collapse of this idea and an understanding of the need for government intervention. Socialism is believed to have caused the crisis of the capitalist system. According to Jean Charles Sismondi, there is no balance between the process of production and consumption. The capitalist process of production is not allowed to increase the subsistence level of the workers at the same rate as production increases. Worker's wages will not be increased according to profit increases with higher productivity in a capitalist system. This paradox will lead to economic crisis. According to Marx, the capitalist system is the cause of the crisis. Furthermore, he has even claimed there will be no end to the business cycle in the capitalist system. Because of the contradictions within the capitalist system, there will be a crisis a decade and each crisis will lead to the next crisis.The next the business cycle will be more severe than the first one. The can be no solution if the capitalist system continues to live.

The business cycle theory of the Austrian school of economics was developed by the second generation's most important name, Ludwing Von Misses, on the basis of theory from representatives of the first generation, Friedrich Wieser. The Theory of Misses was developed and given its final shape by Hayek. The key point of this theory is monetary policy. The problem begins with the fall in interest rates by expansionary monetary policy so that two types of interest occur, like the natural interest rate and the market interest rates. These mismatches between the two interest rates will cause both an increased intention to save by reducing consumption and an increase in production opportunities. Despite the expansion in the economy experienced in the short-term, investment imbalance will cause stagflation. Expansionary policies will be taken against unemployment which will increase unemployment and inflation. Hayek proposes the control of the money supply for the solution of the crisis.

The classical school of confidence lost popularity with the Great Depression and Keynes' ideas became popular. J. M. Keynes ideas were constructed on crisis solution. According to Keynes, the cause of the crisis is pessimism. So, individuals invest with the expectation of high returns but the real value of the investment is below expectations. The solution is to take serious steps for the provision of redistribution by stimulating income-consumption trends. This can be achieved by the government's application of fiscal policy. John Hicks and Alvin Hansen, representatives of the neo-Keynesian thought, sought solutions in active composition of fiscal and monetary policy. According to them, there are strengths and weaknesses of monetary policy and fiscal policy. There are also some side effects of the two policies.

Post Keynesian economist Hyman Minsky explained the business cycle by his financial instability hypothesis. According to the hypothesis, the cause of business cycles is the accumulation of debt. There are three types of borrowers in the financial system: These are, hedge borrowers, speculative borrowers and Ponzi borrowers. Hedge borrowers can pay both the capital and interest of the amount of current cash flow of investments. Speculative borrowers can pay only interest on the interest of debt capital by the current cash flow of investments, She/he has to borrow again from the same source for the payment of capital. Ponzi borrowers can pay neither the capital nor interest by current cash flow of investments. She/he relies on the increase in the value of financial assets. If the economy is dominated by hedge borrowers, then the economy is in equilibrium or near-equilibrium. But if the economy speculative borrowers or Ponzi dominate, the economy will move away from balance. The long term balance [1]will lead to a greater risk for banks and other financial institutions and will encourage more risk. Hedge borrowers will turn into speculative borrowers and even to Ponzi borrowers.

According to Milton Friedman, the reason of the move away from balance is monetary shocks stemming from the central bank playing withth money supply. An increase in money supply leads to a temporary cyclical expansion and cut down on money supply leads to cyclical economic contraction. In an economy in which meeting the requirements of full competition is a condition, unless monetary shocks are not alive, the business cycle will be minimal. To avoid this business cycle, transparent and accountable central banks should be established. Central banks should remain loyal to a constitutional increase rate of money supply equal to the rate of economic growth and should follow a policy of quantitative easing.

Representatives of New Keynesian thinking, Nobel Prize winner George Akerlof and Joseph Stiglitz, argued that different players will have different levels of access to the information in the market. Asymmetric information will adversely affect function of the market when all players do not have full information. Players with better access to information will hold onto good stocks, which are undervalued and sell overvalued bad stocks. Players with limited access to the information will end up buying overvalued bad stocks. The result is that capital markets cannot work effectively. The same situation will happen in the debt markets and productive investments will be abandoned. Theapparent market failures due to asymmetric information can be solved by government intervention. The government should increase opportunities of information and should punish people who benefit from the result of asymmetric information.

Major Global Crises

Three major global crises influenced this theory. The first is the Great Depression. The Great Depression is a result of the devastating effects of World War I in defeated countries. The USA was the winner in this war which was not domestic and was protected from the destructive effects of the war. In addition, USA was in a superior condition because of technological developments in the country and held a significant portion of the world's gold reserves. The USA had provided financing for the needs of defeated countries. During this period, total receivables of the U.S. were 11.563 million dollars together with interest from 15 countries. This golden age in the U.S has led to extreme volatility in production, consumption and financial sectors. Stock prices had increased excessively in 1923-29 period despite two banks being bankrupted on average per day. In 1928, the Dow-Jones Index reached 191 and 382 in 1929. (Bakırtaş and Tekinşen, 2004,) Investors were pulling out their savings from banks, remortgaging their houses. Stocks were purchased with 10% down payment. Even new stocks were purchased based on previously purchased stocks as collateral. There were no regulations on the money market at that time. The banking system was not regulated by laws.There were no basic laws on minimum capital to open a bank or how much of the cash reserve could be loaned. 4000 banks went bankrupt rapidly following Black Tuesday, since they invested all their deposits in the New York Stock Exchange. (Açıkgöz and Özkan, 2009)

In the real sector there was an increase in rapid monopolization. This was caused by both the fragility of the real sector and financial markets. Also, in the period of 1928-29, the U.S. increased its production of wheat by 17% and, correspondingly, the USSR highly increased its production and exports of wheat. This led to fluctuations in international markets. President Hoover insisted on collecting gold post-war receivables, and did not accept payments of debts with goods or services. Moreover, they saw this as a threat for their domestic markets and created customs practices to narrow foreign trade. This attitude had become the general attitude of the state and from the beginning of the crisis until 1932, world trade declined by 60%. (Açıkgöz and Özkan, 2009)

The crisis began with the collapse of the real estate market. First the stock market, then the financial sector collapsed. This was followed by the real estate sector. When the crisis began in the US, it spread to developed countries such as Germany, England and France, then the whole world, because the U.S. was producing more than 42% of world output. It was the largest exporter in the world and also the biggest importer in the world after England. The US alone was producing 40%of the imports of the 15 most developed countries. After the Great Depression, the imports and exports of the U.S. decreased by 70%. The U.S. unemployment rate increased from 3% to 25%, the GDP decreased by1/3 percent. In 1932, until it reached the lowest point in the business cycle, government economical policies were based on classical economics. (Bocutoglu, 2011) Budget balances, costs to be minimized, the gold standard of protection and strict monetary policy were adopted. However, this policy led to the further deepening of the crisis. For this reason, both tax reductions and subsidies were applied and the markets held with the law.

This program was known as the New Deal. These applications were implemented in two packages per hundred days. The first 100 days in applications was for improving labor, regulation of the banking system, agricultural and industrial reforms. In addition, the tax of presence from upper-income people was increased to 25% from 63%. Thus, the improvement of income inequality was targeted. The Creation of employment by increasing public spending in the second pack was at work. For that purpose, public expenditures of $ 5 billion were undertaken. Deregulation policies caused the Great Depression and regulation policies ended the depression. (Bocutoglu, 2011)

The policy of regulation was continued until the crisis of OPEC. A crisis arose because of a cut in production of oil-exporting countries. In 1971, The United States left the Bretton-Woods agreement and put the dollar at a floating exchange rate. This led to decrease in the real oil revenues of OPEC countries. From then on, these countries indexed oil prices at gold and cut production. This caused high oil prices in oil importing countries, collapse of the monetary system, and fluctuation in international goods prices. There there was an embargo on countries with a a Pro-Israel stance due to Pro-Israel stance in the Arab-Israeli wars. The embargo led to the energy crisis and the subsequent collapse of the New York Stock Exchange. While the oil-importing industrialized countries dragging a crisis, the oil exporting Arab countries deposited 70% of their oil export revenue in the U.S., European and Japanese banks. Increased bank reserves in the developed countries caused a debt crippling trade in developing countries due to oil crisis. In 1978, the third oil shock once again raised the oil price. There were fluctuations in money and the real estate sector, where profits descreased. Financial abundance increased thanks to hedge funds in the financial market. This created fragilility in the financial markets. These emerging imbalances caused current account deficit and rising inflation. To tackle these problems,the U.S. raised excessive interest rates. Developing countries could not sustain principal debt and interest obligations because of the 70% interest rate, Developing countries had variable rate interest.

The increased borrowing needs of many developing countires (particularly Latin American countries) decreased the ability to pay back their debts. In the second half of the 1970s, debtor countries paid interest expense via 10% of export incomes. In 1974-79 interest rates rose from 18% to 30% and became 51.5% in 1982. Mexico declared a moratorium in 1982.Then, 34 developing countries became insolvent because of developed countries cutting off financial flows to developing countries. The protectionist policies of the developed countries did not allow developing countries to increase their exports, which would have allowed them to pay their depts and reduce their financing needs. At commercial banks in developing countries there was an extraordinary expansion and exports of commercial debt ratio increased from 60% to 130% due to developing countries adopting foreign borrowing as a cheap method of financing. From 1975-1976, foreign borrowing was about 70% of the total current account deficit of developing countries. The original sin of the decision-makers in these countries and the lack of regulation caused the debt crisis in the 1980s and was a provocative factor for Asian and Russian crises. By financial assistance from international authorities, the crisis was terminated. (Bakırtaş and Tekinşen, 2004)

The OPEC crisis did not cause only the debt crisis of the developing countries. It also stopped the falling rate of profit in the real sector and to address financial markets. The technology crisis in the 2000s and actions of the Fed by cutting interest rates with hopes of stimulating the economy has deepened the crisisin financial markets further. The OPEC crisis was initiated by deregulation policies, which kept financial markets away from intervention and control. Some marketable securities assets without sufficient capital have evaluated the own risk and set their own capital requirements. In addition, subprime bank lending was removed from the balance sheets by securitizing them. 50% of subprime loans were securitized in 2001. Obligations collateralized debts were developed to reduce the risk of securitized mortgage loans and were introduced into the domestic and foreign markets. Risk diversification has led to risk going out of control and the increase of credit problems. Besides, rating agencies were misled and individuals were given higher safety rankings despite high-risk in financial markets.

Asian countries (especially China) bought bonds of developed countries, including the U.S., with a saving of 40% of GDP. This caused excess global liquidity. Abundance of global liquidity caused expansion of consumer credit and excessive rise in housing prices. Bank lending began in order to buy more credit in high-risk groups. This process was supported by the federal home ownership provider. Therefore, assets of banks in bad debts increased steadily.Eventually, bad debts turned into toxic assets. In the year 2000, hedge funds were $ 500 billion and had reached $ 2 trillion at the end of 2007. Likewise, derivative products amounted to between $20 trillion and 120 trillion dollars. (Bocutoglu, 2011)

The deepening of the crisis lead to an increase in unethical behavior. The first of these was a Ponzi scheme. MadBernard L. Madoff an owner of Madoff Investment Securities, Wall Street's sixth largest company, had a Ponzi scheme valued at $ 60 billion. Allen Stanford had a Ponzi scheme valued at $ 8 billion. Another example of unethical behavior was what took place with the counter derivatives. These bonds were bonds that carry a value above what was written. Banks did not use this paper for giving credit due to the fact that they could not know its real value. The result of these insecurities was narrowed loans and the credit crunch. These bonds became toxic assets and their value was $ 14 trillion. That is 44 times the total GDP of the United States and 10 times the total GDP of the world. (Kazgan, 2012)

All this negativity in financial markets in the spring of 2007 and the bankruptcies of major investment companies has created a crisis. The recession began in developed countries, including the USA with bankruptcies in the financial sector. Against the recession, tax deduction were undertaken in the USA by an act of economic stimulus in 2008. The $ 787 billion fiscal expansion was launched by The American Recovery and Reinvestment Act. Public spending increased by investment and subsidy applications. Large firms in the American economy such as General Motors, Chrysler and banks have recovered due to rescue packages. After the U.S., Britain was the next country that implemented deregulation policies and had done so since the days of Margaret Thatcher. Bankrupt banks were nationalized in the UK and were insured against toxic capital assets. Other European countries have applied expansionary policies and nationalization. Japan has applied interest rate cuts and support programs for the real sector. (Kazgan, 2012)

One of the EU countries most affected by the crisis is Greece, since it could not reduce public spending or increase public revenue. Ireland entered into the great recession with a real estate sector crisis. Lack of regulatory and supervisory mechanisms in the Irish banking sector was another cause of the crisis. The Irish government was forced to request additional EU-IMF aid despite the 45 billion Euros supplied to banks internally. Portugal is another country experiencing a crisis. In 2009, the budget deficit was 288.5%. An EU-IMF rescue package was also given to Portugal. Similarly, Spain and Cyprus were also in a debt crisis. The EU has put mechanisms in place in the face of events and gave financial support to Hungary, Latvia, Romania, and Portugal, Germany, France, Italy, Austria, Portugal, Romania, Spain, and Russia. (Bocutoglu, 2011)

The crisis impacted the labor market the most. The number of unemployed in the world has risen to 7 million in 2008, 27 million in 2009 and 212 million in 2010-11. An Employment Summit in Prague on 7 May 2009 was held for the avoidance of unemployment in the EU. Within the framework of the decisions taken, various tax cuts and subsidies were applied. In the same manner, OECD countries applied tax cuts and subsidies and, furthermore, gave job search assistance and counseling. (Erdönmez, 2009)

HOMO ECONOMICUS

When we examine the Great Depression, the Financial Crisis of 2008and 1980 debt crisis we find deregulation policies as one of the causes of the crisis. Especially for developing countries, there are two reasons for the policies of deregulation: First, market players put pressure on decision-makers to not apply deregulation policies. They especially do not want innovation-restrictive controls in the financial sector. The second reason is the influence of the uncontrolled free market approach starting with Adam Smith. According to this understanding, the invisible hand is the largest contributor to the home economics that will bring balance to the economy.The economy reaches an equilibrium while individuals try to maximize their profits and benefits. This theory does not explain the crisis since there are many dilemmas due to home economics. The first is that individuals may take high risk when they are using other people's money. In the Financial Crisis of 2008, of the 6845 "hedge" funds in the U.S., only 1471 had sunk to 21% in 2008, while others made a profit of 12% in the first 7 months of 2009. Fund managers had their own money in the hedge funds, which retained their values in contrast to the hedge funds, which performed poorly. This is because individuals are more careful in risk prediction when they use their own money in the game. However, there was not the same care for someone else's money. (Kazgan, 2012) In the debt crisis, decision-makers thought of cheap sources of finance through foreign debt and we're addicted. The reason for this was the same.

Another dilemma of Homo Economicus is that it cannot control the desire of winning after a certain point. Vernon Smith did a laboratory experiment on investors. The subjects were asked to exchange a bond, which was imaginary but the real value of which could be understood. Subjects began exchanging under the actual value but continued to increase the price of the bonds to a bubble, which eventually burst. Subjects were asked to process on bond a second time. Even if they knew the outcome of a previous experiment, the balloon was inflated and blown again. Just this once, they increased the speed of business andthe balloon exploded in a shorter time. In the third experiment, a number of participants did not repeat the mistakes while others continued the error. (Kazgan, 2012) Before the Great Depression,people bought bonds with the bank deposits and all their assets. However, in the Financial Crisis of 2008 people became Ponzi debtors and players of Ponzi schemes.

Another dilemma of home economics is unethical behavior. We have seen these behaviors in the Ponzi scheme, playing with the national figure of some EU countries, in which ratings agency gave wrong ratings. Adam Smith claims that Homo Economicus does not avoid unethical behavior in fear of condemnation in society. The player of Ponzi schemes, Bernard Madoff, is Jewish and had a respectable place in the Jewish community. In the Jewish community to deceive Jew is reason to be excluded from the community. Nevertheless, Madoff also deceived people from his own community.

Another dilemma of Homo Economicus is everyone cannot equally act rationally. For example, according to renowned investor George Soros, prices of financial instruments are not true any time prices are at either excessive or deficient levels. He founded the Quantum Fund in 1969 for proving this theory. He found an increase from $ 10,000 to $ 4 million until 2000. This is a capacity for predictiveability.But not everyone has this ability. Soros also used his ability in the 1992 economic crisis in Britain and was the sole reason for 1/3rd of the total losses in the crisis. Another reason that individuals do not behave rationally is social structure. Samuel Bowles and Herbert Gintis have proven this in their experiments. They worked with people from different communities by playing the ultimatum game.

"In the ultimatum game, under conditions of anonymity, two players are shown a sum of money, say $10. One of the players, called the "proposer," is instructed to offer any number of dollars, from $1 to $10, to the second player, who is called the "responder." The proposer can make only one offer. The responder, again under conditions of anonymity, can either accept or reject this offer.

If the responder accepts the offer, the money is shared accordingly. If the responder rejects the offer, both players receive nothing. Since the game is played only once and the players do not know each other's identity, a self-regarding responder will accept any positive amount of money. Knowing this, a self-regarding proposer will offer the minimum possible amount, $1, and this will be accepted. However, when actually played, the self-regarding outcome is never attained and never even approximated." (Bowle&Gintis, 2004)

In Ghana and in AU socitey, to accept an expensive gift means to accept that the receiver is inferior. If a person accepts the expensive gift she/he declares that he accepts the superiority of the giver. For this reason, a high offer is never accepted in games of this society. Among the whale hunting Lamalera, 63% of the proposers in the ultimatum game divided the pie equally, and most of those who did not, offered more than 50%. This is because whale hunting is done all together and the hunted whale is shared equally in this society.

SOLUTIONS AND RECOMMENDATIONS

It is not possible to prevent the faults of the Homo Economicus by thoroughly annihilating it. Individuals giving up their liberties by making their own economic decisions and transfering it to a dominant power will not remove Homo Economicus. The desire to earn more, one of the main human instincts, will always be present. That is why the dominant power which has grasped the individuals' decision making right in their hand, will sooner or later use this power to maximize its own interests. Thus, the socialist state established in the USSR and Eastern Block was criticized by some intellectuals such as Rose Luxemburg and Trotsky, after the Leninist period. It was claimed that the socialist state led by Lenin was transformed to an oligarchy by the ruling class (nomenclature) or to a corrupt labor state. On the other hand, even if the individuals' desire to earn more were possible to be removed exactly, it would not be efficient. As is known, Malthus, in his book "Study on Population Growth" which he first published in 1789 and then revised and republished in 1803, asserted that population grows in a geometric progression (2,4,8,16,32,64,..) and food materials grow in arithmetical progression (1,2,3,4,5,6...).So humankind would suffer misery approximately 50 years later. But this prophecy of Malthus did not come true. The reason of this is that people developed new production technologies with the desire to earn more with them.

Both extreme and non existant Homo Economicus will lead to ineffectiveness. The Zoon Politikon and the moderate person is a virtuous person. The midpoint of the two extreme bad behaviors is a virtue. For example, finding the middle point between being a coward or being brave to an aggressive level is a virtue. In the same way, a person neither should refrain from profit nor behave unethically while making profits. The tendency to seek maximum advantage of Homo economics should be limited in such a way as to remain within ethical boundaries. The person who Aristotle called Zoon Politikon, and NasiruddinTusi and Kınalızade Ali Efendi called the 'moderate human' is the solution of the problem that originates with the homo economicus.

Finding the virtuous middle economical way is done by restricting the homo economicus by laws. Laws are financial rules and monetary policy choices. Financial rules restrict budget deficits, total or net public debts, some expenditures and tax load. The regulations of these principles are adopted in the constitution. E.g. Knut Wicksell worked on public expenditures. For him, all rises in public expenditures should be met by taxes and be subject to the approval of the legislative organ. Another rule which is prescribed in the constitution is that tax income should be specified at the rate of GSYIH or GSMH. Also, maximum tax rates can be specified in the constitution. Another suggestion is that generality principle should be put in the constitution. An allocation principle in order to prevent misuse of tax is another suggestion. Another constitutional tax principle was adopted by G. Brennan and J.M. Buchanan. They set forth that the equal tax rates should be applied to all citizens and these taxes should be specified in the constitution. Not only tax rates but also tax subjects should be specified in the constitution. This financial rule began to be applied in many countries after the debt crisis in 1970. Several financial rules are applied in the USA, Japan, Canada, Latin America and EU countries.

Another application discussed after the 1970s is Tobin tax. This tax, which targets short-term capital movements, intends to prevent the instability which can be raised from the speculative movements and fluctuations in exchange. This low-rate and tariff-decreasing tax is supposed to not affect the direct capital investments and transactions related to merchandise trade. The Tobin tax came to the fore in many countries after being applied in France, Chile, Brazil and Malaysia after big recessions. Another application regarding monetary policies is the Taylor rule. In this rule, the short-term lending rate of the central bank should be changed in the same direction as the difference between actual GDP and potential GDP(the difference between actual inflation and potential inflation). M. Friedman defended the view that central banks should pursue a monetary expanding policy at the rate of economic growth. He wanted to put the principle of increasing the money supply at the rate of 3-5% every year in the constitution. In literature, another monetary policy option is optimal money area. According to this theory, regions in which a single monetary unit is used (and so a common monetary policy are applied) must be created. In this way, national currencies will be prevented from excessively gaining value and crises based on currency speculations will be avoided.

FUTURE RESEARCH DIRECTIONS

Economic stability issues were approached from different angles and a solution was sought. Mostly, the internal dynamics of the economy and state intervention have been questioned. But for us, there are people at the basis of the problem. Scientists must think holistically. In the future, social psychologists, behavioral scientists, sociologists, lawyers and economists can resolve these ancient problems by creating a collective perspective.

CONCLUSION

In conclusion, we see that when we analyze the reasons for the three big global crises and the ways to overcome crisis, the reason for the crisis is the unethical and irrational behavior of homo economicus. That is why Homo Economicus has to be encouraged to stay at a point at which it cannot display such harmful behavior and should be made to obey constitutional fiscal and monetary rules.

REFERENCES

Açıkgöz, Ö., & Bülent, Ö. (2009). *1929 Dünya Ekonomik Buhranı ve Türkiye Ekonomisine Etkileri*. Turkey: Mevzuat Dergisi.

Aktan, C. C. (2008). *Yeni İktisat Okulları*. Ankara, Turkey: SeçkinYayınevi.

Avrupa Birliği Genel Sekreterliği. (2011). Avrupa Birliği'nde Küresel Finansal Krize Karşı Alınan Önlemler ve Birliğin Rekabet Gücünün Arttırılmasına Yönelik Girişimler. In *Euro RekabetPaktı*. Ankara, Turkey: Avrupa Birliği Genel Sekreterliği Yayınları.

Bakırtaş, İ., & Tekinşen, A. (2004). Dünya Savaşları ve Büyük Buhran Arasındaki Etkileşimin Ekonomik Politiği. Ankara, Turkey: Palme Yayıncılık.

Bocutoğlu, E. (2011). *Krizin Makro İktisadından Makro İktisadın Krizine: Eleştirel bir Değerlendirme*. Ankara, Turkey: Turk Ekonomi Kurumu.

Bowles, S., & Gintis, H. (2006). Homo economicus and zoon politikon:Behavioral game theory and political behavior. In R. E. Goodin & C. Tilly (Eds.), *The Oxford handbook of contextual political analysis*. Oxford, UK: Oxford University Press.

Duman, K. (2004). *Finansal Krizlere Karşı Politika Tercihleri*. Antalya, Turkey: Akdeniz İktisadi ve İdari Bilimler Fakültesi Yayınları.

Erdönmez, P. A. (2009). *Küresel Kriz ve Ülkeler Tarafından Alınan Önlemler Kronolojisi*. İstanbul, Turkey: Bankacılar Dergisi.

Erim, N. (2007). *İktisadi Düşünce Tarihi*. Ankara, Turkey: Palme Yayıncılık.

Kazgan, G. (2002). *Küreselleşme ve Ulus-Devlet Yeni Ekonomik Düzen*. İstanbul, Turkey: İstanbul Bilgi Üniversitesi Yayınları.

Kazgan, G. (2012). *2008 Küresel Krizi: Nedenleri, Etik Ilkeleri ve Iktisat Eğitimi*. Ankara, Turkey: Turkish Economic Association.

Telatar, F. (2004). *Politik İktisat Politikası*. Ankara, Turkey: İmaj Yayınevi.

World Development Report. (1984). World Bank.

KEY TERMS AND DEFINITIONS

Constitutional Fiscal Rules: Government's fiscal policy decisions and practices are limited by constitutional rules.

Constitutional Monetary Rules: Government's monetary policy decisions and practices are limited by constitutional rules.

Economic Crisis: Shocking economic events that occur suddenly, adversely affectin both the state and companies.

Homo Economicus: She/he is a human that behaves rationally and selfish, has a desire forbenefit maximization

Moderate Human: She/he is an ethical person that does not prefer excessive or insufficient belief, chooses the middle way. This term was used by Islamic philosophers

Zoon Politikon: She/he is an ethical person that does not prefer excessive or insufficient lifestyle, chooses the middle way. This term was used by Aristotle.

Chapter 13
Fiscal Paradises and G-20 as a Global Decision Maker

Alper Dogan
Izmir Katip Celebi University, Turkey

ABSTRACT

Fiscal Paradises are described as the "dark side of globalization" because of the negative role they have been playing in the global economy. Today, they are an extremely important reason of tax evasion and tax avoidance, financial instability, money laundering, terrorist finance, and other issues. Recent actions by G-20 have focused on fiscal paradise countries, targeting tax evasion and avoidance issues, because of the fact that the economic crisis in 2008 has showed the destructive influence of fiscal paradises in the economy not only on national but also on international level. The following year, in 2009, struggling with the fiscal paradises was the main focus of the G-20 London Summit. In addition, the following four G-20 summits refined the issue concern in fiscal paradises. This chapter aims to explain what has been achieved regarding the fiscal paradise problems at G-20 summits since the economic crisis of 2008.

INTRODUCTION

It's all the more suprising because nobody has yet offered a description of 'tax haven' on which everyone can agree (Palan, Murphy, Chavagneux, 2010). The IMF, the OECD and the other international agencies tend to adopt the language they think acceptable to their own area. The term 'tax haven' is clear meaning, as the French translation (paradis fiscal) makes more clear. "Offshore" also point to island paradises, but for example Switzerland, Liechtenstein not close to even seasides.. We use "Fiscal Paradises" in this study for description of the places concern in.

Globalisation is designing new tasks hard to cope with in tax policy. Harmful fiscal competiton between govenments carries negative outcomes like distorting trade and investment and can cause to erosion of national tax bases. Govenments support in a powerful manner the OECD to actively follow its work in this area, aimed at developing a multilateral approach under which goverments

DOI: 10.4018/978-1-4666-7308-3.ch013

can manage individually and collectively to limit the increasing of these harmful tax practices. In addittion govenment are going to follow in a close manner the progress by the OECD, that is because of produce a report in 1998' (regards to G7 summit in Lyon 1996). Actually, this was agreed decision from the OECD ministers had taken in May 1996 (OECD, 1998).

Fiscal paradise countries, become a specialist on attracting financial action and investment from other countries, so mainly catching use of less tax rates, and weak regulation (Palan, Murphy, Chavagneux, 2010). International integrations such as International Monetary Fund (IMF), Organisation for Economic Cooperation and Development (OECD), G-7 (G-20), and national governments examing that countries since about 15 years. For reason that they play a negative function on global economy on the other hand related to financial instability, money laundering, terrorist finance, and tax evasion.

Fiscal paradises allow multinational enterprises (MNEs) to shift profits out of high tax jurisdictions into low tax jurisdictions most commonly via transfer pricing (Eden, 2009). The issue of corporate tax avoidance is popular on the political platforms. Last media news regarding the tax affairs of some of the world's most famous MNEs such as Amazon, Apple, Google and Starbucks have made much hostility from civil society, non-governmental organisations (NGOs) and the general public. Arround 21 to $32 trillion has been invested virtually tax-free through the world's more than 80 offshore secrecy jurisdictions estimated by The Tax Justice Network. In June 2012 the G20[1] explicitly referred to "the need to prevent base erosion and profit shifting" (OECD, 2013). Most important advantages of MNEs financial strategy is regard to its tax issues, by nature its transfer pricing activities. MNEs pay lower corporate income taxes by means of transfer pricing. Working with fiscal paradises lets corporates to use useful plans for tax avoidance for them. Such kind of activities could be used by management to develope a competitive advantage by international differences in the tax rates so that diminish corporate tax costs compare with single country firms (Oxelheim, 1998).

Governments lose income tax not only on individual tax level both also corporate tax level on revenue by rotating of income and profits to fiscal paradise countries. The revenue losses of governments from this tax evasion are difficult to caluculate, and there is no proper estimation method yet. Though its easy to say tax evasion on the international area may crop up by international companies and rich investors nevertheless this arise can brings both legal and illegal actions as a consequence.

Results of an ampiric study suggest that high home country corporate tax rates will drive firms offshore. Also, high technology MNEs from both the manufacturing and services sector have a real tendency to do this activity. Furthermore, there is important country heterogeneity with MNEs from the liberal market economies showing a greater tendency to do so (Jones&Temouri, 2014).

WHERE FISCAL PARADISES ARE LOCATED?

OECD prepared a report in 1998 regards to against special tax regimes and multinational cooperations in OECD member countries. According to this report, main reasons of fiscal paradises are lack of transparency, lack of detailed information exchange, no sufficient activities. A blacklist and a list of enforcement against fiscal paradises explained in this report. Tiny fiscal paradises in the Caribbean and Pasific had lobbied to large extend in a successful manner by Anglo-Saxon side of the world, by means of that increase of development regarding to this situation in the OECD made a strong barrier in front of their financial centres. Same approach supported by USA, after Presiden

G. W. Bush came into power in 2001. Moreover OECD began to make pressure on two fiscal paradises countries, Luxemburg and Switzerland. Also this kind of fiscal activities removed from target jurisdiction. Sanctions on international platform also dropped to end of the list. Since OECD select his operation in the direction of Global Forum on Transparency and Exchange of Information. Member and non-member countries (Switzerland, Luxemburg etc.) discussed on fair sharing in a sensitive way (Sharman, 2006). Despite more fiscal paradises revealed by OECD then, realization of specifications are inadequate.

The reality is that there are at least four primary uses for 'fiscal paradise' locations (Murphy, 2008):

- First, they are used by those wishing to avoid or evade their obligation to pay tax. Tax avoidance is legal, but outside the spirit of taxation law, while tax evasion is always an illegal activity involving the non-disclosure of a source of income to a taxation authority that has a legal right to know about it.
- Second, they are used to hide criminal activities from view. That criminal activity may be tax evasion itself, but may also be money-laundering or crimes creating cash that needs to be laundered – theft, fraud, corruption, insider dealing, piracy, financing of terrorism, drug trafficking, human trafficking, counterfeiting, bribery and extortion etc.
- Third, they are used by those who want their activities to be anonymous, even if they are entirely legitimate. Some people wish to keep secret their wealth from their spouses, for example; others may want to conduct trade which, though legitimate, might risk their reputation.
- Fourth, they are used by those searching somewhere less expensive to do business; in these locations they can usually let the costly obligation to comply with legal regulations that would apply if the transaction concern in were undertaken.

REASON OF FINANCIAL CRISES: FISCAL PARADISES

Concern in financial problematic events in 2008 and 2009 years public debts and budgetary deficits are followed more tentyfly at global level, after increasing effectively in volume, in the time of the financial crisis and the recession, based on increase of the expenses and diminish of the budgetary incomes (Dobreschu, Pociovalisteanu, 2011). In the same years French and German goverments get angry to fiscal paradises in Europe like Switzerland and Liechtenstein due to their harmful financial institutions. All over the world

Table 1. Countries listed on various fiscal paradises lists

Caribbean/West Indies: Anguilla, Antigua and Barbuda, Aruba, Bahamas, Barbados, British Virgin Islands, Cayman Islands, Dominica, Grenada, Montserrat, Netherlands Antilles, St. Kitts and Nevis, St. Lucia, St. Vincent and Grenadines, Turks and Caicos, U.S. Virgin Islands
Central America: Belize, Costa Rica, Panama
Coast of East Asia: Hong Kong, Macau, Singapore
Europe/Mediterranean: Andorra, Channel Islands (Guernsey and Jersey), Cyprus, Gibralter, Isle of Man, Ireland, Liechtenstein, Luxembourg, Malta, Monaco, San Marino, Switzerlanda
Indian Ocean: Maldives, Mauritius, Seychellesa
Middle East: Bahrain, Jordan, Lebanona
North Atlantic: Bermudae
Pacific, South Pacific: Cook Islands, Marshall Islands, Samoa, Nauru, Niue, Tonga, Vanuatu

Source: United States Government Accountability Office. (2008). Report to Congressional Requesters, Retrieved June 19, 2014, from http://www.gao.gov/new.items/d09157.pdf

funds flow these countries without paying taxes to their origin countries. After Obama became into power, USA government also changed its manner against fiscal paradises aswell. For sure financal crises incriesed the pressure on fiscal paradises at the same time too. Fiscal paradises described as one of the main reason of the crises. On the international platform, their weak regulations make possible the roaming of risky financial products as black money and hard to caluculate to size of these funds. Govenments are all enhusiastic to recover tax revenue from fiscal paradises funds.

Actually, recent development regards to fighting with fiscal paradises began in a meeting in Paris, organised by Germany and France in 2008. 17 countries goverments attended the meeting. Main thema of the meeting was fiscal paradises. OECD policy against fiscal paradises goes so slow and fiscal paradises are al resist against the OECD implications (Kubosova, 2008). Same year in at the first G20 summit by presidency of G. Bush, underlined that lack of transperancy and inadeque information exchange is main barriers in front of fighting with fiscal paradises (G20, 2008).

Then G20 has put the issue of fiscal paradises to top of the political agenda on international platform is the conclusion of several developments. Firstly the G20 initiative reflects that the financial crisis and the global recession which began in 2008 has placed a huge burden on goverment finances, so that efforts to crowd back tax evasion and collect revenue are necessary. At the same time, fiscal paradises are seen like a main actor by allowing financial institutions to run away financial regulation and supervision. Transparency in taxation and regulation are widely considered as mutually reinforcing. Secondly a debate continues concern in implications of international tax competition for goverment finances. The beginning point was a report by OECD in 1998, its argued that certain forms of tax competition are harmful for global economy as a whole due to they undermine goverment finances. Cases where countries seem to invite investors by offering bank secrecy and protection against information exchange in tax matters (maybe its about harmful tax competition). For support the exchange of tax information between OECD countries o forum created. "Global Forun on Transperancy and Exchange of Information for the Tax Purposes" is the name of the forum. Its giving info not only OECD member countries but also non-member countries too. Its role is to provide a framework for global cooperation in the issue of information exchange concern in tax issue. Many fiscal paradises have reacted to this political pressure by changing their policies concern in bank secrecy and information exchange (Bilicka&Fuest, 2012).

LEADERSHIP OF G20

In 2009 G20 summit in London also focused on fiscal paradises too. Two biggest power of G20, Germany and France sustained their pressure concern in fighting with fiscal paradises. Althought a fiscal paradises in their territories as Isle of Man, British governmet also started to move together with Germany and France after 2008 (BBC, 2008). At the same year USA increased their fight with Swiss Banks which has accounts belong to US taxpayers to large extent. But in this summit European fiscal paradiese Switzerland, Monaco, Liechtenstein and Luxemburg declared that they would obey the standards of OECD concern in transparency, information exchange (Willis 2009). European fiscal paradises not want to be in a new punishment list as Black List and thats why they would obey the standards of OECD then.

G20 leaders had an agreement to create a new system in the global financial system. The financing package of 1.1 trillion $ to support commercial global flows was voted by leaders of the world that are present in the London, at G20 summit. The British Prime Minister Gordon Brown stated that G20 leaders had an agreement to enforce legislation linked to investment funds, fiscal paradises and to strictly settle the global financial system (Dobreschu, Pociovalisteanu, 2011).

At the end of G20 summit in London, US president B. Obama stated that the obtained agreement represents "a turning point in our effort to realize a recovery of global economy". Obama made these explanations after the G20's leaders declared an crucial plan for the activation of the world economy, including the fortification of the legislation concern in investment funds and fiscal paradise, also more strict settlement of the financial international system. Among the most important ideas of the leader from the White House have been: the G20 agreement representing a turning point in the effort of member countries to notice a recovery of the international economy; to prevent causing a worse crisis, it was planned the increase the transparency and protection of the capital of financial institutions from member countries; in life there ais no warranty, and there are always risks. And the measures taken are sufficient to prevent an economic depression. If are sufficient, we should wait and see. In 2-3 years we will look back and we will see if these decisions are fruitful. It is very important to be aware of the crisis. Generally, it was a constructive approach from all the leaders (Dobreschu, Pociovalisteanu, 2011).

In London Summit, OECD standards explained followingly (OECD: 2010):

- Exchange of information on request where it is "foreseeably relevant" to administration and enforcement of the domestic laws of the treaty partner.
- No restrictions on exchange caused by bank secrecy or domestic tax interst requiremnts.
- Availability of reliable information and powers to obtain it.
- Respect for taxpayer's rights.
- Strict confidentiality of information exchanged.

G20 countries decided to take a synchronized action against fiscal paradises and non-cooperative jurisdictions (G20 2009a). They created a toolkit for possible situations (G20 2009b):

- Increased disclosure requirements on the part of taxpayers and financial institutions to report transactions involving non-cooperative jurisdictions;
- Witholding taxes in respect of wide variety of payments;
- Deniying deductions in respect of expense payments to payees resident in non-cooperative jurisdictions;
- Reviewing tax treaty policy;
- Asking international institutions and regional development banks to review their investment policies;
- Giving extra weight to the principles of tax transperancy and information exchange when designing bilateral aid programs.

As well three list prepared by the G20 that contained all countries in the world. First list, named as white list containes countries that agreed tax standards of the OECD. This white list countries exchanging information without bank secrecy, respecting taxpayer's right concern in all financial activities according to OECD standards. Most of the OECD countries are in white list. Second list, named as grey list containes countries that have accepted OECD's tax standards but not implemented yet. Grey list has 30 fiscal paradises and 8 other financial centres such as Chilie, Singapore, Belgium, Luxembourg, Austria and Switzerland. Last list is named black list containes countries not commited to agreed tax standards of OECD, as Costa Rica, Malaysia, Philippines and Ururguay (OECD 2009a).

These three list cant move without goverments support. One of the biggest power in OECD, China is not enhusiastic to support these three list owing to countries that in its territory as Macau and Hong Kong in grey list . On the other hand The

EU members Austria, Luxemburg and Belgium are not supporter of these three list too but they allowed publication of these lists and this shows even though EU is member of the G20 formally, neverthless single member countries like Belgium for example are not power to change decisions aswell (Wintour, 2009, Luce, 2009, Mason, 2009).

WORK IN PROCESS

Acouple days after London summit, countries in black list accepted the standards (OECD, 2009b). This reaction shows the positive development of OECD's pressure on fiscal regulation. National juridistictions predict that if they not accept and obey the tax standards they could meet new negative fraction by OECD, because samples in Delaware, or Hong Kong shows posibilities.

An empty black list was a impressive result for G20 until 2009. 9 fiscal paradises and 5 financila centre was still in the grey list when Pittsburg summit 2009. Switzerland, Austria, Belgium nad Luxemburg moved in white list.

OECD's tax departmant head J. Owens, stated in 2010 that process moved from political stage to implementation stage (Houlder, 2010). So G20 was thinking that their duty is almost done. But bilateral agreements were able to create problems. Because its not reliable way to create a tax regime for information exchange only with 12 bilateral agreements, need more agreements for widespread tax regime (G8, 2009). Neverthless more problems concern in bilateral agreements can occure due to heavy procedures to caluculate request in spite of legal regulations and administrative obstructions. Besides OECD principles process hampered or impossible because of technical issues that are not detailed in bilateral agreements (Tax Justice Network, 2009). If G20/OECD succesfully adress the problems in next summits solutions can be find.

The G-20 and the OECD for promoting a Tax Information Exchange Agreement (TIEA) with limited effectiveness. The G-20 countries realized that the supporter countries of international tax evasion and aggressive tax avoidance wont change their political attitude easily. In addittion they notice that their own financial services industries are aggressive enablers of international tax evasion also accounting fraud and lots of other bad practices. The economic crisis and deep recession brought on by the abuses of the international financial industry have fostered a completely change in public economy toward that industry. Banks surely will become subject to new transparency regulations, and political pressure to prevent a repeat of past abuses is not going away. For the first time in world history, the opponents of fiscal paradises abuses have a real opportunity to foster important change (Mclntyre, 2009).

Due to all of these reasons aforementioned before a new better approach designed by an expert group as multilateral automatic information exchange. Automaticty is obviously more effective because it obliges all juridiction involved to collect important information in their borders, could bring cases of fraud to light of which tax autorities were not yet aware of and has therefore am major deterrrence effect. Thought avaiable technological means and regulatory know-how, this approach is technically is feasible not only develeped but also developing jurisdictions. Automatic information exchange for tax matters on multilateral basis is not all science-fiction: EU already applies it throught its Saving Directive among 24 of its member states (Tax Justice Network, 2009). It seems international information exchange regime will be more effective with such kind of serious measures.

CONCLUSION

The main measure established in the meetings of the G20 member states, reconfirmed at London during September 2009, was that banks should collect more money to increase the capital basis, a measure that is necessary to equilibrate their accountant balance sheets

G20 have done a great work regarding global political mood on tax avasion and bank secrecy. But information exchange mainly throught bilateral agreements that not may work. Their autority can chamge course whenever that appears necessary. Then the current way of commitments to the OECD standard and the rapid proliferation of bilateral agreements is to be considered as another important point in the right direction (Lesage, 2010).

First of all, by means of G20 commits Germany, France and OECD secretary had chance to express their politic concerns about fiscal paradises on the top of the global political agenda. By the way G20 commitments prepared an infrastructure about solving the fiscal paradises problem. Without G20 this would be much more harder or ineffectiveness. Second, the prospect of a G20 summits publishing blacklists and coordinating sanctions, had a major impact on fiscal paradises, which rapidly started to make commitments and negotiate bilateral agreements, in particular in the run-up to the London summit and the months that followed. Third, probably listing countries grey, black and white, threatening with sanctions, can more easily be undertaken by heads of state and government, in consultation with each other. For that reason the G20 summit again provides a suitable format. Fourth, the awareness that following and heavily mediatized summits of leaders will evaluate each step of the process, encourages all actors at the lower levels in the process to deliver. Fifth, this case shows again a interesting interplay between summitry and multilateral organizations such as the OECD. The G7/G8/G20 and the OECD have been closely cooperating for a very long time on taxation and many other issues. It seems difficult to ascertain, though, who is actually guiding whom with intellectual and entrepreneurial leadership. Is it the G-x that gives instructions to the OECD, or is it the OECD that precooks what the leaders have to say? In any case, it seems that there is a close symbiosis, with G- members and OECD secretariat simultaneously feeding the process with new ideas. Sixth, G20 summits is growth with politics power (Lesage, 2010).

Inexplicably, expert economists have almost entirely denied the issue of fiscal paradises. Small population of tax academics who have inspected them argue that fiscal paradises are useful (James R Hines). Anyway it is clear that fiscal paradises, by rejecting access to information, are an disorder in neoclassical economic theory bound to result in the misallocation of resources in a capitalism. To some in the market fiscal paradises are, needless to say, of enormous benefit. Those who have reach to them will, given the prices charged, be those with reach to important wealth. They diminish their effective tax rates by cloaking their tax avoidance and tax evasions in secrecy; their capital increases exponentially quicker than others' at the end; this reason is hidden from view and, as a result, does not attract comment. Undoubted tax paradises continue to survive (Murphy, 2011).

Today information exchange is far from complete but growing networks make tax evasion harder and costly compare with ten years ago.

REFERENCES

BBC. (2008). *Anger at darling island criticism*. Retrieved March 19, 2014, from http://news.bbc.co.uk/2/hi/europe/isle_of_man/7713258.stm

Bilicka, K., & Fuest, C. (2012). *With which countries do tax havens share information? EUI Working Paper, RCAS 2012/6*. Retrieved April 21, 2014, from http://cadmus.eui.eu/bitstream/handle/1814/20618/RSCAS_2012_06.pdf?sequence=1

Dobrescu, M. E., Pociovalistenau, D. M., & Brancusi, C. (n.d.). *One the slide of public deficiency and financial settlements.* Retrieved April 25, 2014, from http://www.ceeol.com/aspx/getdocument.aspx?logid=5&id=f34457f4-8d6d-402f-8ad0-8dc6ef971b30

Eden, L. (2009). Taxes, transfer pricing and the multinational enterprise. In A. M. Rugman (Ed.), *The Oxford handbook of international business* (2nd ed.). Oxford University Press. doi:10.1093/oxfordhb/9780199234257.003.0021

G20. (2008). *Declaration.* Summit on Financial Markets and the World Economy. Retrieved March 19, 2014, from http://www.g20.org/Documents/g20_summit_declaration.pdf

G7 Summit. (1996). *Economic communiqué: Making a success of globalization for the benefit of all, Lyon, 18.06.1996.* Retrieved March 30, 2014, from http://europa.eu/rapid/press-release_DOC-96-5_en.htm

Gravelle, J. (2013). *Tax havens: International tax avoidance and evasion, CRS report for congress.* Retrieved April 19, 2014, from https://www.fas.org/sgp/crs/misc/R40623.pdf

Hines, J. R. Jr. (2010, Fall). Treasure islands. *The Journal of Economic Perspectives, 24*(4), 103–126. doi:10.1257/jep.24.4.103

Houlder, V. (2010b). Tax haven drive will mean greater scrutiny. *Financial Times.* Retrieved March 20, 2014, from http://www.ft.com/cms/s/0/385490cc-336b-11df-bc32-00144feabdc0.html

Jones, C., & Temouri, Y. (2014). *FDI in tax havens: Do corporate tax rates matter?* Retrieved April 1, 2014, from http://www.etsg.org/ETSG2013/Papers/105.pdf

Kubosova, L. (2008). *EU states crack down on tax evasion.* Retrieved March 19, 2014, from http://euobserver.com/9/26976

Lesage, D. (2010). *The G20 and tax havens: Maintaining the momentum?* Retrieved March 30, 2014, from www.g20.utoronto.ca/biblio/lesage-tax-havens.pdf

Mclyntyre, J. M. (2009). *How to end the charade information exchange.* Tax Notes, Tax Analysists.

Murphy, R. (2008). *Creating turmoil, tax justice network.* Retrieved April 24, 2014, from http://www.taxresearch.org.uk/Documents/Creating-Turmoil.pdf

Murphy, R. (2011). Tax havens, secrecy jurisdictions and the breakdown of corporation tax. *Real-World Economics Review,* (57), 56-59. Retrieved April 20, 2014, from http://www.paecon.net/PAEReview/issue57/Murphy57.pdf

OECD. (1998). *Harmful tax competition: An emerging global issue.* Retrieved April 15, 2014, from http://www.oecd.org/tax/transparency/44430243.pdf

OECD. (2009a). *A progress report on the jurisdictions surveyed by the OECD Global Forum in implementing the internationally agreed tax standard: Progress made as at 2nd April 2009.* Retrieved March 20, 2014, from http://www.oecd.org/dataoecd/38/14/42497950.pdf

OECD. (2009b). *Four more countries commit to OECD tax standards.* Retrieved March 20, 2014, from http://www.oecd.org/document/0/0,3343,en_2649_33767_42521280_1_1_1_1,00.html

OECD. (2010). *Promoting transparency and exchange of information for tax purposes: A background information brief.* Retrieved Mach 20, 2014, from http://www.oecd.org/dataoecd/32/45/43757434.pdf

OECD. (2013). *Addressing base erosion and profit shifting.* Retrieved April 21, 2014, from http://www.oecd-ilibrary.org/

Oxelheim, L., Stonehill, A., Randøy, T., Vikkula, K., Dullum, K. B., & Mode'n, K.-M. (1998). *Corporate strategies to internationalise the cost of capital*. Copenhagen Business School Press.

Palan, R., Murphy, R., & Chavagneux, C. (2010). *Tax havens: How globalisation really works*. Ithaca, NY: Cornell University Press.

Sharman, J. C. (2006). *Havens in a storm: The struggle for global tax regulation*. Ithaca, NY: Cornell University Press.

Tax Justice Network. (2009). *Tax information exchange agreements: Tax justice briefing*. Retrieved March 16, 2014, from http://www.taxjustice.net/cms/upload/pdf/TJN_0903_Exchange_of_Info_Briefing_draft.pdf

United States Government Accountability Office. (2008). *Report to congressional requesters*. Retrieved June 19, 2014, from http://www.gao.gov/new.items/d09157.pdf

Willis, A. (2009). *Switzerland, Austria and Luxembourg relax banking secrecy*. Retrieved March 20, 2014, from http://euobserver.com/?aid=27775

KEY TERMS AND DEFINITIONS

Financial Crises: A situation in which the value of financial institutions or assets drops rapidly. It can hit a single sector of an economy and not necessarily affect the other sectors.

Fiscal Paradises: A country, state or territory that offers foreign individuals and businesses low rate tax or no tax liability in stable environment concern in politically and economically.

Harmful Tax Practice: An activity to diminishes global welfare andundermines taxpayer confidence in the integrity of tax systems.

Money Laundering: Is the process of concealing the source of illegally gotten money.

Tax Avoidance: The practice of diminishing tax liabilities to a minimum by legal means.

Tax Evasion: An illegal activity to lower or avoid the taxes that one owes.

Tax Information Exchange Agreement: A type of an agreement developed by OECD Global Forum Working Group on Effective Exchange of Information to promote international co-operation in criminal or civil tax matters under investigation through exchange of information.

Transfer Pricing: Is the main device for corporate tax avoidance. While unrealistic transfer prices do not affect the overall enterprise directly, they become a concern when they are misused to lower profits in a division of an enterprise that is located in a country that levies high taxes and raise profits in a country that is a fiscal paradises that levies no or low taxes.

ENDNOTES

1 The G20 refers to the group of 20 leading industrialized countries: the United States, the United Kingdom, France, Italy, Canada, Germany, Japan, Russia, Australia, Saudi Arabia, India, South Africa, Turkey, Argentina, Brazil, Mexico, China, Indonesia, South Korea and EU.

Chapter 14

From Keynes's Proposition to the Robin Hood Tax:

Historical Development and the Current Situation of the Financial Transaction Taxes

Abdülkadir Işık
Namık Kemal University, Turkey

Özge Selvi Yavuz
Namık Kemal University, Turkey

Gamze Yıldız Şeren
Namık Kemal University, Turkey

Davuthan Günaydın
Namık Kemal University, Turkey

ABSTRACT

Along with the overthrow of the Bretton Woods system in the early 1970s, financial liberalization process started to be active in the whole world. The developing countries joined in the process by removing the obstacles on the capital flows in the 1980s. However, this process triggered subsequent crises and had destructive effects in these countries. Accordingly, the thought of excising the speculative capital movements, which were developed by J. Tobin through taking the idea of excising of security transactions of J.M. Keynes, came forward again. Then the feasible alternatives as two-staged Tobin tax of P.B. Spahn were suggested. After 2008 financial crisis, an implementation of financial transactions tax that has been drafted to be implemented across the EU has been brought to the agenda. In this chapter, it is aimed to discuss financial transaction taxes in the context of the European Union and Turkey from a historical view.

INTRODUCTION

Although a new world order has been established with Bretton Woods system, financial liberalization process has influenced all markets after that system collapsed. While it is hoped that, with financial liberalization policies, economic growth would be ensured in developing countries by providing desired savings, these policies proved to be a failure in 1990s. The removal of obstacles affecting the capital has made way for speculative movements and spurts of short-term speculative movements resulted in financial crises in developing countries which liberated their "shallow" markets. At this specific point, Tobin Tax, proposed by Nobel-awarded economist James Tobin in year 1912 but which didn't attract much attention especially if we consider that the trad-

DOI: 10.4018/978-1-4666-7308-3.ch014

ing volume in the markets back then was not as high as it was in 1990s, has become a subject of discussion because the main actor in crises was speculative short term capital movements. Tobin has been followed by Spahn's proposition and Robin Hood Tax which maintains its popularity specifically in today's world.

When it is looked from today's window, world markets experienced shocks with 2008 Global crisis. The crisis which has originated from US financial sector has inflicted immense damage specifically on European economies. Thus, the hazards of capital movements which we thought we left in 90s led economic authorities to look for new solutions. Although EU submitted a proposal regarding the implementation of a financial transactions tax within this area in 28 September 2011 in a period where neoliberal understanding is questioned 11 of member states established an "Empowered Cooperation" and accepted the implementation of FTT (Financial Transaction Tax) after no unanimity was achieved in ECOFIN Council.

The purpose of this paper is to evaluate financial transaction taxes by also considering its historical development. In this context, in the first section of this paper we will examine the process necessitating the financial transaction taxes; consider financial transaction taxes from a historical perspective in the second section, and in the last section we will evaluate the financial transaction taxes implemented in Turkey and EU.

THE PROCESS NECESSITATING THROWING SOME SAND IN THE WELL-LUBRICATED WHEELS: FINANCIAL LIBERALIZATION AND CRISES

Since 1960's, while the replacement of fixed rate syste00m with floating rate system and liberalization of financial markets have been the primary factor of financial globalization, electronic communication have been the secondary factor in this process. With these developments, transaction processes in financial markets accelerated but the global financial bubble was followed by many macroeconomic imbalances and dramatic increases in financial crises. Floating rate and the liberalization of financial markets which yield negative results also disproved the prediction of economists who promote these policies (Felix, 1995).

The globalization of financial markets deeply affected bank loans, deposits, assets, debts, securities and physical capital but, when compared with others, the globalization of assets and debts was achieved much easier. After all, with the revolution in communication performing these transactions has become easier, faster and cheaper. The only obstruction standing before financial transactions is national regulations. After all countries were liberalized step by step, no obstacles stood before international financial flows (Tobin, 2000). These flows can be not only an instrument to channel savings of developed capitalist democracies into developing regions such as Asia, Africa, Latin America as productive capital investments but it also cause financial crises, depression, recession, or unemployment (Tobin, 2000).

20th century was a period which was not supported by gold or a similar real asset and where exchange value of national currency had a nominal size. Indeterminacy in the terms of exchange of national currencies encourages speculative earnings and lead financial capital flow to be stimulated independent from real production world. However, capital flows transformed national markets into areas of speculative interest and caused instabilities. After all, the hot money attracted by relatively high interest rate provided foreign exchange accumulation and therefore overvalued national currency and created current deficit by causing recession in export and decrease in prices of imported goods. Disruption of balances between real interest and exchange lead to collapses (Yeldan, 2011).

The justification regarding the internationalization of asset markets is to facilitate the movement of productive capital in rich and developed economies towards poor developing countries. However, the matter here is the net flow of the capital rather than the gross volume of transactions (Tobin, 2000).

In this context, 1990s became a decade of international financial discrepancies. The process started in Europe in 1992, followed by Mexico in 1994-1995 and Eastern Asia in 1997-1998 and peaked with Russia and Brazil in 1998 (Tobin, 2000).

In the early 90s, countries in Asia, Eastern Europe, Latin America, and some of the ex-soviet republics experienced fluctuations in capital flows. External factors such as interest rates and internal factors such as structural reforms were shown as the cause regarding the capital flows' movement into the developing market economies (Montieland&Reinhart, 2001). Despite these various causes brought forward, following the financial liberalization short term speculative flows have done destructive impacts on economies of developing countries.

After the consecutive financial crises occurred as an inevitable result of capital flows capital supervision, which was expected to reduce the risk of crisis, became a topic of discussion (Edwards, 2000). However if the saving deficit of developing countries is considered, it would be obvious that there is a need for foreign resources. In this case, it seems more rational to prevent the outflow of speculative capital. After the crises in 90s, the idea that a low rate tax obstructing the capital outflow might be an effective deterrent, which was described as "throwing some sand to the well lubricated wheels" by Nobel-awarded economist James Tobin, became a topic of discussion.

At this point, Tobin questioned the ways to both preserve long term foreign investments and deter speculative flows (Tobin, 2000). Tobin proposed an international system to slow down the money flow without obstructing trade and productive investments. The small tax imposed on these foreign exchange transactions must be implemented with a common rate established by all countries. At this point, 3-tierfloating exchange rates slow down foreign capital entries; make them more expensive and lead to greater national dominance. Although this combination will not eliminate crises entirely, it will decrease its frequency, make them less costly, and reduce its impact (Tobin, 2000).

FINANCIAL TRANSACTION TAXES IN THE PAST AND TODAY

Several tax instruments are named generally as financial transaction tax. In a way, financial transaction tax is a general name for taxes acquired from instruments in question. Here, Matheson (2011) classified financial transaction taxes as follows; currency transaction tax, which is also called Tobin tax, is a securities tax imposed on currency transactions and derivatives. Another tax is Capital Levy which is imposed on loan/stock and bond issue increases. Bank Transaction Tax (BTT) is imposed on money withdrawals from savings or bank accounts and it is advalorem. Latin America and Asia used it frequently. The last one is Real Estate Transaction Tax imposed on the value of land or construction sales (Matheson, 2011).

Following the 2008 Global Crisis many proposals were made regarding Robin Hood tax or financial transaction taxes for banks. According to this, a tax with a rate of 0.05% to be collected from the total value of financial transactions include currency transactions, derivatives agreements, bonds and other financial assets (Daniels, 2010). Even though financial transaction taxes were discussed after 2008 Global crisis, its origin can be found in Keynes.

The idea behind financial transaction taxes goes back to J.M. Keynes. Keynes expressed that a transaction tax established in 1936 would empower stock market in long term against speculators short term behaviors. This proposal of Keynes is also applicable for exchange market. After all, speculators are interested in how markets react to the developments and not economic signs (Eichengreen, Tobin & Wyplosz, 1995). Thus excessive volatility would be reduced with a transaction tax and the market actors will tend towards long term investors and this would play a deterrent role over speculators. The main purpose of tax is to increase the autonomy of national monetary policies (Eichengreen, Tobin & Wyplosz, 199).

For Keynes' book "General Theory for Money, Interest, and Employment", James Tobin, in his presidency speech at American Economic Association, said: "The book that shapes the minds of economists of my generation" (Grossman, 1975). In this context James Tobin was influenced by Keynes' ideas and the taxation of short term currency transactions which he proposed in 1972 was based upon the Keynes' idea of transaction tax.

Tobin tax proposed by Nobel-awarded economist James Tobin; will throw sand to the wheels of global financial markets[11], and thus, with the famous statement of Keynes, ensure that "the dominance of speculation over enterprises shall be reduced" (Felix, 1995a.)

The characteristics of Tobin tax, which is imposed on exchange transactions, can be listed as such; the tax must be advalorem, must be implemented in one type, all payments made by residents must be collected and managed by the government, tax incomes must be deposited to a central fund controlled by IMF or World Bank

With a small tax imposed on exchange transactions Tobin aimed to punish short term speculators and not long term investors and the idea based on the establishment of market stability by deterring speculative movements. Since this proposal, financial transaction taxes has been continued to be discussed until today. While some people assert that the tax cannot be implemented others propose financial transaction taxes such as Robin Hood tax campaigns against big financial crises (Mcculloch&Pocillo, 2011).

According to Tobin, a low rate tax to be imposed on all currency transactions would be sufficient to make most of the daily transaction amount to be non-profitable. The decrease depends on the tax rates and estimated reactions of market actors. According to the experts, a tax of 0.25% will reduce the transaction volume at least by 1/3. Tobin's first suggestion regarding the rates is 1% (see: Tobin, 1978). At this point, 2/3 of the trade will move on (Wahl, 2005).

Spahn, asserted that high and/or varying tax rates must be implemented to prevent instability in exchange rates and advocated a two stage structure against exchange rate instability which disrupts the functioning of international financial markets (Spahn, 1996). In this context, Tobin's proposal was improved by Paul Bernd Spahn and proposed in 1995 with a version that is more suitable to today's market conditions. In this context, Spahn, in addition to the available tax, stated that there is need for a secondary tax with a much higher rate to be engaged against big speculative indications. Thus, the second stage of the tax will play a deterrent role where the low rate tax cannot affect speculative flows (Erdoğdu&Balseven, 2006).

Spahn's two stage Tobin tax includes; continually implemented low rate transaction tax, low standard rate of 0,2% for spot currency transactions, taxation of derivative transactions with the rate of 0.1% which is half of the standard rate, additional currency tax to be implemented in speculative periods (Patterson and Galliano,1998). The proposal of tax with varying rates may yield some unwanted results. One of these results is that in case where the tax affecting the market behaviors has no volatility it may lead to indeterminacy in the financial markets, which ultimately would disrupt the taxation. Another unwanted result is the additional encumbrance on tax payers and offices caused by varying tax rates (Stotsky, 1996).

Robin Hood, designed with the philosophy of collecting from the rich and handing it to the poor, follows the same logic. Although the tax had a go after Adoin Turner's speech and Brown's intervention towards G20 Ministers of Finance, it can be described as an outdated idea from various aspects. After all, Keynes proposed the first transaction tax in 1936 and Tobin proposed the currency transaction tax in 1973. What is relatively new is Financial Transaction Taxes being a topic of discussion after the rapid growth of derivatives market. As the IMF reported, various financial transaction taxes are implemented for the last 10 years at least by 16 countries of G20 economies (Robin Hood Tax). According the proponents who use the slogans "small change for banks, big change for people", "It's not tax on the people, tax for the people" the tax to be implemented can help the social security network throughout the USA and the world and the taxation of finance sector can be fairer. With a tax of less than half of 1% of Wall Street transactions millions of dollars can be saved in US each year. Thus, sufficient amount of investments can be made on education, health and climate change. This is a tax to be imposed on Wall Street Banks, hedge funds and other financial institutions causing big crises. And it will contribute to the limitation of speculations which threaten financial stability. According to the economists' estimation the income which can be established by financial transaction taxes with a rate of less than half of 1% is 350 billion dollars (Robin Hood Tax).

The income in the amount of billions of dollars acquired from financial sector by tax can stop austerity policies that obstruct public services and help global efforts against poverty, AIDS and other diseases, and climate change. In order to set these in motion, financial transaction taxes are the right way to go. The rate of Robin Hood tax, which is a small tax imposed on derivatives markets, bonds and currency transactions, varies around 0.005%-0.5% and a quite small percentage of trade value is collected as tax. The tax aims excessive banking activities and not savings and regular investors (Robin Hood Tax, (b)) with a tax to be collected in USA 9 million people can be employed, unemployment can be reduced by %60, more than 1.75 million pledged house can be saved, 41 million families can be provided with health services and an R&D budget can be established. And as a global effect, all the children can be placed into primary school with 6.5 billion dollar, a considerable progress can be made to resolve global AIDS crisis with 6 billion dollars, 1333 wind turbines can be provided with 2 billion dollars to establish clean energy (Robin Hood Tax (b)).

Robin Hood tax; is supported by 82% of German citizens and 72% of French citizens. Another reason why two-third of people in EU supports the tax is the agreement between 11 European countries, including Germany, France, Spain, and Italy, to impose a financial transaction tax with a rate of 0.01%-1% on stock, bond, and derivatives. Although the tax brought a lot of discussions along; it is possible with this tax to make the financial sector safer and channel the income towards reinvestments and public services. (The Robin Hood Tax Rides Forth, 2014).

Although efforts which will contribute to the human life to be carried out with the income acquired from Robin Hood tax receive some support, there are also some critiques.

- **Lack of International Coordination**: In order for the tax to be successful, the establishment of an international coordination is required. Otherwise, financial institutions may shift into areas where tax is not applied. In this context, the lack of coordination may lead to the emigration of institutions or transactions. Even though a union such as EU may establish coordination within, it would be difficult to coordinate with non-Member States (Daniels, 2010).

- **Deviations to Occur in Financial Markets:** Even this is implemented universally, taxed transactions would be punished in a way and the transaction volume would be reduced. (Daniels, 2010).
- **Income Problems:** According to CEPR, increase in transaction costs may reduce transactions by 35-50%. This situation also means reduction in taxes imposed on transactions (Daniels, 2010).
- **The Fact that it is Impossible to Both Regulate the Markets and Ensure Revenue:** Another critique is that it is not possible to both regulate markets and ensure revenue with financial transaction tax. However, just like tobacco or green taxes, they are quite viable. In addition to the stamp tax in UK, many financial transaction taxes are widely implemented around the world (The Robin Hood tax rides forth, 2014).

EVALUATION OF FINANCIAL TRANSACTION TAXES IN TURKEY AND EU CONTEXT

In this section financial transaction taxes practices was examined in Turkey and EU.

Financial Transaction Taxes in Turkey

Encumbrance on financial transactions in Turkey can be expressed as BITT (Banking and Insurance Transaction Tax) and RUSF (Resource Utilization Support Fund), which is acquired as a fund. Accordingly, BITT based on expenditure taxes law no 6902 and dated 23.07.1956 was in effect as a basic indirect tax law until VAT entered into force and as of 01.01.1985 most parts of the law was abolished and replaced with VAT. Transactions within the scope of VAT and which is subject to BITT exempted from VAT with a special provision. BITT; in addition to its aim to tax banking transactions and insurance transactions it has also defined persons engaged in certain transactions as bankers as well and some transactions subjected to BITT (Çakıcı&Ceylan, 2014).

The taxation of transactions regarding derivatives and some other capital market transactions with regard to banking and insurance transactions tax (BITT) (Expenditure Taxes General Notification with serial no 89) is defined in article 28 of Expenditure Tax Law no 6802 and dated 13/7/1956 which regulates the subject of bank and insurance transactions tax and the event incurring the tax: with the exemption of transactions performed as per Financial Leasing Law no. 3226 and dated 10/6/1985[2], all money received to their own name as a result of all transactions are subject to banking and insurance transaction tax. All money received in cash or through accounts by bankers related to the banking transactions and services are subject to banking transaction tax. Arbitrage transactions and options and transactions related to option agreements and money benefited as a result of these transactions are exempted from BITT. According to this:

- As of 1/9/1998, BITT rate regarding benefited money as a result of deposit transactions between banks is 1%.
- As of 1/5/2008 BITT rate regarding sales amount in currency transactions is zero.
- To be valid as of 2/9/1998, general BITT rate (for all other transactions the rate of which is set differently by cabinet decree) is 5%.

While a separate transaction tax other than VAT is implemented for all banking transaction in Turkey, in EU pure banking transactions are not taxed with VAT or other transaction tax. In this context, regarding financial transactions, transactions subject to BITT in Turkey and transactions exempted from VAT in EU directive are not in full correspondence. However, the regulations concerning the status of financial transactions with regard to VAT present similarities (Çakıcı &Ceylan, 2014).

RUSF, which can be described as another financial transaction tax, is imposed on transactions regarding loan and loan exports used both domestically and abroad by banks and finance companies. In this case, since there is no provision regarding VAT exemption, a transaction within the scope of RUSF and VAT is subject to both financial encumbrances (Çakıcı&Ceylan, 2014).

According to this, as per article 75, paragraph 2, item 7 and 12, 18% in drawing and call accounts and time deposit accounts with up to 6 month term, 15% in time deposit accounts with up to 1 year term, and 13% in time deposit accounts with more than 1 year term will be collected as Resource Utilization Support Fund from securities capital revenues; interests in exchange deposit accounts, and royalties paid for participation accounts in participation banks. The situation in deposit interests is as follows: There will be cutbacks with a rate of 15% in drawing and call accounts and time deposit accounts with up to 6 months term, 12% in time deposit accounts with up to 1 year term, and 10% time deposit accounts with more than 1 year term. In royalties paid as participation account charge in participation banks, there will be cutbacks with a rate of 15% in call and private current accounts and time deposit accounts with up to 6 months term, 12% in time deposit accounts with up to 1 year term, and 10% time deposit accounts with more than 1 year term[3]

Although taxes are collected from effective or currency transactions, stock trade income, loans acquired from foreign countries, there is no financial transaction tax implementation in a conventional sense (Güler, Keleş &Uçar, 2012).

According to the recent researchs, there are fewer fluctuations in the exchange markets of developed countries when compared to developing countries. In this context, when taken into account that the financial markets in Turkey is shallow, it will be clear that it would cause fluctuations in stock trade markets which would risk small investors and the stability of the market. Therefore transaction taxes are not sufficient on their own. When we consider that capital flows are mainly depend on short term flows serious measures must be taken against the speculative movements (Balseven, 2003). A tax similar to Tobin tax or Robin Hood tax should be taken into consideration.

Financial Transaction Taxes in EU

2008 Global crisis seriously affected EU economies and public finance and the finance sector has played an important role in the economic crisis. Both in Europe and international arena, there has been a strong consensus that finance sector must be taxed to make greater contributions to the crisis-related costs (European Commission(a),2013) Financial transaction taxes, which has become a topic of discussion especially in recent periods, can be implemented on all financial transactions such as stocks, bonds, derivatives, currency etc. and will be implemented with a relatively low rate and will be always applicable on processed assets (European Commission(b),2010).

In this context, on 28 September 2001 the commission discussed the Council Directive in detail for the implementation of a common financial transaction tax, and the directive aimed the harmonization of the regulation on taxation of financial transactions in order for financial instrument transactions to operate properly in the domestic market (European Commission (b), 2013).

EU anticipates that the financial transactions tax to be implemented in early 2014. Financial transaction tax attracted attention due to its possible impact on outside its boundaries. Although UK did not participate in financial transactions tax, they took legal action and applied to European Court of Justice due to the tax' possible negative effect on London's status as an important center of finance (Erdoğdu & Balseven, 2006). However,

European Court of Justice rejected UK's application because the details of the tax were not yet finalized (BBC News).

In September 2011, European Commission first proposed a financial transactions tax to be implemented throughout the EU. Two main reasons of EU's justification regarding the practice of financial transaction tax were to ensure that finance sector contributes to the rescue operations which financed by the taxpayers and to empower the EU market. Although some countries such as Germany and France favored financial transactions tax; the UK and some other countries opposed the implementation of tax in EU unless it is implemented internationally (Macleod & Gaut, 2013). In this context, financial transaction tax originally planned to be implemented throughout the EU couldn't provide the required unanimous support of 27 member states. However, since some of the countries wanted to implemented the tax, in the early 2013 EU Council allowed 11 countries to implement financial transactions tax under the name of "Empowered Cooperation"(Macleod & Gaut, 2013). The 11 member states are; Belgium, Germany, Estonia, Greece, Spain, France, Italy, Austria, Slovenia and Slovakia. Financial transaction implementations in some of EU member states are given in the table below.

Financial transaction taxes is not a new practice and limited FTT versions were implemented in developed economies throughout the post-war period. Countries such as Belgium, Holland, Sweden, and Germany imposed tax on publicly listed stocks. However, most of these taxes were lifted in 1990s but UK, as the only country among member states, maintained the stamp tax collected from stock transfers. However limited nature of UK's taxation, made it easier to avoid. Investors could prefer to purchase an untaxed derivative rather than buying the stocks directly (EU Briefings, 2012).

Hungarian government could not receive the predicted amount of revenue from FTT in the first quarter of 2013 (While the expectation was HUF 82 billion, the actual result was 38 billion Euros. Additionally some of the companies moved their financial activities to foreign countries (PWC, 2013)

Belgium, too, is another EU country that imposes tax on its financial instruments. Stock transactions tax has been imposed mostly on currency trade and 0.17% tax from derivatives such as option-futures transactions and 0.07% tax from OTC instruments such as company bonds is collected. The tax is applicable on secondary market transactions The tax, which is collected equally from purchaser and seller, that is, both parties in the transaction, cannot exceed 500 Euro per person (Brondolo,2011: 10)Belgium has approved Tobin tax in 2004. However, its implementation depends on the same tax implementation in the EU. Although the Tobin tax in Belgium was addressing spot currency transactions, Belgium accepted financial transaction tax without a discussion under empowered cooperation. Today Belgium imposes taxes on tradable securities transactions. However, the fact that its scope has increased number of limited exceptions caused the tax to be encumbered on individual investors (Allen & Overy, 2013)

Italy supported the financial transaction tax throughout the EU and it is one of the 11 countries establishing the FTT area. In 24 December 2012 Italy passed the budget law where the financial transaction tax is introduced.

Although it is early to make a conclusion regarding Italy, FTT caused reduction in the trade volume of Italy. Between the early 2013 and 12.03.2013 daily average revenue increased by 2.64% throughout the EU while it decreased by 38% in Italy. Undoubtedly, the political transition that Italy experienced had negative impacts on investment decisions in the market (PWC, 2013)

The FTT experienced of Sweden in the late 1980, too, emphasized by academicians and politicians. The government collected taxes from both stock and bond issues and the tax collection carried out via Brokers in Sweden. Here, investors avoided

Table 1. Financial transaction taxes In EU

	UK	France	Sweden	Italy	Hungary
Term	Implemented -currently implemented-	August 2012 -implemented	December 1991 January 1984	March 2013 -present	January 2013 -Present
Scope	-Registered equities in England -options and rights -convertible and profit-linked bond issues	-CDS acquired from public debts -Frequently done cancellations and changes -The market value of shares issued by French companies to be > €1bn	-Related derivations such as interest rate futures -Fixed revenue 0.5% -Stocks and stock options	-Derivations and HFT as of September 2013 -High frequency stock trade as of 1 March -Exported stocks in Italy	-Deposits -Money Withdrawal transactions -Direct debt -Effects -Bank transfers
Ratio	0.5%	-Stock 0.2% -Frequently done cancellation or change 0.01% -CDS acquired from public debts 0.01%	-Fixed revenue depending on its maturity 0.002%- 0.015% -Stock, for startup 0.5% and %0.1 in the sequel	-Lump sum price on stock derivations varying according to the instrument type and nominal value -OTC stock trade 0.2%, and 0.22% as of 1 January 2014 term HFT 0.02% as of 1 September 2013 -Publicly listed stocks 0.1%, it was 0.12% prior to 1 January 2014	-HUF 6,000 (≈ €20) all transactions except money withdrawal subject to taxing -Cash withdrawal 0.6% -All transactions other than cash withdrawal 0.3%
Exceptions	-Transactions carried out by a Omedium quoted in the exchange in UK -Primary Market Transactions - UK public debts - Temporary transfer of securities including repo transactions - Bond issues with no profit-relation -Non-convertible bond issues	-Securities acquisition within the scope of employees' saving management -Transactions for market building purposes - Central securities receivables -Primary market transactions -Transactions performed within liquidity agreements -Transactions within groups - Temporary transfer of securities including repo transactions	-Sweden bonds -Transformation of warranties into stocks -Floating rate bond Forward rate agreement -Interim transactions such as intermediary services after 1987	-Transactions under liquidity agreements -Transactions for market building purposes -Transactions with corporate parties -Pension funds or obligatory social security institutions in member states of EEA or EU	-Transfers between accounts held by same individuals in same banks -Cash repository in the bank account held by companies in the same institution -Transactions between current and investment accounts held by same individual in the same institution

Source: (PWC, 2013)

making extra payments by performing transaction through foreign brokers. And in a couple of years more than 50% of stock transactions in Sweden were moved to London. In 1991, the tax has been lifted. It can be said that this negative experience in Sweden, proved a ground for EU countries who are opposing FTT. Swede Prime Minister Frederick Reinfeldt who opposed the EU tax proposal in 2011, attended to show that Sweden is the only country who can talk about the negative results of the tax (EU Briefings, 2012)

France, too, favored a global practice of financial transaction tax. Before November 2011, Nicholas Sarkozy, then president of France, urged member states in G20 summit for the implementation of financial transaction tax to prevent financial speculation and support countries that are deep in debt. In March 2012, three financial transaction package was approved. According to this, financial transaction tax will be imposed on frequent exchange orders, default swaps with no hedge status in public bonds, and purchase of French stocks (Allen&Overy, 2013). However, FTT in France remained below the expectations. Although the expectation was 530 billion Euros, in August-November 2012 200 billion Euro was collected from the tax. Additionally, it was expressed that FTT had limited impact on stock transaction volume (PWC, 2013)

Germany adopted FTT for several years but its general opinion was that the tax must be implemented worldwide or throughout the EU. Germany also accepted FTT proposal in 2012 under the empowered cooperation. Today, Germany imposes no FTT/stamp tax on securities or derivatives transactions. Although there was a transfer tax for securities it was lifted in 1990s (Allen&Overy, 2013).

CONCLUSION

When the president Nixon stated that US Dollar broke it ties with gold standard in the speech he delivered on 15 August 1971, the period of Bretton Woods system came to an end. Keynesian policies were replaced with neoliberal policies. However, the removal of all obstructions standing before the capital and deregulation of markets, caused speculative flows to overwhelm markets in developing countries and shook them with crises in 1990s. In 2008 global crisis and after that, neoliberal policies started to be questioned and financial transactions taxes became a matter of discussion as a measure which would empower markets and provide revenue for the public. Although EU discussed a FTT proposal in detail to be implemented throughout the area, not all countries had interested and finally an "empowered cooperation" was formed with the participation of 11 countries. But at this point two main critiques are directed to FTT. According to critics when FTT is implemented globally there might be a capital flight or loss of competitiveness caused by the increasing of capital costs. On the other side, maintaining stability in financial markets, allocating more resources for public services with the revenue acquired are some of the advantages of FTT's implementation. The implementation of FTT, it can be whether Tobin, Spahn or Robin Hood, is a political issue rather than a technical one.

REFERENCES

Allen & Overy. (2013). *Global tax practice, financial transaction tax*. Retrieved from http://www.allenovery.com/SiteCollectionDocuments/Global%20Tax_FTT%20Brochure%20(email).pdf

Balseven, H. (2003). Dünya Uygulamalarında ve Türkiye'de Finansal Piyasalardaki İşlem Vergileri. *Vergi Dünyası*, *365*, 171–178.

BBC News. (2014). Europe rejects UK's financial transaction tax challenge. *BBC NEWS*. Retrieved from http://www.bbc.com/news/business-27218615

Brondolo, J. D. (2011). *Taxing financial transactions: An assessment of administrative feasibility*. IMF Working Paper.

Çakıcı, Ö., & Ceylan, M. (2014). Banka ve Sigorta Muameleleri Vergisi, Teori-Uygulama-Mevzuat. TBB: Publication No.301.

Daniels, B. (2010). *The "Robın Hood" tax: A rejection.* TWS Policy Paper. Retrieved from http://thewilberforcesociety.co.uk/wp-content/uploads/2011/10/The-Robin-Hood-tax-A-rejection-Ben-Daniels.pdf

Edwards, S. (2000). Exchange rate regimes, capital flows and crisis prevention. *NBER*. 1-67.

Eichengreen, B., Tobin, J., & Wyplosz, C. (1995). Two cases for sand in the wheels of international finance. *The Economic Journal*, *428*(105), 162–172. doi:10.2307/2235326

Erdoğdu, M., & Balseven, H. (2006). How effective is the Tobin tax in coping with financial volatility? *Anadolu Üniversitesi Sosyal Bilimler Journal*, (1). Retrieved from http://www.asosindex.com/journal-article-abstract?id=849

European Commıssıon. (2010). *Financial sector taxation.* Working Paper No.25. Retrieved from http://ec.europa.eu/taxation_customs/resources/documents/taxation/gen_info/economic_analysis/tax_papers/taxation_paper_25_en.pdf

European Commıssıon. (2013). *Proposal for a council directive implementing enhanced cooperation in the area of financial transaction tax {SWD(2013) 28 final} {SWD(2013) 29 final}. Brussels, 14.2.2013, COM(2013) 71 final, 2013/0045(CNS).* Retrieved from http://ec.europa.eu/taxation_customs/resources/documents/taxation/com_2013_71_en.pdf

European Union Center of North Carolina. (2012). *The politics of an EU financial transactions tax.* EU Briefings. Retrieved from http://europe.unc.edu/wp-content/uploads/2013/08/Brief1206-ftt.pdf

Expenditure Tax General Communique No 89. (2012). Retrieved from http://www.gib.gov.tr/index.php?id=1079&uid=dPD8ZomGh2rFg1SH&type=teblig

Felix, D. (1995a). Financial globalization and the Tobin tax. *Challenge*, 56–59.

Felix, D. (1995b). The Tobin tax proposal, background, issues and prospects. *Furures*, *2*(27), 195–208.

Grossman, H. I. (1975). Tobin on macroeconomics: A review article. *The Journal of Political Economy*, *83*(4), 829-848.

Güler, B. (2012). *Keleş.,E. & Uçar.,Ö.* Ankara: Finansal İşlem Vergileri ve Avrupa Birliği Uygulaması.

Macleod, N. (2013). *Robert Gaut.* The Proposed EU Financial Transaction Tax. FriedFrank.

Matheson, T. (2011). *Taxing financial transactions: Issues and evidence.* IMF Working Paper. Retrieved From https://www.imf.org/external/pubs/ft/wp/2011/wp1154.pdf

McCulloch, N., & Pacillo, G. (2011). *The Tobin tax: A review of the evidence.* IDS Research Report 68.

Montiel, P., & Reinhart, C. M. (2001). The dynamics of capital movements to emerging economies during the 1990s. In S. Griffith-Jones, M. F. Montes, & A. Nasution (Eds.), *Short-term capital flows and economic crises.* Oxford Publication. doi:10.1093/acprof:oso/9780198296867.003.0001

Patterson, B., & Galliano, M. (1998). *The feasibility of an international "Tobin tax".* European Parliament Directorate-General For Research Working Paper,Economic Affairs Series, ECON-107 En. Retrieved from http://www.europarl.europa.eu/workingpapers/econ/pdf/107_en.pdf

PWC. (2013). *Financial transaction tax: The impacts and arguments, a literature review.* Retrieved from www.pwc.co.uk

Robin Hood Tax. (n.d.c). Retrieved from http://www.robinhoodtax.org/sites/default/files/Robin%20Hood%20Tax%20FAQ.pdf

Robin Hood Tax. (n.d.a). *The big idea*. Retrieved from http://www.robinhoodtax.org/sites/default/files/Robin%20Hood%20Tax%20FAQ.pdf

Robin Hood Tax. (n.d.b). *Everything you need to know*. Retrieved from http://www.robinhoodtax.org/how/everything-you-need-to-know

Robin Hood Tax Rides Forth. (2014). International Tax Review, 25(1).

Spahn, P. B. (1996). The Tobin tax and exchange rate stability. *Finance & Development*, *33*(2). Retrieved from http://www.imf.org/external/pubs/ft/fandd/1996/06/pdf/spahn.pdf

Stotsky, J. G. (1996). Why a two-tier Tobin tax won't work. *Finance & Development*, *33*(2). Retrieved from http://www.imf.org/external/pubs/ft/fandd/1996/06/pdf/stotsky.pdf

Tobin, J. (2000). Financial globalization. *World Development*, *6*(28), 1101–1104. doi:10.1016/S0305-750X(00)00008-5

Wahl, P. (2005). *International taxation regulating globalisation – Financing development* (W. E. E. D. Thomas Kalinowski, Ed.). Berlin.

Yeldan, E. (2011). *Küreselleşme Sürecinde Türkiye Ekonomisi, Bölüşüm, Birikim ve Büyüme*. İstanbul: İletişim Publishing.

KEY TERMS AND DEFINITIONS

Financial Liberalization: Disappearance of boundary separating among the national financial markets.

Financial Transaction Tax: Generally very low rate tax which applied for financial transactions.

Globalization: Process of increased integration and interaction to aspects of economic, social, technological, cultural, political and ecological balance.

Robin Hood Tax: Low rate tax (less than half of %1) on transactions Wall Street, big banks and investment houses which was launched on 10 February 2010.

Short Term Capital Flows: Maturity of up to one year, which are private and official capital flows in nature.

Tobin Tax: Tobin tax is a lower international tax on the foreign currency transfers which suggested by American Economist James Tobin.

Two Tier Spahn Tax: Spahn tax which is a kind of Tobin tax, designed as two step and two rate by Paul Bernd Spahn in 1995.

ENDNOTES

1 For the article which James Tobin used the expression " "throw some sand in the wheels of our excessively efficient international money markets" to describe the tax he proposed see: James Tobin,"A Proposal For International Monetary Reform",Cowles Foundation Discussion Paper,No.495(Acquired from Eastern Economic Journal, 4 (3-4), July/October 1978 and republished), Cowles Foundation, Yale University, http://cowles.econ.yale.edu/P/cp/p04b/p0495.pdf, (Date of Access:20.05.2011), s.154

2 Financial Leasing Law no. 3226, Official Gazette dated 28 June 1985, Issue. 18975,Acceptance Date:10.06.1985,http://www.alomaliye.com/finansal_kiralama_kanunu.htm

3 24.12.2012 Date and 2012/4116 Appendix to the Decree, http://www.gib.gov.tr/fileadmin/mevzuatek/20130101-1-1.pdf

Chapter 15
Relationships between Financial Development, Trade Openness, and Economic Growth: Empirical Evidence for Turkey

Fahri Seker
University of Bozok, Turkey

Birol Topcu
Namik Kemal University, Turkey

Murat Cetin
Namik Kemal University, Turkey

Gamze Yıldız Seren
Namik Kemal University, Turkey

ABSTRACT

The aim of this chapter is to investigate the cointegration and causal relationship between financial development, trade openness, and economic growth in Turkey for the period of 1980-2012. To analyze the data, the bounds testing and Johansen-Juselius approaches to cointegration and Granger causality test based on vector error-correction model are employed. The cointegration tests suggest that there is a long-run relationship between the variables. The Granger causality test reveals long-run bidirectional causality between trade openness and economic growth. The findings also indicate unidirectional causality running from financial development to trade openness and economic growth in the long run as well as a bi-directional causality between financial development and economic growth in the short run. The results support supply-leading and trade-led growth hypotheses. Therefore, it can be suggested that Turkey can accelerate its economic growth by improving its financial systems and encouraging foreign trade.

INTRODUCTION

In empirical growth literature, degree of financial development (FD) and level of trade openness are amongst the most significant variables which affect growth performance (Barro, 1997; Beck, 2002). Particularly, over the last few decades, the relationship between finance and economic growth has attracted considerable attention in economic development literature. After 2007-2008 global economic crises, policy-makers and researchers have paid more attention to financial systems of the countries (Pan, 2013). Actually, the theoretical foundation of this relationship can be traced back

DOI: 10.4018/978-1-4666-7308-3.ch015

to the work of Schumpeter (1911) defending that financial development encourages new production techniques. Recently, there is growing empirical evidence that FD contributes significantly to economic growth. The leading studies such as those of Goldsmith (1969), McKinnon (1973) and Shaw (1973), along with some recent important works, indicated that well-functioning financial systems can contribute to economic growth in positive ways (see e.g. King & Levine, 1993; Demetriades & Hussein, 1996; Levine, 1997; Rajan & Zingales, 1998; Aghion, Howitt & Mayer-Foulkes, 2005). Some prominent theoretical studies also explain the positive effects through various functions of financial intermediaries (see e.g. Goldsmith, 1969; Patrik, 1966; Levine, Norman & Thorsten, 2000). For instance, according to Levine (1997), financial intermediaries (i) facilitate the trading and pooling of risk, (ii) allocate resources effectively, (iii) monitor managers and exert corporate control, (iv) mobilize savings, and (v) facilitate the exchange of goods and services. On the other hand, Robinson (1952) claims that financial development has no effect on economic growth. Moreover, economic growth may encourage the financial industry to provide better services, and thus economic growth can cause financial development rather than the other way. In addition, the evidences gained from many empirical studies on finance-growth nexus have been mixed and ambiguous depending on the choice of methodology employed and special features of the countries.

As the effect of financial development and trade openness on economic growth varies according to the political systems and economic structures of the countries, studies on individual countries have been gaining more significance in the empirical literature. This study on Turkey, a developing country and a candidate for EU membership, aims at contributing to the current literature in two aspects. Firstly, unlike the other studies on Turkey, the trade openness variable is included in the analyses in addition to the financial development variable. Otherwise, disregarding trade openness and taking only the financial development into account as an independent variable can lead to inaccurate predictions about the degree of the relationship between financial development and economic growth (Wolde-Rufael, 2009; Baltagi, Panicos & Siong, 2009; Beck, 2002). Such an approach as the one adopted in this study allows us to separately examine the effects of financial development and trade openness on economic growth. Moreover, the simultaneous equations system can provide information on how financial development affects trade openness and vice versa (Kim, Shu-Chin & Yu-Bo, 2012). Secondly, following FED's inclusion of Turkey as the most fragile country among the fragile five (Turkey, Brazil, India, South Africa and Indonesia) in early 2014, concerns about Turkey's financial markets and economic stability have increased. For this reason, by expanding the current perspective in the literature on Turkish economy and the financial markets, this study is expected to contribute to the policy-makers' decision making processes.

For the reasons mentioned above, the current study investigates the cointegration and causal relationships between financial development, trade openness and economic growth in Turkey for the period 1980-2012, during which the country experienced fast economic growth and rapid expansion of financial intermediation. We employ the bounds testing and Johansen-Juselius approaches to cointegration and Granger causality test based on vector error-correction model to conduct the analysis. The cointegration tests suggest that there is a long-run relationship between the variables. The Granger causality test reveals a long run bi-directional causality between trade openness and economic growth. The findings also indicate a unidirectional causality running from financial development to trade openness and economic growth in the long run as well as a bi-directional causality between financial development and economic growth in the short run.

The remainder of this paper is organized as follows. Section 2 presents a brief literature review. The data and empirical model are described in Section 3. Section 4 lays out the econometric methodology. The empirical findings are presented in Section 5. Finally, Section 6 offers a brief summary of the major findings and some concluding remarks.

LITERATURE REVIEW

The relationships between financial development, international trade and economic growth have been extensively studied in both theoretical and empirical literatures (Levine et al., 2000; Ang, 2008; Wachtel, 2003; Shan, 2005 and Baltagi et al., 2009).

The theoretical studies can be classified mainly under two categories: supply-leading hypothesis and demand-following hypothesis. According to Patrick (1966) supply-leading hypothesis has two functions: to transfer resources from traditional sectors to modern sectors and to stimulate an entrepreneurial response in these modern sectors. Accordingly, financial institutions encourage innovation and promote growth through the process of capital accumulation, which is reflected in saving and productive investments. Supply-leading hypothesis is supported by prominent studies by Beck (2002), Goldsmith (1969), King & Levine (1993), Levine (1997). A growing body of empirical analyses, including firm, industry, and individual-country studies, and broader cross-country comparisons, demonstrate a strong positive relationship between the functioning of the financial system and long-run economic growth (Levine, 1997). For instance, Levine et al. (2000) demonstrated that the external component of financial development is positively associated with economic growth. More recently, the study of Bojanic (2012) has revealed the presence of a long-run equilibrium relationship and unidirectional Granger causality running from the indicators of financial development and trade openness to economic growth. Similarly, Dritsaki & Dritsaki (2013) have demonstrated a unidirectional causality from financial development and trade openness to economic growth as well as one from financial development and economic growth to trade openness in the long-run. Hsueh, Yu-Hau & Chien-Heng (2013) analyzing the causality between financial development and economic growth among ten Asian countries between 1980 and 2007 found that the direction of causality between financial development and economic growth is sensitive to the financial development variables.

As implied by the demand-following hypothesis, finance in the growth process is essentially passive and permissive (Patrick, 1966). In her fundamental works, Robinson (1952) argues that an increase in the demand for financial services is what economic development favors, as it leads to the development of the financial sector. Some recent studies including Zang & Kim (2007); Chimobi (2010), Shan (2005), Demetriades & Hussein (1996) provide evidence for the demand-following approach. More recently, Menyah, Nazlioglu & Wolde-Rufael (2014) and Gries, Manfred & Meierrieks (2009) found limited support for supply-leading hypothesis in African countries. According to Atindéhou, Pierre & Kossi (2005) the impact of economic growth on finance has received less support in the literature. As in empirical cases on other countries, there is no consensus on direction of causality between financial development and economic growth in Turkey. Unalmis (2002) suggests that causality runs from financial development to economic growth in the short-run, except for one of the proxies used. In the long-run, the test results in the context of VECM for the coefficients of all cointegrated series show a two way causality between financial deepening and economic growth for the period 1970-2001 in Turkey. Ozcan & Ari (2011) analyzed the issue by estimating a VAR Model over the 1998-2009 period in Turkey. They found unidirectional relationship between financial development and economic growth in Turkey according to Granger causality test. The direction of this relationship is from economic growth to financial development, which consequently, has confirmed the demand-following hypothesis. On the other hand, in another research on Turkey, Yucel (2009) found a positive relationship between trade openness and growth and a negative relationship between financial development and growth.

In recent empirical literature, it is widely acknowledged that financial development is a potentially important mechanism for long-run growth. For this reason, in the related literature there is a shift towards providing answers to the question of why some countries are more financially developed than others (Baltagi et al., 2009). One of the pioneer contributions in this literature comes from the interest-group hypothesis put forward by Rajan & Zingales (2003). In line with their hypothesis, trade openness, especially when combined with financial liberation, weakens the incentives of incumbent business firms or financial intermediaries hindering financial development in order to reduce entry and competition. In addition, the relative political power of incumbents could decrease with foreign trade as well. Then, trade has a beneficial impact on financial development (Rajan & Zingales, 2003). Several recent papers suggest that trade is strongly linked to financial development. For instance, using a 30-year panel for 65 countries, Beck (2002) shows that financial development exerts a large causal impact on the level of both exports and the trade balance of manufactured goods. Baltagi et al. (2009) provide statistical evidence for the contention that banking sector development is determined by trade openness. Employing the pooled mean group approach to study the dynamic effects of trade openness on financial development in 88 countries over a time period of 1960-2005, Kim et al. (2010) indicated that a positive long-run relationship between trade openness and financial development coexists with a negative short-run relationship. Bojanic (2012) analyzed with annual time-series data for Bolivia during the 1940-2010 period. The empirical results demonstrate that there is a long-run equilibrium relationship. In addition, there is a unidirectional Granger causality running from the indicators of financial development and trade openness to economic growth.

DATA AND EMPIRICAL MODEL

The reason for investigating the period of 1980-2012 in the current study was due to the essential developments in both financial sector and trade openness in Turkey between these years. As a financial development indicator, we use private credit, which is defined as credit to the private sector by deposit money banks and other financial institutions as a share of GDP. This indicator is expected to adequately capture the developments in the financial sector of Turkey, as the financial sector is mainly dominated by the banking sector in Turkey. This proxy is also widely used in the literature (see, Shahbaz & Lean, 2012; Islam et al. 2013; Levine et al, 2000; Pan & Whang, 2013; Abu-Bader & Abu-Qarn, 2008; Rousseau & D'onofrio, 2013). According to Gregorio & Guidotti (1995), this indicator is superior to the measures of real interest rates or monetary aggregates such as Ml, M2, or M3, in the sense that it more accurately exposes the actual volume of funds channeled to the private sector. Therefore, it can be argued that there is more direct link between the ratio of bank credit to the private sector and the investment and economic growth.

The following empirical model describes the long-run relationship between financial development, trade openness and economic growth. Modified from Menyah et al. (2014), the basic framework for economic growth can be expressed as

$$lnGDP_t = \alpha_0 + \beta_1 FD_t + \beta_2 TRADE_t + \varepsilon_t \quad (1)$$

where *GDP* is per capita real income (constant 2005 international dollars); *FD* is financial development proxied by domestic credit to private sector as share of GDP and *TRADE* is trade openness (foreign trade, % of GDP). α_0 is the constant; β_1 *and* β_2 are the slope coefficients and ε_t is the standard error term. All data are from World Development Indicators (WDI) online data base. Table 1 reports the summary statistics and correlation matrix of the variable used in the empirical analysis. The correlation matrix shows that there is a positive link between the variables.

ECONOMETRIC METHODOLOGY

Cointegration analysis is the appropriate technique to investigate the long-run relationship between financial development, openness and economic growth. To do that, we have first investigated the stationarity properties of the variables. We adopt the recently developed panel unit root tests suggested by the Phillips & Perron (1988) (PP), Elliott, Rothenberg & Stock (1996) (DF-GLS), Ng & Perron (2001). Secondly, the bounds testing approach to cointegration developed by Pesaran, Shin & Smith (2001) is used to investigate the presence of cointegration. Finally, we employ Granger causality test based on vector error correction model (VECM) to examine the causal relationship between mentioned variables.

Unit Root Tests

The analysis begins by examining the unit root test of variables using the Phillips & Perron (1988) (PP), Elliott et al. (1996) (DF-GLS), Ng & Perron (2001) tests. In the first two tests and Ng-Perron MZa and MZt tests, the null hypothesis of the series has a unit root is tested against the alternative of stationarity. Whereas, in Ng-Perron MSB and MPT tests, the null hypothesis is that the series are stationary.

Under the null hypothesis, the PP statistics have the same asymptotic distributions as the ADF *t*-statistic and normalized bias statistics. The PP tests are robust to general forms of heteroskedasticity in the error term. Another advantage is that the user does not have to specify a lag length for the test regression. However, Harris & Sollis (2003) argue that due to their poor size and power

Table 1. Descriptive Statistics and Correlation Matrix (Time Series Data: 1980-2012, Observations=33)

Statistics	*GDP*	*FD*	*TRADE*
Mean	5746.201	22.455	40.706
Median	5687.244	17.941	41.750
Maximum	8482.614	54.395	57.995
Minimum	3700.797	13.588	17.089
Std. dev.	1405.040	10.187	10.478
Skewness	0.381	1.909	-0.307
Kurtosis	2.115	2.218	2.218
GDP	1.000		
FD	0.756	1.000	
TRADE	0.867	0.586	1.000

properties, these tests are not reliable for small sample size. According to them Ng-Perron tests are superior and more powerful as compared to traditional unit root tests

Cointegration Tests

In this study, the bounds testing approach to cointegration developed by Pesaran et al. (2001) is used to investigate the presence of cointegration among financial development, trade openness and economic growth in Turkey. This procedure has been widely used in the economic growth literature (Shahbaz, Zeshan & Afza, 2012; Uddin & Shahbaz, 2013) because it has important advantages over the classical cointegration methods such as Engle-Granger (1987) and Johansen-Juselius (1990). It can be used to test the presence of cointegration relationship even if the regressors are $I(0)$ or $I(1)$ (Pesaran & Shin, 1999).

The bounds testing approach to cointegration can be applied by estimating the following autoregressive distributed lag (ARDL) equation which is known as the unrestricted ECM using the ordinary least squares (OLS) technique:

$$\Delta lnGDP_t = \gamma_0 + \sum_{i=1}^{p}\gamma_{1i}\Delta lnGDP_{t-i} + \sum_{i=0}^{p}\gamma_{2i}\Delta FD_{t-i} + \sum_{i=0}^{p}\gamma_{3i}\Delta TRADE_{t-i} + \lambda_1 lnGDP_{t-1} + \lambda_2 FD_{t-1} + \lambda_3 TRADE_{t-1} + \varepsilon_t \tag{2}$$

where γ_0 is the drift component and ε_t is error term assumed to be independently and identically distributed. The coefficients of λ_1, λ_2 and λ_3 denote the long run relationship while the coefficients of γ_1, γ_2 and γ_3 represent the error correction dynamics in Equation (2).

Firstly, equation (2) is estimated by the OLS method. Secondly, we calculate the F-statistic for joint significance of the coefficients of the lagged level of the variables. Here, the null hypothesis of no cointegration $H_0 : \lambda_1 = \lambda_2 = \lambda_3 = 0$ is tested against the alternative of $H_1 : \lambda_1 \neq \lambda_2 \neq \lambda_3 \neq 0$. Thirdly, the calculated F-statistic is compared with the critical bounds developed by Pesaran *et al.* (2001) to examine the existence of a cointegration relationship among the variables. If the calculated F-statistic is higher than the upper critical bound (UCB), then there is a long-run relationship between the variables. If the calculated F-statistic is less than the lower critical bound (LCB), then there is no a long-run relationship between the variables. If the calculated F-statistic falls between the LCB and UCB, then the result is inconclusive. Finally, the goodness of the bounds testing approach is investigated by applying several diagnostic tests. These tests are conducted to test the serial correlation, functional form, normality of error term and heteroscedisticity in the model.

As well as the bounds testing approach to cointegration, we also apply the Johansen-Juselius (1990) cointegration test to provide a sensitivity check for the cointegration results. This procedure is based on the vector autoregression (VAR) of order p given by

$$\Delta y_t = \mu + \Pi y_{t-1} + \sum_{i=1}^{p-1}\Gamma_i \Delta y_{t-i} + Bz_t + \varepsilon_t \tag{3}$$

where y_t is a vector of variables that are integrated of order one, ε_t is a vector of innovations and Bz_t is a vector of deterministic variables. $\Pi = \sum_{i=1}^{p} A_i - I$ and $\Gamma_i = -\sum_{j=i+1}^{p} A_j$. Johansen-Juselius estimates the significance of the canonical correlations and the reduced rank of the Π matrix. This procedure presents two different likelihood ratio tests: the trace test and maximum eigenvalue test, shown in equations (4) and (5) respectively.

$$J_{iz} = -T\sum_{i=r+1}^{n}\ln(1-\hat{\lambda}i) \tag{4}$$

$$J_{max} = -Tln\left(1-\hat{\lambda}_{ir+1}\right) \quad (5)$$

where T is the sample size and $\hat{\lambda}_i$ is the ith largest canonical correlation. In the trace test, the null hypothesis is r cointegrating vectors which is tested against its alternative of n cointegrating vectors. In the maximum eigenvalue test, the null hypothesis is r cointegrating vectors which is tested against its alternative of $(r+1)$ cointegrating vectors.

VECM Granger Causality Test

The bounds testing and Johansen-Juselius approaches to cointegration do not indicate the direction of causality between variables. We employ Granger causality test based on vector error correction model (VECM) to examine the causal relationship between mentioned variables. This test includes the Error-Correction Term (ECT) as an additional variable to the VAR system. So, it is known the augmented Granger causality test. This model is as follows:

$$(1-B)\begin{bmatrix}\ln GDP_t\\ FD_t\\ TRADE_t\end{bmatrix} = \begin{bmatrix}C_1\\ C_2\\ C_3\end{bmatrix} + \sum_{i=1}^{p}(1-B)\begin{bmatrix}d_{11,i}\,d_{12,i}\,d_{13,i}\\ d_{21,i}\,d_{22,i}\,d_{23,i}\\ d_{31,i}\,d_{32,i}\,d_{33,i}\end{bmatrix}\begin{bmatrix}\ln GDP_{t-i}\\ FD_{t-i}\\ TRADE_{t-i}\end{bmatrix} + \begin{bmatrix}\lambda_1\\ \lambda_2\\ \lambda_3\end{bmatrix}\left[ECM_{t-1}\right] + \begin{bmatrix}\varepsilon_{1t}\\ \varepsilon_{2t}\\ \varepsilon_{3t}\end{bmatrix} \quad (6)$$

where (1-B) is the lag operator and ECM_{t-1} is the lagged error correction term generated from the long run equation. The significant t-statistics on the coefficients of the ECM_{t-1} show that there is a long run causality between the variables. The existence of a significant relationship in first differences of the variables presents evidence on the direction of short run causality.

EMPIRICAL FINDINGS

Table 2 reports the outcome of the PP, DF-GLS and Ng-Perron unit-root tests on the levels and the first differences of the series. The results suggest that all series are stationary in their first differences, indicating that they are $I(1)$. Hence, this validates the use of bounds testing and Johansen-Juselius approaches to cointegration.

The bounds testing procedure requires appropriate lag order of the variable to calculate F-statistic. The results presented in Table 3 show that the optimum lag is 3 based on AIC. The results of the bounds testing analysis are also reported in Table 3. We find that there is a long run relationship between financial development, trade openness and economic growth because calculated F-statistic (4.944) is higher than the UCB (4.85) at 5% level of significance. The results of diagnostic tests such as serial correlation, functional form, normality and heteroscedasticity presented in the lower part of Table 3 show that the underlying model passes all the tests. We also apply the Johansen-Juselius cointegration test to investigate the robustness of long run results. The results indicate one cointegrating vector confirming that there is a long run relationship between the variables.

The presence of cointegration between financial development, trade openness and economic growth implies that there is at least one way directional causal relationship between the variables. The results of short and long-run Granger causality based on VECM are reported in Table 4. In both short and long run, we find unidirectional Granger causality running from financial development and trade openness to real income for case

Table 2. Unit root tests

Variables/Statistics	Ng-Perron				DF-GLS	PP
	MZa	MZt	MSB	MPT	t	Adj. t
ln*GDP*	1.587	1.433	0.903	64.359	0.728	-0.139
FD	2.233	0.688	0.308	14.333	0.720	2.056
TRADE	-0.477	-0.210	0.441	15.079	-0.700	-1.749
Δln*GDP*	-15.169[a]	-2.748[a]	0.181[b]	1.635[b]	-6.332[a]	-7.636[a]
Δ*FD*	-12.576[b]	-2.482[b]	0.197[b]	2.045[b]	-3.425[a]	-3.517[b]
Δ*TRADE*	-15.340[a]	-2.768[a]	0.180[b]	1.601[a]	-5.114[a]	-7.762[a]
Critical values*						
1%	-13.800	-2.580	0.174	1.780	-2.641	-3.653
5%	-8.100	-1.980	0.233	3.170	-1.952	-2.957
10%	-5.700	-1.620	0.275	4.450	-1.610	-2.617

Note: * Critical values are taken from Ng & Perron (2001) and McKinnon (1996). [a] and [b] denote significance at 1 and 5% levels, respectively. The model with constant is used to estimate the unit root tests. The optimal lag length for DF-GLS and Ng-Perron tests is determined by AIC, while the bandwidth for the PP test is determined using the Bartlett-Kernel procedure.

Table 3. Cointegration test results

A: Multivariate Johansen-Juselius Cointegration Test		
Number of Cointegrating Equations (null hypotheses)	**Max-Eigen Statistics**	**Trace Statistics**
$r = 0$	19.522[b]	30.871[c]
$r \leq 1$	11.137	11.316
$r \leq 2$	0.178	0.178
B: Bounds Testing Approach to Cointegration		
Model	**Optimal Lag (AIC)**	**Calculated F-Statistics**
$F_{\ln GDP}$[ln*GDP*|*FD, TRADE*]	[2, 2, 2]	4.944[b]
Significance level	Lower bounds, I (0)	Upper bounds, I (1)
1%	5.15	6.36
5%	3.79	4.85
10%	3.17	4.14
Diagnostic tests		
R^2	0.536	
Adjusted-R^2	0.367	
F-statistics	3.180(0.014)[b]	
Jarque-Bera normality	3.227(0.199)	
Breusch-Godfrey LM	0.151(0.860)	
ARCH LM	0.420(0.521)	
Ramsey Reset	1.795(0.191)	

Note: Values in parenthesis are p-values. [b] and [c] denote significance at 5 and 10% levels, respectively. Both optimal lag orders for the VAR and ARDL models are selected based on AIC. The critical values are obtained from Peseran *et al.* (2001), critical values for the bounds test: case III: unrestricted intercept and no trend.

Table 4. Results of the VECM granger causality test

Dependent Variable	Short-Run Granger Causality F-Statistics		Long-Run Granger Causality
Case 1. $F_{\Delta lnGDP}[\Delta lnGDP \mid \Delta FD, \Delta TRADE]$ Lag 1			
	ΔFD	$\Delta TRADE$	ECT_{t-1} (t-statistics)
	2.905[a]	-1.985[b]	-0.195[-2.392][b]
Diagnostic tests			
R^2		0.312	
Adjusted-R^2		0.207	
F-statistics		2.959(0.038)[b]	
Jarque-Bera normality		1.322(0.516)	
Breusch-Godfrey LM		0.769(0.474)	
ARCH LM		0.015(0.903)	
Ramsey Reset		1.617(0.118)	
Case 2. $F_{\Delta FD}[\Delta FD \mid \Delta lnGDP, \Delta TRADE]$ Lag 1			
	$\Delta lnGDP$	$\Delta TRADE$	ECT_{t-1} (t-statistics)
	-1.799[c]	-1.521	-0.035[-0.380]
Diagnostic tests			
R^2		0.297	
Adjusted-R^2		0.188	
F-statistics		2.747(0.049)[b]	
Jarque-Bera normality		35.902(0.000)	
Breusch-Godfrey LM		0.360(0.700)	
ARCH LM		0.117(0.733)	
Ramsey Reset		1.369(0.183)	
Case 3. $F_{\Delta TRADE}[\Delta TRADE \mid \Delta FD, \Delta lnGDP]$ Lag 1			
	ΔFD	$\Delta lnGDP$	ECT_{t-1} (t-statistics)
	0.439	0.363	-0.578[-3.064][a]
Diagnostic tests			
R^2		0.321	
Adjusted- R^2		0.217	
F-statistics		3.085(0.033)[b]	
Jarque-Bera normality		0.655(0.720)	
Breusch-Godfrey LM		0.358(0.702)	
ARCH LM		0.558(0.461)	
Ramsey Reset		0.862(0.396)	

Note: [a], [b] and [c] denote significance at 1, 5 and 10% levels, respectively. Values in parenthesis are p-values. VECMs are selected based on AIC.

1. This indicates that financial development and trade openness cause economic growth. Table 4 reveals that the estimate of ECM_{t-1} is negative and statistically significant in case 1 implying the existence of cointegration relationship between the variables. We also find short run unidirectional Granger causality running from trade openness to real income for case 2. This implies that trade openness causes economic growth. Table 4 also reports long run unidirectional Granger causality running from financial development and real income to trade openness for case 3 indicating that financial development and real income cause trade openness. As seen from the table, the underlying models pass the diagnostic tests. The results of Granger causality movements are also summarized in Table 5.

CONCLUSION AND POLICY IMPLICATIONS

This study examines the cointegration relationships and direction of causality between financial development, trade openness and economic growth over the period 1980-2012 for Turkish economy. For this purpose, the bounds testing and Johansen-Juselius approaches to cointegration and VECM Granger causality test are employed. The results show that the series are cointegrated implying a long-run relationship between the variables and bidirectional causality between trade openness and economic growth. Additionally, the results demonstrate long run unidirectional causality running from financial development to trade openness and economic growth. In the short run, bidirectional causality between financial development and economic growth is also observed. So, this study provides an empirical evidence for the validity of trade-led growth and financial development-led growth hypotheses in the Turkish economy.

Although individual-country case studies offer a crucial insight to be used as a reference for policy formulation, the findings of these case studies are not sufficient to confirm or refute the prevailing views on the finance, openness and growth relationship. The results obtained from any specific country cannot be generalized to the contexts of different countries. Hence, the use of single-country time series analyses could solely be relevant to the policy formulation for the specific country under investigation (Ang, 2008). In this sense, in accordance with the key findings of this study, caution is recommended in the choice of financial development indicators as policy instruments in the implementation of growth policies in Turkey.

On the basis of the above mentioned findings, to reach high employment rate, more per capita incomes and sustainable economic growth, policies that improve access by the private sector to affordable credit would stimulate innovation and capacity increases in industry and manufacturing. Overall, to remove barriers in front of financial markets operations and thus enhance their efficiency, it can be suggested that policymakers in

Table 5. Summary of the results of the VECM granger causality approach

Direction of Causality	Short Run (F-Statistics)	Long Run (ECM_{t-1})
FD causes ln*GDP*	At 1% significance level	At 5% significance level
TRADE causes ln*GDP*	At 5% significance level	At 5% significance level
ln*GDP* causes *FD*	At 10% significance level	No
TRADE causes *FD*	No	No
FD causes *TRADE*	No	At 1% significance level
ln*GDP* causes *TRADE*	No	At 1% significance level

Turkey should encourage financial market development through appropriate taxes, and legal and regulatory policies. Further research can broaden the analyses of the variables of finance, openness and growth by obtaining additional measures of legal, supervisory, and regulatory factors that determine the level of financial intermediary development.

REFERENCES

Abu-Bader, S., & Abu-Qarn, A. S. (2008). Financial development and economic growth: The Egyptian experience. *Journal of Policy Modeling*, *30*(5), 887–898. doi:10.1016/j.jpolmod.2007.02.001

Aghion, P., Howitt, P., & Mayer-Foulkes, D. (2005). The effect of financial development on convergence: Theory and evidence. *The Quarterly Journal of Economics*, *120*(1), 173–222.

Ang, J. B. (2008). A survey of recent developments in the literature of finance and growth. *Journal of Economic Surveys*, *22*(3), 536–576. doi:10.1111/j.1467-6419.2007.00542.x

Atindéhou, R. B., Pierre, G. J., & Kossi, E. (2005). Financial intermediation and economic growth: Evidence from Western Africa. *Applied Financial Economics*, *15*(11), 777–790. doi:10.1080/09603100500108030

Baltagi, B. H., Panicos, O. D., & Siong, H. L. (2009). Financial development and openness: Evidence from panel data. *Journal of Development Economics*, *89*(2), 285–296. doi:10.1016/j.jdeveco.2008.06.006

Barro, R. J. (1997). *Determinants of economic growth: A cross-country empirical study*. Cambridge, MA: The MIT Press.

Beck, T. (2002). Financial development and international trade: Is there a link? *Journal of International Economics*, *57*(1), 107–131. doi:10.1016/S0022-1996(01)00131-3

Bojanic, A. N. (2012). The impact of financial development and trade on the economic growth of Bolivia. *Journal of Applied Econometrics*, *15*(1), 51–70.

Chimobi, O. P. (2010). The causal relationship among financial development, trade openness and economic growth in Nigeria. *International Journal of Economics and Finance*, *2*(2), 137–147. doi:10.5539/ijef.v2n2p137

Demetriades, P. O., & Khaled, A. H. (1996). Does financial development cause economic growth? Time-series evidence from 16 countries. *Journal of Development Economics*, *51*(2), 387–411. doi:10.1016/S0304-3878(96)00421-X

Dritsaki, M., & Chaido, D. (2013). Bounds testing approach for cointegration and causality between financial development, trade openness and economic growth in Bulgaria. *Journal of Applied Econometrics*, *52*(1), 50–67.

Elliott, G., Rothenberg, T. J., & Stock, J. H. (1996). Efficient tests for an autoregressive unit root. *Econometrica*, *64*(4), 813–836. doi:10.2307/2171846

Engle, R., & Granger, C. W. J. (1987). Cointegration and error-correction representation, estimation and testing. *Econometrica*, *55*(2), 251–276. doi:10.2307/1913236

Goldsmith, R. W. (1969). *Financial structure and development*. New Haven, CT: Yale University Press.

Gregorio, J. D., & Pablo, E. G. (1995). Financial development and economic growth. *World Development, 23*(3), 433–448. doi:10.1016/0305-750X(94)00132-I

Gries, T., Manfred, K., & Meierrieks, D. (2009). Linkages between financial deepening, trade openness, and economic development: Causality evidence from Sub-Saharan Africa. *World Development, 37*(12), 1849–1860. doi:10.1016/j.worlddev.2009.05.008

Harris, R., & Sollis, R. (2003). *Applied time series modeling and forecasting*. West Sussex, UK: Wiley.

Hsueh, S. J., Yu-Hau, H., & Chien-Heng, T. (2013). Economic growth and financial development in Asian countries: A bootstrap panel Granger causality analysis. *Economic Modelling, 32*, 294–301. doi:10.1016/j.econmod.2013.02.027

Islam, F., Shahbaz, M., Ahmed, A. U., & Alam, M. M. (2013). Financial development and energy consumption nexus in Malaysia: A multivariate time series analysis. *Economic Modelling, 30*, 435–441. doi:10.1016/j.econmod.2012.09.033

Johansen, S., & Juselius, K. (1990). Maximum likelihood estimation and inference on cointegration with application to the demand for money. *Oxford Bulletin of Economics and Statistics, 52*(2), 169–210. doi:10.1111/j.1468-0084.1990.mp52002003.x

Kim, D. H., Shu-Chin, L., & Yu-Bo, S. (2010). Dynamic effects of trade openness on financial development. *Economic Modelling, 27*(1), 254–261. doi:10.1016/j.econmod.2009.09.005

Kim, D. H., Shu-Chin, L., & Yu-Bo, S. (2012). The simultaneous evolution of economic growth, financial development, and trade openness. *The Journal of International Trade & Economic Development, 21*(4), 513–537. doi:10.1080/09638199.2010.497933

King, R. G., & Levine, R. (1993). Finance, entrepreneurship and growth. *Journal of Monetary Economics, 32*(3), 513–542. doi:10.1016/0304-3932(93)90028-E

Levine, R. (1997). Financial development and economic growth: Views and agenda. *Journal of Economic Literature, XXXV*, 688–726.

Levine, R., Norman, L., & Thorsten, B. (2000). Financial intermediation and growth: Causality and causes. *Journal of Monetary Economics, 46*(1), 32–77. doi:10.1016/S0304-3932(00)00017-9

McKinnon, J. G. (1996). Numerical distribution functions for unit root and cointegration tests. *Journal of Applied Econometrics, 11*(6), 601–618. doi:10.1002/(SICI)1099-1255(199611)11:6<601::AID-JAE417>3.0.CO;2-T

McKinnon, R. I. (1973). Money and capital in economic development. Brookings Institution.

Menyah, K., Nazlioglu, S., & Wolde-Rufael, Y. (2014). Financial development, trade openness and economic growth in African countries: New insights from a panel causality approach. *Economic Modelling, 37*, 386–394. doi:10.1016/j.econmod.2013.11.044

Ng, S., & Perron, P. (2001). Lag length selection and the construction of unit root tests with good size and power. *Econometrica, 69*(6), 1519–1554. doi:10.1111/1468-0262.00256

Ozcan, B., & Ari, A. (2011). An empirical analysis of relationship between financial development and economic growth: The Turkish case. *Business and Economics Research Journal, 2*(1), 121–142.

Pan, H., & Chun, W. (2013). Financial development and economic growth: A new investigation. *Journal of Economic Development, 38*(1), 27–46.

Patrick, H. T. (1966). Financial development and economic growth in underdeveloped countries. *Economic Development and Cultural Change*, *14*(2), 174–189. doi:10.1086/450153

Pesaran, M. H., & Shin, Y. (1999). *An autoregressive distributed lag modeling approach to cointegration analysis: Econometrics and economic theory in 20th century: The Ragnar Frisch centennial symposium* (S. Strom, Ed.). Cambridge, UK: Cambridge University Press.

Pesaran, M. H., Shin, Y., & Smith, R. (2001). Bounds testing approaches to the analysis of level relationships. *Journal of Applied Econometrics*, *16*(3), 289–326. doi:10.1002/jae.616

Phillips, P. C. B., & Perron, P. (1988). Testing for unit roots in time series regression. *Biometrika*, *75*(2), 335–346. doi:10.1093/biomet/75.2.335

Rajan, R. G., & Luigi, Z. (1998). Financial dependence and growth. *The American Economic Review*, *88*(3), 559–586.

Rajan, R. G., & Luigi, Z. (2003). The great reversals: The politics of financial development in the twentieth century. *Journal of Financial Economics*, *69*(1), 5–50. doi:10.1016/S0304-405X(03)00125-9

Robinson, J. (1952). *The generalization of the general theory: The rate of interest and other essays*. London: Macmillan.

Rousseau, P. L., & Alexandra, D. (2013). Monetization, financial development, and growth: Time series evidence from 22 countries in Sub-Saharan Africa. *World Development*, *51*, 132–153. doi:10.1016/j.worlddev.2013.05.016

Schumpeter, J. A. (1911). *The theory of economic development*. Oxford, UK: Oxford University Press.

Shahbaz, M., & Lean, H. H. (2012). Does financial development increase energy consumption? The role of industrialization and urbanization in Tunisia. *Energy Policy*, *40*, 473–479. doi:10.1016/j.enpol.2011.10.050

Shahbaz, M., Zeshan, M., & Afza, T. (2012). Is energy consumption effective to spur economic growth in Pakistan? New evidence from bounds test to level relationships and Granger causality tests. *Economic Modelling*, *29*(6), 2310–2319. doi:10.1016/j.econmod.2012.06.027

Shan, J. (2005). Does financial development lead economic growth? A vector autoregression appraisal. *Applied Economics*, *37*(12), 1353–1367. doi:10.1080/00036840500118762

Shaw, E. (1973). *Financial deepening in economic development*. London: Oxford University Press.

Uddin, G. S., & Shahbaz, M. (2013). The causal nexus between financial development and economic growth in Kenya. *Economic Modelling*, *35*, 701–707. doi:10.1016/j.econmod.2013.08.031

Unalmis, D. (2002). *The causality between financial development and economic growth: The case of Turkey*. The central bank of the republic of Turkey research department working paper, No: 3.

Wachtel, P. (2003). How much do we really know about growth and finance? *Federal Reserve Bank of Atlanta Economic Review,* 33-47.

Wolde-Rufael, Y. (2009). Re-examining the financial development and economic growth nexus in Kenya. *Economic Modelling*, *26*(6), 1140–1146. doi:10.1016/j.econmod.2009.05.002

Yucel, F. (2009). Causal relationships between financial development, trade openness and economic growth: The case of Turkey. *Journal of Social Sciences*, *5*(1), 33–42. doi:10.3844/jssp.2009.33.42

Zhang, J., Lanfang, W., & Susheng, W. (2012). Financial development and economic growth: Recent evidence from China. *Journal of Comparative Economics*, *40*(3), 393–412. doi:10.1016/j.jce.2012.01.001

KEY TERMS AND DEFINITIONS

Cointegration: When two or more series integrated on by one (in the time series sense) but some of their linear combination has a lower integration order, these series are called to be cointegrated. The case of the individual series are first-order integrated (I(1)) but some (cointegrating) vector of coefficients exists to form a stationary linear combination of them is a prevalent example.

Demand-Following Hypothesis: This hypothesis is an increase in the demand for financial services in favor of economic development, because it causes to the development of the financial sector.

Economic Growth: Economic growth means a process by which a nation's wealth increases over time. The increase in a country's productive capacity is measured by comparing gross domestic product GDP in a year with the GDP in the previous year.

Financial Development: Financial development is usually characterized as a period which specifies improvement in quantity, quality and effectiveness of financial intermediary services. The interaction of many activities and institutions occur in this process and probably it is related with economic growth.

Granger Causality Test: This is a statistical hypothesis test. It is used to determine if one time series is useful in forecasting another. Causality in economics could be reflected by measuring the ability of predicting the future values of a time series using past values of another time series.

Supply-Leading Hypothesis: Financial institutions incite innovation and support growth through the process of capital accumulation, which is reflected in saving and productive investments.

Trade Openness: Trade openness is stated as the degrees to which countries or economies allow or have trade with other countries or economies. Import and export, foreign direct investment, borrowing and lending, and repatriation of funds abroad are included in trading activities.

Chapter 16
The Sustainable Development Approach in the Economy–Ecology Dilemma

Gökhan Tenikler
Dokuz Eylül University, Turkey

Gamze Yıldız Şeren
Namık Kemal University, Turkey

ABSTRACT

The managerial model of cooperation and dialogue-driven, international, and supranational efforts during the past half-century form one of the most important topics within the "sustainable development" concept. Rapidly growing human population, together with the unsustainable pattern of consumption of renewable natural resources for future generations, also leads to the transfer of resources. The concept of development in keeping with ecological concerns about the impact of the dynamic approach should be reformulated. Faced with such dilemmas, these debates illustrate the need for a rational approach. Without jeopardizing the needs of future generations, to meet the demands of today's resource usage, the authors envision a sustainable development approach that seeks to balance protection and use. This approach should be addressed in the context of an understanding.

INTRODUCTION

The world we live in entered into a recent flurry of ends which can be estimated even today. However, this haste is not likely to be fulfilled only by those living in the present time, but needs to reach into future time.

So what's all the fuss about; what is the reason for this concern? Actually it is not too difficult to answer this question; the answer is very clear: Unsustainability. This concept corresponds to the expression: END OF LIFE.

It is mandatory to ensure continuity of natural resources, the living and non-living environment that constitutes the environmental components. So it is possible to separate these resources into two categories: living and nonliving resources (Keleş, Hamamcı & Çoban, 2012).

Live natural resources are biologically diverse and are composed of plants, animals and micro-

DOI: 10.4018/978-1-4666-7308-3.ch016

organisms. Humans are also a part of biodiversity and the life chain. Extinction of one of these species endangers other species which complement all the types generating the chain. If the Protection-usage balance cannot be established in a healthy way, the shortened chain may eliminate humans in the future. Commissioned by the United Nations Environment Program (UNEP), in 1995 the "Global Biodiversity Assessment" scientific report disclosed that about 1000 generations of species could rapidly become extinct (Türkman, 1998). Again, in 2010, declared the Year of Biodiversity by the United Nations, the International Union for Conservation of Nature (IUCN) reported that 44% face this danger, while 2% were also completely accounted for as extinct, of a total of 47,677 species on the IUCN's Red List (United Nations Environment Program [UNEP], 2010).

Essential and gradually decreasing living resources for food and agriculture are among the important advantages a country can have these days. The world's arable lands and water resources are rapidly becoming polluted and destroyed. Scientists agree that people will face a serious food and water problem in the near future. In the light of these developments, a country's biological diversity, particularly in terms of genetic resources, confers the status of a great power, because wild living resources are utilized to develop varieties with high production potential and resistance to environmental pressures (Convention on Biological Diversity [CBD], http://www.bcs.gov.tr/biodiversity/biodiversity.php).

Nonliving natural resources needed to sustain biological diversity are air, water, soil habitats and the subterranean base. The relative importance of these resources has an economic rather than ecological basis. As a result of unlimited economic growth, resource depletion has accelerated, creating the danger that the resources will fail to perform their functions due to global warming, soil erosion, and atmospheric pollution.

The exit point of the problems of living and non-living natural resources is related to conservation vs use, or "ecology" vs "economy", and reconciliation of these conflicting values.

The term "ecology" was first used by the German biologist Ernst Haeckel in 1866 (Keleş et al., 2012). He combined the Ancient Greek "Oikos", meaning "house, home, dwelling place, habitation" with the word "Logia", which means "speaking, discourse, treatise, doctrine, theory, science" (Okologie). In this respect, the word "ecology", derived from a discipline that identifies the subject areas of creatures' lives, encompasses the meaning "home science".

The etymological root of the word "economy" is similar to that of ecology. It (oikonomia) is derived from a combination of the Ancient Greek word for "home" (oikos) with the word for "law, management" (nomos). Economy might thus denote "thrifty household management", because in this context it incorporates the meanings "household management" and "being frugal, being thrifty".

However, the word "economy" has moved away from this meaning nowadays. Modern economics has lost its roots in the Greek word oikonomia (household management). It has instead absorbed chrematistics, or the maximization of short-run gain (Pearce, 1998, from Hayward, 1995).

SUSTAINABILITY OF RESOURCES

The famous Greek philosopher Plato is remarkable for his unconscious insight into the use of natural resources. In his work "Kritias" he wrote that, as a result of cutting trees, fertile soil is lost to excessive erosion, so that water resources are depleted. The slogan of today's environmentalists, "Let's protect biological diversity", has its source in the "abundance, productivity, diversity" principle put forward by Plato. The ancient Roman Tacitus is one of the most important environmental thinkers. Today he can be regarded as the pioneer of green values and of natural areas, as well as the person who first came up with the idea of leaving natural areas as they are. Tacitus particularly opposed dam construction and the modification of river channels (Tont, 1997).

A pessimistic approach to this aspect of the world, of course, depends on many factors which might arise. Two of these factors are located at the heart of the problem.

The first factor is "non-sustainable" consumption (Keating, 1993). Largely because of this problem, continuity can only be assured by the balanced use of resources. The second factor is the tremendous increase of the human population worldwide. In particular, the rapid population growth in the least developed and developing countries raises the prospect of impoverishment and degradation. In this sense the unplanned consumption of resources by the population has increased.

Unsustainable consumption patterns in a world with a growing population continues to put increasing pressure on natural resources. Former United States Vice President Al Gore declared in the documentary film "An Inconvenient Truth" (Isaacs, 2009):

We are witnessing a collision between our civilization and the Earth. And there are three factors that are causing this collision, and the first is population. When my generation, the baby boom generation, was born after World War II, the (world) population had just crossed the two billion mark. Now, I'm in my 50's, and it's already gone to almost six and a half billion. And if I reach the demographic expectation for the baby boomers, it'll go over nine billion.So, if it takes 10.000 generations to reach two billion and then in one human lifetime, ours, it goes from two billion to nine billion, something profoundly different is going on right now. We're putting pressure on the Earth. Most of it's in the poorer nations of the world. This puts pressure on food demand. It puts pressure on water demand. It puts pressure on vulnerable natural resources, and this pressure is one of the reasons why we have seen all the devastation of the forest, not only tropical, but elsewhere.

United Nations population projections in 2012 confirm Al Gore's statement. According to calculations made in 2013, the world population of 7,162,119 will reach 9,550,945 in 2050, and 10,853,849 in the year 2100 (United Nations [UN], 2013a).

Physical and biological properties of natural resources around the world in countries with existing assets are not unlimited. Renewable natural resources face the danger of misuse as a result of disruptive activities. Rapidly growing human populations are placing ecological and social pressure on these natural resources, leading to concern about a livable environment, especially for future generations, and even about the end of available resources, let alone their sustainability.

At Stanford University, biologist Petr Vitousek and his team stated that 40% of the annual net primary production on the earth's land is used directly to meet people's requirements, or used and destroyed indirectly by human activities. According to a simple calculation based on this statement, for the human species to survive on earth only 60% will remain of the millions of species. However, the speed of population growth threatens to increase the current rate of net primary production to 80% in 2030. In addition, the increase in per capita consumption may shorten this period. The earth's people, increasingly usurping the dynamics of ongoing life, will further accelerate the collapse of natural systems. However, as indicated by Vitousek and his team, "it seems that the limits of growth today will be of interest to decision-makers who think it is so far away, unaware of this biological reality" (Brown, Flavin, & Postel, 1998).

Nowadays, the system of consumption of water, air and soil that we regard as "renewable" leads to the pollution of natural resources, the alternative being to reduce utilization. It should be noted that the resources of world are not compliant with this outlook; they are not enough.

All societies, especially in the developed countries, have a tendency to more and more consumption. In short, these societies have built their future scenarios on a world in which "they consume more than they produce", without being aware of the problems they may encounter as a result.

At this point, in the context of unsustainability, an imbalance emerges between the consumption of developing or less developed societies, and that of developed societies. First of all, continuity of supply represents a balance. Sustainability, ensuring a balance between the long-term integrated and systematic economic, environmental and cultural resources, is necessary and inevitable.

United States President Thomas Jefferson, on September 6, 1789, asked in a letter to the next president James Madison, "whether a generation, have the right to bind provisions of the next generation", and answered in the negative that the world belonged to the living not the dead and that therefore those currently living should not leave a debt to future generations (Boyd (ed.), 1950):

Would the present generation be obliged to apply the produce of the earth and of their labor to replace their dissipations? Not at all.

Former United States Vice President Al Gore, again, expressed the imbalance in consumption in the following way (Karaca, 1995): that every American child consumes and produces waste up to the equivalent of every 30 Indian children born.

The World Bank Development Indicators report for 2008 showed that, according to 2005 data, 20% of the richest countries in the world are consuming about 76.6% more than the rest of the world. However, constituting 20% of the world's population, the poor countries, despite being equally proportional in size to the rich countries, consumed just 1.5% (World Bank, 2008).

In the early 1990s, Mathis Wackernagel developed the methodology for the "Ecological Footprint" along with his doctoral advisor Professor William E: Rees at the University of British Colombia in Canada. This is a natural resource accounting tool that measures how much of nature we have, how much we use and who uses what (Amend et al. (eds), 2010).

It is a measure of how much area of biologically productive land and water an individual, a population or an activity requires to produce all the resources it consumes and to absorb the corresponding waste (such as carbon dioxide emissions from fossil fuel use), using prevailing technology and resource management practices. The Ecological Footprint is usually measured in global hectares (gha), and includes the area of built-up land (Wackernagel et al., 2012).

According to ecological footprint calculations in 2008, our planet's biocapacity was 12.0 billion gha, or 1.8 gha per person, while humanity's ecological footprint was 18.2 billion gha, or 2.7 gha per person. This indicates a biocapacity deficit of 0.9 gha per person. Biocapacity per capita continuously declines as population increases (World Wildlife Fund [WWF], 2012).

Every country of the world has a different ecological footprint. For example, if all humanity lived like an average Indonesian, only two-thirds of the planet's biocapacity would be used; if everyone lived like an average Argentinean, humanity would demand more than half an additional planet, and if everyone lived like an average American, a total of four Earths would be required to regenerate humanity's annual demand on nature (WWF, 2012).

Advanced societies not only consume their own natural resources quickly but also consume those natural resources of less-developed societies which are not used or operated due to lack of money.

Thus has emerged an imbalance of natural resources, on the one hand those developed by cultures grown better able to achieve their targets, and on the other hand those in cultures of developed societies that have reached a level of rapid rationalization leading to destruction.

While this disparity lasts, people living in poverty-ridden societies will find it difficult to wait for the protection of natural resources. However, one of the most important steps is to establish a balance between the positive and the moderate in seeking sustainability of natural resources and human resources.

Hence, all countries are obliged to create sustainable consumption patterns, the goal being pursued by a sincere effort under the leadership of developed countries. So, arising from unsustainable consumption of natural resources, we are required to review and limit the addiction that minimizes the world's resources and carrying capacity, in line with a more accurate understanding of consumption (Keating, 1993).

After a general statement about the elements of sustainability that should be seen as a threat, there is the question of what the concept of "sustainability" means and what its scope is.

PROTECTION AND USAGE BALANCE: SUSTAINABLE POLICY

The purpose of economic development since the 1950s, over 10-year periods, has been defined by a variety of changing catchwords. For example, in the 1950s it was "Industrial Development", and shortly afterwards, "Agricultural Development" (Agricultural Development); the 1970s brought in the concepts of "Poverty" and then "Basic Needs", when determining economic purposes; finally, "Sustainability" is added to the list in the middle of the 1980s (Bennett, 2002).

Along with the concept of sustainability as based in ecology, development-based approaches are also seen. Naturally, the question "Sustainability of what?" arises.

Scope of Sustainability

Sustainability embodies issues of environmental values as well as the question of the scope of democracy (International Council for Local Environmental Initiatives [ICLEI], 1997).

The environmental management principle and the democratic decision-making principle are the indispensable conditions of sustainability. The environmental management principle is applied within the time available and as long as each generation continues to achieve sustainability. However, sustainability cannot be realized independently of the principle of democratic decision-making. In an environment conducted independently of this principle it can only be managed to a certain level.

Likewise, when adopting the concepts of democracy and equality within the idea of sustainability, namely environmental values in the geographic and spatial sense, rejecting democracy and equality is unthinkable.

Sustainability, in the context of a rational use of resources, is also intended to address issues of intergenerational democracy and social equality. Over time, the understanding of democracy and equality presents a case extending well into future generations. In not separating future needs from those of today, sustainability represents a democratic element in terms of time. Likewise, when adopting the concept of democracy and equality within the idea of environmental sustainability in the geographic and spatial sense, it would be out of the question to reject democracy and equality.

Sustainability as a concept does not target a single point within the community. The aim of creating a sustainable life requires a joint effort by all institutions of the society. For example, an improvement to be made in consumption patterns cannot be separated from the population. Again, the selection of technology appropriate to the idea of sustainability cannot be independent of the social and cultural structure of the society. Hence, in forming a global community of interdependent parts, sustainability alone is unthinkable.

Sustainability is a broad concept in scope. The proposal entails provisions affecting many elements of society: population is kept under control by reducing poverty, alternative technology is introduced, consumption patterns are improved, hunger/famine issues affect biodiversity, the adequate apportionment of resources is established.

So the concept of sustainability involves not only the outlook of the ecological movement which aims to prevent environmental pollution, but also has much wider societal implications. However, the application of this insight is not possible solely within the concept of sustainability. The success of its implementation and realization of its purposes depends on management of the social and political struggle.

Transformation of Development Approach

The history of mankind's struggle with nature offers many examples. Some authors have asserted that societies must struggle with Nature in order to create civilization.

The famous historian Arnold Toynbee described the struggle of humanity with nature in his "Challenge and Response Theory", according to which, in the emergence and development of civilizations, the available geographical environment determines the status of the constant human "challenge". But it should be noted that the struggle against nature undoubtedly involves taking advantages of the resources given by nature. As early as 3000 BC, the oldest written epic, the Sumerian Gilgamesh Epic, relates how the King of Gilgamesh fought to kill the monster Huwawa, a protector of a forest containing cedar trees, which provide timber, an important raw material in meeting his country's development needs (George, 2003).

The human–nature struggle that went on through the historical process has been reshaped as further growth in the developed countries today, and the further development, as reflexes, of the developing countries.

The 18th century classical economist Adam Smith promoted economic growth on the assumption that natural resources are unlimited. Especially in the 19th century, marked by the Industrial Revolution, natural resources were under pressure, as they provided the input to intensive production.

The effect of imperialist values on the use and allocation of resources should not be underestimated. For example, in 1855, the Indian Chief Seattle, whose natural resources the white man wished to purchase, made a speech which is impossible not to heed. This letter may be considered among the "first civilian protests against imperialism bearing the ecological label" (Toprak, 2012).

Although the ideas of the Industrial Revolution and the Enlightenment are the main source of the increase in prominent ecological problems, they also played a major role in the increase in environmental and ecological sensitivity. Awareness of nature began with the problems of industrial society. In the United Kingdom the Alpine Club (founded 1857), the Open Spaces Society (1865) and the Royal Society for the Protection of Birds (1889), were among the organizations that displayed such sensitivity (Görmez, 2010).

In the second half of the 20th century, intense debate over intergenerational obligations became the subject of the period, though in the first half of this century, highlights from the work and comments of the economist Pigou on "Wealth and Welfare" (1912) are noteworthy. Indeed, Pigou was one of the earliest economists to robustly defend the interests of future generations, who are likely suffer harm due to the indulgence of present generations (Kula, 1998).

Especially in the period after the Second World War, states and governments revived moves to continue within the framework of the their intense development efforts up to 1960, so that, to ensure the legitimacy of these efforts, natural resources were neglected.

Problems related to the rational use of natural resources began to be noticed by 1960. However, this awareness had not yet spread throughout the world.

In 1962, the ideas of Rachel Carson's "Silent Spring" and Garrett Hardin's "The Tragedy of the Commons" were among the first examples of effective efforts towards sustainable development. Paradigm-breaking books and articles such as these galvanized individual countries and the international community into action (UNEP, http://www.unep.org/geo/GEO3/english/pdfs/chapter1.pdf).

Carson's work, discussing the impact of the use of the chemicals, especially DDT, and the nature of jamming, saw the beginning of the modern environmentalist movement, while Garrett Hardin's discussion of the pressure on natural resources created by population growth in public areas is considered an important contribution to environmental understanding in the 1970s.

The "Environmentalist years", as the 1970s were called, along with development of the "green management" approach, were building the tendency towards non-rational use of resources based on this awareness.

The concept of development has become one that needs to be reformulated, after evaluating the managerial approach within the framework of economic perceptions, along with the impact of the approach based on ecological concerns.

Looking both Responsive to Development and Sensitive to the Environment

In the 70s, Western scientists and industrialists, observing the process of environmental problems arising and necessary measures not being taken, resulting in greater risks to vibrant life, began to offer responses having universal dimensions.

In 1971, MIT (Massachusetts Institute of Technology) professionals were commissioned by the Rome Club and in 1972, as a suggestion offered by developed countries to less developed countries in "The Limits to Growth" report, originated the "Zero Growth" model (Meadows, Meadows, Randers, Behrens, 1972).

The model's basic logic rested on the view that a stage of developed countries' economies and a certain level of welfare had to be reached before the environment was destroyed. Starting from that idea, developing countries could be prevented from making similar mistakes, so that at least in other parts of the world the environment would remain intact.

At that time the model seemed Utopian and exaggerated, containing elements contrary to equality in developing countries, and rightly evoked strong reactions. It was suggested that the Rome Club report was a "trap" for the development efforts of less developed or developing countries. Developed countries following such a model encouraged the establishment of polluting industries in less developed countries, thus indirectly threatening the latter while allowing their own capital in these countries to increase, but without the risk of contamination.

The reaction created by this concept, in a sense has led to the countries' search for a more realistic use of resources.

In 1972, the world experienced a development that would be recognized as a turning point in environmental policy: the Stockholm Conference on the Human Environment.

Recognizing the environment as a right for the first time, this conference took an important step towards sustainable development. Maurice Strong, secretary-general of the conference, who first used the maxim "environment does not exclude development" (Eco development), intended to adopt a development strategy from local sources, expressing the concept of equitable benefit (Keleş et al., 2012).

At the end of the conference, the Stockholm Declaration was issued, highlighting the relationship between the two principles for present and future generations, as the basis for recognition of sustainable development in the near future (UN, 1972):

- "Man has the fundamental right to freedom, equality and adequate conditions of life, in an environment of a quality that permits a life of dignity and well-being, and he bears a solemn responsibility to protect and improve the environment for present and future generations." (Principle 1)
- "The non-renewable resources of the earth must be employed in such a way as to guard against the danger of their future exhaustion and to ensure that benefits from such employment are shared by all mankind." (Principle 5)

In 1973, in Ernst Friedrich Schumacher's book "Small is Beautiful", underlining scarce resources in terms of production and consumption relations and the reorganization of necessity, criticized the capitalist perspective which defends growth and increases consumption (Schumacher, 1973).

In 1973, establishment of the United Nations Environment Program (UNEP) was among the first steps formulated in the corporate sense of environment–development relationships.

The most important of these concrete steps was the World Conservation Strategy (WCS) certificate, prepared and published in 1980 by UNEP, in partnership with the International Union for the Conservation of Nature and Natural Resources (IUCN) and the World Wildlife Fund (WWF).

The document was entitled "World Conservation Strategy – Living Resource Conservation for Sustainable Development". As can be seen, the "sustainable development" concept, first used in this strategy document with its current meaning, meant that the handling of its present meaning would take place in subsequent years.

WCS emphasizes the need for conservation and development to be dealt with so as to achieve a sustainable society. The document's definitions of development and conservation are as follows (International Union for Conservation of Nature [IUCN], UNEP, WWF, 1980):

Development is defined here as: the modification of the biosphere and the application of human, financial, living and non-living resources to satisfy human needs and improve the quality of human life. For development to be sustainable it must take account of social and ecological factors, as well as economic ones; of the living and non-living resource base; and of the long term as well as the short term advantages and disadvantages of alternative actions.

Conservation is defined here as: the management of human use of the biosphere so that it may yield the greatest sustainable benefit to present generations while maintaining its potential to meet the needs and aspirations of future generations. Thus conservation is positive, embracing preservation, maintenance, sustainable utilization, restoration, and enhancement of the natural environment. Living resource conservation is specifically concerned with plants, animals and microorganisms, and with those non-living elements of the environment on which they depend. Living resources have two important properties the combination of which distinguishes them from non-living resources: they are renewable if conserved; and they are destructible if not.

The issue highlighted in this strategy document is the conservation of living resources. Accordingly, living resource conservation has three specific objectives:

- To maintain essential ecological processes and life-support systems (such as soil regeneration and protection, the recycling of nutrients, and the cleansing of waters), on which human survival and development depend;

- To preserve genetic diversity (the range of genetic material found in the world's organisms), on which depend the breeding programs necessary for the protection and improvement of cultivated plants and domesticated animals, as well as much scientific advance, technical innovation, and the security of the many industries that use living resources;
- To ensure the sustainable utilization of species and ecosystems (notably fish and other wildlife, forests and grazing lands), which support millions of rural communities as well as major industries.

"Sustainable utilization" is introduced to international literature in this document along with other concepts.

This first formulation of the sustainable development approach, foregrounding the more ecological approach and conservation of living resources, will consider reasons such as opposition to perceived improvement and the criticism that each activity will adversely affect the environment. The narrow perspective brought forward in WCS on the relationship between economy and ecology has created the need for reformulation of the concept of sustainable development. Development in a sustainable manner, without destroying natural resources and realizing the principles and decisions concerning the infrastructure, was outlined in the Brundtland Report of 1987 and has become effective.

1987 Brundtland Report (Our Common Future)

Unconscious and unplanned results of the use of natural resources, furthering the process of destruction, was an issue to be addressed once again, gaining importance in the international arena. By 1983 the United Nations created the UN World Environment and Development Commission (UN World Commission on Environment and Development); by 1987, it organized a meeting at the Kenyan capital Nairobi, where the principles for a sustainable future were applied and decisions were made. Here, the concept of sustainability, which today is used literally, was expressed by the Commission at the "Our Common Future" meeting, chaired by the UN Secretary General, former Norwegian Prime Minister Gro Harlem Brundtland. Hence the name "Brundtland report" entered the world agenda.

The most valid approach to the concept of sustainable development is found in the official definition of its scope provided by UNWCED (United Nations World Commission on Environment and Development) in 1987, in the Brundtland Report (Our Common Future):

According to the report, Sustainable development is development that meets the needs of the present without compromising the ability of future generations to meet their own needs (United Nations World Commission on Environment and Development [UNWCED], 1987). Development, thus, includes not only rising aggregate consumption or output, but also environmental quality, social factors, and the distribution of income (Bretschger & Egli, 2001).

It contains within it two key concepts:

- The concept of "needs", in particular the essential needs of the world's poor, to which overriding priority should be given; and
- The idea of limitations imposed by the state of technology and social organization on the environment's ability to meet present and future needs.

Critical objectives for environmental and developmental policies that follow from the concept of sustainable development include:

- Reviving growth;
- Changing the quality of growth;
- Meeting essential needs for jobs, food, energy, water, and sanitation;
- Ensuring a sustainable level of population;
- Conserving and enhancing the resource base:
- Reorienting technology and managing risk; and
- Merging environment and economics in decision making.

Sustainable development requires:

- A political system that secures effective citizen participation in decision making;
- An economic system that is able to generate surpluses and technical knowledge on a self-reliant and sustained basis;
- A social system that provides solutions to the tensions arising from disharmonious development;
- A production system that respects the obligation to preserve the ecological base for development;
- A technological system that can search continuously for new solutions;
- An international system that fosters sustainable patterns of trade and finance; and
- An administrative system that is flexible and has the capacity for self-correction.

This report counted as priority issues population, food, agriculture, energy, industry, health, human settlements, and environmental cooperation in international relations.

The concept of sustainability has been introduced to the world's agenda in a way that has not been top-down. This concept in the international sense of addressing, on the basis of "development carried out for every legitimate action and development for the sake of resources consumed in an unconsciously destructive process" was unquestioned in the 1960s, when a developmentalist ideology appeared, and the environmental movement, emerging as a response in the 1970s, had its effects. Here the Brundtland Report, in the 1980s, served the purpose of the 1960s developmentalist ideology, reconciling it with the environmental understanding of the 1970s.

The report does not offer policy recommendations, but instead focuses on current problems and preventative challenges. The report indicates the need for an integrated planning approach that no country's sustainable development can perform while abstracting itself from other countries. Thus the report reveals the necessity of change in international relations, mentioning the importance of the World Bank's leadership role in sustainable development.

The principles in the report were turned into a declaration by the UN General Assembly. Such a transformation in the form of recommendations is an important step in the creation of binding international environmental policy.

Despite the ideas it presented, the report has been subject to various criticisms (Erdoğan & Ejder, 1997). For example, some developed countries, especially in Germany, where the environmental groups were combined under the name "Alliance for Sustainable Development", presented their own reports. One such report, while praising the Brundtland Report, which drew attention to useful information and created an international debate about the environment, stated that the report would not bring fundamental change. The idea of showing environmental degradation as poverty and offering expansion as a remedy was rejected. The concept of Western-type growth and development from outside was a fallacy, since they should come from within the country. As an example, in answer to a question about the chances of India reaching Britain's living standards, Gandhi asserted: "this wealth of England was required to reach half of the world's resources. How many planets does a country like India want?"

The United Nations Conference on Environment and Development – Earth Summit

The Brundtland report provides a wealth of information on the concept of sustainable development, as well as paving the way to a global action plan for its implementation. However, the report has fallen far short of the expected "participation" that increasingly began to gain importance in the world (Emrealp, 2005).

Hence, the sustainable development approach adopted in 1987 must seek concrete implementation in terms of action-oriented policy, through arrangement of a global meeting to discuss need.

Indeed, in 1972, in Stockholm the world's first environmental conference was held, known as the "Human Environment Conference"; and on its 20th anniversary, the second largest world conference was held, on 3-14 June 1992 in Rio de Janeiro, the capital of Brazil.

For the development of environmentally compatible development policy, the summit aims at "a collective association", including representatives of the heads of state and governments as well as of non-governmental organizations (NGOs), considered as partners.

Meetings were carried out in two stages: the "Conference on Environment and Development (UNCED; 3 to 11 June 1992)" and "Earth Summit (12 to 14 June 1992)". Over 30,000 people from 172 countries participated in the well-attended conference, which brought together heads of state and government representatives at the global level for the first time to consider issues of environment and development.

As a result of UNCED, the Rio Declaration was published without a binding clause specifying the rights and obligations of countries in regard to environment–development issues.

The United Nations Conference on Environment and Development released, as one of the conference's five[1] documents, a declaration of principles containing 27 points.

The decisions taken and principles identified at the 1972 Stockholm Conference on Human Environment were reaffirmed; global environment and development systems would be studied for their protective agreements and the need to address these for the world as a whole was indicated. In addition, the creation of a new level was targeted, in order to establish a new and unbiased partnership of global cooperation between people and key sectors of society.

We can specify 27 principles directly related to the "sustainable development" concept adopted in the Rio Declaration on Environment and Development (UN, 1992):

- **The Right to a Healthy Life:** Human beings are at the center of concerns for sustainable development. They are entitled to a healthy and productive life in harmony with nature.
- **Jurisdiction and Responsibility:** States have, in accordance with the Charter of the United Nations and the principles of international law, the sovereign right to exploit their own resources pursuant to their own environmental and developmental policies, and the responsibility to ensure that activities within their jurisdiction or control do not cause damage to the environment of other States or of areas beyond the limits of national jurisdiction.
- **The Right to Development:** The right to development must be fulfilled so as to equitably meet developmental and environmental needs of present and future generations.

- **Integration of Environment and Development:** In order to achieve sustainable development, environmental protection shall constitute an integral part of the development process and cannot be considered in isolation from it.
- **Poverty Eradication:** All States and all people shall cooperate in the essential task of eradicating poverty as an indispensable requirement for sustainable development, in order to decrease the disparities in standards of living and better meet the needs of the majority of the people of the world.
- **Special Priority to Developing Countries:** The special situation and needs of developing countries, particularly the least developed and those most environmentally vulnerable, shall be given special priority. International actions in the field of environment and development should also address the interests and needs of all countries.
- **Global Partnership and Cooperation:** States shall cooperate in a spirit of global partnership to conserve, protect and restore the health and integrity of the Earth's ecosystem. In view of the different contributions to global environmental degradation, States have common but differentiated responsibilities. The developed countries acknowledge the responsibility that they bear in the international pursuit of sustainable development in view of the pressures their societies place on the global environment and of the technologies and financial resources they command.
- **Patterns of Production–Consumption:** To achieve sustainable development and a higher quality of life for all people, States should reduce and eliminate unsustainable patterns of production and consumption and promote appropriate demographic policies.
- **Exchange of Knowledge:** States should cooperate to strengthen endogenous capacity-building for sustainable development by improving scientific understanding through exchanges of scientific and technological knowledge, and by enhancing the development, adaptation, diffusion and transfer of technologies, including new and innovative technologies.
- **Participation of Women:** Women have a vital role in environmental management and development. Their full participation is therefore essential to achieve sustainable development.
- **Importance of Youth:** The creativity, ideals and courage of the youth of the world should be mobilized to forge a global partnership in order to achieve sustainable development and ensure a better future for all.
- **Support to Local Communities:** Indigenous people and their communities and other local communities have a vital role in environmental management and development because of their knowledge and traditional practices. States should recognize and duly support their identity, culture and interests and enable their effective participation in the achievement of sustainable development.
- **Respect for International Law:** Warfare is inherently destructive of sustainable development. States shall therefore respect international law providing protection for the environment in times of armed conflict and cooperate in its further development, as necessary.
- **Good Faith and Spirit of Partnership:** States and people shall cooperate in good faith and in a spirit of partnership in the fulfilment of the principles embodied in this Declaration and in the further development of international law in the field of sustainable development.

As seen earlier, many issues not addressed in a global dimension were discussed at Rio and agreed in principle. However, a full consensus could not be reached on all the policies raised, because of disagreements, particularly between developed countries and developing countries. No definitive consensus can be asserted on principles such as powers and responsibilities, the right to development, poverty alleviation, collaboration, and production-consumption-population.

The Rio Conference was a milestone of the world environmental movement, not only bringing the "sustainable development" concept into our lives, but also enhancing it, taking into account the participatory mechanisms and processes of the United Nations, and of all governments and other agencies and organizations. The Rio Conference reveals resources and dimensions in terms of environmental problems, and also includes a feature which enabled ideas and activities arising quite late in the history of mankind to be discussed on an international scale as comprehensive property. A basic common understanding of the principles adopted and expressed in the contracts signed at the conference is required; countries that have a common future cannot be unresponsive to environmental challenges, pollutants emitted into the global environment at different levels must be in amounts that do not endanger the environmental balance, and resources must renew themselves according to an ecologically sustainable conservation–use balance.

In order to take action on the topics discussed at Rio, an action plan has been prepared under the name of "Agenda 21".

The document presenting the Agenda of the 21st century, which features an action plan, is intended to form the basis for an understanding on sustainable development and environmental protection within the "global partnership". Agenda 21, which is one of the best-known documents of the United Nations, sets out the basic principles established in Rio about environmental protection and community development issues, based on their own residential properties.

The "global partnership" concept is introduced in the Agenda 21 Action Plan to meet basic requirements, improve living standards, better protect and manage ecosystems, and lay the building blocks for a more secure path to the future.

The Agenda 21 Action Plan consists of four main sections[2]:

- Social and Economic Dimensions
- Conservation and Management of Resources for Development
- Strengthening the Role of Major Groups
- Means of Implementation

At the Conference in Rio de Janeiro, world leaders signed three international treaties – the United Nations Framework Convention on Climate Change (UNFCCC) (followed by the Kyoto Protocol in 1997), the Convention on Biological Diversity (CBD), and the Convention to Combat Desertification (UNCCD) – which pursue one common goal: sustainable human development. All three Conventions are of equal status in terms of their relevance to the preservation of our natural life-support systems, poverty reduction, and achieving greater global justice (Amend et al. (eds), 2010).

The United Nations Conference on Environment and Development in 1992 recognized the important role that the indicators could play in helping countries make informed decisions concerning sustainable development. As a matter of fact, Chapter 40 of Agenda 21 has called on countries, as well as international, governmental and non-governmental organizations, to develop indicators of sustainable development that can provide a solid basis for decision-making at all levels. Agenda 21 also has called for the harmonization of efforts to develop such indicators (UN, 2007).

Founded in 1992, the Commission on Sustainable Development (CSD) has since 1995 initiated the international sustainable development indicators, of which the main and sub-themes are as follows (UN, 2007):

- **Poverty:** Income Poverty, Income Inequality, Sanitation, Drinking Water, Access to Energy, Living Conditions
- **Governance:** Corruption, Crime
- **Health:** Mortality, Life Expectancy at Birth, Health Care Delivery, Immunization against Infectious Childhood Diseases, Nutritional Status, Health Status and Risks
- **Education:** Education Level, Literacy
- **Demographics:** Population, Tourism
- **Natural Hazards:** Vulnerability to Natural Hazards, Disaster Preparedness and Response
- **Atmosphere:** Climate Change, Ozone Layer Depletion, Air Quality
- **Land:** Land Use and Status, Desertification, Agriculture, Forests
- **Oceans, Seas, and Coasts:** Coastal Zone Fisheries, Marine Environment
- **Freshwater:** Water Quantity, Water Quality
- **Biodiversity:** Ecosystem, Species
- **Economic Development:** Macroeconomic Performance, Sustainable Public Finance, Employment, Information and Communication Technologies, Research and Development, Tourism
- **Global Economic Partnership:** Trade, External Financing
- **Consumption and Production Patterns:** Material Consumption, Energy Use, Waste Generation and Management, Transportation

These indicators are intended to give guidance to countries on how to create national sustainable development indicators.

Despite all these efforts, Agenda 21 failed to reach an agreement on all the issues up for discussion. These issues can be summarized as orientation of technology from rich countries to poor countries, transfer of financial resources, the protection of water resources, chemicals and hazardous waste management, data and information flow (Keleş & Hamamcı, 1993). It is not surprising that sharp differences of opinion on "sustainable development" have emerged between the developed countries who have used enhanced levels of access to natural resources rashly and caused a very large portion of current environmental problems, and those who are oppressed under the weight of the rapid urbanization process and whose natural resources are being depleted by development (Emrealp, 2005).

Similar efforts were made after 1992, with similar topics carried over to the following years.

Millennium Development Goals

The United Nations Millennium Development Goals were considered in September 2000 at the UN Millennium Summit in New York City by 192 members of the United Nations, who scheduled eight goals to be met by 2015:

The Millennium Development Goals for 2015 (UNEP):

1. Eradicate extreme hunger and poverty
2. Achieve universal primary education
3. Promote gender equality and empower women
4. Reduce child mortality
5. Improve maternal health
6. Combat HIV/AIDS, malaria and other diseases
7. Ensure environmental sustainability
8. Develop a global partnership for development

In 2015 the eighth goal was to be achieved, as the United Nations 2013 Millennium Development Goals Assessment Report discussed poverty reduction, wider access to clean water, improvement of living conditions in poor urban neighborhoods, and achievement of gender equality in primary schools, and stated that millions of people had realized improvement; as of 2015 it has become possible to achieve far more within the Millennium Development Goals (UN, 2013b).

However, one of the most important factors affecting the achievement of targets is the reduction of aid to developing countries. The report declares that the poorest countries received the biggest blow from this reduction. In 2012, net aid disbursements from developed to developing countries totaled $126 billion. This represents a 4 per cent drop in real terms compared to 2011, which was 2 per cent below 2010 levels. The decline affected least developed countries the most (UN, 2013b).

Rio+10, Rio+20

In 1992 was the Rio Environment and Development Summit; in 1997, the fifth annual assessment meeting was held in New York City, the Rio +5 Conference, following 10-year aims to be evaluated; and Rio +10, known as the World Sustainable Development Summit, 26 August to 4 September 2002, in Johannesburg was arranged.

The summits were followed by more than 104 heads of government and state as well as 20.000 participants, among them representatives of civil society organizations.

According to the Plan of Implementation of the World Summit on Sustainable Development, poverty eradication, changing consumption and production patterns, and protecting and managing the natural resource base for economic and social development are overarching objectives of and essential requirements for sustainable development (UN, 2002).

To achieve the objectives of Sustainable Development a new World summit was added, known as the Rio+20 Conference on Sustainable Development, aimed at a 20-year review of the 1992 Rio Summit. Held in Rio de Janeiro, "Sustainable development and the green economy" were established as the most important items on the agenda of the conference. In particular it was to lead to countries making the transition to a green economy, while realistic and implementable solutions for public and private sectors were also put forward.

The outcome of the Rio +20 Earth Summit, the "Future We Want" document, discussed limitations and failures, despite the activities of the last 20 years, in meeting the objectives of sustainable development. According to the document, poverty is still the world's biggest problem. Poverty eradication, highlighting the aspects of sustainable consumption and production, and conservation and management of natural resources in economic and social areas of development, are confirmed once again as objectives of basic and comprehensive sustainable development. As of 2015, it was necessary to accelerate the achievement of development goals, including the Millennium Development Goals, by making repeated efforts to show commitment (UN, 2012).

Key to Ecology-Economy Dilemma: Sustainable Development

The idea of economic growth had the dominant role in the development process of the country until the 1970s, when the idea of Sustainable Development was first put forward.

Backward countries never had to handle economic development in relation to the environment. However, the concepts of environment and development are not independent of or opposed to each other.

Development sustainability and acceptability are connected to adoption of the idea that the environment is the source of economic development and has limits. In this spirit, the sustainability of economic development makes the maintenance of environmental health also necessary. Each of these two cases can seem, at first glance, to have a property which endangers the existence of the other.

Within the framework of the international efforts mentioned above, today's three basic elements of sustainable development, economy, environment and society, have experienced a major transformation in their relationship.

Sustainable development within this vision requires:

Economic competition within the world market, ensuring that basic needs such as education, people's housing, health, and clean drinking water are met in an appropriate manner, raising the level of welfare; Socially equitable policies, inclusive of disadvantaged groups and boosting the quality of life, From an environmental perspective, environmental pollution prevention and protection of the natural systems that support life in mutually supportive and complementary ways. A balanced planning, implementation and management process, between generations and inter generations (Republic of Turkey, Ministry of Development, 2012)

1992 and later events showed that development begins first at the local level. It would not be possible to think of economy as separate from environment, environment from community, and community from the economy. The elements of economy, community and environment complement each other and each one has its own specific requirements (see Figure 1[3]).

Economic development also includes stable economic growth. It is necessary in the search for new markets that production capacity will inevitably need to grow. Community development requires an egalitarian social structure. Participation in decision-making should be improved. The presence of a social structure which is self-sufficient, able to meet basic needs and improve the quality of life is required. Ecological development demands resource utilization, reproduction of sources and less development, through technologies that respect the carrying capacity of nature. In fact, some aspects of community development will take place in a more effective in a way with the establishment of a healthy balance between economy and ecology.

So are these three requirements of the development process in conflict within each other? The answer to this question is yes, by the shortest path. Economic production resource needs will put pressure on the idea of conservation of natural resources. The basic needs of society as well as individuals within the framework of luxury consumption habits can support economic development at the expense of ecological development.

Figure 1. The sustainable development challenge

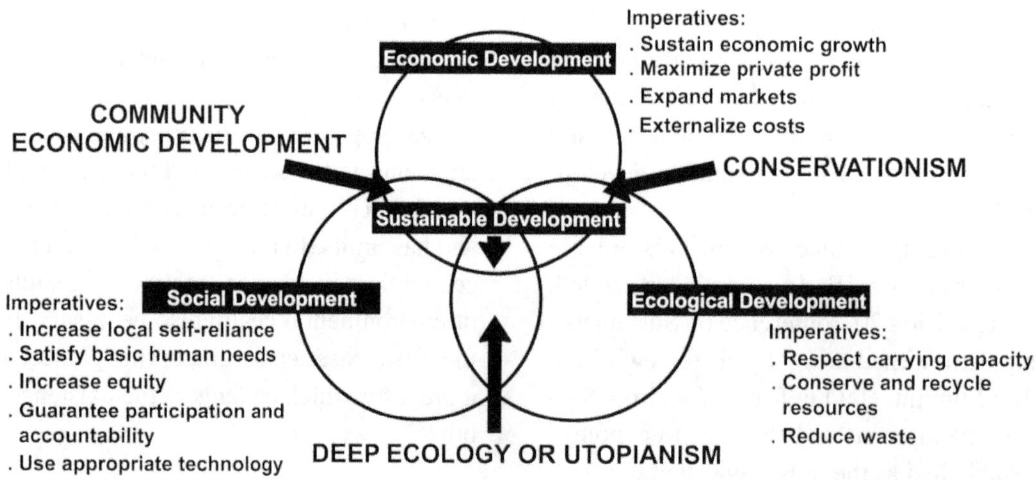

Economically prosperous sectors of society will increase inequality in income distribution in relation to impoverished segments of society. These contradictions, as can be seen within a single society, can also be clearly observed between countries.

In this regard, sustainable development is a process of bringing these three development processes into balance with each other. The implementation of a sustainable development strategy therefore involves negotiation among the primary interest groups (stakeholders) involved in these three development processes (ICLEI, 1996).

The current perception of the three dimensions of sustainable development is shown in Figure 2[4]. There is little belief in sustainable development as a mechanism for adaptation of these three dimensions, in an environment that has not produced effective solutions despite efforts taking place over the last 40 years. The presence of conflicting or crosscutting aspects render these three elements insufficient for the creation of a healthy harmony.

In a new perception, environment is evaluated in society and from the economy-wide perspective. Namely, the environmental conditions will acquire sustainability features or will weaken according to the community's economic preferences within their own lives. Developed at Rio +20, the "green economy" concept aims at catalyzing a reformulation of the environment rather than seeing environmental and economic thought as two separate, intersecting or conflicting, elements.

Sustainability means improving the quality of life concept in accordance with the carrying capacity of the area. The concept of sustainability is designed to provide sustainable development.

In fact, sustainability is meant to include the environmental sustainability of natural resources as components. The concept of sustainability, resource use, not only takes into account the needs of the present generation but also those of future generations.

Environment, earlier perceived narrowly as short-term solutions to contamination problems and their elimination, today has begun to present itself in terms of natural, economic, social and cultural values as a whole. The most important factor determining this outlook is the destruction of the resources used to carry out social and economic development by rapid and irreversible methods.

Sustainable development as a concept popular in recent years is not, however, actually a new concept. In one respect, it upholds one of the basic elements of classical growth theory. It is possible to trace the original roots of this concept to Ricardo and Malthus. Both asserted that there were "natural

Figure 2. Evolution of sustainable development thought

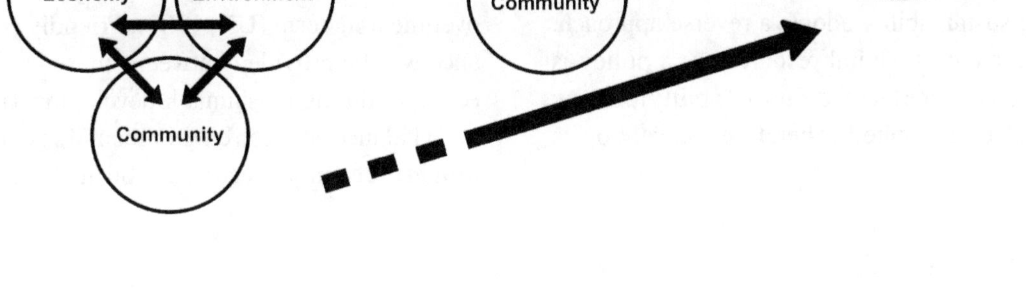

limits" to economic growth. Ricardo argued that land resources are limited, while Malthus argued that in the relation between increasing population and resources, there were limits to the growth of the "natural", and that, once these limits were reached, producing goods would not be possible (Aruoba, 1992). The basis of this idea is that progression of population growth is geometric, while the increase in natural resources is subject to an arithmetic progression. So while population multiplies greatly over 25 years, natural resources increase only slightly (Keleş et al., 2012)

The question to discuss in seeking an approach to resource allocation, in view of the "Environment-Production" problem, is whether to allow the use of sources of growth to continue at a rapid pace, if they are also to be used in the future.

The question to be asked at this point is: how long will this development continue?

Long-term and steady development, if adopted as a goal to be achieved at the expense of short-term goals embodying a wasteful attitude to consumption of natural resources, will bring us to the point of blockage. In the future, if it is not possible to replace exhaustible resources with other sources, sustainable development will be out of the question.

In this context, two different perceptions of sustainability have been suggested: Weak and Strong Sustainability (Pearce, 1999).

These two concepts are shaped by the substitution relationship between natural resources and man-made capital. According to the weak sustainability concept, there is an unlimited opportunity for substitution between natural resources and man-made capital. Natural resources are not endangered, therefore do not require protection. Growth continues with only partial restrictions. Strong sustainability adopts a reverse approach. Replacement of natural resources as a policy is inadequate, since these resources' ability to renew themselves is limited. Therefore, prevention is required.

In some sources a third definition of sustainability is added: Environmental Sustainability (Tietenberg, 2003). By this definition, it is not only the total value of natural resources that is important; protection of the individual is connected. For example, if a lot of fish are caught on a regular basis, more than the total number of fish caught are taken into account in protecting them.

In this context, if physical or human capital can be substituted by natural resources, the total natural resource base will not decrease (Ertürk, 2011). Indeed, sustainable development depends on the sustainability of renewable natural resources. In this regard the production of renewable energy needs to be more involved in the process.

Accordingly, the ideas brought forward by the concept of sustainable development can be summarized as economic development that does not consume natural capital, does not take away the possibility for future generations to meet their own needs, protects the balance between the economy and the ecosystem, and is ecologically sustainable (Berkes & Kışlalıoğlu, 1990).

Environment, in terms of natural resources, is the foundation of the economy needed to sustain the lives of people living in the surrounding area, and thus coexists with it. With the close connections between the environment and economic stability, ensuring the sustainability of human life is of vital importance.

However, economic growth always brings the risk of environmental damage, as it puts increased pressure on environmental resources. But policy makers guided by the concept of sustainable development will necessarily work to ensure that growing economies remain firmly attached to their ecological roots and that these roots are protected and nurtured so that they may support growth over the long term (UN, 1987). Friendly compliance will be provided between environment and economy through sustainable development policy.

A balance between environmental sustainability and the economy can be established only when communities, with fewer resources, can take "a precautionary approach" to prevent environmental problems before they occur, rejecting the principle of "the development concept despite everything" and to that extent reducing the uneven development and prosperity gap between countries.

Against the concept of sustainable development, some other approaches have emerged. One of the most important is "rather than sustainable development, sustainable living" (Karaca, 1998). On this understanding, sustainable development means depletion and pollution. Depletion and pollution risks all life, should these goals be pursued. Because development means production, consumption means contamination. It is necessary to seek the concept of a life that will guarantee of the survival of all living things in the future.

Another topic of discussion is whether the sensitivity that governments show in the international conventions is adequately reflected in their internal legal order.

In relation to this issue, some examples are found in provisions of the 1982 Constitution of the Republic of Turkey[5].

In the 1982 Constitution of the Republic of Turkey, "Social and Economic Rights and Duties" are listed under the headings of Article 56 and 65, as follows:

A. Health services and protection of the environment ARTICLE 56. Everyone has the right to live in a healthy and balanced environment. It is the duty of the State and citizens to improve the natural environment, to protect environmental health and to prevent environmental pollution. ....

XIII. The Extent of Social and Economic Rights (Before 2001) ARTICLE 65. The State shall fulfill its duties as laid down in the Constitution in the social and economic fields within the limits of its financial resources, taking into consideration the maintenance of economic stability.

XIII. The extent of social and economic duties of the State (After 2001) ARTICLE 65 (As amended on October 3, 2001; Act No. 4709): The State shall fulfill its duties as laid down in the Constitution in the social and economic fields within the capacity of its financial resources, taking into consideration the priorities appropriate with the aims of these duties.

As seen in Article 56, protecting the environment is located among the social obligations of the government and citizens.

Hence, as of today, according to Article 65 entitled "The extent of social and economic duties of the State", before the 2001 amendments, the state was looking out for economic stability in the social and economic performance of its duties. So that is one of the social obligations of environmental protection activities, should they adversely affect the economic stability of the state in carrying out its task. This application strengthened the state's discretion.

By the change made in 2001, "the maintenance of economic stability" was removed, and "the priorities appropriate with the aims of these duties" were added. In this case the government now will not only oversee economic stability to protect the environment, but the observance of environmental protection is expressed as a priority issue by the administration; if accepted, the government will fulfill this duty, but in fact, it is still at the discretion of the administration. However, the government's duty to protect the environment will not get caught on obstacles to economic stability alone.

As can be seen in the work of national legislation, taking into account the international approach to intellectual transformation, more is needed.

CONCLUSION AND REMARKS

The concepts of economy and ecology are not irreconcilable opposites. Greater competition between countries and the search for growth creates this dilemma. The only concern is for countries to exhibit a friendly attitude when discussing sustainable policies.

At the point of implementation of the principle of sustainable development, although it is not a full consensus even after a period of over 40 years, it is going ahead. The starting point of discussion is the developed countries which do not respect the balance of claims between protection and use. Those countries which destroyed the ecology are also trying to partner with less developed countries on the invoice.

With declarations and contracts signed after prolonged discussion by several governments, it remains to be seen to what extent sustainable life will be achieved. However, in reflecting on the application of these universal efforts, it appears that delays and conflicts of interest under the influence of forces might allow possible violations to occur.

Today all mankind are connected to each other more than ever because of the problems faced in relation to a common destiny. So far, all the national and international entities have combined to serve the common destiny and to find solutions to the problems on a national and international basis. For this reason, international organizations and governments have to be more responsible and responsive to the opinions and expectations of the people of the whole world.

There isn't a single mould for sustainability, because economic systems and ecological conditions vary greatly between countries. Therefore, each nation must determine for itself its own concrete policy requirements. But regardless of these differences, environmentally sensitive, sustainable development is seen as a global objective.

No country cannot develop apart from the others. Hence, in the quest for sustainable development, a new orientation to international relations is required. Long-term and environmentally sensitive sustainable development ensures that necessary changes of great magnitude are also inevitable, with trade, capital and technology flowing more equitably and more in sync with the environment.

As a result, environment and development depend on how each one is clear on the relationship between ecology and economy. In this respect, protection and use preferences should be implemented in a harmonious balance. In fact, the relationship between ecology and economy, as elements indicating a contradiction, reflect how developed and developing countries embody non-harmonized preferences. When these two approaches reject each other, communities are interconnected willy-nilly. Instead of criticizing so as to trivialize the sustainable development approach, finding the solution to practical problems by joint action on economic, social and ecological issues, and eliminating inequalities, are the most important responsibilities of today's society.

International responsibilities to guarantee a sustainable future will vary according to the development level of countries and sectors. What's important is to manage sustainability in a common format, for a common future of all nations. Because humanitarian needs have common characteristics, a multilateral system is required. This system must accept that the world is one.

REFERENCES

Amend, T., Barbeau, B., Beyers, B., Burns, S., Eißing, S., Fleischhauer, A. ... Poblete, P. (Eds.). (2010). *A big foot on a small planet? Accounting with the ecological footprint: Succeeding in a world with growing resource constraints.* Deutsche Gesellschaft für Technische Zusammenarbeit (GTZ) GmbH, Eschborn. Available from http://www.conservation-development.net/?L=2&ds=313

Aruoba, Ç. (1992). *Çevre Ekonomisi, Gelişme Ekonomisi, İnsan Çevre Toplum, Prepared for publication by: Ruşen Keleş*. Ankara: İmge Publishing House.

Bennett, J. W. (2002). Human ecology as human behaviour: Essays in environmental and development anthropology. Academic Press.

Berkes, F., & Kışlalıoğlu, M. (1990). *Ekoloji ve Çevre Bilimleri*. Istanbul: Remzi Publishing House.

Boyd, J. P. (Ed.). (1950). *The papers of Thomas Jefferson*. Princeton, NJ: Princeton University Press. Retrieved May 12, 2014, from http://press-pubs.uchicago.edu/founders/documents/v1ch2s23.html

Bretschger, L., & Egli, H. (2001). Sustainable growth in open economies. In G. G. Schulze & H. W. Ursprung (Eds.), International environmental economics-A survey of the issues (pp. 183-208). New York: Oxford University Press.

Brown, L. R., Flavin, C., & Postel, S. (1998). Convention on Biological Diversity, Turkey National Website, Retrieved May 6, 2014, from http://www.bcs.gov.tr/biodiversity/biodiversity.php

Emrealp, S. (2005). *Türkiye Yerel Gündem 21 Programı, Yerel Gündem 21 Uygulamalarına Yönelik Kolaylaştırıcı Bilgiler El Kitabı*. Istanbul: IULA-EMME Publications.

Erdoğan, İ., & Ejder, N. (1997). *Çevre Sorunları; Nedenler, Çözümler-Egemen ve Marksist Anlayışın İlettikleri Üzerine*. Ankara: Doruk Publications.

Ertürk, H. (2011). *Çevre Politikası*. Bursa: Ekin Publications.

George, A. R. (Ed.). (2003). The Babylonian Gilgamesh epic: Introduction, critical edition and cuneiform texts (vol. 1). Oxford.

Görmez, K. (2010). *Çevre Sorunları*. Ankara: Nobel Publications.

Hayward, T. (1995). *Ecological Thought: An Introduction*. Cambridge, MA: Polity Press.

International Council for Local Environmental Initiatives. (1996), Local agenda 21 planning guide: An introduction to sustainable development planning. Author.

International Council for Local Environmental Initiatives. (1997). Avrupa Yerel Gündem 21 Planlama Rehberi. (T., Albayrak, G.Celik & G.Okyay, Trans.). Author.

International Union for Conservation of Nature-United Nations Environment Program-World Wildlife Fund. (1980). *World conservation strategy-Living resources conservation for sustainable development*. Retrieved May 14, 2014, from http://cisdl.org/biodiversity-biosafety/public/docs/wcs.pdf

Isaacs, D. (2009). *The extinction of evolution*. Bridge-Logos.

Karaca, H. (1995). *Sürdürülebilir Bir Yaşam İçin İnsan Verimliliği* (Vol. 1-5). Ankara: Yeni Türkiye.

Keating, M. (1993). *Yeryüzü Zirvesinde Değişimin Gündemi*. Ankara: Publications of Environment Foundation of Turkey/UNEP National Committee.

Keleş, R., & Hamamcı, C. (1993). *Çevrebilim*. Ankara: İmge Publishing House.

Keleş, R., Hamamcı, C., & Çoban, A. (2012). *Çevre Politikası*. Ankara: İmge Publishing House.

Kula, E. (2003). *History of environmental economic thought*. London: Routledge.

Meadows, D. H., Meadows, D. L., Randers, J., & Behrens, W. W. (1972). *The limits to growth-A report for the club of Rome's project on the predicament of mankind*. Universe Books. Retrieved May 13, 2014, from http://www.donellameadows.org/wp-content/userfiles/Limits-to-Growth-digital-scan-version.pdf

Pearce, D. (1999). *Economic and environment-Essays on ecological economics and sustainable development.* Edward Elgar Publishing.

Republic of Turkey, Ministry of Development. (2012). Rio'dan Rio'ya: Türkiye'de Sürdürülebilir Kalkınmanın Mevcut Durumu. Ankara: Author.

Schumacher, E. F. (1973). *Small is beautiful-Economics as if people mattered.* London: Blond & Briggs.

Secretariat of the Convention on Biological Diversity. (2010). *Global biodiversity outlook 3.* Available from http://www.cbd.int/GBO3/

The Grand National Assembly of Turkey. (1982). *Constitution of the Republic of Turkey-1982.* Retrieved May 13, 2014, from http://global.tbmm.gov.tr/docs/constitution_en.pdf

Tietenberg, T. (2003). *Environmental and natural resource economics* (6th ed.). Addison Wesley.

Tont, S.A. (1997). *Sulak Bir Gezegen'den Öyküler.* Ankara: Publications of TUBITAK.

Toprak, Z. (2012). *Çevre Yönetimi ve Politikası.* İzmir: Albi Publications.

Türkman, A. (1998). *Yaşanabilir Bir Çevre İçin* (vol. 45). Izmir: Publications of Izmir Chamber of Commerce.

United Nations. (1972). *Report of the United Nations conference on the human environment, 5-16 June 1972.* United Nations Publications, A/CONF/48.14/Rev.1. Retrieved May 8, 2014, from http://www.un-documents.net/aconf48-14r1.pdf

United Nations. (1992). *The Rio declaration on environment and development.* United Nations Publication, A/CONF.151/26 (Vol. 1), Retrieved May 8, 2014, from http://www.un.org/documents/ga/conf151/aconf15126-1annex1.htm

United Nations. (2002). *Plan of implementation of the world summit on sustainable development.* A/CONF.199/20. Retrieved May 14, 2014, from http://www.un-documents.net/jburgpln.htm

United Nations. (2007). Indicators of sustainable development: Guidelines and methodologies (3rd ed.). New York: Author.

United Nations. (2012). *World population 2012.* Retrieved May 11, 2014, from http://www.un.org/en/development/desa/population/publications/pdf/trends/WPP2012_Wallchart.pdf

United Nations. (2012). *Future we want.* A/RES/66/288. Retrieved May 13, 2014, from http://www.un.org/ga/search/view_doc.asp?symbol=A/RES/66/288&Lang=E

United Nations. (2013a). *World population prospects: The 2012 revision-Key findings and advance tables.* Department of Economic and Social Affairs-Population Division, New York, ESA/P/WP.227. Retrieved May 14, 2014, from http://esa.un.org/wpp/Documentation/pdf/WPP2012_%20KEY%20FINDINGS.pdf

United Nations. (2013b). *The millennium development goals report 2013.* New York: Author. Retrieved May 14, 2014, from http://www.un.org/millenniumgoals/pdf/report-2013/mdg-report-2013-english.pdf

United Nations Environment Program. (n.d.). *Global environment outlook 3.* Retrieved May 10, 2014, from http://www.unep.org/geo/GEO3/english/pdfs/chapter1.pdf

United Nations World Commission on Environment and Development. (1987). *Report of the world commission on environment and development-Our common future.* Retrieved May 16, 2014, from http://www.un-documents.net/our-common-future.pdf

Wackernagel, M., Galli, A., Moore, D., Cranston, G., Kalem, S., Devranoğlu, S., & Ayas, C. (2012). *Turkey's ecological footprint report*. World Wildlife Fund, WWF-Turkey. Retrieved May 6, 2014, from http://www.footprintnetwork.org/images/uploads/Turkey_Ecological_Footprint_Report_Executive_Summary-Conclusion.pdf

World Bank. (2008). *World development indicators-08*. Washington, DC: Author.

World Wildlife Fund. (2012). *Living planet report 2012-Biodiversity, biocapacity and better choices*. Available from http://www.worldwildlife.org/publications/living-planet-report-2012-biodiversity-biocapacity-and-better-choices

KEY TERMS AND DEFINITIONS:

Brundtland Report: This report established the "sustainable development" term.

Eco Development: This means that "environment does not exclude development".

Ecological Footprint: It refers to a measurable concept of the impact of production and consumption activities on the natural environment.

Resource Management: It refers to management of resources by considering the protection and usage balance.

Rio Conference: This was the second largest earth summit, held in 1992 in Rio de Janeiro, the capital of Brazil. It is known as the United Nations Conference on Environment and Development Earth Summit.

Stockholm Conference: This was the first largest global conference on environment under the leadership of the United Nations, held in 1972.

Sustainable Development: The development approach which envisages the use of today's resources by considering the needs of future generations.

Zero Growth: It is the Roma Club's utopian approach which aimed to limit growth and development, at the beginning of the 1970s.

ENDNOTES

1 The other four documents are Agenda 21, the Statement of Forest Principles, the United Nations Framework Convention on Climate Change and the United Nations Convention on Biological Diversity.

2 Social and Economic Dimensions: International cooperation to accelerate sustainable development in developing countries, and related aims of Combating poverty, Changing consumption patterns, Demographic dynamics and sustainability, Protecting and promoting human health conditions, Promoting sustainable human settlement development, Integrating environment and development in decision-making; also: Conservation and Management of Resources for Development: Protection of the atmosphere, Integrated approach to the planning and management of land resources, Combatting deforestation, Managing fragile ecosystems: combatting desertification and drought, plus sustainable mountain development, Promoting sustainable agriculture and rural development, Conservation of biological diversity, Environmentally sound management of biotechnology, Protection of the oceans and all kinds of seas, including enclosed and semi-enclosed seas and coastal areas and the protection, rational use and development of their living resources, Protection of the quality and supply of freshwater resources: application of integrated approaches to the development, management and use of water resources, Environmentally sound management of toxic chemicals, including preven-

tion of illegal international traffic in toxic and dangerous products, Environmentally sound management of hazardous wastes, Environmentally sound management of solid wastes and sewage-related issues, Safe and environmentally sound management of radioactive wastes; also: Strengthening the Role of Major Groups: Global action for women towards sustainable and equitable development, Children and youth in sustainable development, Recognizing and strengthening the role of indigenous people and their communities, Strengthening the role of non-governmental organizations: partners for sustainable development, Local authorities' initiatives in support of the Agenda, Strengthening the role of workers and their trade unions, Strengthening the role of business and industry, Scientific and technological community, Strengthening the role of farmers; also: Means of Implementation: Financial resources and mechanisms, Transfer of environmentally sound technology, cooperation and capacity-building, Science for sustainable development, Promoting education, public awareness and training, National mechanisms and international cooperation for capacity-building in developing countries, International institutional arrangements, International legal instruments and mechanisms, Information for decision-making.

3 To see the original figure: International Council for Local Environmental Initiatives (1996). Local Agenda 21 Planning Guide, An Introduction to Sustainable Development Planning, Canada.

4 To see the original figure: Republic of Turkey, Ministry of Development (2012). Rio'dan Rio'ya: Türkiye'de Sürdürülebilir Kalkınmanın Mevcut Durumu, Ankara.

5 To see the 1982 Turkish Republic Constitution (in English), http://global.tbmm.gov.tr/docs/constitution_en.pdf

Chapter 17
The Impact of Trade Openness on Environmental Pollution:
A Panel Cointegration and Causality Analysis

Murat Cetin
Namik Kemal University, Turkey

Fahri Seker
University of Bozok, Turkey

Hakan Cavlak
Namik Kemal University, Turkey

ABSTRACT

This chapter analyzes the impact of trade openness on environmental pollution in the newly industrialized countries that have focused on trade over the period 1971-2010 by using recently developed panel unit root, cointegration, and causality tests. The results indicate a cointegration relationship between the variables. The results also show that trade openness increases carbon dioxide emissions with the elasticity of 0.53 and there is a Granger causality running from trade openness to carbon dioxide emissions in the long run. These findings may provide some policy implications. Without taking into account impact of trade on pollutions, optimistic environmental Kuznets curve hypothesis would be invalid. Therefore, policymakers who decide on environment policies should pay attention to not only growth effects but also trade effects on pollutions. Future empirical analysis would expose the new evidences for governmental policies and environmental regulations to change these effects positively.

INTRODUCTION

In this study, the impact of trade openness on environmental pollution is investigated in a sample of 10 newly industrialized countries for the period 1971-2010 by conducting a panel data analysis. For this purpose, panel unit root, cointegration and causality methods are employed. Several studies (e.g. Baumol, 1971; Baumol & Oates, 1988; Anderson & Blackhurst, 1992; Tsai, 1999; Gallagher & Ackerman, 2000; Savard & Bohman, 2003; Saunders & Cagatay, 2004) examined the

DOI: 10.4018/978-1-4666-7308-3.ch017

link between trade and environment by developing the partial equilibrium models. On the other hand, several studies (e.g. Walter, 1974; Pethig, 1976; Asako, 1979; Siebert, 1992; Perroni & Wigle, 1994; Lee & Roland-Holst, 1997; and Beladi & Oladi, 2011) contributed to the theoretical literature within the framework of general equilibrium models.

Baumol & Oates (1988) analyzing the effects of environment on trade suggested that the international pollution problems may discredit the idea of free trade. They concluded that tariffs may be appropriate to improve resource allocation in the world. Anderson & Blackhurst (1992) examined the relationship between trade liberalization and environment in a small and large country which have open economy. They exhibited that when a suitable environmental policy is applied the welfare and environmental quality of these countries could be improved. Unlike Baumol (1971), Baumol & Oates (1988) and Anderson & Blackhurst (1992), Perroni & Wigle (1994) developing a general equilibrium model suggested that the trade has a weak effect on environmental quality.

Antweiler, Copeland & Taylor (2001) investigated the relationship between trade and environmental quality by considering the scale, composition and technique effects of trade. Later on, this work was developed by several studies (e.g. Dean, 2002; Cole & Elliot, 2003 and Frankel & Rose, 2005) with the help of some methodological and conceptual modifications.

Empirical evidences related to this topic are not conclusive. Lucas, Wheeler & Hettige (1992) investigating rapidly growing countries found that trade-distorting policies may increase pollution. Dean (2002), Antweiler et al. (2001) and Copeland & Taylor (2003) concluded that liberalization has a beneficial effect on the environment. Frankel & Rose (2005) indicated no evidence for a detrimental effect on the environment. Using standard and generalized OLS techniques, Feridun (2006) found that pollution is positively related to trade openness in Nigeria. Managi, Hibiki & Tsurumi (2009) indicated that trade benefit to the environment in OECD countries by using the instrumental variables technique. Kukla-Gryz (2009) estimating the Structural Equation Model in the developing countries suggested that international trade and per capita income increase air pollution. Baek, Cho & Koo (2009) analyzing developed and developing countries showed that the impact of trade on environmental quality is positive developed countries. They also showed that trade negatively affects environmental quality in most developing countries. Finally, in G-20 economies Baek & Kim (2011) found similar results with Baek et al. (2009) by using a CVAR framework.

It can be said that the empirical findings are different depending upon research methods, time and sample of the studies. These studies examine a long-run relationship between the variables by employing different estimation techniques. But, they do not conduct cointegration and causality analyses. Using the methods of panel unit root, cointegration and causality, the present study investigates the relationship between trade and environmental pollution. It does not consider decomposed effects of trade as in the studies of Managi (2004) and Frankel & Rose (2005). This study uses the panel unit root tests presented by Levin, Lin & Chu (2002); Im, Pesaran & Shin (2003) and Pesaran (2007). CIPS statistics developed by Pesaran (2007) takes into consideration cross-sectional dependency. Here, Breusch-Pagan (1980) and Pesaran (2004) LM tests are employed to investigate whether the variables or model have cross-sectional dependency.

This study uses Westerlund & Edgerton (2007) cointegration method based on a bootstrap test to test for the presence of the long-run relationship between the variables. It bases on the LM test developed by McCoskey & Kao (1998). This technique allows us for accommodating correlation within and between the cross-sectional units. The main characteristic of this test is to reduce the distortions of the asymptotic test. In estimation of the long-run cointegration vector, this study also employs Pedroni (2000) group-mean DOLS and FMOLS estimators. These methods correct the classical pooled OLS for the problems of serial correlation and regressors' endogeneity. Finally, panel VECM is used to investigate the short and long-run causality between the variables. Empirical results of the study may provide some policy implications.

The remainder of the paper is organized as follows. Section 2 presents the model and data used in the study. Section 3 considers the econometric methodology. Section 4 reports the empirical findings. Final remarks are provided in Section 5.

MODEL AND DATA

In the analyzing of the relationship between trade openness and environmental pollution by incorporating a balanced panel from 10 newly industrialized countries the study considers the linear panel data specification as fallows

$$LNCO_{2it} = \beta_0 + \beta_1 LNTRADE_{it} + u_{it} \quad (1)$$

where CO_2 and TRADE are per capita carbon dioxide emission and trade openness (measured as exports and imports divided by GDP), respectively. The annual data is used. The data covers the period of 1971 to 2010 derived from World Bank's World Development Indicators, 2013. This sample is determined based on the data availability. The variables are converted to natural logarithms. The countries dealt with in this study are Brazil, China, India, Malaysia, Mexico, Philippines, Singapore, South Africa, Thailand and Turkey.

Table 1 presents the variables and their descriptive statistics. The cross-sectional dimension is 10 units and the time dimension is 40 years. In total, there are 400 observations for each variable. For all variables, it is seen that there are no strong outliers.

ECONOMETRIC METHODOLOGY

The study examines the cointegration and causality relationship between trade openness and carbon dioxide emissions over the period. Firstly, the =existence of cross-sectional dependence is investigated. Secondly, the order of integration in the variables is examined. Thirdly, the study tests for panel cointegration. Fourthly, the long-run parameters are estimated and finally, the Granger causality between trade openness and carbon dioxide emissions is tested.

In this study, Breusch-Pagan test (1980) CD_{LM1}, Pesaran (2004) CD_{LM} and CD_{LM2} tests are employed to examine the existence of cross-sectional dependence in the model. Generally, two specifications are considered in cross-sectional dependence which bases on the assumed persistence of the dependence. The first one assumes weak dependence and ignores the common factors. In this specification, the cross section units are allowed to be correlated through only the cross correlations in the errors. The second specification is a factor model which assumes strong dependence (Sarafidis & de Hoyos, 2006).

Table 1. Descriptive statistics

Balanced Panel: N=10, T=40, Observations=400						
Variable	Unit	Mean	Median	Std. Dev.	Min.	Max.
$LNCO_2$	Metric ton per capita	0.916	0.879	0.947	-1.012	2.950
LNTRADE	Trade/GDP	3.917	3.872	0.968	1.754	6.132

Breusch-Pagan (1980) test bases on the average of the squared pair-wise correlation of the residuals. According to Pesaran (2004) standard techniques is not available in cases where N is large. The tests developed by Pesaran (2004) are centered for fixed N and T. The main feature of these tests is that they have the correct size in very small samples.

The study uses the panel unit root tests presented by Levin et al. (2002) and Im et al. (2003) to investigate stationarity properties of the series. The main feature of these methods known as the first generation unit root tests is that they have an assumption of the independence of cross-section units. Banerjee, Marcellino & Osbat (2004) and Breitung & Pesaran (2008) indicate that this assumption of the first-generation unit root tests may cause size distortions and produce results in favor of the series' stationarity. Therefore, CADF test developed by Pesaran (2007) is also employed. It is known as a second-generation unit root test.

Pesaran (2007) considers a simple model for a panel data covering N cross-sectional units and T time series observations. This model is given by

$$Y_{it} = \left(1 - \rho_i\right)\mu_i + \rho_i Y_{it-1} + u_{it} \tag{2}$$

where the error term u_{it} has a common factor structure as

$$u_{it} = \gamma_i f_t + e_{it} \tag{3}$$

where f_t, γ_i and e_{it} are an unobserved common factor, the corresponding factor loading and an idiosyncratic error term independent across i and independent of the common factor, respectively. (2) and (3) can be rewritten as

$$\Delta Y_{it} = \alpha_{0i} + \alpha_{1i} Y_{it-1} + \gamma_i f_t + e_{it} \tag{4}$$

where $\alpha_{oi} = (1 - \rho_i)\mu_i$, $\alpha_{1i} = (\rho_i - 1)$ and $\Delta Y_{it} = Y_{it} - Y_{it-1}$. Pesaran (2007) puts forward cross-sectional augment test equation (4) with cross-sectional averages of the first differences and the lagged levels to explain the cross-sectional dependence. The cross-sectional augmented Dickey-Fuller test known as CADF uses the following equation

$$\Delta Y_{it} = \alpha_i + \beta_i Y_{it-1} + \gamma_i \bar{Y}_{t-1} + \lambda_i \Delta \bar{Y}_t + \varepsilon_{it} \tag{5}$$

where $\bar{Y}_t = \frac{1}{N}\sum_{i=1}^{N} Y_{it}, \Delta \bar{Y}_t = \frac{1}{N}\sum_{i=1}^{N} \Delta Y_{it}$ and ε_{it} is the regression error. For the hypothesis $H_{0i} : \rho_i = 1$ for a given i the individual specific test statistic is the t-statistic of β_i in (5) represented by $CADF_i$. For the panel unit root the null hypothesis $H_o : \rho_i = 1$ for all i is tested against the heterogeneous alternative $H_1 : \rho_i < 1$ for some i given by the cross-sectional average of the $CADF_i$ tests, such that

$$CIPS = \frac{1}{N}\sum_{i=1}^{N} CADF_i \tag{6}$$

Pesaran (2007) presents the critical values for the CIPS tests in Tables 2(a)-2(c).

Panel cointegration tests can be classified into two major types such as residual and maximum-likelihood-oriented tests. The first residual-oriented tests are developed by McCoskey & Kao (1998), Kao (1999) and Pedroni (1999). In these tests, the null hypothesis has no cointegration in cross-sectional independent panels. On the other hand, the cointegration methods developed by Larsson & Lyhagen (1999), Larsson, Lyhagen & Lothgren (2001), Groen & Kleibergen (2003), Breitung (2005), and Anderson, Qian & Rasche (2006) are the best examples for the maximum-likelihood-oriented tests.

Table 2. Results for panel unit root and cross-sectional dependence tests

Series	Model	IPS	LLC	CIPS
Panel 1: Level				
$LNCO_2$	Constant Constant and trend	1.191 -0.000	-0.837 -0.389	-1.603 -2.188
LNTRADE	Constant Constant and trend	0.898 1.460	-1.460 1.564	-1.506 -1.377
Panel 2: First difference				
$\Delta LNCO_2$	Constant Constant and trend	-13.483[a] -12.427[a]	-14.001[a] -13.062[a]	-3.444[b] -3.525[c]
$\Delta LNTRADE$	Constant Constant and trend	-12.117[a] -10.868[a]	-13.642[a] -13.089[a]	-3.421[b] -3.508[c]
Breush-Pagan CD_{LM1}	193.49[a]			
Pesaran CD_{LM2}	15.61[a]			
Pesaran CD_{LM}	2.25[a]			

Note:Δ is the first difference operator. The LLC test uses Newey-West bandwidth selection with Bartlett kernel. Schwarz Bayesian Criterion is used to select the optimal lag length. [a], [b] and [c] denote significance at the 1, 5, and 10% level, respectively.

The present study employs a relatively new test presented by Westerlund & Edgerton (2007). This panel bootstrap cointegration test bases on LM test of McCoskey & Kao (1998) which does not enable to the cross-sectional dependency. According to Westerlund (2005, 2006) an important disadvantage of the asymptotic distribution is that it has a poor predictor of the empirical distribution. This cointegration test considers the cross-sectional dependence. Here, the bootstrap statistics are derived from the joint empirical distribution of the regression errors and have effective results in small samples.

In Westerlund & Edgerton (2007) test, a finite AR process of order *pi* for $i = 1, \ldots, N$ approximates the equilibrium errors. Let

$$\sum_{j=0}^{\infty} \phi_{ij} w_{it-j} = e_{it} \tag{7}$$

which constitutes the basis for residual-oriented resampling of the bootstrap test. This test consists of five steps. The first step is to estimate ϕ_{ij} in (4) by using $\hat{w}_{it} = (\hat{z}_{it}, \Delta x'_{it})'$ instead of w_{it} and p_i lags. The residuals are computed by

$$\hat{e}_{it} = \sum_{j=0}^{p_i} \hat{\phi}_{ij} \hat{w}_{it-j} \tag{8}$$

here, $\hat{\phi}_{ij}$ are determined by using the empirical Yule-Walker equations to assure the invertibility of (8). In the second step, a random sample e^*_t is derived from the empirical distribution, which puts mass $1/T$ on each of the centered residuals $\hat{e}_t - \frac{1}{T}\sum_{j=1}^{T} \hat{e}_j$. Then w^*_{it} is generated recursively from e^*_t using (8) with w^*_{it} and e^*_{it} in place of $\hat{w}_{it}$ and $\hat{e}_{it}$, respectively.

In the third step, w^*_{it} is partitioned $w^*_{it} = (z^*_{it}, \Delta x^{*\prime}_{it})'$ and bootstrap samples x^*_{it} and y^*_{it} are generated by

$$y^*_{it} = \alpha i + x^*_{it}\beta i + z^*_{it} \text{ and } x^*_{it} = \sum_{j=1}^{t} \Delta x^*_{ij} \tag{9}$$

where $\hat{\alpha}_i$ and $\hat{\beta}_i$ are the fully modified estimates of α_i and β_i, respectively.

In the fourth step, the LM test statistic is calculated with y^*_{it} and x^*_{it}.

$$LM^{+} = \frac{1}{NT^{2}} \sum_{t=1}^{N} \sum_{t=1}^{T} \hat{w}_{i}^{-2} S_{it}^{2} \tag{10}$$

where $\hat{w}_i^2$ and S_{it} denote the long-run variance of u_{it} conditional on w_{it} and the partial sum process of $\hat{e}_{it}$, respectively. The stages from 1 to 4 are reiterated *R* times. In the final step, the critical values are computed from the bootstrap distribution. So, the bootstrap critical values are employed in place of the asymptotic critical values.

The study also employs the estimation methods presented by Pedroni (2000) to estimate long-run parameter in equation (1). Pedroni (2000) provides the "group mean" DOLS and FMOLS estimators. These estimators allow for greater flexibility in the existence of heterogeneity of the cointegrating vectors. The test statistics are derived from the between-dimension estimator. Here, the null hypothesis $H_0 : \beta_i = \beta_0$ for all *i* is tested against the alternative $H_1 : \beta_i \neq \beta_0$. The following cointegrated system for a panel of *i = 1, 2,....N* members, can be taken into consideration

$$Y_{it} = \alpha_i + \beta X_{it} + \mu_{it} \tag{11}$$

$$X_{it} = X_{it-1} + \varepsilon_{it} \tag{12}$$

where $Z_{it} = (Y_{it}, X_{it}) \sim I(1)_{it}$ and $\xi_i = (\mu_{it}, \varepsilon_{it}) \sim I(0)$, with long run covariance matrix $\Omega_i = L_i L_i'$. In this system, β and α_i denote the cointegrating vector and member specific fixed effect, respectively. The covariance matrix may also be expressed as $\Omega_i = \Omega_i^0 + \Gamma_i + \Gamma_i'$, where Ω_i^0 is a weighted sum of autocovariances. The Panel FMOLS estimator for the coefficient β is expressed as follows:

$$\beta_{NT}^{*} = N^{-1}\left(\sum_{i=1}^{N} (X_{it} - \bar{X}_{it})^{2} ((\bar{X}_{it} - \bar{X}_{i})\, Y_{it}^{*} - T\hat{\tau} i)\right) \tag{13}$$

where

$$Y_{it}^{*} = \left(Y_{it} - \bar{Y}_{i}\right) - \frac{\hat{L}_{21i}}{\hat{L}_{22i}} \Delta X_{it}\,, \quad \hat{\tau}_{i} = \hat{\Gamma}_{21i} + \hat{\Omega}_{21i}^{0} - \frac{\hat{L}_{21i}}{\hat{L}_{22i}} \left(\hat{\Gamma}_{22i} - \hat{\Omega}_{22i}^{0} \right)$$

and Li is a lower triangular decomposition of Ωi expressed as $\Omega_i = \begin{bmatrix} \Omega_{11i} \Omega_{21i}' \\ \Omega_{21i} \Omega_{22i} \end{bmatrix}$

For the panel DOLS estimation, the augmented cointegration equation is given by:

$$Y_{it} = \alpha_i + \beta_i X_{it} + \sum_{j=-k_i}^{k_i} \gamma_{ik} X_{it-k} + \mu_{it} \tag{14}$$

and the estimated coefficient β is given by:

$$\hat{\beta}_{GD}^{*} = \left[N^{-1} (\sum_{i=1}^{N} Z_{it} Z_{it}') (\sum_{i=1}^{N} Z_{it} Y_{it}^{*}) \right] \tag{15}$$

where $Z_{it} = \left(X_{it} - \bar{X}_i, \Delta X_{it-k}, \ldots\ldots, \Delta X_{it+k} \right)$ is the 2 (*K+1*) x 1 vector of regressors.

The cointegration tests do not inform about direction of causality between the variables. Therefore, in the final step of this panel study the direction of causality between the variables are examined. The study uses a panel-based error correction model (PVECM). In this test the Error-Correction Term (ECT) is included to the VAR system as an additional variable. The short-run and long-run Granger causality can be distinguished in this model. So, PVECM can be specified as follows:

$$\Delta Y_{it} = \theta_{1i} + \gamma_{1i} ECT_{it-1} + \sum_{k=1}^{p} \theta_{11ik} \Delta Y_{it-k} + \sum_{k=1}^{p} \theta_{12ik} \Delta X_{it-k} + \varepsilon_{1t} \tag{16}$$

where *Δ*, *ECT* and *p* represent the first difference of the variable, the error-correction term and the lag length, respectively. *ECT* are the estimated residuals from the long-run model in Equation (1), $\gamma_{1i} ECT_{it}$ reflects the long-run equilibrium relationship among the variables. If θ_{12} or γ_{1i} are not equal to zero, it is determined to be a short run or long run causal relationship.

EMPIRICAL RESULTS

The results from Breusch-Pagan (1980) CD_{LM1}, Pesaran (2004) CD_{LM} and CD_{LM2} tests are reported in Table 2. The null hypothesis for all tests is cross-sectional independence. All tests strongly reject the null, and hence indicate that the error terms are correlated across cross-sectional units. Table 2 also presents panel unit root test results. The findings show that the series are not stationary in level. After taking the first difference, the series are stationary. So, it is concluded that all variables are integrated at order of *I(1)*.

As seen from the table 3, the results of asymptotic and bootstrap p-value clearly indicate that there is a cointegration relationship between LNTRADE and $LNCO_2$. These findings mean that there is a long-run relationship between trade openness and environmental pollution over the period. Pedroni DOLS and FMOLS estimation results are reported in Table 4. For the DOLS model, the coefficient on the trade openness is significantly positive in cases of Brazil, China, India, Malaysia, Mexico, Philippines, Thailand and Turkey. Results for the FMOLS model, the coefficient on the trade openness is significantly positive in cases of China, India, Malaysia, Mexico, Philippines, Thailand and Turkey. So, based on the country-by-country estimation results trade openness seems to be a fundamental determinant of carbon dioxide emissions. On the other hand, the panel coefficients provide that trade openness has statistically significant parameter. Specifically, a 1% increase in trade openness increases carbon dioxide emissions by 0.53%. Panel findings suggest that trade openness is an important determinant of carbon dioxide emissions in these countries over the period. These are in agreement with Managi (2004), Tsurumi & Managi (2011) investigating the relationship between trade liberalization and environment using panel data.

Finally, the causal relationship between LNTRADE and $LNCO_2$ is investigated in this study. The Granger causality results seen from Table 5 suggest that there is no causal relationship between the variables in the short run. The results also suggest that ECT_{t-1} is negative and statistically significant at 5% level. This indicates a causality running from trade openness to carbon dioxide emissions in the long run. The results provide an evidence that there is a joint causal relationship between the variables.

CONCLUSION AND POLICY IMPLICATIONS

The interaction between trade and environment is one of the vital topics for the national and international policy makers. This study has examined the impact of trade openness on the carbon dioxide

Table 3. Results for Westerlund-Edgerton test

Statistic	Constant	Constant Trend
LM	0.112	-0.351
Bootstrap p-value	0.210	0.160
Asymptotic p-value	0.455	0.637

Note: LM denotes Lagrange Multiplier. Yule-Walker is used for sieve estimation. The null hypothesis is that there is a cointegration. The bootstrap is basedon1000 replications.

Table 4. Results for Pedroni DOLS and FMOLS estimation (Dependent variable: $LNCO_2$)

Country	DOLS	FMOLS
Brazil	0.44[a] (3.05)	0.23 (1.31)
China	0.63[a] (14.44)	0.61[a] (10.75)
India	0.87[a] (10.71)	0.81[a] (7.55)
Malaysia	1.46[a] (23.70)	1.40[a] (15.57)
Mexico	0.19[a] (3.80)	0.21[a] (3.02)
Philippines	0.38[a] (4.56)	0.38[a] (3.66)
Singapore	-0.56 (-1.58)	-0.26 (-0.67)
South Africa	-0.27 (-1.63)	-0.14 (-0.69)
Thailand	1.65[a] (20.37)	1.59[a] (14.94)
Turkey	0.55[a] (12.81)	0.50[a] (6.83)
Panel	0.53[a] (28.54)	0.53[a] (19.69)

Note: Numbers in parentheses are the estimates are the absolute values of *t*-statistics. [a] denote significance at the 1% level.

Table 5. Results for Panel Granger Causality Test (Dependent variable: $LNCO_2$)

Series	Short run	Long run	Joint (Short Run and Long Run)
ΔLNTRADE	0.972 (0.331)		
ECT_{it-1}		-0.012[a] (0.014)	
ΔLNTRADE/ECT			3.712[a] (0.025)

Note: Akaike's Information Criterion (AIC) is used to select the optimal lag length. [a] denote significance at the 5% level. The values in parenthesis are p-values.

emissions for 10 newly industrialized countries over the period 1971-2010 using panel data in the context of cointegration and causality analyses.

Empirical results show that i) there is a cross-section dependence in the model, ii) the variables are stationary in the first difference, iii) there is an evidence of a long run relationship between the variables, iv) the estimated trade openness elasticity of carbon dioxide emissions is 0.53 meaning that carbon dioxide emissions are positively correlated with trade openness, v) there is a causality running from trade openness to carbon dioxide emissions in the long run.

The empirical results may provide some policy implications. Policy makers can take a variety of measures without compromising on trade liberalization. Firstly, environmentally-sensitive trade subsidies can be performed. Secondly, optimal environmental taxes can be applied to pollution-intensive industries. Thirdly, those countries should fulfill the requirements of the Kyoto protocol.

On the other hand, the present study cannot exhibit what the trade-based determinants of environmental pollution are in detail. This reveals the necessity of an empirical study taking into consideration the scale, technical and composition effects of trade for those countries as Cole and Elliott (2003).

REFERENCES

Anderson, K., & Blackhurst, R. (1992). The greening of world trade issues. Ann Arbor, MI: University of Michigan Press.

Anderson, R., Qian, H., & Rasche, R. (2006). *Analysis of panel vector error correction models using maximum likelihood, bootstrap and canonical-correlation estimators*. Federal Reserve Bank of St. Louis, Working Paper No 50A.

Antweiler, W., Copeland, B., & Taylor, M. S. (2001). Is free trade good for the environment? The American Economic Review, 91(4), 877–908. doi:10.1257/aer.91.4.877 doi:10.1257/aer.91.4.877

Asako, K. (1979). Environmental pollution in an open economy. The Economic Record, 55(4), 359–367. doi:10.1111/j.1475-4932.1979.tb02241.x doi:10.1111/j.1475-4932.1979.tb02241.x

Baek, J., & Kim, H. S. (2011). Trade liberalization, economic growth, energy consumption and the environment: Time series evidence from G-20 economies. Journal of East Asian Economic Integration, 15(1), 3–32. doi:10.11644/KIEP.JEAI.2011.15.1.224 doi:10.11644/KIEP.JEAI.2011.15.1.224

Baek, J., Cho, Y., & Koo, W. W. (2009). The environmental consequences of globalization: A country-specific time-series analysis. Ecological Economics, 68(8-9), 2255–2264. doi:10.1016/j.ecolecon.2009.02.021 doi:10.1016/j.ecolecon.2009.02.021

Banerjee, A., Marcellino, M., & Osbat, C. (2004). Some cautions on the use of panel methods for integrated series of macro-economic data. The Econometrics Journal, 7(2), 322–340. doi:10.1111/j.1368-423X.2004.00133.x doi:10.1111/j.1368-423X.2004.00133.x

Baumol, W. J., & Oates, W. E. (1988). The theory of environmental policy. Cambridge: Cambridge University Press. doi:10.1017/CBO9781139173513 doi:10.1017/CBO9781139173513

Baumol, W.J. (1971). *Environmental protection, international spillovers, and trade*. Stock-holm: Almquit and Wixell.

Beladi, H., & Oladi, R. (2011). Does trade liberalization increase global pollution? Resource and Energy Economics, 33(1), 172–178. doi:10.1016/j.reseneeco.2010.04.009 doi:10.1016/j.reseneeco.2010.04.009

Breitung, J., & Pesaran, M. (2008). Unit roots and cointegration in panels. In L. Matyas & P. Sevestre (Eds.), The econometrics of panel data: Fundamentals and recent developments in theory and practice. Kluwer Academic Publishers.

Breitung, J. (2005). A parametric approach to the estimation of cointegration vectors in panel data. Econometric Reviews, 24(2), 151–173. doi:10.1081/ETC-200067895 doi:10.1081/ETC-200067895

Breusch, T. S., & Pagan, A. R. (1980). The LaGrange multiplier test and its applications to model specification in econometrics. The Review of Economic Studies, 47(1), 239–254. doi:10.2307/2297111 doi:10.2307/2297111

Cole, M. A., & Elliott, R. J. (2003). Determining the trade-environment composition effect: The role of capital, labour and environmental regulations. Journal of Environmental Economics and Management, 46(3), 363–383. doi:10.1016/S0095-0696(03)00021-4 doi:10.1016/S0095-0696(03)00021-4

Copeland, B. R., & Taylor, M. S. (2003). Trade and the environment: Theory and evidence. Princeton, NJ: Princeton University Press.

Dean, J. (2002). Does trade liberalization harm the environment? A new test. The Canadian Journal of Economics. Revue Canadienne d'Economique, 35(4), 819–842. doi:10.1111/0008-4085.00155 doi:10.1111/0008-4085.00155

Feridun, M. (2006). Impact of trade liberalization on the environment in developing countries: The case of Nigeria. Journal of Developing Societies, 22(1), 9–56. doi:10.1177/0169796X06062965 doi:10.1177/0169796X06062965

Frankel, J. A., & Rose, A. K. (2005). Is trade good or bad for the environment? Sorting out the causality. The Review of Economics and Statistics, 87(1), 85–91. doi:10.1162/0034653053327577 doi:10.1162/0034653053327577

Gallagher, K., & Ackerman, F. (2000). *Trade liberalization and pollution intensive industry in developing countries*. Global Development and Environment Institute, Working Paper No 3.

Groen, J. J. J., & Kleibergen, F. (2003). Likelihood-based cointegration analysis in panels of vector error correction models. Journal of Business & Economic Statistics, 21(2), 295–318. doi:10.1198/073500103288618972 doi:10.1198/073500103288618972

Im, K. S., Pesaran, M. H., & Shin, Y. (2003). Testing for unit roots in heterogeneous panels. Journal of Econometrics, 115(1), 53–74. doi:10.1016/S0304-4076(03)00092-7 doi:10.1016/S0304-4076(03)00092-7

Kao, C. (1999). Spurious regression and residual-based tests for cointegration in panel data. Journal of Econometrics, 90(1), 1–44. doi:10.1016/S0304-4076(98)00023-2 doi:10.1016/S0304-4076(98)00023-2

Kukla-Gryz, A. (2009). Economic growth, international trade and air pollution: A decomposition analysis. Ecological Economics, 68(5), 1329–1339. doi:10.1016/j.ecolecon.2008.09.005 doi:10.1016/j.ecolecon.2008.09.005

Larsson, R., & Lyhagen, J. (1999). *Likelihood-based inference in multivariate panel cointegration models*. Working Paper Series in Economics and Finance 331, Stockhholm School of Economics.

Larsson, R., Lyhagen, J., & Lothgren, M. (2001). Likelihood-based cointegration tests in heterogeneous panels. The Econometrics Journal, 4(1), 109–142. doi:10.1111/1368-423X.00059 doi:10.1111/1368-423X.00059

Lee, H., & Roland-Holst, W. D. (1997). Trade and the environment. In J. F. Francois & K. A. Reinert (Eds.), Applied methods for trade policy analysis-A handbook. Cambridge, UK: Cambridge University Press. doi:10.1017/CBO9781139174824.018 doi:10.1017/CBO9781139174824.018

Levin, A., Lin, C., & Chu, C. (2002). Unit root tests in panel data: Asymptotic and finite sample properties. Journal of Econometrics, 108(1), 1–24. doi:10.1016/S0304-4076(01)00098-7 doi:10.1016/S0304-4076(01)00098-7

Lucas, R. E. B., Wheeler, D., & Hettige, H. (1992). Economic development, environmental regulation, and the international migration of toxic industrial pollution 1960-88. The World Bank.

Managi, S. (2004). Trade liberalization and the environment: Carbon dioxide for 1960-1999. Economic Bulletin, 17(1), 1–5.

Managi, S., Hibiki, A., & Tsurumi, T. (2009). Does trade openness improve environmental quality? Journal of Environmental Economics and Management, 58(3), 346–363. doi:10.1016/j.jeem.2009.04.008 doi:10.1016/j.jeem.2009.04.008

McCoskey, S., & Kao, C. (1998). A residual-based test for the null of cointegration in panel data. Econometric Reviews, 17(1), 57–84. doi:10.1080/07474939808800403 doi:10.1080/07474939808800403

Pedroni, P. (1999). Critical values for cointegration tests in heterogeneous panels with multiple regressors. Oxford Bulletin of Economics and Statistics, 61(4), 653–670. doi:10.1111/1468-0084.61.s1.14 doi:10.1111/1468-0084.61.s1.14

Pedroni, P. (2000). Fully modified OLS for heterogeneous cointegrated panels. Advances in Econometrics, 15, 93–130. doi:10.1016/S0731-9053(00)15004-2 doi:10.1016/S0731-9053(00)15004-2

Perroni, C., & Wigle, R. M. (1994). International trade and environmental quality: How important the linkages? The Canadian Journal of Economics. Revue Canadienne d'Economique, 27(3), 551–567. doi:10.2307/135783 doi:10.2307/135783

Pesaran, H. M. (2004). *General diagnostic tests for cross section dependence in panels*. Cambridge Working Paper in Economics, No 435.

Pesaran, M. H. (2007). A simple panel unit root test in the presence of cross-section dependence. Journal of Applied Econometrics, 22(2), 265–312. doi:10.1002/jae.951 doi:10.1002/jae.951

Pethig, R. (1976). Pollution, welfare and environmental policy in the theory of comparative advantage. Journal of Environmental Economics and Management, 2(3), 160–169. doi:10.1016/0095-0696(76)90031-0 doi:10.1016/0095-0696(76)90031-0

Sarafidis, V., & De Hoyos, R. E. (2006). On testing for cross sectional dependence in panel data models. University of Cambridge.

Saunders, C. S., & Cagatay, S. (2004). Trade and the environment: Economic and environmental impacts of global dairy trade liberalization. International Journal of Environmental Assessment Policy and Management, 6(3), 339–365. doi:10.1142/S1464333204001766 doi:10.1142/S1464333204001766

Savard, M., & Bohman, M. (2003). Impacts of trade, environmental and agricultural policies in the North American hog/pork industry on water quality. Journal of Policy Modeling, 25(1), 77–84. doi:10.1016/S0161-8938(02)00197-7 doi:10.1016/S0161-8938(02)00197-7

Siebert, H. (1992). Economics of the environment. New York: Springer Verlag. doi:10.1007/978-3-662-02842-1 doi:10.1007/978-3-662-02842-1

Tsai, P.-L. (1999). Is trade liberalization harmful to the environment? An alternative view. Journal of Economic Studies (Glasgow, Scotland), 26(3), 201–209. doi:10.1108/01443589910284381 doi:10.1108/01443589910284381

Tsurumi, T., & Managi, S. (2011). *The effect of trade openness on deforestation: Empirical analysis for 142 countries*. MPRA Paper No. 35805.

Walter, I. (1974). International trade and resource diversion: The case of environmental management. Weltwirtschaftliches Archiv, 110(3), 482–493. doi:10.1007/BF02696706 doi:10.1007/BF02696706

Westerlund, J., & Edgerton, D. L. (2007). A panel bootstrap cointegration test. Economics Letters, 97(3), 185–190. doi:10.1016/j.econlet.2007.03.003 doi:10.1016/j.econlet.2007.03.003

Westerlund, J. (2005). A panel CUSUM test of the null of cointegration. Oxford Bulletin of Economics and Statistics, 67(2), 231–262. doi:10.1111/j.1468-0084.2004.00118.x doi:10.1111/j.1468-0084.2004.00118.x

Westerlund, J. (2006). Reducing the size distortion of the panel LM test for cointegration. Economics Letters, 90(3), 384–389. doi:10.1016/j.econlet.2005.09.002 doi:10.1016/j.econlet.2005.09.002

World Bank World Development Indicators Database. (2014). Retrieved January 14, 2014, from http://data.worldbank.org/data-catalog/world-development-indicators

KEY TERMS AND DEFINITIONS

Environmental Pollution: Environmental pollution implies the undesired spread of toxic chemicals into the aquatic habitats of the world. The most common types of pollution are water, air and land pollution. Today, environmental pollution is correlated with economic growth and other economic variables.

Newly Industrialized Countries (NIC): These countries have moved away from an agriculture based economy and into a more industrialized economy. They are China, India, Brazil, Malaysia, Mexico, Philippines, South Africa, Thailand, and Turkey.

Panel Cointegration Test: Panel cointegration tests are often used to investigate the presence of the long run (cointegration) relationship between the variables. If the results are positive, this implies that there exists an evidence of a long run relationship between the variables.

Panel Data: Panel data are a type of longitudinal data at different points in time. This data are generally used for states, companies, individuals or countries.

Panel Estimation Methods: Panel estimation methods are frequently used to estimate the presence of a long run relation between panel data. These are the pooled OLS estimator, dynamic OLS estimator and Fully Modified OLS estimator.

Panel Granger Causality Test: This test is generally employed to examine the existence of causality relations between the variables. Classical Granger causality test and Vector error correction based causality test are well known in empirical theory.

Trade Openness: Trade openness refers to the degrees to which countries have trade with other countries. This variables is usually used to measure the importance of international transactions relative to domestic transactions. This is computed for each country as the simple average of total trade relative to GDP.

Section 4
Globalization of Regionalism

Chapter 18
Economic Crisis and its Impact on Regionalism and Globalism

Baris Kablamaci
Istanbul University, Turkey

Giray Gozgor
Dogus University, Turkey

ABSTRACT

This chapter reviews the financial crisis of 2008-09 and its impacts on the international trade in terms of regionalism and globalism. The chapter glances over different aspects of globalism and regionalism as well as looks on historical pattern and recent developments of regionalism and globalism. The data used in the chapter indicates that the financial crisis of 2008-09 negatively affected both globalization and regionalization trends. In addition, the EU has experienced an interesting transformation from regionalism to globalism. This chapter suggests that the issue is not only related with the great trade collapse of 2008-09 but also the sovereign debt crisis of 2010-12.

INTRODUCTION

In 2009, according to the World Trade Organization (WTO) (2010), world trade volume and Gross Domestic Product (GDP) growth respectively decreased 12.2 per cent and 2.3 per cent, after the 10-year average increase of 4.1 per cent and 3.0 per cent. This sharp fall in the trade growth of the world economy came up with a quick recovery in 2010 but fell again in 2011 and 2012, 3.8 per cent, 2.4 per cent, and 2.1 per cent, respectively. Therefore, an experience in international trade caused countries to give a reaction to the financial crisis of 2008-09 in various ways, the analyses on regionalism and globalism got a possession of significant importance.

International trade has always been a significant issue for both developed and developing countries in order to integrate to the global markets to increase growth and welfare. This process make more vulnerable to the external shocks through the export dependence of economy and bring the protection necessities subject to bilateral or regional agreements (Whalley, 2008). While some empirical studies in literature suggest that there is a significant positive correlation between trade liberalization and growth (Wacziarg and Welch, 2008), the issue is still much debated and seems

DOI: 10.4018/978-1-4666-7308-3.ch018

to be complex. However, some other studies argue the deeper roots of this relation, a developing country's economy can be more unstable subject to the relative impact of trade liberalization on exports and imports performance and its balance of payments (shock)–or terms-of-trade shocks that reflect the trade balance, and be more vulnerable to external shocks, particularly for commodity exporters (Cavallo and Frankel, 2008). However, significance of the distance is associated with the substitutability of goods and the level of trade costs, rather than changes in tariff levels or transportation costs (Berthelon and Freund, 2008).

By the short time after the second war, globalization process had begun in an institutional route that conducts the negotiations under the General Agreement on Tariffs and Trade (GATT) in 1947, leading to a unified global economy. For reaching such an objective, globalism requires the path of multilateralization. However, nearly in sixty years, it was experienced that the GATT arrangements, which are the fundamental structure of the multilateral trade liberalization, was supported much less than the arrangements in regional economic integrations. In this context, particularly by the mid-1990s multilateral and regional solutions for global trading system became a considerable issue that if the relation between them is complementary or substitutive. The WTO firstly stated in 1995 that the linkage between regional and multilateral integrations have characteristics of complementary and reinforced its statement by the conception of "multilateralizing regionalism" in 2007 (World Trade Organization, 2010).

The regional economic integration was first suggested by Viner (1950) as a customs union theory. This approach of economic regionalism is termed as "old" or "first" regionalism that represents a "closed" and "shallow" economic integration by trade agreements. Cadot et al. (1999) suggest that "deep" regional tend to strengthen the protectionist feature of the region and free trade agreements have mostly "shallow" integration structure, the competition in the tariff-revenue and consumer arbitrage possibilities in region lead member countries to set trade agreements with non-members separately. Following Viner (1950), Meade (1955) (the Nobel Memorial Laureate in 1977), Lipsey and Lancaster (1956), and Lipsey (1960) evolve and contribute to his approaches. In the customs unions, trade barriers in the region should be eliminated and made one tariff of imports from non-member countries. Viner (1950) examines the effects of customs unions and argues whether regional integration agreements rely on either trade creation or trade diversion that has positive and negative influence respectively on the welfare of a member country. He also suggests that the influence of such these agreements like customs unions on trade and welfare of a country is ambiguous and depends on the balance between trade creating and trade diverting effects. If a member country that sign the regional agreements cause to a high-cost domestic production to low-cost import, this situation turns out to be a trade creating effect. On the other hand, this agreements cause low-cost production from previous a non-member partner to high-cost partner and this situation generates trade-diverting effect.

From an economic development point of view, regional integration provides developing countries lower barriers to intra–regional trade, and an economic interaction between countries that have open development strategies, promoting trade in the region and in international markets, improving technology transfers, variation in the structure of the production and trade, increased foreign direct investments (FDI), and rapid economic growth. There are two different regional integration patterns that make the differentiation between "regionalism" and "regionalization". While the former term represents the integration between countries through agreements among formal governments under not only economic also political and cultural conditions have importance such as the European Union (EU), the North American Free Trade Agreement (NAFTA), and the Association of Southeast Asian Nations

(ASEAN), the latter term represents integration of economies under the market–driven structure without formal agreements between governments, such as the Asia-Pacific Economic Cooperation (APEC) (McDonald et al., 2008). On the other hand, according to the United Nations Conference on Trade and Development (UNCTAD) (2007), "external integration" considerably depends on process of the "internal integration" of the country that reflects the industrial division of labor in economic activities and the relationship between sectors under institutionalized economic structure. The main purposes of entering into a regional trade agreements country to have an accession to foreign markets with low or removed tariff barriers, to take attention for new investments, to reinforce liberalization of the economy and the stabilization of the political structure the country, to increase the competitiveness in global economy against trade giants and to raise the power in international community as well as in negotiations.

There are also two regional economic integration regimes that constraint the countries' economic and political policy space on their own accounts. The agreements signify the characteristic of the regional integration whether it is a "shallow" or a "deep" integration. The shallow regional integration implies the quota liberalization and the elimination of trade barriers by preferential trade agreements (PTA) and free trade agreements (FTA). FTAs represent the majority of these integration regimes, such as the US-Canada FTA (CUSFTA), the North American FTA (NAFTA), the MERCOSUR, the ASEAN and other regional integrations that have only lowering trade barriers and consist of zero tariffs between member countries but positive tariffs with non-members. On the other hand, deep regional integration regimes, such as the EU involves the institutional change of the linkage of trade through liberalization of capital, labor, firms, and services movements besides product standards and regulations among economies within the region for increasing the efficiency of markets.

The objective of this chapter is to analyze the great collapse of 2008-2009 and its impacts on regionalism and globalism. For this purpose, we investigate several regional trade integrations and the recent developments in world trade using data from the UNCTAD. The main research question in this chapter is that the collapse in international worldwide whether has homogeneous or heterogonous effects on regional integrations. We suggest that our overview in this chapter would be important for theoretical considerations and policy implications. The remainder of this chapter is organized as follows. Section 2 presents the historical background of the economic regionalism by classifying into two main periods. Section 3 describes the data set and discusses the overview and assessment of the recent developments in several international trade measures. Section 4 concludes.

HISTORICAL BACKGROUND OF THE ECONOMIC REGIONALISM

In the late 1940s, the GATT was negotiated and came into force by industrialized countries for increasing world trade and reducing trade volatility. The Article XXIV of the GATT and the Enabling Clause in and the Article V of the General Agreement on Trade in Services (GATS) that were entered into force in 1948, as a result of Tokyo Round in 1979, and as well as result of Uruguay Round in 1995, respectively, enable the WTO member countries to participate in regional trade agreements, custom unions, and free-trade areas in area of trade in goods and services. While, the former Article generated standard procedure for becoming a member in FTAs, the second arrangement gave permission to developing and least developed countries that are ineligible to meet the criteria in the Article XXIV of the GATT for regional trade agreements. On the other hand, the third one identified the economic integration rules involving trade in services that were arranged in the GATS negotiations. According to the WTO, over 400 arrangements made after the establishment of the WTO in 1995 in comparison with 124 notifications of RTAs under the GATT between 1948 and 1994. Within this period, global economy had experienced a dual structure in international trade through regionalism and multilateralism that made the entire trading system as a famous term, "spaghetti bowl" in Bhagwati's words (Bhagwati, 1993).

The Economic Regionalism of the 1950s-1970s

In 1947, after the Second World War, reconstruction of Europe by the aid program of the Marshall Plan, which was brought about by the US conducted to European integration in political and economic ways. In 1951, by the Treaty of Paris, West Germany, France, Italy, Belgium, Netherlands, and Luxembourg became together to form the European Coal and Steel Community (ECSC) that was an international institution toward a united Western Europe, having supranational features. The main motivation under this integration was not only economic but also especially political. These countries made an achievement to establish new communities in 1957, by signing the Treaty of Rome as named the European Atomic Energy Community (EURATOM) to develop a nuclear energy market in Europe for energy dependence and the European Economic Community (EEC) to form a common market having a common trade tariffs and policies against non-member countries, including agriculture sector and transportation, and free mobilization of goods, services, labor, and capital. On the other hand, in 1960 by the Stockholm Convention, the European Free Trade Association (EFTA) was established in the leading of the United Kingdom as an alternative regional trade bloc, including Switzerland, Sweden, Norway, Portugal, Denmark, and Austria. While it made a significant progress in the beginning, it lost importance by leaving of Denmark and the UK in 1973.

In 1967, by the Merger Treaty, three separate communities became together in a unique organization that holds characteristic structures of every community as termed the European Community (EC). The process of European regional integration was significantly depended on political motivations making a control mechanism for each of the devastated great powers of the continent in presence of two economic and political superpowers, the US and the Soviet Union. The collapse of the Bretton Woods system (the fixed US Dollar to gold system) in 1971 and the oil crises in 1973 and in 1979 led the integration of Europe into an unexpected break till 1986.

There were also several regional groupings among developing countries in the first era of the economic regionalism that tend to make free trade areas and customs unions with the inspiration of the regional progress in Europe, such as the Central American Common Market (CACM) in 1960, the Latin American Free Trade Association (LAFTA) in 1960, the Arab Common Market (ACM) in 1964, the Customs and Economic Union of Central Africa (CEUCA) in 1966, the Association of Southeast Asian Nations (ASEAN) in 1967, the South African Customs Union (SACU) in 1969, the Andean Community of Nations (CAN) in 1969, the Caribbean Community (CARICOM) in 1973. Although, the European integration had significantly political motivations, these integration arrangements between developing countries had mainly economic motivations, considering such as import substitution industrialization strategy with high external trade barriers toward the achievement of national economic development. The characteristic features of these agreements were mainly protectionist and interventionist, considering restrictions on the economic activity on member countries (Schiff and Winters, 2003).

New Regionalism

The economic regionalism was seen by the mid-1980s, so called as the "second wave" regionalism by Bhagwati et al. (1999) also termed as "new regionalism" especially began with the Single European Act, which was signed in 1986, toward a unified Europe, had totally changed attention to economic regionalism in a new way. Through this Act, the EC moved forward for being a single market implying removal of trade barriers across the Europe with also the intention of common policies, such as monetary, foreign policy, environmental for harmonization of member countries. The emergence of the new global economic order involved the reduction of determinant economic and political power of the US and the accretion of economic factors in global politics in this new era.

In the meantime, the US, which was the dominant economic and political power of the previous global economic period, transformed the pattern of its regionalism by making a regional agreement with Canada in 1987 and by adding Mexico, generated a regional trade bloc entered in force in 1994, called as the NAFTA. According to Cai (2010), the NAFTA was a response to the new challenging conditions that implies intense competitive environment of the new world trading system as European "deep" regional integration and increasing competitive power of Asian countries in the world economy by the US and also the likelihood of failure in the Uruguay Round reflecting the process of multilateralism towards a global integration. Opposite of the EU, the NAFTA was established to become mainly from economic motivations forming a regional trade bloc that depends on a trade union instead of a customs union, reflecting a common external tariffs. Although the NAFTA stand for an economic alternative regional integration against the EU, there are major differences between these influential global powers. The main difference is where the EU has an institutionalized supranational economic and political structure; the NAFTA is still away from political integration, which is significantly driven by economic initiatives. The changing path of the US on regionalism rather than multilateral arrangements also affects the trend of international trade system, that could be seen the uncertainty of the state of affairs of the Doha Round, which was started in 2001 and is still negotiating till the present time.

In the early years of 1990s, significant changes had occurred in the international political conditions as the collapse of the Soviet Union that has the meaning of end of the Cold War between the communist bloc and the liberal Western Hemisphere. Such a change switched the political and economic structure of the European integration, due to the reunification of Germany. In line with these new geopolitical developments in the continent, besides the objective to be a major competitive unified region against the US, Japan, and emerging markets, the EC turned into the EU in 1993 by the Treaty of Maastricht.

According to Baldwin (1997), while developed countries object to trade liberalization in the agricultural sector, developing countries object to tariff-cuts on manufacturing goods in multilateral and regional agreements. He also argues that due to having a high possession of global trade, regional agreements among North Atlantic countries have significant consequences on trade partners with non-member countries (Baldwin, 1997). Even as Summers (1991) addresses regionalism has a positive impact, Bhagwati and Krueger (1995) argue whether this is an important constraint on multilateral global trading system. In a recent empirical study, Geldi (2012) finds that member countries in the EU have to increase intra-regional trade. For the NAFTA, exports to excluded-countries substantially diverted, in spite of that member countries of the MERCOSUR and the AFTA are considerably dependent on extra-union imports. Moreover, Romalis (2007) suggests that NAFTA has a significant impact on the international trade but a moderate impact on prices and welfare. However, Ornelas (2008) states that due to governments have political motivations and concerns, free trade is unattainable in the global economy. He also shows that the GATT/WTO negotiating rules are suitable for achieving equilibrium, which indicates a politically efficient, is economically inefficient. On the other hand, he argues that due to by lowering trade barriers within the region, members are also prone to lower their multilateral tariffs, regional trade agreements increase world welfare (Ornelas, 2008). According to Schultz (1996), in spite of multilateral negotiations, due to be managed more easily by member countries, regional liberalization agreements are proliferating and much more attractive for non-member countries, thus global trading system follows a slow pace subject to regional liberalization. The harmonization of standards on the goods among a regional integration have effects both member and non-member countries. Standardization of the tradable goods causes a reduction in the exports of non-member countries. The excluded-country's exports are positively associated with the capability to meet the standards of regional agreements (Chen and Mattoo, 2008).

The firms in countries that are early entrant to regional trade arrangements have the opportunity of first-mover advantages for increasing growth in these economies. The firms in non-member economies had to challenge with insider firms by fixed expenses at the initial point (Freund, 2000). The regional integration could damage non-member countries by trade diversion through high external tariffs and preferential liberalization. However, Freund (2010) shows that there is no evidence on those trade preferences in Latin America would not generate any decrease imports from excluding countries. The main determinant of the effects of regionalism on welfare of a member country relies on how reacts to trade barriers and this situation shape the trade policy of a member country while generating the trade diversion against non-member countries. Freund (2000) also indicates that regionalism is a way toward to integration of the global economy. Welfare effects of regional integration do not only come up with the trade structure of member countries with trade barriers, but also these integration agreements effect significantly and positively FDI flows by increasing investment diversion, employment rate in these nations. In an empirical study, Kreinin and Plummer (2008) show that FDI is a substitute for trade in a considerable amount of cases than be in complimentary for international trade.

International trade faced with a new system since 1947. This new system tried to generate a trade liberalization multilateralization, due to the GATT rounds over forty years until these rounds ended up with a new global institution as the WTO. The early professions are Jacob Viner, James Meade, and Richard Lipsey who gave their attention to regionalism in the world trading system as a trade policy in the 1940s and 1950s. Until Canada and Mexico made a decision to make FTAs between their giant trading power and the US in the late 1980s, regionalism was seen as a widely effective customs union among developing countries which figured in a small ratio in the global trade. The relationship between regionalism and multilateralism had always taken attention not only from professions in economics and especially international trade, but also from policy makers and governments in either developed or developing countries. While some scholars, such as Summers (1991) and Bergsten (1991) see this relation as a complimentary; and other ones, such as Krugman (1991) and Bhagwati (1991) see the relation as a substitution and tend to make regional trade blocs that hinders free trade in the world economy. The regional arrangements between the US and Mexico induced to make bilateral FTAs between the US and Latin American countries and also lead to regional agreements among and make a regional trading bloc, such as the MERCOSUR among these countries. North American regionalism has followed three main events that shaped global economy, which were the first one, the collapse of the Uruguay Round in 1990 that represents the failure of the GATT negotiations and multilateralism; the second one was the conversion of the EC to the EU in 1992, and the third one was the collapse of the Soviet Union in 1991.

On the other hand, the EU had already started to regional arrangements in 1951 by six states as the ECSC and 1957 Treaty of Rome for became an institutionalized regional structure covering not only economic issues, as trade policies or monetary union, but also adopting similar laws for across European countries until the establishment of the EU in 1992. In parallel with the regional developments in Europe and North America, developing countries also seek to integrate to global markets through regionalism rather than multilateralism while observing slow progress of the GATT negotiations and the sequential international institutionalized organization as the WTO. For developing countries, being in an economic regional integration reflects the motivation to achieve economic development and the reduction of poverty. Regional integration leads to increase trade due to extended market opportunities along with the technology transfer, and increasing efficiency. Trade integration became a driving force for the underdeveloped or developing countries to challenge with the giant trade blocs in an increasing severe competitive environment in the global economy. For instance, we understand this idea from following sentences in the trade and development report of the UNCTAD in 2007 as such: "As individual developing countries become more vulnerable and lose national policy autonomy in the process of globalization, regional economic cooperation can also be a defensive response in the hope that a regional partnership will soften the impact of global factors and help them to cope with globalization. From this perspective, regional institutions could also fill gaps in global economic governance structures." (UNCTAD, Trade and Development Report, 2007: 53).

One of major economic regional integrations, depends mainly on the agreement of "Argentina-Brazil Integration and Economic Cooperation" in 1985 led to the regional integration arrangement that was established by Argentina, Brazil, Uruguay, and Paraguay under the Treaty of Asunción in 1991, called as the MERCOSUR, abbreviation of the "Mercado Común del Sur" in Spanish (Southern Common Market) and expanded accession of Venezuela and Bolivia in 2012. Similar with the EU, the MERCOSUR was founded for achievement of a "deep" regional integration to build a common external tariff policy, customs union, and political motivation to challenge with the competitiveness and security needs that are caused in era of globalization. As the regional integration in Europe reflects the agreement of France and West Germany in the 1950s, the MERCOSUR also depends on the relation between Argentina and Brazil that is the dominant economic power within the region providing economic benefits to other countries in the region. Correspondingly, in a recent empirical model Domingues et al. (2008) examine the sensitivity to the trade shocks and welfare gains for trade were in Brazil, Argentina, and Uruguay and find that as Brazil is well-conditioned to various degrees of trade liberalization and this influence welfare gains in which Argentina and Uruguay are highly dependent to the terms-of-trade shocks, due to high degree of trade liberalization.

Within this process of the economic integration in Americas, currency union, common trade policy and a unified macroeconomic policy is one of the objectives of this intergovernmental structure. While regional trade agreements tend to make a bloc against global economic powers, they also lead to export opportunities and upgrade technology through the removal of tariffs of the trading partner and increasing revenues for exporting countries, as falling Brazil's tariffs induce the Argentinean firms to adopt new technologies, which generate a positive effect on the Argentinean firms by revenues and performance (Bustos, 2011).

Another regional integration, the Association of Southeast Asian Nations (ASEAN) was established in 1967 in the Bangkok Declaration by Indonesia, Malaysia, the Philippines, Singapore, and Thailand, has been growing rapidly in East Asia from the mid-1980s with Brunei. Especially, in 1990s, after establishment of the WTO, Vietnam, Myanmar, Laos, and Cambodia enter to a new regional trade bloc. Following the accession to the WTO in December 2001, the ASEAN and China made Free Trade Area Agreement that came into force in 2010 moving forward to be a significant economic collaboration in the global economy (Park, 2009). Although major currencies have impacts on the individual ASEAN currencies, their impact levels are different in a long-run relationship. In a distinctive manner, the UK pound has an importance on these currencies (Click, 2009). The ASEAN currencies either is not tracing a global currency standard or having a tendency for adopting a common currency (Krapohl and Fink, 2013). The rationale of economic regional integration of the ASEAN is an export-promoting development strategy of individual countries that depends on the trade liberalization within the region. This type of the way to regional economic integration promotes the reliance on trade with non-member countries. Extra-regional trade has a significant importance for these countries to achieve their economic development objectives (Krapohl and Fink, 2013).

The regional integration within the ASEAN countries especially after the mid-1990s, provided member countries to have a reduction in trade costs relatively to non-members and allow them both regional and global trade advantages (Sourdin, 2009). Asian regionalism relies on four major determinants that form the increasing number of FTAs in the region, as follows: first of all, market-driven economic integration that states the trade liberalization, FDI, supply-chains, and the standardization of trade and rules across the region. Second, the rising global power of the EU and the NAFTA toward dominance in international trade through their economic integrations give a tendency to reduce trade costs and raise the bargaining power in order to be much competitive in the global trading system. Third, the Asian financial crisis in the late 1990s led the countries in the region to act together to achieve individual economic growth and increase the interdependence for stabilizing macroeconomic issues. Fourth, the slow pace of the negotiations in the multilateral level, as the WTO Doha Round, guided the economic integration in Asia into a regional trade bloc (Kawai and Wignaraja, 2011).

Another economic regional integration is generated in Africa in several arrangements such as the Common Market of Eastern and Southern Africa (COMESA) and the Economic Community of West African States (ECOWAS), which are founded in 1993 with its origins in 1960s and 1975, relatively. Although 12 of 19 and 10 of 17 countries respectively, most of the African countries are classified as the Least Developed Countries (LDCs) by the United Nations (UN) in these integrations, challenging with the economic underdevelopment, weak institutional structure, and potential conflicts or wars in the region, countries endeavors not to be marginalized from the world economy. There are two significant objectives of the COMESA, instead of small economic gains for member countries. One is that to support peace and security in the region by trade liberalization between member countries. The other one is that to provide the resource allocation more efficiently by trade agreements rather than weak featured institutions. According to Mayda and Chad (2009), for instance Uganda did not get significant benefits from the tariff liberalization through arrangements in the COMESA.

Besides with these processes at both regional groups and global economy, we know the great global recession of 2008-09 heavily and negatively affected openness to trade in all open economies in general but developed economies in particular. The severe effects of the great global recession 2008-09 on the welfare is mainly explained by the decreasing volume of international trade in big rich countries (Levchenko et al., 2010). Actually, the great global recession of 2008-09 was also related with a dramatic collapse in world international trade and this significantly larger than the fall in GDP in world (Gopinath et al., 2012). Therefore, there could be a significant effects of the great global recession 2008-09 on both regional and global aspects of international trade, namely in the terms of "regionalism" and globalism". We now look through the related data in terms of economic aspects of regionalism and globalism.

DATA AND OVERVIEW

In this section, we overview developments of outlook trade pattern in world and regional groups. For this purpose, we analyze the roots of "regionalism" and "globalism" using trade statistics data of the UNTCAD. In particular, we focus on the periods of the pre-crisis, the crisis, and the post-crisis.

In Table 1, we report the nominal trade openness of the goods and services over the period 1980-2012. We consider the measure of percentage of gross domestic product. Data in Table 1 remark that world trade openness is significantly diminished from 64.2 to 54.2 in the great global recession of 2008-09. In 2012, the level of world nominal trade openness (62.6) is still behind times of the pre-crisis. These data in Table 1 reveal that globalization process is negatively affected by the global financial crisis of 2008-09.

On the other hand, we observe that there is a similar trade collapse in regional groups. In 2012, trade openness levels of the ANCOM, the ASEAN, the COMESA, the ECO, and the MERCOSUR also fall astern in times of the pre-crisis levels. Trade openness levels of the NAFTA and the GCC recover relatively fast but their growths are still lower than the world nominal trade openness. However, the most remarkable display is that the trade openness levels of the EU27 and the Euro area act jointly with the world trade openness but their rates of increase are greater than the world's as well as the rest of regional groups. Shortly, the global financial crisis has unfavorable impression on globalization in worldwide. In addition, to evaluate effects of the great global recession on the "regionalism", we will look into intra-trade patterns of regional groups in Table 2 and in Table 3.

In Table 2, we report the progress of the intra-trade total exports of regional groups for the period from 1995 to 2012. The data show that the global crisis of 2008-09 has not significant impacts on the exports pattern of the ASEAN, the EFTA, and the GCC. However, the great global recession of 2008-09 decreased the intra-exports in the ANCOM, the EU, the Euro area, and the NAFTA. On the contrary, the intra-exports has increased aftermath the global crisis of 2008-09 in the COMESA, the ECO, and the MERCOSUR. The data present interesting patterns in intra-exports in both developing and developed economies: First, the exports patterns of the developing Southern Asia and Pacific economies have not been significantly affected by the global trade collapse of 2008-09. However, the Southern American regional groups have divided into two parts: The MERCOSUR, which is originated by free marketer developing economies, has concentrated on the intra-exports. However, the ANCOM, which is originated by more protectionist developing economies, try to export more on rest of the world.

Second, the developed economies those are generally substantial in the EU and the NAFTA export more to rest of the world after the global crisis of 2008-09. In short, if we leave aside the developing large Asian economies, the data state that developed economies seem to be more "global" and majority of large developing economies seem to be more "regional" in the patterns of exports. For a closer look, we analyze the total imports in regional groups in Table 3.

In Table 3, we report the progress of the intra-trade total imports of regional groups for the period from 1995 to 2012. The data in Table 3 indicate that the great global recession of 2008-09 do not significantly affect on the imports pattern of the most of regional groups but the exceptions are the

Table 1. Goods and services trade openness, percentage of gross domestic product, 1980-2012

Year and Economy	1980	1990	2000	2005	2006	2007	2008	2009	2010	2011	2012
World	39.7	38.4	49.1	56.1	59.4	61.3	64.2	54.2	59.1	63.2	62.6
ANCOM	33.9	30.9	35.3	41.7	45.3	44.9	47.5	40.7	42.4	47.6	46.1
ASEAN	81.5	96.3	159.0	159.8	154.0	147.4	148.7	122.7	126.4	128.5	126.7
COMESA	67.6	51.6	46.4	69.8	70.1	73.7	75.6	61.7	64.9	59.3	62.0
ECO	24.0	30.9	46.1	55.6	57.1	57.2	60.1	52.5	52.7	56.6	52.2
EFTA	85.4	76.4	83.8	84.7	87.8	91.2	94.0	88.5	93.9	97.9	97.0
EU27	54.4	53.0	71.6	73.1	78.0	79.0	81.7	72.8	80.8	86.6	87.8
Euro area	53.5	53.0	73.3	74.4	79.2	81.2	82.7	72.7	81.3	87.4	89.2
GCC	97.8	79.5	81.5	100.1	103.3	112.1	115.5	111.1	110.1	115.1	120.8
MERCOSUR	32.4	21.5	25.4	34.1	33.4	32.8	34.3	27.0	26.9	30.3	31.7
NAFTA	23.1	23.3	31.0	31.3	32.7	33.8	35.9	29.9	33.8	36.8	36.7

Notes: Measure is the US Dollars at current prices. Data source: UNCTAD, UNCTADstat.

Table 2. Intra-trade of regional groups, total exports, 1995-2012

Economy and Year	1995	2000	2005	2008	2009	2012
World	5121053	6366950	10447270	16110246	12509705	18351468
	100	100	100	100	100	100
ANCOM (Andean Community)	1804	2039	4574	7174	5977	9948
	8.5	7.8	9.0	7.6	7.6	7.1
ASEAN (Association of South-East Asian Nations)	80081	98189	165406	250620	198943	325513
	24.9	23.0	25.3	25.5	24.5	26.0
COMESA (Common Market for Eastern and Southern Africa)	1363	1404	3399	6930	6833	9297
	5.6	4.7	5.2	5.5	7.2	6.9
ECO (Economic Cooperation Organization)	4908	4693	14565	31025	23786	48430
	8.1	5.7	7.4	7.9	8.4	11.1
EFTA (European Free Trade Association)	927	842	1220	2962	2108	2970
	0.7	0.6	0.5	0.8	0.7	0.8
EU27 (European Union)	1412003	1607599	2725738	3963196	3028790	3576710
	65.9	67.5	67.6	67.0	66.3	61.8
Euro area	883190	956886	1619956	2312535	1792902	2038696
	51.7	51.6	51.5	50.0	50.1	45.7
GCC (Gulf Cooperation Council)	7041	8340	19453	37102	32281	51191
	6.8	4.8	4.9	4.9	6.4	5.0
MERCOSUR (Mercado Común Sudamericano)	17677	21042	26970	56477	44051	66614
	19.5	18.0	12.2	14.9	15.7	14.9
NAFTA (North American Free Trade Agreement)	392902	681263	824515	1012592	768105	1150305
	46.0	55.7	55.7	49.5	48.0	48.5

Notes: Measure is the US Dollars at current prices and current exchange rates in millions. We also report the percentage by total intra-trade in regional groups. Source: UNCTAD, UNCTADstat.

Table 3. Intra-trade of regional groups, total imports, 1995-2012

Economy and Year	1995	2000	2005	2008	2009	2012
World	5186545	6562546	10705057	16371584	12585416	18439112
	100	100	100	100	100	100
ANCOM (Andean Community)	1799	2168	5233	7922	6453	11613
	6.6	8.9	11.5	8.5	8.7	8.7
ASEAN (Association of South-East Asian Nations)	63986	83642	154268	233722	181682	286870
	18.0	22.0	25.6	24.9	24.9	23.5
COMESA (Common Market for Eastern and Southern Africa)	1391	1678	3946	6926	6804	10231
	4.2	4.9	6.0	5.6	5.9	5.8
ECO (Economic Cooperation Organization)	4602	5399	12964	27153	19279	33958
	6.4	5.9	6.1	7.3	6.8	7.8
EFTA (European Free Trade Association)	1002	920	1378	2461	1892	2671
	0.9	0.8	0.7	0.9	0.8	0.9
EU27 (European Union)	1329511	1503393	2524158	3682368	2785451	3273535
	63.8	61.7	61.5	59.6	60.3	56.3
Euro area	819093	879048	1470089	2107916	1615172	1818919
	50.4	47.8	47.8	45.5	46.2	42.4
GCC (Gulf Cooperation Council)	6435	7775	16687	33617	26759	48974
	9.1	9.1	9.0	8.3	8.0	9.6
MERCOSUR (Mercado Común Sudamericano)	16992	21262	27573	56687	42650	66097
	18.1	20.6	20.6	18.8	19.1	17.2
NAFTA (North American Free Trade Agreement)	380081	664472	782101	952739	707692	1065988
	37.7	39.6	34.5	33.1	32.8	33.7

Notes: Measure is the US Dollars at current prices and current exchange rates in millions. We also report the percentage by total intra-trade in regional groups. Source: UNCTAD, UNCTADstat.

EU and the Euro area. The global financial crisis of 2008-09 decreased the patterns of intra-imports in the EU and the Euro area. Similar with the appearance in Table 1 and Table 2, our data in Table 3 demonstrate that there is a growing globalization process in both the EU and the Euro area aftermath the great global recession of 2008-09.

For more detailed analysis on the aspects of regionalism aftermath the great global recession of 2008-09, we focus on the services trade and the merchandise trade in regional groups. In Table 4 and Table 5, we report the share of services exports and imports by service-category for the period from 1980 to 2013, respectively. We consider the percentages of total world for the share of services exports and services imports, due to this would be better measure of "regionalism" and "globalism" regards to aspects in the services trade.

We report the progress of services trade progress in world and regional groups in Table 4 and Table 5. We focus on total services and their sub-groups: Transport, travel, and other services (i.e., communications, construction, insurance, financial services, computer and information, royalties and license fees, other business services, personal, cultural and recreational services, and

Table 4. Share of services exports by service-category, percentage of total world, 1980-2013

Economy and Year		1980	1990	2000	2005	2008	2009	2013
ANCOM	Total services	0.63	0.37	0.31	0.25	0.25	0.27	0.31
	Transport	0.60	0.49	0.34	0.30	0.28	0.32	0.43
	Travel	0.91	0.33	0.49	0.46	0.51	0.57	0.62
	Other services	0.49	0.33	0.17	0.12	0.12	0.12	0.14
	Communications	..	..	1.07	0.68	0.65	0.65	0.48
	Construction	..	..	-	0.00	0.00	0.00	0.00
	Insurance	..	..	0.56	0.31	0.33	0.34	0.46
	Financial services	..	..	0.09	0.02	0.04	0.04	0.03
	Computer and information	..	..	0.01	0.02	0.04	0.03	0.10
	Royalties and license fees	..	..	0.01	0.01	0.01	0.02	0.03
	Other business services	..	..	0.07	0.08	0.09	0.10	0.11
	Personal, cultural and recreational services	..	..	0.43	0.35	0.33	0.32	0.74
	Government services n.i.e.	0.45	0.42	0.81	0.50	0.47	0.51	0.53
ASEAN	Total services	2.45	3.55	4.53	4.63	5.06	4.72	5.86
	Transport	1.90	2.43	5.57	5.94	6.36	6.71	6.93
	Travel	3.12	5.11	5.64	4.99	6.23	6.17	9.10
	Other services	2.47	3.08	3.26	3.87	3.95	3.39	4.05
	Communications	..	..	3.25	5.25	4.00	4.07	4.36
	Construction	..	..	2.63	3.86	3.14	2.88	4.51
	Insurance	..	..	3.04	3.39	2.89	3.41	3.99
	Financial services	..	..	2.58	2.94	3.61	4.16	5.40
	Computer and information	..	..	1.31	1.18	2.03	2.54	2.43
	Royalties and license fees	..	..	0.13	0.77	0.73	0.55	0.66
	Other business services	..	..	4.95	5.38	5.57	4.15	5.03
	Personal, cultural and recreational services	..	..	-	8.07	4.43	4.61	2.62
	Government services n.i.e.	1.86	1.57	1.80	1.63	1.85	1.89	2.13
COMESA	Total services	1.13	1.14	0.97	0.90	0.98	0.95	0.83
	Transport	1.54	1.59	1.18	1.25	1.35	1.48	1.77
	Travel	1.07	0.85	1.27	1.44	1.64	1.72	1.18
	Other services	0.83	1.09	0.64	0.45	0.52	0.43	0.36
	Communications	..	..	1.21	1.22	2.50	1.72	1.61
	Construction	..	..	0.45	0.97	1.25	0.71	0.87
	Insurance	..	..	0.47	0.32	0.37	0.27	0.28
	Financial services	..	..	0.28	0.21	0.19	0.16	0.20
	Computer and information	..	..	0.09	0.08	0.15	0.13	0.13
	Royalties and license fees	..	..	0.08	0.11	0.13	0.09	0.05

Table 4. Continued

Economy and Year		1980	1990	2000	2005	2008	2009	2013
	Other business services	..	..	0.79	0.34	0.33	0.33	0.18
	Personal, cultural and recreational services	..	..	0.16	0.40	0.31	0.52	0.54
	Government services n.i.e.	1.40	4.33	2.69	2.81	3.21	2.87	-
ECO	Total services	0.65	1.29	1.75	1.57	1.51	1.68	1.69
	Transport	-	0.95	1.64	1.80	2.03	2.60	2.63
	Travel	0.57	1.37	1.87	2.90	2.76	2.99	2.99
	Other services	0.73	1.45	1.73	0.75	0.70	0.78	-
	Communications	..	..	1.09	1.55	1.25	1.60	1.47
	Construction	..	..	4.68	4.52	2.80	3.80	3.65
	Insurance	..	..	0.21	0.85	1.20	0.97	1.18
	Financial services	..	..	0.43	0.27	0.41	0.41	0.42
	Computer and information	..	..	0.09	-	0.21	-	-
	Royalties and license fees	..	..	0.02	-	-	-	-
	Other business services	..	..	1.90	-	0.30	-	0.52
	Personal, cultural and recreational services	..	..	17.79	4.96	4.92	3.63	3.78
	Government services n.i.e.	0.90	1.13	3.12	4.27	4.48	4.23	4.46
EFTA	Total services	3.99	4.02	3.25	3.16	3.17	3.30	2.92
	Transport	5.86	5.28	4.23	3.63	3.18	3.19	2.60
	Travel	3.82	3.10	1.87	1.96	2.06	2.14	1.90
	Other services	2.52	3.91	3.70	3.60	3.69	3.85	3.49
	Communications	..	..	3.44	2.64	2.07	2.18	1.31
	Insurance	..	..	6.02	7.49	7.40	6.07	6.14
	Financial services	..	..	11.29	8.21	6.92	6.79	5.46
	Royalties and license fees	..	..	3.16	5.75	5.25	6.68	7.14
	Personal, cultural and recreational services	..	..	1.04	1.60	1.96	1.73	0.93
	Government services n.i.e.	0.57	2.60	5.09	2.82	2.90	3.36	2.97
EU27	Total services	54.05	48.73	43.18	46.75	46.14	46.08	42.37
	Transport	49.34	44.41	43.74	46.06	45.96	46.34	42.81
	Travel	54.06	47.73	41.58	42.12	40.56	38.69	33.57
	Other services	58.03	52.31	44.01	49.59	48.78	49.28	46.21
	Communications	..	..	41.56	53.63	50.83	49.23	51.92
	Construction	..	..	52.50	52.24	41.67	42.28	37.30
	Insurance	..	..	46.44	46.14	50.81	59.96	55.05
	Financial services	..	..	47.18	52.19	54.67	50.87	47.33
	Computer and information	..	..	50.22	60.20	57.42	57.14	54.01

continued on following page

Table 4. Continued

Economy and Year		1980	1990	2000	2005	2008	2009	2013
	Royalties and license fees	..	..	23.24	30.62	32.99	36.95	35.30
	Other business services	..	..	47.71	52.46	50.26	51.05	46.84
	Personal, cultural and recreational services	..	..	53.45	61.62	59.00	62.83	65.01
	Government services n.i.e.	43.86	51.55	35.17	35.74	33.18	31.01	26.79
Euro area	Total services	39.87	37.47	30.35	32.99	32.49	33.03	30.36
	Transport	32.59	32.38	30.69	31.30	31.28	32.11	29.11
	Travel	43.81	38.56	32.39	33.10	31.46	30.37	25.86
	Other services	43.44	39.93	28.79	33.69	33.45	34.53	32.82
	Communications	..	..	28.10	35.26	35.73	35.43	38.67
	Construction	..	..	46.98	45.82	35.76	35.97	30.79
	Insurance	..	..	22.67	38.20	36.15	32.72	29.62
	Financial services	..	..	24.82	27.10	28.43	27.10	27.81
	Computer and information	..	..	35.90	44.57	43.24	43.34	41.71
	Royalties and license fees	..	..	11.73	18.48	22.90	27.41	28.33
	Other business services	..	..	32.68	36.78	35.45	37.34	33.62
	Personal, cultural and recreational services	..	..	34.21	35.04	35.90	41.04	43.56
	Government services n.i.e.	35.46	43.86	26.41	26.44	23.77	22.69	19.62
GCC	Total services	-	-	0.69	1.10	1.02	1.09	-
	Transport	-	-	1.03	1.38	1.35	1.48	-
	Travel	-	-	0.64	1.44	1.61	1.80	-
	Other services	-	-	0.56	0.79	0.61	0.65	-
	Communications	..	..	2.63	3.76	7.33	8.56	4.45
	Insurance	..	..	2.34	3.20	1.45	1.66	1.55
	Financial services	..	..	1.68	1.41	0.31	0.45	0.16
	Other business services	..	..	0.04	0.25	0.06	-	0.06
	Personal, cultural and recreational services	..	..	-	-	-	-	0.59
	Government services n.i.e.	-	-	1.95	4.06	3.80	2.40	-
MERCOSUR	Total services	1.27	1.01	1.16	1.03	1.24	1.25	1.28
	Transport	1.51	1.46	0.99	0.96	0.98	1.01	1.07
	Travel	1.10	1.20	1.26	1.16	1.34	1.38	1.23
	Other services	1.18	0.58	1.19	0.99	1.31	1.28	1.38
	Communications	..	..	1.13	1.02	1.11	0.95	0.72
	Construction	..	..	0.78	0.10	0.05	0.03	0.07
	Insurance	..	..	1.53	0.40	1.09	0.49	0.60
	Financial services	..	..	0.47	0.33	0.45	0.64	0.93
	Computer and information	..	..	0.44	0.40	0.65	0.75	0.80

continued on following page

Table 4. Continued

Economy and Year		1980	1990	2000	2005	2008	2009	2013
	Royalties and license fees	..	..	0.40	0.23	0.37	0.23	0.23
	Other business services	..	..	1.61	1.45	2.00	2.00	2.07
	Personal, cultural and recreational services	..	..	0.63	1.14	1.98	1.33	1.22
	Government services n.i.e.	2.02	0.78	2.90	2.61	3.01	3.04	3.16
NAFTA	Total services	15.06	21.07	22.54	17.47	15.89	16.68	16.67
	Transport	12.86	19.06	15.63	11.14	9.88	10.47	11.08
	Travel	15.78	23.66	25.16	18.87	17.58	17.01	17.29
	Other services	16.45	20.39	24.18	19.51	17.72	18.74	18.34
	Communications	..	..	19.59	12.73	13.44	13.91	15.86
	Construction	..	..	6.77	2.72	3.67	3.99	3.53
	Insurance	..	..	26.60	24.96	23.47	18.16	19.26
	Financial services	..	..	23.70	23.17	22.15	25.48	25.90
	Computer and information	..	..	20.66	12.55	9.29	10.24	8.51
	Royalties and license fees	..	..	58.86	48.35	45.96	43.22	42.96
	Other business services	..	..	17.27	13.55	12.38	13.90	13.38
	Personal, cultural and recreational services	..	..	13.11	11.56	10.31	10.59	7.07
	Government services n.i.e.	34.89	28.42	25.77	25.70	26.56	29.53	31.22

Notes: Measure is the US Dollars at current prices. Source: UNCTAD, UNCTADstat.

Table 5. Share of services imports by service-category, percentage of total world, 1980-2013

Economy-Year		1980	1990	2000	2005	2008	2009	2013
ANCOM	Total services	0.67	0.46	0.48	0.43	0.45	0.45	0.55
	Transport	0.84	0.59	0.68	0.69	0.73	0.70	0.73
	Travel	0.58	0.37	0.42	0.38	0.42	0.46	0.55
	Other services	0.57	0.43	0.40	0.31	0.31	0.34	0.47
	Government services n.i.e.	0.35	0.44	0.45	0.31	0.26	0.23	0.41
ASEAN	Total services	3.15	3.29	5.79	5.61	5.64	5.55	6.52
	Transport	3.75	5.16	8.00	8.34	8.48	8.28	9.26
	Travel	1.91	2.21	3.56	3.66	4.20	4.60	5.70
	Other services	3.33	2.71	5.87	5.09	4.78	4.82	5.61
	Government services n.i.e.	0.95	0.97	1.41	1.20	1.31	1.30	1.78
COMESA	Total services	1.96	1.13	0.95	0.94	1.05	1.00	-
	Transport	2.50	1.58	1.29	1.48	1.65	1.85	-
	Travel	1.22	0.48	0.55	0.62	0.82	0.83	-
	Other services	1.90	1.28	0.97	0.78	0.82	0.69	-

continued on following page

Table 5. Continued

Economy-Year		1980	1990	2000	2005	2008	2009	2013
	Government services n.i.e.	1.73	2.55	1.53	2.31	2.53	2.15	-
ECO	Total services	1.67	1.20	1.23	1.69	1.75	1.74	-
	Transport	2.11	1.71	1.47	1.76	2.00	2.13	1.93
	Travel	1.91	-	0.80	1.40	1.74	1.91	-
	Other services	1.08	1.24	1.38	1.82	1.64	1.53	1.50
	Government services n.i.e.	0.95	1.46	3.03	2.37	2.20	2.46	2.91
EFTA	Total services	2.71	2.46	1.91	2.22	2.07	2.13	2.21
	Transport	3.15	2.97	2.16	1.95	1.83	1.68	1.45
	Travel	3.62	3.41	2.38	3.06	2.98	3.00	2.94
	Other services	1.71	1.37	1.43	1.91	1.83	2.00	2.33
	Government services n.i.e.	0.13	0.44	0.52	1.04	0.83	0.56	0.61
EU27	Total services	42.19	43.08	41.54	44.24	43.03	42.73	37.52
	Transport	38.63	38.59	36.17	36.61	34.89	34.67	29.65
	Travel	49.27	46.69	43.61	45.52	44.44	42.19	33.62
	Other services	41.21	43.74	43.59	48.11	45.99	45.65	42.31
	Government services n.i.e.	19.54	21.22	18.77	25.01	24.85	21.78	20.11
Euro area	Total services	32.19	33.31	30.43	32.16	30.74	31.00	27.22
	Transport	26.31	28.61	25.74	26.20	25.54	25.33	21.68
	Travel	39.48	35.20	30.33	31.53	30.87	30.51	24.03
	Other services	33.36	35.43	33.49	36.12	34.19	34.58	32.39
	Government services n.i.e.	12.69	12.55	12.11	8.62	6.52	5.69	5.13
GCC	Total services	-	-	2.82	2.83	3.99	4.07	-
	Transport	-	-	2.32	3.21	5.09	5.50	-
	Travel	-	-	1.87	3.47	4.47	4.89	-
	Other services	-	-	3.78	2.23	3.19	3.12	-
	Government services n.i.e.	-	-	28.18	17.36	22.98	24.21	22.35
MERCOSUR	Total services	3.08	1.64	2.11	1.59	2.02	2.17	2.93
	Transport	3.42	2.02	2.25	1.48	1.97	1.94	2.49
	Travel	4.11	1.50	2.23	1.43	2.11	2.24	3.36
	Other services	2.10	1.45	1.95	1.75	2.04	2.30	3.03
	Government services n.i.e.	1.58	2.49	2.93	2.78	3.07	3.07	4.13
NAFTA	Total services	12.99	17.86	18.46	15.69	13.79	14.37	13.24
	Transport	12.14	16.66	18.10	14.87	11.44	11.26	11.19
	Travel	15.50	20.70	19.45	15.44	14.19	14.20	13.13
	Other services	12.23	16.61	18.05	16.35	15.26	16.27	14.76
	Government services n.i.e.	29.03	38.68	28.18	32.72	25.62	28.18	26.38

Notes: Measure is the US Dollars at current prices. Data source: UNCTAD, UNCTADstat.

government services). The data in Table 4 and Table 5 state that the global financial crisis of 2008-09 do not significantly affect on services exports and services imports of the most of regional groups. Once more, the exceptions are the EU and the Euro area. The great global recession of 2008-09 decreased both services exports and services imports in the EU and the Euro area. These facts state that globalism is even more issue than regionalism in the EU and the Euro-area because the growth pattern in worldwide trade is greater than theirs. For more detailed analysis, we also look over the merchandise exports and the merchandise imports in Table 6 and Table 7.

We report the improvements of merchandise trade of regional groups in Table 6 and Table 7. We focus on the share of merchandise exports and merchandise imports as percentage of total world over the period 1960-2013, respectively. The data in Table 6 and Table 7 indicate that the great global recession of 2008-09 do not significantly affect on merchandise exports and merchandise imports of the most of regional groups. However, the exceptions are the EU and the Euro area yet again. Global financial crisis of 2008-09 decreased both

Table 6. Shares of merchandise exports, percentage of total world, 1960-2013

Year and Economy	1960	1980	1990	2000	2005	2008	2009	2010	2011	2012	2013
ANCOM	0.8	0.5	0.4	0.4	0.5	0.6	0.6	0.6	0.7	0.8	0.7
ASEAN	3.6	3.5	4.1	6.7	6.3	6.1	6.5	6.9	6.7	6.8	6.8
COMESA	1.9	1.7	0.7	0.5	0.6	0.8	0.7	0.8	0.5	0.7	0.6
ECO	1.1	0.9	1.1	1.3	1.8	2.4	2.2	2.3	2.4	2.3	2.2
EFTA	2.2	2.4	2.8	2.2	2.3	2.3	2.3	2.2	2.2	2.1	2.1
EU27	43.5	41.5	44.7	38.0	38.7	36.7	36.6	33.8	33.2	31.5	32.2
Euro area	28.1	30.7	35.4	29.7	30.3	28.7	28.7	26.2	25.5	24.3	24.6
GCC	1.7	8.0	2.5	2.7	3.8	4.7	4.2	4.3	5.2	5.8	5.7
MERCOSUR	3.7	2.4	1.9	1.9	2.1	2.4	2.2	2.3	2.5	2.4	2.4
NAFTA	20.1	15.2	16.1	19.0	14.1	12.6	12.8	12.8	12.4	12.9	12.9

Notes: Measure is the US Dollars at current prices. Data source: UNCTAD, UNCTADstat.

Table 7. Shares of merchandise imports, percentage of total world, 1960-2013

Year and Economy	1960	1980	1990	2000	2005	2008	2009	2010	2011	2012	2013
ANCOM	0.8	0.5	0.3	0.4	0.4	0.6	0.6	0.6	0.7	0.7	0.7
ASEAN	3.4	3.1	4.5	5.7	5.6	5.7	5.7	6.2	6.3	6.6	6.6
COMESA	2.0	1.1	0.8	0.5	0.6	0.7	0.9	0.9	0.8	0.9	0.9
ECO	1.5	1.3	1.4	1.4	2.0	2.3	2.2	2.3	2.3	2.3	2.4
EFTA	2.7	2.6	2.7	1.8	1.7	1.7	1.8	1.7	1.6	1.6	1.6
EU27	44.6	45.5	45.1	37.7	38.4	37.6	37.0	34.4	33.8	31.6	31.3
Euro area	28.1	30.7	35.4	29.7	30.3	28.7	28.7	26.2	25.5	24.3	24.6
GCC	0.6	2.5	1.3	1.3	1.7	2.5	2.5	2.3	2.3	2.6	2.8
MERCOSUR	3.1	2.4	1.0	1.6	1.3	1.9	1.8	2.0	2.1	2.1	2.2
NAFTA	17.2	16.3	19.0	25.3	21.2	17.7	17.2	17.4	16.8	17.2	17.0

Notes: Measure is the US Dollars at current prices. Data source: UNCTAD, UNCTADstat.

merchandise exports and s merchandise imports in the EU and the Euro area relative to merchandise exports and merchandise imports in world. For more detailed analysis, we look at the growth rates of merchandise exports and merchandise imports in quarterly data.

We report the volume index and the growth rates of merchandise exports and merchandise imports in quarterly data for the period from Q32008 to Q42013 in Table 8 and Table 9, respectively. The data in Table 8 and Table 9 demonstrate that the great global recession of 2008-09 significantly affect on merchandise exports and merchandise imports in the all of regional groups as well as the world. In addition, the growth rates in the EU27 are lower than the other regional groups. Global financial crisis of 2008-09 decreased both merchandise exports and merchandise imports in all regional groups and the world economy; however, the recovery in the EU27 and the Euro area is relatively weak, when it is compared to the world economy and other regional groups.

Finally, we also discuss the goods and services trade balance over the period 1980-2012 in Table 11. We consider a measure of the percentage of gross domestic product. The world economy has an increasing surplus in the external goods and services trade balance in 2000s and this trend has not been affected by the great global recession of 2008-09. In the crisis period, surplus in trade balance in the ASEAN is soared but the in the post-crisis period surplus in trade balance goes towards a balance. However, there is a reverse accretion in the COMESA, because their trade balances are getting more instable after the great global recession of 2008-09. The MERCOSUR is followed same trend in the trade balance and their trade surplus has steadily declined in the crisis and the post-crisis period. The NAFTA has also a far amount reduced the trade balance deficit. On the other hand, the EU27, the Euro area, and

Table 8. Volume index and growth rates of merchandise exports, quarterly, Q3 2008-Q4 2013

	Measure	Q3 2008	Q4 2008	Q1 2009	Q2 2009	Q3 2009	Q4 2009	Q1 2013	Q2 2013	Q3 2013	Q4 2013
World	Volume growth rate over previous period	-0.6	-7.1	-14.9	3.7	5.1	6.5	-3.4	5.1	-0.7	2.6
	Volume growth rate over corresponding period of previous year	4.6	-7.1	-18.5	-18.5	-13.8	-1.2	0.7	1.7	3.0	3.6
	Volume Index (2005=100)	129.1	120.0	102.1	105.9	111.2	118.5	132.7	139.5	138.6	142.2
ASEAN	Volume growth rate over previous period	2.3	-11.9	-11.0	4.8	9.9	4.8	-4.2	5.3	3.9	2.4
	Volume growth rate over corresponding period of previous year	2.2	-10.8	-17.4	-15.9	-9.6	7.5	0.8	2.3	5.7	7.4
	Volume Index (2005=100)	125.9	111.0	98.8	103.5	113.8	119.3	131.9	138.9	144.4	147.8
EU27	Volume growth rate over previous period	-5.5	-4.4	-12.6	1.1	1.4	6.7	-0.9	4.0	-3.0	2.6
	Volume growth rate over corresponding period of previous year	1.4	-8.3	-19.3	-20.2	-14.4	-4.5	-1.5	2.6	2.3	2.5
	Volume Index (2005=100)	116.5	111.4	97.3	98.4	99.7	106.4	118.6	123.3	119.5	122.6
MERCOSUR	Volume growth rate over previous period	7.4	-16.2	-17.0	22.0	-1.5	-5.6	-15.3	24.2	0.3	-4.9
	Volume growth rate over corresponding period of previous year	4.4	-9.2	-14.8	-8.9	-16.4	-5.8	-5.5	7.1	3.8	0.3
	Volume Index (2005=100)	130.6	109.4	90.8	110.8	109.1	103.1	99.1	123.0	123.3	117.3
NAFTA	Volume growth rate over previous period	-1.8	-5.3	-14.4	0.7	3.7	8.9	-3.5	5.9	-1.9	4.8
	Volume growth rate over corresponding period of previous year	3.6	-4.8	-16.4	-19.9	-15.4	-2.7	0.0	2.3	3.8	5.1
	Volume Index (2005=100)	122.6	116.1	99.3	100.0	103.7	112.9	129.5	137.2	134.6	141.1

Notes: Q1 2005=100. Measure is the US Dollars at current prices. Data source: UNCTAD, UNCTADstat.

Table 9. Volume index and growth rates of merchandise imports, quarterly, Q3 2008-Q4 2013

	Measure	Q3 2008	Q4 2008	Q1 2009	Q2 2009	Q3 2009	Q4 2009	Q1 2013	Q2 2013	Q3 2013	Q4 2013
World	Volume growth rate over previous period	-0.6	-7.1	-14.9	3.7	5.1	6.5	-3.4	5.1	-0.7	2.6
	Volume growth rate over corresponding period of previous year	4.6	-7.1	-18.5	-18.5	-13.8	-1.2	0.7	1.7	3.0	3.6
	Volume Index (2005=100)	129.1	120.0	102.1	105.9	111.2	118.5	132.7	139.5	138.6	142.2
ASEAN	Volume growth rate over previous period	2.3	-11.9	-11.0	4.8	9.9	4.8	-4.2	5.3	3.9	2.4
	Volume growth rate over corresponding period of previous year	2.2	-10.8	-17.4	-15.9	-9.6	7.5	0.8	2.3	5.7	7.4
	Volume Index (2005=100)	125.9	111.0	98.8	103.5	113.8	119.3	131.9	138.9	144.4	147.8
EU27	Volume growth rate over previous period	-5.5	-4.4	-12.6	1.1	1.4	6.7	-0.9	4.0	-3.0	2.6
	Volume growth rate over corresponding period of previous year	1.4	-8.3	-19.3	-20.2	-14.4	-4.5	-1.5	2.6	2.3	2.5
	Volume Index (2005=100)	116.5	111.4	97.3	98.4	99.7	106.4	118.6	123.3	119.5	122.6
MERCOSUR	Volume growth rate over previous period	7.4	-16.2	-17.0	22.0	-1.5	-5.6	-15.3	24.2	0.3	-4.9
	Volume growth rate over corresponding period of previous year	4.4	-9.2	-14.8	-8.9	-16.4	-5.8	-5.5	7.1	3.8	0.3
	Volume Index (2005=100)	130.6	109.4	90.8	110.8	109.1	103.1	99.1	123.0	123.3	117.3
NAFTA	Volume growth rate over previous period	-1.8	-5.3	-14.4	0.7	3.7	8.9	-3.5	5.9	-1.9	4.8
	Volume growth rate over corresponding period of previous year	3.6	-4.8	-16.4	-19.9	-15.4	-2.7	0.0	2.3	3.8	5.1
	Volume Index (2005=100)	122.6	116.1	99.3	100.0	103.7	112.9	129.5	137.2	134.6	141.1

Notes: Q1 2005=100. Measure is the US Dollars at current prices. Data source: UNCTAD, UNCTADstat.

Table 10. Terms-of-trade indices and purchasing power indices of exports, 2005-2012

Economy	Measure	2005	2008	2009	2010	2011	2012
World	Terms-of-trade indices	101.8	102.6	103.1	103.3	103.6	103.3
	Purchasing power indices of exports	129.3	153.0	133.3	152.2	160.6	162.9
ANCOM	Terms-of-trade indices	112.2	137.9	124.3	142.3	159.1	157.7
	Purchasing power indices of exports	170.9	238.7	217.5	253.2	312.0	323.2
ASEAN	Terms-of-trade indices	95.8	95.2	94.7	95.9	95.5	94.7
	Purchasing power indices of exports	136.1	160.5	143.6	172.5	179.3	181.8
COMESA	Terms-of-trade indices	128.9	163.1	138.0	154.0	166.1	167.8
	Purchasing power indices of exports	175.6	251.0	201.1	238.7	169.5	239.9
ECO	Terms-of-trade indices	114.5	131.1	112.1	122.2	134.0	133.4
	Purchasing power indices of exports	174.3	253.6	202.5	228.9	259.8	249.5
EFTA	Terms-of-trade indices	99.9	108.6	102.4	105.2	106.2	111.5
	Purchasing power indices of exports	126.5	157.9	134.6	145.2	151.8	157.9
EU27	Terms-of-trade indices	98.4	95.5	98.3	95.9	93.9	93.0
	Purchasing power indices of exports	115.2	124.8	109.4	119.2	123.1	121.6
Euro area	Terms-of-trade indices	97.4	93.9	97.3	94.8	92.6	91.8
	Purchasing power indices of exports	114.2	122.9	108.2	117.0	119.8	119.2
GCC	Terms-of-trade indices	150.7	205.8	151.5	174.4	205.1	207.7
	Purchasing power indices of exports	194.8	296.1	208.0	254.7	321.2	345.3
MERCOSUR	Terms-of-trade indices	112.3	138.9	128.0	144.5	158.4	154.3
	Purchasing power indices of exports	160.0	205.8	171.6	206.8	236.4	229.2
NAFTA	Terms-of-trade indices	102.5	101.2	103.1	103.9	103.4	103.0
	Purchasing power indices of exports	108.8	124.3	108.7	124.9	131.8	136.4

Notes: 2000=100. Measure is the US Dollars at current prices. Data source: UNCTAD, UNCTADstat.

Table 11. Goods and services trade balance, percentage of gross domestic product, 1980-2012

Year and Economy	1980	1990	2000	2005	2008	2009	2010	2011	2012
World	-0.11	0.01	-0.03	0.31	0.53	0.65	0.68	0.78	1.01
ANCOM	0.84	2.43	0.36	1.46	-0.08	0.84	0.13	0.76	0.33
ASEAN	-0.40	-0.88	7.64	7.12	5.78	7.99	7.24	6.30	4.13
COMESA	2.62	-3.82	-1.99	-0.36	0.43	-4.90	-2.56	-7.27	-8.79
ECO	-4.98	-3.18	0.27	-1.05	0.45	0.74	0.26	2.25	1.02
EFTA	0.17	3.40	11.02	11.23	14.48	11.13	12.31	12.29	11.44
EU27	-0.97	0.25	0.14	0.72	0.11	1.08	1.03	1.20	2.99
Euro area	-1.58	0.64	0.58	1.56	0.97	1.46	1.50	1.59	2.92
GCC	32.01	8.14	17.76	27.97	24.74	13.52	19.82	30.45	30.95
MERCOSUR	-1.44	4.35	0.20	6.17	2.39	1.42	0.70	1.14	0.44
NAFTA	-0.58	-1.25	-3.07	-4.65	-4.14	-2.55	-3.15	-3.34	-3.09

Notes: Measure is the US Dollars at current prices. Data source: UNCTAD, UNCTADstat.

the GCC have enhanced their trade and balance surplus in terms of the period of post great global recession of 2008-09. In short, there is a different trend in the goods and services trade balance in regional groups; however, the world economy has a steadily increasing trade balance surplus.

CONCLUSION

In this chapter, we briefly review the financial crisis of 2008-09 and its impacts on the international trade in terms of regionalism and globalism. We analyze different aspects of globalism and regionalism. We look on historical pattern and recent developments of regionalism and globalism. The statistical data in this chapter reveals that the great trade collapse of 2008-09 negatively affect both globalization and regionalization trends. The EU has experienced an interesting transformation from regionalism to globalism. We think that the issue is not only related with the great trade collapse of 2008-09, but also the sovereign debt crisis of 2010-12.

The chapter emphasizes that regional integration is a vital phenomenon for developing countries and LDCs in general. In particular, regional integration is even more issue in developing or least developed countries, which are more open to the terms-of-trade shocks. The vulnerability due to terms-of-trade shocks is especially related with the dependence of primary exports. Developing countries, which are significantly primary commodity exporter, of course more vulnerable in terms-of-trade shocks. They seek to protect from external shocks with getting involve to regional integration. At this point the role of the Chinese economy with regional groups would be important to understand future of regional groups and globalization trends.

Last but not least, a further study can examine effects of currency unions on regionalism and globalism. Even though developing countries try to avoid the negative impacts of terms-of-trade shocks by using regional integrations, real value of the US Dollar will be determining the patterns of international trade. Regional groups can provide preservation from external shocks; however, the currency, which they will use in international trade, would still create vulnerability in developing economies. At this stage, possible impacts of the currency unions (particularly related with the Chinese Renminbi) on regionalism and globalism will be examined in a future research.

REFERENCES

Baldwin, E. R. (1997). The causes of regionalism. *World Economy*, *20*(7), 865–888. doi:10.1111/1467-9701.00107

Bergsten, C.F. (1991, November). Commentary: The move toward free trade zones. *Economic Review,* 27-35.

Berthelon, M., & Freund, C. (2008). On the conservation of distance in international trade. *Journal of International Economics*, *75*(2), 310–320. doi:10.1016/j.jinteco.2007.12.005

Bhagwati, J. (1991). *The world trading system at risk*. New York: Princeton University Press. doi:10.1515/9781400861590

Bhagwati, J. (1993). Regionalism and multilateralism: An overview. In J. de Melo & A. Panagariya (Eds.), *New dimensions in regional integration* (pp. 22–51). New York: Cambridge University Press. doi:10.1017/CBO9780511628511.004

Bhagwati, J., Krishna, P., & Panagariya, A. (1999). *Trading blocs: Alternative approaches to analyzing preferential trade agreements*. Cambridge, MA: MIT Press.

Bhagwati, J., & Krueger, A. O. (1995). *The dangerous drift to preferential trade agreements*. Washington, DC: AEI Press.

Bustos, P. (2011). Trade liberalization, exports, and technology upgrading: Evidence on the impact of MERCOSUR on Argentinean firms. *The American Economic Review*, *101*(1), 304–340. doi:10.1257/aer.101.1.304

Cadot, O., de Melo, J., & Olarreaga, M. (1999). Regional integration and lobbying for tariffs against non members. *International Economic Review*, *40*(3), 635–657. doi:10.1111/1468-2354.00032

Cai, K. G. (2010). *The politics of economic regionalism*. New York: Palgrave Macmillan. doi:10.1057/9780230277267

Cavallo, E. A., & Frankel, J. A. (2008). Does openness to trade make countries more vulnerable to sudden stops, or less? Using gravity to establish causality. *Journal of International Money and Finance*, *27*(8), 1430–1452. doi:10.1016/j.jimonfin.2007.10.004

Chen, M. X., & Mattoo, A. (2008). Regionalism in standards: Good or bad for trade? *The Canadian Journal of Economics. Revue Canadienne d'Economique*, *41*(3), 838–863. doi:10.1111/j.1540-5982.2008.00488.x

Click, R. W. (2009). The ASEAN Dollar standard in the post-crisis era: Reconsideration. *Journal of Asian Economics*, *20*(3), 269–279. doi:10.1016/j.asieco.2009.02.005

Domingues, E. P., Haddad, E. A., & Hewings, G. (2008). Sensitivity analysis in applied general equilibrium models: An empirical assessment for MERCOSUR free trade areas agreements. *The Quarterly Review of Economics and Finance*, *48*(2), 287–306. doi:10.1016/j.qref.2006.12.018

Freund, C. (2000). Different paths to free trade: The gains from regionalism. *The Quarterly Journal of Economics*, *115*(4), 1317–1341. doi:10.1162/003355300555088

Freund, C. (2010). Third-country effects of regional trade agreements. *World Economy*, *33*(11), 1589–1605. doi:10.1111/j.1467-9701.2010.01283.x

Geldi, H. K. (2012). Trade effects of regional integration: A panel cointegration analysis. *Economic Modelling*, *29*(5), 1566–1570. doi:10.1016/j.econmod.2012.05.017

Gopinath, G., Itskhoki, O., & Neiman, B. (2012). Trade prices and the global trade collapse of 2008-09. *IMF Economic Review*, *60*(3), 303–328. doi:10.1057/imfer.2012.17

Kawai, M., & Wignaraja, G. (2011). Asian FTAs: Trends, prospects and challenges. *Journal of Asian Economics*, *22*(1), 1–22. doi:10.1016/j.asieco.2010.10.002

Krapohl, S., & Fink, S. (2013). Different paths of regional integration: Trade networks and regional institution-building in Europe, Southeast Asia and Southern Africa. *Journal of Common Market Studies*, *51*(3), 472–488. doi:10.1111/jcms.12012

Kreinin, M. E., & Plummer, M. G. (2008). Effects of regional integration on FDI: An empirical approach. *Journal of Asian Economics*, *19*(5-6), 447–454. doi:10.1016/j.asieco.2008.09.005

Krugman, P. (1991, November). The move toward free trade zones. *Economic Review,* 5-25.

Levchenko, A. A., Lewis, L. T., & Tesar, L. L. (2010). The collapse of international trade during the 2008-09 Crisis: In search of the smoking gun. *IMF Economic Review*, *58*(2), 214–253. doi:10.1057/imfer.2010.11

Lipsey, R. G. (1960). The theory of customs unions: A general survey. *The Economic Journal*, *70*(279), 496–513. doi:10.2307/2228805

Lipsey, R. G., & Lancaster, K. (1956). The general theory of second best. *The Review of Economic Studies*, *24*(1), 11–32. doi:10.2307/2296233

Mayda, A. M., & Chad, S. (2009). Do south-south trade agreements increase trade? Commodity-level evidence from COMESA. *The Canadian Journal of Economics. Revue Canadienne d'Economique*, *42*(4), 1361–1389. doi:10.1111/j.1540-5982.2009.01548.x

McDonald, S., Robinson, S., & Thierfelder, K. (2008). Asian growth and trade poles: India, China, and East and Southeast Asia. *World Development*, *36*(2), 210–234. doi:10.1016/j.worlddev.2007.06.013

Meade, J. E. (1955). *Trade and welfare*. London: Oxford University Press.

Ornelas, E. (2008). Feasible multilateralism and the effects of regionalism. *Journal of International Economics*, *74*(1), 202–224. doi:10.1016/j.jinteco.2007.05.006

Park, I. (2009). Regional trade agreements in East Asia: Will they be sustainable? *Asian Economic Journal*, *23*(2), 169–194. doi:10.1111/j.1467-8381.2009.02008.x

Romalis, J. (2007). NAFTA's and CUSFTA's impact on international trade. *The Review of Economics and Statistics*, *89*(3), 416–435. doi:10.1162/rest.89.3.416

Schiff, M., & Winters, A. (2003). Regional integration and development. Washington, DC: World Bank Publications. doi:10.1596/0-8213-5078-1

Schultz, S. (1996). Regionalisation of world trade dead end or way out? In M. P. Van Dijk & S. Sideri (Eds.), *Multilateralism versus regionalism: Trade issues after the Uruguay round* (pp. 23–43). London: Frank Cass Publishers.

Sourdin, P., & Pomfret, R. (2009). Have Asian trade agreements reduced trade costs? *Journal of Asian Economics*, *20*(3), 255–268. doi:10.1016/j.asieco.2009.02.007

Summers, L. H. (1991). Regionalism and the world trading system, In *Proceedings-Economic Policy Symposium Sponsored by the Federal Reserve Bank of Kansas City*. The Federal Reserve Bank of Kansas City.

United Nations Conference on Trade and Development (UNCTAD). (2007). *Trade and development report 2007: Regional cooperation for development*. Geneva: United Nations Conference on Trade and Development.

United Nations Conference on Trade and Development (UNCTAD). (n.d.). *UNCTADstat database*. Retrieved from http://unctadstat.unctad.org/wds/ReportFolders/reportFolders.aspx

Viner, J. (1950). *The customs union issue*. New York: Carnegie Endowment for International Peace.

Wacziarg, R., & Welch, K. H. (2008). Trade liberalization and growth: New evidence. *The World Bank Economic Review*, *22*(2), 187–231. doi:10.1093/wber/lhn007

Whalley, J. (2008). Recent regional agreements: Why so many, why so much variance in form. Why coming so fast, and where are they headed? *World Economy*, *31*(4), 517–532. doi:10.1111/j.1467-9701.2008.01094.x

World Trade Organization (WTO). (2010). *World trade report 2010: Trade in natural resources*. Geneva: World Trade Organization.

KEY TERMS AND DEFINITIONS

Deep Integration: The integration of economies that consists institutionalized trade structure through liberalization of capital, labor, firms and services movements.

Globalization: The integration of economies through open international trade and financial systems through which goods and services are traded and international flows of capital, technology, labor and knowledge occur.

Regionalism: The structure of economic, political and social integration between formal governments of the concerned countries.

Regionalization: The structure of market integration between regional economies without formal agreements.

Shallow Integration: The integration of economies that involves quota liberalization and the removal of trade barriers.

Spaghetti Bowl: The complex trading system, particularly originated in the rules and regulations of various FTAs.

The Financial Crisis of 2008-09: The global recession that began in the mid-2008 and sharp decline in international trade and financial markets.

Chapter 19
Sino-Russian Strategic Partnership:
The Shanghai Cooperation Organization

Cagri Erdem
Dogus University, Turkey

ABSTRACT

The colossal economic transformations and political intrusions had been affecting brutally China and the Soviet Union in the final decades of the twentieth century. Currently, Russia is a gigantic power struggling to rebuild its economic base in an era of globalization. On the other hand, the economic rise of China has attracted a great deal of attention and labeled as a success story by the Western world. China and Russia have made a number of efforts to strengthen bilateral ties and improve cooperation on a number of economic/political/diplomatic fronts. Since the mid-1990s, the Shanghai Cooperation Organization (SCO) has been an important feature of Eurasian politics and a vehicle to forge a new sort of cooperation between China and Russia. A number of issues related to geopolitics, security, the economy, and regional politics have been handled by the SCO member states.

INTRODUCTION

Since the end of the Cold War, several scholars have suggested that the regions of the world have gained increased importance in the current international system and they act as an emerging potent force in the process of globalization (Holm & Sørensen, 1995; Mittelman, 2000). The Westphalian state is referred as a system of political authority based on territory and autonomy and it has been the dominant form in the international system up to the 1990s (Caporaso, 2000). In the past decade, however, the underpinnings of this system have been challenged by the creation of new regional unions or the restructuring of already existing ones. Consequently, the international system has witnessed a cohabitation of multiple forms of governance at multi level. Regions are the building blocks of this new international system and inherently, changes that take place within them affect the international system overall. To certain extend the regions and their development provides a context for the explanation of newly emerged systemic trends.

DOI: 10.4018/978-1-4666-7308-3.ch019

This chapter will argue that the 21st century saw the strengthening of the existing regional systems or the naissance of many loose and new regional systems. The chapter will discuss regional integration theories while providing examples from the Shanghai Cooperation Organization (SCO).

In distinction from European Union, the SCO as a regional system is characterized by the absence of democracy and the continuation of authoritarian leadership (Ambrosio, 2008). The nature of the regime in place limits the possibility of interest and preference formation from bottom-up. Consequently, regional integration theories utilized to explain European integration becomes blurry when applied to the SCO. Finally, the chapter will evaluate the development of the SCO over the past decade by taking in consideration Chinese and Russian approaches. Yet, the contention of this chapter is that since most of the developed conceptual framework as well as the case studies vis-à-vis the regional systems are Eurocentric, the application of these lenses to the growing number of regional systems in other parts of the globe remains at best problematic, and at worst elusive.

BACKGROUND

Definitions of Region, Regionalism, Regionalization

There are multiple definitions of the region and each reflects the peculiarities of a specific historical period of the international system and adjusts itself to the changing environment. In the first half of the 20th century, certain definitions referred to geostrategic regions (Mackinder, 1919), to physiographic characteristics (Vance, 1951), or to homogeneity of economic and social structures within a national context (Odum, 1936; Odum & Moore, 1938). In the Cold War era, Bruce Russett illustrated the complex process of identifying a "region". He emphasized a number of criteria such as cultural similarity, common political orientation, institutional membership, transaction flows, and proximity. A region is determined as such if it attained a certain minimum score when measured quantitatively against these criteria (Russett, 1967). Several scholars developed an approach of region as subsystems based mostly on geographic region such as either side of the North Atlantic (Hoffmann, 1963), Southeast Asia (Brecher, 1963; Modelski, 1963) or Africa (Zartman, 1973).

In the post-Cold War era, International Relations (IR) scholars started to redefine these concepts along with the concept of globalization. Holm and Sorensen provide four different definitions of the concept of region: geographical units with natural barriers (e.g., the Caucasus and Africa); social or cultural entities (e.g., Polynesia and Iberian peninsula); organized political units (e.g., the European Union and the North American Free Trade Area); regions of identity (e.g., Central Asia and Latin America). Andrew Hurrell (Fawcett & Hurrell, 1995), with regard to regionalism identifies four categories. First, regionalization refers to the growth of societal integration within a region that takes in consideration an increasing flow of people and the intensification of market interaction. Second, regional identity is associated with an increase in its awareness, which in turn facilitates the regionalism. Third, regional interstate cooperation refers to the formation and intensification of intergovernmental and institutional relations. Finally, regional cohesion represents the ultimate manifestation of regionalism and incorporates the full development of the above mentioned categories. Hurrel's definition also implies that regionalism is understood as an integral part of globalization. It is assumed that regionalism is a unifying process rather than fragmenting on international level. Bjorn Hettne after identifying three models of region—trading blocs, geopolitical division, and process of regionalization—claims that the "new regionalism" is the outcome of the process of regionalization and represents a version of "extended nationalism". Subsequently, he develops five levels of regionness or regional complexity with an evolutionary logic—geographical unit or ecological unit, social system organize cooperation, regional civil society, and region as an acting subject. This new regionalism differs from the old one in three important ways. The new one is the product of a multipolar world order, created 'from within', and represents a multidimensional process. On the other hand, the old one was the product of the bipolar Cold War context, created 'form above', and specific in terms of objectives (Farrell, Hettne, & Langenhove, 2005; Hettne, Inotai, & Sunkel, 1999).

In addition, it is essential to address the mystery surrounding the question of regional/global dialectic or dichotomy. The growth of regional systems in the past decade does not constitute a threat to trends of globalization. Regional systems can be conceptualized as a component of globalization, challenge to globalization or as a parallel process of globalization (Kacowicz, 1998; Mittelman, 1996, 2000). However, in this essay, the growth of regional systems is assumed to be an important step within the process of globalization.

Theories of International Relations

Theories of regional integration find their origins in functionalism and neofunctionalism. David Mitrany the main proponent of functionalism, proposed the development of activities in the areas of agreement such as the growth of specialized technical organizations that cross national borders (Mitrany, 1946). According to this approach, technological and economic development lead to more supranational structures as states seek practical means to fulfill necessary functions (Deutsch, 1957; Mitrany, 1966, 1976). Due to the devastating effects of the Second World War, Mitrany was concerned with the problem of war and saw the solution in the reordering of international relations along functional lines.

Neofunctionalism presented a refined and further elaborated version of functional theory to explain the development of more general and more political supranational bodies (Haas 1961). The argument was that the major actors are situated at both the subnational level (e.g., labor unions and political parties) and at the supranational level. The governments' role are to be responsive to the demands from subnational or supranational actors. Neofunctionalism aims to reach a political community larger than a nation-state and looked for the conditions in which this new type of political community would evolve. The method of integration pursued by neofunctionalism is, indeed, taken from functionalism. Similar to functionalism, it proposed a step-by-step method starting from economic sectors and spreading through political fields for creating a supranational political community. Neofunctionalists argued that economic integration generates a political dynamic that drives integration further. Closer economic ties require more political coordination in order to operate effectively and eventually would lead to political integration and this process was called "functional spillover" (Burley & Mattli, 1993; Mattli, 1999). This political integration is most likely if the countries in question maintain a high degree of economic and social transactions, possess a similar economic size and development level and have similar pluralist domestic institutions (Schmitter & Haas, 1964). However, due to the empirical developments in the European integration process, neofunctionalism has been discredited. Three major problems were recognized with the neofunctionalist approach of integration by its critics: that a definable institutional pattern must mark the outcome of integration, that integration will move in one direction, and that incrementalism is the major form of decision-making (Haas & Whiting, 1975). However, several scholars argued that despite the empirical evidence from the European integration process, the framework was not wrong but just less relevant (Caporaso, 1998).

Neoliberal intergovermentalism, on the other hand, like realism, puts states at the center of analysis but still take into consideration the impact of interests groups through domestic preference formation. Also, heads of the states are considered central players, which make it different from neo-functionalism. The process of interest aggregation, intergovernmental bargaining and enforcement of decisions are considered as essential elements of this approach of integration. Major advocate of this approach, Andrew Moravcsik developed a three step-process (Moravcsik, 1998). First, interests are recognized and mobilized to become active in politics (preference formation). Second step refers to political process of interests' aggregation at regional level through intergovernmental bargaining in order to reach favorable results for foreign counterparts and domestic constituencies. The last phase, after ratification, is institutional lock-in of the agreements. The liberal intergovernmental approach provides more sophisticated theory of preference formation than neofunctionalism (Choi & Caporaso, 2002). However, by focusing on intergovernmental bargaining neglect the ongoing social process. Paul Pierson calls this a "snapshot view of integration that is distorted in crucial respects." (Pierson, 1995).

Realism and regional integration may seem to be at odds at first glance. However, particularly after the end of the Cold War, realism has something to say about regional integration. The core of realist arguments is shaped by a number of assumptions (Grieco, 1993): states are the most important actors (Morgenthau, 1948; Waltz, 1979); international anarchy is the principal force shaping the motives, preferences and actions of states (Waltz, 1979), states are unitary rational agents, states facing the conditions of anarchy are preoccupied with power and security and often fail to cooperate even in the face of common interests (Waltz, 1979), international institutions affect the prospects for cooperation only marginally (Gilpin, 1986). The sub-national and supranational actors are not important in the preference formation in regional integration. Along the same line of logic, the realists' argument would be that the international institutions glorified by functionalist or neofunctionalist approaches cannot diminish anarchy's constraining effects on interstate cooperation. The preferences of the states are formed by the position of the state in the international system. Under certain circumstances, realism can explain integration. For instance, Joanne Gowa's 1989 study shows that the stability of bipolarity after the Second World War facilitated the deep integration within Europe (Gowa, 1989). On the other hand, at the end of the Cold War along the realist thinking, Mearsheimer developed arguments about the absence of Soviet threat and the return of multipolar international system with mounting anxiety that would increase concerns about security and relative gains among the European partners (Mearsheimer, 1990). Grieco's extensive studies on the European integration and particularly on the Maastricht treaty indicate that weaker states used the European Monetary Union to increase their influence by binding the strong states into an institutional framework. Relatively weak states would ensure that they have an effective "voice opportunity" while negotiating the nature of new international institutions (Grieco, 1995).

In the 1990s, the inability of rationalist theories—neoliberal and neorealist— to explain the change in the international system increased the eminence of reflectivist (Keohane & Martin, 1995) theories—critical theory, post-modernism, constructivism, and feminist theories. For instance, the constructivist framework of regional integration is mostly directed to the role of ideas, norms and identities in the integration process. The constructivist literature on regional integration noticeably is in the rise. For instance, Adler and Barnett updated and reinterpreted Deutsch's work on security communities (Deutsch, 1957) and the values behind it (Adler & Barnett, 1998). Jefferey Checkel offers various hypotheses on the preference changes and identities in the integration process (Checkel, 1999). On the other hand, Moravcsik admits that constructivists present an interesting and important set of questions about the effects of an integration process on individuals and states but they fail to make significant contributions to the empirical understanding of the integration process due to their unwillingness to take any risk of empirical disconfirmation (Moravcsik, 1999). But, constructivist approaches are mostly in the metatheoretical stage and have not yet developed recognized puzzles and common research strategies (Choi & Caporaso, 2002).

Most of the developments of the European integration process over the past decade have been asserted in the previous section through the studies of Mearsheimer, Grieco, Checkel, Moravcsik. The impressive course throughout the 1990s consisting of the 1992 Masstricht Treaty, and the subsequent deepening of integration by the 1997 Amsterdam treaty and the 2001 Nice treaty can be considered as an indication of the reemerging importance of regional systems as a prominent form of governance after the end of the Cold War.

Yet, it is interesting to observe that all the theoretical frameworks outlined above—functionalism/neofunctionalism, liberal intergovernmentalism, realism, and constructivism— are limited mostly to the European system and the European integration process. However, the rise of regional governance over the past decade is not just restricted to Europe. Certainly, the unique nature of its integration process, its economic/political influence in the international system and its cultural impact on global norm/value formation represents the rationale behind its appeal to scholars around the world. This chapter will, now, reflect on the SCO in contrast to European system, while showing the shortcomings of the *eurocentric* bias of these approaches.

THE SHANGHAI COOPERATION ORGANIZATION (SCO)

The Shanghai Cooperation Organization is a permanent intergovernmental international organization founded on 15 June 2001 in Shanghai by the People's Republic of China, the Russian Federation, the Republic of Kazakhstan, the Kyrgyz Republic, the Republic of Tajikistan and the Republic of Uzbekistan. The four observer states are Mongolia, India, Pakistan and Iran. The main goals of the SCO are strengthening mutual confidence and good neighborly relations between the member countries; promoting effective cooperation in politics, trade and economy, science and technology, culture as well as education, energy, transportation, tourism, environmental protection and other fields; making joint efforts to maintain and ensure peace, security and stability in the region. The Council of Heads of State Council (HSC) is the highest decision-making body in the SCO. It meets once a year to take decisions and give instructions on all important issues of the SCO activity.

The SCO is an emerging regional organization in post-Soviet Central Asia. It has become an important part of both Russia's and China's regional strategy towards Central Asia and the security and economic policies of the newly independent former Soviet Central Asian states—Kazakhstan, Kyrgyzstan, Tajikistan and Uzbekistan. Moreover, the development of the SCO is of wider significance to global politics, security and economics due to the fact that the core member states with 30 million km^2 forms one fifth of earth's landmass, have one fourth of global population and one sixth of global GDP. Russia and China are two of the most prominent states of the international system as permanent members of the UN Security Council.

At present, the SCO's full membership stretches from the Baltic Sea to the Pacific Ocean, covering most of the territory of the Eurasian continent. China, Russia, Kazakhstan, Kyrgyzstan, Tajikistan and Uzbekistan have all been full members of the SCO since its formation in 2001. In addition to full membership, India, Pakistan, Iran and Mongolia has being accepted as official observer-members, while in 2009 a further associate-member status was introduced, allowing Sri Lanka and Belarus to become official 'dialogue partners'. Turkey, a member of NATO, was granted dialogue partner status in the SCO at the group's 2012 summit in Beijing. However, it would be fair to argue that in spite of these two categories of associate membership, the SCO is overpoweringly centered on its core full membership. The SCO's agenda now encompasses a wide range of issue areas from security to economic to cultural and humanitarian collaboration between its member states.

CHINA'S APPROACH TO THE SCO

China's rapid rise to global power status changed the parameters of the strategic chest game in global politics. Consequently, its relationship with Russia is also frequently renegotiated due to the fact that Russia is an important neighbor and a crucial resource base in a time of ever growing Chinese energy hunger (Eder, 2014). The development of the SCO has provided a number of regional policy benefits for China. First, the development of these links has served to facilitate China's policy of ensuring the stability of the country's vulnerable western frontier in and around Xinjiang. Despite the remoteness of the province and the considerable amount of resources required by China to maintain it, the area is vital to Chinese security interests, since it provides a buffer zone between China's core provinces and unstable greater Central Asia (Song, 2014). It contains natural resources deemed important to Chinese economic growth and it provides a wanted/desirable window into Soviet Central Asia that began to grow in importance after the collapse of the USSR. Retaining good relations with Russia and Central Asia is absolutely critical to guarantee the safety of China's Xinjiang region (Lanteigne, 2010).

However, China has also demonstrated increasing reservations about the prospect of color revolutions being exported from the ex-Soviet territory to China itself. The Chinese government's view of those events—Georgian Rose Revolution in 2003, Ukrainian Orange Revolution in 2004, Kyrgyz Tulip Revolution in 2005—were that they were the outcomes of external intrusion intended to weaken the regimes. The Chinese government has been worried about Western attempts to destabilize its legitimacy, and the above mentioned Revolutions in the former Soviet space have further intensified those concerns (Lanteigne, 2010; Yuan, 2010).

Although the revolutions in Georgia and Ukraine took place in areas distant enough for China to be concerned about it, the Tulip Revolution just next to the Chinese unstable Xinjiang region created a good deal of internal discussions in Beijing. The SCO has been seen as promoting both regime security as well as state security in the wake of those revolutions. The SCO has uncompromisingly accentuated the non-interference in the internal affairs of the member states (Lanteigne, 2010).

Central Asian relations are a natural prolongation of Chinese strategy of developing more harmonious and friendly relations in the international system, otherwise known as peripheral diplomacy. This proclivity began in the 1980s, when the Chinese government began developing its policy of building a stable periphery in Asia and encouraging more cordial relations with its neighbors in order to facilitate its ongoing economic and security policy reforms, to gain insight from the newly industrializing economies in East Asia such as South Korea or Taiwan and to discourage any developments in terms of security threats on Chinese borders (Baizakova, 2013; Lanteigne, 2010).

To a certain extent, the SCO has confirmed China's new regional friendship policies, enhancing further the Chinese government's policy of presenting a more businesslike and congenial face both to its periphery and to the world as a whole, in keeping with its stated goal of peaceful development. Moreover, China's desire to obtain a responsible great power status has been linked with productive co-operation and engagement with international institutions such as the UN and regional economic and strategic organizations (Lanteigne, 2010).

Evidently, a fundamental element vis-à-vis China's peripheral diplomatic plan has been the aspiration to re-establish friendly relations with the Russian Federation. The relations between those two giants had been placed in a deep freeze for decades following the Sino-Soviet split in the 1960s after the Great Leap Forward catastrophe. Due to the extensive border between the two states—the world's sixth-longest international border with 4,195 km—any Chinese undertaking to create a stable periphery along its western frontier would not succeed without more cordial relations with the government in Moscow (Baizakova, 2013; Cheng, 2011; Dadabaev, 2013; Lanteigne, 2010; Movkebaeva, 2013).

However, the end of the Cold War did bring with it some major alterations to global politics. Russian or Chinese foreign policy concerns became increasingly closer to alignment, which in turn were influenced by both countries' concern about American power in Eurasia as well as a joint preference for the development of a multipolar international system rather than a system based on US hegemony. The SCO was a great vehicle to realize their strategic goals for both countries. (Baizakova, 2013; Lanteigne, 2010; Zhuangzhi, 2004).

The government in Moscow in the 1990s sought to increase economic ties with the Asia-Pacific region based on the Russian Far East's energy supplies and its strategic location as a transport corridor, as well as it being both a destination for foreign laborers and a source of scientific expertise (Poussenkova, 2009). China has played an important role in that engagement process as it became worried after 9/11 that Russian regional interests were experiencing a strategic contraction, which allowed the USA swiftly to augment its presence in Afghanistan and elsewhere in the Eurasian region. However, China's relationship with Russia is not without its difficulties. There are a number of controversial issues on the table between two countries such as trade imbalances in favor of China, illegal and unregulated cross-border trade, high levels of Chinese immigration into the Russian Far East, and persistent historical distrust. (Alexeeva, 2008; Arsenov, Artemkina, & Zaboev, 2005; Barkovsky, 2006; Kangas, 2007; Kuhrt, 2012; Lanteigne, 2010; Rozman, 2008; Sullivan & Renz, 2010; Troyakova, 2007).

On the other hand, although both countries have shown some signs of anxiety to publicize their growing levels of harmonious relationship, equally, it is unlikely that the two countries will enter into an alliance comparable to one that existed before the Sino-Soviet split in the 1960s. China just wants to keep Russia engaged in the North East Asia as a key regional actor and the SCO represents a great framework to do so. Conversely, there are also signs of mounting tension between the respective Russian and Chinese governments' view vis-à-vis the direction of the SCO. Moscow envisions an Organization with significantly improved military capabilities and desires greater cooperation between the SCO and the Collective Security Treaty Organization. However, Chinese government has been more inclined towards an Organization that develops into a more multifaceted community and has resisted adamantly any Russian efforts to link too narrowly both organizations. (Cheng, 2011; Lanteigne, 2010).

The Soviet Central Asia is another point of friction between Russia and China within the framework of the SCO. The fascinating aspect of Central Asian system is that it became to exist as a region composed by nation-states along the Westphalian logic only after the end of the Cold War. Even more captivating phenomenon is that nation building and region building have developed simultaneously. In December 1991, five new Central Asian states—Kazakhstan, Kyrgyzstan, Tajikistan, Turkmenistan, and Uzbekistan— emerged after the collapse of the Soviet Union (Allworth,

1995). In modern times, these five countries have never enjoyed the status of independent actors in the international arena.

There are several features corresponding to the concepts of region / regionalism / regionalization highlighted in the first part this essay. First, Central Asian states form a logical geopolitical unit. It is isolated by a range of high mountains, the Caspian Sea and steppes at the core of the Eurasian continent. Second, they share a common Muslim heritage, a common history and a common language—the only exception being Tajik—and similar social structures. Nowhere are the states of the former Soviet Union more closely bound with one another than in Central Asia.

Less than one year after their independence, these states engaged in the integration of their policies in the domains of the environment, energy, illicit drug trafficking, the economy and security. However, the dimensions of the ecological catastrophe in the region have important repercussions on all five states. The awareness of the issue gave birth to the signing of an agreement, in February 1992 dealing with the establishment of a basic institutional framework. The agreement is designed to govern activities of the two interstate Basin Water Management Bodies—*Bassejnovoe Vodnoje Ob'edinenie-BVO*. Over the past decade, many other agreements have been reached to form a common front with the aim of producing an effective regional response to the problem. Currently, the Interstate Council for the Aral Sea (ICAS) is designated as the principal regional organization responsible for formulating broad and long-term policies and implementing programs for addressing various aspects of the ecological crisis. On the other hand, the regional cooperation over the environmental issues initiated the creation of a "Central Asian Union" in 1993.

In the early years after the collapse of the Soviet system, the development of Central Asian relations has offered China the opportunity to establish a diplomatic and strategic foothold in an increasingly important region. With the overlap between NATO partners and the SCO membership, it was suggested that the Shanghai group might act as bridge between Chinese and Atlantic security interests. Obviously, the need for this connection has grown since 9/11 attacks in the US. The strategic engagement of global power gets in Central Asia due to its proximity to Afghanistan has presented to China a window of opportunity to get firmly engaged not only in the core of Eurasia but also well beyond. In addition, China's engagement with both Russia and Central Asia can be seen as an attempt to weaken further Western influence at the core of Eurasia. Although the Chinese government has insisted that it is not in a position to challenge Western interests in Central Asia, its growing diplomatic and political power cannot be discounted when examining the future of Central Asian foreign relations. There is no doubt that the 2005 closure of American air force base at Karshi-Khananbad (K2) in Uzbekistan and another closure in 2014 at Manas in Kyrgyzstan after more than 12 years of flying troops and cargo in and out of Afghanistan were indications of a power shift between the USA, the SCO member states at the heart of Eurasia. (Lanteigne, 2010).

China's relations with the Central Asian states have been also based on the creation of a more comprehensive set of tools with which to address non-security issues, most notably increased economic and energy cooperation. The establishment of SCO Business Council and Interbank Consortium intend to coordinate and finance joint projects among regional entrepreneurs. The Chinese government has been especially committed to developing the trade potential of the SCO. Consequently, Chinese trade with Kazakhstan, Kyrgyzstan and Uzbekistan has increased considerably since the 1990s. This development did not only allow Chinese goods and services compete with those of Russia and Europe but also permitted a greater access to Chinese markets by Central Asian countries. Moreover, China provides a great deal of financing and technical know-how to important infrastructure projects such as improvement of the transportation links and pipelines (Lanteigne, 2010; Movkebaeva, 2013).

However, it would be fair to assert that the SCO's image is largely associated with its anti-colonial and anti-imperial initiatives, and that's the reason why smaller member states enthusiastically participate in this organization. There is an increasing concern that smaller members of the SCO are not considered to be equal players but are only taken advantage of by economically and demographically superior China. This current perceived image of China complicates the process of SCO identity formation. Consequently, there is a need for a closer and more clearly defined SCO area identity formation based on shared visions and opportunities for all member states without distinction (Dadabaev, 2013).

Equally, it is important to remember that Central Asian energy resources also play a central role in the Chinese government's strategic calculations, especially as China is very much concerned with developing a steady external energy supply that cannot be easily interrupted by Western pressures or politics, or subject to any maritime interference or blockades—which may be the case for the fossil fuels imported from the Middle East through the Malacca strait. This explains why the Chinese government has been anxious to develop energy trade with the landlocked Central Asian states, while also ensuring that it has its own pipeline projects capable of transporting oil and natural gas from Kazakhstan and Turkmenistan to offset Western and Russian projects (Song, 2014). Undeniably China is seeking alternative energy resources in various regions around the globe but the proven reserves of Central Asia's Caspian region takes a central place in those strategic calculations. The country's increasing dependence upon imported oil and natural gas as a result of steady/continuous economic development has increased China's uneasiness about energy security/insecurity. As a logical outcome of those concerns, respective Chinese governments signed a number of energy development and transport agreements with Central Asian states since 1993, as the country became net oil importer for the first time (Lanteigne, 2010).

RUSSIA'S APPROACH TO THE SCO

For Russia, the SCO is above all a framework for cooperation with China. The scale of cooperation between Moscow and Beijing reached unprecedented levels not just within the framework of the SCO but also on bilateral level (Lukin, 2006). For instance, the recent China/Russia natural gas deal worth around $400 billion represents a major step not only in global energy markets but also in Eurasian geopolitics. Moreover, Russia and China held a series of joint large-scale military exercises, made a joint declaration on world order in the 21st century, and have used the SCO to counter US military presence in Central Asia. However, there is also some remarkable competition with and distrust vis-à-vis each other. The Russian military community views the promotion of cooperation with China within the framework of the SCO as indispensable, but remains divided over the extent of such strategic military cooperation in light of possible rivalry between the two (Laumullin, 2006).

Russian ambitions for economic cooperation within the SCO are limited to certain sectors and predominately to large-scale infrastructural and energy projects. The Russian leadership considers that the strength of the Chinese economy means that a free trade agenda in the SCO would lead to Chinese domination of the other member states' economies. This concern also plays an important role in Russia's approach to bilateral economic relations with China. Moscow is seen as restricting the development of the huge trade potential between the economically weak regions of Russia's Far East and North-Western China because of political considerations about growing Chinese influence in these regions. It is absolutely true that the Russian Far East (RFE) is considered as a region in crisis due to troubled economic conditions, corrupt governance, and problem-ridden cross-border relations with China, Japan, and both Koreas (Rozman, 2008). Due to the some fears that the Russian Far East might disengage itself from the center and other regional/global powers may end up having a major grip in the region, Moscow started to show some genuine interest in those eastern border provinces. The region in question covers a large geographical area from Siberia to Russia's Pacific coast, forming the northeastern corner of Asia. Although the Far East constitutes one-third of Russia's total landmass, it has only 6.6 million residents—4.7 percent of the total population. The low population density, just over one person per square kilometer, makes the region one of the most sparsely populated places in the world. The scarcity of residents exists alongside a wealth of natural resources that have attracted the interest of the Russian central government as well as foreign investors. Evidently, Russian politicians, bureaucrats/technocrats are all concerned about the level of socioeconomic development in that region (Troyakova, 2007). However, it would be fair to assert that the developmental troubles of the RFE partly related to the region's history and location. Moreover, the USSR did also neglect socio-economically the region until its collapse in 1991. After the disintegration of the Union, the RFE, like many other regions, was to a great extent abandoned by the financially struggling central government in Moscow Moscow's extended negligence to the region has left the RFE provinces economically underdeveloped, demographically challenged, and geographically exposed. Yet Moscow has recently begun to focus specifically on revitalizing the RFE, as years of dynamic economic growth and surging global trade in neighboring China have pulled the international community's attention to developments in the Pacific Rim. This change in the international political and economic climate, especially in light of the RFE's rich supplies of natural resources and strategic location in the North Pacific, has brought about a rethinking of Moscow's policy in Russia's Far East (Alexeeva, 2008; S. Blank, 2011).

There is no doubt that the Russian Far East has many barriers to economic development. It is very important, for China and Russia, to establish a friendly and mutually beneficial relationship by following the converging interests of the two countries. While discussing long term prospects of cooperation in the Russian Far East with China, it is possible to envisage some scenarios of economic development that may be useful to policymakers. An active involvement of China in the economy of the Russian Far East seems to be the best way to accelerate the economic development of the region. It is possible to generate powerful arguments for such a policy regarding the region (Arsenov et al., 2005). First, the Chinese economy is very dynamic and shows remarkable strength not only in the region but also all over the world. According to some estimations done by the Russian Academy of Sciences, Gross National Product (GNP) of China will be more than twice the size of Japanese economy—another economic giant of the region—by 2015. Secondly, the length of territorial border between Russia and China in the Russian Far East makes possible the development of joint production facilities by creating *"frontier zones"* of economic interaction. Thirdly, this economic interaction could make the region more attractive for Chinese labor, which in turn would promote stable/friendly interstate and interregional Russian-Chinese relations. Moreover, the relationship between China and Russia can also be a role model for a new type of relationship between great powers, characterized by mutual security, cooperation and mutual economic development. There is no doubt that those two countries in question have different political/economic systems and social structures. Consequently, there are often misapprehensions regarding a number of issues. But, both sides by getting familiar with these situations may circumvent misreading each other. The strategic partnership between China and

Russia should be forged on interests, rationality and rule of law by avoiding the sentiments of fantasizing or idealizing each other. The Russian Far East can present a good opportunity to create that environment where the mutual interests for both sides would come together.

Russian foreign policy under the leadership of Vladimir Putin has focused on recapturing the lost great power status after the collapse of the Soviet Union in 1991 (Billon, 2005; Goldman, 2008; Perovic, Orttung, & Wenger, 2009; Spechler, 2010). As part of this agenda, the reclaiming of Russia's place as the leading power in the former Soviet space has been seen as a priority. This focus on the post-Soviet space is interpreted by many as one part of a wider program aimed at recapturing the status of a 'great power'. Russia always considered Soviet Eurasia space as its privileged interest area. However, Chinese scholars (Yi-chong, 2006; Zhao, 2008; Zweig & Jianhai, 2005) persistently underline the centrality of Soviet Central Asia to Chinese energy security and describe Sino-Central Asian energy relations as "natural" and "inevitable". There is little doubt that China will eventually replace Russia as the dominant economic force in Central Asia (Eder, 2014).

The development and deepening of bilateral/multilateral cooperation with Commonwealth of Independent States (CIS) has always been a priority for Russia's foreign policy. In this context, the Russian decision makers view Central Asia as a pivotal region (Allison, 2004; Bahgat, 2006; S. J. Blank, 2006; Buszynski, 2005; Ebel, 2009; Jaffe & Soligo, 2009; Johnson, 2009; Mankoff, 2009; O'Hara, 2005; Specher & Specher, 2009). Consequently, the SCO is considered by Russian elites to be one of its key tools for expanding its relations with the Central Asian states. Moreover, the Russian leadership sees the SCO as an important element in its security policy in a number of respects. It views its own security as directly related to Central Asia, because Russia shares a long porous border with the region. Issues such as illegal narcotics and the activities of Islamic fundamentalist groups in Central Asia have been identified as major security challenges with the potentiality to spread north over the border into Russia. As well as engaging with Central Asia for security purposes, the Russian leadership also interprets economic cooperation as important for ensuring its predominant place in the region, and its position as the Central Asian Republics' most important trade partner. Russia values the SCO as a means for cooperation in infrastructure development and for coordination of its energy policies among itself, China, Kazakhstan and Uzbekistan. This focus on energy is also born out of the perceived need to increase Russia's role in the wider East Asian economy, in order to assert itself as an important energy supplier to the rapidly growing states of the region (Aris, 2011).

CONCLUSION

Since the revival of relations between Russia and China at the end of the Cold War, both countries have established a degree of solidarity on interpretations of the current contemporary international system, with both perceiving that alternative models to the Western liberal-democratic international system are necessary. Both countries want to show the real possibility of a "Eurasian integration" model that is independent from, and an alternative to, its political dialogue with the European Union (EU) and the North Atlantic Treaty Organization (NATO). The SCO can be viewed by Russia and China as having contributed to presenting their viewpoint on a number of significant international events, especially when this viewpoint is contrary to the position taken by the EU or the US.

In distinction from the EU, the SCO as a regional system is characterized by the absence of democracy and the continuation of Soviet style authoritarian leadership. The nature of the regimes in place limits the possibility of interest and preference formation from bottom-up. Consequently, regional integration theories utilized to explain European integration becomes blurry when applied to the Shanghai Cooperation Organization.

The emerging international system is characterized by regional diversity and not by uniformity. Consequently, it is fair to argue that since the regional differences in the structure of the world exist, such differences should matter theoretically also. Current state of field in regional integration theories indicates more "European exceptionalism" than 'a' regional integration theory. However, it might appear to be quite challenging task to develop a theoretical structure encompassing such regional diversity, but attempts has to be made.

Furthermore, the growth of regional systems after the Cold War suggests that it is plausible to treat regions as unit of analysis and generate middle range theories that can be tested. That would be useful to detect certain trends in systemic changes since the dominant theories of International Relations show certain limitation regarding that matter.

The SCO is a very loose organization: it is not a military-strategic alliance, nor a full-fledged economic union, nor is it a political organization in the conventional sense. Taking into account various aspects, the possibility of creating an effective regional organization out of the SCO—comparable to NATO in terms of military or the EU in terms of political/economic decision making—may be an impressive undertaking. No doubt that still the major issues/problems are mostly handled at the bilateral level. And even if the SCO did succeed in developing into such an effective organization, the China's extraordinary growth would confine the other member states into little more than a supply-base for China's natural resources (Laumullin, 2006). To this end, May 2014 Sino-Russian deal of $400-billion gas supply opens up a new market for Moscow as it risks losing European customers over the Ukraine/Crimea crisis.

Russian and Chinese leadership increasingly interprets the approach of leading Western powers towards the SCO as negative. Furthermore, both countries have encountered a number of disagreements with Western states and organizations over normative issues, which in turn gave birth to a number of criticisms about the 'double standards' of Western powers vis-à-vis international affairs. In that sort of global political context, both China and Russia would use the SCO as a valuable tool to assert themselves in global affairs.

REFERENCES

Adler, E., & Barnett, M. (Eds.). (1998). *Security communities*. Cambridge University Press. doi:10.1017/CBO9780511598661

Alexeeva, O. (2008). Chinese migration in the Russian far east. [Article]. *China Perspectives, 2008*(3), 20-32.

Allison, R. (2004). Strategic reassertion in Russia's central Asia policy. *International Affairs, 80*(2), 277–293. doi:10.1111/j.1468-2346.2004.00383.x

Allworth, E. A. (1995). *Central Asia: One hundred thirty years of Russian dominance, a historical overview* (3rd ed.). Duke University Press.

Ambrosio, T. (2008). Catching the 'Shanghai spirit': How the Shanghai cooperation organization promotes authoritarian norms in central Asia. *Europe-Asia Studies, 60*(8), 1321–1344. doi:10.1080/09668130802292143

Aris, S. (2011). *Eurasian regionalism: The Shanghai cooperation organisation*. Palgrave Macmillan. doi:10.1057/9780230307643

Arsenov, V. I., Artemkina, E. V., & Zaboev, A. I. (2005). Rossiya v sisteme mejdunarodnih evroaziatiskih transportnih koridorov: sovremennoy sostoyanie, problemi, perspektivi i konkurentosposobnost. *Rossiskiy Vneshneekonomicheskiy Vestnik,* (1).

Bahgat, G. (2006). Central Asia and energy security. *Asian Affairs, 37*(1), 1–16. doi:10.1080/03068370500456819

Baizakova, K. I. (2013). The Shanghai cooperation organization's role in countering threats and challenges to central Asian regional security. *Russian Politics and Law*, *51*(1), 59–79. doi:10.2753/RUP1061-1940510104

Barkovsky, A. N. (2006). Obrechen li Rossisky Dalny Vostok na sudbu tranzitnoy territoriy? *Rossiskiy Vneshneekonomicheskiy Vestnik,* (3).

Billon, P. L. (Ed.). (2005). *The geopolitics of resource wars: Resource dependence, governance and violence*. New York: Routledge. doi:10.4324/9780203323229

Blank, S. (2011). Russia's geo-economic future; The security implications of Russia's political and economic structure. [Article]. *Journal of Slavic Military Studies*, *24*(3), 351–395. doi:10.1080/13518046.2011.598723

Blank, S. J. (2006). The Eurasian energy triangle: China, Russia, and the Central Asian states. *The Brown Journal of World Affairs*, *XII*(2).

Brecher, M. (1963). *The new states of Asia, a political analysis*. London: Oxford University Press.

Burley, A.-M., & Mattli, W. (1993). Europe before the court: A political theory of legal integration. *International Organization*, *47*(1), 41–76. doi:10.1017/S0020818300004707

Buszynski, L. (2005). Russia's new role in central Asia. *Asian Survey*, *45*(4), 546–565. doi:10.1525/as.2005.45.4.546

Caporaso, J. A. (1998). Regional integration theory: Understanding our past and anticipating the future. In W. Sandholtz & A. S. Sweet (Eds.), *Supranational governance: The institutionalization of the European Union* (pp. 334–351). New York: Oxford University Press. doi:10.1093/0198294646.003.0012

Caporaso, J. A. (2000). *The European Union: Dilemmas of regional integration*. Boulder, Colo.: Westview Press.

Checkel, J. T. (1999). Norms, institutions, and national identity in contemporary Europe. *International Studies Quarterly*, *43*(1), 84–111. doi:10.1111/0020-8833.00112

Cheng, J. Y. S. (2011). The Shanghai co-operation organisation: China's initiative in regional institutional building. *Journal of Contemporary Asia*, *41*(4), 632–656. doi:10.1080/00472336.2011.610618

Choi, Y. J., & Caporaso, J. A. (2002). Comparative regional integration. In W. Carlsnaes, T. Risse, & B. A. Simmons (Eds.), *Handbook of international relations* (pp. 480–499). London: Sage Publications. doi:10.4135/9781848608290.n25

Dadabaev, T. (2013). Shanghai cooperation organization (SCO) regional identity formation from the perspective of the central Asia states. *Journal of Contemporary China*, *23*(85), 102–118. doi:10.1080/10670564.2013.809982

Deutsch, K. W. (1957). *Political community and the North Atlantic area; International organization in the light of historical experience*. Princeton, NJ: Princeton University Press.

Ebel, R. E. (2009). *The geopolitics of Russian energy: Looking back, looking forward*. Washington, DC: Center for Strategic & International Studies.

Eder, T. S. (2014). *China-Russia relations in Central Asia: Energy policy, Beijing's new assertiveness and 21st century geopolitics*. Wiesbaden, Germany: Springer. doi:10.1007/978-3-658-03272-2

Farrell, M., Hettne, B., & Langenhove, L. v. (Eds.). (2005). *Global politics of regionalism: Theory and practice*. Pluto Press.

Fawcett, L. L. E., & Hurrell, A. (1995). *Regionalism in world politics: Regional organization and international order*. New York: Oxford University Press.

Gilpin, R. G. (1986). The richness of the tradition of political realism. In R. O. Keohane (Ed.), *Neorealism and its critics* (pp. 301–322). Columbia University Press.

Goldman, M. I. (2008). *Petrostate: Putin, power, and the new Russia*. New York: Oxford University Press.

Gowa, J. (1989). Bipolarity, multipolarity, and free trade. *The American Political Science Review*, *83*(4), 1245–1256. doi:10.2307/1961667

Grieco, J. (1993). Understanding the problem of international cooperation: The limitations of neoliberal institutionalism and the future of realist theory. In D. Baldwin (Ed.), *Neorealism and neoliberalism: The contemporary debate*. New York: Columbia University Press.

Grieco, J. (1995). The Maastricht treaty, economic and monetary union, and the neorealist research programme. *Review of International Studies*, *21*(01), 21–40. doi:10.1017/S0260210500117504

Haas, E. B., & Whiting, A. S. (1975). *Dynamics of international relations*. Westport, CT: Greenwood Press.

Hettne, B., Inotai, A., & Sunkel, O. (1999). *Globalism and the new regionalism*. Palgrave Macmillan.

Hoffmann, S. (1963). Discord in community: The North Atlantic area as a partial international system. *International Organization*, *17*(3), 521–549. doi:10.1017/S0020818300034536

Holm, H. H., & Sørensen, G. (1995). *Whose world order? Uneven globalization and the end of the Cold War*. Boulder, CO: Westview Press.

Jaffe, A. M., & Soligo, R. (2009). Energy security: The Russian connection. In D. Moran & J. A. Russell (Eds.), *Energy security and global politics: The militarization of resource management* (pp. 112–135). New York: Routledge.

Johnson, T. H. (2009). Central Asia: Energy resources, politics, and security. In D. Moran & J. A. Russell (Eds.), *Energy security and global politics: The militarization of resource management* (pp. 135–155). New York: Routledge.

Kacowicz, A. M. (1998). *Zones of peace in the third world: South America and West Africa in comparative perspective*. Albany, NY: State University of New York Press.

Kangas, R. (2007). The changing face of the Russian far east: Cooperation and resource competition between Japan, Korea, and China in Northeast Asia. *Perspectives on Global Development and Technology*, *6*(1-3), 441–460. doi:10.1163/156914907X207829

Keohane, R., & Martin, L. (1995). The promise of institutional theory. *International Security*, *20*(1), 39–51. doi:10.2307/2539214

Kuhrt, N. (2012). The Russian far east in Russia's Asia policy: Dual integration or double periphery? [Article]. *Europe-Asia Studies*, *64*(3), 471–493. doi:10.1080/09668136.2012.661926

Lanteigne, M. (2010). Security, strategy and the former USSR: China and the Shanghai cooperation organisation. In S. Breslin (Ed.), *Handbook of China's international relations*. New York: Routledge.

Laumullin, M. (2006). *The Shanghai cooperation organization as "geopolitical bluff?" A view from astana* (Vol. 12). Paris: Institut Français des Relations Internationales.

Lukin, A. (2006). The Russian approach to China under Gorbachev, Yeltsin, and Putin. In G. Rozman, K. Togo, & J. P. Ferguson (Eds.), *Russian strategic thought toward Asia*. New York: PALGRAVE MACMILLAN.

Mackinder, H. J. (1919). *Democratic ideals and reality; A study in the politics of reconstruction*. London: Constable and Company, Ltd.

Mankoff, J. (2009). *Eurasian energy security* (Vol. 43). New York: Council on Foreign Relations.

Mattli, W. (1999). *The logic of regional integration: Europe and beyond*. New York: Cambridge University Press. doi:10.1017/CBO9780511756238

Mearsheimer, J. J. (1990). Back to the future: Instability in Europe after the Cold War. *International Security, 15*(1), 5-56.

Mitrany, D. (1946). *A working peace system; An argument for the functional developmental of international organization* (4th ed.). London: National Peace Council.

Mitrany, D. (1966). *A working peace system*. Chicago: Quadrangle Books.

Mitrany, D. (1976). *The functional theory of politics*. London: St. Martin's Press.

Mittelman, J. H. (1996). *Globalization: Critical reflections*. Boulder, CO: Lynne Rienner Publishers.

Mittelman, J. H. (2000). *The globalization syndrome: Transformation and resistance*. Princeton, NJ: Princeton University Press. doi:10.1515/9781400823697

Modelski, G. (1963). *The new emerging forces; Documents on the ideology of Indonesian foreign policy*. Canberra, Australia: Dept. of International Relations, Research School of Pacific Studies, Institute of Advanced Studies, Australian National University.

Moravcsik, A. (1998). Integration theory. In D. Dinan (Ed.), *Encyclopedia of the European Union*. Boulder, CO: Lynne Rienner.

Moravcsik, A. (1999). Is something rotten in the state of Denmark? Constructivism and European integration. *Journal of European Public Policy, 6*(4), 669–681. doi:10.1080/135017699343531

Morgenthau, H. J. (1948). *Politics among nations: The struggle for power and peace*. Alfred A. Knopf.

Movkebaeva, G. A. (2013). Energy cooperation among Kazakhstan, Russia, and China within the Shanghai cooperation organization. *Russian Politics and Law, 51*(1), 80–87. doi:10.2753/RUP1061-1940510105

O'Hara, S. L. (2005). Great game or grubby game? The struggle for control of the Caspian. In P. L. Billon (Ed.), *The geopolitics of resource wars: Resource dependence, governance and violence* (pp. 138–161). New York: Routledge.

Odum, H. (1936). *Southern regions of the United States*. Chapel Hill, NC: The University of North Carolina Press.

Odum, H., & Moore, H. E. (1938). *American regionalism: A cultural-historical approach to national integration*. New York: Holt.

Perovic, J., Orttung, R. W., & Wenger, A. (2009). *Russian energy power and foreign relations: Implications for conflict and cooperation*. London: Taylor & Francis.

Pierson, P. (1995). Fragmented welfare states: Federal institutions and the development of social policy. *Governance: An International Journal of Policy, Administration and Institutions, 8*(4), 449–478. doi:10.1111/j.1468-0491.1995.tb00223.x

Poussenkova, N. (2009). Russia's future customers: Asia and beyond. In J. Perovic (Ed.), *Russian energy power and foreign relations: Implications for conflict and cooperation* (pp. 132–154). New York: Routledge.

Rozman, G. (2008). Strategic thinking about the Russian far east: A resurgent Russia eyes its future in northeast Asia. [Article]. *Problems of Post-Communism, 55*(1), 36–48. doi:10.2753/PPC1075-8216550104

Russett, B. M. (1967). *International regions and the international system; A study in political ecology*. Chicago: Rand McNally.

Schmitter, P. C., & Haas, E. B. (1964). *Mexico and Latin American economic integration*. Berkeley, CA: Institute of International Studies, University of California.

Song, W. (2014). Interests, power and China's difficult game in the Shanghai cooperation organization (SCO). *Journal of Contemporary China*, *23*(85), 85–101. doi:10.1080/10670564.2013.809981

Specher, M., & Specher, D. (2009). *Is Russia winning in Central Asia?* (Vol. 1). Private University of Applied Sciences.

Spechler, D. R. (2010). Russian foreign policy during the Putin presidency. [Article]. *Problems of Post-Communism*, *57*(5), 35–50. doi:10.2753/PPC1075-8216570503

Sullivan, J., & Renz, B. (2010). Chinese migration: Still the major focus of Russian Far East/Chinese North East relations? [Article]. *The Pacific Review*, *23*(2), 261–285. doi:10.1080/09512741003624450

Troyakova, T. (2007). The Russian Far East: Isolation or Integration? *Problems of Post-Communism*, *54*(2), 61–71. doi:10.2753/PPC1075-8216540206

Vance, R. B. (1951). The regional concept as a tool for social research. In M. Jensen (Ed.), *Regionalism in America* (pp. 119–140). Madison, WI: Univ. of Wisconsin Press.

Waltz, K. N. (1979). *Theory of international politics*. Addison-Wesley Pub. Co.

Yi-chong, X. (2006). China's energy security. *Australian Journal of International Affairs*, *60*(2), 265–286. doi:10.1080/10357710600696175

Yuan, J.-D. (2010). China's role in establishing and building the Shanghai cooperation organization (SCO). *Journal of Contemporary China*, *19*(67), 855–869. doi:10.1080/10670564.2010.508587

Zartman, I. W. (1973). *Man, state, and society in the contemporary Maghrib*. New York: Praeger Publishers.

Zhao, S. (2008). China's global search for energy security: Cooperation and competition in Asia–Pacific. *Journal of Contemporary China*, *17*(55), 207–227. doi:10.1080/10670560701809460

Zhuangzhi, S. (2004). New and old regionalism: The Shanghai cooperation organization and Sino-Central Asian relations. *The Review of International Affairs*, *3*(4), 600–612. doi:10.1080/1475355042000241548

Zweig, D., & Jianhai, B. (2005). China's global hunt for energy. *Foreign Affairs*, *84*(5), 25–38. doi:10.2307/20031703

KEY TERMS AND DEFINITIONS

Central Asia: The core region of the Eurasian continent stretching from the Caspian Sea in the west to China in the east and from Afghanistan in the south to Russia in the north.

Energy Security: The relationship between national security and the accessibility to natural resources for energy consumption/production.

Eurasia: Combined continental landmass of Europe and Asia.

International Security: A number of measures such as military action/treaties/conventions taken by nations/international organizations to guarantee the survival and safety of international order.

People's Republic of China: The world's most populous country, with one fifth of global population. A rising power and key player in global political/economic/military relations.

Regionalism: The common sense of identity/purpose combined with the creation of institutions that express a particular identity and shape collective action within a geographical region.

Russian Far East: The extreme eastern parts of the Russian federation and the Eurasian continent, located between Lake Baikal in Eastern Siberia and the Pacific Ocean.

Russian Federation: The largest country in the world, covering more than one-third of Eurasia. A key player in global political/economic/military relations.

The Shanghai Cooperation Organization: A Eurasian political, economic and military organization established in 2001 in Shanghai by the leaders of China, Russia, Kazakhstan, Kyrgyzstan, Tajikistan and Uzbekistan.

Chapter 20
The TTIP and the SCO in the Light of the Success Conditions for Economic Integration

Engin Sorhun
Istanbul 29 Mayıs University, Turkey

ABSTRACT

The last global economic crisis has prompted new dynamics in the scope of economic integration: On the one hand, the Transatlantic economy witnessed the formation of the largest economic integration in the human history: the Transatlantic Trade and Investment Partnership (TTIP). On the other hand, Shanghai Cooperation Organization (SCO) recently adopted the economic vision for initiating an economic integration. Since both integration projects were recently launched, this chapter is intended to make a small contribution to the limited scientific resources available to policymakers, academicians, NGOs, etc. In this respect, this chapter first presents a set of political, economic, institutional, and natural conditions suggested in the principal economic integration literature for the success of a regional economic bloc. Second, it aims at evaluating the TTIP and the SCO in the light of these success conditions.

INTRODUCTION

The whole is bigger than the sum of its parts -Aristotle

One of the major dynamics in the international relations is international economic integration. However, though it has a long history dating back to ancient times (colonial empires, merchant associations, religious empires, criminal empires) [1] this dynamics has never shaped the world as powerfully as it does in the modern times. Its evolution and its variation may tell us the story of the international economic integration in last two centuries from the Zollverein to the European Union. Together with the foundation of inter-governmental organizations in the form of regional economic bloc the notion "economic integration" has developed both on theoretical ground and empirical ground.

In modern times, the theoretical basis of the economic integration is, as many economists acknowledged, laid by Viner (1950) which defined trade creation and trade diversion. Questioning Viner's notion of trade diversion, Meade (1955)

DOI: 10.4018/978-1-4666-7308-3.ch020

conclude that even though there is trade diversion, a customs union can cause a "trade expansion" under condition of elastic demand. Meade (1955) examined conditions under which trade blocs made member countries better off and conditions under which it did not. He suggested that a customs union may be welfare increasing if the partner countries are actually competitive but potentially complementary, if the initial tariff levels were very high, and if each partner is the principle supplier to the other partner of the traded products. Meade's general equilibrium model that analyzes the welfare effect of trade blocs from a worldwide perspective is further developed by Lipsey (1957), Balassa (1961), Vanek (1965), McMillan and McCann (1981). Lipsey (1957) tested Viner's arguments through statistical data. Balassa (1961) argued that the forms of integration other than Customs Union may be possible and produced a model with five steps (free exchange area, customs union, common market, economic union, economic and monetary union) in order to evaluate European Integration. Vanek (1965) proved that setting a common external tariff with the rest of the world and eliminating the barriers to internal trade do not necessarily lead a regional bloc to the situation where trade diversion is greater than trade creation. Vinner's trade creation-trade diversion approach was challenged by Lipsey (1970) that initially developed the terms of trade-volume of trade approach. This alternative approach stresses on the impacts of a regional economic bloc on individual countries as integration occurs, instead of on world welfare. McMillan and McCann (1981) prove in a three-good model that two partners within the same trade bloc may prefer an intra-union tariff or subsidy to internal free trade to obtain volume-of-trade gains through increased imports from the non-partner country.

On the one hand, the traditional theory of economic integration deals with the issue from the static effect point of view. On the other hand, the new theory of economic integration deals with the issue including dynamic effects into the analysis. Balassa (1961, 1965) added a new dimension by introducing the concept of dynamic effect into the theory of economic integration. Since the trade creation and trade diversion are not solely able to explain the whole potential gain from integration he listed a set of additional effects (larger scale economies, technology transfer, and an increase in competition, investment flows, productivity and growth) that is uneven and obtained over time. Balassa's argument is developed through partial equilibrium models and empirically tested principally by Corden (1972), Krugman (1979, 1980), Lancaster (1980), Helpman (1981).

Since economic integration is a multidimensional process, political, institutional and historical perspectives of this process are analyzed throughout successful and unsuccessful integration projects by Strange (1995), Edblad (1996), Rooyen (1998), Mattli (1999), Durina (2006), McCarty (2006), Salvatore (2009).

Economic integration literature suggests that a bloc may be welfare generating for the cooperating countries depending on some conditions. Various conditions for a successful economic integration have been suggested in different partial equilibrium models or in empirical tests of these models. In this chapter, the suggested conditions in the revised literature will further be dealt with under four subtopics: namely political conditions, economic conditions, institutional conditions, and natural conditions. Subsequently, these success conditions for economic integration, tackled in previous literature, will be used in order to evaluate the potential of the Transatlantic Trade and Investment Partnership (TTIP) and an eventual economic integration project within the Shanghai Cooperation Organization (SCO). Since these two integration projects were recently launched, the concerned policymakers, academicians, NGOs etc. have a very limited scientific resource. This study is intended to make a small contribution to studies in this field.

This chapter is organized as follows: in the next section the theoretical background and developments in economic integration literature are discussed. In the third section, eighteen conditions for successful economic integration are categorized and explained under four subtopics. Following a brief descriptions about the TTIP and the SCO, in the fourth section the two economic integration projects are examined in the light of the success condition for economic integration. However, since the two projects in question have not been finalized yet, some conditions are left out of assessment. Finally, conclusions and remarks are given.

THEORETICAL BACKGROUND AND DEVELOPMENTS

If the history of economic integration dates back to 3rd millennium B.C. the process of the Zollverein matches to Industrial Revolution and the process of the European Union to the computer age. The Zollverein is often considered as the first modern economic integration process that starting as a custom union in 1881 helped the political unification of Germany. Due to its success the Zollverein has had become inspiring model for following economic integration projects, one of them is European Union. As McCarty (2006) suggests, the Zollverein has left nine general lessons for the process of international economic integration.: (1) Central motivating idea (Developed by Friedrich List and others, this idea was that a combination of states could reduce barriers that were limiting trade among them); (2) underlying force with deep emotional wellsprings (German nationalism), (3) a vision (political unification and customs union); (4) a major leadership (Otto von Bismarck of Prussia); (5) overcoming hostile forces (enemies, competitors); (6) alignment of geography with economics; (7) steadfastness (big things take time), (8) sequencing (do not do too much at once); (9) realistic goals. Some of these principles seem to still keep their validities for the other integration projects.

Customs union is one of the forms of economic integration. Especially as from the World War II some new forms of integration from Preferential Trade Area[2] to Political Union have appeared. "Most economic integration projects are bilateral and do not proceed from a customs union type agreement." (Snorrason, 2012). The process of economic integration may take any of the following forms: (1) Free trade area (FTA), which is the complete removal of trade barriers among member countries, while each member-country maintains separate trade policies with non-members (Example: European Free Trade Area -EFTA). (2) Customs union, which allows member countries to go beyond the removal of trade barriers among them and to adopt a common external trade policy with all non-members (Example: Arab Customs Union will start in 2015). (3) Common market, which involves the removal of all barriers to the movement of factors of production (particularly labor and capital) among member countries in addition to the requirements of a customs union (Example: Southern Common Market –MERCOSUR). (4) Economic union, which requires member-countries to unify the economic institutions of the member-countries, and the coordination of their economic, fiscal, monetary[3] and socioeconomic policies (Example: European Union – EU). (5) Political union, among countries assumes union with a single economic policy and a supranational government akin to a nation-state or federal government with greater economic authority by creating centralized political institutions, including a regional parliament.

Table 1 presents theoretical forms of international economic integration arrangements. However, there are two main points of view about the question whether the forms of integration are the stages that member countries skip over time. On the one hand, theoretically these various schemes are characterized by different intensities of cooperation. For Horvart (1999) the lowest intensity, practiced in FTA, consists of *co-operation*, which means voluntary and unenforceable alignments of national policies in various fields. *Harmonization* is the second degree of co-ordination and involves agreements on how member countries will exercise policy instruments over which they retain control. This is practiced in (3), Customs Union and Common Market. If various policy instruments are assigned to Economic Union, this is *integration*. Besides, Gerber (2013) has referred to the first two stages or forms of integration as '*shallow integration*,' while the last three represent what he has designated as '*deep integration*.' Essentially, the term 'shallow integration' refers to any form or stage of economic integration whose scope is limited to border-related issues—that is, tariffs and non-tariff trade barriers (NTBs). 'Deep integration,' on the other hand, goes beyond border-related issues; among other things, it entails harmonization of member-countries' important economic institutions, as well as legal, product-safety, labeling, environmental, and technical standards. In this respect, each of form of integration represents a different stage of integration if member countries have a desire to pursue the integration of their national economies to its logical conclusion.

On the other hand, what is the most critical point, in practice, for understanding of forms of integration is that the process of integration does not necessarily have to be gradual from one type to another. The establishment of any of these types depends on the agreement among the participating countries. There is substantial historical evidence to support this consideration. A group of countries can start a regional bloc by establishing a customs union just because this is, they consider, the most appropriate integration framework for them (like NAFTA) while another group of countries can start a basic framework and subsequently deepen it (like EU).

Beside five level of economic integration at regional level, another economic integration path started through the GATT in 1948. This represents the integration at global level. The GATT provided a framework for the multilateral trade system, subsequently incorporated into an organization for international trade, the World Trade Organization (WTO). "If the world trading system has a constitution, it is embodied in the Articles of the GATT and its successor organization, the WTO" (Bagwell and Staiger, 2002). The WTO defined its main goal as "to reduce trade barriers among its members (154 countries)" and itself as "an organization for liberalizing trade".

The presence of two international integration paths (regional and multilateral scales) leads to the theory of second best: Adam Smith and David Ricardo view free trade and the unimpeded movements of factors as the first best policy in a world which does not have any distortions. Free trade among all nations of the world would, according to international trade theory, optimize the allocation of the world's resources[4], and ultimately maximize global output, as well as improve welfare worldwide. However, creation of

Table 1. Forms of international integration

Policy Action	Free Trade Area (1)	Customs Union (2)	Common Market (3)	Economic Union (4)	Political Union (5)
Removal of Tariffs	Yes	Yes	Yes	Yes	Yes
Common External Tariffs	No	Yes	Yes	Yes	Yes
Factor Mobility	No	No	Yes	Yes	Yes
Harmonization of Economic Policies	No	No	No	Yes	Yes
Total unification of economic and monetary policies and supranational government	No	No	No	No	Yes

regional trading blocs would, therefore, not lead to such a scenario, since it would not precipitate into complete liberalization of global trade. In other words, a global economy that is composed of regional trading blocs would still have tariffs and non-tariff trade barriers and would, therefore, not generate maximum welfare gains. Nevertheless, in a world, where all distortions cannot be removed, the removal of some of the distortions constitutes the second best. The rational is that since total trade liberalization maximizes world welfare regional scale integration that represents a move towards free trade therefore increases welfare, although it does not maximize it[5]. In Meade's words, 'any move towards economic union covering a large number of countries would undoubtedly serve to raise standards of living.' (Meade, 1955).

For the traditional economic theory there are two important questions relating to regionalism (integration at regional scale) and globalism (integration at global scale): What is the welfare effect on each member country? ; And, what is the welfare impact on the bloc as a whole and the rest of the world? These questions keep their validity. However since the international economic integration is a dynamic process answers to these questions have been subject to the change in theoretical developments and empirical findings in this field.

The classical trade theory looks at these questions throughout the static gains (trade creation, trade diversion, administrating savings, grater bargaining power, improvement in member countries' collective terms of trade) from integration since the theoretical framework of economic integration was mostly based on the FTA and CU; and we have had a little idea about the effect of "deep integration" (such as economic union) and the dynamic effect that it extracted until the 1980s. What was known until then is that "both customs unions and free trade areas can generate potential gains in terms of the national income of the bloc by encouraging specialization amongst the member countries on the basis of comparative advantage. A common market can generate additional gains in real income by overcoming the barriers to factor mobility that allows differences in factor productivities to exist in the bloc." (Robson, 2003). In the world of Viner (1950), Meade (1955) Lipsey (1957), Mundell (1964), Vanek (1965), Corden (1976) and McMillan and McCann (1981), the term regional integration was used as the synonym of FTA and CU; and trade liberalization worldwide was better than the second best in terms of static gains.

However, the new trade theory pays attention to the dynamic effects of integration (economies of scale, intra-industry specialization, emergence of competition, increase in bilateral foreign investment, stable financial market). If static gain is obtained in the short term just following integration, dynamic effects are unevenly distributed among members and can only be obtained in the long term. "With economies of scale and imperfect competition (monopolistic competition model), there are no unconditional expectations that all countries will gain from integration, even less that they will gain equally. Under imperfect market conditions the new trade theory suggest that integration profoundly changes the economic structure of participating countries which must modify, and even abandon, the established domestic monopolies and autarkic traditions. So that the potential gain related to dynamic effects is efficiently realized a set of well-designed adjustment policies must be implemented throughout the bloc. In the absence of adjustment policies, such as industrial, regional, cohesion and social policies, integration may impose costs on some countries, rather than give them benefits. It may take decades to reach a new, higher and stable steady state. Unfriendly policies can cancel out all the beneficial effects which accrue from an improved access to a larger market. In this respect international economic integration is never more than a useful supporting tool that only supports (rather than replaces) a sound domestic macroeconomic policy and structural reforms. If these domestic policies (fiscal monetary and exchange rate policy etc.) are not healthy, integration cannot be their substitute." Jovanović (2005). The dynamic effect makes economic integration a dynamic, rather than static, process whose the success depends on the self-transformation capacity of member countries. In sum, obtaining the additional gain stemming from the dynamic effects depends on well-designed policies and adequately implementations of them.

Whether it is at regional level or at global level all kinds of arrangement for international economic integration explicitly require the acceptance of constraints on national policy making. And the farther along the road between free trade area and political union that countries progress, the greater those constraints become. What motivations induce countries to accept such constraints? What are expected economic benefits that provide the motivation for forgoing policy independence in relation to trade, factor movements and other major policy areas?

International economic integration increases the significant potential in economic welfare. Thus, countries organise themselves to reap these gain. Specialisation and increase in the export potentials in order to pay for the imports are necessary conditions for success. Jovanović (2005) listed the main economic motivations, suggested by traditional and new trade theories, for what countries integrate:

- First and foremost, countries integrate in order to secure access to markets of partner countries;
- They also want to secure and solidify domestic market-oriented reforms;
- Increased investment opportunities as expectations may be established with an increased degree of security;
- Improved efficiency in the use of resources;
- An elimination of trade barriers reduces the cost of trade;
- Increased competition on internal market puts a downward pressure on prices;
- Facilitation of exchange of technical information;
- Competition forces firms to implement new ideas and technologies;
- Due to the enlarged market, producers may better exploit and benefit from economies of scale;
- Potential for coordination of certain economic policies in order to increase their effectiveness;
- Improved bargaining position with external partners;
- Research and innovation may be stimulated because of tougher competition on a larger market and a possibility to share fixed costs in such a market environment;
- Market of the integrated group provides more opportunities for a wider range of goods and services that can be offered to consumers, hence there is an improvement in individuals' utility function; and reduction in inefficiency which moves the production activities of firms closer to best-practice business organisation.

Though the motivations for economic integration are more or less clearly defined in theory, the realization of these advantages that international economic integration presents for participating countries depends on several conditions both in theory and in practice.

CONDITIONS FOR SUCCESFUL ECONOMIC INTEGRATION

As Viner (1950), Balassa (1961, 1986), Johnson (1962), Vanek (1965), Lipsey (1957 and 1970), Meade (1955), McMillan and McCann (1981), Leistner (1997), Mattli (1999), Rooyen (1998), Duina (2006), Simms and Simms (2006), Salvatore (2009), Snorrason (2012) among numerous other notable economists, have maintained, several conditions need to be met in order for any form of integration among the national economies of cooperating countries to be viable; they include the following:

Political Conditions

1. **Peace and Stability:** Sustained peace and stability in all cooperating countries, and transparency and popular participation in the generation of important inter-governmental organization (IGO) related decisions, protocols and treaties in each of the cooperating countries.
2. **Sustained Political Will and Pubic Support:** A genuine desire among leaders of each and every cooperating country to create a successful economic bloc, and willingness to compromise on sensitive issues and matters relating to national sovereignty. If decision makers, especially at highest levels (governments, parliaments etc.), does not take the interests of the nation as a whole we do not talk about any political will and popular support to integration. In the absence of these, the possibility of failure of an economic integration project is very high. If social and ideological diversity and social stratification within the nation are considered public support to integration seems to depend on culture of compromise that evolved through the history of this nation. Political will and public support first and foremost are fed by economic gains. Casella (2010) notes that the European Union's first focus was on forming economic ties and breaking down barriers to the movement of goods, before it was possible to forge political linkages and to deal with issues such as: a single currency, collective security policy and human rights policy. We can deal with political will issue from two perspectives: politic support and public support for integration: First, the integration agenda should not be subject to arbitrary arrangement by changes in political leadership of the member countries. Second, participation of public (citizens, sectors, lobbies, civil society, local governments etc.) to the decision making process or taking adequately peoples' views into consideration make easier to overcome the sovereignty issues.

Economic Conditions

3. **Competitive Economies:** The economies of cooperating countries need to be *initially* competitive rather than complementary in order to provide for a competitive business environment in the regional economy which may eventually be created. In other words, each member-country's economy should initially have the capacity to compete in cross-border trade by itself with little or no dependence on other countries' economies to complement its competitive position. Whether member countries' economies are competitive or not primarily depend on their production and demand structures.
4. **Similarity in Production:** This can be dealt with from the classical trade theory and the new trade theory: (i) The classical trade theory explains international trade among members through technological differences between nations and suggests that each country has to specialize in the industries in which they produce less costly and leave the production in the other industries. If countries initially having similarity in production move factor of production form abandoned industries to the specialized ones this yields an increase in productivity and gives them comparative advantage. Trade between two countries can benefit both countries if each country exports the goods in which it has a comparative advantage. In this case integration process serve to determine which

member specialize in which set of products and export them to other members. However, when member countries produce *completely* different goods, as seen in integration among low income countries, there is little scope for further complementary specialization. (ii) The new trade theory suggests that demand for differentiated products grows as per capita income (Linder, 1961) and differentiated products allows consumer to satisfy their preference for variety (Krugman 1979; Lancaster 1980; Helpman 1981). Since the preference for variety and product differentiation are larger in developed countries than in low income countries a regional bloc with similar developed economies yields more gain than a regional bloc with similar low income countries. In this case, although integration does not require members to leave completely the production in the same industry, instead, they have to leave one variety and specialize in another in each industry in order to achieve economies of scale; and they exports the specialized varieties of product each other. However, this competitive process can lead some firms in each country to failure. Thus, economic similarity does not necessarily guarantee success for a regional bloc. Integration process serves to minimize the post-integration stress and to monitor implementation of adjustment policies such as industrial, regional policies integration by member countries' governments that may alleviate the post-competition effect.

5. **Trade Creation Larger Than Trade Diversion**: The more different they are from the outside world, the more likely it is for member countries to gain from the union because possible losses from trade diversion are smaller (Johnson, 1962). The formation of a regional bloc encourages trade creation as the result of a shift from a dearer to a cheaper source of supply. Other things being equal, this is a potential move towards free trade because a less efficient protected domestic supplier is replaced by a more efficient foreign one.
6. **Similar Stage of Development:** The national economies of cooperating countries also need to be generally at similar stages of industrial development in order to circumvent problems pertaining to the following: (i) mass-emigration of people from low-income to high-income member-countries, (ii) dominance by one or a few member-countries in the supply of manufactured goods or industrial inputs, and/or (iii) differences in labor, environmental and product safety standards. Countries at similar stages of economic development (similar GNP per capita) will find it easier to equalize tariff rates and harmonize economic policies because of similar productivity and similar organizational experience. An advanced country in a less developed environment would enjoy monopoly position and exert disruptive influences on the union. A less developed country in a developed environment would not be able to compete successfully when internal tariffs are eliminated and so would create both economic and political problems.
7. **Size of Countries:** There is a negative correlation between country size difference (difference countries' arithmetic mean of their GDP) and gain from integration since countries with similar size will trade similar goods (Balassa, 1986 and Balassa and Bauwens, 1987). Thus, as the country size difference among members increases (i) potential gain from integration decreases or (ii) potential gain from integration is unevenly distributed among members. For example, countries tend to specialise and export goods for which they have a relatively large domestic market. It is this domestic demand or 'home market' effect (Linder, 1961; Krugman, 1980) that

induces production, rather than domestic factor endowment. The response by firms to strong local demand for a product is so powerful that it leads this country to export that product. Countries have a competitive edge in the production of these goods and thus gain an advantage in foreign markets, while they import goods demanded by a minority of the home population. These are standardized goods for mass consumption[6]. Snorrason (2012) confirms the asymmetry between the impact of regional blocs on trade flow and sizes of countries: depending on the size classification, the effects of regional blocs are least on the trade flow, imports and exports, of large countries, and exports of micro countries; and the effect of regional bloc are most on the trade flow, imports and exports, of small countries. He concludes that ex post, the effect of economic integration agreements is asymmetric between countries of different sizes; small countries are the bigger gainers of ex post economic integration agreements.

8. **Pre-Integration Trade Ties:** Strong pre-integration trade ties (which would reflect the existence of specialization by cooperating countries in the production of divergent commodities), harmonious and protracted political relations, and similarity of economic systems between and among cooperating countries.
9. **High Pre-Integration Trade Barriers:** Much mutual trading among prospective members so that gains can be achieved by eliminating internal tariffs of formerly separated countries. High pre-integration tariffs and non-tariff trade barriers between and among cooperating countries, so that the eventual scaling down or complete removal of trade barriers can result in very low prices of tradable products in the regional economy that is to be created and ultimately lead to trade creation.
10. **Low Post-Integration Trade Barriers:** Low tariffs and non-tariff trade barriers on the integrated region's imports from non-member countries so that trade with such countries is sustained in order to promote the generation of tariff revenues by member-countries;

Institutional Conditions

11. **Optimum Number of Countries:** Involvement of a large number of countries in the creation of an IGO in order to broaden the potential for inclusion of many countries which have low-cost industries in the IGO, as well as create a larger economic region in terms of both market size and investment opportunities. The larger the union, the greater its bargaining power and so, unlike a small country, may benefit from improved terms of trade or at least not suffer from imposed upon conditions for trade. Large internal market, brought about by the union, makes for more efficient allocation of production and consumption (for instance, the elimination of empty stretches along former borders), more efficient transportation network, more effective competition lowering costs and prices and possibilities for exploiting economies of scale. On the other hand, trust among the participating countries and decision making process within a bloc is particularly important. A relatively small number of participants may create cosy relationships, make monitoring and enforcement of the deal easier, settle disputes more quickly and efficiently while a large group of countries may have many conflicting objectives.
12. **Sharing of Gains and Losses:** presence of an acceptable mechanism for assessing both qualitative and quantitative costs associated with cooperating countries' membership in an IGO, and ensuring that the benefits of integration—including revenues generated from tariffs that are levied on imports from

non-member countries— are distributed both fairly and efficiently among member-countries; and

13. **Regional Leadership:** This suggests a country's leadership or visionary leaders within a regional bloc. A visionary leadership helps to surmount thorny issues in decision making process while adopting rules, regulations and policies. Besides, acting as a paymaster within the bloc a regional leader may support the relatively poorer members or new members during their transition period to cope with competition pressure within the bloc. For example, "Germany emerged as the undisputed leader of the EC. Germany's leadership can also be seen in its role as 'paymaster of the EC'; the Germans by virtue of their strong economy were able to contribute the most to the EC Budget and to provide assistance to poorer countries as they integrated into the competitive EC market. This again was invaluable in the successful development of the EC economy." (Mattli, 1999). Beside its economic pre-eminence, the *Zollverein* experience bestowed Germany an undisputable advantage for leadership. On the other hand, pre- and post- stages of formation of a bloc require a hard work by countries' leaders. Issues like "national sovereignty" may often hinder regional institutionalization schemes as the formation of regional integration area forces members to partly relinquish economic and political sovereignty in favor of the supranational entity. Visionary leaders undertake seminal role in unblocking the blockages in thorny negotiations. Charles de Gaulle and Conrad Adenauer in laying the foundation of the future EU; Carlos Menem and Fernando Henrique Cardoso in establishing the MERCOSUR played a role of "founding faders". Every IGO need some leadership to deal with collective action problems. This leadership may take different shapes like single leadership or a joint leadership by two or more countries. What is the most important as to leadership is that at least one member must take charge of integration efforts, especially those relating to income distribution, policy formation and institution building.
14. **Commitment Institutions:** In addition to regional leadership the presence of commitment institutions which execute a monitoring function over the member countries and their national institutions are indispensable so that they satisfy their obligations due to integration agreement and also provide enforcement procedures against states and individuals which violate treaty obligations is necessary for efficient functioning of a regional integration bloc. Both Mattli (1999) and Duina (2006) are of the view that "commitment institutions" are necessary to sustain integration movements – but the form and extent of these "commitment institutions" is not rigid but depends on the historical and cultural realities of the particular trading bloc. However, comparing EU, NAFTA and MERCOSUR Duina (2006) emphasizes the role of regional law as a facilitator of economic integration and points out that "the approach of the interaction between law and the rules of trade in NAFTA is quite different from the approach in the EU and MERCOSUR". He hereby describes two approaches: minimalist and interventionist approach[7]. A half century regional blocking experience suggests that which approach member countries adopt while establishing commitment institution on which a regional integration area will be promoted depends on the national sensibility (sovereignty). For example, one institution MERCOSUR does not want is a supranational court independent of national system. For this purposes the

member governments decided in the 1991 Protocol of Brazil to establish a tribunal to which every member country send a judge. Member countries believe this approach will protect their national sovereignty in legal matters. We may see the pre-eminence of the leader country when members of a regional bloc shape the framework of the commitment institutions. For example, "its economic superiority led Germany be able to shape the formation of the EU institutions. This is illustrated by the widespread acceptance of the Bundesbank as the model for the statute for the European Central Bank. In the area of technical standards, the German national standards-setting organization, Deutsches Institut fur Normen (DIN), influenced the European standards-setting organizations, European Standards Committee (CEN) and European Electrical Standards Committee (CENELEC)" (Simms and Simms, 2006).

15. **Fair Distribution of Regional Institutions:** Evenly and fairly dispersed commercial, industrial, administrative, educational, training, health, and other essential and communal facilities and institutions in the economic bloc lead member counties to be more engaged with strategic targets of the bloc. However, note that it is necessary that the existence of a regional leader (or joint leadership) neither harms the fair distributions of the institution nor disrupts the functioning of these institutions.

Natural Conditions

16. **Geographical Proximity:** Geographical distance has a negative impact on trade as it increases transport, communications and transaction costs; consumers are likely to trade product diversity for price. However, countries sharing common border are likely to trade more. There is a need for geographical proximity among cooperating countries to make it possible for them to create a well-developed and efficient transportation system for distributing industrial inputs and finished products within their regional economy.
17. **Cultural Proximity:** Sharing cultural values, common language and long historical contacts facilitate cooperation even if at some earlier times countries were involved in bloody confrontation. Mutual understanding is crucial for successful communication.
18. **Preferential Treatment:** An inclination by each and every member-country to import relatively more commodities from cooperating countries than from nonmembers. Large volumes of foreign trade in relation to total expenditures- an indicator for this inclination- so that the elimination of trade impediments generates large gains.

THE TTIP AND THE SCO IN THE LIGHT OF THE SUCCESS CONDITIONS FOR ECONOMIC INTEGRATION

The Transatlantic Trade and Investment Partnership (TTIP)

The transatlantic economy is the largest and wealthiest market in the world, accounting for 40% of world GDP, 28% of world trade, 60% of world FDI stock, and 45% of total merger and acquisition of firms in the world. "However, as globalization proceeds and emerging markets rise, transatlantic markets are shifting from pre-eminence position to predominance position – still considerable, but less overwhelming than in the past" (Hamilton and Quinlan, 2013). This results from three developments: 1) The USA and the EU have a growing trade deficit with the emerging market, especially with China. 2) The USA and the EU have lower growth rate than their potential competitors. 3) The FDI share of developing countries increases more rapidly than that of the USA and the EU.

Rooted in centuries of shared history, transatlantic economic relationship gets a new dimension. If successful the TTIP would become the world's largest free trade agreement. This project aims to develop and introduce a new set of rules in addition to that of WTO to govern international economic relations. Greater gain is estimated to be realized through reduction in non-tariff barriers and aligning regulatory standards (technical regulations, standardizations, conformity assessment procedures, mutual recognition, Sanitary and Phytosanitary Measures etc.) since average tariff rate between the USA and the EU is very low[8].

Shanghai Cooperation Organization (SCO)

The security concerns in Post-Soviet period were initially the main motivation of six countries (China, Russia, Kazakhstan, Kyrgyzstan, Tajikistan, and Uzbekistan) for the SCO. However, economic cooperation gradually became an area of growing interest for its members. Though economic cooperation has always been on the agenda of the SCO since its foundation it has only come to fore following the completion of the SCO's institution-building and agenda expansion phase. In 2006 an Action Plan for the realization of the SCO Programme of Multilateral Trade and Economic cooperation was initiated. It has been observed since a decade that the expectations of the member countries from the Organization have evolved. Since they reached a consensus on the initial concerns like security and border issues the economic cooperation has gradually gotten more importance. Especially, the global financial crisis engendered an accelerating impact on the economic ambitions of the SCO to cope with its negative effects as well as to enhance economic cooperation. During the discussion in the recent submits the Chinese leadership proposed the removal of tariff barriers and to opening-up of its market to the other members. Additionally, the Russian leadership proposed the introduction of a common unit of currency among the SCO members (Aris, 2011). Intention of forming a regional economic community on the basis of a free trade area (and further a customs union) has gained ground.

The TTIP and the SCO in the Light of the Political Conditions

On the one hand, the rise of emerging markets that have gradually taken a growing share in the world economy creates economic pressure on the developed nations. This fact feeds political will in the USA and the EU, especially following the global economic crisis as from 2008, to counterbalance this pressure coming from the Asia. On the other hand, emerging markets like China and Russia want to reinforce through politic cooperation and economic integration the advantage that they have taken since two decades. This fact feed political will in the SCO's members to enlarge the cooperation ground. However, the reflection of the political will on the policy action process varies in the TTIP's participants and the SCO's participants. Culture of democracy constitutes the main reason for this situation.

Comparatively the TTIP's negotiating parties (the USA and the EU's members) can be said to have taken a long way in terms of transparency, good governance, institution quality, state of law and participating democracy. However, the SCO's parties (China, Russia, Kazakhstan, Kyrgyzstan, Tajikistan, and Uzbekistan) are mostly transition countries where the mentioned elements tumultuously function.

Both the TTIP's parties and the SCO's members have sustained political support for economic integration. However, the fact that this will appears top-down instead of bottom-up leads to arbitrariness in decision-making process. This fact, mainly observed in the discussions among SCO members, constitutes a political risk for the future of the bloc.

The TTIP and the SCO in the Light of the Economic Conditions

As the Final Project Report, prepared by Center for Economic Policy Research (Francois et al., 2013) for European Commission, indicates through twenty good and services subheadings, the USA and the EU intensively trade wide varieties of similar goods and services with each other. In spite of the obstacles resulting from the presence of tariffs and non-tariff barriers, two parties exchange similar products in each industry and services group. In this respect the USA and the EU can be defined to be competitive economies.

However, it is difficult to say at first sight that the SCO is composed of competitive economies while considering six member countries. On the one hand, there is a dependency relation among members: (i) Russia and Kazakhstan are the important providers of energy commodities to China, Kyrgyzstan, Tajikistan, and Uzbekistan. (ii) The Central Asian members of the SCO suffer from being economic enclave and they need to use

Table 2. The TTIP and the SCO in the light of the Condition for Successful Economics Integration

Condition for Success of Integration		TTIP	SCO
Political Conditions	*Peace and stability*	Yes	Partially
	Sustained political will	Yes	Yes
Economic Conditions	*Competitive economies*	Yes	No
	Similarity in production	Mostly	No
	Trade creation larger than trade diversion	Yes	N/A
	Similar stage of development	Yes	No
	Sizes of countries	No if the EU's members are considered individually; Yes if the EU is considered as a whole.	No
	Pre-integration trade ties	Yes	No
	High pre-integration trade barriers	No if tariffs considered; Yes if NTB considered	Yes
	Low post-integration trade barriers	-	-
Institutional Conditions	*Optimum number of countries*	No if considered as two blocs	Yes
	Sharing of gains and losses	-	-
	Regional leader	No	China and Russia
	Commitment institutions	-	-
	Fair distribution of IGO institutions	-	-
Natural Conditions	*Geographical proximity*	No	Partially due to the surface of the region
	Cultural proximity	Partially	No
	Preferential treatment	Yes	No

transport roots of Russia and China to get access to alternative markets. (iii) Compared with the other members, Russia and China have comparative advantage, by far, in the industries (manufactured commodities, machinery and transport equipment) accounting for the largest part of the bilateral trade flows (Sorhun, 2014). This latter stresses on the presence of a dichotomy within the SCO and the weak capacity of the other members to cope with competitive pressures vis-à-vis the dominant economies like Russia and China.

An economic integration project offers two kinds of potential gain for its participating countries: static gain and dynamic gain. The former which is primarily linked to non-tariff barriers reveals when trade creation effect is greater than trade diversion effect. However, though some forms of integration such as FTA and CU are associated rather with static gains, instead a potential FTA to be launched by the TTIP aims to reveal dynamic gains.

Francois et al. (2013) evaluate according to different scenarios[9] the eventual impact of the TTIP's FTA on the markets of the cooperating countries and the markets of the non-member countries. A critical point of the report is about trade diverted from intra-EU trade: "the lower barrier to trade with the USA will cause a shift in relative costs leading to diverting some trade away from intra-EU partners towards new partners." (Francois et al., 2013). However, it forecasts that trade creation within the TTIP will be greater than the trade diversion of the two parties of the block with the rest of the world[10]. And the same report underlines that "the benefits for the EU and US would not be able at the expense of the rest of the world" (Francois et al., 2013).

In the absence of any estimation about the SCO's future FTA we are not able to express any opinion. However, studies measuring both trade creation effect and trade diversion effect of this FTA will be illuminating for policymakers and stimulating for researchers.

Whatever index is taken as indicator of development stage (Development Indicators by the World Bank, Human Development Index by the United Nations or Better Life Index by the OECD) it is undisputedly the case that the participating countries of the TTIP have similar patterns whereas the participating countries of the SCO have different patterns. However, the regional socioeconomic differences that the EU struggles to correct throughout regional policies may be a concern if it provokes immigration between two sides of the Atlantic. Even so, the past EU enlargement experiences strengthen the opposite opinion that inter-Atlantic immigration would be limited since immigration from relatively low income countries to higher income countries within the EU has been limited due to regional policies. When the difference in terms of standard of living, industrialization among the SCO participants, China, Russia, Kazakhstan on the one hand and Kirgizstan, Tajikistan, Uzbekistan on the other hand, is taken into consideration an eventual mass immigration seems inevitable. To give an example, intensive immigration flows from the Central Asia to the Russian Federation have already become actual concern. Considering the importance of the immigration issue, there is a need to scientifically evaluate the impact of a future FTA, launched by the SCO, on immigration flows as well as to question whether immigration flows threaten this FTA.

Another point about sage of development concerns the SCO, particularly. China with its dominant role in trade has already had monopoly position in the organization. And this poses an obstacle for the other partners to compete with China. Similarly, if each EU country acted individually and the USA enjoyed monopoly position within the bloc, the TTIP would be exposed to the same pressure. However, the fact that the EU acts as a unified bloc with its interlocutor will reduce the obstacles that the dominant position of the USA can create.

When the TTIP and the SCO are compared from the standpoint of competitiveness, development stage and production and trade structure, explicitly the new trade theory for the TTIP and the classic trade theory for the SCO presumptively appear to be theoretical grounds to analyze these two possible entities.

Having similar economic size is an important matter for the potential members of an economic bloc since empirical evidence suggest that the larger the economic size difference among cooperating countries is, the lower the potential gain from an eventual integration is; or the more unevenly this potential gain is distributed among members.

When the EU is considered as a whole the economic size of the two entities is similar. It can be expected to generate an extra gain for the TTIP partners from future integration. Nevertheless, the asymmetric economic size distribution, when the EU's member countries are considered individually, can lead to an uneven distribution of gain for the TTIP members from future integration. This can be dealt with from two perspectives: first, if home market effect is active within the TTIP the USA and a few EU members with greater local demand and production capacity would get a greater gain from future FTA. Second, empirical evidence (Snorrason, 2012) shows that the bigger gainers of economic integration are primarily small countries and then large countries while micro countries are disadvantageous in benefiting from integration.

The membership composition of the SCO indicates an asymmetric distribution of economic size. It can be expected that the SCO's future FTA will generate uneven distribution of gain from trade. Sorhun (2014) points out that China and Russia on the one side and Kazakhstan, Kyrgyzstan, Tajikistan, and Uzbekistan on the other side diverge from each other due to production and trade structure, geographical access to alternative markets. Thus "home market effect" and large-small-micro country issue matter for the SCO, too.

Conventionally the two sides of the Atlantic manage intensive trade flows for centuries. Besides, many European countries works with the USA under the same international organizations like World Trade Organization, International Labor Organization and are subject to the similar set of rules, adopted by the international organizations in question. In this respect, is can be explicitly said that the two parties of the TTIP have pre-integration trade ties. The Transatlantic trade volume, the share of transatlantic trade in the total trade of the USA and the EU and the low tariff rate between them are the major sign of this transatlantic economic relationship. If the tariffs are considered, the USA and the EU appear to be almost integrated. However, differently from conventional FTAs, the efforts for the TTIP mainly focus on the non-tariff barriers. Compared with the other regional blocs it can be clearly observed that the TTIP has relatively low pre-integration trade barriers.

The SCO has high pre-integration trade barriers due to the factors such as relatively high tariff rates, transportation infrastructure, weak economic relations in the past, geographical impediments etc. However, elimination or reduction of high pre-integration trade barriers will generate a great potential gain from trade in the SCO. As economic integration project the SCO is relatively more advantageous than the TTIP since it is easier to reduce tariffs (priority of the SCO) than to reduce non-tariff barriers (main objective of the TTIP). In other words, elimination (or a great reduction) of tariffs proportionally increases more inter-regional trade in the SCO than in the TTIP.

The TTIP and the SCO in the Light of the Institutional Conditions

Neither the TTIP nor the SCO have any institutional body that a regional bloc need for economic integration. However, both of them have intergovernmental institutions that pursue economic purposes.

Before starting negotiations the USA and the EU decided to establish the High Level Working Group on Jobs and Growth, composed of government experts, to better understand the impact of a Free Trade Agreement between the two economic powers on their economic prosperity. In this group the US Trade Representative and the EU Trade Commissioner represents the USA and the EU, respectively. As Leaders requested in 2011, the High Level Working Group has evaluated a wide range of scenarios for expanding transatlantic trade and investment: elimination or reduction of tariffs, elimination or reduction of non-tariff barriers, alignment of regulation and standards, enhancement of cooperation for the development of rules and principles on global issues of common concern. And it concluded that among different scenarios a comprehensive agreement covering all sectors would boost bilateral trade, growth, job creation on the both side of the Atlantic. It recommended launching negotiations. If the negotiations end up with an agreement the European Parliament in the name of the EU and the US Congress in the name of the USA will approve or reject it.

As for the SCO, The Heads of State Council (HSC) and The Heads of Government Council (HGC) together constitute the highest decision-making body in the SCO. Leaders of the SCO members meet once every year to take important decisions. Besides sessions of the HSC and the HGC there are also parallel meetings at ministerial level. The annual meeting of the ministers of Economy and Transportation is considered as governmental body while the annual session of the Business Consul is considered as non-governmental body. This later brings together the most influential members of the business communities of the six members with the goal of encouraging cooperation, establishing direct links and dialogue among business and financial circles and assisting multilateral projects determined in the Programme of Trade and Economic Cooperation in 2003. Since 2006 the Business Consul has focused on harmonization of national legislation in economic field. In this respect, the Consul prepares recommendations and proposals for the HSC and the HGC.

It is difficult for now to conclude which integration project (the TTIP or the SCO) is close to which institutional approach (minimalist or interventionist). However, when we consider the course of decisions taken until now we may have preliminary observation: First, the SCO's procedure evokes minimalist approach. Second, although the TTIP's procedure invokes rather minimalist approach there are two different institutional cultures between the USA and the EU coming from the NAFTA experience and the European integration. Historical experiences of the two blocs show that the USA inclines to minimalist approach while the EU inclines to interventionist approach.

Russia and China are together undisputed regional leaders within the SCO while due to the supranational structure of the EU, the leadership is assumed by neither the USA nor any member of the EU within the TTIP. However, it is observed that the USA and Germany on the side of the EU play an active role in the TTIP's works.

The TTIP and the SCO in the Light of the Natural Conditions

Although border-neighborhood give an advantage to an economic bloc, remoteness and ruggedness between production-centers, intra-bloc transportation connection and transportation infrastructure take precedence over it. If the TTIP and the SCO are compared in this respect, the USA and the EU seem to be more advantageous although they are not next-door neighbor. However, the impact of transportation issue and geographical obstacle on these two economic integration projects is worth an academic work.

Fundamentally economic integration projects aim to develop the natural inclination of potential partners to trade more each other. To do it cooperating countries expand intra-bloc preferential treatment through legislation and institutional body, reduction of tariff and non-tariff barriers, investment incentives. If this natural inclination that is linked to geographical, cultural, ideological proximity is not present in a group of countries an economic integration agreement has limited capacity to reveal their economic potential as a bloc through common rules and institutions.

Intra-bloc trade in relation to the bloc's total trade or total intra-regional trade in relation to the bloc's GDP shows the inclination of preferential treatment among cooperating. Historically the two sides of the Atlantic trade more intensively than they do with the other parts of the world. In 1012 the EU is the first trading partner of the US with 18% of trade in goods (Canada being the second and China the third). And the US is the EU's second largest trading partner with 14% of the EU's total trade in goods (China being the first). However, the relative share of bilateral trade has been in decline over the past decade[11]. This decline became one of the motivations for the TTIP.

On the other hand, revealing a very weak intra-bloc trade among the six members of the SCO at an average of 20% of the total trade, compared with the intra-regional trade of the NAFTA with 40% and the intra-regional trade of the EU with 60% between 2001 and 2012, Sorhun (2014) conclude that "the SCO's economies have not managed to concentrate their trade but they need to develop it within themselves".

CONCLUSION AND REMARKS

Regional economic integration issue is previously tackled in the concerned literature. Both partial models and general equilibrium models account for success or failure of the economic integration under some conditions. In this chapter, first, revising the principal studies the eighteen conditions for successful economic integration that are treated in the previous literature are specified. Of course, it is possible to increase or decrease the number of conditions depending on the body of revised literature. On the other hand, it is important to emphasize that there is no guarantee for an economic integration project to be successful even if the whole success conditions are completely satisfied by cooperating countries. And contrarily, satisfaction of fewer conditions may be sufficient for some blocs. Likewise, for different group of country, different success conditions may be prioritized. Second, these conditions are used to examine the potential FTAs that are expected to be found within the TTIP and the SCO. Main results are summarized under four categories as follows:

Both intergovernmental organizations are motivated for an economic integration. This motivation results primarily from the need of counterbalancing external pressure: Asian Giants for the USA and the EU; and vice versa. However, their motivations concretize in different perspective while decision making process matters: the TTIP's short experience shows that the USA and the EU implement bottom-up strategy due to the long democracy culture whereas the SCO implements top-down strategy due to socialist experience and transition period.

One of the economic gains for integrating markets results from being competitive with each other. In this respect it is expected that an integrated transatlantic market will yield extra gain since the USA and the EU have already approved capacity to cope with competitive pressure stemming from each other's markets. Contrarily, a dependency relation is present among the SCO's members due to difference in production structure, development stage and economic enclave of some members. In the case of the TTIP production and demand structures and development stages follow a similar path.

Compositions of the two blocs in terms of economic size are expected to generate an extra gain from integration. However, there is high probability that this gain will be more unevenly dispersed within the SCO than within the TTIP.

China and Russia will be the bigger gainers of the SCO's economic integration. As for the TTIP, whether the dispersion of this extra gain is mostly even or mostly uneven depends on whether EU members act as a whole or individually within the bloc. Acting as a union increases not only the probability that EU members will be beneficiary but also the probability that the TTIP project will be successful.

Taking into consideration the economic conditions together it is clear that the classical trade theory is assumedly more convenient to explain the SCO when the new trade theory is assumedly more convenient to explain the TTIP.

The two blocs have not established any institutional body but a kind of supreme board: The High Level Working Group of the TTIP and the Heads of State Council and the Heads of Government Council of the SCO. Preliminary observation shows that the SCO distinctly suggests minimalist approach while the TTIP to some extent suggests minimalist. The position of the TTIP results from the past experience of the USA (NAFTA) and the EU.

The two sides of the Atlantic have historically concentrated trade flows thanks to longstanding cultural, political, economic ties. Although the transatlantic bilateral trade in relation to the total trade of the USA and the EU has declined since last decade they are still natural partners. In 2013, the transatlantic trade share in the total trade of the TTIP region is about 32%. However, weak but increasing intraregional trade share in the total trade of the SCO (20%) shows the SCO has intraregional trade bias to reduce.

Some success conditions are ignored both because it is very early to deal with them and because there are not sufficiently data and academic study and report. For example, the issues like "the impact of the transport infrastructure on the intra bloc trade within the SCO", "the impact of the asymmetric economic size distribution on the potential gain from the SCO's integration" and "the trade creation and trade diversion effect of the potential FTA of the SCO" are worth studying.

REFERENCES

Aris, S. (2011). *Eurasian regionalism: The Shanghai cooperation organization*. London, UK: Palgrave Macmillan. doi:10.1057/9780230307643

Bagwell, K., & Staiger, R. W. (2002). *The economics of the world trading system*. Cambridge, MA: MIT Press.

Balassa, B. (1961). *The theory of economic integration*. London: Allew and Unwin.

Balassa, B. (1965). *Economic development and integration*. Mexico: Centro De Estudios Monetario Latinoamericanos.

Balassa, B. (1986). The determinants of intra-industry specialization in United States trade. *Oxford Economic Papers*, *38*, 220–233.

Balassa, B., & Bauwens, L. (1987). Intra-industry specialization in a multi-country and multi-industry framework. *The Economic Journal*, *97*(388), 923–939. doi:10.2307/2233080

Casella, P. B. (2010). The common market of the south (MERCOSUR): Models and qualitative mutations for consolidating an integrated economic area. *Annual Survey of International & Comparative Law*. *9*(1), Article 2. Retrieved Avril 8, 2014, from http://digitalcommons.law.ggu.edu/cgi/viewcontent.cgi?article=1070&context=annlsurvey

Commission, E. U. (2013). *Impact assessment report on the future of EU-US trade relation*. Commission Staff Working Document, 12.3.2013, SWD(2013), Strasbourg. Retrieved February 12 2014 from http://trade.ec.europa.eu/doclib/docs/2013/march/tradoc_150759.pdf

Corden, M. (1972). Economies of scale and customs union theory. *Journal of Political Economy*, *80*(3), 465–475. doi:10.1086/259899

Corden, M. (1976). Customs unions theory and the non-uniformity of tariffs. *Journal of International Economics*, *6*(1), 99–106. doi:10.1016/0022-1996(76)90026-X

Davis, D. R., & Weinstein, D. E. (2003). Market access, economic geography and comparative advantage: An empirical test. *Journal of International Economics*, *59*(1), 1–23. doi:10.1016/S0022-1996(02)00088-0

Duina, F. (2006). *The social construction of free trade: The European Union, NAFTA, and MERCOSUR*. Princeton, NJ: Princeton University Press.

Edblad, J. (1996). *The political economy of regional integration in developing countries.* CERUM-Centre for Regional Science Working Paper No. 3/1996. Retrieved February 10 2014 from http://www.diva-portal.org/smash/get/diva2:227410/FULLTEXT01.pdf

Francois, J., Manchin, M., Norberg, H., Pindyuk, O., & Tomberger, P. (2013). *Reducing transatlantic barriers to trade and investment: an economic assessment.* London: Center for Economic Policy Research. Retrieved March 29 2014 from http://trade.ec.europa.eu/doclib/docs/2013/march/tradoc_150737.pdf

Frank, A. G. (1998). *ReOrient: Global economy in the Asian age*. Berkeley, CA: University of California Press.

Gerber, J. (2013). International economics. Prentice Hall.

Hamilton, D. S., & Quinlan, J. P. (2013). *The transatlantic economy 2013 annual survey of jobs, trade and investment between the United States and Europe.* Center for Transatlantic Relations and Transatlantic Business Consul, Washington, D.C., USA. Retrieved April 14 2014 from http://transatlantic.sais-jhu.edu/publications/books/Transatlantic_Economy_2013/TE2013%20volume%201.pdf

Helpman, E. (1981). International trade in the presence of product differentiation, economies of scale and monopolistic competition: A Chamberlin-Heckscher-Ohlin approach. *Journal of International Economics*, *11*(3), 305–340. doi:10.1016/0022-1996(81)90001-5

Horvat, B. (1999). *The theory of international trade: An alternative approach.* London, UK: Palgrave Macmillan. doi:10.1057/9780333983386

Johnson, H. G. (1962). *The economic theory of customs unions in money, trade and economic growth.* London: George Allen and Unwin.

Jovanović, M. N. (2005). *The economics of European integration: Limits and prospects.* Edward Elgar Pub.

Krugman, P. R. (1980). Scale economies, product differentiation, and the pattern of trade. *The American Economic Review*, *70*(5), 950–959.

Kurugman, P. R. (1979). Increasing returns, monopolistic competition and international trade. *Journal of International Economics*, *9*(4), 469–479. doi:10.1016/0022-1996(79)90017-5

Lancaster, K. (1980). Intra-industry trade under perfect monopolistic competition. *Journal of International Economics*, *10*(2), 151–175. doi:10.1016/0022-1996(80)90052-5

Leistner, E. (1997). Regional cooperation in Sub-Saharan Africa. *Africa Insight*, *27*(2), 112–123.

Linder, S. B. (1961). *An essay on trade and transformation*. Stockholm: Almqvist and Wiksell.

Lipsey, R. G. (1957). The theory of customs unions: Trade diversion and welfare. *Economica*, *24*(93), 40–46. doi:10.2307/2551626

Lipsey, T. G. (1970). *The theory of customs unions: A general equilibrium analysis*. London, UK: Weidenfeld & Nicolson.

Mattli, W. (1999). *The logic of regional integration: Europe and beyond*. Cambridge, UK: Cambridge University Press. doi:10.1017/CBO9780511756238

McCarty, D. M. (2006). *International economic integration in historical perspective*. New York, NY: Routladge.

McMillan, J., & McCann, E. (1981). Welfare effects in customs unions. *The Economic Journal*, *91*(363), 697–703. doi:10.2307/2232833

Meade, J. E. (1955). *The theory of customs unions*. Amsterdam: North Holland.

Mundell, R. A. (1964). Tariff preferences and the terms of trade. *The Manchester School of Economic and Social Studies*, *32*(1), 1–13. doi:10.1111/j.1467-9957.1964.tb01029.x

Robson, P. (2003). *The economics of international integration*. London: Routledge.

Rooyen, C. (1998). Regional integration as a development strategy: The case of the SADC. *Africa Insight*, *28*, 125–132.

Salvatore, D. (2009). *International economics* (10th ed.). London, UK: Wiley.

Simms, R., & Simms, E. (2006). *The building block of successful regional integration: Lessons for the CSME from other regional integration schemes*. Retrieved March 15 2014 from http://sta.uwi.edu/conferences/salises/documents/Simms%20R%20-%20Simms%20E.pdf

Snorrason, S. T. (2012). *Asymmetric economic integration: Size characteristics of economies, trade cost and welfare*. Berlin: Physca-Verlag. doi:10.1007/978-3-7908-2861-0

Sorhun, E. (2014). What kind of trade integration would the SCO's further FTA be? In H. Dincer & U. Hacioglu (Eds.), *Globalization and government in the international political economy* (pp. 63–74). Hershey, PA: IGI-Global. doi:10.4018/978-1-4666-4639-1.ch005

Strange, S. (1995). Political economy and international relations. In K. Booth & S. Smith (Eds.), *International relations theory today* (pp. 154–174). Cambridge, MA: Polity Press.

Vanek, J. (1965). *General equilibrium of international discrimination: The case of customs unions*. Cambridge, MA: Harvard University Press.

Viner, J. (1950). *The customs union issue*. New York, NY: Carnegie Endowment for International Peace.

KEY TERMS AND DEFINITIONS

EU: The European Union.

FTA: Free Trade Area.

SCO: The Shanghai Cooperation Organization.

TTIP: The Transatlantic Trade and Investment Partnership.

ENDNOTES

1 See McCarty, D.M. (2006), "International Economic Integration in Historical Perspective", Routladge, New York.

2 Preferential trade arrangements (PTA) which represent the form of loose economic integration whereby participating countries agree to reduce import duties on the mutual trade (arrangements between imperial centers and their former colonial dependencies). Since the General Agreement on Tariffs and Trade (GATT) rules do not authorize PTAs this kind of integration is excluded from the forms of integration.

3 However, a monetary union may be established solely: The member-countries, in addition to satisfying the requirements of an economic union, adopt a common currency, as well as create and use a common, supranational central bank. For example, African Financial Community (*Communité Financière d'Afrique*) of which the members have colonial ties with France was a currency union with a money unit pegged to French franc until 1999 when Euro replaced franc. East Caribbean Currency Union is a valid example for monetary union.

4 "An allocation of resource is said to be Pareto optimal if there does not exist another feasible allocation in which some agents would be better off (in a welfare sense) and no agents worse off. Pareto optimality is achieved exclusively under free trade that other cases where there are distortions – e.g. tariffs, subsidies, taxes, monopolies etc. – are sub-optimal." (Snorrason, 2012).

5 This rational lies behind the GATT rules which permit the formation of a regional trading bloc such as FTA, CU. However, the same set of rules does not allow any form of regional integration leading international discrimination. GATT XXIV article states that a group of countries may form a trading bloc by reducing barriers in the group, is subject to several requirements: First, substantially all barriers among members must be removed. Second, trade barriers against non-members are not made more restrictive than before the formation of the trading bloc. The new external tariffs must be no more than the weighted average of the pre-integration tariffs. Third, the process of the formation of a regional bloc and along with the implementations of the defined rules must not exceed ten years.

6 Empirical investigation by Davis and Weinstein (2003) found support for the existence of home market effects, as well as for the role and importance of increasing returns in determining the production structure for the OECD countries.

7 For Duina, the NAFTA with less voluminous laws and regulations adopted minimalist approach while the EU and MECOSUR with more voluminous laws and regulations that standardize every aspect of political and economic interaction among members adopted interventionist approach. However, although less costly than the interventionist approach the minimalist approach makes it more difficult for member countries and firms to compete with each other in a greater market since they are not subject to the same set of homogenized regional laws. The presence of less written body of regulation under the minimalist approach generates uncertainties about economic interactions among members and involves potential risks for conflicts between States or between firms.

8 The European Parliament Commission Staff Working Document (2013) noted that "In general, both the USA and the EU have low tariffs on goods with simple average MFN tariff rates of 5,2% and 3,5%. Trade-weighted tariff protection in the USA for the EU is estimated at 2,1, while the trade-weighted

tariff rate for exports to the EU is estimated at 2,8%."

9 Narrow FTA Scenario evaluates a 98% reduction of tariffs, a 10% reduction of NTBs on services and a 25% reduction of NTB on procurement market, separately. Less ambitious scenario evaluates a 98% reduction of tariffs, a 10% reduction of NTBs on goods and services, a 25% reduction on procurement market. And ambitious scenario evaluates total elimination of tariffs, a 25% reduction of NTBs on goods and services, a 50% reduction of NTBs on procurement market.

10 According to the report (on the 2027 benchmark basis), only tariff reduction will lead to 6.6% increase of EU exports to the USA and to a 12.4% increase of US exports to the EU. And, if comprehensive scenario becomes fact, then the total exports from the EU to the USA are estimated to increase by 16.16% in the less ambitious scenario and 28.03% in the ambitious scenario, respectively while the total exports from the USA to the EU are estimated to increase by 23.20% in the less ambitious scenario and by 36.57% in the ambitious scenario. On the other hand, as for the estimated changes in the EU's total external trade (out of the USA) with the rest of the world, only tariff reduction will cause total imports and exports of the EU to increase by 1.18% and 1.00%, respectively. And overall imports and exports are both estimated to increase by 3.37% and 5.11% in the less ambitious and ambitious scenarios, respectively. As for the estimated changes in the US's total external trade (out of the EU) with the rest of the world, only tariff reduction will lead US imports and exports to increase by 1.91% and 1.13%, respectively. And overall imports and exports are both estimated to increase by 4.75% and 8.02% in the less ambitious and ambitious scenarios, respectively.

11 According to the EU Commission (2013) assessment report "This relative decline is particularly sharp when looking at EU trade in goods. Between 2000 and 2011, EU exports of goods to the world increased by 7.6%. But EU exports to the US only grew by 1%. As a result, the share of the US in total EU exports declined from 28% in 2000 to 17% in 2011. In the period from 2000-2011, the EU exports to the US and the US exports to the EU have stagnated in absolute terms. This stands in sharp contrast with the significant increase of EU and US exports to China over the same period. The share of transatlantic trade is slowly diminishing, due to the high growth in emerging economies like China, Brazil and India. The recent financial and economic crisis has accelerated this trend." "A number of factors have contributed to the stagnation and relative decline in trade between the EU and the US: (1) the EU's 2004 and 2007 enlargements as well as the EU's Neighborhood Policy have boosted trade with the neighboring regions. (2) the North American Free Trade Agreement (NAFTA), which entered into force 1994, promoted stronger trade linkages between the US, Canada and Mexico. (3) The major driver is obviously the rapid rise of emerging market economies in developing countries, particularly China. In the last decade, the emerging economies of Asia have been growing faster than the EU and the US".

Chapter 21
Understanding The Political Economy of Novel Metropolitan Governance Schemes of Turkish Local Management System:
An Elaboration of Impact of Regionalism and Globalization

Buğra Özer
Celal Bayar University, Turkey

Hakan Ay
Dokuz Eylül University, Turkey

Mehmet Emin Merter
Celal Bayar University, Turkey

ABSTRACT

This chapter tackles with different dimensions the new brave world of Turkish metropolitan policymaking within the context of Law No: 6360, namely the administrative aspects, the public financial characteristics, along with the political dimensions. The problematization of the work, simply, follows how regionalism and globalization have come and interacted to render such a reform in Turkish local management units, under the rule of the Justice and Development Party (JDP-Adalet ve Kalkınma Partisi). The effort shall also tackle the philosophy and the rationale of the new system in reference to regionalism and globalization with the need to underline the ramifications of the implementation of the new scheme in Turkey.

DOI: 10.4018/978-1-4666-7308-3.ch021

LOCAL GOVERNANCE AND METROPOLITAN POLICY PROCESSES IN POST-1980s TURKEY: INTRODUCTORY REMARKS

Local governance in Turkey has been a sine *quo non* item of systematic reform and retrenchment since the heydays of the Republic promulgated in 1923. Yet, in a country characterized by a strong center with tutelage powers over the periphery[1](Eryılmaz, 2011, 292; Eryılmaz, 1992), and strong state tradition inherent (Heper, 1985; Heper and Keyman, 1992), the local governance policy making has been less than developed and the issue gets to be more and more complicated in terms of her historical experience left behind when compared with her Western counterparts (Öner, 2006). Given the deficits of the Turkish politico-economic transformation, characterized by a problematic urban transformation since the early 1950's the metropolitan governance, has been an object of attention for the Turkish policy-makers (Eryılmaz, 1997).[2] The arduous attempts to restructure and to retrench the Turkish landscape for governance of urban regions since the early 1980s, entered a new phase, and paved a way to rethink urban governance in a political economic setting struggling with different financial, political and economic problems (For elaborations from such a perpective see Ökmen and Parlak, 2009; for a constitutional law perspective see Bozlağan, 2012).

Indeed, faced with the need to respond to the overhaul of global economic and political systems and the obligation to integrate the Turkish political-economic setting to the global web of international capitalist system (Ramazanoğlu 1985), Turkish governments responded to the challenges in regard to metropolitan governance with a zealous project of transformation and restructuring. In such respect, the neoliberal restructuring and retrenchment policies which came to be implemented since the late 1970s Turkey gained a new momentum for the prospects of Turkish metropolitan policy making along which an overall transformation of political economic transformation was running under the auspices of the Motherland Party's (*Anavatan Partisi*) coming into office in the aftermath of the introduction of multi-party politics in 1983 (Ökmen and Parlak, 2009, 292-293).

The 1982 Constitution, prepared under the shadow of a military takeover, took the primary step for a constitutional arrangement for the very existence of metropolitan governance with the 127th Article of the Constitution stipulating that specific administrative arrangements could be realized for metropolitan zone to deal with the problems of urban economic growth given the constraints of administrative priorities (Ökmen and Parlak, 2013, 210). However, the cadre, behind the 1982 Constitution, was far away of locating the governance-based democratic notion of local governance system. The whole issue of establishing metropolitan governance schemes was quite technical, rather than being motivated to deal with the shortcuts in regard to participation and multi-actors involvement in processes. In a new age of depoliticization throughout the 1980s and 1990s, metropolitan governance issues were solely evaluated from a managerial perspective. Along with the values of the Zeitgeist of the 1980s, Erkip describes the system as such, (2000, 374), until the late 1990s the Turkish metropolitan system was based on "(...) a two-tier system with greater and district municipalities since 1984" as an outcome of governments striving to have a decentralization perspective which intended to attain a formidable budget increases. As Erkip again (2000, 374) carefully notes in relation to the experiences of Turkish metropolitan policy making until the 2000s: "Although it seemed to be a managerial effort to provide services more efficiently, the performance has been disappointing as the service responsibilities were shared between greater and district municipalities on the basis of service size, rather than the characteristics of the services and the citizens."

Despite the delays in restructuring processes within Turkish politico-economic setting, extending from the mid-1980s to the late 1990s, Turkish metropolitan policy-making came to handle different problems in a setting of reform characterized by the use of market-type mechanisms, organizational restructuring, and a focus on performance, all being essential components of New Public Management (NPM)-(for a discussion on the Turkish experience in NPM see Sözen and Shaw, 2002, Sözen, 2012). Indisputedly, privatization and liberalization became the motto of the day that came to be more and more pronounced by the triumph of the Justice and Development Party in 2002.

It was a brave new era, yet, with challenges to be confronted as Göymen (2006, 264) correctly identifies the actors and other dynamics of local governance in Turkey as such "The structural changes in the economy, the transition from an autarkic, closed economy to a market-oriented one open to international competition created and/or reinforced the position of new actors. These new actors emphasized efficiency/effectiveness; questioned size and role of the state; and demanded a new societal division of labor, with a smaller, more efficient state, and enhanced role for private sector and civil society. These demands not only reinforced the dynamics of local governance in general but also provided support for local government bodies (representing all colors of politics) wishing to be freed from the tutelage of central government."

The JDP handling the unfinished project of Turkish neoliberalism added up different autonomous regulatory bodies onto the present body of regulatory organizations that emerged in the mid-1990s with outsourcing of public service delivery field on an extensive array of fields. Moreover, managerial types of reforms were added onto the list by means of The Law (No. 5018) on Public Financial Management and Control (Kamu Mali Yönetimi ve Kontrol Kanunu, KMYKK) in 2003, that introduced "strategic plans and performance-based budgeting with the aim of ensuring economic, efficient and effective use of the resources and increasing fiscal transparency and accountability." (Sözen, 2012,169)

Additionally, decentralization came to be a major theme in metropolitan policy making to deal with the need "to be responsive to the needs of the citizens." As Sözen (2012,169) carefully remarks in regard to the making of the restructuring of Turkish local governance scheme along with the perquisites of New Public Management. "In this context, the former laws regulating local governments were totally changed and the duties, responsibilities and powers of local governments were expanded with the Law (No. 5302) on Provincial Special Administration, and the Law (No. 5393) on Municipalities, Law (No. 5216) on Greater City Municipalities and the Law (No. 5355) on Local Government Unions. The new laws, approved in the middle of 2000s, narrowed the administrative tutelage control of the central government on local governments and also included provisions providing participatory mechanisms for local community. Besides, local government bodies are also granted the legal authority for outsourcing almost every service in their spectrum of tasks."

Besides, JDP governments supported the making of this new public governance systematic with a second-tier of NPM reforms namely by means of governance related schemes. In such respect, legislations such as Ethics Committee for Civil Servants in 2004 with the Law (Number. 5176) aiming to set up standards for the ethical conduct of government employees; the Law on the Right to Information (*Bilgi Edinme Hakkı Kanunu,* BEHK) in 2003 calibrating to increase public trust of citizens in governmental schemes and to inform people on government activities and the Law (Number 5548) on Public Inspection

Authority in 2006, which set up a public inspection body to investigate the actions of both local and central government's action on the basis of public reviews and complaints (Parlak and Sobacı, 2012, 375-379).

In addition to the steps mentioned above, in terms of local democratic governance City Councils were introduced with in 2005 by the Law Number. 5393 on Municipalities (art. 76) (Sözen 2012, 169-170; Parlak and Sobacı, 2012, 375-379). These newly created bodies were geared to increase local participation at each and every step, henceforth creating opportunities for a multi-actor approach in terms of both involvement and participation. Moreover Constitution Amendments in 2001, 2004 and 2010 formed a new basis for a more formidable human rights system that would render universal standards for Turkey.

Given the numerous restructuring of Turkish metropolitan policy making in the aftermath of the 1980 coup d'état as stated above, the transformation of governmental arrangements for central and local governments has been more than colossal. Yet, Legislation Number 6360signified a new era how governments redefined the scaling of important metropolitan centers on a whole basis of provincial basis, henceforth, taking the step to define the Turkish metropolitan policy on the basis of regions. Indeed, the legislation 6360 has been a major step in tackling with those tendencies shaping metropolitan policy making that aims to balance two axes, namely, the scaling at which local service- delivery shall be carried out effectively and efficiently on the one hand and the scale whereby local democratization shall be put into practice on the other. This poses a quiet perplexing task which this work will present an overview of globalization and new regionalism in relation to local government and metropolitan policy making, followed by a discussion of Legislation Number 6360. Finally, the attempt will render a section of concluding remarks where Turkey will go from here after the implementation of the new scheme

UNDERSTANDING THE IMPACT OF GLOBALIZATION AND NEW REGIONALISM ON METROPOLITAN POLICY MAKING: A THEORATICAL OVERVIEW

To be able to have a good reading of transformation of local governance schemes, two terms will be of quintessential importance, namely globalization and new regionalism As for globalization, throughout the past quarter of the last century, a wide array of overwhelming changes emerged on social, political economic levels (Ökmen and Parlak, 2009). These changes influenced the whole set of global political economic setting integrating new structures and processes in a rapid pace. From such a perspective globalization became an omnipotent and omnipresent force as fundamental determinant, beacon; direction and depth of changes. Henceforth, in a process of transformation of industrial societies to information societies, the concept-'State'-centric discussions and developments affected the administrative and managerial approaches, organizations, principles, roles of organizations in a substantial and radical way (Ökmen and Özer, 2007, 20-23; Parlak and Sobacı, 2012, 215-223). The rapid and effective impact of such transformation came to be concrete and visible at how public administrations and local administrations operate and interact with each other.

In more concrete terms, newly emerging universal understandings and rationales directly affected local governments as dispensable elements of democratic governance and local service delivery leading to vital changes and breaks in relation to management rationales and methods of public service delivery. The rapid and effective impact of such transformation was concrete and visible at how public administrations and local administrations handled and defined their modus vivendi. Newly emerging universal understandings and rationales directly affected local governments as in dispensable elements of democratic governance and local services delivery, which paved the way to overwhelming changes and breaks in relation to management rationales and methods of public service delivery (Parlak and Sobacı, 2012, 223-231).

NPM became a systematic for all operations for public delivery of social services and governmental structuring and operations. The basic idea behind these novel application was simple by means of NPM approaches market oriented management of the public sector will lead to greater cost-efficiency for governments, without having negative side-effects on other objectives and considerations. In such regard, not only convergence of economic and political systems and their policies but also of different sets of countries' political and economic systems and their respective policies came onto stakes, thereby converging social and political agendas and policies globally (See for a more thorough and elaborate account on the link between globalization and public administration, refer to Ökmen and Parlak, 2009, Chapter III).

One can witness the globalization of social values such as development of human rights, democratization of state and society relationships and the empowerment of civil society elements. This grand transformation took place as a result of societal demands for more human rights and democratization, calling for an overall review of government functions bringing for inevitable changes at political and social actions led by governments (Ökmen and Parlak,2009, Chapter III) Localization defined as a reaction in relation local units' needs to define themselves and forms new dimensions for localities has given birth to regionalization to deal with negative externalities and repercussions of globalization in a stronger and a more effective way. Globalization affected the organizational structures and functioning bringing forth radical breaks at representative government schemes and governing rationales. National, regional and global scale changes discussed so far called for the remaking of national state understanding and international system (Parlak and Sobacı, 2012, 216).

In a process whereby globalization and localization take place simultaneously and paradoxically, the very tension transformed the structure of nation state. In such regard, monolithic and centralized government structures were substituted by new organizations reproducing and integrating local identities based on historical, cultural and physical traits, thereby contributing to a multi-level political systematic combining local, national and supranational components of policymaking (Ökmen and Özer, 2007, 26-39).

Localization accompanied by globalization changed the classical understanding of democracy, pushing a mosaic democracy leaving the mass-based democracies on the way to information societies. Changing our assumptions in regard to classical democracy, the process subjugated most societal centers of power to change with radical changes of communication means and political relation patterns. In one sense tan evolution was in progress from mass based democracy as a by-product of industrial societies (representative democracy) to a more pluralistic democratic scheme (Parlak and Ökmen, 2009, Chapter III).

Localization of democratization processes and administration and organization has been an outstanding characteristics of the globalization processes contributing to the making of information societies. Transforming the centralization and representative democracy based structure of industrial societies, globalization leads to a decentralized, pluralistic and participatory social and political system with more limitations on the central governments 'jurisdictions and more powers granted to the local management bodies by means of decentralization (Ökmen and Özer, 2007,25-28).

The term 'subsidiarity' has been a remedy to deal with the drawbacks of centralization and to handle the needs of localization tendencies. In such regard, there has been an international consensus on the need to empowerment and development of local administrations. Developments on the way to empowerment of local administrations, more autonomies granted to the units, the minimization of centralization on local managements have found their ways and places on internationally signed agreements and constitutions globally speaking. In relation to a basic concept in regard to globalization and localization dynamic the term subsidiarity is backed by the rationale that the related cases are limited by the rule that a matter ought to be handled by the smallest, lowest, or least centralized authority capable of addressing that matter effectively when centralized authorities are far from dealing with it. .Beyond being a simple organizing principle, the term is applied to first individual and society and at lateral stages to the institutions and society, requiring the transfer of resources of individuals to societies (Parlak and Ökmen, 2009, Chapter III).

As the study attempts to develop a reading of macro perspective of local governance and metropolitan policy making within a general framework of globalization, we will link the changes and reform movements within metropolitan policy making to the perspective of 'New Regionalism." New Regionalism calls for comprehending the transformation of metropolitan policy making by means of the arguments that metropolitan policy with a notion of a government based on metropolitan units would be better endowed with tools to deal with local, national and supranational elements relative to those disjointed government units.

New regionalism therefore becomes and approach which multi-layer politics defines the cities and/or metropolitan as competitive units leaving room for the interaction both local and national state actors and non-state actors i.e. multinational corporations, non-governmental organizations, and other interested social groups. Suffice it to say that both of these actors collaborate with each other by means of national and transnational coalitions through the creation of formal and information partnerships with each other. From the perspective of new regionalism it is rather better to say different partners and different stake holders will be likely to have different preferences thereby demonstrating sectoral selectivity (Loewendahl-Ertugal, 2004;4;Sarkar, 2009)

The new regionalism depicts peculiarities such that as a process it is inclusive of more spontaneities as a result of tendencies of regions' characteristics and problems. In such regard, new regionalism is argued to be bestowed with capacities to deal with the question of complexity. Different problems maybe emergent at different levels of analyses starting from the inmal structures of regions defined within the organization and structure of nation state, ethnically defined subgroups and transnational micro regions. Regional identity becomes of paramount importance with emphasis on market-based and open economies. (Hettne and Soderbaum, 2007, Sarkar 2009).

New regionalism from the perspective of metropolitan policy making emerges as reaction to two basic strands of literature, first being the hierarchical approach whose academic roots can be traced back to the logic of economies of scale and second being the public choice approach that considered metropolitan policy making as the entity of a multi-jurisdictional area with a need for rational organization. In such regard, the hierarchical approach calls for the suggestion that institutional boundaries match the scale of functional metropolitan territory (Kübler, 2012;11).

Therefore, Kübler (2012,11) explains the dynamics of the hierarchical approach as follows: "Such consolidation can be achieved, it is argued, through the annexation of suburbs by core-cities, city-county consolidation (in the American context), or by the creation of metropolitan governments, i.e., two-tier institutions with extensive competencies and autonomy. Metropolitan reformers claim that a more centralized and integrated governing system would reduce social segregation within metropolitan areas, allow to address the spatial mismatch of expenditure needs and fiscal capacities, as well as ensure the supply of metropolitan-wide policies designed to enhance equity and promote economic growth."

The second approach is the public choice approach that is built on the Tiebout's renowned theory of voting with their feet which suggest that autonomous local constituencies create competition bringing forth meeting an effective match of service demands and a better level of efficacy. The public choice school will lay emphasis on lower taxes with better services along with responsiveness rendered for the citizens.

Self-governance, accordingly, with strong sense of localities will be better endowed with means to negotiate on their differences in terms of conflicts. While pursuing after efficiency in public delivery of social services, they will inevitably to foster collaboration with their partners therefore sustain area-wide coordination. In the words of Kübler (2012, 12) concrete prescription of public choice school will materialize as such: "The prescriptive implications of the public choice perspective are straightforward: it makes a strong case for institutional fragmentation – rather than consolidation - as well as for self-governance by autonomous localities - rather than centralized government."

New Regionalism emphasized the role of negotiation of multi-layer actors relative to hierarchic decision making and competition as the previous strands of literature drew attention. Voluntary cooperation and joint decision systems become important "means to coordinate policy-making across state levels in a context of increasing interdependencies." (Kübler, 2012, 13) On the assumption that design of territorial institutions relates matching actors to produce policies that will enhance international competitiveness, voluntary cooperation between autonomous localities become of paramount importance (Savitch and Vogler, 2000; Savage and Vogler, 2009).

The given theoretical discussions regarding the changes in metropolitan policy making bring up an important question in regard to scaling. The very raison d'étre of local governance has been the need of localities for the functional effectiveness which is inclusive of sustainability of both effectiveness and efficiency of local service delivery and the need for democracy resting upon concepts of participation and representation of local interests which have come to cover terms like freedoms, autonomy and redistribution. The functional effectiveness and the democracy as two planes of foundations for the making of local governance converge at a point of scale which poses itself as an important problem for the metropolitan policy making. In such regard, when magnitude of scale for local governance gets larger and bigger, it will be more feasible to attain functional effectiveness whereas such a proposal of magnitude of scale will diminish the chances of getting a better level of democratic attainment (Eryılmaz, 2011;171-176 and İzci and Turan, 2013,120).

As the scale of local governance gets smaller, prospects for attainment of governance and democratic schemes will ameliorate, yet, leading to the inefficacies and an ineffective resultant outcome for the question of functional effectiveness. In such regard, when the whole question of magnitude of scale for local governance boils down to which one is a better alternative, New Regional and Regional Approaches claim and call for a much broad and bigger scale in which regions defined on a broad geographical space will be better suiting with localities and territorial local governing bodies rather than a state-led process.

Once again returning to the main argumentation of New Regional approach as Loewendahl-Ertugal (2004, 4) states: "the regional level is the best strategic level at which to organize networks and build linkages between firms, arrange enterprise support facilities, enhance trust, attract inward investment, and provide training with a view to the strategic positioning of the regional economy within the global economy." In contrast, Regional Cities approach argues that by means of larger magnitude of scale it will be possible to call off the distinction between the rural and urban therefore uniting the whole under the metropolitan region while the Public Choice School will propose a much more fragmented magnitude of scale leaving more rooms for competition among localities (İzci and Turan, 2013, 121).

A DISCUSSION OF LEGISLATION NUMBER 6360 ON A BASIS OF NEO-REGIONALISM AND GLOBALIZATION

With the advent of the legislation dated December 6th 2012 Number 6360 on the Establishment of Thirteen Metropolitan Municipalities in Thirteen Provinces and Twenty-six Districts and Amending Certain Laws and Decree-laws, the effectiveness and productive public services once again has been a reference point for the revision of the delimitation of the boundaries of metropolitan municipalities. The legislation's preamble also clearly stated that the strengthening of local democracy at the local level, happens to be a major theme in the study while the efficiency of local services and provision of better services were accepted to be accompanying vales (Ökmen and Parlak, 2013, 312-320).

The new legislation converted 14 municipalities thereby adding onto the existing 16 metropolitan municipalities existing until 2012, to metropolitan municipalities' state and provincial borders were declared as the borders of metropolitan municipalities which became the spatial dimensions of the jurisdiction of novel metropolitan zones. (İzci and Turan, 2013)Yet the legal arrangement resorted to the abolishment of a great multitude of neighborhoods and villages and the administrative units in question were converted into districts. The legislation foresaw substantial increases in the financial resources allocated to metropolitan units. It has been rather in this legislation that Special Provincial Administrations (SPAs) based on the French administrative system became history throughout the metropolitan (For a brief history on the SPAs see Aytaç, 1995, Başsoy 1995; Dedeoğlu, 1997); and while the whole array tasks carried out by the SPAs were transferred to metropolitan governance bodies.

As stated earlier, one of the most important objective of the legislation as stated by the Law strengthening of local democracy was underlined while the legislation italicized an integral component to realize the objective by means of institutionalizing an effective local governance structuring (İzci and Turan, 2013, 119). A coordinating body known as the Department of Monitoring Investment and Coordination under the Governor was also created in metropolitan governance and policy making to facilitate the following tasks: "to efficiently provide, monitor and coordinate the investment and services of the public institutions and organizations, coordinate and conduct the emergency calls, disasters and emergency aid services, to provide the publicity of the province, to provide and coordinate the investments which the central administration will make in province when required, to provide the services of representation, ceremony, reward and protocol, to guide and inspect the public institutions and organizations in the province ." (T.C. Avrupa Birliği Bakanlığı, 2013, 23)

The perspective brought about by the Legislation Number 6360 is argued by many scholars including Keleş(2012) and Eke(1982) may be deemed to presenting a historical continuity in terms of policies advocated by Turkish government in the aftermath of 1980 coup d'état. Keleş's argument (2012) follows that central governments happened to be the main decision makers of determination of the magnitude of scale for metropolitan governance mechanism without resorting to a governance-based scheme with the localities. In such regard, the initiative of central governments upon shaping the scaling of metropolitan management units became a preferred action method rather than collaboration of smaller units to determine the scale of certain local services delivered in metropolitan regions materializing of localities unions. Indeed, the Legislation Number 6360 by means of defining the scale on a broad geographical basis in the dimensions of provincial borders delegated all essential strategic functions such as management, training to the upper tier of local governance scheme while rendering all other infra-structure services to a lower echelon of local governance units under the tutelage of the higher echelon of the system.

It may be argued that this new scheme of metropolitan governance by means of unifying a whole set of local management and representative bodies on the basis of regions on a permanent basis has been backed by new regional concerns. In other words, the JDP governments deemed it necessary that provincial borders be defined as economic regions to foster economic growth where international competitiveness will be of the basic reference with other measures to foster governance based schemes. Yet, the basic rationale of legislation has been calibrated to deal with the functional effectiveness targeting the attainment of efficiency and effectiveness of local service delivery at each and every level (İzci and Turan, 2012)

Here, it must be once again remarked, that determination of the scale for the new metropolitan governance schemes has been more than problematic. In more concrete terms, the legislators took the population of provinces as an integral criterion for the establishment of new metropolitan units. Still, when viewed from the historical experience of post-1980s Turkish metropolitan policy making, it was, again, yet, the decision of central governments to declare the metropolitan scale on the condition that a province should have at least two sub-provinces within the borders of the central provincial municipality borders rather than population as portrayed in the Legislation Number 3030 passed in 1982. It was in the lateral years that economic growth considerations along with the creation of artificial sub provinces came to play more important role in the making of metropolitan zones as seen in the conversion of Gaziantep Konya, Adana, and Bursa municipalities into metropolitan bodies of governance. In 1990s, central government turned to the creation of lower echelon municipalities within metropolitan governance schemes by decrees in the force laws as experienced in the cases of Mersin, Eskisehir, Diyarbakır, Antalya, Samsun, İzmit and Erzurum in 1993 (Ökmen and Parlak, 2013, 281-297).

The Legislation Number 5216 in 2004 of metropolitan governance opted for more specific criteria for the establishment of metropolitan regions, requiring centers to be endowed with a certain level of economic growth along with population criteria, henceforth laying the basis for the question of scaling (Parlak ans Sobacı, 2012, 169-181). Yet, due to several problems that emerged at lateral stage, a new arrangement legislation number 5747 in 2008 came into being, envisaging to broaden the borders of some sub-province without abiding by the borders specified in the provincial division, yet, with being more and more specific for the metropolitan region scale such as the condition of a center having a population of 750.000 and a convenient physical location. The 2008 revisions also made it necessary that establishment of metropolitan zones be only done by laws not by any other legislative means(İzci and Turan, 2013).

Given the adventure of Turkish metropolitan policy-making, the Turkish experience depicts the making of such a system which is under the direct control and initiative of the Central Governments. The Legislation Number 6360 presents no exception to this very finding which central governments whilst it undertook a more challenging task to convert 14 municipalities into the metropolitan zones defined on the basis of provincial boundaries, toppling these centers onto the existing 16 metropolitan zones and to transform the very functioning of the new metropolitan governance schemes in 30 centers. While new administrative changes took the form of transforming all villages and neighborhoods to districts, local management unions, SPAs and sub-districts within the borders of new metropolitan administrations were abolished along with major changes introduced in the functioning and structure of SPAs laying outside the metropolitan municipalities (Ökmen and Parlak, 2013, 315-16).

The very final changes in regard to the abolishment of SPAs within the total coverage of metropolitan governance mechanism became the hotspot for criticism by main-opposition party, namely the Republican People's Party along with the other opposition partner Nationalist Action Party along with different sections of civil society. The new regionalist rationale and design of the system was indeed in the center of the debate which many social circles that a vast geography of provincial border-based metropolitan governance was ill equipped to respond the needs of rural communities which are scattered throughout the provinces (For the older framework of SPAs by Legislation Number 5302 and the one that precedes Legislation Number 5302,see Koçak and Kavsara, 2012, Parlak; 2005; Sobacı, 2005).

The older configuration of SPAs were designed to deal with the challenges faced by local management units that were located outside municipal boundaries of both provinces and sub province, in particular infrastructural, social and economic needs of rural regions. Indeed the final fine-tuning of SPAs was realized by the Legislation Number 5302 passed in 2005 giving a clear task definition and bringing forth remedies to the question of administrative tutelage with curbing the powers of the central government on the system thereby rendering a more democratic system of representation (Ökmen and Parlak, 2013-205-239) Given overwhelming changes put forth by the 6360 configuration, the optimal scale theme once again became a matter of discussion. The criticism followed that the scaling problem that the Legislation Number 6360 posed an important challenge for Turkish metropolitan and local governance schemes (Turan and İzci, 2013).

Yet, according to the critiques with a scale that was designed for urban metropolitan governance the new system was incapable of solving the potential problems inherent in the rural zones of new metropolitan regions. While some scholars argued that there existed no rural governance scheme designed and realized under the dominance of rural governance schemes, others put the proposition that the novelties of the new governance regime was in fact a governance scheme of Regions (Ökmen and Parlak, 2013, 212-220).

In terms of public financial arrangements, the new devised system proposed a system that would grant 1.50% of the total realized tax incomes of general budget to those municipalities other than the metropolitan municipalities, 4, and 50% of the sub provincial municipalities within the metropolitan regions and the 0, 5% to SPAs. With exception of private expenditure taxation, 6% of all tax budgetary incomes attained within the borders of metropolis regions and %30 percent of all tax budgetary incomes realized in sub provinces of metropolitan boundaries were transferred to the metropolitan municipalities. Despite substantial increases in public financial bodies, the costs of devising the system as foreseen by the 6360 reconfiguration would levy a burden of financing a population of 56.5 million with new increases in metropolitan taxation (İzci and Turan, 2013, 142).

Other concerns in regard to the arrangements of the Legislation Number 6360 merge in relation to the federalism debate in Turkey. As some argue that the 6360 is a gradual step to a transformation to a federal system of governance, others believe the 6360 proposes no outlook for a transformation to federalism as the legislation was far away from distributing legislative powers with the federally defined unit. On the other hand, the Legislation Number 6360 was criticized on the basis that the arrangement left little room for substantial participation and governance related practices as metropolitan governance mechanisms became obliged to deal with a great bulk of affairs defined on a vast geographic dimension. These criticisms were backed by the inadequate consultation of central government in the preparation of the legislation leading to alienation of so many sections of civil societal components (Ökmen and Parlak, 2013, 312-320).

RATHER THAN CONCLUSION: WHERE DOES TURKISH METROPOLITAN GOVERNANCE PROCESS GO FROM HERE?

As reiterated many times in the present work, the novelties brought forth by the Legislation Number 6360 demonstrate a total continuity in terms of reforms and restructuring oriented to shape the metropolitan governance since the early 1980s. Living in a world of complexities backed by neoliberal prerequisites globally, Turkey finds herself obliged to develop a new systematic for her metropolitan governance on the basis of regions. To ensure that the country will keep up with notions of competitive advantage, the metropolitan governance scale become an important and heated debate of discussions. In light of developments after local elections carried out on March 30th, 2014, there still remain a number of ambiguities surrounding the system. First and foremost, the country faces a need to relocate and to redefine the Legislation Number 6360 in a constitutional setting due to the fact that the provincial division which was taken as the sole basis of scaling in 6360 was an outcome of the social, economic and political realities of 1920s' Turkey.

In such regard, to whatever extent the present legal existing scheme of metropolitan scheme is based on an ambiguous scale of region, the systematic remains ill-equipped with challenges in regard to efficient and effective delivery of local services in the rural regions. Thus, we all require a clearer picture in relation to what constitutes a scale of province that will embrace the political economic reality of contemporary Turkey. Secondly but not the least, democratic and governance related aspects of the system would need to be developed with other means. Otherwise a country striving to be a part of the European Union would fall way from the European and Western civil participation.

Finally, governance related schemes would not be limited with the political and business elites but also extended to the masses and ordinary citizens of metropolitan regions. Suffice it to say, this poses no easy task as attainment of functional effectiveness and democracy as two main pillars of local management systems would paradoxically have to enter a tradeoff process as some aspects of each other may be sacrificed.

REFERENCES

Aktel, M. & Gül, H. (2004). Tarihsel Bir Bakış Açısıyla Kamu Ve Yerel Yönetimler Reformu, Yerel Yönetimler Kongresi Dünden Bugüne Yerel Yönetimlerde Yeniden Yapılanma. *Çanakkale Onsekiz Mart Üniversitesi Biga İktisadi Ve İdari Bilimler Fakültesi*, 79-90.

Aktel, M., & Memişoğlu, D. (2005). Yerel Yönetim Reformlarının Başarısızlık Nedenleri. In İ. H. Özgür & M. Kösecik (Eds.), Yerel Yönetimler Üzerine Güncel Yazılar-I Reform (pp. 21-38). Ankara: Academic Press.

Avrupa Birliği Bakanlığı, T. C. (2012). *Turkey's progress report prepared by Turkey, 2013*. Retrieved from http://www.abgs.gov.tr/files/IlerlemeRaporlari/2012/2012_tr_progress_report_en.pdf

Aytaç, F. (1995). İl Özel İdareleri Hakkında Düşünceler. *Yeni Türkiye*, *1*(4), 377–389.

Başsoy, A. (1995). İl Özel İdarelerimiz. *Yeni Türkiye*, *1*(4), 390–397.

Bozlağan, R. (2012). *Anayasalarda Mahalli İdareler Ve Yeni Anayasa Yapım Sürecinde Mahalli İdarelere Dair Düzenlemeler, Lider Ülke Türkiye*. İstanbul: AK Parti.

Dedeoğlu, E. (1997). İl Özel İdarelerinin Tarihi Gelişimi Ve Bugünkü Durumu. *Yerel Yönetim Ve Denetim Dergisi*, *2*(1).

Eke, A. E. (1982). *Anakent Yönetimi ve Yönetimlerarası İlişkiler*. Ankara: AÜ SBF Yayınları.

Erkip, F. (2000). Global transformations versus local dynamics in Istanbul: Planning in a fragmented metropolis. *Cities (London, England)*, *17*(5), 371–377. doi:10.1016/S0264-2751(00)00033-0

Eryilmaz, B. (1992). *Tanzimat Ve Yönetimde Modernleşme*. İstanbul: İşaret Yayınları.

Eryilmaz, B. (1997). *Yerel Yönetimlerin Yeniden Yapılanması*. İstanbul: Birleşik Yayıncılık.

Eryilmaz, B. (2011). *Kamu Yönetimi*. Ankara: Okutman.

Göymen, K. (2006). Dynamics of changes in Turkish local governance. *Demise of the Bureaucratic Ruling Tradition Society and Economy*, *28*(3), 245–266.

Heper, M. (1992). The strong state as a problem of democracy: Turkey and Germany compared. *Comparative Political Studies*, *25*(2), 169–194. doi:10.1177/0010414092025002002

Heper, M., & Keyman, F. (1998). Double-faced state: Political patronage and the consolidation of democracy in Turkey. *Middle Eastern Studies*, *34*(4), 259–277. doi:10.1080/00263209808701251

Hettne, B., & Soderbaum, F. (2014, May 2). *The new regionalism approach: The new regionalism and north-south trade agreements*. United Nations Conference on Trade and Development. Retrieved from http://www.Unctad.Org/En/Docs/Tdr2007ch3_En.Pdf

İzci, F., & Turan, M. (2013). Türkiye'de Büyükşehir Belediyesi Sistemi ve 6360 Sayili Yasa İle Büyükşehir Belediyesi Sisteminde Meydana Gelen Değişimler. *Van Örneği Süleyman Demirel Üniversitesi İktisadi ve İdari Bilimler Fakültesi Dergisi*, *18*(1), 117–152.

Keleş, R. (2012). *Yerinden Yönetim Ve Siyaset*. İstanbul: Cem.

Koçak, S. Y., & Kavsara, V. (2012). 5302 Sayılı Kanun Sonrasında İl Özel İdarelerinde Yaşanan Sorunlar Ve Çözüm Önerileri. *Yönetim Bilimleri Dergisi*, *10*(20), 61–92.

Kübler, D. (2014, May 7). *Megacities and the challenge of governance*. Zurich Open Repository and Archive, University of Zurich Main Library Winterthurerstrasse. Retrieved from www.zora.uzh.ch

Loewendahl-Ertugal. (2014, April 29). *Ebru regions and European integration: Prospects for regional governance in Turkey*. Paper presented at Second Pan-European Conference Standing Group on EU Politics. Bologna, Spain. Retrieved from http://www.jhubc.it/ecpr-bologna/docs/471.pdf

Ökmen, M., & Özer, B. (2007). Küreselleşme-Yerelleşme Dikotomisinin Açılımları Üzerine Bir Tartışma. In A. Yılmaz & Y. Bozkurt (Eds.), *Türk Kamu Yönetimi*. Ankara: Gazi.

Ökmen, M., & Parlak, B. (2009). *Kuramdan Uygulama Yerel Yönetimler İlkeler, Yaklaşımlar Ve Mevzuat*. Bursa: Alfa Aktüel.

Ökmen, M., & Parlak, B. (2013). *Yerel Yönetimler*. Ankara: Orion.

Öner, Ş. (2006). *Yeni Mevzuat Çerçevesinde Türkiye'de Belediye Yönetimi*. Ankara: Academic Press.

Ortayli, İ. (1974). *Tanzimattan Sonra Mahalli İdareler (1840-1878)*. Ankara: Todaie Yayınları.

Ortayli, İ. (1978). İmparatorluk Döneminde Mahalli İdarelerin Ve Belediyeciliğin Evrimi. In İ. E. Türkcan (Ed.), *Türkiye İdare Tarihi*. Ankara: Todaie Yayını.

Ortayli, İ. (1985). *Tanzimattan Cumhuriyete Yerel Yönetim Geleneği*. İstanbul: Hil Yayınları.

Parlak, B. (2005). *Tarihi Perspektifte Ve Reform Sürecinde İ.Ö.İ. In Yerel Yönetimler Üzerine Güncel Yazılar I Reform* (pp. 175–200). Ankara: Nobel Yayıncılık.

Parlak, B., & Sobacı, Z. (2012). *Ulusal ve Küresel Perspektif.* Bursa: MKM.

Sarkar, P. (2014, May 7). *Unpublished course notes: A comparison of old and new regionalism*. Retrieved from https://www.academia.edu/2103291/Old_vs_New_Regionalism

Savitch, H., & Vogel, R. K. (2000). Paths to new regionalism. *State & Local Government Review*, *32*(1), 158–168. doi:10.1177/0160323X0003200301

Savitch, H., & Vogel, R. K. (2009). Regionalism and urban politics. In J. S. Davies & D. L. Imbroscio (Eds.), *Theories of urban politics*. London: Sage. doi:10.4135/9781446279298.n8

Sobaci, M. Z. (2005). Yeniden Yapılanma Süreci İ.Ö.İ. Dünü, Bugünü, Geleceği Üzerine Değerlendirme. *Çağdaş Yerel Yönetimler Dergisi*, *14*, 5.

Sobacı, Z. (2009). Regional development agencies in Turkey: Are they examples of obligated policy transfer? *Public Organization Review*, *9*(1), 51–65. doi:10.1007/s11115-008-0069-0

Sözen, S. (2012). Recent administrative reforms in Turkey: A preliminary assessment. *International Journal of Business and Social Science*, *3*(9), 168–173.

Sözen, S., & Shaw, I. (2002). The international applicability of "new" public management: Lessons from Turkey. *International Journal of Public Sector Management*, *15*(6), 475–486. doi:10.1108/09513550210439625

Sözen, S., & Shaw, I. (2003). Turkey and the European Union: Modernizing a traditional state? *Social Policy and Administration*, *37*(2), 108–120. doi:10.1111/1467-9515.00328

Ulusoy, A., & Tekin, A. (2010). *Mahalli İdareler Teori, Maliye Ve Uygulama*. Ankara: Seçkin Yayıncılık.

KEY TERMS AND DEFINITIONS

Centralization: The term refers to the concentration of power in both political and geograhical terms into one central government's organization.

Decentralization: A term that refers to a scheme where government distributes and disperses Powers, priveleges and other means from a location and/or unit centrally defined.

Globalization: A process of international deepening integration due to exchange and inter change of cultures, products, ideas and other related means.

Governance: A process of government whereby multiactor involvement is more and mor eemphasized.

Metropolitan Region: The terms refers to densely populated regions with a urban core and center surrounded by regions identified with common industry, infrastructure and housing.

Policy: A term that refers to the ways and protocoles of doing something in a rational manner.

Regionalism: An economic and administrative scheme of development where interests of a particular region or group of region become basic matters of reference.

ENDNOTES

1 For a thorough discussion of Turkish modernity and Turkish administrative history please also see Ortayli, İ. (1974). *Tanzimattan Sonra Mahalli İdareler (1840-1878).* Ankara: Todaie Yayınları, Ortayli, İ. (1985). *Tanzimattan Cumhuriyete Yerel Yönetim Geleneği.* İstanbul: Hil Yayınları.and Ortayli, İ.(1978). İmparatorluk Döneminde Mahalli İdarelerin Ve Belediyeciliğin Evrimi. İçinde E. Türkcan (Ed.) *Türkiye İdare Tarihi*, Ankara: Todaie Yayını.

2 For a more detailed account of reform in local governance reforms in the post-1980s perspective please refer to Aktel, M. & Gül, H. (2004). Tarihsel Bir Bakış Açısıyla Kamu Ve Yerel Yönetimler Reformu, Yerel Yönetimler Kongresi Dünden Bugüne Yerel Yönetimlerde Yeniden Yapılanma. *Çanakkale Onsekiz Mart Üniversitesi Biga İktisadi Ve İdari Bilimler Fakültesi*, 79-90. andAktel, M. & Memişoğlu, D. (2005). Yerel Yönetim Reformlarının Başarısızlık Nedenleri. İçinde H. Özgür & M. Kösecik (Ed.), *Yerel Yönetimler Üzerine Güncel Yazılar-I Reform* (Ss.21-38). Ankara: Nobel Yayın Dağıtım as succinct accounts on the proceses.

Compilation of References

Abu-Bader, S., & Abu-Qarn, A. S. (2008). Financial development and economic growth: The Egyptian experience. *Journal of Policy Modeling*, *30*(5), 887–898. doi:10.1016/j.jpolmod.2007.02.001

Abuhanoğlu, H. C., & Ayanoğlu, Y. (2011). Mezuniyet Oncesi Tıp Egitimi Maliyetlerinin Belirlenmesi: Tıp Fakültesinde Bir Uygulama. *Sağlıkta Performans ve Kalite Dergisi, 4.*

Açıkgöz, Ö., & Bülent, Ö. (2009). *1929 Dünya Ekonomik Buhranı ve Türkiye Ekonomisine Etkileri*. Turkey: Mevzuat Dergisi.

Adanu, K. (2005). A cross-province comparison of Okun's coefficient for Canada. *Applied Economics*, *37*(5), 561–570. doi:10.1080/0003684042000201848

Adler, E., & Barnett, M. (Eds.). (1998). *Security communities*. Cambridge University Press. doi:10.1017/CBO9780511598661

Aghion, P., Howitt, P., & Mayer-Foulkes, D. (2005). The effect of financial development on convergence: Theory and evidence. *The Quarterly Journal of Economics*, *120*(1), 173–222.

Aidis, R. (2014). *Why don't we see more small- and medium-sized enterprises (SMEs) in Lithuania? Institutional impediments to SME development*. Retrieved, May 17, 2014, from http://papers.ssrn.com/sol3/papers.cfm?abstract_id=314201

Akcapar, B. (2006). Perspectives on Turkey's EU accession: The long road from Ankara to Brussels. *Yale Journal of International Affairs*, *1*(2), 50–57.

Akçay, B. (2013). Avro Bölgesinin Yapısı ve Yönetimi. In B. Akçay (Ed.), *Avrupayı Saran Kriz Avro Bölgesi* (pp. 31–52). Ankara: Seçkin Yayıncılık.

Akiş, E. (2011). In the process of globalization developments in regional development approach and regional development agencies. *Journal of Sociology Conference*, (s. 239).

Aktan, C. C. (2008). *Yeni İktisat Okulları*. Ankara, Turkey: SeçkinYayınevi.

Aktel, M. & Gül, H. (2004). Tarihsel Bir Bakış Açısıyla Kamu Ve Yerel Yönetimler Reformu, Yerel Yönetimler Kongresi Dünden Bugüne Yerel Yönetimlerde Yeniden Yapılanma. *Çanakkale Onsekiz Mart Üniversitesi Biga İktisadi Ve İdari Bilimler Fakültesi*, 79-90.

Aktel, M., & Memişoğlu, D. (2005). Yerel Yönetim Reformlarının Başarısızlık Nedenleri. In İ. H. Özgür & M. Kösecik (Eds.), Yerel Yönetimler Üzerine Güncel Yazılar-I Reform (pp. 21-38). Ankara: Academic Press.

Albert, E. (2013, November 29). Londres défie l'Union européenne sur la libre circulation. *Le Monde*. Retrieved July 3, 2014, from http://www.lexisnexis.com/hottopics/lnacademic

Albert, E. (2014, July 1). Londres pris dans l'engrenage du "Brexit". *Le Monde*. Retrieved July 3, 2014, from http://www.lemonde.fr/europe/article/2014/06/30/londres-pris-dans-l-engrenage-du-brexit_4447850_3214.html

Alexeeva, O. (2008). Chinese migration in the Russian far east. [Article]. *China Perspectives, 2008*(3), 20-32.

Alganer, Y., & Çetin, M.Ö.(2007). Avrupa'da birlik ve bütünleşme hareketleri-I, *Journal of Marmara University İ.İ.B.F., 23*(2), 285-309.

Ali, T. M. (2012). The impact of the sovereign debt crisis on the eurozone countris. *Procedia: Social and Behavioral Sciences*, *62*, 424–430. doi:10.1016/j.sbspro.2012.09.069

Allen & Overy. (2013). *Global tax practice, financial transaction tax*. Retrieved from http://www.allenovery.com/SiteCollectionDocuments/Global%20Tax_FTT%20Brochure%20(email).pdf

Allison, R. (2004). Strategic reassertion in Russia's central Asia policy. *International Affairs*, *80*(2), 277–293. doi:10.1111/j.1468-2346.2004.00383.x

Allworth, E. A. (1995). *Central Asia: One hundred thirty years of Russian dominance, a historical overview* (3rd ed.). Duke University Press.

Alter, A., & Schüler, Y. S. (2012). Credit spread interdependencies of European states and banks during the financial crisis. *Journal of Banking & Finance*, *36*(12), 3444–3468. doi:10.1016/j.jbankfin.2012.08.002

Altman, E., Sabato, G., & Wilson, N. (2014, May 20). *The value of non-financial information in SME risk management*. Academic Press.

Amariei, C., & Eaton, K. A. (2009). Systems for the provision of oral health care in the Black Sea countries part 1: Romania. *Oral Health and Dental Management in the Black Sea Countries*, *8*, 3–6.

Ambrosio, T. (2008). Catching the 'Shanghai spirit': How the Shanghai cooperation organization promotes authoritarian norms in central Asia. *Europe-Asia Studies*, *60*(8), 1321–1344. doi:10.1080/09668130802292143

Amend, T., Barbeau, B., Beyers, B., Burns, S., Eißing, S., Fleischhauer, A. … Poblete, P. (Eds.). (2010). *A big foot on a small planet? Accounting with the ecological footprint: Succeeding in a world with growing resource constraints*. Deutsche Gesellschaft für Technische Zusammenarbeit (GTZ) GmbH, Eschborn. Available from http://www.conservation-development.net/?L=2&ds=313

Anderson, K., & Blackhurst, R. (1992). The greening of world trade issues. Ann Arbor, MI: University of Michigan Press.

Anderson, R., Qian, H., & Rasche, R. (2006). *Analysis of panel vector error correction models using maximum likelihood, bootstrap and canonical-correlation estimators*. Federal Reserve Bank of St. Louis, Working Paper No 50A.

Angelillo, I. F., Nobile, C. G., & Pavia, M. (1996). Oral health status and treatment needs in immigrants and refugees in Italy. *European Journal of Epidemiology*, *12*(4), 359–365. doi:10.1007/BF00145298 PMID:8891539

Ang, J. B. (2008). A survey of recent developments in the literature of finance and growth. *Journal of Economic Surveys*, *22*(3), 536–576. doi:10.1111/j.1467-6419.2007.00542.x

Anonymous. (2006). *The law abaout the establisment coordination and duties of development agencies*. Author.

Antweiler, W., Copeland, B., & Taylor, M. S. (2001). Is free trade good for the environment? The American Economic Review, 91(4), 877–908. doi:10.1257/aer.91.4.877 doi:10.1257/aer.91.4.877

Araujo, M. W., Dermen, K., & Connors, G. (2004). 0ral and dental health among inpatients in treatment for alcohol use disorders: A pilot study. *Journal of the International Academy of Periodontology*, *6*, 125–130. PMID:15553979

Arghyrou, M. G., & Kontonikas, A. (2011). *The EMU-sovereign debt crisis: Fundemantals, expectetion and contagion*. Brussels: European Commision.

Aris, S. (2011). *Eurasian regionalism: The Shanghai cooperation organisation*. Palgrave Macmillan. doi:10.1057/9780230307643

Arsenov, V. I., Artemkina, E. V., & Zaboev, A. I. (2005). Rossiya v sisteme mejdunarodnih evroaziatiskih transportnih koridorov: sovremennoy sostoyanie, problemi, perspektivi i konkurentosposobnost. *Rossiskiy Vneshneekonomicheskiy Vestnik*, (1).

Arslan, E. (2010). Development agencies and development agency expected contribution to the economy of Turkey. *Kamu İş*, 93.

Aruoba, Ç. (1992). *Çevre Ekonomisi, Gelişme Ekonomisi, İnsan Çevre Toplum, Prepared for publication by: Ruşen Keleş*. Ankara: İmge Publishing House.

Asako, K. (1979). Environmental pollution in an open economy. The Economic Record, 55(4), 359–367. doi:10.1111/j.1475-4932.1979.tb02241.x doi:10.1111/j.1475-4932.1979.tb02241.x

Aspinwall, M. (2000). Structuring Europe: Powersharing institutions and British preferences on European integration. *Political Studies*, *48*(3), 415–442. doi:10.1111/1467-9248.00268

Atik, H. (2013). AB Türkiye'yi Neden Tam Üyeliğe Kabul Etmiyor? *Ankara Strateji Enstitüsü*. Retrieved from http://www.ankarastrateji.org/yazar/prof-dr-hayriye-atik/ab-turkiye-yi-neden-tam-uyelige-kabul-etmiyor/

Atindéhou, R. B., Pierre, G. J., & Kossi, E. (2005). Financial intermediation and economic growth: Evidence from Western Africa. *Applied Financial Economics*, *15*(11), 777–790. doi:10.1080/09603100500108030

Australian Institute of Health and Welfare. (2010). *Australia's health in 2010: Twelth biennial health report of the Australian Institute of Health and Welfare*. Retrieved from: www.aihw.gov.au/W0rkArea/DownloadAsset.aspx?id=6442452962 on O1/07/2012

Avaro, M., & Sterdyniak, H. (2014). Banking union: A solution to the Euro Zone crisis? *Revue de l'OFCE*, *132*, 195–241.

Avrupa Birliği Bakanlığı, T. C. (2011). *Türkiye-AB İlişkilerinin Tarihçesi*. Retrieved from http://www.abgs.gov.tr/index.php?p=111&l=1

Avrupa Birliği Bakanlığı, T. C. (2012). *Turkey's progress report prepared by Turkey, 2013*. Retrieved from http://www.abgs.gov.tr/files/IlerlemeRaporlari/2012/2012_tr_progress_report_en.pdf

Avrupa Birliği Genel Sekreterliği. (2010). *Türkiye'nin Üyeliği Perspektifinden Kaynaklanan Hususlar*. Retrieved from http://www.mfa.gov.tr/data/AB/etki_degerlendirme.pdf

Avrupa Birliği Genel Sekreterliği. (2011). Avrupa Birliği'nde Küresel Finansal Krize Karşı Alınan Önlemler ve Birliğin Rekabet Gücünün Arttırılmasına Yönelik Girişimler. In *Euro RekabetPaktı*. Ankara, Turkey: Avrupa Birliği Genel Sekreterliği Yayınları.

Ay, H. (2013). *AB Mali Yapısı* (p. 237). İzmir: Kanyılmaz Matbaası.

Aytaç, F. (1995). İl Özel İdareleri Hakkında Düşünceler. *Yeni Türkiye*, *1*(4), 377–389.

Baas, T., & Schrooten, M. (2014). *Relationship banking and SMEs: A theoretical analysis*. Retrieved, May 17, 2014, from http://papers.ssrn.com/sol3/papers.cfm?abstract_id=788344

Bacik, G., & Aras, B. (2004). Turkey's inescapable dilemma: America or Europe? *Alternatives: Turkish Journal of International Affairs*, *3*(1), 56–74.

Baek, J., & Kim, H. S. (2011). Trade liberalization, economic growth, energy consumption and the environment: Time series evidence from G-20 economies. Journal of East Asian Economic Integration, 15(1), 3–32. doi:10.11644/KIEP.JEAI.2011.15.1.224 doi:10.11644/KIEP.JEAI.2011.15.1.224

Baek, J., Cho, Y., & Koo, W. W. (2009). The environmental consequences of globalization: A country-specific time-series analysis. Ecological Economics, 68(8-9), 2255–2264. doi:10.1016/j.ecolecon.2009.02.021 doi:10.1016/j.ecolecon.2009.02.021

Bagwell, K., & Staiger, R. W. (2002). *The economics of the world trading system*. Cambridge, MA: MIT Press.

Bahgat, G. (2006). Central Asia and energy security. *Asian Affairs*, *37*(1), 1–16. doi:10.1080/03068370500456819

Baizakova, K. I. (2013). The Shanghai cooperation organization's role in countering threats and challenges to central Asian regional security. *Russian Politics and Law*, *51*(1), 59–79. doi:10.2753/RUP1061-1940510104

Bakırtaş, İ., & Tekinşen, A. (2004). Dünya Savaşları ve Büyük Buhran Arasındaki Etkileşimin Ekonomik Politiği. Ankara, Turkey: Palme Yayıncılık.

Balassa, B. (1961). *The theory of economic integration*. London: Allew and Unwin.

Balassa, B. (1965). *Economic development and integration*. Mexico: Centro De Estudios Monetario Latinoamericanos.

Balassa, B. (1986). The determinants of intra-industry specialization in United States trade. *Oxford Economic Papers*, *38*, 220–233.

Balassa, B., & Bauwens, L. (1987). Intra-industry specialization in a multi-country and multi-industry framework. *The Economic Journal*, *97*(388), 923–939. doi:10.2307/2233080

Baldwin, E. R. (1997). The causes of regionalism. *World Economy*, *20*(7), 865–888. doi:10.1111/1467-9701.00107

Baldwin, R., & Wyplosz, C. (2012). *The economics of European integration*. London: McGraw-Hill.

Balseven, H. (2003). Dünya Uygulamalarında ve Türkiye'de Finansal Piyasalardaki İşlem Vergileri. *Vergi Dünyası*, *365*, 171–178.

Baltagi, B. H., Panicos, O. D., & Siong, H. L. (2009). Financial development and openness: Evidence from panel data. *Journal of Development Economics*, *89*(2), 285–296. doi:10.1016/j.jdeveco.2008.06.006

Banerjee, A., Marcellino, M., & Osbat, C. (2004). Some cautions on the use of panel methods for integrated series of macro-economic data. The Econometrics Journal, 7(2), 322–340. doi:10.1111/j.1368-423X.2004.00133.x doi:10.1111/j.1368-423X.2004.00133.x

Banking Union – Single Resolution Mechanism (SRM). (n.d.). *European Commission*. Factsheet. Retrieved June 1, 2014, from http://ec.europa.eu/internal_market/finances/docs/banking-union/dg-markt-factsheets-srm_en.pdf

Banks' Riskier Trading Activities to be Curbed, EU Proposes. (2014, January 29). *BBC*. Retrieved April 20, 2014, from http://www.bbc.com/news/business-25941075

Barker, A. (2014, March 17). France and Germany squabble over who pays for EU banking union. *Financial Times*. Retrieved April 20, 2014, from http://www.ft.com/intl/cms/s/0/4ab7c61a-adcb-11e3-9ddc-00144feab7de.html

Barkovsky, A. N. (2006). Obrechen li Rossisky Dalny Vostok na sudbu tranzitnoy territoriy? *Rossiskiy Vneshneekonomicheskiy Vestnik,* (3).

Barnier Launches EU Bid to Ban Risky Bank Trades. (2014, January 29). *EUobserver*. Retrieved May 12, 2014, from http://euobserver.com/news/122919

Barro, R. J. (1997). *Determinants of economic growth: A cross-country empirical study*. Cambridge, MA: The MIT Press.

Basilico, E., Maestroni, M., & Mantovani, G. M. (2014). *The relation between corporate governance, firm performance and the merit of credit in SMEs*. Retrieved, May 25, 2014, from http://papers.ssrn.com/sol3/papers.cfm?abstract_id=2403166

Başsoy, A. (1995). İl Özel İdarelerimiz. *Yeni Türkiye*, *1*(4), 390–397.

Bauer J., Neumann T. & Saekel R. (2009). *Zahnmedizinische Versorgung in Deutschland*. Verlag: Hans Huber.

Baum, A., Westphal, C. C., & Rother, P. (2013). Debt and growth: New evidence for the euro area. *Journal of International Money and Finance*, *32*, 809–821. doi:10.1016/j.jimonfin.2012.07.004

Baumol, W. J., & Oates, W. E. (1988). The theory of environmental policy. Cambridge: Cambridge University Press. doi:10.1017/CBO9781139173513 doi:10.1017/CBO9781139173513

Baumol, W.J. (1971). *Environmental protection, international spillovers, and trade*. Stock-holm: Almquit and Wixell.

Baygun, S. (2005). *EU – Turkey customs union*. Retrieved from: http://www.dtm.gov.tr/ab/ingilizce/gbnot.htm

BBC News. (2014). Europe rejects UK's financial transaction tax challenge. *BBC NEWS*. Retrieved from http://www.bbc.com/news/business-27218615

BBC. (2008). *Anger at darling island criticism*. Retrieved March 19, 2014, from http://news.bbc.co.uk/2/hi/europe/isle_of_man/7713258.stm

Beach, D. (2006). The commission and the council secretariat: How they gained some influence. In F. Laursen (Ed.), *The treaty of Nice: Actor preferences, bargaining and institutional choice* (pp. 369–406). Leiden: Martinus Nijhoff Publishers.

Beck, T. (2002). Financial development and international trade: Is there a link? *Journal of International Economics*, *57*(1), 107–131. doi:10.1016/S0022-1996(01)00131-3

Bekmez, S. (2002). Sectoral impacts of Turkish accession to the European Union. *Eastern European Economics*, *40*, 57–84.

Beladi, H., & Oladi, R. (2011). Does trade liberalization increase global pollution? Resource and Energy Economics, 33(1), 172–178. doi:10.1016/j.reseneeco.2010.04.009 doi:10.1016/j.reseneeco.2010.04.009

Bennett, J. W. (2002). Human ecology as human behaviour: Essays in environmental and development anthropology. Academic Press.

Bergmann, J., & Niemann, A. (2013). Theories of European integration and their contribution to the study of European foreign policy. In *Proceedings of8th Pan-European Conference on International Relations*. Warsaw: Academic Press.

Bergsten, C.F. (1991, November). Commentary: The move toward free trade zones. *Economic Review,* 27-35.

Berkes, F., & Kışlalıoğlu, M. (1990). *Ekoloji ve Çevre Bilimleri*. Istanbul: Remzi Publishing House.

Berthelon, M., & Freund, C. (2008). On the conservation of distance in international trade. *Journal of International Economics, 75*(2), 310–320. doi:10.1016/j.jinteco.2007.12.005

Bhagwati, J. (1991). *The world trading system at risk*. New York: Princeton University Press. doi:10.1515/9781400861590

Bhagwati, J. (1993). Regionalism and multilateralism: An overview. In J. de Melo & A. Panagariya (Eds.), *New dimensions in regional integration* (pp. 22–51). New York: Cambridge University Press. doi:10.1017/CBO9780511628511.004

Bhagwati, J., Krishna, P., & Panagariya, A. (1999). *Trading blocs: Alternative approaches to analysing preferential trade agreements*. Cambridge, MA: MIT Press.

Bhagwati, J., & Krueger, A. O. (1995). *The dangerous drift to preferential trade agreements*. Washington, DC: AEI Press.

Bhanot, K., Burns, N., Hunter, D., & Williams, M. (2014). News spillovers from the Greek debt crisis: Impact on the Eurozone financial sector. *Journal of Banking & Finance, 38*, 51–63. doi:10.1016/j.jbankfin.2013.09.015

Bickerton, C. J. (2011). Crisis in the Eurozone: Transnational governance and national power in European integration. *Political Geography, 30*(8), 415–416. doi:10.1016/j.polgeo.2011.03.004

Bilicka, K., & Fuest, C. (2012). *With which countries do tax havens share information? EUI Working Paper, RCAS 2012/6*. Retrieved April 21, 2014, from http://cadmus.eui.eu/bitstream/handle/1814/20618/RSCAS_2012_06.pdf?sequence=1

Billon, P. L. (Ed.). (2005). *The geopolitics of resource wars: Resource dependence, governance and violence*. New York: Routledge. doi:10.4324/9780203323229

Biseau, G., & Alemagna, L. (2014, February 19). Hollande et Merkel, plus unis que jamais. *Libération*. Retrieved May 12, 2014, from http://www.liberation.fr/politiques/2014/02/19/hollande-et-merkel-toujours-plus-proches_981468

Blair, D. (2013, January 9). US publicly voices concerns over Britain leaving EU. *The Telegraph*. Retrieved July 5, 2014, from http://www.telegraph.co.uk/news/worldnews/europe/eu/9791484/US-publicly-voices-concerns-over-Britain-leaving-EU.html

Blank, S. (2011). Russia's geo-economic future; The security implications of Russia's political and economic structure.[Article]. *Journal of Slavic Military Studies, 24*(3), 351–395. doi:10.1080/13518046.2011.598723

Blank, S. J. (2006). The Eurasian energy triangle: China, Russia, and the Central Asian states. *The Brown Journal of World Affairs, XII*(2).

Blot, W. J., McLaughlin, J. K., Winn, D. M., Austin, D. F., Greenberg, R. S., & Preston-Martin, S. (1998). Smoking and drinking in rela-tion to oral and pharyngeal cancer. *Cancer Research, 4*(23282), 7.

Bocutoğlu, E. (2011). *Krizin Makro İktisadından Makro İktisadın Krizine: Eleştirel bir Değerlendirme*. Ankara, Turkey: Turk Ekonomi Kurumu.

Bojanic, A. N. (2012). The impact of financial development and trade on the economic growth of Bolivia. *Journal of Applied Econometrics, 15*(1), 51–70.

Bomberg, E., Peterson, J., & Corbett, R. (2012). *The European Union: How does it work?* (3rd ed.). Oxford University Press.

Borger, J., Traynor, I., & Watt, N. (2013, January 10). Britain should stay in European Union, says Obama administration. *The Guardian*. Retrieved July 2, 2014, from http://www.theguardian.com/world/2013/jan/09/us-warns-uk-european-union

Borrow Foundation. (n.d.). Retrieved from: http://wwwborrowfoundation.org/why-fluoridate-milk

Boston, W. (2012, September 18). Merkel backs bond-buying program. *The Wall Street Journal*. Retrieved April 24, 2014, from http://online.wsj.com/news/articles/SB10000872396390444450004578002150260399228

Bounds, A. (2014, June 30). Pro-EU strategy at risk of failing, warns head of Siemens UK. *Financial Times*. Retrieved July 14, 2014, from http://www.ft.com/intl/cms/s/0/b172bf28-fe1a-11e3-b4f1-00144feab7de.html#axzz37QWUcfdo

Bowles, S., & Gintis, H. (2006). Homo economicus and zoon politikon:Behavioral game theory and political behavior. In R. E. Goodin & C. Tilly (Eds.), *The Oxford handbook of contextual political analysis*. Oxford, UK: Oxford University Press.

Boyd, J. P. (Ed.). (1950). *The papers of Thomas Jefferson*. Princeton, NJ: Princeton University Press. Retrieved May 12, 2014, from http://press-pubs.uchicago.edu/founders/documents/v1ch2s23.html

Boyer, P., & Ponce, J. (2012). Regulatory capture and banking supervision reform. *Journal of Financial Stability*, *8*(3), 206–217. doi:10.1016/j.jfs.2011.07.002

Boyle, P., & Levin, B. (2008). *World cancer report*. Lyon: International Agency for Research on Cancer.

Bozlağan, R. (2012). *Anayasalarda Mahalli İdareler Ve Yeni Anayasa Yapım Sürecinde Mahalli İdarelere Dair Düzenlemeler, Lider Ülke Türkiye*. İstanbul: AK Parti.

Brecher, M. (1963). *The new states of Asia, a political analysis*. London: Oxford University Press.

Breitung, J. (2005). A parametric approach to the estimation of cointegration vectors in panel data. Econometric Reviews, 24(2), 151–173. doi:10.1081/ETC-200067895 doi:10.1081/ETC-200067895

Breitung, J., & Pesaran, M. (2008). Unit roots and cointegration in panels. In L. Matyas & P. Sevestre (Eds.), The econometrics of panel data: Fundamentals and recent developments in theory and practice. Kluwer Academic Publishers.

Breitung, J. (2000). The local power of some unit root tests for panel data. In B. Baltagi (Ed.), *Nonstationary panels, panel cointegration, and dynamic panels, advances in econometrics, 15* (pp. 161–178). Amsterdam: JAI. doi:10.1016/S0731-9053(00)15006-6

Bretschger, L., & Egli, H. (2001). Sustainable growth in open economies. In G. G. Schulze & H. W. Ursprung (Eds.), International environmental economics-A survey of the issues (pp. 183-208). New York: Oxford University Press.

Breusch, T. S., & Pagan, A. R. (1980). The LaGrange multiplier test and its applications to model specification in econometrics. The Review of Economic Studies, 47(1), 239–254. doi:10.2307/2297111 doi:10.2307/2297111

Breuss, F. (2013). European banking union. *WIFO Working Papers*, No 454.

Brexit Could Cost UK its UN Security Council Seat, Warns Leading Tory. (2014, June 20). *Euractiv*. Retrieved June 30, 2014, from http://www.euractiv.com/sections/uk-europe/brexit-could-cost-uk-its-un-security-council-seat-warns-leading-tory-302920

Brexit or Brinfluence? Britain and Europe. (2013, July 17). *The Economist*. Retrieved June 30, 2014, from http://www.lexisnexis.com/hottopics/lnacademic

Brock, W. (2009). Comments in collapse in world trade: A symposium of views. *The International Economy*, (2009), 28-38.

Brondolo, J. D. (2011). *Taxing financial transactions: An assessment of administrative feasibility*. IMF Working Paper.

Brown, L. R., Flavin, C., & Postel, S. (1998). *Gezegenimizi Kurtarmak-Küresel Ekonominin Çevresel Olarak Sürdürülebilirliği*. Ankara: Tübitak-Tema Vakfı Yayınları. Retrieved May 6, 2014, from http://www.bcs.gov.tr/biodiversity/biodiversity.php

Brunsden, J., & Christie, R. (2013, July 10). EU unveils bank-crisis plan with 55 billion-Euro fund. *Bloomberg*. Retrieved June 12, 2014, from http://www.bloomberg.com/news/2013-07-09/eu-steels-for-battle-over-bank-resolution-plans-led-by-germany.html

Buiter, W., & Rahbari, E. (2012). The European Central Bank as lender of last resort for sovereigns in the Eurozone. *Journal of Common Market Studies, 50*, 6–35. doi:10.1111/j.1468-5965.2012.02275.x

Burfisher, M., Robinson, S., & Thierfelder, K. (2003). Regionalism: Old and new, theory and practice. In *Proceedings of Conference of International Agricultural Trade Research Consortium (IATRC)*. Capri, Italy: IATRC.

Burley, A.-M., & Mattli, W. (1993). Europe before the court: A political theory of legal integration. *International Organization, 47*(1), 41–76. doi:10.1017/S0020818300004707

Bustos, P. (2011). Trade liberalization, exports, and technology upgrading: Evidence on the impact of MERCOSUR on Argentinean firms. *The American Economic Review, 101*(1), 304–340. doi:10.1257/aer.101.1.304

Buszynski, L. (2005). Russia's new role in central Asia. *Asian Survey, 45*(4), 546–565. doi:10.1525/as.2005.45.4.546

Cadot, O., de Melo, J., & Olarreaga, M. (1999). Regional integration and lobbying for tariffs against non members. *International Economic Review, 40*(3), 635–657. doi:10.1111/1468-2354.00032

Cai, K. G. (2010). *The politics of economic regionalism*. New York: Palgrave Macmillan. doi:10.1057/9780230277267

Çakıcı, Ö., & Ceylan, M. (2014). Banka ve Sigorta Muameleleri Vergisi, Teori-Uygulama-Mevzuat. TBB: Publication No.301.

Calculated in Accordance with Dış Ticaret İstatistikleri: 1995. (1997). Ankara, pp. 191-220. quoted from Natalia Ulchenko, p. 140.

Çalışkan, Z. (2009). Saglık Hizmetlerinde Önceliklerin Belirlenmesinde Ekonomik Degerlendirme Yontemi Olarak Maliyet-Etkililik Analizi. *Süleyman Demirel Üniversitesi İktisadi ve İdari Bilimler Fakültesi Dergisi, 14*, 311–332.

Cameron, D. (2013, November 26). Free movement within Europe needs to be less free. *Financial Times*. Retrieved July 7, 2014, from http://www.ft.com/cms/s/0/add36222-56be-11e3-ab12-00144feabdc0.html#axzz37SWR98FG

Campos, N. F., Coricelli, F., & Moretti, L. (2014, April 5). The eye, the needle and the camel: Rich countries can benefit from EU membership. *Vox*. Retrieved July 12, 2014, from http://www.voxeu.org/article/how-rich-nations-benefit-eu-membership

Caporaso, J. A. (1998). Regional integration theory: Understanding our past and anticipating the future. In W. Sandholtz & A. S. Sweet (Eds.), *Supranational governance: The institutionalization of the European Union* (pp. 334–351). New York: Oxford University Press. doi:10.1093/0198294646.003.0012

Caporaso, J. A. (2000). *The European Union: Dilemmas of regional integration*. Boulder, Colo.: Westview Press.

Case of Kohll and Decker, C-120/95; C-158/96 (ECJ 4 28, 1998).

Casella, P. B. (2010). The common market of the south (MERCOSUR): Models and qualitative mutations for consolidating an integrated economic area. *Annual Survey of International & Comparative Law. 9*(1), Article 2. Retrieved Avril 8, 2014, from http://digitalcommons.law.ggu.edu/cgi/viewcontent.cgi?article=1070&context=annlsurvey

Cavallo, E. A., & Frankel, J. A. (2008). Does openness to trade make countries more vulnerable to sudden stops, or less? Using gravity to establish causality. *Journal of International Money and Finance, 27*(8), 1430–1452. doi:10.1016/j.jimonfin.2007.10.004

Cechetti, S., Fender, I., & McGuire, P. (2010). Towards a global risk map. *Bank for International Settlements Working Papers*, No 309.

Celasun, M. (1986). A general equilibrium model of the Turkish economy. *SIMLOG-1 METU Studies in Development, 13*(1-2), 29-64.

Central Intelligence Agency. (2013). *The world factbook: Turkey*. Retrieved from https://www.cia.gov/library/publications/the-world-factbook/geos/tu.html

Cervellati, E., & Fioriti, E. (2007). *Financial supervision in EU countries.* Paper presented at the EFMA Annual Meeting, Vienna, Austria.

Ceylan, S., & Sahin, B. Y. (2010). Asymmetry in the relationship between unemployment and economic growth. *The Journal of Dogus University, 11*(2), 157–165.

Checkel, J. T. (1999). Norms, institutions, and national identity in contemporary Europe. *International Studies Quarterly, 43*(1), 84–111. doi:10.1111/0020-8833.00112

Cheng, J. Y. S. (2011). The Shanghai co-operation organisation: China's initiative in regional institutional building. *Journal of Contemporary Asia, 41*(4), 632–656. doi:10.1080/00472336.2011.610618

Chen, M. X., & Mattoo, A. (2008). Regionalism in standards: Good or bad for trade? *The Canadian Journal of Economics. Revue Canadienne d'Economique, 41*(3), 838–863. doi:10.1111/j.1540-5982.2008.00488.x

Childsmile. (n.d.). Retrieved from: http://www.childsmile.org.uk

Chimobi, O. P. (2010). The causal relationship among financial development, trade openness and economic growth in Nigeria. *International Journal of Economics and Finance, 2*(2), 137–147. doi:10.5539/ijef.v2n2p137

Choe, C. (2014). *The political economy of SME financing and Japan's regional bank problems.* Retrieved, May 21, 2014, from http://papers.ssrn.com/sol3/papers.cfm?abstract_id=902791

Choi, Y. J., & Caporaso, J. A. (2002). Comparative regional integration. In W. Carlsnaes, T. Risse, & B. A. Simmons (Eds.), *Handbook of international relations* (pp. 480–499). London: Sage Publications. doi:10.4135/9781848608290.n25

Christensen, L., Twetman, S., & Sundby, A. (2010). Oral health in children and adolescents with different socio-cultural and socio-economic backgrounds. *Acta Odontologica Scandinavica, 68*(1), 34–42. doi:10.3109/00016350903301712 PMID:19878044

Christopoulos, D. K. (2004). The relationship between output and unemployment: Evidence from Greek regions. *Regional Science, 83*(3), 611–620. doi:10.1111/j.1435-5597.2004.tb01928.x

Chuang, S. C., Jenab, M., Heck, J. E., Bosetti, C., Talamini, R., Matsuo, K., & Hashibe, M. et al. (2012). Diet and the risk of head and neck cancer: A pooled analysis in the INHANCE consortium. *Cancer Causes & Control, 23*(1), 69–88. doi:10.1007/s10552-011-9857-x PMID:22037906

Cini, M., Perez, N., & Borragan, S. (2013). *European Union politics* (4th ed.). Oxford University Press.

Cizre, Ü., & Yeldan, E. (2000). Politics, society and financial liberalization: Turkey in the 1990s. *Development and Change, 31*(2), 488.

Click, R. W. (2009). The ASEAN Dollar standard in the post-crisis era: Reconsideration. *Journal of Asian Economics, 20*(3), 269–279. doi:10.1016/j.asieco.2009.02.005

Colak, H., Serdaroglu, L., & Dulgergil, C. (2010). Temel Agız Ve Dis Saglıgı Hizmetinde Restorasyon Uygulamalarının Yeri Önemi ve Sonucları. *Saglıkta Performans ve Kalite Dergisi,* (1).

Cole, M. A., & Elliott, R. J. (2003). Determining the trade-environment composition effect: The role of capital, labour and environmental regulations. Journal of Environmental Economics and Management, 46(3), 363–383. doi:10.1016/S0095-0696(03)00021-4 doi:10.1016/S0095-0696(03)00021-4

Collignon, S. (2011, March 24). Eurobonds: The financial equivalent of the single currency. In *Eurobonds: Concepts and implications: Compilation of notes for the monetary dialogue.* European Parliament, Directorate-General for Internal Policies. Retrieved June 20, 2014, from http://www.europarl.europa.eu/document/activities/cont/201201/20120130ATT36516/20120130ATT36516EN.pdf

Collomp, F. (2014, June 30). Le Royaume-Uni peut-il quitter l'UE? Argument de négociation agité par Londres face à ses partenaires européens, la perspective d'un « Brexit » (British exit) n'est pas seulement rhétorique. *Le Figaro.* Retrieved July 1, 2014, from http://www.lexisnexis.com/hottopics/lnacademic

COM(2011) 900 final (a Communication on a Quality Framework for Services of General Interest (SGI) in the EU 12 20, 2011).

Commemorating 60th Anniversary of Allied Landing on D-Day. (2004). *Deutsche aussenpolitik*. Retrieved May 12, 2014, from http://www.deutsche-aussenpolitik.de/daparchive/dateien/2002/06082004xxx24.html

Commission of the European Communities. (2009). *Reducing health inequalities in the EU. COM(2009) 567*. Retrieved from: http://ec.europa.eu/health/ph_determinants/socio_economics/documents/com2009_en.pdf

Commission, E. U. (2013). *Impact assessment report on the future of EU-US trade relation*. Commission Staff Working Document, 12.3.2013, SWD(2013), Strasbourg. Retrieved February 12 2014 from http://trade.ec.europa.eu/doclib/docs/2013/march/tradoc_150759.pdf

Constancio, V. (2013). *Speech of Vice-President of the ECB*. Paper presented at the 2nd FIN-FSA Conference "Banking and Supervision under Transformation", Helsinki, Finland.

Constancio, V. (2014). The European crisis and the role of the financial system. *Journal of Macroeconomics, 39* (Part B), 250-259.

Copeland, B. R., & Taylor, M. S. (2003). Trade and the environment: Theory and evidence. Princeton, NJ: Princeton University Press.

Corbet, E. (2007). Public health aspects of oral diseases and disorders — Periodontal diseases. In C. Pine & R. Harris (Eds.), *Community oral health* (2nd ed.). Surrey, UK: Quintessence.

Corden, M. (1972). Economies of scale and customs union theory. *Journal of Political Economy*, *80*(3), 465–475. doi:10.1086/259899

Corden, M. (1976). Customs unions theory and the non-uniformity of tariffs. *Journal of International Economics*, *6*(1), 99–106. doi:10.1016/0022-1996(76)90026-X

Council of European Chief Dental Officers. (n.d.). *Database*. Retrivied from: http://www.cecdo.org/pages/database%20intro.html

Council of European Dentists. (2009). *EU manual of dental practice: Version 4.1*. Retrivied from: http://www.eudental.eu/index.php?lD=35918 on O2/04/2012

Council of European Dentists. (2011). *CED resolution 'for better oral health ofall EU citizens: Mutual integration of oral and general health*. Retrivied from: http://wwweudental.eu/inde><.php?lD=2741 on 25/O3/2012

Cruz, J. D., & Stamps, J. (2014). *Small and medium-sized enterprises: U.S. and EU export activities, and barriers and opportunities experienced by U.S. firms*. Retrieved, January 4, 2014, from http://www.usitc.gov/publications/332/pub4169.pdf

Dadabaev, T. (2013). Shanghai cooperation organization (SCO) regional identity formation from the perspective of the central Asia states. *Journal of Contemporary China*, *23*(85), 102–118. doi:10.1080/10670564.2013.809982

Daniels, B. (2010). *The "Robın Hood" tax: A rejection*. TWS Policy Paper. Retrieved from http://thewilberforcesociety.co.uk/wp-content/uploads/2011/10/The-Robin-Hood-tax-A-rejection-Ben-Daniels.pdf

Danzinger, N. L., Felicitaz, D. H., Inmaculada, M. Z., & Vollme, S. (2005). The impact of a customs union between Turkey and the EU on Turkey's exports to the EU: A reassessment of the paradox. *DIW's Working Papers Series*, No. 483.

David Cameron's EU Speech – Full Text. (2013, January 23). *The Guardian*. Retrieved June 12, 2014, from http://www.theguardian.com/politics/2013/jan/23/david-cameron-eu-speech-referendum

Davies, C., & Wintour, P. (2013, May 17). CBI chief John Cridland issues warning over European Union exit. *The Guardian*. Retrieved July 12, 2014, from http://www.theguardian.com/politics/2013/may/17/cbi-john-cridland-european-union-exit

Davis, D. R., & Weinstein, D. E. (2003). Market access, economic geography and comparative advantage: An empirical test. *Journal of International Economics*, *59*(1), 1–23. doi:10.1016/S0022-1996(02)00088-0

de Santis, R. A. (2001). The 1990 trade liberalisation policy of Turkey: An applied general equilibrium assessment. *International Economic Journal*, *15*(2), 115–132.

de Waal, M. (2014). *The choice for Euro: the treaty on stability, coordination and governance through a liberal intergovernmentalist lens (2012-2014).* (Unpublished master dissertation). University of Twente, Faculty of Management and Governance, Netherland.

Dean, J. (2002). Does trade liberalization harm the environment? A new test. The Canadian Journal of Economics. Revue Canadienne d'Economique, 35(4), 819–842. doi:10.1111/0008-4085.00155 doi:10.1111/0008-4085.00155

Dedeoğlu, E. (1997). İl Özel İdarelerinin Tarihi Gelişimi Ve Bugünkü Durumu. *Yerel Yönetim Ve Denetim Dergisi, 2*(1).

Dellas, H. (1997). European monetary union: A new approach. *Journal of International Money and Finance, 16*(4), 581–594. doi:10.1016/S0261-5606(97)00019-3

Demetriades, P. O., & Khaled, A. H. (1996). Does financial development cause economic growth? Time-series evidence from 16 countries. *Journal of Development Economics, 51*(2), 387–411. doi:10.1016/S0304-3878(96)00421-X

Demurger, S., Sachs, J. D., Woo, W. T., Bao, S., Chang, G., & Mellinger, A. (2014). *Geography, economic policy and regional development in China.* Retrieved, May 16, 2014, from http://post.economics.harvard.edu/hier/2002papers/2002list.html

Deshpande, A., & Jadad, A. R. (2008). The impact of polyol-containing chewing gums on dental caries: A systematic review of original randomized controlled trials and observational studies. *The Journal of the American Dental Association, 139*(12), 1602–1614. doi:10.14219/jada.archive.2008.0102 PMID:19047666

Deutsche Bank- DB Research. (2013). *Do all roads lead to fiscal union? Options for deeper fiscal integraton in the Eurozone.* Frankfurt am Main: Author.

Deutsch, K. W. (1957). *Political community and the North Atlantic area; International organization in the light of historical experience.* Princeton, NJ: Princeton University Press.

Directive 65/65/EEC (Council Directive on the approximation of provisions laid down by Law, Regulation or Administrative Action relating to proprietary medicinal products 1 26, 1965).

Directive 93/16/EEC (Council Directive to facilitate the free movement of doctors and the mutual recognition of their diplomas, certificates and other evidence of formal qualifications 4 5, 1993).

Dobrescu, M. E., Pociovalistenau, D. M., & Brancusi, C. (n.d.). *One the slide of public deficiency and financial settlements.* Retrieved April 25, 2014, from http://www.ceeol.com/aspx/getdocument.aspx?logid=5&id=f34457f4-8d6d-402f-8ad0-8dc6ef971b30

Doğan, B. G. (2007). Toplum Agız ve Dis Saglıgı Göstergeleri. *Toplum Hekimligi Bulteni, 26*(2).

Dogru, B. (2013). The link between unemployment rate and real output in Eurozone: A panel error correction approach. *Procedia: Social and Behavioral Sciences, 99,* 94–103. doi:10.1016/j.sbspro.2013.10.475

Domingues, E. P., Haddad, E. A., & Hewings, G. (2008). Sensitivity analysis in applied general equilibrium models: An empirical assessment for MERCOSUR free trade areas agreements. *The Quarterly Review of Economics and Finance, 48*(2), 287–306. doi:10.1016/j.qref.2006.12.018

Dritsaki, M., & Chaido, D. (2013). Bounds testing approach for cointegration and causality between financial development, trade openness and economic growth in Bulgaria. *Journal of Applied Econometrics, 52*(1), 50–67.

Droz, D., Guéguen, R., Bruncher, P., Gerhard, J. L., & Roland, E. (2006). Epidemiological study of oral dental health of 4-year-old children in french nursery schools. *Archives of Pediatrics & Adolescent Medicine, 13,* 122Z–9. PMID:16860544

DTM. (2007). *Turkiye'nin Dis Ticareti ve AB'nin Payi.* Retrieved from: http://www.dtm.gov.tr/dtmweb/index.cfm?action=detay&yayinID=376&icerikID=475&dil=TR

Duina, F. (2006). *The social construction of free trade: The European Union, NAFTA, and MERCOSUR.* Princeton, NJ: Princeton University Press.

Duman, K. (2004). *Finansal Krizlere Karşı Politika Tercihleri*. Antalya, Turkey: Akdeniz İktisadi ve İdari Bilimler Fakültesi Yayınları.

Dura, C., & Atik, H. (2003). *Avrupa Birligi, Gumruk Birligi ve Turkiye*. Ankara: Nobel Yayin Dagitim.

Eaton, J., Kortum, S., Neiman, B., & Romalis, J. (2013). Trade and the global recession. NBER *Working Paper*, No:16666.

Eaton, K. A., Newman, H. N., & Bulman, J. S. (2003). National mean DMFF scores for Western European 12 year-olds — Are they Comparable? *Journal of Dental Research*, *82*(519), 334. PMID:12709497

Ebel, R. E. (2009). *The geopolitics of Russian energy: Looking back, looking forward*. Washington, DC: Center for Strategic & International Studies.

EC. (2009). Lisbon Treaty. *Article 168*.

EC. (2009). Lisbon Treaty. *Article 18, 39, 43, 28 and 49*.

Economic and Financial Affairs - European Commission. (2013). *Turkey from soft landing to renewed upturn*. Retrieved from http://ec.europa.eu/economy_finance/eu/forecasts/2013_spring/cc_turkey_en.pdf

Economic Benefits of EU Membership – Vox Views with Nauro Campos. (n.d.). *Vox*. Retrieved July 12, 2014, from http://www.voxeu.org/content/economic-benefits-eu-membership-vox-views-nauro-campos

Edblad, J. (1996). *The political economy of regional integration in developing countries*. CERUM-Centre for Regional Science Working Paper No. 3/1996. Retrieved February 10 2014 from http://www.diva-portal.org/smash/get/diva2:227410/FULLTEXT01.pdf

Eden, L. (2009). Taxes, transfer pricing and the multinational enterprise. In A. M. Rugman (Ed.), *The Oxford handbook of international business* (2nd ed.). Oxford University Press. doi:10.1093/oxfordhb/9780199234257.003.0021

Eder, M. (2003). Implementing the economic criteria of the EU membership: How difficult is it for Turkey? *Turkish Studies, Vol*, *4*(1), 219–244. doi:10.1080/714005711

Eder, T. S. (2014). *China-Russia relations in Central Asia: Energy policy, Beijing's new assertiveness and 21st century geopolitics*. Wiesbaden, Germany: Springer. doi:10.1007/978-3-658-03272-2

Edwards, S. (2000). Exchange rate regimes, capital flows and crisis prevention. *NBER*. 1-67.

Edwards, D. M., & Watt, R. G. (1997). Oral health care in the lives of Gypsy travellers in east Hertfordshire. *British Dental Journal*, *183*(252), 7. PMID:9364092

Eichengreen, B., Tobin, J., & Wyplosz, C. (1995). Two cases for sand in the wheels of international finance. *The Economic Journal*, *428*(105), 162–172. doi:10.2307/2235326

Eke, A. E. (1982). *Anakent Yönetimi ve Yönetimlerarası İlişkiler*. Ankara: AÜ SBF Yayınları.

Ekonomi Bakanlığı, T. C. (2014). Ekonomik Görünüm Nisan 2014: Kişi Başına Düşen GSYH Oranları. Academic Press.

Elliott, G., Rothenberg, T. J., & Stock, J. H. (1996). Efficient tests for an autoregressive unit root. *Econometrica*, *64*(4), 813–836. doi:10.2307/2171846

Elshamy, H. (2013). The relationship between unemployment and output in Egypt. *Procedia: Social and Behavioral Sciences*, *81*, 22–26. doi:10.1016/j.sbspro.2013.06.381

Emrealp, S. (2005). *Türkiye Yerel Gündem 21 Programı, Yerel Gündem 21 Uygulamalarına Yönelik Kolaylaştırıcı Bilgiler El Kitabı¸*. Istanbul: IULA-EMME Publications.

Engle, R. F., & Granger, C. W. J. (1987). Co-integration and error correction: Representation, estimation and testing. *Econometrica*, *55*(2), 251–276. doi:10.2307/1913236

Entre les marchés et l'Europe, le Royaume-Uni a choisi. (2014, December 10). *RTL*. Retrieved July 14, 2014, from http://www.rtl.fr/actu/international/entre-le-marche-et-l-europe-le-royaume-uni-a-choisi-7740381990

Erdoğan, İ., & Ejder, N. (1997). *Çevre Sorunları; Nedenler, Çözümler-Egemen ve Marksist Anlayışın İlettikleri Üzerine*. Ankara: Doruk Publications.

Erdoğdu, M., & Balseven, H. (2006). How effective is the Tobin tax in coping with financial volatility? *Anadolu Üniversitesi Sosyal Bilimler Journal*, (1). Retrieved from http://www.asosindex.com/journal-article-abstract?id=849

Erdönmez, P. A. (2009). *Küresel Kriz ve Ülkeler Tarafından Alınan Önlemler Kronolojisi*. İstanbul, Turkey: Bankacılar Dergisi.

Ericsson, J. S., Abrahamsson, K. H., & Ostberg, A. L. (2009). Periodontal health status in Swedish adolescents: An epidemiological, cross-sectional study. *Swedish Dental Journal*, *33*, 131–139. PMID:19994563

Erim, N. (2007). *İktisadi Düşünce Tarihi*. Ankara, Turkey: Palme Yayıncılık.

Erkip, F. (2000). Global transformations versus local dynamics in Istanbul: Planning in a fragmented metropolis. *Cities (London, England)*, *17*(5), 371–377. doi:10.1016/S0264-2751(00)00033-0

Ersayin, Z. (2012). Assessment of additiveness in public intervention. In *Assessment of additiveness in public intervention*. Ankara, Turkey: Ministery of Development.

Ertürk, H. (2011). *Çevre Politikası*. Bursa: Ekin Publications.

Eruygur, H. O., & Cakmak, E. H. (2005). Trade implications of extending Turkey-EU customs union to agricultural products. In *Proceedings of the Conference of 'Middile East and North African Economies: Past Perspectives and Future Challenges*. Brussels, Belgium: Academic Press.

Eryilmaz, B. (1992). *Tanzimat Ve Yönetimde Modernleşme*. İstanbul: İşaret Yayınları.

Eryilmaz, B. (1997). *Yerel Yönetimlerin Yeniden Yapılanması*. İstanbul: Birleşik Yayıncılık.

Eryilmaz, B. (2011). *Kamu Yönetimi*. Ankara: Okutman.

EU Poll Battle Bus in Town. (2012, May 16). *Birmingham Evening Mail*. Retrieved July 14, 2014, from http://www.lexisnexis.com/hottopics/lnacademic

EU Referendum 'Unlikely' under Labour, says Ed Miliband. (2014, March 12). *BBC*. Retrieved July 9, 2014, from http://www.bbc.com/news/uk-politics-26538420

EU. (2013). *The new SME definition*. Retrieved, December 30, 2013, from http://ec.europa.eu/enterprise/policies/sme/files/sme_definition/sme_user_guide_en.pdf

EUNİDA. (n.d.). Retrieved, October 30, 2013, from http://www.eunida.eu/

Euroactiv. (2006). *EU-Turkey negotiations*. Retrieved from: http://www.euractiv.com/en/enlargement/eu-turkey-negotiations/article-145219

Eurobaromoter 72.3 Oral Health. Special Eurobarometer 330. (2010). Retrivied from: http://eceuropa.eu/public_opinion/archives/ebs/ebs_330_en.pdf

Europe Backs Down in Bid to Tackle Mega-Banks. (2014, January 29). *Reuters*. Retrieved April 14, 2014, from http://uk.reuters.com/article/2014/01/29/uk-eu-banks-idUKBREA0S0PY20140129

European Central Bank. (2011). *The Eurosystem: The European system of the central banks*. Luxembourg: European Central Bank.

European Commıssıon. (2010). *Financial sector taxation*. Working Paper No.25. Retrieved from http://ec.europa.eu/taxation_customs/resources/documents/taxation/gen_info/economic_analysis/tax_papers/taxation_paper_25_en.pdf

European Commission. (2012). *A roadmap towards a banking union, COM(2012)510*. Retrieved from http://ec.europa.eu/internal_market/finances/banking-union/index_en.html

European Commıssıon. (2013). *Proposal for a council directive implementing enhanced cooperation in the area of financial transaction tax {SWD(2013) 28 final} {SWD(2013) 29 final}. Brussels, 14.2.2013, COM(2013) 71 final, 2013/0045 (CNS)*. Retrieved from http://ec.europa.eu/taxation_customs/resources/documents/taxation/com_2013_71_en.pdf

European Commission. (2013). *Turkey 2013 progress report*. Retrieved from http://ec.europa.eu/enlargement/pdf/key_documents/2013/package/brochures/turkey_2013.pdf

European Commission. (2013). *Enlargement: Chapters of the acqius*. Retrieved from http://ec.europa.eu/enlargement/policy/conditions-membership/chapters-of-the-acquis/index_en.htm

European Commission. (2013). *From 6 to 28 members*. Retrieved from http://ec.europa.eu/enlargement/policy/from-6-to-28-members/index_en.htm

European Commission. (2013). *Steps towards joining*. Retrieved from http://ec.europa.eu/enlargement/policy/steps-towards-joining/index_en.htm

European Commission. (2014). *EU-Albania: Solid argument for candidate status*. Retrieved from http://ec.europa.eu/commission_2010-2014/fule/headlines/news/2014/06/20140604_en.htm

European Commission. (2014). *Countries preparing to join*. Retrieved from http://ec.europa.eu/enlargement/countries/check-current-status/index_en.htm

European Commission. (2014). *Detailed country information: Serbia*. Retrieved from http://ec.europa.eu/enlargement/countries/detailed-country-information/serbia/index_en.htm

European Commission. (2014). *Detailed country information: Montenegro*. Retrieved from http://ec.europa.eu/enlargement/countries/detailed-country-information/montenegro/index_en.htm

European Commission. (2014). *Detailed country information: Former Yugoslav Republic of Macedonia*. Retrieved from http://ec.europa.eu/enlargement/countries/detailed-country-information/fyrom/index_en.htm

European Commission. (2014). *Detailed country information: Iceland*. Retrieved from http://ec.europa.eu/enlargement/countries/detailed-country-information/iceland/index_en.htm

European Commission. (2014). *Detailed country information: Turkey*. Retrieved from http://ec.europa.eu/enlargement/countries/detailed-country-information/turkey/index_en.htm

European Council Conclusions. (2012, October 9). *EUCO 156/12*. Retrieved June 1, 2014, from http://www.consilium.europa.eu/uedocs/cms_data/docs/pressdata/en/ec/133004.pdf

European Council. (1993). *Press release: Copenhagen criteria*. Retrieved from http://europa.eu/rapid/press-release_DOC-93-3_en.htm?locale=en

European Union Center of North Carolina. (2012). *The politics of an EU financial transactions tax*. EU Briefings. Retrieved from http://europe.unc.edu/wp-content/uploads/2013/08/Brief1206-ftt.pdf

European Union Finances 2013: Statement on the 2013 EU Budget and Measures to Counter Fraud and Financial Mismanagement (2013, November). *HM Treasury*. Retrieved July 12, 2014, from https://www.gov.uk/government/uploads/system/uploads/attachment_data/file/259692/EU_Finances_2013.pdf

Eurostat. (2013). *Smarter, greener, more inclusive? Indicators to support the Europe 2020 strategy*. Luxembourg: Eurostat.

EUROSTAT. (2014). *Selected principal European economic indicators*. Retrieved April 22, 2014, from http://epp.eurostat.ec.europa.eu/cache/ITY_PUBLIC/3-08012014-BP/EN/3-08012014-BP-EN.PDF

EU Treaties. (n.d.). Retrieved July 10, 2014, from http://europa.eu/about-eu/basic-information/decision-making/treaties/index_en.htm

Expenditure Tax General Communique No 89. (2012). Retrieved from http://www.gib.gov.tr/index.php?id=1079&uid=dPD8ZomGh2rFg1SH&type=teblig

Farrell, M., Hettne, B., & Langenhove, L. v. (Eds.). (2005). *Global politics of regionalism: Theory and practice*. Pluto Press.

Fawcett, L. L. E., & Hurrell, A. (1995). *Regionalism in world politics: Regional organization and international order*. New York: Oxford University Press.

Felix, D. (1995). Financial globalization and the Tobin tax. *Challenge*, 56–59.

Felix, D. (1995). The Tobin tax proposal, background, issues and prospects. *Furures*, *2*(27), 195–208.

Feridun, M. (2006). Impact of trade liberalization on the environment in developing countries: The case of Nigeria. Journal of Developing Societies, 22(1), 9–56. doi:10.1177/0169796X06062965 doi:10.1177/0169796X06062965

Ferlay, J., Parkin, D. M., & Steliarova-Foucher, E. (2010). Estimates of cancer incidence and mortality in Europe in 2008. *European Journal of Cancer*, *46*(4), 765–781. doi:10.1016/j.ejca.2009.12.014 PMID:20116997

Ferry, J. P. (2013). The known unknowns and unknown unknowns of European Monetary Union. *Journal of International Money and Finance*, *34*, 6–14. doi:10.1016/j.jimonfin.2012.11.002

Filiztekin, A. (2008). *Regional differences and policies in Turkey. (s. 97)*. TUSİAD.

Fontagne, L., Foure, J., & Keck, A. (2014). Stimulating world trade in the decades ahead: Driving forces and policy implications. *World Trade Organisation Working Paper* ERSD-2014-05.

Fox, E. M. (2012). Competition, development and regional integration: In search of a competition law fit for developing countries, law & economics research paper series working paper. *Economic Research Paper Series Working Paper*, s. 2-3.

France and Germany Propose EU 'Competitiveness Pact'. (2011, February 4). *BBC*. Retrieved June 12, 2014, from http://www.bbc.co.uk/news/world-europe-12368401

Francois, J. (2005). Accession of Turkey to the EU: Implications for the transport sector. In Turkey economic reform and accession to the European Union. Washington, DC: The World Bank.

Francois, J. F., McQueen, M., & Wignaraja, G. (2003). An overview of EU FTAs. In *Proceedings of the Vienna World Economic Institute Workshop on WTO Issues*. Vienna: Academic Press.

Francois, J., Manchin, M., Norberg, H., Pindyuk, O., & Tomberger, P. (2013). *Reducing transatlantic barriers to trade and investment: an economic assessment*. London: Center for Economic Policy Research. Retrieved March 29 2014 from http://trade.ec.europa.eu/doclib/docs/2013/march/tradoc_150737.pdf

Frank, A. G. (1998). *ReOrient: Global economy in the Asian age*. Berkeley, CA: University of California Press.

Frankel, J. A., & Rose, A. K. (2005). Is trade good or bad for the environment? Sorting out the causality. The Review of Economics and Statistics, 87(1), 85–91. doi:10.1162/0034653053327577 doi:10.1162/0034653053327577

Freeman, D. G. (2001). Panel tests of Okun's law for ten industrial countries. *Economic Inquiry*, *39*(4), 511–523. doi:10.1093/ei/39.4.511

Freiling, J. (2014). *SME management – What can we learn from entrepreneurship theory?* Retrieved, May 21, 2014, from http://papers.ssrn.com/sol3/papers.cfm?abstract_id=984658

Freund, C. (2000). Different paths to free trade: The gains from regionalism. *The Quarterly Journal of Economics*, *115*(4), 1317–1341. doi:10.1162/003355300555088

Freund, C. (2010). Third-country effects of regional trade agreements. *World Economy*, *33*(11), 1589–1605. doi:10.1111/j.1467-9701.2010.01283.x

G20. (2008). *Declaration*. Summit on Financial Markets and the World Economy. Retrieved March 19, 2014, from http://www.g20.org/Documents/g20_summit_declaration.pdf

G7 Summit. (1996). *Economic communiqué: Making a success of globalization for the benefit of all, Lyon, 18.06.1996*. Retrieved March 30, 2014, from http://europa.eu/rapid/press-release_DOC-96-5_en.htm

Gallagher, K., & Ackerman, F. (2000). *Trade liberalization and pollution intensive industry in developing countries*. Global Development and Environment Institute, Working Paper No 3.

GB. risques accrus d'une sortie de l'UE après la défaite de Cameron contre Juncker. (2014, June 28). *Agence France Presse*. Retrieved June 30, 2014, from http://www.lexisnexis.com/hottopics/lnacademic

GDP Growth (Annual %). (n.d.). *The World Bank*. Retrieved June 4, 2014, from http://data.worldbank.org/indicator/NY.GDP.MKTP.KD.ZG/countries?display=default

Geldi, H. K. (2012). Trade effects of regional integration: A panel cointegration analysis. *Economic Modelling*, *29*(5), 1566–1570. doi:10.1016/j.econmod.2012.05.017

George, A. R. (Ed.). (2003). The Babylonian Gilgamesh epic: Introduction, critical edition and cuneiform texts (vol. 1). Oxford.

Geradin, D. (2014). *The development of european regulatory agencies: What the EU should learn from Amerıcan experience*. Retrieved, May 24, 2014, from http://papers.ssrn.com/sol3/papers.cfm?abstract_id=877922

Gerber, J. (2013). International economics. Prentice Hall.

Germany Insists no Eurobonds to Solve Debt Crisis. (2012, May 21). *Fox News*. Retrieved May 19, 2014, from http://www.foxnews.com/world/2012/05/21/germany-insists-no-eurobonds-to-solve-debt-crisis/

Gifford, C. (2006). The rise of post-imperial populism: The case of right-wing Euroscepticism in Britain. *European Journal of Political Research*, *45*(5), 851–869. doi:10.1111/j.1475-6765.2006.00638.x

Gifford, C. (2014). The people against Europe: The Eurosceptic challenge to the united kingdom's coalition government. *JCMS: Journal of Common Market Studies*, *52*(3), 512–528.

Gilpin, R. G. (1986). The richness of the tradition of political realism. In R. O. Keohane (Ed.), *Neorealism and its critics* (pp. 301–322). Columbia University Press.

Glassman, P., & Miller, C. E. (2003). Preventing dental disease for people with special needs: The need for practical preventive protocols for use in community settings. *Special Care in Dentistry*, *23*(5), 165–167. doi:10.1111/j.1754-4505.2003.tb00305.x PMID:14965180

Glencross, A. (2014). The Eurozone crisis as a challenge to democracy and integration in Europe. *Orbis*, *58*(1), 55–68. doi:10.1016/j.orbis.2013.11.003

Gökbunar, R., Yanıkkaya, H., & Cura, S. (2008). *Avrupa Birliği'nin Türkiyeli Geleceği Umutlar ve Korkular*. Ankara: Nobel Yayıncılık.

Goldman, M. I. (2008). *Petrostate: Putin, power, and the new Russia*. New York: Oxford University Press.

Goldsmith, R. W. (1969). *Financial structure and development*. New Haven, CT: Yale University Press.

Gonul, F. D. (2010). Economy of development. In F. D. Gonul içinde (Ed.), Economy of development (pp. 237-298). Ankara: Efil Bookstore.

Gooch, B. F., Griffin, S. O., Gray, S. K., Kohn, W. G., Rozier, R. G., Siegal, M., & Zero, D. T. et al. (2009). Preventing dental caries through school-based sealant programs: Updated recommendations and reviews of evidence. *The Journal of the American Dental Association*, *140*(11), 1356–1365. doi:10.14219/jada.archive.2009.0070 PMID:19884392

Goodhart, C., & Schoenmaker, D. (2009). Fiscal burden sharing in cross-border banking crisis. *International Journal of Central Banking*, *5*(1), 141–165.

Gopinath, G., Itskhoki, O., & Neiman, B. (2012). Trade prices and the global trade collapse of 2008-09. *IMF Economic Review*, *60*(3), 303–328. doi:10.1057/imfer.2012.17

Görmez, K. (2010). *Çevre Sorunları*. Ankara: Nobel Publications.

Gould, J. E. (2014, January 8). Roadmap to a banking union. *The Financialist*. Retrieved May 18, 2014, http://www.thefinancialist.com/roadmap-to-a-banking-union/

Gowa, J. (1989). Bipolarity, multipolarity, and free trade. *The American Political Science Review*, *83*(4), 1245–1256. doi:10.2307/1961667

Göymen, K. (2006). Dynamics of changes in Turkish local governance. *Demise of the Bureaucratic Ruling Tradition Society and Economy*, *28*(3), 245–266.

Gravelle, J. (2013). *Tax havens: International tax avoidance and evasion, CRS report for congress*. Retrieved April 19, 2014, from https://www.fas.org/sgp/crs/misc/R40623.pdf

Greer, S. (2006). Uninvited Europeanization: Neofunctionalism and the EU in health policy. *Journal of European Public Policy*, *13*(1), 134–152. doi:10.1080/13501760500380783

Gregorio, J. D., & Pablo, E. G. (1995). Financial development and economic growth. *World Development*, *23*(3), 433–448. doi:10.1016/0305-750X(94)00132-I

Grieco, J. (1993). Understanding the problem of international cooperation: The limitations of neoliberal institutionalism and the future of realist theory. In D. Baldwin (Ed.), *Neorealism and neoliberalism: The contemporary debate*. New York: Columbia University Press.

Grieco, J. (1995). The Maastricht treaty, economic and monetary union, and the neorealist research programme. *Review of International Studies*, *21*(01), 21–40. doi:10.1017/S0260210500117504

Gries, T., Manfred, K., & Meierrieks, D. (2009). Linkages between financial deepening, trade openness, and economic development: Causality evidence from Sub-Saharan Africa. *World Development*, *37*(12), 1849–1860. doi:10.1016/j.worlddev.2009.05.008

Groen, J. J. J., & Kleibergen, F. (2003). Likelihood-based cointegration analysis in panels of vector error correction models. Journal of Business & Economic Statistics, 21(2), 295–318. doi:10.1198/073500103288618972 doi:10.1198/073500103288618972

Groom, B. (2014, July 7). Political risks top concerns for UK company finance chiefs. *Financial Times*. Retrieved July 14, 2014, from http://www.ft.com/intl/cms/s/0/bf097006-037d-11e4-9195-00144feab7de.html#axzz37QWUcfdo

Gros, D. (2013). Banking union with a sovereign virus. *Inter Economics*, *48*(2), 93–97. doi:10.1007/s10272-013-0449-8

Grossman, H. I. (1975). Tobin on macroeconomics: A review article. *The Journal of Political Economy*, *83*(4), 829-848.

Growth, Competitiveness, Employment: The Challenges and Ways Forward into the 21st Century. (1993, December 5). *European Commission.* White Paper. COM(93) 700.

Guiso, L., Sapienza, P., & Zingales, L. (n.d.). *Does local financial development matter*. Retrieved, May 17, 2014, from http://papers.ssrn.com/sol3/papers.cfm?abstract_id=308569

Güler, B. (2012). *Keleş.,E. & Uçar.,Ö.* Ankara: Finansal İşlem Vergileri ve Avrupa Birliği Uygulaması.

Haas, E. B. (1958). *The uniting of Europe: Political, social, and economic forces, 1950-1957*. Stanford, CA: Stanford University Press.

Haas, E. B., & Whiting, A. S. (1975). *Dynamics of international relations*. Westport, CT: Greenwood Press.

Hall, M. (2012, January 31). MPs urged to back EU referendum ballots. *The Daily Express*. Retrieved July 14, 2014, from http://www.express.co.uk/news/uk/299080/MPs-urged-to-back-EU-referendum-ballots

Hamilton, D. S., & Quinlan, J. P. (2013). *The transatlantic economy 2013 annual survey of jobs, trade and investment between the United States and Europe.* Center for Transatlantic Relations and Transatlantic Business Consul, Washington, D.C., USA. Retrieved April 14 2014 from http://transatlantic.sais-jhu.edu/publications/books/Transatlantic_Economy_2013/TE2013%20volume%201.pdf

Hansen, E. D. (2001). *European economic history*. Copenhagen Bussines School Press DK.

Harrison, G.W., Rutherford, T.F. & Tarr, D.G. (1996). *Economic implications for Turkey of a customs union with the European Union.* The World Bank, International Economics Department, International Trade Division.

Harrison, G. W., Rutherford, T. F., & Tarr, D. G. (1993). Trade reform in the partially liberalised economy of Turkey. *The World Bank Economic Review*, *7*(2), 191–217. doi:10.1093/wber/7.2.191

Harrison, G. W., Rutherford, T. F., & Tarr, D. G. (1997). Economic implications of Turkey of a customs union with the European Union. *European Economic Review*, *41*(3-5), 861–870. doi:10.1016/S0014-2921(97)00043-3

Harrison, G., Rutherfold, T., & Tarr, D. (1997). Quantifying the Uruguay round. *The Economic Journal*, *107*(444), 1405–1430. doi:10.1111/j.1468-0297.1997.tb00055.x

Harris, R., & Sollis, R. (2003). *Applied time series modeling and forecasting*. West Sussex, UK: Wiley.

Hashibe, M., Brennan, P., & Chuang, S. C. (2009). Interaction between tobacco and alcohol use and the risk of head and neck cancer: Pooled analysis in the INHANCE consortium. *Cancer Epidemiology, Biomarkers & Prevention, 18*, 541–550. PMID:19190158

Hayward, T. (1995). *Ecological Thought: An Introduction*. Cambridge, MA: Polity Press.

Helpman, E. (1981). International trade in the presence of product differentiation, economies of scale and monopolistic competition: A Chamberlin-Heckscher-Ohlin approach. *Journal of International Economics, 11*(3), 305–340. doi:10.1016/0022-1996(81)90001-5

Heper, M. (1992). The strong state as a problem of democracy: Turkey and Germany compared. *Comparative Political Studies, 25*(2), 169–194. doi:10.1177/0010414092025002002

Heper, M., & Keyman, F. (1998). Double-faced state: Political patronage and the consolidation of democracy in Turkey. *Middle Eastern Studies, 34*(4), 259–277. doi:10.1080/00263209808701251

Hervey, T. (2002). Mapping the contours of European Union health law and policy. *European Public Law, 8*(1), 69–105. doi:10.1023/A:1014542608569

Hervey, T., & McHale, J. (2004). *Health law and the European Union*. Cambridge, UK: Cambridge University Press. doi:10.1017/CBO9780511617553

Hettne, B., & Soderbaum, F. (2014, May 2). *The new regionalism approach: The new regionalism and north-south trade agreements*. United Nations Conference on Trade and Development. Retrieved from http://www.Unctad.Org/En/Docs/Tdr2007ch3_En.Pdf

Hettne, B., Inotai, A., & Sunkel, O. (1999). *Globalism and the new regionalism*. Palgrave Macmillan.

Hines, J. R. Jr. (2010, Fall). Treasure islands. *The Journal of Economic Perspectives, 24*(4), 103–126. doi:10.1257/jep.24.4.103

Hoekman, B. M., & Togan, S. (2005). *Turkey: Economic reform & accession to the European Union*. Washington, DC: World Bank and the Centre for Economic Policy Research. doi:10.1596/978-0-8213-5932-0

Hoffmann, S. (1963). Discord in community: The North Atlantic area as a partial international system. *International Organization, 17*(3), 521–549. doi:10.1017/S0020818300034536

Holhausen, C., & Ronde, T. (2004). Cooperation in international banking supervision. *ECB Working Paper*, No 245.

Hollande à Cameron: "Pas possible de négocier l'Europe". (2013, January 23). *Le Figaro*. Retrieved July 15, 2014, from http://www.lefigaro.fr/international/2013/01/23/01003-20130123ARTFIG00343-fabius-previent-cameron-pas-d-europe-a-la-carte.php

Hollande Proposes Eurozone 'Government' as Differences with Merkel Show. (2013, May 17). *Deutsche Welle*. Retrieved June 1, 2014, from http://www.dw.de/hollande-proposes-eurozone-government-as-differences-with-merkel-show/a-16819966

Hollande, M. (2012, June 22). Merkel et Rajoy tentent de s'accorder avant le sommet Européen. *France24*. Retrieved May 18, 2014, from http://www.france24.com/fr/20120622-zone-euro-sommet-plan-anti-crise-rencontre-monti-merkel-hollande-rajoy/

Holm, H. H., & Sørensen, G. (1995). *Whose world order? Uneven globalization and the end of the Cold War*. Boulder, CO: Westview Press.

Honkapohja, S. (2014). The Euro area crisis: A view from the north. *Journal of Macroeconomics, 39*, 260–271. doi:10.1016/j.jmacro.2013.08.004

Horvat, B. (1999). *The theory of international trade: An alternative approach*. London, UK: Palgrave Macmillan. doi:10.1057/9780333983386

Houlder, V. (2010). Tax haven drive will mean greater scrutiny. *Financial Times*. Retrieved March 20, 2014, from http://www.ft.com/cms/s/0/385490cc-336b-11df-bc32-00144feabdc0.html

HSCB Bank A.ş. (2013, March). Almanya Türk Yatırımcısına Büyük Fırsatlar Sunuyor. *Turkish Time Global Export*, p. 5.

Hsueh, S. J., Yu-Hau, H., & Chien-Heng, T. (2013). Economic growth and financial development in Asian countries: A bootstrap panel Granger causality analysis. *Economic Modelling*, *32*, 294–301. doi:10.1016/j.econmod.2013.02.027

Huang, H. C., & Lin, S. C. (2008). Smooth-time-varying Okun's coefficients. *Economic Modelling*, *25*(2), 363–375. doi:10.1016/j.econmod.2007.06.009

Hughes, K. (2004). Turkey and the European Union: Just another enlargement. *A Friends of Europe Working Paper*.

Hugo, V. (n.d.). *Les états-Unis d'Europe, Discours prononcé le21août1849lors du Congrès de la paix*. Retrieved June 8, 2014, from http://www.oasisfle.com/culture_oasisfle/etats_unis_d_europe.htm

Iain Mansfield named winner of €100.000 IEA Brexit Prize. (2014, April 8). Retrieved July 8, 2014, from http://www.iea.org.uk/in-the-media/press-release/iain-mansfield-named-winner-of-%E2%82%AC100000-iea-brexit-prize

IMF Country Report. (2012). *Euro area policies - 2012 article IV consultation- No.12/181*. Washington, DC: Author.

IMF Working Paper. (2012). *Fiscal rules in response to the crisis—Toward the "next-generation" rule*. Washington, DC: Author.

Im, K. S., Pesaran, M. H., & Shin, Y. (2003). Testing for unit roots in heterogeneous panels. *Journal of Econometrics*, *115*(1), 53–63. doi:10.1016/S0304-4076(03)00092-7

Inman, P. (2012, May 24). Eurobonds: An essential guide. *The Guardian*. Retrieved May 18, 2014, from http://www.theguardian.com/business/2012/may/24/eurobonds-an-essential-guide

International Council for Local Environmental Initiatives. (1996), Local agenda 21 planning guide: An introduction to sustainable development planning. Author.

International Council for Local Environmental Initiatives. (1997). Avrupa Yerel Gündem 21 Planlama Rehberi. (T., Albayrak, G.Celik & G.Okyay, Trans.). Author.

International Monetary Fund (IMF) Working Paper. (2001). *Is fiscal policy coordination in EMU desirable?* Washington, DC: Author.

International Union for Conservation of Nature- United Nations Environment Program-World Wildlife Fund. (1980). *World conservation strategy-Living resources conservationfor sustainable development*. Retrieved May 14, 2014, from http://cisdl.org/biodiversity-biosafety/public/docs/wcs.pdf

Ioannou, D., & Stracca, L. (2014). Havethe euro area and EU governance worked? Just the facts. *European Journal of Political Economy*, *34*, 1–17. doi:10.1016/j.ejpoleco.2013.11.009

Isaacs, D. (2009). *The extinction of evolution*. Bridge-Logos.

Işık, A., & Mutlu, A. (2011). *Saglık Ekonomisine Giris*. Ekin Basım Yayın.

Islam, F., Shahbaz, M., Ahmed, A. U., & Alam, M. M. (2013). Financial development and energy consumption nexus in Malaysia: A multivariate time series analysis. *Economic Modelling*, *30*, 435–441. doi:10.1016/j.econmod.2012.09.033

İstanbul, E. (2014). Retrieved, January 07, 2014, from http://borsaistanbul.com/urunler-ve-piyasalar/piyasalar/pay-piyasasi

Itoh, M., & Urata, S. (2014). *Small and medium size enterprise support policy in Japan*. Retrieved, May 25, 2014, from http://papers.ssrn.com/sol3/papers.cfm?abstract_id=604918

İzci, F., & Turan, M. (2013). Türkiye'de Büyükşehir Belediyesi Sistemi ve 6360 Sayili Yasa İle Büyükşehir Belediyesi Sisteminde Meydana Gelen Değişimler. *Van Örneği Süleyman Demirel Üniversitesi İktisadi ve İdari Bilimler Fakültesi Dergisi*, *18*(1), 117–152.

Jackson, A. (2012, October 26). *The Financialist*. Retrieved June 10, 2014, http://www.thefinancialist.com/euro-area-banking-union-gains-momentum-axel-lang-credit-suisse/

Jacques Delors suggère au Royaume-Uni de quitter l'UE. (2012, December 28). *Le Monde*. Retrieved July 15, 2014, from http://www.lemonde.fr/europe/article/2012/12/28/jacques-delors-suggere-au-royaume-uni-de-quitter-l-ue_1811217_3214.html. http://labourforareferendum.com. Retrieved July 9, 2014.

Jaffe, A. M., & Soligo, R. (2009). Energy security: The Russian connection. In D. Moran & J. A. Russell (Eds.), *Energy security and global politics: The militarization of resource management* (pp. 112–135). New York: Routledge.

Johansen, S., & Juselius, K. (1990). Maximum likelihood estimation and inference on cointegration with application to the demand for money. *Oxford Bulletin of Economics and Statistics*, *52*(2), 169–210. doi:10.1111/j.1468-0084.1990.mp52002003.x

Johnson, H. G. (1962). *The economic theory of customs unions in money, trade and economic growth*. London: George Allen and Unwin.

Johnson, T. H. (2009). Central Asia: Energy resources, politics, and security. In D. Moran & J. A. Russell (Eds.), *Energy security and global politics: The militarization of resource management* (pp. 135–155). New York: Routledge.

Jones, C., & Temouri, Y. (2014). *FDI in tax havens: Do corporate tax rates matter?* Retrieved April 1, 2014, from http://www.etsg.org/ETSG2013/Papers/105.pdf

Jovanović, M. N. (2005). *The economics of European integration: Limits and prospects*. Edward Elgar Pub.

Juzhong Zhuang, O. (2014). *Financial sector development, economic growth, and poverty*. Retrieved, May 21, 2014, from http://www.adb.org/publications/financial-sector-development-economic-growth-and-poverty-reduction-literature-review

Kacowicz, A. M. (1998). *Zones of peace in the third world: South America and West Africa in comparative perspective*. Albany, NY: State University of New York Press.

Kangas, R. (2007). The changing face of the Russian far east: Cooperation and resource competition between Japan, Korea, and China in Northeast Asia. *Perspectives on Global Development and Technology*, *6*(1-3), 441–460. doi:10.1163/156914907X207829

Kant, I. (1795). *Perpetual peace: A philosophical sketch*. Retrieved June 7, 2014, from http://isites.harvard.edu/fs/docs/icb.topic248058.files/March%2017%20readings/Kant%20Perpetual%20Peace%20section%20II.pdf

Kao, C. (1999). Spurious regression and residual-based tests for cointegration in panel data. *Journal of Econometrics*, *90*(1), 1–44. doi:10.1016/S0304-4076(98)00023-2

Karaca, H. (1995). *Sürdürülebilir Bir Yaşam İçin İnsan Verimliliği* (Vol. 1-5). Ankara: Yeni Türkiye.

Kawai, M., & Wignaraja, G. (2011). Asian FTAs: Trends, prospects and challenges. *Journal of Asian Economics*, *22*(1), 1–22. doi:10.1016/j.asieco.2010.10.002

Kaya, K. (2007). *A new model of regional development*. Ankara: Develeopment Agencies and Applicability in Turkey.

Kayasü, S., & Yaşar, S. S. (2006). *Development policies in the EU accession process: Legal and institutional transformation*. Paper presented at the Regional Development and Governance Symposium, Ankara, Turkey.

Kazgan, G. (2002). *Küreselleşme ve Ulus-Devlet Yeni Ekonomik Düzen*. İstanbul, Turkey: İstanbul Bilgi Üniversitesi Yayınları.

Kazgan, G. (2012). *2008 Küresel Krizi: Nedenleri, Etik Ilkeleri ve Iktisat Eğitimi*. Ankara, Turkey: Turkish Economic Association.

Keating, M. (1993). *Yeryüzü Zirvesinde Değişimin Gündemi*. Ankara: Publications of Environment Foundation of Turkey/UNEP National Committee.

Keleş, R. (2012). *Yerinden Yönetim Ve Siyaset*. İstanbul: Cem.

Keleş, R., & Hamamcı, C. (1993). *Çevrebilim*. Ankara: İmge Publishing House.

Keohane, R., & Martin, L. (1995). The promise of institutional theory. *International Security*, *20*(1), 39–51. doi:10.2307/2539214

Kim, D. H., Shu-Chin, L., & Yu-Bo, S. (2010). Dynamic effects of trade openness on financial development. *Economic Modelling*, *27*(1), 254–261. doi:10.1016/j.econmod.2009.09.005

Kim, D. H., Shu-Chin, L., & Yu-Bo, S. (2012). The simultaneous evolution of economic growth, financial development, and trade openness. *The Journal of International Trade & Economic Development*, *21*(4), 513–537. doi:10.1080/09638199.2010.497933

King, R. G., & Levine, R. (1993). Finance, entrepreneurship and growth. *Journal of Monetary Economics*, *32*(3), 513–542. doi:10.1016/0304-3932(93)90028-E

Koçak, S. Y., & Kavsara, V. (2012). 5302 Sayılı Kanun Sonrasında İl Özel İdarelerinde Yaşanan Sorunlar Ve Çözüm Önerileri. *Yönetim Bilimleri Dergisi*, *10*(20), 61–92.

Koivusilta, L., Honkala, S., Honkala, E., & Rimpela, A. (2003). Toothbrushing as part of the adolescent lifestyle predicts education level. *Journal of Dental Research*, *82*(5), 361–366. doi:10.1177/154405910308200507 PMID:12709502

Kollmann, R., Ratto, M., Roeger, W., & Veld, J. i. (2013). Fiscal policy, banks and the financial crisis. *Journal of Economic Dynamics & Control*, *37*(2), 387–403. doi:10.1016/j.jedc.2012.09.007

Konig, J., Holtfreter, B., & Kocher, T. (2010). Periodontal health in Europe: Future trends based on treatment needs and the provision of periodontal services-position paper. *European Journal of Dental Education*, *1*, 4–24. doi:10.1111/j.1600-0579.2010.00620.x PMID:20415972

Kousenidis, D. V., Ladas, A. C., & Negakis, C. I. (2013). The effects of the European debt crisis on earnings quality. *International Review of Financial Analysis*, *30*, 352–362. doi:10.1016/j.irfa.2013.03.004

Krapohl, S., & Fink, S. (2013). Different paths of regional integration: Trade networks and regional institution-building in Europe, Southeast Asia and Southern Africa. *Journal of Common Market Studies*, *51*(3), 472–488. doi:10.1111/jcms.12012

Kreinin, M. E., & Plummer, M. G. (2008). Effects of regional integration on FDI: An empirical approach. *Journal of Asian Economics*, *19*(5-6), 447–454. doi:10.1016/j.asieco.2008.09.005

Krotz, U., & Schild, J. (2013). *Shaping Europe: France, Germany, and embedded bilateralism from the Elysée Treaty to twenty-first century politics*. Oxford, UK: Oxford University Press.

Krugman, P. (1991, November). The move toward free trade zones. *Economic Review,* 5-25.

Krugman, P. R. (1980). Scale economies, product differentiation, and the pattern of trade. *The American Economic Review*, *70*(5), 950–959.

Kübler, D. (2014, May 7). *Megacities and the challenge of governance*. Zurich Open Repository and Archive, University of Zurich Main Library Winterthurerstrasse. Retrieved from www.zora.uzh.ch

Kubosova, L. (2008). *EU states crack down on tax evasion*. Retrieved March 19, 2014, from http://euobserver.com/9/26976

Kuhrt, N. (2012). The Russian far east in Russia's Asia policy: Dual integration or double periphery?[Article]. *Europe-Asia Studies*, *64*(3), 471–493. doi:10.1080/09668136.2012.661926

Kukla-Gryz, A. (2009). Economic growth, international trade and air pollution: A decomposition analysis. Ecological Economics, 68(5), 1329–1339. doi:10.1016/j.ecolecon.2008.09.005 doi:10.1016/j.ecolecon.2008.09.005

Kula, E. (2003). *History of environmental economic thought*. London: Routledge.

Kurugman, P. R. (1979). Increasing returns, monopolistic competition and international trade. *Journal of International Economics*, *9*(4), 469–479. doi:10.1016/0022-1996(79)90017-5

Lammers, K. (2006). The EU and Turkey – Economic effects of Turkey's full membership. *Inter Economics*, *41*(5), 282–288. doi:10.1007/s10272-006-0198-z

Lancaster, K. (1980). Intra-industry trade under perfect monopolistic competition. *Journal of International Economics*, *10*(2), 151–175. doi:10.1016/0022-1996(80)90052-5

Lane, P. R. (2012). The European sovereign debt crisis. *The Journal of Economic Perspectives*, *26*(3), 49–68. doi:10.1257/jep.26.3.49

Lanteigne, M. (2010). Security, strategy and the former USSR: China and the Shanghai cooperation organisation. In S. Breslin (Ed.), *Handbook of China's international relations*. New York: Routledge.

Larsson, R., & Lyhagen, J. (1999). *Likelihood-based inference in multivariate panel cointegration models*. Working Paper Series in Economics and Finance 331, Stockhholm School of Economics.

Larsson, R., Lyhagen, J., & Lothgren, M. (2001). Likelihood-based cointegration tests in heterogeneous panels. The Econometrics Journal, 4(1), 109–142. doi:10.1111/1368-423X.00059 doi:10.1111/1368-423X.00059

Laumullin, M. (2006). *The Shanghai cooperation organization as "geopolitical bluff?" A view from astana* (Vol. 12). Paris: Institut Français des Relations Internationales.

Lawrence, R. Z. (1996). *Regionalism, multilateralism and deeper integration*. Washington, DC: Brookings Institute.

Lazer, H. (1976). British populism: The Labour Party and the common market parliamentary debate. *Political Science Quarterly*, *91*(2), 259–277. doi:10.2307/2148412

Lee, H., & Roland-Holst, W. D. (1997). Trade and the environment. In J. F. Francois & K. A. Reinert (Eds.), Applied methods for trade policy analysis-A handbook. Cambridge, UK: Cambridge University Press. doi:10.1017/CBO9781139174824.018 doi:10.1017/CBO9781139174824.018

Leistner, E. (1997). Regional cooperation in Sub-Saharan Africa. *Africa Insight*, *27*(2), 112–123.

Lejárraga, I., & Shepherd, B. (2013). *Quantitative evidence on transparency in regional trade agreements (OECD Trade Policy Papers No. 153)*. Paris: OECD. doi:10.1787/18166873

Lejour, A., & de Mooij, R. A. (2005). Turkish delight: Does Turkey's accession to the EU bring economic benefits? *Kyklow*, *58*(1), 87–120. doi:10.1111/j.0023-5962.2005.00279.x

Lellouche, P. (2012). France-allemagne: Le double déni. *Politique Etrangere*, *4*(Hiver), 739–754. doi:10.3917/pe.124.0739

Les Gouvernements Européens ont une Marge de Manoeuvre Limitée pour Stimuler la Croissance – Merkel. (2013, June 28). *Les Echos*. Retrieved June 5, 2014, from http://bourse.lesechos.fr/infos-conseils-boursiers/actus-des-marches/infos-marches/les-gouvernements-europeens-ont-une-marge-de-manoeuvre-limitee-pour-stimuler-la-croissance-merkel-892386.php

Lesage, D. (2010). *The G20 and tax havens: Maintaining the momentum?* Retrieved March 30, 2014, from www.g20.utoronto.ca/biblio/lesage-tax-havens.pdf

Levchenko, A. A., Lewis, L. T., & Tesar, L. L. (2010). The collapse of international trade during the 2008-09 Crisis: In search of the smoking gun. *IMF Economic Review*, *58*(2), 214–253. doi:10.1057/imfer.2010.11

Levin, A., Lin, C., & Chu, C. (2002). Unit root tests in panel data: Asymptotic and finite sample properties. Journal of Econometrics, 108(1), 1–24. doi:10.1016/S0304-4076(01)00098-7 doi:10.1016/S0304-4076(01)00098-7

Levine, R. (1997). Financial development and economic growth: Views and agenda. *Journal of Economic Literature*, *XXXV*, 688–726.

Levine, R., Norman, L., & Thorsten, B. (2000). Financial intermediation and growth: Causality and causes. *Journal of Monetary Economics*, *46*(1), 32–77. doi:10.1016/S0304-3932(00)00017-9

Levin, K. A., & Currie, C. (2010). Adolescent toothbrushing and the home environment: Sociodemographic factors, family relationships and mealtime routines and disorganisation. *Community Dentistry and Oral Epidemiology*, *38*(1), 10–18. doi:10.1111/j.1600-0528.2009.00509.x PMID:19845713

Liikanen, E. (2012). *Final report of the high-level expert group on reforming the structure of the EU banking section*. Retrieved from http://ec.europa.eu/internal_market/bank/docs/hihl-level_expert_group/report_en.pdf

Lindberg, L. N. (1963). *The political dynamics of European economic integration*. Stanford, CA: Stanford Univeristy Press.

Linder, S. B. (1961). *An essay on trade and transformation*. Stockholm: Almqvist and Wiksell.

Lipsey, R. G. (1957). The theory of customs unions: Trade diversion and welfare. *Economica*, *24*(93), 40–46. doi:10.2307/2551626

Lipsey, R. G. (1960). The theory of customs unions: A general survey. *The Economic Journal*, *70*(279), 496–513. doi:10.2307/2228805

Lipsey, R. G., & Lancaster, K. (1956). The general theory of second best. *The Review of Economic Studies*, *24*(1), 11–32. doi:10.2307/2296233

Lipsey, T. G. (1970). *The theory of customs unions: A general equilibrium analysis*. London, UK: Weidenfeld & Nicolson.

Loewendahl-Ertugal. (2014, April 29). *Ebru regions and European integration: Prospects for regional governance in Turkey*. Paper presented at Second Pan-European Conference Standing Group on EU Politics. Bologna, Spain. Retrieved from http://www.jhubc.it/ecpr-bologna/docs/471.pdf

Lucas, R. E. B., Wheeler, D., & Hettige, H. (1992). Economic development, environmental regulation, and the international migration of toxic industrial pollution 1960-88. The World Bank.

Lukin, A. (2006). The Russian approach to China under Gorbachev, Yeltsin, and Putin. In G. Rozman, K. Togo, & J. P. Ferguson (Eds.), *Russian strategic thought toward Asia*. New York: PALGRAVE MACMILLAN.

Ly, K. A., Milgrom, P., & Rothen, M. (2008). The potential of dental-protective chewing gum in oral health interventions. *The Journal of the American Dental Association*, *139*(5), 553–563. doi:10.14219/jada.archive.2008.0215 PMID:18451371

Machlup, F. (1975). *The history of thought on economic integration*. New York: New York University Press.

Mackinder, H. J. (1919). *Democratic ideals and reality; A study in the politics of reconstruction*. London: Constable and Company, Ltd.

Macleod, N. (2013). *Robert Gaut*. The Proposed EU Financial Transaction Tax. FriedFrank.

Maddala, G. S., & Wu, S. (1999). A comparative study of unit root tests with panel data and a new simple test. *Oxford Bulletin of Economics and Statistics*, *61*(Special Issue), 631–652. doi:10.1111/1468-0084.61.s1.13

Managi, S. (2004). Trade liberalization and the environment: Carbon dioxide for 1960-1999. Economic Bulletin, 17(1), 1–5.

Managi, S., Hibiki, A., & Tsurumi, T. (2009). Does trade openness improve environmental quality? Journal of Environmental Economics and Management, 58(3), 346–363. doi:10.1016/j.jeem.2009.04.008 doi:10.1016/j.jeem.2009.04.008

Manganelli, S., & Wolswijk, G. (2009). What drives spreads in the Euro area government bond market? *Economic Policy*, *24*(58), 191–240. doi:10.1111/j.1468-0327.2009.00220.x

Mankoff, J. (2009). *Eurasian energy security* (Vol. 43). New York: Council on Foreign Relations.

Mansfield, I. (2014). A blueprint for Britain: Openness not isolation. *IEA Brexit Prize*. Retrieved June 20, 2014, from http://www.iea.org.uk/sites/default/files/publications/files/Brexit%20Entry%20170_final_bio_web.pdf

Marinho, V. C. C., Higgins, J. P. T., Logan, S., & Sheiham, A. (2003). Fluoride toothpastes for preventing dental caries in children and adolescents. *Cochrane Database of Systematic Reviews*, 1.

Marr, A. (2007). *A history of modern Britain*. Macmillan.

Masciandaro, D. (2007). Divide et impera: Financial supervision unification and central bank fragmentation effect. *European Journal of Political Economy*, *23*(2), 285–315. doi:10.1016/j.ejpoleco.2006.02.001

Matheson, T. (2011). *Taxing financial transactions: Issues and evidence*. IMF Working Paper. Retrieved From https://www.imf.org/external/pubs/ft/wp/2011/wp1154.pdf

Mattli, W. (1999). *The logic of regional integration: Europe and beyond*. New York: Cambridge University Press. doi:10.1017/CBO9780511756238

Mayda, A. M., & Chad, S. (2009). Do south-south trade agreements increase trade? Commodity-level evidence from COMESA. *The Canadian Journal of Economics. Revue Canadienne d'Economique*, *42*(4), 1361–1389. doi:10.1111/j.1540-5982.2009.01548.x

McCarty, D. M. (2006). *International economic integration in historical perspective*. New York, NY: Routladge.

McCoskey, S., & Kao, C. (1998). A residual-based test for the null of cointegration in panel data. Econometric Reviews, 17(1), 57–84. doi:10.1080/07474939808800403 doi:10.1080/07474939808800403

McCulloch, N., & Pacillo, G. (2011). *The Tobin tax: A review of the evidence*. IDS Research Report 68.

McDonald, S., Robinson, S., & Thierfelder, K. (2008). Asian growth and trade poles: India, China, and East and Southeast Asia. *World Development*, *36*(2), 210–234. doi:10.1016/j.worlddev.2007.06.013

McKinnon, R. I. (1973). Money and capital in economic development. Brookings Institution.

McKinnon, J. G. (1996). Numerical distribution functions for unit root and cointegration tests. *Journal of Applied Econometrics*, *11*(6), 601–618. doi:10.1002/(SICI)1099-1255(199611)11:6<601::AID-JAE417>3.0.CO;2-T

McKinsey & Company. (2008). *Mapping global capital markets: Fifth annual report*. Retrieved from http://www.mckinsey.com/insights/global_capital_markets/mapping_global_capital_markets_fifth_annual_report

Mclyntyre, J. M. (2009). *How to end the charade information exchange*. Tax Notes, Tax Analysists.

McMillan, J., & McCann, E. (1981). Welfare effects in customs unions. *The Economic Journal*, *91*(363), 697–703. doi:10.2307/2232833

Meade, J. E. (1955). *The theory of customs unions*. Amsterdam: North Holland.

Meade, J. E. (1955). *Trade and welfare*. London: Oxford University Press.

Meadows, D. H., Meadows, D. L., Randers, J., & Behrens, W. W. (1972). *The limits to growth-A report for the club of Rome's project on the predicament of mankind*. Universe Books. Retrieved May 13, 2014, from http://www.donellameadows.org/wp-content/userfiles/Limits-to-Growth-digital-scan-version.pdf

Mearsheimer, J. J. (1990). Back to the future: Instability in Europe after the Cold War. *International Security, 15*(1), 5-56.

Menyah, K., Nazlioglu, S., & Wolde-Rufael, Y. (2014). Financial development, trade openness and economic growth in African countries: New insights from a panel causality approach. *Economic Modelling*, *37*, 386–394. doi:10.1016/j.econmod.2013.11.044

Mercenier, J., & Yeldan, E. (1997). On Turkey's trade policy: Is a customs union with Europe enough? *European Economic Review*, *41*(3-5), 871–880. doi:10.1016/S0014-2921(97)00044-5

Miller Llana, S. (2014, May 1). A decade after the EU's first expansion, open borders still rankle. *The Christian Science Monitor*. Retrieved July 14, 2014, from http://www.lexisnexis.com/hottopics/lnacademic

Miller, V. (2010, October 13). How much legislation comes from Europe? *House of Commons*. Research Paper 10/62. Retrieved July 8, 2014, from http://www.parliament.uk/business/publications/research/briefing-papers/RP10-62/how-much-legislation-comes-from-europe

Miller, V. (2011). *The EU's acquis communautaire*. Retrieved May 20, 2014, from www.parliament.uk/briefing.../sn05944.pdf

Minc, A. (2011, August 23). *Le Figaro*. Retrieved April 14, 2014, from http://www.lefigaro.fr/conjoncture/2011/08/23/04016-20110823ARTFIG00548-alain-minc-le-aaa-de-la-france-est-un-tresor-national.php

Mini-Sommet de la Zone Euro: 130 Milliards Pour la Relance. (2012, June 22). *La Chaine Info*. Retrieved June 22, 2014, from http://lci.tf1.fr/economie/conjoncture/merkel-hollande-rajoy-et-monti-s-accordent-sur-la-croissance-7380147.html

Ministery of Foreign Affairs. (n.d.). *Turkey-EU relations*. Retrieved from http://www.mfa.gov.tr/relations-between-turkey-and-the-european-union.en.mfa

Mink, M., & De Haan, J. (2013). Contagion during the Greek sovereign debt crisis. *Journal of International Money and Finance*, *34*, 102–113. doi:10.1016/j.jimonfin.2012.11.006

Mitrany, D. (1946). *A working peace system; An argument for the functional developmental of international organization* (4th ed.). London: National Peace Council.

Mitrany, D. (1966). *A working peace system*. Chicago: Quadrangle Books.

Mitrany, D. (1976). *The functional theory of politics*. London: St. Martin's Press.

Mittelman, J. H. (1996). *Globalization: Critical reflections*. Boulder, CO: Lynne Rienner Publishers.

Mittelman, J. H. (2000). *The globalization syndrome: Transformation and resistance*. Princeton, NJ: Princeton University Press. doi:10.1515/9781400823697

Modelski, G. (1963). *The new emerging forces; Documents on the ideology of Indonesian foreign policy*. Canberra, Australia: Dept. of International Relations, Research School of Pacific Studies, Institute of Advanced Studies, Australian National University.

Montébourg, A. (2011). *Votez pour la démondialisation*. Paris: Flammarion.

Montiel, P., & Reinhart, C. M. (2001). The dynamics of capital movements to emerging economies during the 1990s. In S. Griffith-Jones, M. F. Montes, & A. Nasution (Eds.), *Short-term capital flows and economic crises*. Oxford Publication. doi:10.1093/acprof:oso/9780198296867.003.0001

Moravcsik, A. (1998). Integration theory. In D. Dinan (Ed.), *Encyclopedia of the European Union*. Boulder, CO: Lynne Rienner.

Moravcsik, A. (1999). Is something rotten in the state of Denmark? Constructivism and European integration. *Journal of European Public Policy*, *6*(4), 669–681. doi:10.1080/135017699343531

Morgenthau, H. J. (1948). *Politics among nations: The struggle for power and peace*. Alfred A. Knopf.

Movkebaeva, G. A. (2013). Energy cooperation among Kazakhstan, Russia, and China within the Shanghai cooperation organization. *Russian Politics and Law*, *51*(1), 80–87. doi:10.2753/RUP1061-1940510105

Müftüler, M. (1995). Turkish economic liberalization and European integration. *Middle Eastern Studies*, *31*(1), 86.

Mundell, R. A. (1964). Tariff preferences and the terms of trade. *The Manchester School of Economic and Social Studies*, *32*(1), 1–13. doi:10.1111/j.1467-9957.1964.tb01029.x

Murphy, R. (2008). *Creating turmoil, tax justice network*. Retrieved April 24, 2014, from http://www.taxresearch.org.uk/Documents/CreatingTurmoil.pdf

Murphy, R. (2011). Tax havens, secrecy jurisdictions and the breakdown of corporation tax. *Real-World Economics Review*, (57), 56-59. Retrieved April 20, 2014, from http://www.paecon.net/PAEReview/issue57/Murphy57.pdf

Nello, S. S. (2012). *The European Union: Economics, policies and history*. McGraw-Hill.

New EU Banking Rules Without Teeth; EU Banking. (2014, January 29). *Business World*. Retrieved June 1, 2014, from http://www.businessworld.ie/livenews.htm?a=3136310

Ng, S., & Perron, P. (2001). Lag length selection and the construction of unit root tests with good size and power. *Econometrica*, *69*(6), 1519–1554. doi:10.1111/1468-0262.00256

Nichols, S. (2004). The challenges of the free movement of health professionals. In *Health policy and European Union enlargement*. Maidenhead, UK: Open University Press.

Nickless, J. (2001). The internal market and the social nature of health care. In *The impact of EU law on health care systems*. Brussels: Peter Lang.

Nikki's Petition Drive. (2012, May 11). *Solihull News*. Retrieved July 14, 2014, from www.lexisnexis.com/hottopics/lnacademic

O'Donnel, J. (2014, February 17). EU's Reding warns Brexit would isolate London's city. *Reuters*. Retrieved July 14, 2014, from http://www.reuters.com/article/2014/02/17/us-eu-britain-city-idUSBREA1G17C20140217

Odum, H. (1936). *Southern regions of the United States*. Chapel Hill, NC: The University of North Carolina Press.

Odum, H., & Moore, H. E. (1938). *American regionalism: A cultural-historical approach to national integration*. New York: Holt.

OECD Library. (2011). *HealthataGlance2011: OECD indicators*. Retrivied from http://www.oecd-ilibrary.org/sites/health_glance2011en/06/06/index.html;jsessionid=3dln9sdrovedm.delta?cOntentType=&itemld=/content/chapter/health_glance201157n&containerltemld=/content/serial/19991312&accessltemlds=/content/book/health_glance-2011-en&mimeType=text/html on 02/04/2012

OECD. (1998). *Harmful tax competition: An emerging global issue*. Retrieved April 15, 2014, from http://www.oecd.org/tax/transparency/44430243.pdf

OECD. (2009). *A progress report on the jurisdictions surveyed by the OECD Global Forum in implementing the internationally agreed tax standard: Progress made as at 2nd April 2009*. Retrieved March 20, 2014, from http://www.oecd.org/dataoecd/38/14/42497950.pdf

OECD. (2009). *Four more countries commit to OECD tax standards*. Retrieved March 20, 2014, from http://www.oecd.org/document/0/0,3343,en_2649_33767_42521280_1_1_1_1,00.html

OECD. (2010). *Promoting transparency and exchange of information for tax purposes: A background information brief*. Retrieved Mach 20, 2014, from http://www.oecd.org/dataoecd/32/45/43757434.pdf

OECD. (2013). *Addressing base erosion and profit shifting*. Retrieved April 21, 2014, from http://www.oecd-ilibrary.org/

Office for Offical Publications of the European Communities. (1987). Treaties establishing the European Communities (ECSC, EEC, EAEC). Brussels: Author.

O'Hara, S. L. (2005). Great game or grubby game? The struggle for control of the Caspian. In P. L. Billon (Ed.), *The geopolitics of resource wars: Resource dependence, governance and violence* (pp. 138–161). New York: Routledge.

Ökmen, M., & Özer, B. (2007). Küreselleşme-Yerelleşme Dikotomisinin Açılımları Üzerine Bir Tartışma. In A. Yılmaz & Y. Bozkurt (Eds.), *Türk Kamu Yönetimi*. Ankara: Gazi.

Ökmen, M., & Parlak, B. (2009). *Kuramdan Uygulama Yerel Yönetimler İlkeler, Yaklaşımlar Ve Mevzuat*. Bursa: Alfa Aktüel.

Ökmen, M., & Parlak, B. (2013). *Yerel Yönetimler*. Ankara: Orion.

Okun, A. (1962). Potential GNP: Its measurement and significance. American Statistical Association. In *Proceedings of the Business and Economic Statistics Section* (pp. 98-104). Academic Press.

Oliveira, L., Curto, J. D., & Nunes, J. P. (2012). The determinants of sovereign credit spread changes in the Euro-zone. *Journal of International Financial Markets, Institutions and Money*, *22*(2), 278–304. doi:10.1016/j.intfin.2011.09.007

Oliver, T. (2013, September). *Europe without Britain*. SWP Research Paper. Stiftung Wissenschaft und Politik / German Institute for International and Security Affairs. Retrieved June 21, 2014, from http://www.swp-berlin.org/fileadmin/contents/products/research_papers/2013_RP07_olv.pdf

Önder, N. (2007). The Turkish political economy: Globalization and regionalism. *Perspectives on Global Development and Technology*, *6*(1), 242–243.

Önder, N. (2008). The Turkish project of globalization and new regionalism. *Turkish Journal of International Relations*, *7*(2-3), 89.

Öner, Ş. (2006). *Yeni Mevzuat Çerçevesinde Türkiye'de Belediye Yönetimi*. Ankara: Academic Press.

Öniş, Z., & Kutlay, M. (2012). Ekonomik Bütünleşme/ Siyasal Parçalanmışlık Paradoksu: Avro Krizi ve Avrupa Birliğinin Geleceği. *Uluslararası İlişkiler*, *9*(33), 3–22.

Organisation for Economic Co-operation and Development. (n.d.). *Better regulation in Europe: An OECD assessment of regulatory: Capacity in the 15 original member states of the EU*. Paris: OECD. Retrieved July 11, 2014, from http://www.oecd.org/gov/regulatory-policy/44952782.pdf

Ornelas, E. (2008). Feasible multilateralism and the effects of regionalism. *Journal of International Economics*, *74*(1), 202–224. doi:10.1016/j.jinteco.2007.05.006

Ortayli, İ. (1974). *Tanzimattan Sonra Mahalli İdareler (1840-1878)*. Ankara: Todaie Yayınları.

Ortayli, İ. (1978). İmparatorluk Döneminde Mahalli İdarelerin Ve Belediyeciliğin Evrimi. In İ. E. Türkcan (Ed.), *Türkiye İdare Tarihi*. Ankara: Todaie Yayını.

Ortayli, İ. (1985). *Tanzimattan Cumhuriyete Yerel Yönetim Geleneği*. İstanbul: Hil Yayınları.

Ottaviano, G., Pessoa, J. P., Sampson, T., & van Reenen, J. (2014, May 13). *The costs and benefits of leaving the EU*. London School of Economics Centre for Economic Performance. Retrieved July 13, 2014, http://cep.lse.ac.uk/pubs/download/pa016_tech.pdf

Oxelheim, L., Stonehill, A., Randøy, T., Vikkula, K., Dullum, K. B., & Mode'n, K.-M. (1998). *Corporate strategies to internationalise the cost of capital*. Copenhagen Business School Press.

Ozcan, B., & Ari, A. (2011). An empirical analysis of relationship between financial development and economic growth: The Turkish case. *Business and Economics Research Journal*, *2*(1), 121–142.

Özen, P. (2005). *Regional development agencies*. Ankara: TEPAV. Retrieved, December 23, 2013,from http://www.tepav.org.tr/upload/files/1271245092r8246.Bolgesel_Kalkinma_Ajanslari.pdf

Ozgen H., Tatar M. (2008). *Saglık Sektorunde Bir Verimlilik Degerlendirme Teknigi Olarak Maliyet-Etkililik Analizi ve Turkiye'de Durum*.

Pain, N., & Young, G. (2004). The macroeconomic impact of UK withdrawal from the EU. *Economic Modelling*, *21*(3), 387–408. doi:10.1016/S0264-9993(02)00068-8

Palan, R., Murphy, R., & Chavagneux, C. (2010). *Tax havens: How globalisation really works*. Ithaca, NY: Cornell University Press.

Pan, H., & Chun, W. (2013). Financial development and economic growth: A new investigation. *Journal of Economic Development*, *38*(1), 27–46.

Park, I. (2009). Regional trade agreements in East Asia: Will they be sustainable? *Asian Economic Journal*, *23*(2), 169–194. doi:10.1111/j.1467-8381.2009.02008.x

Parlak, B., & Sobacı, Z. (2012). *Ulusal ve Küresel Perspektif*. Bursa: MKM.

Parlak, B. (2005). *Tarihi Perspektifte Ve Reform Sürecinde İ.Ö.İ. In Yerel Yönetimler Üzerine Güncel Yazılar I Reform* (pp. 175–200). Ankara: Nobel Yayıncılık.

Patrick, H. T. (1966). Financial development and economic growth in underdeveloped countries. *Economic Development and Cultural Change*, *14*(2), 174–189. doi:10.1086/450153

Patterson, B., & Galliano, M. (1998). *The feasibility of an international "Tobin tax"*. European Parliament Directorate-General For Research Working Paper, Economic Affairs Series, ECON-107 En. Retrieved from http://www.europarl.europa.eu/workingpapers/econ/pdf/107_en.pdf

Pearce, D. (1999). *Economic and environment-Essays on ecological economics and sustainable development*. Edward Elgar Publishing.

Pedroni, P. (2000). Fully modified OLS for heterogeneous cointegrated panels. Advances in Econometrics, 15, 93–130. doi:10.1016/S0731-9053(00)15004-2 doi:10.1016/S0731-9053(00)15004-2

Pedroni, P. (1999). Critical values for cointegration tests in heterogeneous panels with multiple regressors. *Oxford Bulletin of Economics and Statistics*, *61*(s1), 653–670. doi:10.1111/1468-0084.61.s1.14

Pentland, C. (1973). *International theory and European integration*. London: Faber and Faber.

People's Pledge. (n.d.). Retrieved from www.thepeoplespledge.org

Perovic, J., Orttung, R. W., & Wenger, A. (2009). *Russian energy power and foreign relations: Implications for conflict and cooperation*. London: Taylor & Francis.

Perroni, C., & Wigle, R. M. (1994). International trade and environmental quality: How important the linkages? The Canadian Journal of Economics. Revue Canadienne d'Economique, 27(3), 551–567. doi:10.2307/135783 doi:10.2307/135783

Perte, A. A. A. (2012, January 13). L'opposition fustige Sarkozy, la majorité temporise. *Le Nouvel Observateur*. Retrieved April 14, 2014, from http://tempsreel.nouvelobs.com/chronique-du-triple-a/20120113.OBS8761/video-perte-aaa-l-opposition-fustige-sarkozy-la-majorite-temporise.html

Pesaran, H. M. (2004). *General diagnostic tests for cross section dependence in panels*. Cambridge Working Paper in Economics, No 435.

Pesaran, M. H. (2007). A simple panel unit root test in the presence of cross-section dependence. Journal of Applied Econometrics, 22(2), 265–312. doi:10.1002/jae.951 doi:10.1002/jae.951

Pesaran, M. H., & Shin, Y. (1999). *An autoregressive distributed lag modeling approach to cointegration analysis: Econometrics and economic theory in 20th century: The Ragnar Frisch centennial symposium* (S. Strom, Ed.). Cambridge, UK: Cambridge University Press.

Pesaran, M. H., Shin, Y., & Smith, R. (2001). Bounds testing approaches to the analysis of level relationships. *Journal of Applied Econometrics*, *16*(3), 289–326. doi:10.1002/jae.616

Pethig, R. (1976). Pollution, welfare and environmental policy in the theory of comparative advantage. Journal of Environmental Economics and Management, 2(3), 160–169. doi:10.1016/0095-0696(76)90031-0 doi:10.1016/0095-0696(76)90031-0

Phillips, P. C. B., & Perron, P. (1988). Testing for unit roots in time series regression. *Biometrika*, *75*(2), 335–346. doi:10.1093/biomet/75.2.335

Pierson, P. (1995). Fragmented welfare states: Federal institutions and the development of social policy. *Governance: An International Journal of Policy, Administration and Institutions*, *8*(4), 449–478. doi:10.1111/j.1468-0491.1995.tb00223.x

Pihlstrom, B. L., Michalowicz, B. S., & Johnson, N. W. (2005). Periodontal diseases. *Lancet*, *366*(9499), 1809–1820. doi:10.1016/S0140-6736(05)67728-8 PMID:16298220

Pisani-Ferry, J. (2006). Only one bed for two dreams: A critical retrospective on the debate over the economic governance of the Euro area. *Journal of Common Market Studies*, *44*(4), 823–844. doi:10.1111/j.1468-5965.2006.00664.x

Polyak, P. (2013). *Fiscal unification going unnoticed? Trends in the European Union's involvement in national tax policies in the onset of the Euro crisis*. (Unpublished master dissertation). Central European University.

Poussenkova, N. (2009). Russia's future customers: Asia and beyond. In J. Perovic (Ed.), *Russian energy power and foreign relations: Implications for conflict and cooperation* (pp. 132–154). New York: Routledge.

Prachowny, M. F. J. (1993). Okun's law: Theoretical foundations and revised estimates. *The Review of Economics and Statistics*, *75*(2), 331–336. doi:10.2307/2109440

Pratley, N. (2012, 23 May). Germany and its Eurobonds resistance. *The Guardian*. Retrieved June 12, 2014, from http://www.theguardian.com/business/nils-pratley-on-finance/2012/may/23/why-germany-doesnt-want-eurobonds

Puig, M. G., & Rivero, S. S. (2014). Causality and contagion in EMU sovereign debt markets. *International Review of Economics & Finance*, *33*, 12–27. doi:10.1016/j.iref.2014.03.003

PWC. (2013). *Financial transaction tax: The impacts and arguments, a literature review*. Retrieved from www.pwc.co.uk

Rajan, R. G., & Luigi, Z. (1998). Financial dependence and growth. *The American Economic Review*, *88*(3), 559–586.

Rajan, R. G., & Luigi, Z. (2003). The great reversals: The politics of financial development in the twentieth century. *Journal of Financial Economics*, *69*(1), 5–50. doi:10.1016/S0304-405X(03)00125-9

Randall, E. (2001). *The European Union and health policy*. Basingstoke, UK: Palgrave.

Real GDP Growth Rate – Volume. (n.d.). *Eurostat*. Retrieved June 10, 2014, from http://epp.eurostat.ec.europa.eu/portal/page/portal/product_details/dataset?p_product_code=tec00115

Reinhardt, C. H., Lopker, N., Noack, M. J., Klein, K., & Rosen, E. (2009). Peer tutoring pilot program for the improvement of oral health behavior in underprivileged and immigrant children. *Pediatric Dentistry*, *31*, 481–485. PMID:20108738

Reinhart, C. M., & Rogoff, K. S. (2010). *From financial crash to debt crisis*. Cambridge, MA: NBER Working Paper No.15795.

Republic of Turkey, Ministry of Development. (2012). Rio'dan Rio'ya: Türkiye'de Sürdürülebilir Kalkınmanın Mevcut Durumu. Ankara: Author.

Republic, T. O. (2006). Retrieved, December 30, 2013, from http://www.kosgeb.gov.tr/Pages/UI/Baskanligimiz.aspx?ref=2

Repullo, R. (2000). Who should act as lender of last resort? An incomplete contracts model. *Journal of Money, Credit and Banking*, *32*(3), 580–605. doi:10.2307/2601196

Rickens, C. (2013, 26 August). Aid debate: Merkel leaves door open to greek debt cut. *Der Spiegel*. Retrieved April 14, 2014, from http://www.spiegel.de/international/europe/merkel-declines-to-rule-out-greek-debt-cut-a-918560.html

Rikkers, F., & Thibeault, A. E. (2014). *The optimal rating philosophy for the rating of SMEs*. Retrieved, May 20, 2014, from http://ssrn.com/abstract=966322

Robin Hood Tax Rides Forth. (2014). International Tax Review, 25(1).

Robin Hood Tax. (n.d.a). *The big idea*. Retrieved from http://www.robinhoodtax.org/sites/default/files/Robin%20Hood%20Tax%20FAQ.pdf

Robin Hood Tax. (n.d.b). *Everything you need to know*. Retrieved from http://www.robinhoodtax.org/how/everything-you-need-to-know

Robin Hood Tax. (n.d.c). Retrieved from http://www.robinhoodtax.org/sites/default/files/Robin%20Hood%20Tax%20FAQ.pdf

Robinson, J. (1952). *The generalization of the general theory: The rate of interest and other essays*. London: Macmillan.

Robson, P. (2003). *The economics of international integration*. London: Routledge.

Romalis, J. (2007). NAFTA's and CUSFTA's impact on international trade. *The Review of Economics and Statistics*, *89*(3), 416–435. doi:10.1162/rest.89.3.416

Roman, A., & Bilan, I. (2012). The Euro area sovereign debt crisis and the role of ECB's monetary policy. *Procedia Economics and Finance*, *3*, 763–768. doi:10.1016/S2212-5671(12)00227-4

Rooyen, C. (1998). Regional integration as a development strategy: The case of the SADC. *Africa Insight*, *28*, 125–132.

Rousseau, P. L., & Alexandra, D. (2013). Monetization, financial development, and growth: Time series evidence from 22 countries in Sub-Saharan Africa. *World Development*, *51*, 132–153. doi:10.1016/j.worlddev.2013.05.016

Rozman, G. (2008). Strategic thinking about the Russian far east: A resurgent Russia eyes its future in northeast Asia.[Article]. *Problems of Post-Communism*, *55*(1), 36–48. doi:10.2753/PPC1075-8216550104

Russett, B. M. (1967). *International regions and the international system; A study in political ecology*. Chicago: Rand McNally.

S&S Group of Companies. (2011). *About Turkey: Turkey to Europe's future*. Retrieved from http://www.ssgroupofcompanies.com/en/index/turkey.php#

Sabbah, W., Sheiham, A., & Bernabé, E. (2010). Income inequality and periodontal diseases in rich countries: An ecological cross-sectional study. *International Dental Journal*, *60*, 370–374. PMID:21141210

Sahin, H. (1998). *Economy of Turkey.* Bursa: Ezgi Bookstore.

Sahinoz. T., Sahinoz. S. (2012). Demografik ve Bazı Saglık Gostergeleri Acısından Turkiye'nin Dunyadaki Durumu. *Gumushane Universitesi Saglık Bilimleri Dergisi, 1.*

Sahyoun, N. R., Lin, C. L., & Krall, E. (2003). Nutritional status of the older adult is associated with dentition status. *Journal of the American Dietetic Association, 103*(1), 61–66. doi:10.1053/jada.2003.50003 PMID:12525795

Salvatore, D. (2009). *International economics* (10th ed.). London, UK: Wiley.

Santis, R. A. (2014). The euro area sovereign debt crisis: Identifying flight-to-liquidity and the spillover mechanisms. *Journal of Empirical Finance, 26*, 150–170. doi:10.1016/j.jempfin.2013.12.003

Sarafidis, V., & De Hoyos, R. E. (2006). On testing for cross sectional dependence in panel data models. University of Cambridge.

Sarkar, P. (2014, May 7). *Unpublished course notes: A comparison of old and new regionalism.* Retrieved from https://www.academia.edu/2103291/Old_vs_New_Regionalism

Saunders, C. S., & Cagatay, S. (2004). Trade and the environment: Economic and environmental impacts of global dairy trade liberalization. International Journal of Environmental Assessment Policy and Management, 6(3), 339–365. doi:10.1142/S1464333204001766 doi:10.1142/S1464333204001766

Savard, M., & Bohman, M. (2003). Impacts of trade, environmental and agricultural policies in the North American hog/pork industry on water quality. Journal of Policy Modeling, 25(1), 77–84. doi:10.1016/S0161-8938(02)00197-7 doi:10.1016/S0161-8938(02)00197-7

Saveanu, C. (2012). For and against a new framework for banking supervision. *Ovidius University Annals, 12*(1), 278–289.

Savitch, H., & Vogel, R. K. (2000). Paths to new regionalism. *State & Local Government Review, 32*(1), 158–168. doi:10.1177/0160323X0003200301

Savitch, H., & Vogel, R. K. (2009). Regionalism and urban politics. In J. S. Davies & D. L. Imbroscio (Eds.), *Theories of urban politics.* London: Sage. doi:10.4135/9781446279298.n8

Sbragia, A., & Stolfi, F. (2008). Key policies. In E. Bomberg, J. Peterson, & A. Stubb (Eds.), *The European Union: How does it work?* Oxford, UK: Oxford University Press.

Scharpf, F. (2002). The European social model: Coping with the challenges of diversity. *Journal of Common Market Studies, 40*(4), 645–670. doi:10.1111/1468-5965.00392

Schiff, M., & Winters, A. (2003). Regional integration and development. Washington, DC: World Bank Publications. doi:10.1596/0-8213-5078-1

Schild, J. (2011). 20 ans après: La France et l'Allemagne dans la nouvelle Europe. *Regards sur l'Economie Allemande, 100*, 11-25.

Schmitter, P. C., & Haas, E. B. (1964). *Mexico and Latin American economic integration.* Berkeley, CA: Institute of International Studies, University of California.

Schnapper, P. (2010). Le Royaume-Uni et l'Europe: Toujours un malentendu? Hérodote. *Revue de Géographie et de Géopolitique, 137*, 135–147.

Schoenmaker, D., & Peek, T. (2014). The state of the banking sector in Europe. *OECD Working Papers*, No 1102.

Schoenmaker, D., & Siegmann, D. (2013). Efficiency gains of a European Banking Union. *Tinbergen Institute Discussion Papers,* No 13-026/IV/DSF51.

Schoenmaker, D., & Wagner, W. (2013). Cross-border banking in Europe and financial stability. *International Finance, 16*(1), 1–22. doi:10.1111/j.1468-2362.2013.12026.x

Schultz, S. (1996). Regionalisation of world trade dead end or way out? In M. P. Van Dijk & S. Sideri (Eds.), *Multilateralism versus regionalism: Trade issues after the Uruguay round* (pp. 23–43). London: Frank Cass Publishers.

Schumacher, E. F. (1973). *Small is beautiful-Economics as if people mattered.* London: Blond & Briggs.

Schumpeter, J. A. (1911). *The theory of economic development*. Oxford, UK: Oxford University Press.

Scotland Decides. (2014). *BBC*. Retrieved September 25, 2014, from http://www.bbc.com/news/events/scotland-decides/results

Scully, C., & Bagan, J. (2009). Oral squamous cell carcinoma overview. *Oral Oncology*, *45*(4-5), 301–308. doi:10.1016/j.oraloncology.2009.01.004 PMID:19249237

Secretariat of the Convention on Biological Diversity. (2010). *Global biodiversity outlook 3*. Available from http://www.cbd.int/GBO3/

Seibt, S. (2011, August 16). Les Euro-obligations sont-elles le remède miracle à la crise? *France24*. Retrieved June 8, 2014, from http://www.france24.com/fr/20110816-sommet-franco-allemand-sarkozy-merkel-zone-euro-crise-eurobond-obligation-dette-marche-speculation/

Shah, A. (n.d.). *Fiscal decentralization in developing and transition economies*. Retrieved, May 21, 2014, from http://elibrary.worldbank.org/doi/book/10.1596/1813-9450-3282

Shahbaz, M., & Lean, H. H. (2012). Does financial development increase energy consumption? The role of industrialization and urbanization in Tunisia. *Energy Policy*, *40*, 473–479. doi:10.1016/j.enpol.2011.10.050

Shahbaz, M., Zeshan, M., & Afza, T. (2012). Is energy consumption effective to spur economic growth in Pakistan? New evidence from bounds test to level relationships and Granger causality tests. *Economic Modelling*, *29*(6), 2310–2319. doi:10.1016/j.econmod.2012.06.027

Shan, J. (2005). Does financial development lead economic growth? A vector autoregression appraisal. *Applied Economics*, *37*(12), 1353–1367. doi:10.1080/00036840500118762

Sharman, J. C. (2006). *Havens in a storm: The struggle for global tax regulation*. Ithaca, NY: Cornell University Press.

Shaw, E. (1973). *Financial deepening in economic development*. London: Oxford University Press.

Sheiham, A. (2006). Dental caries affects body weight, growth and quality of life in preschool children. *British Dental Journal*, *201*(910), 625–626. doi:10.1038/sj.bdj.4814259 PMID:17128231

Sheiham, A., & Nicolau, B. (2005). Evaluation of social and psychological factors in periodontal disease. *Periodontol*, *Z00039*(1), 118–131. doi:10.1111/j.1600-0757.2005.00115.x PMID:16135067

Shiau, H. J., & Reynolds, M. A. (2010). Sex differences n destructive periodontal disease: Exploring the biologic basis. *Journal of Periodontology*, *81*(11), 1505–1517. doi:10.1902/jop.2010.100045 PMID:20594052

Siebert, H. (1992). Economics of the environment. New York: Springer Verlag. doi:10.1007/978-3-662-02842-1 doi:10.1007/978-3-662-02842-1

Simms, R., & Simms, E. (2006). *The building block of successful regional integration: Lessons for the CSME from other regional integration schemes*. Retrieved March 15 2014 from http://sta.uwi.edu/conferences/salises/documents/Simms%20R%20-%20Simms%20E.pdf

Snorrason, S. T. (2012). *Asymmetric economic integration: Size characteristics of economies, trade cost and welfare*. Berlin: Physca-Verlag. doi:10.1007/978-3-7908-2861-0

Sobaci, M. Z. (2005). Yeniden Yapılanma Süreci İ.Ö.İ. Dünü, Bugünü, Geleceği Üzerine Değerlendirme. *Çağdaş Yerel Yönetimler Dergisi*, *14*, 5.

Sobacı, Z. (2009). Regional development agencies in Turkey: Are they examples of obligated policy transfer? *Public Organization Review*, *9*(1), 51–65. doi:10.1007/s11115-008-0069-0

Song, W. (2014). Interests, power and China's difficult game in the Shanghai cooperation organization (SCO). *Journal of Contemporary China*, *23*(85), 85–101. doi:10.1080/10670564.2013.809981

Sorhun, E. (2014). What kind of trade integration would the SCO's further FTA be? In H. Dincer & U. Hacioglu (Eds.), *Globalization and government in the international political economy* (pp. 63–74). Hershey, PA: IGI-Global. doi:10.4018/978-1-4666-4639-1.ch005

Sourdin, P., & Pomfret, R. (2009). Have Asian trade agreements reduced trade costs? *Journal of Asian Economics*, *20*(3), 255–268. doi:10.1016/j.asieco.2009.02.007

Sözen, S. (2012). Recent administrative reforms in Turkey: A preliminary assessment. *International Journal of Business and Social Science*, *3*(9), 168–173.

Sözen, S., & Shaw, I. (2002). The international applicability of "new" public management: Lessons from Turkey. *International Journal of Public Sector Management*, *15*(6), 475–486. doi:10.1108/09513550210439625

Sözen, S., & Shaw, I. (2003). Turkey and the European Union: Modernizing a traditional state? *Social Policy and Administration*, *37*(2), 108–120. doi:10.1111/1467-9515.00328

Spahn, P. B. (1996). The Tobin tax and exchange rate stability. *Finance & Development*, *33*(2). Retrieved from http://www.imf.org/external/pubs/ft/fandd/1996/06/pdf/spahn.pdf

Specher, M., & Specher, D. (2009). *Is Russia winning in Central Asia?* (Vol. 1). Private University of Applied Sciences.

Spechler, D. R. (2010). Russian foreign policy during the Putin presidency.[Article]. *Problems of Post-Communism*, *57*(5), 35–50. doi:10.2753/PPC1075-8216570503

Spillius, A. (2012, December 18). Britain will be weaker without EU, says USA. *The Telegraph*. Retrieved July 5, 2014, from http://www.telegraph.co.uk/news/worldnews/europe/eu/9754042/Britain-will-be-weaker-without-EU-says-USA.html

Split Persists between Berlin and Paris. (2013, May 17). *Der Spiegel*. Retrieved June 3, 2014, from http://www.spiegel.de/international/europe/germany-and-france-will-not-create-joint-statement-ahead-of-eu-summit-a-900514.html

Standard & Poor's Takes Various Rating Actions on 16 Eurozone Sovereign Governments. (2012, 13 January). *S&P*. Retrieved May 19, 2014, from http://www.standardandpoors.com/ratings/articles/en/us/?articleType=HTML&assetID=1245327294763

Stark, H. (2012). Le couple Franco-Allemand à l'épreuve de la crise de la zone Euro. *Questions Internationales*, *54*(March-April), 76–78.

Steichen, A. (2002). Tax competition in Europe or the taming of leviathan. *General Report at the EATLP Seminar.* Retrieved July 12, 2014, from http://www.eatlp.org/uploads/Members/GeneralReportSteichen.pdf

Stewart, H. (2012, May 22). Hollande pushes case for Eurobonds. *The Guardian*. Retrieved June 19, 2014, from, http://www.theguardian.com/business/2012/may/22/eurozone-crisis-eurobonds-hollande-merkel

Stoica, O., & Scântee. (2012). Financial supervision and banking competition in European Union. *Acta Universitatis Danubius*, *8*(6), 56–67.

Stotsky, J. G. (1996). Why a two-tier Tobin tax won't work. *Finance & Development*, *33*(2). Retrieved from http://www.imf.org/external/pubs/ft/fandd/1996/06/pdf/stotsky.pdf

Strange, S. (1995). Political economy and international relations. In K. Booth & S. Smith (Eds.), *International relations theory today* (pp. 154–174). Cambridge, MA: Polity Press.

Structural Reform of the EU Banking Sector. (2014, January 29). *European Commission.* Retrieved April 18, 2014, from http://europa.eu/rapid/press-release_IP-14-85_en.htm?locale=FR

Strüning, F. (2012). Turks in Germany in 2012: Study on German-Turkish life and values. *Citizen Times*. Retrieved from http://www.citizentimes.theEU/2012/08/23/turks-in-germany-2012/

Sulamaa, P. &Widgren, M. T. (2005). Turkish EU membership: A simulation study on economic effects. *VATT Discussion Papers from Government Institute for Economic Research*, No. 410.

Sullivan, J., & Renz, B. (2010). Chinese migration: Still the major focus of Russian Far East/Chinese North East relations?[Article]. *The Pacific Review*, *23*(2), 261–285. doi:10.1080/09512741003624450

Summers, L. H. (1991). Regionalism and the world trading system, In *Proceedings-Economic Policy Symposium Sponsored by the Federal Reserve Bank ofKansas City*. The Federal Reserve Bank of Kansas City.

Sunar, İ. (1990). Populism and patronage: The democrat party and its legacy in Turkey. Academic Press.

Sweet, A. S. (2012). Neofunctionalism and supranational governance. *Faculty Scholarship Series*, 1.

Tabellini, G. (n.d.). *Culture and institutions: Economic development in the regions of Europe*. Retrieved, May 20, 2014, from http://SSRN.com/abstract=754086

Tambunan, T. (n.d.). *SME development in Indonesia: Do economic growth and government supports matter*. Retrieved, May 16, 2014, from http://ijaps.usm.my/?page_id=312

Tamer, A. (2012). *Legislation of development agencies*. Ankara: Adalet Bookstore.

Tanzi, V., & Schuknecht, L. (2000). Public spending. In *The 20th century a global perspective*. Cambridge, UK: Cambridge University Press. doi:10.1017/CBO9780511625800.017

Tatoglu, F. Y. (2011). The long and short run effects between unemployment and economic growth in Europe. *The Journal of Dogus University*, *12*(1), 99–113.

Tax Justice Network. (2009). *Tax information exchange agreements: Tax justice briefing*. Retrieved March 16, 2014, from http://www.taxjustice.net/cms/upload/pdf/TJN_0903_Exchange_of_Info_Briefing_draft.pdf

TC. (n.d.a). Kültür ve Turizm Bakanlığı. 2011-2014 Turizm Gelir, Gider ve Ortalama Harcamaları: Turizm Gelirleri. Academic Press.

TC. (n.d.b). Kültür ve Turizm Bakanlığı: Turizm Raporları: Dünya'da ve Türkiye'de Turizm 2009. Araştırma ve Değerlendirme Daire Başkanlığı. Academic Press.

Teica, R. A. (2012). Analysis of the public debt sustainability in the economic and monetary union. *Procedia Economics and Finance*, *3*, 1081–1087. doi:10.1016/S2212-5671(12)00277-8

Telatar, F. (2004). *Politik İktisat Politikası*. Ankara, Turkey: İmaj Yayınevi.

The Grand National Assembly of Turkey. (1982). *Constitution of the Republic of Turkey-1982*. Retrieved May 13, 2014, from http://global.tbmm.gov.tr/docs/constitution_en.pdf

The World Bank. (2014). *Table: GDP growth rate of all countries (2009 – 2013)*. Retrieved from http://data.worldbank.org/indicator/NY.GDP.MKTP.KD.ZG

Thompson, G., & Harari, D. (2013, September 17). *The economic impact of EU membership on the UK*. House of Commons. SN/EP/6730. Retrieved July 8, 2014, from http://www.parliament.uk/business/publications/research/briefing-papers/SN06730/the-economic-impact-of-eu-membership-on-the-uk

Tietenberg, T. (2003). *Environmental and natural resource economics* (6th ed.). Addison Wesley.

TISK (Confederation of Turkish Employers Union). (2002). *Comparative report on candidate countries to the EU*. Ankara: Author.

TMMOB. (1996). 95 Sanayi Kongresi, Bildiriler Kitabı. Academic Press.

Tobin, J. (2000). Financial globalization. *World Development*, *28*(6), 1101–1104. doi:10.1016/S0305-750X(00)00008-5

Togan, S. (2005). Economic implications of EU accession for Turkey. In Turkey economic reform and accession to the European Union. Washington, DC: The World Bank.

Tont, S.A. (1997). *Sulak Bir Gezegen'den Öyküler*. Ankara: Publications of TUBITAK.

Toprak, Z. (2012). *Çevre Yönetimi ve Politikası*. İzmir: Albi Publications.

Tranholm-Mikkelsen, J. (1991). Neo-functionalism: Obstinate or obsolete? A reappraisal in the light of the new dynamism of the EC millennium. *Journal of International Studies*, *20*(1), 1–22.

Traynor, I., & Wintour, P. (2012, May 24). Eurozone crisis: Germany and France clash over Eurobonds at summit. *The Guardian*. Retrieved May 19, 2014, from http://www.theguardian.com/business/2012/may/23/eurozone-crisis-france-germany-divide

Treasury, H. M. (2013). *European Union finances 2013: Statement on the 2013 EU budget and measures to counter fraud and financial mismanagement*. Retrieved July 13, 2014, from https://www.gov.uk/government/uploads/system/uploads/attachment_data/file/220966/foi_eumembership_fdi.pdf

Troyakova, T. (2007). The Russian Far East: Isolation or Integration? *Problems of Post-Communism*, *54*(2), 61–71. doi:10.2753/PPC1075-8216540206

Tsai, P.-L. (1999). Is trade liberalization harmful to the environment? An alternative view. Journal of Economic Studies (Glasgow, Scotland), 26(3), 201–209. doi:10.1108/01443589910284381 doi:10.1108/01443589910284381

Tserakhava T., Shakavets N., & Smirnoy A. (2011). Systems for the provision of oral health care in the black sea countries part 9: Belarus. *Oral Health and Dental Management, 10*, 115-118.

Tsurumi, T., & Managi, S. (2011). *The effect of trade openness on deforestation: Empirical analysis for 142 countries*. MPRA Paper No. 35805.

TUIK. (n.d.). *News bulletin*. Retrieved, December 30, 2013, from http://www.tuik.gov.tr/PreHaberBultenleri.do?id=13146

Tuliuc, D., & Popovici, A. (2013). Towards the European Banking Union. *SEA Practical Application of Science*, *1*(1), 221–229.

Turk Dishekimleri Birligi Dishekimlerinin Calısma Sekilleri. (n.d.). *Kurumlarda ve Ilcelerde.*

Turkish State Planning Institute. (1990, March). Article. *European Communities Bulletin*, *1*(3/4), 15–16.

Türkiye İstatistik Kurumu. (2014). *Adrese Dayalı Nüfus Kayıt Sistemi Sonuçları: 2013. No:15974*. Retrieved from http://www.tuik.gov.tr/PreHaberBultenleri.do?id=15974

Türkman, A. (1998). *Yaşanabilir Bir Çevre İçin* (vol. 45). Izmir: Publications of Izmir Chamber of Commerce.

Uddin, G. S., & Shahbaz, M. (2013). The causal nexus between financial development and economic growth in Kenya. *Economic Modelling*, *35*, 701–707. doi:10.1016/j.econmod.2013.08.031

UE. Berlin prêt à discuter avec Londres. (2013, January 23). *Le Figaro*. Retrieved July 15, 2014, from http://www.lefigaro.fr/flash-eco/2013/01/23/97002-20130123FILWWW00450-ue-berlin-pret-a-discuter-avec-londres.php

UK must maintain a strong voice in Europe says automotive industry. (2014, April 2). *SMMT*. Retrieved July 14, 2014, from http://www.smmt.co.uk/2014/04/uk-automotive-industry-europe/

Ulchenko, N. (1988). Turkey-EU economic relations: problems and prospects. *The Turkish Yearbook of International Relations*, *18*, 141.

Ulgen, S., & Zahariadis, Y. (2004). The future of Turkey-EU trade relations: Deepening vs widening. *CEPS EU-Turkey Working Papers*, 5.

Ulusoy, A., & Tekin, A. (2010). *Mahalli İdareler Teori, Maliye Ve Uygulama*. Ankara: Seçkin Yayıncılık.

Unalmis, D. (2002). *The causality between financial development and economic growth: The case of Turkey*. The central bank of the republic of Turkey research department working paper, No: 3.

United Nations Conference on Trade and Development (UNCTAD). (2007). *Trade and development report 2007: Regional cooperation for development*. Geneva: United Nations Conference on Trade and Development.

United Nations Conference on Trade and Development (UNCTAD). (n.d.). *UNCTADstat database*. Retrieved from http://unctadstat.unctad.org/wds/ReportFolders/reportFolders.aspx

United Nations Environment Program. (n.d.). *Global environment outlook 3*. Retrieved May 10, 2014, from http://www.unep.org/geo/GEO3/english/pdfs/chapter1.pdf

United Nations World Commission on Environment and Development. (1987). *Report of the world commission on environment and development-Our common future*. Retrieved May 16, 2014, from http://www.un-documents.net/our-common-future.pdf

United Nations. (1972). *Report of the United Nations conference on the human environment, 5-16 June 1972*. United Nations Publications, A/CONF/48.14/Rev.1. Retrieved May 8, 2014, from http://www.un-documents.net/aconf48-14r1.pdf

United Nations. (1992). *The Rio declaration on environment and development.* United Nations Publication, A/CONF.151/26 (Vol. 1), Retrieved May 8, 2014, from http://www.un.org/documents/ga/conf151/aconf15126-1annex1.htm

United Nations. (2002). *Plan of implementation of the world summit on sustainable development.* A/CONF.199/20. Retrieved May 14, 2014, from http://www.un-documents.net/jburgpln.htm

United Nations. (2007). Indicators of sustainable development: Guidelines and methodologies (3rd ed.). New York: Author.

United Nations. (2012). *Future we want.* A/RES/66/288. Retrieved May 13, 2014, from http://www.un.org/ga/search/view_doc.asp?symbol=A/RES/66/288&Lang=E

United Nations. (2012). *World population 2012.* Retrieved May 11, 2014, from http://www.un.org/en/development/desa/population/publications/pdf/trends/WPP2012_Wallchart.pdf

United Nations. (2013). *World population prospects: The 2012 revision-Key findings and advance tables.* Department of Economic and Social Affairs-Population Division, New York, ESA/P/WP.227. Retrieved May 14, 2014, from http://esa.un.org/wpp/Documentation/pdf/WPP2012_%20KEY%20FINDINGS.pdf

United Nations. (2013). *The millennium development goals report 2013.* New York: Author. Retrieved May 14, 2014, from http://www.un.org/millenniumgoals/pdf/report-2013/mdg-report-2013-english.pdf

United States Government Accountability Office. (2008). *Report to congressional requesters.* Retrieved June 19, 2014, from http://www.gao.gov/new.items/d09157.pdf

Ureche-Rangau, L., & Burietz, A. (2013). One crisis, two crises...the subprime crisis and the European sovereign debt problems. *Economic Modelling, 35,* 35–44. doi:10.1016/j.econmod.2013.06.026

Us, V. (2007). Türkiye-AB Bütünleşmesi Sürecine İlişkin Karşılaştırmalı Analiz: EMR2 İçin Yol Haritası. *Ankara Çalışmaları Dergisi, 6*(2), 123.

Uysal, Y. (2014). *Temel Ekonomik Göstergeler: Türkiye Ekonomisine İlişkin Temel Göstergeler.* Retrieved from http://kisi.deu.edu.tr/yasar.uysal/site/temel-gostergeler.html

Vallée, S. (2014). From mutual insurance to fiscal federalism: Rebuilding the Economic and Monetary Union after the demise of the Maastricht architecture. *Inter Economics, 138,* 49–62. doi:10.1016/j.inteco.2013.11.003

Van Rompuy, H. (2012). Towards a genuine economic and monetary union. *Report by President of the European Council.* Retrieved from http://www.consilium.europa.eu/uedocs/cms_data/docs/pressdata/en/ec/134069.pdf

Vance, R. B. (1951). The regional concept as a tool for social research. In M. Jensen (Ed.), *Regionalism in America* (pp. 119–140). Madison, WI: Univ. of Wisconsin Press.

Vanek, J. (1965). *General equilibrium of international discrimination: The case of customs unions.* Cambridge, MA: Harvard University Press.

Velayos, F., Barreix, A., & Villela, L. (2008). *Regional integration and tax harmonization: issues and recent experiences.* Retrieved July 12, 2014, from http://siteresources.worldbank.org/INTTPA/Resources/Velayos-Villela-Barreix.pdf

Vereecken, C. A. (2005). The Relative influence of individual and contextual socioeconomic status on consumption of fruit and soft drinks among adolescents in Europe. *European Journal of Public Health, 15*(3), 224–232. doi:10.1093/eurpub/cki005 PMID:15905182

Viegnes, M. (2005). The French vision of Europe from Victor Hugo's United States of Europe to the no to the constitution. *Europe's Journal of Psychology.* Retrieved May 30, 2014, from http://ejop.psychopen.eu/article/view/376/279

Villaverde, J., & Maza, A. (2009). The robustness of Okun's law in Spain, 1980-2004 regional evidence. *Journal of Policy Modeling, 31*(2), 289–297. doi:10.1016/j.jpolmod.2008.09.003

Vina, G. (2013, April 14). Almost one in five U.K. companies favor leaving EU. *Businessweek*. Retrieved July 7, 2014, from http://www.businessweek.com/news/2013-04-14/almost-one-in-five-u-dot-k-dot-companies-favor-leaving-eu

Viner, J. (1950). *The customs union issue*. New York: Carnegie Endowment for International Peace.

Volkery, C. (2012, May 24). *France dominates EU summit: Hollande steals the show from Merkel*. Retrieved April 15, 2014, from http://www.spiegel.de/international/europe/euro-bond-discussion-dominates-european-union-summit-a-834865.html

Wachtel, P. (2003). How much do we really know about growth and finance? *Federal Reserve Bank of Atlanta Economic Review*, 33-47.

Wackernagel, M., Galli, A., Moore, D., Cranston, G., Kalem, S., Devranoğlu, S., & Ayas, C. (2012). *Turkey's ecological footprint report*. World Wildlife Fund, WWF-Turkey. Retrieved May 6, 2014, from http://www.footprintnetwork.org/images/uploads/Turkey_Ecological_Footprint_Report_Executive_Summary-Conclusion.pdf

Wacziarg, R., & Welch, K. H. (2008). Trade liberalization and growth: New evidence. *The World Bank Economic Review*, *22*(2), 187–231. doi:10.1093/wber/lhn007

Wagstyl, S., Parker, G., & Barker, A. (2014, June 4). Angela Merkel seeks to dispel fears of Brexit. *Financial Times*. Retrieved July 15, 2014, from http://www.ft.com/intl/cms/s/0/f091232e-ec05-11e3-a9e3-00144feabdc0.html#axzz37QTMXh00

Wahl, P. (2005). *International taxation regulating globalisation – Financing development* (W. E. E. D. Thomas Kalinowski, Ed.). Berlin.

Wallace, W. (1991). Foreign policy and national identity in the United Kingdom. *International Affairs*, *67*(1), 65–80. doi:10.2307/2621219

Walter, I. (1974). International trade and resource diversion: The case of environmental management. Weltwirtschaftliches Archiv, 110(3), 482–493. doi:10.1007/BF02696706 doi:10.1007/BF02696706

Waltz, K. N. (1979). *Theory of international politics*. Addison-Wesley Pub. Co.

Watt, N. (2014, July 1). Nick Clegg defeats Lib Dem bid to guarantee EU referendum. *The Guardian*. Retrieved July 9, 2014, from http://www.theguardian.com/politics/2014/jul/01/clegg-lib-dems-no-in-out-referendum-eu

Watt, R., & Sheiham, A. (1999). Inequalities in oral health: A review of the evidence and recommendations for action. *British Dental Journal*, *187*, 6–12. PMID:10452185

Watt, R., & Sheiham, A. (2012). Integrating the common risk factor approach into a social determinants framework. *Community Dentistry and Oral Epidemiology*, *40*(4), 289–296. doi:10.1111/j.1600-0528.2012.00680.x PMID:22429083

Weathill, S., & Beaumont, P. (1999). *EU law*. London: Penguin.

Westerlund, J. (2005). A panel CUSUM test of the null of cointegration. Oxford Bulletin of Economics and Statistics, 67(2), 231–262. doi:10.1111/j.1468-0084.2004.00118.x doi:10.1111/j.1468-0084.2004.00118.x

Westerlund, J. (2006). Reducing the size distortion of the panel LM test for cointegration. Economics Letters, 90(3), 384–389. doi:10.1016/j.econlet.2005.09.002 doi:10.1016/j.econlet.2005.09.002

Westerlund, J., & Edgerton, D. L. (2007). A panel bootstrap cointegration test. Economics Letters, 97(3), 185–190. doi:10.1016/j.econlet.2007.03.003 doi:10.1016/j.econlet.2007.03.003

Whalley, J. (2008). Recent regional agreements: Why so many, why so much variance in form, why coming so fast and where are they headed? *World Economy*, *31*(1), 31–66.

Whalley, J. (2008). Recent regional agreements: Why so many, why so much variance in form. Why coming so fast, and where are they headed? *World Economy*, *31*(4), 517–532. doi:10.1111/j.1467-9701.2008.01094.x

Widstrom, E., & Eaton, K. A. (2004). Oral healthcare systems in the extended European Union. *Oral Health & Preventive Dentistry*, *2*, 155–194. PMID:15641621

Wignall, A. B. (2011). Solving the financial and sovereign debt crisis in Europe. *Financial Market Trends- OECD Journal,* (2), 1-23.

Willis, A. (2009). *Switzerland, Austria and Luxembourg relax banking secrecy.* Retrieved March 20, 2014, from http://euobserver.com/?aid=27775

Willis, A. (2011, February 4). Franco-German 'pact for competitiveness' hits immediate opposition. *EUobserver.* Retrieved April 14, 2014, from, http://euobserver.com/economic/31755

Willsher, K., & Chu, H. (2011, December 5). France, Germany see budget discipline as key in crisis. *Los Angeles Times.* Retrieved May 22, 2014, from, http://articles.latimes.com/2011/dec/05/world/la-fg-eu-merkel-sarkozy-20111206

Wintour, P. (2013, January 4). Cameron promises voters 'a real choice' over relations with Europe. *The Guardian.* Retrieved July 7, 2014, from http://www.theguardian.com/politics/2013/jan/04/cameron-promises-real-choice-eu

Wolde-Rufael, Y. (2009). Re-examining the financial development and economic growth nexus in Kenya. *Economic Modelling, 26*(6), 1140–1146. doi:10.1016/j.econmod.2009.05.002

World Bank World Development Indicators Database. (2014). Retrieved January 14, 2014, from http://data.worldbank.org/data-catalog/world-development-indicators

World Bank World Development Indicators Database. (2014). Retrieved May 5, 2014 from http://data.worldbank.org/data-catalog/world-development-indicators

World Bank. (2008). *World development indicators-08.* Washington, DC: Author.

World Bank. (n.d.). *World databank.* Retrivied from http://databank.worldbank.org

World Development Report. (1984). World Bank.

World Health Organisation. (2012). *Oral health fact sheet N°318.* Retrivied from: http://www.who.int/media-centre/factsheets/fs318/en/index.html on 14/04/2012

World Health Organisation. (2012). Oral health country/area profile programme. WHO Collaborating Centre, Malmo University, Sweden. Retrivied from: http://www.mah.se/CAPP/Country-Oral-Health-Profiles/EURO/

World Trade Organization (WTO). (2010). *World trade report 2010: Trade in natural resources.* Geneva: World Trade Organization.

World Wildlife Fund. (2012). *Living planet report 2012-Biodiversity, biocapacity and better choices.* Available from http://www.worldwildlife.org/publications/living-planet-report-2012-biodiversity-biocapacity-and-better-choices

WTO. (2014). *The trend towards increased regionalism could be reversed, new WTO research suggests.* Retrieved from http://www.wto.org/english/news_e/news14_e/rese_23apr14_e.htm

WTO. (2014). *Regional trade agreements.* Retrieved from http://www.wto.org/english/tratop_e/region_e/region_e.htm

WTO. (2014). *Regionalism: Friends or rivals?* Retrieved from http://www.wto.org/english/thewto_e/whatis_e/tif_e/bey1_e.htm

Yardımcıoğlu, M., Kocamaz, H., & Sezal, N. (2012). *Regional development policiy and development in Turkey.* Paper presented at the *Regional Development and Governance Symposium,* Kahramanmaraş, Turkey.

Yeldan, E. (1989). Structural adjustment and trade in Turkey: Investigating the alternatives beyond export-led growth. *Journal of Policy Modeling, 11*(2), 273–296. doi:10.1016/0161-8938(89)90018-5

Yeldan, E. (2011). *Küreselleşme Sürecinde Türkiye Ekonomisi, Bölüşüm, Birikim ve Büyüme.* İstanbul: İletişim Publishing.

Yeung, C. A. (2011). Efficacy of salt fluoridation. *Evidence-Based Dentistry, 12*(1), 17–18. doi:10.1038/sj.ebd.6400776 PMID:21436859

Yi-chong, X. (2006). China's energy security. *Australian Journal of International Affairs, 60*(2), 265–286. doi:10.1080/10357710600696175

Yiğidim, A. (2012). *Growing policy: Evaluation in terms of Turkey economy*. Retrieved, January 10, 2014, from http://www.tek.org.tr/dosyalar/buyume6.pdf

Yıldırım I., Dulgergil C., & Serdaroglu. (2010). Aile Hekimligi Uygulamalarında Erken Donem Koruyucu Dis Hekimligi Uygulamaları ve Önemi. *Saglıkta Performans ve Kalite Dergisi, 2.*

Yılmaz, G., & Alganer, Y. (2010). Avrupa Birliği müktesebatı bağlamında katma değer vergisinde yakınlaştırma ve uyumlaştırma çalışmaları. *Journal of Marmara University İ.İ.B.F., 27*(1), 135-160.

YouGov/The Sun Survey Results. (2014). Retrieved July 1, 2014, from http://yougov.co.uk/news/categories/politics/

Yousouf, H. (2012). S&P downgrades Europe bailout fund. *CNN International*. Retrieved April 15, 2014, from http://money.cnn.com/2012/01/16/markets/sandp_efsf_downgrade/index.htm

Yuan, J.-D. (2010). China's role in establishing and building the Shanghai cooperation organization (SCO). *Journal of Contemporary China, 19*(67), 855–869. doi:10.1080/10670564.2010.508587

Yucel, F. (2009). Causal relationships between financial development, trade openness and economic growth: The case of Turkey. *Journal of Social Sciences, 5*(1), 33–42. doi:10.3844/jssp.2009.33.42

Yüksel, A. (2011). *Access to bank loans of SMEs in Turkey*. Ankara, Turkey: Minister of Development .

Zahariadis, Y. (2005). The economic implications of deep integration in the EU-Turkey customs union. *GTAP Paper Resource*. No 1668.

Zartman, I. W. (1973). *Man, state, and society in the contemporary Maghrib*. New York: Praeger Publishers.

Zhang, J., Lanfang, W., & Susheng, W. (2012). Financial development and economic growth: Recent evidence from China. *Journal of Comparative Economics, 40*(3), 393–412. doi:10.1016/j.jce.2012.01.001

Zhao, S. (2008). China's global search for energy security: Cooperation and competition in Asia–Pacific. *Journal of Contemporary China, 17*(55), 207–227. doi:10.1080/10670560701809460

Zhuangzhi, S. (2004). New and old regionalism: The Shanghai cooperation organization and Sino-Central Asian relations. *The Review of International Affairs, 3*(4), 600–612. doi:10.1080/1475355042000241548

Zigon, G., Berrino, F., Gatta, G., Sanchez, M. J., Van Dijk, B., Van Eycken, E., & Francisci, S.EUROCARE Working Group. (2011). Prognoses for head and neck cancers in Europe diagnosed in 1995-1999: A population-based study. *Annals of Oncology, 22*(1), 165–174. doi:10.1093/annonc/mdq306 PMID:20587510

Zweig, D., & Jianhai, B. (2005). China's global hunt for energy. *Foreign Affairs, 84*(5), 25–38. doi:10.2307/20031703

About the Contributors

Engin Sorhun is an assistant professor of international economics and vice-chairman of economics department at Istanbul 29 University. He received MA in Transition Economics from Sorbonne University Paris I (2003) and PhD in International Economic from University of Strasbourg with his thesis entitled "Integration of Turkey to the EU in the Light of Three-Regularity of Geographical Economics". He has work experience in private sector in addition to his academic career. Economic Integration, Geographical Economics, International Trade are the main pillars of his interdisciplinary studies. As a visiting-lecturer, he gave lectures, seminars, conferences on economic integration in several European universities. His recent studies investigate the potential economic impacts of the Organization of Islamic Cooperation, the Shanghai Cooperation Organization, and the Transatlantic Trade and Investment Partnership.

Ümit Hacıoğlu is an associate professor at Istanbul Medipol University, Turkey. Dr. Hacıoğlu has BAs in Business Administration and International Relations (2002). He received PhD in Finance and Banking with his thesis entitled "Effects of Conflict on Equity Performance". Finance and Banking, Strategic Management, and International Political Economy are the main pillars of his interdisciplinary studies. He is the executive editor of *International Journal of Research in Business and Social Science* (IJRBS) and the founder member of the Society for the Study of Business and Finance (SSBF).

Hasan Dinçer is an associate professor at Istanbul Medipol University, Turkey. Dr. Dinçer has BAs in Financial Markets and Investment Management at Marmara University. He received PhD in Finance and Banking with his thesis entitled "The Effect of Changes on the Competitive Strategies of New Service Development in the Banking Sector". He has work experience in finance sector as portfolio specialist and his major academic studies focusing on financial instruments, performance evaluation, and economics. He is the executive editor of *International Journal of Finance and Banking Studies* (IJFBS) and the founder member of the Society for the Study of Business and Finance (SSBF).

* * *

Yalçın Alganer is an assistant professor of Finance at Marmara University, Faculty of Economics, Istanbul, Turkey. Dr. Alganer has BAs in Public Finance (1973). He received MA degree from Marmara University of Public Finance (1975). He finished the PhD program at the Public Finance, Fiscal Law in Marmara University with his thesis entitled as "Income Redistribution and the Role of the Government and Public Finance Instruments". His major academic studies focusing on European Union (History, Creation, Financial Rules, Harmonization, Enlargement...), Global and National Income Distribution and Redistribution, International Finance, Globalization, Taxation of the Multinational Enterprises and Transfer Pricing, are the main pillars of his interdisciplinary studies. He has a work experience in private finance sector especially in a taxation and budgeting domains. Presently, he is a head of the Budgeting and Planning Department.

Hakan Ay is an associate professor of public finance at the Dokuz Eylül University, Faculty of Economics and Administrative Sciences, İzmir-Turkey. Dr. Ay has BAs in Public Finance, (1986). He received a PhD in Public Finance with his thesis entitled as "The Role of Economic Interest Group on the Implementation of Tax Policy Case of Turkey". He has worked as a controller at Agricultural Credit Cooperatives of Turkey at 1987-1990 periods. In 1990, He has been appointed as a research assistant at the Dokuz Eylul University Faculty of Economics and Administrative Sciences Department of Finance. In 1997, He has been appointed as an Assistant Professor at the same university. He served as Vice President of Finance Department at 1999-2003 periods. He has been situated George Mason University (USA) as Guest Lecturer at 1999-2000 period. He has been deputy director of DEU-ATMER (European Community Research and Application Center of International Economic Relations) since 2002.

Hakan Cavlak is an assistant professor of international relations at Namık Kemal University, Faculty of Economics and Administrative Sciences, Tekirdağ, Turkey. Dr. Cavlak has BAs in International Relations at Istanbul University (2000). He received PhD in EU Politics and International Relations with his thesis entitled as "Europeanization of Environmental Policy in Turkey". European Policies, Integration Theories, Enlargement of the EU, EU-Turkey Relations are his main research areas. He is the editor in chief of *Balkan Journal of Social Sciences* (BJSS).

Murat Cetin is an Associate Professor of Economic Development at Faculty of Economics and Administrative Sciences in Namik Kemal University, Tekirdag, Turkey. Assoc. Prof. Cetin teaches Economic Growth and Development, Macroeconomics, Monetary Policy related courses. He received the B.S. degree in Economics Karadeniz Teknik University, 1994, M.S. degree in Economics, Karadeniz Teknik University, 1996, and PhD degree in Economics Karadeniz Teknik University, 2000. His main research areas focus on growth economics, energy economics, time-series, and panel data analyses.

Serkan Cura is an assistant professor of public finance at Celal Bayar University, Faculty of Economics and Administrative Sciences, Manisa-Turkey. Dr. Cura has BAs in Public Finance (2004). He received PhD in Public Finance with his thesis entitled as "The Efficiency of Health Systems and Public Health Expenditures in The World and Turkey: A Comparative Analysis". Public budgeting, public finance, poverty, economic crises and stability, foreign direct investments and European Union are the main pillars of his interdisciplinary studies. He is the assistant editor of *Journal of Management and Economics.*

Alper Doğan is an assistant professor of public finance at Izmir Katip Çelebi University, Faculty of Economics and Administrative Sciences, Izmir-Turkey. Dr. Doğan has BAs in Public Finance (2003). He received Ph.D in Public Finance with his thesis entitled as "Gender Budgets: An Evaluation for Turkey". Fiscal Theory, Gender Studies, Government Budgets, Fiscal Economics, Taxation are the main pillars of his interdisciplinary studies.

Giray Gozgor is an associate professor at Dogus University, Department of Economics and Finance in Istanbul-Turkey. Dr. Gozgor has received PhD in Economics with the thesis entitled: "The Application of Stochastic Processes in Exchange Rate Forecasting: Benchmark Tests for Developed and Emerging Markets" from Istanbul University. He has published at peer-reviewed international journals, including *Emerging Markets Review, Economic Modeling*, and the *Journal of International Trade & Economic Development*.

Armağan Gözkaman (joint Ph.D. in Strasbourg University & Marmara University) is an Assistant Professor of Political Sci-ence and International Relations at Beykent University. He had his BA degree in Galatasaray University (Istanbul) and his MA degree in Galatasaray University and Strasbourg (Robert Schuman) University. His research interests center on European and international security studies. His Ph.D. thesis on Turkey's reaction to international crises was published by LAP Lambert Academic Publishing and he is currently co-editing a book on the Arab Spring. He is currently one of the reviewers of the journal entitled International Relations and Diplomacy.

Davuthan Gunaydın is an Assistant Professor of Labor Economics at Faculty of Economics and Administrative Sciences in Namik Kemal University, Tekirdag, Turkey. Assist. Prof. Gunaydın teaches social policy, sociology of work and regional development related courses. He received the B.S. degree in Economics Anadolu University, 2003, M.S. degree in Operations Research, Marmara University, 2006, and PhD degree in Labor Economics Marmara University, 2011. His main research areas focus on health policies regional development policies and social policies.

Berkay Habiboğlu is a specialist at Thrace Development Agency, Program Coordination Unit, Tekirdag-Turkey. He has BAs in Economics (2006). He studies at Galatasaray University to receive his MSc degree in Business Administration. He has a work experience on Marketing and on Government Supports which aims to stimulate entrepreneurship, investment and development.

Abdülkadir Işık was born in 1972 Ahlat-Bitlis, Turkey. He is a professor at Namık Kemal University, Faculty of Economics and Administrative Sciences, Tekirdag, Turkey. He completed undergraduate degree from Anadolu University, Faculty of Economics and Administrative Sciences, Department of Public Finance. He completed master's degree (MA) in Public Finance at Marmara University and he holds a Ph.D in Public Finance from Marmara University. He was a visiting researcher at Sussex University, UK, and a post doctoral researcher at New York State University, USA. His main research fields focus on public finance, public sector economics, taxation, and health care economics.

Baris Kablamaci is an assistant professor at Istanbul University, Department of Economics in Istanbul- Turkey. Dr. Kablamaci has BAs in Economics (2000). He received PhD in Economics with the thesis entitled: "The Macroeconomic Effects of Crude Oil Price Changes: A Turkish Experience" from Istanbul University. He was the Turkish editor of the book *Modern Macroeconomics* that was written by Brian Snowdon and Howard R. Vane.

Mehmet Emin Merter is an assistant professor at the Akhisar Vocational College, Department of Marketing, Celal Bayar University Manisa, Turkey. Dr. Merter received his BA in Business Administration, Faculty of Economics and Administrative Sciences, 9 Eylül University, İzmir Turke in 1987. Having acquired his MA in Public Finance from 9 Eylül University, Graduate School of Social Sciences in 1995, Dr. Merter received his Ph.D. from 9 Eylül University with his dissertation work on tax auditing and total quality management. Having worked as instructor at Vocational Colleges at Süleyman Demirel University and Celal Bayar University, he was appointed as an assistant professor to the Akhisar Vocational College at Celal Bayar University as the head of Marketing Program at this very unit. Merter has several works on Total Quality Management including a book with the authorship of many book chapters.

Abdullah Önder Özkul graduated from Karadeniz Technical Univ. Department of Finance in 2001. Özkul's master education has been complated at Beykent Univ. Department of Banking and Finance. Between the years of 2003-2009, he worked Department of Financal Analysis and Intelligence at a Private Bank in Ankara, respectively as a Specialist Assistant, Specialist and Director. As of November 2009, he is working at Karacadag Development Agency in Diyarbakır as a Head of Monitoring and Evaluation Unit. The Agency responsible for TRC2 region (Diyarbakir- Sanliurfa).

Buğra Özer received his BA from the Department of Political Science and Public Administration, Middle East Technical University, Ankara, Turkey in 1996. Dr. Özer gained his MA from Bilkent University, Department of Political Science and Public Administration, Ankara with his dissertation on the transformation of public bureaucracy in 1998. He continued his Ph.D. studies in Public Policy Program of Carleton University Ph.D. Program in Public Policy of Ottawa, Ontario, Canada between 1999 and 2004. He got his Ph.D. in Economics, Celal Bayar University, Manisa, Turkey in 2010 with his work on health care economics and health care policy making. Dr. Özer was appointed as an assistant professor to Department of Public Administration, Faculty of Economics and Administrative Sciences, Celal Bayar University Manisa. He presently serves as an associate professor the head of Department of Political Science and International Relations at Celal Bayar University, FEAS, Manisa alongside with the vice-directorship of Graduate School of Social Sciences, Manisa, Turkey. He was also a visting fellow at the Reagant's University, London, United Kingdom for the summer of 2013. Dr. Özer's reserach interest lays in the field of contemporary policy making and democratization along with democratization participation theories with emphasis on the processes of remaking of Turkish public policy making in line with the accession talks of Turkey to the European Union along with local administrations in Turkey.

Christophe Schalck is an associate professor of Economics and head of economics department at ESG Management School, Paris- France. He received PhD in Economics with his thesis entitled as "Fiscal policies as a stabilization in the euro zone: estimates and prospects". He has a work experience in the banking sector as economist in the Central Bank of France and his major academic studies focusing on European public finance, energy economics, and economics. He is also lecturer at the University of Paris West (France) and was member of organizing committee of several international conferences.

Fahri Seker is an Assistant Professor of Economic Development at Faculty of Economics and Administrative Sciences in Bozok University, Yozgat, Turkey. Ass. Prof. Seker teaches Economic Growth and Development, Macroeconomics, Monetary Policy related courses. He received the B.S. degree in Economics Marmara University, 1997, M.S. degree in Economics, Marmara University, 2001, and PhD degree in Economics Erciyes University, 2007. His main research areas focus on development economics, environmental economics, applied time-series econometrics.

Gamze Yıldız Şeren was born in 1987 Gaziantep, Turkey. She is a research assistant at Namık Kemal University, Faculty of Economics and Administrative Sciences, Tekirdag-Turkey. She completed undergraduate degree from Marmara University, Faculty of Economics and Administrative Sciences, Department of Public Finance (2008). She completed master's degree (MA) in Public Finance at Marmara University (2011). She continues to work on PhD Thesis in Public Theory, at Marmara University. Her studies on public sector economics, taxation, and public finance.

Yontem Sonmez is an assistant professor of international economics at Manchester Metropolitan University, Faculty of Business and Law, Manchester, UK. Dr. Sonmez has a BA in Economics at Cyprus International University and MSc in Economics at University of Manchester. She received her PhD in International Economics at Sheffield University with her thesis entitled as "Turkey on the Way to EU Accession: Migration and Trade Issues". Empirical international trade, international migration of labour and workers' remittances, FDI, development and labour economics under the broad umbrella of the economics of globalisation are the main pillars of her interdisciplinary studies. She is an editorial board member of *International Journal of Economic Perspectives* and member of the European Trade Study Group and European Association of Labour Economists.

Seda Suat is a student of Namık Kemal University, Faculty of Economics and Administrative Sciences, also she is a dentist and manager of Sevgi Dental Clinic, Tekirdağ. She graduated from Dentistry Faculty of Marmara University,İstanbul.

Gokhan Tenikler graduated from Department of Public Administration (Dokuz Eylul University-Turkey) in 1996 and received his master degree in Public Administration (Division of Urbanization and Environmental Problems) from Dokuz Eylul University in 2001. He got Ph.D. in Public Administration (Division of Urbanization and Environmental Problems) from Dokuz Eylul University (Turkey) in 2007. He is an Assistant Professor of Public Administration at the Dokuz Eylul University (Izmir/Turkey). His current research and teaching interests include: urbanization, environment, sustainable development, international and supranational organizations, and strategical planning. Dr. Tenikler has academical researches and works on environmental policies, urban administration, European Union and he has had editorships of several books. He has invited to conferences, training seminars on his branch by different governerships, municipalities and universities.

Birol Topcu is an Assistant Professor of Biostatistics at Faculty of Medicine in Namik Kemal University, Tekirdag, Turkey. Assist. Prof. Topcu teaches Statistics, Biostatistics, Mathematical Statistics related courses. He received the B.S. degree in Mathematics Ankara University, 1995, M.S. degree in Mathematics, Afyon Kocatepe University, 1997, and PhD degree in Statistics Ankara University, 2003. His main research areas focus on dependence, statistics, biostatistics and mathematical statistics.

Öznur Uçar is a BAs student of public finance at The Dokuz Eylül University, Institute of Social Sciences, Izmir-Turkey. She is a student of sociology at The Anadolu University, Open Education Faculty. She worked as a specialist in foreign trade for 5 years. She has been working as an English teacher since 2008.

Özge Selvi Yavuz is a Research Assistant at Faculty of Economics and Administrative Sciences in Namık Kemal University, Tekirdağ Turkey. She received the B.S degree in Economics, İstanbul University, 2011, M.S degree in Economic Theory, İstanbul University, 2014. Her main research areas focus on flexibility, public finance, public sector expenditures and health economics.

Eren Alper Yılmaz is research assistant of public administration at Dokuz Eylül University, Faculty of Economics and Administrative Sciences, İzmir-Turkey. Yılmaz studied Political Sciences at Bilkent University in English and graduated in 2011. He also studied economics at Anadolu University Faculty of Open University. He made intern at Center for Middle Eastern Strategic Studies and Republic of Turkey Prime Ministry Undersecretariat of Treasury. He received his Master with thesis entitled as "Public Diplomacy Methods Used by Global Actors within the Context of Propaganda: USA Case". Foreign Policy, Political History and Economy are the main pillars of his interdisciplinary studies.

Güneş Yılmaz is an assistant professor of Customs Business at Trakya University, Keşan Yusuf Çapraz School of Applied Sciences, Edirne-Turkey. Dr. Yılmaz has BAs in Public Finance (2002). She received MA degree from Marmara University of Public Finance–Fiscal Law (2004). She finished the PhD program at the Public Finance, Fiscal Law in Marmara University with her thesis entitled as "Supply of Goods as a Chargeable Event in Value Added Tax". Her major academic studies focusing on Public Finance, Public Economics, Tax Law, Turkish and EU Tax Systems. Presently, she is a head of the Department of Custom Business.

Index

A

B

C

D

E

F

G

H

I

J

L

M

N

P

R

S

T

U

V

W

Z

www.ingramcontent.com/pod-product-compliance
Lightning Source LLC
LaVergne TN
LVHW062142200926
848484LV00007B/1846
* 9 7 8 1 4 6 6 6 7 3 0 8 3 *